Fraudulent Conveyances

Fraudulent Conveyances

A Treatise Upon Conveyances Made by Debtors to Defraud Creditors

Containing References to All the Cases
Both
English and American

By

ORLANDO F. BUMP

BeardBooks

Washington, D.C.

PREFACE.

THE subject which is considered and treated in this work is one that has never been made the object of a special treatise or discussed in the light of a thorough and exhaustive collection of the authorities. It is more than seventy years since the last edition of Roberts on Fraudulent Conveyances was printed. May's Voluntary and Fraudulent Conveyances and Hunt's Fraudulent Conveyances are of a later date. These works, however, treat of the statute of 27th Eliz. as well as the statute of 13th Eliz., and are confined to the English cases. It is manifest that the subject of conveyances to defraud creditors is of sufficient importance to require a separate treatise, and those who are at all familiar with the subject, or who will take the trouble to examine this work, will know or see that the American authorities are very numerous and important. This work is therefore confined to conveyances to defraud creditors, and contains references to all the cases upon the subject.

The first difficulty to be overcome in such a work arises from the fact that various statutes have been passed in the different States. These, however, have been copied in the main from the statute of 13 Eliz., and that statute has always been considered as merely declaratory of the common law. Unity and symmetry has, therefore, been attained by considering the law of Fraudulent Conveyances as simply a part of the common law, and as the same in every country where Anglican law prevails. It is manifest, however, that whether a conveyance can defraud creditors is a question that will sometimes depend upon the condition and character of the remedies afforded by the various States. It is no part of this work to treat of local statutes affecting remedies, or relating to any thing else. Each practitioner is to be presumed to be familiar with the statutes of his own State. This work simply considers the subject as it was at common law with the remedies afforded by the common law. Cases, however, that vary from the common law have been cited as opposed to the doctrine in the text merely to warn the practitioner that the text is not applicable to his particular State, and the apparent conflict of authorities can sometimes be explained on this ground. The author preferred, as a rule, to leave such conflict of authority without explanation rather than encumber his work with explanations which would not interest the profession generally.

But after all the conflicting cases have been eliminated that depend upon local statutes, there still remain a large number of opposing authorities, a larger number in fact than can be found in any other branch of the law. The relation of debtor and creditor is one that appears to be simple, and to rest simply upon the duty of common honesty. It is thus a question of morals, and a question of morals is frequently made a question of public policy. About forty independent courts are thus called upon to consider and determine a question of morals and of public policy. The result is manifest and inevitable. Different minds do and inevitably must reach different conclusions, and the doctrine of each court is the law within its jurisdiction.

A work could have been written covering every point of the law, and selecting only those cases which were consistent with the author's theory of the law. Such a work, however, would have been merely theoretical, and would have been useless and misleading in those States where a contrary doctrine prevails. To avoid this objection, and render the work practical, the plan has been adopted of presenting a theory of the law in the text and citing all the authorities, so that each practitioner can tell at a glance whether any proposition is accepted in his own State.

The author will also add that he does not expect that his views will be adopted. Where eminent courts, after careful discussion, have reached different conclusions, it would be presumptuous to assert that he has accepted the better opinion, for he also is fallible. All that he has aimed to do has been to present a systematic and consistent theory of the law, and to so arrange and classify the authorities as to unfold that theory. Conflict was there before he began his investigations, and will continue after his labors have ceased. All the merit he claims is simply that of presenting the law in a compact, accessible shape, and thus lightening the labors of a profession whose toils are arduous amid the ever increasing multiplication of reports.

The author takes this opportunity to return his thanks to his friends for the assistance they have so kindly rendered him in the preparation of this work. To know that others sympathize with his labors, and to feel that some benefit, no matter how slight, may be conferred in return, is no inconsiderable relief to the tediousness of an author's self-imposed task.

ORLANDO F. BUMP.

Baltimore, Nov. 1st, 1872.

CONTENTS.

CHAPTER IX.

CHAPTER X.

CHAPTER XI.

CHAPTER XII.

CHAPTER XIII.

CHAPTER XIV.

CHAPTER XV.

CHAPTER XVI.

CHAPTER XVII.

CHAPTER XVIII.

CHAPTER XIX.

CHAPTER XX.

CHAPTER XXI.

CHAPTER XXII.

CHAPTER XXIII.

CHAPTER XXIV.

―――

TABLE OF CASES.

2

3*

FRAUDULENT CONVEYANCES.

CHAPTER I.

ORIGIN OF COMMERCE.—In the earliest stages of society property has no value, and the transfer of it from one to another does not give rise to the idea of an obligation. There is no commerce, and loans are unknown. *Gaudent muneribus sed nee data imputant nee acceptis obligantur.*[1] *Fœnus agitare et in usuras extendere ignotum.*[2] Even after property has acquired a value, there is at first no facility of intercourse and no commerce. The difficulties in the way of the transfer of property are very great, conveyances are in a high degree ceremonious, requiring many symbolical acts and a great number of witnesses. Not an item of this ceremony can be safely omitted—not a gesture, not a syllable, not a witness. If there is an omission the conveyance is void. The early Roman law affords a ready and apt illustration of the customs of primitive times. The Roman *mancipium* or *mancipatio* required the presence of the parties, the vendor and the vendee, of five witnesses, and the *libripens,* who brought with him a pair of scales to weigh the uncoined copper money of ancient Rome.[3] The vendor brought the prop-

---

[1] Tacit Germ. c. 21.
[2] Tacit Germ. c. 26.
[3] Maine's Ancient Law, 198.

4

erty which he intended to sell, and the purchaser attended with the rough ingots of copper which served
for money. The property, with certain fixed formalities,
was delivered to the vendee, and the copper was weighed
by the *libripens* and passed to the vendor. In ancient
times this transaction, so long as it lasted, was called a
nexum, and the parties were *nexi*. The earliest use of
the *nexum* was to give proper solemnity to the alienation of property. At that period, therefore, the exchange of property was merely barter. Contracts and
commerce were unknown.[1]

TRANSITION FROM BARTER TO COMMERCE.—The next
step in the progress towards commerce is the rise of
contracts. These came naturally from conveyances.
If the property, under the primitive Roman law, was
transferred without the payment of the money, the
nexum was finished, so far as the vendor was concerned.
When he had delivered the property he was no longer
nexus; but, in regard to the vendee, the *nexum* continued. The transaction as to his part was incomplete,
and he was considered to be *nexus*. The same term,
therefore, at that period described the conveyance by
which the right of property was transmitted, and the
personal obligation of the debtor for the unpaid purchase money. The next step in the line of progress was
a proceeding wholly formal, in which nothing was delivered and nothing paid, and thus executory contracts
were introduced.[2] "*Nexum*," therefore, which originally
signified a conveyance of property, came insensibly to
denote a contract also, and ultimately the association
between this word and the notion of a contract became

---

[1] Maine's Ancient Law, 309.
[2] Maine's Ancient Law, 310.

so constant that a special term, *mancipium* or *mancipatio*, had to be used for the purpose of designating the true *nexum*, or transactions in which the property was really transferred. This illustration is drawn from the Roman law, but appears to present the true and natural theory of the transition from barter to commerce. Conveyances are first in order of time; contracts, credit and commerce come afterward. Barter is the primitive mode of exchange, and precedes the era of commercial enterprise.

SEVERITY OF ANCIENT LAWS.—The commission of fraud, however, depends upon the power which creditors have over their debtors. The existence of commerce alone is not sufficient. There must be some temptation or impunity before frauds will be committed. If the laws are severe and rigorous there will be no frauds; if the laws are lax there will be a temptation, and trickery and dishonesty will arise. In primitive times the laws were exceedingly harsh. If the debt was not paid the creditor had the right to reduce his debtor to slavery. Such was the ancient law in Greece, Italy, Asia[1] and Germany.[2] The custom was, in fact, so universal that it may be regarded as a part of the *jus gentium barbarorum*.

ROMAN LAW.—The Roman law was especially severe. The best resource of a debtor who found himself involved in a debt which he could not pay was to sell himself to his creditor, on the condition that, unless the debt was previously discharged, the creditor at the expiration of

---

[1] Grote's Hist. of Greece, vol. 3, pp. 95, 110, 159.
[2] Hallam's Hist. Middle Ages, vol. 1, pp. 196, 317; Hume's Hist. of Eng. vol. 1, p. 176.

a stated term should enter into the possession of his purchase. When the day came the creditor claimed possession and the prætor awarded it, and the debtor, thus given over to his purchaser, passed into his power. If the debtor, resolved not to sacrifice his liberty by his own act, refused thus to sell himself, he risked a fate still more fearful. If he was unable to discharge the claim within thirty days after its justice had been allowed, his creditor might arrest him and bring him before the prætor, and, if no one then offered to be his security, he was given over to his creditor, who kept him in private custody, bound with a chain of not less than fifteen pounds weight, and fed him with a pound of corn daily. If he still could not or would not come to any terms with his creditor, he was thus confined for sixty days, and during this period he was brought into the comitium before the prætor on three successive market days, and the amount of his debt declared, in order to see whether any one would yet come forward in his behalf. On the third market day, if no friend appeared, he was either put to death or sold as a slave into a foreign land beyond the Tiber; or, if there were several creditors, they might actually cut his body into pieces, and no creditor incurred any penalty by taking a part greater or smaller than in proportion to his debt.[1]

MODERN LAW.—Villenage was the resource of insolvent debtors in the Middle Ages,[2] but after the institutions of the country became settled this practice fell into disuse. It was inconsistent with the duties of war-

---

[1] A. Gellius, XX, 1, § 45, *et seq*; Gibbon's Hist. of Rome, vol. 4, 372; Niebuhr's Hist. of Rome, vol. 2, p. 599; Arnold's Hist. of Rome, p. 52.

[2] Hallam's Hist. of Middle Ages, vol. 1, pp. 196, 317; Hume's Hist. of Eng. vol. 1, p. 176.

like service to which every man was bound under the feudal system.[1] Imprisonment for debt, however, took the place which had formerly been filled by the power to enslave. This was unknown at the common law except in cases of trespass with force.[2] It was first given by statute against bailiffs,[3] and was subsequently extended by other acts.[4] Although this power was not as stern as the Roman law, yet it was always severe, and even harsh.[5]

EFFECT OF RIGOROUS LAWS.—The effect of these rigorous provisions, though contrary to the dictates of a humane policy, and repugnant to the teachings of the wisdom of an enlightened age capable of discriminating between fraud and misfortune, may be readily traced. The law of fraudulent conveyances is not to be found in the Twelve Tables. It had its origin in a later age, when the right of the creditor to enslave his debtor had been abrogated. The cases upon the subject in England prior to the commencement of the present century are comparatively few. On the other hand, the great expansion and development of this branch of the law in America is undoubtedly due to the abolition of imprisonment for debt and the absence of a general bankrupt law. It is also worthy of notice that fraud abounded even in England as long as debtors could fly to privileged places and be there exempt from arrest and the service of civil process.

---

[1] 2 Bell Com. 538.

[2] 1 Reeve's Hist. by Fin. 511; 2 Ib. 71; 2 Bell Com. 538; 2 Kent Com. 398; Herbert's Case, 3 Co. 11.

[3] 1 Reeve's Hist. by Fin. 511.

[4] 2 Reeve's Hist. by Fin. 71; 2 Kent Com. 398.

[5] 2 May's Const. Hist. 268; 1 Benton's Thirty Years in Sen. 291.

ROMAN LAW OF FRAUDULENT CONVEYANCES.—The
Roman law is the oldest law upon the subject of fraudulent conveyances, and embodies all the leading principles. *Ait prætor: Quae fraudationis causa gesta erunt,
cum eo qui fraudem non ignoraverit de his curatori bonorum vel ei cui de ea re actionem dare oppertebit infra
annum quo experiundi potestas fuerit, actionem dabo;
idque etiam adversus ipsum qui fraudem fecit, servabo.
Haec verba generalia sunt et continent, in se omnem omnino in fraudem factam vel alienationem vel quemcunque contractum; nam late ista verba patent.*[1] *Hoc
edictum eum coercet qui sciens eum in fraudem creditorum hoc facere, suscepit quod in fraudem creditorum
fiebat. Quare si quid in fraudem creditorum factum sit,
si tamen is qui cepit ignoravit, cessare videntur verba
edicti.*[2] *Simili modo dicimus, et si cui donatum est non
esse quærendum an sciente eo cui donatum gestum sit,
sed hoc tantum an fraudentur creditores.*[3] *Sciendum,
Julianum scribere, eoque jure nos ueti, ut qui debitam
pecuniam recepit antequam bona debitoris possidentur,
quamvis sciens prudensque solvendo non esse recipiat, non
timere hoc edictum; sibi enim vigilavit.*[4] *Quæsitum est
an secundus emptor conveniri potest? Sed verior est
Sabini sententia bona fide emptorem non teneri; quia
dolus ei duntaxat nocere debeat qui eum admisit.*[5] These
principles are sound law even at the present time.

DERIVATION OF THE ANGLICAN LAW.—Anglican con-
stitutional[6] and criminal law[7] is derived from the Anglo-

---

[1] Dig. Lib. 42, tit. 9, § 1.
[2] Dig. Lib. 42, tit. 9, § 8.
[3] Dig. Lib. 42, tit. 9, § 11.
[4] Dig. Lib. 42, tit. 9, § 7.
[5] Dig. Lib. 42, tit. 9, § 9.
[6] Stubbs' Select Charters, Part I.
[7] 1 Reeves' Hist. by Fin. 24, note C; 39, note C.

Saxons, but Anglican civil law is founded upon the Roman law.[1] By this it must not be understood that Anglican civil law is merely a servile copy or imitation of the Roman law, but that it has borrowed the principles of the latter by the nobler process of assimilation and incorporation. How far the law of fraudulent conveyances is founded upon the Roman law it is impossible to determine, on account of the paucity of the materials for forming an opinion, yet the similarity of the principles raises a suspicion which is strengthened by the other circumstances connected with the early history of Anglican law. Derivation, however, is not necessary to account for the similarity, for the law of fraudulent conveyances is founded upon the principles of common honesty, demanded by and adapted to the exigencies of commerce, and, if every memorial of the present law were blotted out, it would spring up again in nearly its present shape.

COMMON LAW.—The cases that were decided prior to the adoption of any statute upon this subject are few and meagre; but, nevertheless, they are sufficient to show that the law of fraudulent conveyances is a part of the common law. A fraudulent conveyance was void as against creditors, and the property might be taken on execution.[2] Whether a gift was fraudulent was deemed a question of fact.[3] After the death of the debtor, the fraudulent grantee could be held as executor *de son tort*,[4] or relief might be had in equity.[5] These principles are

---

[1] 1 Reeves' Hist. Introduction by Fin.

[2] As fol. 101, pl. 72; Rol. Abr. Covin. 549; Brook, Abr. 139; Collusion pl. 9; Fitz. Abr. Execution, 108.

[3] 13 H. IV, 4, pl. 9.

[4] 13 H. IV, 4, pl. 9, Rol. Abr. Covin. 549.

[5] 16 Edw. IV, 9.

sufficient to show that the foundation of the existing law upon the subject had already been laid, and perhaps in the course of time the necessities of commercial enterprise and the quickened sense of justice would have reared a symmetrical system without legislative aid.

STATUTES.—The statutes form an important part of this branch of the law, and show the peculiar shape which fraud assumed in ancient times. Uses had gradually been developed, and were becoming common. No device could be better adapted to facilitate a fraudulent design, for by it the legal title could be placed in another, and the profits only which were not liable to execution at law could be reserved to the debtor.[1] The first statute upon the subject in its recitals sets forth the evil devices of the times in full. It declares as a fact and a matter of notoriety that debtors gave their tenements and chattels to their friends by collusion, thereof to have the profits at their will, and afterwards fled to privileged places, and there lived a great time, of high countenance, till the creditors were compelled to take a small part of their debts and release the balance.[2] The next statute[3] upon this subject recites the same practice of a conveyance to the use of the debtor and a withdrawal to a privileged place, where he could not be served with process, and provides a means of obtaining a judgment after a proclamation once a week for five successive weeks at the gate of the privileged place, and thus reaching the property of the debtor, whether held in trust or not. The third statute in the order of events sets forth the same practice of a fraudulent gift and a

---

[1] 2 Reeves' Hist. by Fin. 283, 457.
[2] 50 E. III, R. 6.
[3] 2 R. 2, c. 3.

seeking of the protection of a sanctuary or other privileged place. The enactment itself is a singular conclusion to its recitals, for, as if it were designed by one vigorous stroke to cut up fraud by the roots, it abolishes all deeds of gift of goods and chattels made to the use of the grantor.[1]

IMPORTANCE OF THE STATUTES.—These statutes and their recitals are important, for they show the form assumed by fraud in those early times, and throw light upon some of the expressions used by the courts in later times. If there had never been a fraudulent conveyance to the use of a debtor, the doctrine of secret trusts would never have arisen. It is to conveyances of this class that Coke refers when he says: " Every gift made upon a trust is out of this proviso, for that which is, betwixt the donor and donee, called a trust, *per nomen speciosum*, is, in truth, as to all the creditors, a fraud, for they are thereby defeated and defrauded of their true and due debts."[2] It has been said that the act of 50 Edw. III, c. 6, is not declaratory of the common law, upon the ground that if the same principles had prevailed at the common law, the statute was in vain, and would never have been made.[3] This doctrine would not be accepted now, though it must be admitted that this multiplication of statutes raises grave doubts as to the vigor and force of the principles acknowledged at the common law upon this subject. If the principles which are now recognized and enforced had been adopted and acted on at common law, there would have been no grievous evils to redress,

---

[1] 3 H. 7, c. 4. Finlason suggests that this is merely a declaratory act. 3 Reeves' Hist. by Fin. 143.

[2] Twyne's Case, 3 Co. 80.

[3] Lyte v. Perry, Dyer, 49 C.

and legislative interferences would not have been necessary. The fact that statutes were passed plainly shows
that there were either doubts as to what the law was or
a lack of vigor in enforcing it.

MERELY DECLARATORY.—The statute of 13 Eliz., c. 5,[1]
is the last in the series, and is the foundation of all the
modern law of fraudulent conveyances. It was extended
to Ireland by 10 Car. I, sess. 2, cap. 3, and is in force in
Maine, New Hampshire, Massachusetts, Delaware, Pennsylvania, Maryland, South Carolina and Iowa. The
various statutes in the other States are modeled after it,
and in the main are simply a reenactment of it. In
this respect the development of the Anglican law presents an analogy to the Roman law. Roman law was
founded upon an edict of the prætor; Anglican law is
founded upon a legislative enactment. This statute, however, is merely declaratory of the common law.[2] By this
expression the courts probably do not mean to say more
than that the statute is founded in common reason, and
common reason has justly been held to be common law.[3]
As far as the actual practice was concerned, it probably
would be more strictly accurate to say that the principles
of the common law, as now understood, are so strong
against fraud in every shape that they will attain every
end proposed by the statute.[4]

COMMON LAW STILL IN FORCE.—This doctrine is of
practical importance, for unless there is a conflict between

---

[1] Made perpetual by 29 Eliz. c. 5.
[2] Co. Litt. 76, a. 290 c.; Twyne's Case, 3 Co. 80; Hamilton v. Russell, 1
Cranch. 309; Peck v. Land, 2 Kelly, 1; Clements v. Moore, 6 Wall, 299;
Hudnal v. Wilder, 4 McCord, 294.
[3] 27 H. 8, fol. 10.
[4] Cadogan v. Kennett, 2 Cowp. 432.

the provisions of a statute and those of the common law relating to the same subject matter, or an evident intent of the legislature to repeal the common law, the latter is considered to be still in force. Consequently, as the act is merely declaratory, resort may always be had to the principles of the common law whenever the statute fails to reach a case of fraud.[1] The act itself is not affected by this doctrine,[2] and will in general be received as a true declaration of what the law was,[3] but, wherever the statute is ineffective, either through a change of custom, or the introduction of a new kind of property, or the concoction of some new device, there the common law intervenes with its pure and elevated principles of morality and justice, and enforces the dictates of common honesty and common sense. In other words, the common law supplements the statute to the end that justice may be done and every species of fraud suppressed.

LIBERAL CONSTRUCTION.—The statute is established for the suppression of fraud, the advancement of justice and the promotion of the public good. Consequently, it should be liberally and beneficially construed to suppress the fraud, abridge the mischief and enlarge the remedy.[4] It must not, however, be so strained as to make it receive an interpretation which it was not intended to bear. Such a construction, moreover, is not to be made in support of creditors as will make third persons sufferers when they act in good faith.[5] These

---

[1] Blackman v. Wheaton, 13 Minn. 326; Fox v. Hills, 1 Conn. 295; State v. Fife, 2 Bailey, 337; Lillard v. M'Gee, 4 Bibb. 165.

[2] Davis v. Turner, 4 Gratt. 422.

[3] Clark v. Douglass, 62 Penn. 408.

[4] Twyne's Case, 3 Co. 80; Gooch's Case, 5 Co. 60; Cadogan v. Kennett, 2 Cowp. 432; McCulloch v. Hutchinson, 7 Watts, 434.

[5] Cadogan v. Kennett, 2 Cowp. 432.

principles are adopted in all the cases, and run through
every branch of the law of fraudulent conveyances.
The statute receives a fair and liberal construction to
carry out the plain intent of the legislature, yet interpretation is not carried to such an extreme as to warp it
from its true meaning. Rather than give a strained
construction to any part of it, the courts prefer to go
back to the liberal principles of the common law. In
this mode the will of the legislature is carried out, and
the principles of the law modified to meet the varying
wants of a progressive civilization.

CHAPTER II.

WHAT CONSTITUTES A FRAUDULENT CONVEYANCE.

OWNER'S ABSOLUTE DOMINION OVER HIS PROPERTY.— By virtue of the absolute dominion which every one has over his own property, he may, according to his good will and pleasure, and within the limits prescribed by law, make any disposition of it which does not interfere with the existing rights of others.[1] The power of courts of justice to interfere with, or in any manner control such disposition, exists only when the right is exercised to the prejudice of third persons. In other respects, he may act according to the dictates of his pleasure, interest, or even caprice.[2] He is permitted to exercise the most liberal and extended discretion as to the time and manner of disposing of his property, investing the proceeds and collecting his debts, provided he exercises that discretion fairly and honestly in reference to the right of his creditors to be paid out of the same, and without any view or intention of delaying, hindering, or preventing them from obtaining their lawful dues and demands. But wherever he exceeds these limits of his legitimate authority and power over his property and funds, the exercise of the power becomes unconscientious and inequitable, and the law then controls and regulates it in such a manner as to compel him to do justice to his creditors. Such an unconscien-

---

[1] Sexton v. Wheaton, 8 Wheat. 229; Thomson v. Dougherty, 12 S. & R. 448.

[2] Pope v. Wilson, 7 Ala. 690.

tious exercise of power by a debtor is considered á fraud upon his creditors.[1]

OWNER'S ABSOLUTE DOMINION NOT DIVERTED BY INDEBTEDNESS.—He is not deprived of his power and dominion over his property by either indebtedness, or even insolvency.[2] His creditors have no right to insist that his resources shall remain in any given shape. He may exchange his property for other property, or sell it and put the proceeds in his pocket or apply them in his discretion, to his debts, his purchases, or his maintenance. He has the right to manage, control, mortgage, pledge, and deal with it, and enter into business contracts in relation to it, in such way and manner as he deems will best conduce to its preservation and increase. His general creditors have no authority to restrain such exercise of his dominion over it, and can only resort to the personal remedies given by law for the coercion of payment.[3] If he is prosecuting an action of ejectment, he may compromise with his adversary in any manner he thinks proper.[4] Simple insolvency does not work a dissolution of a partnership, or divest the partners of their dominion over the partnership property.[5]

OWNER'S ABSOLUTE DOMINION INVOLVES THE RIGHT OF ANOTHER TO PURCHASE.—His right to sell, or otherwise dispose of his property, involves the correspond-

---

[1] Weed v. Pierce, 9 Cow. 722 ; Pope v. Wilson, 7 Ala. 690.

[2] Frank v. Peters, 9 Ind. 344 ; Waddams v. Humphreys, 22 Ill. 661 Barrow v. Bailey, 5 Fla. 9.

[3] Davis v. Turner, 4 Gratt. 422 ; Paper Co. v. Willett, 1 Robt. 131 ; Stanley v. Robbins, 36 Vt. 422 ; Frank v. Levie, 5 Robt. 599 ; Carter v. Neal, 24 Geo. 346.

[4] Richardson v. Stewart, 2 S. & R. 84.

[5] Siezel v. Chidsey, 22 Penn. 279.

ing right of another to purchase, or receive it.[1] The only limitation upon the exercise of these rights, is that the transfer shall be in good faith. Creditors who take no specific security from the debtor, trust him upon the general credit of his property and a confidence that he will not diminish it to their prejudice. They therefore have an equitable claim upon and interest in his property, so that any disposition of it in violation of their confidence is a fraud upon their rights.[2] If another receives it with notice of the fraud, he is aiding the debtor to cheat his creditors, and this the law never tolerates.[3] A person desiring to purchase, however, has a right to trust to the debtor's dominion over his property, and if he purchases in good faith for a valuable consideration, he should be protected. Having parted with his money in good faith, he holds the legal title, and has an equal equity with the creditors, and, consequently, has a paramount right to retain the property.[4]

THE ELEMENTS OF A FRAUDULENT CONVEYANCE.— The statute is founded upon these principles. It vitiates all transfers made "to the end, purpose, and intent to delay, hinder, or defraud creditors," but protects all "estates or interests which are conveyed on good consideration and *bona fide*." An inquiry into the validity of a transfer under the statute, therefore, involves three points: the existence of an intent to delay, hinder, or defraud, the consideration, and the *bona fides* of the transfer.

---

[1] Barrow v. Bailey, 5 Fla. 9.

[2] Eppes v. Randolph, 2 Call, 103; Seymour v. Wilson, 19 N. Y. 417.

[3] Cadogan v. Kennett, 2 Cowp. 432.

[4] Eppes v. Randolph, 2 Call, 103; Seymour v. Wilson, 19 N. Y. 417.

CHAPTER III.

FRAUDULENT INTENT.

THE CHARACTER OF THE INTENT.—The statute renders void all feoffments, gifts, grants, alienations, conveyances, bonds, suits, judgments and executions which are devised and contrived of malice, fraud, covin, collusion or guile to the end, purpose and intent to delay, hinder or defraud creditors and others of their just and lawful actions, suits, debts, accounts, damages, penalties, forfeitures, heriots, mortuaries and reliefs. It will be observed that there is no other description of the intent in the enacting clause except by reference to the preamble " the intent before declared and expressed."[1] This reference however, makes the intent essential to invalidate the transaction, by thus incorporating it in the body of the statute. The introduction of the term "purpose" into the Act does not impart to it any additional potency. It is only a synonym for design, intention—a mere expletive, intended to convey the idea which the Legislature had in view more strikingly and might be stricken from the Act without affecting its interpretation in any manner.[2]

WHAT KIND OF FRAUD IS WITHIN THE STATUTE.—No fraud is within the statute unless it is directed against those who have just and lawful actions, suits, debts, accounts, damages, penalties, forfeitures, heriots, mortuaries,

---

[1] Walker v. Burrows, 1 Atk. 93.
[2] Anderson v. Hooks, 9 Ala. 704.

or reliefs. An intent to deceive and defraud the public without any intent to delay, hinder or defraud the creditors of the grantor does not bring a conveyance within the act.[1] The fraud, moreover, must be a fraud against general creditors and not a mere intent to defeat a prior unrecorded deed.[2]

It must also be aimed at creditors and not at the grantor. The creditors of a party defrauded have no right even though the fraud has the effect to diminish his means of paying them, to look into such fraud or unravel it. It is for him and him alone, to do so and if he chooses to acquiesce in the fraud or suffers himself to be concluded of his right to investigate or undo it, his creditors must be content to abide by the legal rights remaining in him. There is a manifest distinction between a fraud upon the debtor and a fraud upon creditors. In the one case the debtor is the victim and guilty of no wrong, while in the other he is himself either in fact or in law the perpetrator of the fraud. In the latter case the creditors who seek to avoid a sale or transfer do not represent the debtor, but exercise rights paramount to his. In the former case the remedy belongs to the debtor alone and they can not interfere when they are not in the contemplation of the author of the wrong and are only affected consequentially.[3] The fraud, moreover, must lie in the transfer and not in the creation of the debt of the creditor who impeaches it.[4] The fraudulent intent must also be an intent to commit a fraud on creditors by making the transfer and not by

---

[1] Griffin v. Stoddard, 12 Ala. 783.

[2] Burgin v. Burgin, 1 Ired. 453.

[3] Pettus v. Smith, 4 Rich. Eq. 197; Garretson v. Kane, 3 Dutch 208; Eaton v. Perry, 29 Mo. 96; Hovey v. Holcomb, 11 Ill. 660; Vide Van Deusen v. Frink, 19 Pick. 449.

[4] Horwitz v. Ellinger, 31 Md. 492. Mattison v. Demarest, 4 Robt. 161.

some entirely independent act which might and probably would have been done had no transfer been made.[1]

WHAT CONSTITUTES FRAUD.— Fraud consists of unlawful conduct that operates prejudicially upon the rights of others.[2] To defraud is to withhold from another that which is justly due to him, or to deprive him of a right by deception or artifice.[3] A fraud upon creditors consists in the intention to prevent them from recovering their just debts by an act which withdraws the property of the debtor from their reach.[4] It does not consist in mere intention, but in intention acted out.[5] In a fraudulent conveyance there is generally an intention to secure some interest in the property to the debtor or some future right in it to the prejudice of the creditors,[6] and therefore it is sometimes said that a fraudulent instrument is one which the parties do not intend to have in operation as a real instrument according to its apparent character and effect.[7] *Dolus est machinatio cum aliud dissimulat aliud agit.*[8] It is manifest, however, that an instrument may be fraudulent although it is intended to operate as a real transfer as in the case of a voluntary conveyance by an insolvent debtor. A feigned conveyance is a fraudulent conveyance, but a fraudulent conveyance is not necessarily fictitious.

DELAY AND HINDERANCE.—It is not necessary, however, that there should be an intent to defraud in order

---

[1] Wilson v. Forsyth, 24 Barb. 105.

[2] Bunn v. Ahl, 29 Penn. 387.

[3] Burdick v. Post, 12 Barb. 168; s. c. 6 N. Y. 522.

[4] McKibbin v. Martin, 64 Penn. 352; Ala. Ins. Co. v. Pettway, 24 Ala. 544.

[5] Bunn v. Ahl, 29 Penn. 387.

[6] Northampton Bank v. Whiting, 12 Mass. 104; Belmont v. Lane, 22. How. Pr. 365.

[7] Eveleigh v. Purrsford, 2 Mood & Rob. 539; Doe v. Routledge, Cowp. 705.

[8] Rex v. Nottingham, Lane, 42.

to render a transfer void. The statute makes void all conveyances made with "intent to delay, hinder or defraud creditors." This language implies that the intent to defraud is something distinct from the mere intent to delay or hinder and that the latter alone will vitiate a transfer.[1] The term fraud imports something of a more vicious character than the mere production of a delay of satisfaction. There is no distinction however, between delaying and hindering. A person who is hindered is effectually delayed. To hinder any one in his course is necessarily to delay him. Many such pleonasms are to be found in old English statutes where they were introduced for caution's sake more than with any precise idea as to what they were intended to effect.[2]

WHAT CONSTITUTES A HINDRANCE OR DELAY. — The term delay refers not merely to time, but to the interposition of obstacles in the way of creditors, with the fraudulent intent to hinder and delay.[3] The statute is to be construed according to its reasonable intent and object, and by a reasonable construction only such hindrance and delay as will operate as a fraud, come within its operation.[4] A delay for all time renders a transfer void, and the principle is the same when it is sought for a limited time. The difference is in degree only. The hindrance or delay of creditors is reprobated by the statute without regard to the duration of the hindrance or delay.[5] The time for the performance of a contract

---

[1] Pilling v. Otis, 13 Wis. 495; Planck v. Schermerhorn, 3 Barb. Ch. 644; Sutton v. Hanford, 11 Mich. 513; Davenport v. Cummings, 15 Iowa, 219; Burt v. McKinstry, 4 Minn. 204.

[2] Read v. Worthington, 9 Bosw. 617; Burdick v. Post, 12 Barb. 168; s. c. 6 N. Y. 522.

[3] Linn v. Wright, 18 Tex. 317; Hefner v. Metcalf, 1 Head, 577.

[4] Hoffman v. Mackall, 5 Ohio St. R. 124.

[5] Quarles v. Kerr, 14 Gratt. 48; Sutton v. Hanford, 11 Mich. 513.

is both in morals and in law an essential part of the
contract itself, and a debtor who attempts to postpone
the time of payment, endeavors to deprive his creditors
of a valuable right, and thus it may justly be said that
á positive intent to defraud always exists where the inducement to a conveyance is to hinder and delay creditors, since the right of creditors to receive their demands when due, is as absolute as their right to receive
them at all.[1] Therefore, where the debtor places his
property beyond the reach of legal process, so as to
delay creditors, this is a legal fraud, although he may
intend ultimately to appropriate it for the benefit of all
or a part of them.[2] The law provides a mode for the
appropriation of a debtor's property to the payment of
his debts, and the interposition of any obstacle to prevent such appropriation in the due course of legal proceedings, is a delay and hindrance within the meaning
of the statute. The obstacle, however, must be interposed between the creditors and the property of the
debtor. If, after a transfer, the property does not,
either in fact or in contemplation of law, belong to the
debtor, or if the interest reserved is merely difficult to
reach on account of its peculiar character, then there is
no hindrance and delay within the statute. It is for
this reason that a preference,[3] or an assignment for the
benefit of creditors,[4] may be made for the express pur-

---

[1] Nicholson v. Leavitt, 6 N. Y. 510; s. c. 10 N. Y. 591; s. c. 4 Sandf. 252.

[2] Wheelden v. Wilson, 44 Me. 1; Borland v. Mayo, 8 Ala. 104; Kimball
v. Thompson, 4 Cush. 441; Stovall v. Farmers' Bank, 8 S. & M. 305; Mc-
Lean v. Lafayette Bank, 3 McLean, 587.

[3] Holbird v. Anderson, 5 T. R. 235; Woods v. Dixie, 53 E. C. L. 892;
s. c. 7 Q B. 892; Darvill v. Terry, 6 H. & N. 807; Hall v. Arnold, 15 Barb.
599; Hartshorne v. Eames, 31 Me. 93; Gassett v. Wilson, 3 Fla. 235;
Wheaton v. Neville, 9 Cal. 41.

[4] Riches v. Evans, 9 C. & P. 640; Johnson v. Osenton, L. R. 4, Ex. 107;
Wilt v. Franklin, 1 Binn. 502; Jackson v. Cornell, 1 Sandf. Ch. 348; Horwitz v. Ellinger, 31 Md. 492.

pose of defeating an execution. The creditor may be baffled, or even eventually lose his debt, but there is no obstacle interposed between him and any property which belongs to the debtor.

How THE FRAUDULENT INTENT IS ASCERTAINED.— The test words by which the validity of a transfer is tried are, "to the end, purpose, and intent to hinder, delay or defraud." The presence of this intent is essential to render a conveyance void.[1] The transfer must also be "devised and contrived of malice, fraud, covin, collusion or guile," and the intent must be marked by these characters or one of them.[2] Every contrivance, however, to the intent to delay, hinder or defraud creditors, is malicious. If the hindrance of creditors forms any part of the actual intent of the act done, so far the act is as against them a malicious contrivance.[3] In some cases the inference of fraud is a mere question of fact, and being a question of fact, can only be found by the tribunal which determines questions of fact.[4] When the existence of the fraudulent intent is thus a question of fact, it must, in an action at law, be expressly found by the jury, for the court can not infer it.[5] When fraud is thus a question of fact, it is called actual fraud, or fraud in fact.

---

[1] Sibly v. Hood, 3 Mo. 290.

[2] Ewing v. Runkle, 20 Ill. 448; Meux v. Howell, 4 East. 1.

[3] Hafner v. Irwin, 1 Ired. 490.

[4] Allen v. Wheeler, 4 Gray, 123; Ewing v. Gray, 12 Ind. 64; Maples v. Burnside, 22 Ind. 139; Banfield v. Whipple, 14 Allen, 13; Green v. Tanner, 8 Met. 411; Bagg v. Jerome, 7 Mich. 145; Jackson v. Mather, 7 Cow. 301.

[5] Tyrer v. Littleton, 2 Brownl. 187; Crisp v. Pratt, Cro. Car. 549; Oxford's Case, 10 Co. 53 b; Seward v. Jackson, 8 Cow. 406; s. c. 5 Cow. 67; Ridler v. Punter, Cro. Eliz. 291; Marden v. Babcock, 2 Met. 99; Ridgway v. Ogden, 4 Wash. C. C. 139; Charlton v. Gardner, 11 Leigh. 281.

Fraud in law.—The existence of the fraudulent intent is not, however, always a question of fact. It is sometimes a question of law. Every man is presumed to intend the necessary consequences of his act, and if an act necessarily delays, hinders or defrauds creditors, then the law presumes that it is done with a fraudulent intent.[1] The legal effect of a written instrument is also a question of law, and the intent of the parties in making it may be gathered from its face, and where the natural and inevitable consequence of its provisions is to delay, hinder or defraud creditors, it is void as a conclusion of law.[2] When the facts on which the fraud depends are well pleaded on one side and admitted by demurrer or otherwise upon the other, the existence of the fraudulent intent is also a question of law.[3]

To justify the inference of a fraudulent intent, however, when no fraud in fact is proved, there must be creditors who may be delayed, hindered or defrauded, and the necessary consequence of the act must be to produce such delay, hindrance or fraud.[4] In the construction of written instruments, also, the existence of fraud is a question of fact whenever their terms and stipulations are by possibility compatible with good faith, and have upon their face the essential elements of a legal contract.[5] Whenever fraud is thus the inevita-

---

[1] Babcock v. Eckler, 24 N. Y. 623; Potter v. McDowell, 31 Mo. 62; O'Connor v. Bernard, 2 Jo. 654; Freeman v. Pope, L. R. 5, Ch. 538; s. c. L. R. 9 Eq. 206; Norton v. Norton, 5 Cush. 524; Freeman v. Burnham, 36 Conn. 469.

[2] Mitchell v. Beal, 8 Yerg. 134; Ashurst v. Martin, 9 Port. 566; Sheldon v. Dodge, 4 Denio, 217; Griffin v. Cranston, 10 Bosw. 1; s. c. 1 Bosw. 281; Young v. Booe, 11 Ired. 347; Johnson v. Thweat, 18 Ala. 741; Bigelow v. Stringer, 40 Mo. 195; Gere v. Murray, 6 Minn. 305; Goodrich v. Downs, 6 Hill, 438; Bartels v. Harris, 4 Me. 146.

[3] Gerrish v. Mace, 9 Gray, 250.

[4] Pope v. Wilson, 7 Ala. 690.

[5] Jones v. Huggeford, 3 Met. 515; Hastings v. Baldwin, 17 Mass. 552.

ble consequence of an act or instrument, it is called con-structive fraud, or fraud in law.[1] A constructive fraud is an act which the law declares to be fraudulent with-out inquiring into the motive, not because arbitrary rules have been laid down upon this subject, but be-cause certain acts carry in themselves irresistible evi-dence of fraud.[2]

No DIFFERENCE BETWEEN FRAUD IN FACT AND FRAUD IN LAW.—There is no difference in principle between fraud in fact and fraud in law. Where the direct and inevitable consequence of an act is to delay, hinder or defraud creditors, the presumption, at once conclusively arises that such illegal object furnished one of the mo-tives for doing it and it is thus upon this ground held to be fraudulent. The result is the same when the ille-gal design is established as a question of fact. The in-quiry is as to the intention of the debtor. When it appears that among the inducements operating upon him there is an intention to violate any of the duties owing by him to any of his creditors, the transfer is tainted and may be set aside at the suit of any creditor.[3]

LEGAL, NOT MORAL INTENT.—The statute refers to a legal and not a moral intent, for one man's right does not depend on another man's moral sense. The moral sense is much stronger in some men than in others. The stat-ute therefore supposes that every one is capable of per-ceiving what is wrong and if he does what is forbidden, intending to do it, he is not allowed to say that he did not intend to do a forbidden act. A man's moral per-

---

[1] Lukins v. Aird, 6 Wall. 78.

[2] M'Broom v. Rives, 1 Stew. 72.

[3] Oliver Lee & Co.'s Bank v. Talcott, 19 N. Y. 146 ; Gere v. Murray, 6 Minn. 305.

ceptions may be so perverted as to imagine an act to be fair and honest which the law justly pronounces fraudulent and corrupt; but he is not therefore to escape from the consequences of it. The law must have a more certain standard for measuring men's intents than each individual's varying and capricious notions of right and wrong. Whatever a man's opinions of his own acts may be, there are certain rules founded in experience and established by law for determining the validity of transfers under the statute and if these rules are transgressed, they are void without regard to the opinion of the parties to it.[1] Fraud therefore, does not necessarily impute a corrupt or dishonorable motive. Parties may do what they consider perfectly fair for the purpose of preventing a sacrifice merely and with the intention of paying all the creditors ultimately, or may be animated merely by motives of affection or compassion;[2] but the law does not sanction any contrivance for either defeating or delaying creditors.[3]

FRAUD IS A QUESTION OF LAW.—It follows, therefore, that what constitutes fraud is a question of law. It is the judgment of law upon facts and intents.[4] Fraud is expressive of a legal idea and admits of a legal definition. It is therefore a matter of law. The expression that when there is no dispute about the facts fraud is a question of law,[5] is not strictly accurate for the intent is

---

[1] Potter v. McDowell, 31 Mo. 62; Grover v. Wakeman, 11 Wend. 187; s. c. 4 Paige. 23.

[2] Sturdivant v. Davis, 9 Ired. 365; Gardiner Bank v. Wheaton, 8 Me. 373; Briggs v. Mitchell, 60 Barb. 288; Trimble v. Turner, 13 S. & M. 348; Flood v. Prettyman, 24 Ill. 597.

[3] Enders v. Swayne, 8 Dana, 103.

[4] Worseley v. Demattos, 1 Burr. 467; Sturtevant v. Ballard, 9 Johns. 337; Planters Bank v. Borland, 5 Ala. 531.

[5] Sturtevant v. Ballard, 9 Johns, 337; Divver v. McLaughlin, 2 Wend. 596.

a material fact,[1] and this is not in all cases an inference of law. But when the intent is ascertained the law pronounces whether it is fraudulent and covinous.[2] Whenever the transfer is tainted with actual and not constructive fraud, it is the province of the tribunal for the ascertainment of facts to find the actual intent. In that sense fraud is sometimes called a mixed question of law and fact.[3] But it is never exclusively one of fact. It has never been held that the jury may give to the intentions such effect as to them may seem proper in each case. That the law declares and the security of creditors depends upon the fixed principles of the law and not on the uncertain judgment of jurors as to what is fraud.[4] In actions at law therefore it is the province of the court to instruct the jury as to what intent is in law fraudulent and to inform them whether certain evidence had a tendency to prove it.[5]

WHAT INTENT IS SUFFICIENT.—The intent which under the statute avoids a transfer as to creditors is an intent to delay, hinder or defraud, and the existence of the particular intent must be established before the transfer can be set aside. The mere intent to prevent a sacrifice is not sufficient.[6] But if the intent to prevent a sacrifice is accompanied with the requisite delay, hinder

---

[1] Geigler v. Maddox, 26 Mo. 575.

[2] Gere v. Murray, 6 Minn. 305 ; Gregory v. Perkins, 4 Dev. 50; Hardy v. Simpson. 13 Ired. 132 ; Keene v. Newell, 2 Mo. 9.

[3] Wilson v. Lott, 5 Fla. 305 ; Hall v. Tuttle, 8 Wend. 375; Haven v. Low, 2 N. H. 13 ; McLaughlin v. Bank of Potomac, 7 How. 220; Dodd v. McCraw, 8 Ark. 83.

[4] Gregory v. Perkins, 4 Dev. 50.

[5] Leadman v. Harris, 3 Dev. 144; Mott v. McNiel, 1 Aik. 162; Durkee v. Mahoney, 1 Aik. 116 ; Gibson v. Love, 4 Fla. 217; Smith v. Henry, 2 Bailey, 118; s. c. 1 Hill, 16; Babb v. Clemson, 12 S. & R. 328 ; Cadbury v. Nolen, 5 Penn. 320; Vide Kane v. Drake, 27 Ind. 29 ; Wynne v. Glidewell, 7 Ind. 446.

[6] Cason v. Murray, 15 Mo. 378.

or defraud, then the transaction is fraudulent and void.[1] It is not necessary, to establish a specific design to delay, hinder or defraud the particular creditor who assails the transfer for the intent to delay, hinder or defraud one particular creditor renders the transfer void as to all.[2] If the object is to delay, hinder or defraud creditors, the transfer will not be purged because the debtor may also have some other purpose in view.[3]

The validity of the transfer, moreover depends upon the intent of the debtor in making it, and not upon the question whether a remedy is or is not open to creditors.[4] As fraud depends upon the intent of the debtor, it must be in the inception of the transfer[5] and is the same in the smallest as in the largest transactions.[6] No man, moreover, can in general be guilty of fraud by accident or mistake.[7] but the parties to a written instrument are conclusively presumed to intend what is expressed upon its face and if its terms are fraudulent, it can not be supported by proof that they were inserted through inadvertence or mistake.[8] It has never been determined that in order to make void the transfer any creditor should be actually hindered or delayed. The

---

[1] Brown v. Osgood, 25 Me. 505; Borland v. Mayo, 8 Ala. 104.

[2] Turbervill v. Tipper, Palm. 415; Rex v. Nottingham, Lane, 42; Warneford Case, Dyer, 193, 267; Winer v. Warner, 2 Grant, 448; Hoke v. Henderson, 3 Dev. 12; Gruber v. Boyles, 1 Brev. 266; Dardenne v. Hardwick, 9 Ark. 482; Warner v. Percy, 22 Vt. 155.

[3] Reed v. Noxon, 48 Ill. 323.

[4] Grover v. Wakeman, 11 Wend. 187; s. c. 4 Paige, 23; Hyslop v. Clark, 14 Johns. 458; Halsey v. Whitney, 4 Mason, 206; Green v. Trieber, 3 Md. 11; Galt v. Dibrell, 10 Yerg. 146.

[5] Stone v. Grubbam, 2 Bulst. 217; Shep. Touch. 66; Weller v. Wayland, 17 Johns. 102; Claytor v. Anthony, 6 Rand. 285; Sommerville v. Horton, 4 Yerg. 541; Pope v. Wilson, 7 Ala. 690.

[6] State v. Benoist, 37 Mo. 500.

[7] Runyon v. Leary, 4 Dev. & Bat. 231; Fuller v. Acker, 1 Hill. 473.

[8] August v. Seeskind, 6 Cold. 166; Hooper v. Tuckerman, 3 Sandf. 311.

statute speaks of those who may be hindered.[1] The verdict of a jury upon a question of fraud is not conclusive, but may be set aside the same as in any other case.[2] A corporation may in judgment of law intend to defraud creditors.[3]

---

[1] Richardson v. Smallwood, Jac. 552.

[2] Dodd v. McCraw, 8 Ark. 83; Vance v. Phillips, 6 Hill, 433; Potter v. Payne, 21 Conn. 361; Marston v. Vultee, 12 Abb. Pr. 143; Edwards v. Currier, 43 Me. 474; Weisiger v. Chisholm, 28 Tex. 480.

[3] Curtis v. Leavitt, 15 N. Y. 9; s. c. 17 Barb. 309.

CHAPTER IV.

BADGES OF FRAUD.

THE TERM "BADGE OF FRAUD EXPLAINED."—A badge
of fraud is sometimes called a sign of fraud,[1] a mark of
fraud,[2] a circumstance of fraud,[3] an evidence of fraud,[4]
and an argument of fraud.[5] These terms are all synon-
ymous and simply denote an act which has a fraudulent aspect. An intent to defraud is an emotion of the
mind and as fraud is usually hatched in secret, *in arbore
cava et opaca*, there are generally no means of ascertaining whether it exists except by observing the acts of
the parties engaged in any transaction and deducing the
intent from those in accordance with certain principles
which have been established by observation and experience. A badge of fraud is simply an inference drawn
by experience from the customary conduct of mankind.[6]
The law adopts and acts upon the known principles of
human action. A badge of fraud may therefore be
defined as a fact calculated to throw suspicion upon a
transaction, and calling for an explanation.[7] It's only
effect in general is to require a more stringent proof of
the consideration for the transfer and the good faith of
the parties than would be demanded where no such
suspicion of unfairness exists.[8]

---

[1] Twynes Case, 3 Co. 80.

[2] Twynes Case, 3 Co. 80.

[3] Cadogan v. Kennett, 2 Cowp. 432.

[4] Cadogan v. Kennett, 2 Cowp. 432.

[5] Cadogan v. Kennett, 2 Cowp. 432.

[6] Terrell v. Green, 11 Ala. 207.

[7] Peebles v. Horton, 64 N. C. 374; Pilling v. Otis, 13 Wis. 495.

[8] Terrell v. Green, 11 Ala. 207.

WHY AN ACT IS A BADGE OF FRAUD.—The reason why any fact is denominated a badge of fraud is either because its natural and probable tendency is to delay, hinder or defraud creditors or because it is not in the usual course in which men acting in good faith transact business. The first ground rests upon the principle that every man is presumed to intend the natural and probable consequences of his act; the second ground is the result of experience. Whatever is out of the usual course betrays contrivance to give color to the transaction.[1] If the departure from the usual course of business consists in an attempt to conceal, it constitutes secrecy, which is an ordinary badge of fraud. If it consists in an excess of precaution, it looks as though it may have been done for effect to give the semblance of reality to that which is fictitious.[2] It evinces a diffidence in the rectitude of the transaction and a correspondent solicitude to provide defences.[3] Whatever may be the form it assumes, it always excites suspicion, for an assumed act is generally prompted by some unusual motive. When men's designs are correct they are usually content to carry them into effect in the usual mode.[4] To raise such a presumption, however, the transfer must be out of the general course of business as to the particular article transferred and not of the class of men to whom the debtor belongs.[5]

---

[1] Sands v. Codwise, 4 Johns. 536; Borland v. Walker, 7 Ala. 269; Kempner v. Churchill, 8 Wall. 362; Sayres v. Fredericks, 1 C. E. Green, 205 Poague v. Boyce, 6 J. J. Marsh, 70; Godfrey v. Germain, 24 Wis. 410; Rothberger v. Gough, 52 Ill. 436. Vide Kane v. Drake, 27 Ind. 29.

[2] Comstock v. Rayford, 12 S. & M. 369.

[3] Sands v. Codwise, 4 Johns. 536.

[4] Potter v. McDowell, 31 Mo. 62.

[5] Derby v. Gallup, 5 Min. 119.

ALL BADGES OF FRAUD NOT OF EQUAL WEIGHT.—All badges of fraud are not, however, entitled to equal weight as evidence. One may be almost conclusive and another may furnish merely a reasonable inference of fraud, yet both would be badges of fraud. The books accordingly speak of strong badges and slight badges of fraud, meaning by the word "badge" nothing more than that the fact relied on has a tendency to show fraud, but leaving its greater or less effect to depend on its intrinsic character.[1] There is not, moreover any ascertained rule of law which fixes and determines what acts or declarations of a party shall in all cases be required to establish fraud, but on the contrary the badges of fraud may and often do vary according to the intellectual character and moral depravity of the perpetrator, the end designed to be obtained and the means by which it is to be accomplished.[2]

EFFECT OF A BADGE OF FRAUD.—A badge of fraud does not constitute fraud itself, but is simply evidence of fraud, a means of establishing a fraudulent intent.[3] It is not necessary, however, in order to condemn a transaction as fraudulent, that two or more of the marks of a collusive design shall be affixed to it, for all presumption becomes conclusive unless explained. Any one badge simply will impeach a conveyance and on the other hand several badges may unite and the transaction still be protected.[4] The concurrence of several badges will, however, always make out a strong case.[5]

---

[1] Pilling v. Otis, 13 Wis. 495.

[2] Richards v. Swan, 7 Gill, 366 ; Schaferman v. O'Brien, 28 Md. 565.

[3] Wilson v. Lott, 5 Fla. 305 ; Allen v. Wheeler, 4 Gray, 123 ; Pilling v. Otis, 13 Wis. 495.

[4] Peck v. Land, 2 Kelly, 1.

[5] Smith v. Henry, 2 Bailey, 118.

Transfer of all.—The tendency *pro tanto* of every transfer that can be made by a debtor is to hinder and delay his creditors, for it diminishes the fund out of which they can enforce payment.[1] A transfer of all the property of the debtor not only diminishes the fund, but is not an ordinary transaction, and is therefore a badge of fraud.[2] *Dolus versatur in universalibus.*[3] Several distinct transfers not so closely connected as to constitute one transaction, is not within the rule.[4] As the universality of the transfer is merely a badge of fraud, the transfer will be good if made in good faith.[5] A transfer of all the debtor's property does not warrant the inference that the grantee is aware of the debtor's

---

[1] Peck v. Land, 2 Kelly, 1.

[2] Twynes' Case, 3 Co. 80; Hawkins v. Alston, 4 Dev. Eq. 137; Tubb v. Williams, 7 Humph. 367; Farmers' Bank v. Douglass, 11 S. & M. 469; Trimble v. Ratcliff, 9 B. Mon. 511; Bozman v. Draughan, 3 Stew. 243; Rollins v. Mooers, 25 Me. 192; Hord v. Rust, 4 Bibb. 231; Lewis v. Love, 2 B. Mon. 345; Venable v. Bank, 2 Pet. 107; Langford v. Fly, 7 Humph. 585; Hartshorne v. Eames, 31 Me. 93; Bean v. Smith, 2 Mason, 252; Harrison v. Campbell, 6 Dana, 263; Enders v. Swayne, 8 Dana, 103; Garland v. Rives, 4 Rand. 282; Pope v. Andrews, 1 S. & M. Ch. 135; Lillard v. McGee, 4 Bibb. 165; Mason v. Baker, 1 A. K. Marsh, 208; Beeler v. Bullitt, 3 A. K. Marsh, 280; Yoder v. Standiford, 7 Mon. 478; Glenn v. Glenn, 17 Iowa, 498; Vandall v. Vandall, 13 Iowa, 247; Adams v. Slater, 19 Ind. 418; Sarle v. Arnold, 7 R. I. 582; Monell v. Sherrick, 54 Ill. 269; Burke v. Murphy, 27 Miss. 167; Wheelden v. Wilson, 44 Me. 1; Bibb v. Baker, 17 B. Mon. 292; Leadman v. Harris, 3 Dev. 144; Kennedy v. Ross, 2 Mills Con. R. (s. c.) 125; Sayre v. Fredericks, 1 C. E. Green. 205; Chappel v. Clapp, 29 Iowa, 161; Clark v. Wise, 39 How. Pr. 97; Forsyth v. Matthews, 14 Penn. 100; Borland v. Walker, 7 Ala. 269; Barr v. Hatch, 3 Ohio, 527; Parsons v. McKnight, 8 N. H. 35; Borland v. Mayo, 8 Ala. 104; Delaware v. Ensign, 21 Barb. 85; Wilson v. Lott, 5 Fla. 305; Constantine v. Twelves, 29 Ala. 607; Meyer v. Simpson, 21 La. An. 591; Hutchinson v. Kelly, 1 Rob. 123; Oakover v. Pettus, Cas. Temp. Finch, 270; Blow v. Maynard, 2 Leigh, 29.

[3] Twyne's Case, 3 Co. 80.

[4] Preston v. Griffin, 1 Conn. 393; Scott v. Winship, 20 Geo. 429.

[5] Alton v. Harrison, L. R. 4 Ch. 662; Planters' Bank v. Borland, 5 Ala. 531; Borland v. Mayo, 8 Ala. 104; Dardenne v. Hardwicke, 9 Ark. 482.

insolvency.[1] *Dolus versatur in generalibus* is also a recognized maxim of the law.[2] Comprehensive generalities in a deed without any particular specifications are a badge of fraud.[3] Men engaged in real transactions do not commonly deal so loosely. A real purchaser is seldom content with anything short of a precise and unequivocal description.

EMBARRASSMENT.—As every transfer by a debtor tends to diminish the fund from which payment can be enforced, embarrassment and heavy indebtedness are badges of fraud.[4] Indebtedness alone does not, however, deprive a debtor of his dominion over his property. It

---

[1] Borland v. Mayo, 8 Ala. 104.

[2] Stone v. Grubbam, 2 Bulst. 217.

[3] Duvall v. Waters, 1 Bland, 567; s. c. 11 G. & J. 37; Delaware v. Ensign, 21 Barb. 85; Gardner v. McEwen, 19 N. Y. 123; Conkling v. Shelley, 28 N. Y. 360; McCain v. Wood, 4 Ala. 258; Lang v. Lee, 3 Rand. 410; Thompson v. Drake, 3 B. Mon. 565.

[4] Duvall v. Waters, 11 G. & J. 37; s. c. 1 Bland, 567; Durkee v. Mahoney, 1 Aik. 116; Tavenner v. Robinson, 2 Rob. 280; Borland v. Walker, 7 Ala. 269; McRea v. Branch Bank, 19 How. 376; Hudgins v. Kemp, 20 How. 45; Callan v. Statham, 23 How. 477; Chappel v. Clapp, 29 Iowa, 161; Borland v. Mayo, 8 Ala. 104; Gibbs v. Thompson, 7 Humph. 179; Comstock v. Rayford, 12 S. & M. 369; Sayres v. Fredericks, 1 C. E. Green, 205; Richards v. Swan, 7 Gill, 336; McNeal v. Glenn, 4 Md. 87; s. c. 3 Md. Ch. 349; Jackson v. Mather, 7 Cow. 301; Phettiplace, 4 Mason, 312; Borland v. Walker, 7 Ala. 269; Merrill v. Locke, 41 N. H. 486; Darden v. Skinner, 2 N. C. L. R. 279; Ringgold v. Waggoner, 14 Ark. 69; Walcott v. Almy, 6 McLean, 23; Barrow v. Bailey, 5 Fla. 9; Satterwhite v. Hicks, Busbee, 105; Overton v. Morris, 3 Port. 249; Planters' Bank v. Walker, 7 Ala. 926; Kinder v. Macy, 7 Cal. 206; Baker v. Bibb, 17 B. Mon. 292; Purkitt v. Black, 17 Cal. 327; Sheppard v. Iverson, 12 Ala. 97; Rollins v. Movers, 25 Me. 192, Blodgett v. Chaplin, 48 Me. 322; Glenn v. Glenn, 17 Iowa, 498; Hartshorne v. Eames, 31 Me. 93; Clark v. Depew, 25 Penn. 509; Harrison v. Campbell, 6 Dana, 263; Tubb v. Williams, 7 Humph. 367; Bulkley v. Buffington, 5 McLean, 457; Dick v. Grissom, 1 Freem. Ch. (Miss.) 428; Beeler v. Bullitt, 3 A. K. Marsh, 280; Enders v. Swayne, 8 Dana, 103; McConnell v. Brown, Litt. Sel. Cas. 459; Pope v. Andrews, 1 S. & M. Ch. 135.

is merely a circumstance that causes all his transactions to be scrutinized closely and carefully. In order to affect a vendee, moreover, the indebtedness must be known to him. Vendors generally are indebted, and if sales by an insolvent were void, a vendee would be compelled to obtain an abstract of his vendor's circumstances as well as of his title.[1]

PENDENCY OF SUIT.—The expectation,[2] or pendency of a suit is a badge of fraud, because a transfer tends to deprive the creditor of the means of enforcing his judgment when he obtains it.[3]

SECRECY.—Secrecy is a badge of fraud because it tends to deceive creditors, and is not in the course in which honest men commonly transact business. *Dona clandestina sunt suspiciosa.*[4] The secrecy which consti-

---

[1] Copis v. Middleton, 2 Madd. 410; Schultin v. Stone, 3 Barb. 634; s. c. 29 How. Pr. 355.

[2] Glenn v. Glenn, 17 Iowa, 498.

[3] Twyne's Case, 3 Co. 80; Merrill v. Locke, 41 N. H. 486; Satterwhite v. Hicks, Busbee, 105; Overton v. Morris, 3 Port. 249; Sheppard v. Iverson, 12 Ala. 97; Johnston v. Dick, 27 Miss. 277; Gibson v. Hill, 23 Tex. 77; Stewart v. Wilson, 42 Penn. 450; Hartshorne v. Eames, 31 Me. 93; Bean v. Smith, 2 Mason, 252; Venable v. Bank, 2 Pet. 107; Steele v. Parsons, 9 Mo. 823; Colquitt v. Thomas, 8 Geo. 258; Clark v. Depew, 25 Penn. 509; Lillard v. McGee, 4 Bibb. 165; Garland v. Rives, 4 Rand. 282; U. S. v. Lottridge, 1 McLean, 246; Thompson v. Drake, 3 B. Mon. 565; Beeler v. Bullitt, 3 A. K. Marsh, 280; Yoder v. Standiford, 7 Mon. 478; Adams v. Slater, 19 Ind. 418; Howard v. Crawford, 21 Tex. 399; Redfield Manuf. Co. v. Dysart, 62 Penn. 62; Godfrey v. Germaine, 4 Wis. 410; Babb v. Clemson, 10 S. & R. 419; Williams v. Lowndes, 1 Hall, 579; Thornton v. Davenport, 1 Scam. 296; Stoddard v. Butler, 20 Wend. 507; s. c. 7 Paige, 163; Jackson v. Mather, 7 Cow. 301; Schaferman v. O'Brien, 28 Md. 565; Streeper v. Eckart, 2 Whart. 302; Paulling v. Sturgus, 3 Stew. 95; Barr v. Hatch, 3 Ohio, 527; Callan v. Statham, 23 How. 477; Sayre v. Fredericks, 1 C. E. Green, 205; Smith v. Henry, 2 Bailey, 118; Forsyth v. Matthews, 14 Penn. 100; Peck v. Land, 2 Kelly, 1; Barr v. Hatch, 3 Ohio, 527.

[4] Twyne's Case, 3 Co. 80; Corlett v. Radcliffe, 14 Moore P. C. 121; McLachlan v. Wright, 3 Wend. 348; Burtus v. Tisdall, 4 Barb. 571; Darden

tutes a badge of fraud is not, however, a mere want of notoriety, but a concealment, or an attempted concealment.[1] It is not, moreover, conclusive proof,[2] and consequently an agreement by a vendee to conceal his purchase is merely evidence of fraud.[3] The declaration of an intention to make an assignment, may produce the mischief which the assignment is intended to prevent, and secrecy may, therefore, be used.[4]

CONCEALMENT.—A deed not at first fraudulent may become so by being concealed, because by its concealment persons may be induced to give credit to the grantor.[5] In such a case the use that is made of it relates back and shows the intent with which it was made.[6] The omission to place a deed on record,[7] or leaving it in the hands of the grantor,[8] or placing it in the hands of a third person to be produced or suppressed

---

v. Skinner, 2 N. C. L. R. 279; Shiveley v. Jones, 6 B. Mon. 274; Barrow v. Bailey, 5 Fla. 9; James v. Johnson, 22 La. An. 195; Stone v. Grubbam, 2 Bulst. 217; s. c. 1 Rol. Rep. 3; Woodham v. Baldock, Gow. 35, note; Vick v. Keys, 2 Hayw. 126; Warner v. Norton, 20 How. 448; Callan v. Slatham, 23 How. 477; Ross v. Crutsinger, 7 Mo. 245; King v. Moon, 42 Mo. 551; Delaware v. Ensign, 21 Barb. 85.

[1] Vick v. Keys, 2 Hay. (N. C.) 126.

[2] Stone v. Grubbam, 2 Bulst. 217; s. c. 1 Rol. Rep. 3.

[3] Gould v. Ward, 4 Pick. 103; s. c. 5 Pick. 291.

[4] Haven v. Richardson, 5 N. H. 113.

[5] Hungerford v. Earle, 2 Vern. 261; Sands v. Hildreth, 2 Johns. Ch. 35; s. c. 14 Johns. 493; Lewkner v. Freeman, 2 Freem. 236; s. c. Prec. Ch. 105; s. c. Eq. Cas. Abr. 149; Hilderbrun v. Brown, 17 B. Mon. 779; Tarback v. Marbury, 2 Vern. 510; Scrivinor v. Scrivinor, 7 B. Mon. 374.

[6] Worsely v. De Mattos, 1 Burr. 467; Constantine v. Twelves, 29 Ala. 607.

[7] Coates v. Gerlach, 44 Penn. 43; Hood v. Brown, 2 Ohio, 267; Scrivinor v. Scrivinor, 7 B. Mon. 374; Law v. Smith, 4 Ind. 56; Hodges v. Blount, 1 Hayw. 414; Bank of U. S. v. Houseman, 6 Paige, 526; Bank v. Gourdin, Speers Ch. 439; Gaither v. Mumford, 1 N. C. T. R. 167.

[8] Eveleigh v. Pursford, 2 Mood. & Rob. 439.

accordingly as exigencies may demand,[1] are instances of secrecy that are within the rule. If secrecy is a part of the consideration for securities obtained from a debtor who is about to abscond, it contaminates them, but if there is no such agreement, those who receive them need not apprise other creditors of his intention.[2]

SECRET TRUST.—A secret trust between the parties is a badge of fraud, for fraud is always apparelled and clad with a trust, and a trust is the cover of fraud. That which is called a trust *per nomen speciosum* as between the grantor and the grantee, is in truth as to all the creditors a fraud, for they are thereby defeated and defrauded.[3] An instrument which misrepresents the transaction that it recites is evidence of a secret trust, and is calculated to mislead and deceive creditors.[4] A false recital is therefore a badge of fraud. Erroneous recitals may however, and often do happen through mistake, inadvertence or carelessness and for this reason are not conclusive evidence of fraud.[5] In order to be conclusive there must be intentional disguise, dissembling or falsehood.[6] When, however, the true character and consideration of a transaction are not fairly and plainly stated, the instrument is open to suspicion, and the question arises whether in misrepresenting the transaction instead of stating the truth, there was not a design to mislead and deceive creditors,[7] but if upon inves-

---

[1] Brown v. McDonald, 1 Hill Ch. 297.

[2] Hafner v. Irwin, 1 Ired. 490.

[3] Twynes' Case, 3 Co. 80; Shaffer v. Watkins, 7 W. & S. 219; McCulloch v. Hutchinson, 7 Watts, 434.

[4] Kempner v. Churchill, 8 Wal. 362; Divver v. McLaughlin, 2 Wend. 596.

[5] Fetter v. Cirode, 4 B. Mon. 482.

[6] Barker v. French, 18 Vt. 460.

[7] McKinster v. Babcock, 26 N. Y. 378; Ingles v. Donalson, 2 Hay. (N. C.) 57.

tigation, the real transaction appears to be fair, though somewhat different from that which is described, it will be valid.[1]

ABSOLUTE DEEDS AS SECURITY.—Taking an absolute deed as a security for money is a mark of fraud, for it is calculated to deceive creditors, and to make them believe that no part of the property is subject to their demands, when in fact it is otherwise.[2] The right to redeem is an interest of value to him who has it, and to reserve it in such a way as leaves it altogether in confidence between the parties, and enables them to perform the trust as between themselves, and at their pleasure to deny its existence, and refuse its execution for the benefit of creditors, is plainly deceptive, and tends to delay, hinder and defraud creditors. It is however merely a badge, and not conclusive evidence of fraud.[3] In this respect there

---

[1] Shirras v. Craig, 7 Cranch. 34.

[2] Ingles v. Donalson, 2 Hay. (N. S.) 57; Gaither v. Mumford, 1 N. C. T. R. 167.

[3] Harrison v. Phillips Academy, 12 Mass. 456; Richards v. Allen, 8 Pick. 405; New England Ins. Co. v. Chandler, 16 Mass. 275; Reed v. Woodman, 4 Me. 400; Stevens v. Hinckley, 43 Me. 440; Gibson v. Seymour, 4 Vt. 518; Smith v. Onion, 19 Vt. 427; Rucker v. Abell, 8 B. Mon. 566; Gaffney v. Signaigo, 1 Dillon, 158; Gibbs v. Thompson, 7 Humph. 179; Bank v. Jacobs, 10 Mich. 349; Chickering v. Hatch, 3 Sumner, 474; Blair v. Bass, 4 Black, 539; Ingles v. Donalson, 2 Hay, (N. C.) 57; Reed v. Jewett, 5 Me. 96; Emmons v. Bradley, 56 Me. 333; Spaulding v. Austin, 2 Vt. 555; Oriental Bank v. Haskins, 3 Met. 332; Cutter v. Dickinson, 8 Pick. 386; Yoder v. Standiford, 7 Mon. 478; Wiley v. Lashlel, 8 Humph. 717; Fletcher v. Willard, 14 Pick. 464; contra, Winkley v. Hill, 9 N. H. 31; Towle v. Hoitt, 14 N. H. 61; Ladd v. Wiggins, 35 N. H. 421; Smith v. Lowell, 6 N. H. 67; Parker v. Pattee, 4 N. H. 176; Tift v. Walker, 10 N. H. 150; Boardman v. Cushing, 12 N. H. 105; McCulloch v. Hutchingson, 7 Watts, 434; Chenery v. Palmer, 6 Cal. 119; King v. Cantrel, 4 Ired. 251; Halcomb v. Ray, 1 Ired. 340; Gregory v. Perkins, 4 Dev. 50; Bryant v. Young, 21 Ala. 264; Hartshorn v. Williams, 31 Ala. 149; Hough v. Ives, 1 Root, 492; Benton v. Jones, 8 Conn. 186; North v. Belden, 13 Conn. 376; Neal v. Glenn, 4 Md. 87; s. c. 3 Md. Ch. 349; vide St. John v. Camp, 17 Conn. 222; Whitaker v. Sumner, 20 Pick. 399;

is no distinction between the conveyance of real and personal estate.[1] If however it appears that the grantee took an absolute conveyance, with a secret trust to hold the surplus for the use of the grantor, with the intention to prevent his creditors from resorting to it, the transfer will be void.[2] A mere understanding that the grantor may repurchase the property at some future time, by paying a sum equal to the original price, if made *bona fide*, is not fraudulent, whether it be by parol or in writing.[3] A note for an absolute sum may be taken to cover a liability as a surety.[4]

FALSE RECITALS.—A false statement of the consideration for a transfer tends to deceive creditors, and is a badge of fraud.[5] This is especially true in regard to a mortgage. Any discrepancy between the amount to be secured and, that which is in form set forth as the debt of the mortgagor is a badge of fraud.[6] If the statement is

---

Waters v. Riggin, 19 Md. 536. Where it is held to.be conclusive, it does not make the deed void as against subsequent creditors, Smyth v. Carlisle, 16 N. H. 464; s. c. 17 N. H. 417.

[7] Oriental Bank v. Haskins, 3 Met. 332.

[2] Barker v. French, 18 Vt. 460; Harrison v. Phillips Academy, 12 Mass. 456.

[3] Phettiplace v. Sayles, 4 Mason, 312; Barr v. Hatch, 3 Ohio, 527; Glenn v. Randall, 2 Md. Ch. 220; Anderson v. Fuller, 1 McMullan, Ch. 27.

[4] Prescott v. Hayes, 43 N. H. 593.

[5] Shirras v. Craig, 7 Cranch. 34; McKinster v. Babcock, 26 N. Y. 378; Gibbs v. Thompson, 7 Humph. 179; Bumpas v. Dotson, 7 Humph. 310; Miller v. Lockwood, 32 N. Y. 293; Peebles v. Horton, 64 N. C. 374; Foster v. Woodfin, 11 Ired. 339; McCaskle v. Amarine, 12 Ala. 17; Thompson v. Drake, 3 B. Mon. 565; Venable v. Bank, 2 Pet. 107; McElfatrick v. Hicks, 21 Penn. 402.

[6] Parker v. Barker, 2 Met. 423; Prince v. Sheppard, 9 Pick. 176; Bailey v. Burton, 8 Wend. 339; Miller v. Lockwood, 32 N. Y. 293; Stover v. Harrington, 7 Ala. 142; Lynde v. McGregor, 13 Allen, 172; Frost v. Warren, 42 N. Y. 204; Beeler v. Bullitt, 3 A. K. Marsh, 280; Tripp v. Vincent, 8 Paige, 176; Wilson v. Horr, 15 Iowa, 489; Wooley v. Fry, 30 Ill. 158;

intentionally false, it is an act of direct fraud, for no devices are more deceptive, and more calculated to baffle delay or defeat creditors, than the creation of incumbrances for debts that are fictitious, or mainly so.[1] A mortgage may, however, include debts due to others, which the mortgagee at the time gives his promise, whether by parol or in writing, to pay.[2] The taking of a judgment,[3] and the issuing of an execution,[4] for more than is due and the antedating of an instrument,[5] are marks of fraud.

INADEQUACY.—A vendee who purchases the property of an insolvent debtor for less than its value thereby deprives the creditors of the difference, and defeats their just expectations. Inadequacy of price thus tends to defraud them, and is a badge of fraud.[6] There is no

---

Foley v. Foley, 1 McCarter, 350; Davenport v. Cummings, 15 Iowa, 219; Ala. Ins. Co. v. Pettway, 24 Ala. 544; Weeden v. Hawes, 13 Conn. 50; Thompson v. Drake, 3 B. Mon. 565; Bumpas v. Dotson, 7 Humph. 310; vide Butts v. Peacock, 23 Wis. 359.

[1] Hawkins v. Alston, 4 Ired. Eq. 137; Marriott v. Givens, 8 Ala. 694.

[2] Carpenter v. Muren, 42 Barb. 300.

[3] Clark v. Douglass, 66 Penn. 408; Felton v. Wadsworth, 7 Cush. 587; Ayres v. Husted, 15 Conn. 504; Shedd v. Bank, 32 Vt. 709; Davenport v. Wright, 51 Penn. 292.

[4] Wilder v. Fondey, 4 Wend. 100; Harris v. Alcock, 10 G. & J. 226.

[5] Wright v. Hancock, 3 Munf. 521; Jones v. Henry, 3 Litt. 427; Lindle v. Neville, 13 S. & R. 227; Patterson v. Bodenhamer, 9 Ired. 96.

[6] Steere v. Hoagland, 39 Ill. 264; Sands v. Hildreth, 14 Johns. 493; s. c. 2 Johns. Ch. 35; Darden v. Skinner, 2 N. C. L. R. 279; Jessup v. Johnston, 3 Jones, (N. C.) 335; Gardiner Bank v. Wheaton, 8 Me. 373; Hamet v. Dundass, 4 Penn. 178; Crary v. Sprague, 12 Wend. 41; Yoder v. Standiford, 7 Mon. 478; Bowles v. Shoenberger, 2 B. Mon. 372; Hubbs v. Bancroft, 4 Ind. 388; Wright v. Stannard, 2 Brock. 311; Williams v. Cheeseborough, 4 Conn. 356; St. John v. Camp, 17 Conn. 222; Wells v. Thomas, 10 Mo. 237; Monell v. Sherrick, 54 Ill. 269; Williamson v. Goodwyn, 9 Gratt. 503; Tubb v. Williams, 7 Humph. 367; Sheppard v. Iverson, 12 Ala. 97; Trimble v. Ratcliffe, 9 B. Mon. 511; s. c. 12 B. Mon. 32; Merry v. Bostwick, 13 Ill. 398; Burke v. Murphy, 27 Miss. 167; Motley v. Sawyer, 38 Me. 68; Doughten v. Gray, 2 Stockt. 323; Taylor v. Moore, 2 Rand. 563; Bray v. Hussey, 24 Ind. 228; Blow v. May-

rule of law as to what disparity between the real value
of property and the consideration paid will in any case
constitute inadequacy of price, but this must be ascertained from the facts and circumstances of each particular case.[1] The value of a thing is what it will produce,
and admits of no precise standard. It must be in its
nature fluctuating and dependent on various circumstances. To justify an inference of fraud from the inadequacy of the price alone, the consideration must be so
clearly below the market value as to strike the understanding at once with the conviction that such a sale
never could have been made in good faith.[2] But when
circumstances exist raising a doubt of the fairness of the
transaction, the vendee must prove the payment of an
adequate consideration. The transaction is scrutinized
more closely and the same disparity is not required as
in controversies between the vendor and vendee.[3] A
fictitious consideration created by a purchase of articles
at high prices from the vendee is not sufficient.[4] The
pressure of circumstances may however, compel a debtor
to sell his property at a sacrifice for the purpose of meet-

---

nard, 2 Leigh. 29; Bay v. Cook, 31 Ill. 336; Smead v. Williamson, 16 B.
Mon. 492; Kinder v. Macy, 7 Cal. 206; Stanton v. Green, 34 Miss. 576;
Gibson v. Hill, 23 Tex. 77; Haney v. Nugent, 13 Wis. 283; Waterman v.
Donalson, 43 Ill. 29; Craver v. Miller, 65 Penn. 456; Tavenner v. Robinson;
2 Rob. 280; Hudgins v. Kemp. 20 How. 45; Callan v. Statham, 23 How.
477; Kempner v. Churchill, 8 Wal. 362; Borland v. Mayo, 8 Ala. 104;
Roach v. Deering, 9 S. & M. 316; Foster v. Pugh, 12 S. & M. 416; Wil-
liams v. Kelsey, 6 Geo. 365; Delaware v. Ensign, 21 Barb. 85.

[1] Barrow v. Bailey, 5 Fla. 9.

[2] Feigley v. Feigley, 7 Md. 537; Kempner v. Churchill, 8 Wal. 362;
Copis v. Middleton, 2 Madd. 410; Ratcliffe v. Trimble, 12 B. Mon. 32;
Borland v. Mayo, 8 Ala. 104; Prosser v. Henderson, 11 Ala. 484.

[3] Barrow v. Bailey, 5 Fla. 9; Seaman v. White, 8 Ala. 656; Bozman v.
Draughan, 3 Stew. 243; Bryant v. Kelton, 1 Tex. 415; Kuykendall v.
Hitchcock, 15 Mo. 416; State v. Evans, 38 Mo. 150.

[4] Reed v. Carl, 3 S. & M. 74.

ing his liabilities, and in such instances a sale for less than the real value is not unusual and does not indicate an impure intention.[1]

EXCESS IN MORTGAGE.—A mortgage interposes an obstacle between creditors and the property of the debtor, and tends to embarrass them in their attempts to realize their claims, and thus hinder and delay them in their efforts to obtain satisfaction. If it includes an excess above what is fairly necessary to secure the mortgage debt it is therefore a circumstance of fraud.[2] A mortgagee is entitled to property of value fully sufficient to cover his demand under any and all contingencies that may be expected, or reasonably apprehended, but the debtor can not, under the pretense of securing a debt, convey much more than is necessary for that purpose, and really with the intent to secure the use to himself and baffle his creditors. Hence the question is always one of intention.[3]

DURATION OF MORTGAGE.—The time which a mortgage has to run is a circumstance to be taken into consideration in determining the fairness of the transaction. If all or a greater portion of the debtor's property is included in the assurance, and if the value is greatly or considerably beyond the amount of the debt secured, the period of indulgence to the debtor is important to

---

[1] Hubbs v. Bancroft, 4 Ind. 388 ; Hale v. Saloon Omnibus Co. 4 Drew, 492.

[2] Bailey v. Burton, 8 Wend. 339; Hawkins v. Allston, 4 Ired. Eq. 137 ; Adams v. Wheeler, 10 Pick. 199; Bennett v. Union Bank, 5 Humph. 612; Mitchell v. Beal, 8 Yerg. 134; Wright v. Hancock, 3 Munf. 521 ; Ford v. Williams, 13 N. Y. 577 ; Davis v. Ransom, 18 Ill. 396 ; Jewett v. Warren, 10 Mass. 300 ; Hickman v. Perrin, 6 Cold. 135 ; *vide* Downs v. Kissam, 10 How. 12 ; Bank of Georgia v. Higginbottom, 9 Pet. 48.

[3] Burgin v. Burgin, 1 Ired. 453.

the creditors, because to the surplus beyond the mortgagee's claims they must look for the satisfaction of their demands. The evidence of a fraudulent purpose is greater in proportion as the excess in value is increased, and the time of indulgence prolonged.[1]

UNUSUAL CREDIT.—Creditors are entitled to sell the property of the debtor for the satisfaction of their demands, according to the mode and terms prescribed by the law, and any expedient adopted by the debtor with the clear intent to prevent that, is fraudulent. It is a hindrance and delay within the meaning of the statute. A sale of his property upon a long and unusual credit has a tendency to delay and hinder creditors, by interposing a legal title between them and the debtor's estate, and compelling them to wait for the expiration of the credit and consequently is a badge of fraud.[2] A sale upon credit may be good, for there is no principle of the law that prevents the debtor from selling on credit, if thereby he is able to obtain a better price,[3] but if the debtor is insolvent, and his intent is to coerce his credit-

---

[1] Bennett v. Union Bank, 5 Humph. 612; Bigelow v. Stringer, 40 Mo. 195; Reynolds v. Crook, 31 Ala. 634; Mitchell v. Beal, 8 Yerg. 134; Farmers' Bank v. Douglass, 11 S. & M. 469; Lewis v. Caperton, 8 Gratt. 148; Montgomery v. Kirksey, 26 Ala. 172; Wiley v. Knight, 27 Ala. 336; Potter v. McDowell, 31 Mo. 62; Henderson v. Downing, 24 Miss. 106; Davis v. Ransom, 18 Ill. 396; Roane v. Bank, 1 Head. 526; Brinley v. Spring, 7 Me. 241.

[2] Tubb v. Williams, 7 Humph. 367; Mills v. Carnley, 1 Bosw. 159; Stanton v. Green, 34 Miss. 576; Baker v. Bibb, 17 B. Mon. 292; Potter v. McDowell, 31 Mo. 62; Gillett v. Phelps, 12 Wis. 392; Pilling v. Otis, 13 Wis. 495; Clark v. Wise, 39 How. Pr. 97; Blodgett v. Chaplin, 48 Me. 322; Ruhl v. Phillips, 2 Daly, 45; Dewey v. Littlejohn, 2 Ired. Eq. 495; Borland v. Mayo, 8 Ala. 104; Roberts v. Shepard, 2 Daly, 110.

[3] Starr v. Strong, 2 Sandf. Ch. 139; Scheitlin v. Stone, 43 Barb. 634; s. c. 29 How. Pr. 355; Pattison v. Stewart, 6 W. & S. 72; McCasland v. Carson, 1 Head. 117; Loeschigk v. Bridge, 42 Barb. 171; s. c. 42 N. Y. 421; Ocole Bank v. Nelson, 1 Cold. 186.

ors to accept notes drawn for a long time, or keep them
at bay until the time of credit expires, the purpose is
fraudulent.[1]　This is especially true when the sale is not
in the continuation of the debtor's business, with an
honest effort to retrieve his fortunes, but is made as an
abandonment of his business, and a relinquishment of
all hope of future success.[2]

PERISHABLE ARTICLES.—If a mortgage or deed of trust
includes perishable articles, or articles consumable in
their use, it is a badge of fraud, for it raises a presumption of a secret trust for the care and favor of the debtor.[3]
It is for the same reason a mark of fraud if the debtor
sell chattels which are subject to a mortgage and converts the avails to his own use.[4]

POSSESSION OF LAND.—The retention of the possession
of land, and the exercise of unequivocal acts of ownership
over it, is a badge of fraud, for it is not in the usual course
of business, and indicates a secret trust for the benefit of
the debtor.[5]　The acts of ownership by the debtor may

---

[1] Kepner v. Burkhart, 5 Penn. 478; Pope v. Andrews, 1 S. & M. Ch.
135; How v. Camp, Walker Ch. 427; Owen v. Arvis, 2 Dutch. 22; Browning v. Hart, 6 Barb. 91; Wash v. Medley, 1 Dana. 269; Borland v.
Walker, 7 Ala. 269; Cooke v. Smith, 3 Sandf.Ch. 333; Downing v. Kelley,
49 Barb. 547.

[2] Nesbitt v. Digby, 13 Ill. 387.

[3] Elmes v. Sutherland, 7 Ala. 262; Hunter v. Foster, 4 Humph. 211;
Harney v. Pack, 4 S. & M. 229; Farmers' Bank v. Douglass, 11 S. & M. 469;
Potter v. McDowell, 31 Mo. 62; Darwin v. Handley, 3 Yerg. 502; Simpson
v. Mitchell, 8 Yerg. 417; Richmond v. Curdup, Meigs. 581; Planters' &
Merchants' Bank v. Clark, 7 Ala. 765; Ewing v. Cargill, 13 S. & M. 79; Shurt-
leff v. Willard, 19 Pick. 202; Ravisies v. Alston, 5 Ala. 297; Googins v.
Gilmore, 47 Me. 9.

[4] Dickenson v. Cook, 17 Johns. 332; McNeal v. Glenn, 4 Md. 87; s. c.
3 Md. Ch. 349; Park v. Harrison, 8 Humph. 412.

[5] Duvall v. Waters, 1 Bland. 567; s. c. 11 G. & J. 37; McNeal v.
Glenn, 4 Md. 87; s. c. Md. Ch. 349; Jackson v. Mather, 7 Cow. 301;

consist either in renting,[1] or collecting rents,[2] or giving receipts for rent in his own name[3] or directing the making of leases,[4] or making sales of the land, even though he acts under a power of attorney from the grantee,[5] or selling timber,[6] or paying ground rent,[7] or paying taxes,[8] or making improvements,[9] or driving the grantee off the land.[10] The grantee may make a *bona fide* lease to

---

Avery v. Street, 6 Watts, 247; Borland v. Walker, 7 Ala. 269; Starr v. Starr, 1 Ohio, 321; Callan v. Statham, 23 How. 477; Gibbs v. Thompson, 7 Humph. 179; Roach v. Deering, 9 S. & M. 316; King v. Moon, 42 Mo. 551; Halbert v. Grant, 4 Mon. 580; Yoder v. Standiford, 7 Mon. 478; How v. Camp, Walker Ch. 278; Brown v. McDonald, 1 Hill Ch. 297; Dick v. Grissom, Freem. Ch. (Miss.) 428; Williamson v. Goodwyn, 9 Grat. 503; Darden v. Skinner, 2 N. C. L. R. 279; Dewey v. Littlejohn, 2 Ired. Eq. 495; Trimble v. Ratcliffe, 9 B. Mon. 511; Johnston v. Dick, 27 Miss. 277; Steele v. Ward, 25 Iowa, 535; Planters' Bank v. Walker, 7 Ala. 926; Rollins v. Mooers, 25 Me. 192; Ringgold v. Waggoner, 14 Ark. 69; Stanton v. Green, 34 Miss. 576; Knox v. Hunt, 34 Miss. 655; Hartshorne v. Eames, 31 Me. 93; Middleton v. Sinclair, 5 Cranch. C. C. 409; Farnsworth v. Bell, 5 Sneed. 531; Purkitt v. Polack, 17 Cal. 327; Sarle v. Arnold, 7 R. I. 582; Clark v. Johnston, 5 Day, 373; Lillard v. McGee, 4 Bibb. 165; U. S. v. Lottridge, 1 McLean, 246; Lewis v. Love, 2 B. Mon. 345; Venable v. Bank, 2 Pet. 107.

[1] Duvall v. Waters, 1 Bland. 567; s. c. 11 G. & J. 37; Callan v. Stathan, 23 How. 477.

[2] Sands v. Hildreth, 14 Johns. 493; s. c. 2 Johns. Ch. 35; Lee v. Hunter, 1 Paige, 519; Lewis v. Love, 2 B. Mon. 345; Wisner v. Farnham, 2 Mich. 472; Walcott v. Almy, 6 McLean, 23; How v. Camp, Walker Ch. 427; Schaferman v. O'Brien, 28 Md. 565.

[3] Duvall v. Waters, 1 Bland. 567; Callan v. Stratham, 23 How. 477.

[4] Schaferman v. O'Brien, 28 Md. 565.

[5] Starr v. Starr, 1 Ohio, 321; Gibbs v. Thompson, 7 Humph. 179; Stanton v. Green, 34 Miss. 576; Glenn v. Glenn, 17 Iowa, 498.

[6] Duvall v. Waters, 1 Bland. 567; s. c. 11 G. & J. 37.

[7] Schaferman v. O'Brien, 28 Md. 565.

[8] Stanton v. Green, 34 Miss. 576; Knox v. Hunt, 34 Miss. 655; Jacks v. Tunno, 3 Des. 1; Sands v. Codwise, 4 Johns. 536; Haskell v. Bakewel l 10 B. Mon. 106; Hutchinson v. Kelly, 1 Rob. 123.

[9] Sands v. Hildreth, 14 Johns. 493; s. c. 2 Johns. Ch. 35; Merry v. Bostwick, 13 Ill. 398; Marshall v. Green, 24 Ark. 410; Gibbs v. Thompson, 7 Humph. 179; Tappan v. Butler, 7 Bosw. 480.

[10] Duvall v. Waters, 1 Bland. 567; s. c. 11 G. & J. 37.

the debtor,[1] but any act which is out of the usual course
in the transaction, such as a nominal rent,[2] or the non-
enforcement of payment of the rent,[3] or an excessive
rent,[4] or any indefiniteness in the character, terms or
length of the tenancy,[5] is a mark of fraud. Executing
a mortgage to secure the grantor's debts,[6] or making
a reconveyance of part for a nominal consideration,[7]
or taking no steps for a long time to foreclose a pretended mortgage,[8] or selling to the debtor's son,[9] or
permitting the grantor to retain possession for a long
time,[10] is a badge of fraud.

OUT OF THE USUAL COURSE.—Anything out of the
usual course of business is a sign of fraud.[11] Unusual
clauses in an instrument excite suspicion. *Clausulæ in-
consuetæ semper inducunt suspicionem.*[12] The same principle applies to the absence of accounts between the parties, when the transfer purports to be in consideration
of a debt due to the grantee,[13] to the retention of the

---

[1] Glenn v. Grover, 3 Md. 212; s. c. 3 Md. Ch. 29; Gardiner Bank v.
Hogdon, 14 Me. 453; Barr v. Hatch, 3 Ohio, 527; Wood v. Shaw, 29 Ill. 444.

[2] Yoder v. Standiford, 7 Mon. 478; Durkee v. Mahoney, 1 Aik. 116;
Bank v. Fink, 7 Paige, 87; Gibbs v. Thompson, 7 Humph. 179.

[3] Bank v. Fink, 7 Paige, 87; Reed v. Blades, 5 Taunt. 212.

[4] Hitchcock v. St. John, Hoff. Ch. 511.

[5] Dick v. Grisson, Freem. Ch. (Miss.) 428.

[6] Schaferman v. O'Brien, 28 Md. 565; Bank of U. S. v. Houseman, 6
Paige, 526; Jacks v. Tunno, 3 Des. 1; Hudgins v. Kemp, 20 How. 45.

[7] Gibbs v. Thompson, 7 Humph. 179.

[8] Gibbs v. Thompson, 7 Humph. 179.

[9] Phittiplace v. Sayles, 4 Mason, 312.

[10] McIntosh v. Bethune, 8 Ired. 139; Bank v. Fink, 7 Paige, 87.

[11] Danjean v. Blacketer, 13 La. An. 595.

[12] Twynes' Case, 3 Co. 80; Harrison v. Campbell, 6 Dana, 263; Langford v. Fly, 7 Humph. 585.

[13] McDowell v. Goldsmith, 6 Md. 319; s. c. 2 Md. Ch. 370; Wil-
liams v. Cheeseborough, 4 Conn. 356; Enders v. Swayne, 8 Dana, 103;
Basey v. Daniel, 1 Smith, 252; Wheelden v. Wilson, 44 Me. 1; Haney v.
Nugent, 13 Wis. 283; Dick v. Grissom, Freem. Ch. (Miss.) 428.

deed,[1] or the mortgage note,[2] by the debtor, to the omission to execute the mortgage note at the same time with the mortgage,[3] to any alteration of a mortgage note,[4] to the alienation of valuable property without payment or security,[5] to the purchase of property for which the grantee has no use,[6] to the grantee's entrances into a business foreign to his own,[7] to the grantee's pecuniary inability to make the purchase,[8] to the grantee's failure to pay taxes,[9] to an immediate transfer to another, in consideration of property conveyed to the debtor's wife,[10] to the absence of pressure by a preferred creditor,[11] to the absence of competition at a public sale,[12] to the vendee's

---

[1] Hungerford v. Earle, 2 Vern. 261; Tarback v. Marbury, 2 Vern. 510; Starr v. Starr, 1 Ohio, 321.

[2] Bullock v. Narrott, 49 Ill. 62.

[3] Prior v. White, 12 Ill. 261.

[4] Merrill v. Williamson, 35 Ill. 529.

[5] Duvall v. Waters, 1 Bland, 567; s. c. 11 G. & J. 37; Hendricks v. Robinson, 2 Johns. Ch. 283; s. c. 17 Johns. 438; Pope v. Andrews, 1 S. & M. Ch. 135; Smead v. Williamson, 16 B. Mon. 492; Owen v. Arvis, 2 Dutch. 22; Seymour v. Lewis, 2 Beasley, 439; Glenn v. Glenn, 17 Iowa, 498.

[6] Grubbs v. Greer, 5 Cold. 160.

[7] Boies v. Henney, 32 Ill. 130.

[8] Sands v. Codwise, 4 Johns. 536; Railroad Co. v. Kyle, 5 Bosw. 587; Jessup v. Johnston, 3 Jones (N. C.), 335; Overton v. Morris, 3 Port. 249; Bredin v. Bredin, 3 Penn. 81; Pope v. Andrews. 1 S. & M. Ch. 135; Enders v. Swayne, 8 Dana, 103; Venable v. Bank, 2 Pet. 107; McIlvoy v. Kennedy, 2 Bibb. 380; McLean v. Morgan, 5 B. Mon. 282; Gordon v. Lowell, 21 Me. 251; Van Winkle v. Smith, 26 Miss. 491; Johnston v. Dick, 27 Miss. 277; Ringgold v. Waggoner, 14 Ark. 69; Smead v. Williamson, 16 B. Mon. 492; Owen v. Arvis, 2 Dutch. 22; Farnsworth v. Bell, 5 Sneed, 531; Seymour v. Lewis, 2 Beasley, 439; Glenn v. Glenn, 17 Iowa, 498; James v. Johnston, 22 La. An. 195; Graham v. Smith, 25 Penn. 323; vide Andrews v. Jones, 10 Ala. 400.

[9] Bulkley v. Buffington, 5 McLean, 457.

[10] Newman v. Cordell, 43 Barb. 448.

[11] Eveleigh v. Purrsford, 2 Mood. & Rob. 539; Leadman v. Harris, 3 Deo. 144; Kennedy v. Ross, 2 Mills, Con. (S. C.) 125.

[12] Tavenner v. Robinson, 2 Rob. 280.

declaration that he is purchasing for the debtor,[1] to the confession of a judgment and the issuing of an execution on the same day,[2] to the grantor's concealment of property,[3] or flight,[4] to an indemnity for sureties whose liabilities are remote and depend upon a contingency,[5] to inconsistent statements,[6] and to other fraudulent transactions between the same parties.[7] The execution of a deed in the absence of the grantee,[8] and the delivery of the deed by the debtor to the recorder, are not marks of fraud.[9] A written transfer of personal property is merely a suspicious circumstance.[10]

UNUSUAL MODE OF PAYMENT.—Whatever is out of the ordinary course in the mode, manner, or time of the payment of the alleged consideration is a mark of fraud. Precision and formality,[11] the pains taken to invite witnesses to see the sale made, and the bantering and negotiation about the price,[12] cautioning them to pay attention and recollect what they hear,[13] telling them that the

---

[1] Tavenner v. Robinson, 2 Rob. 280.

[2] Floyd v. Goodwin, 8 Yerg. 484.

[3] Avery v. Street, 6 Watts, 247; Comstock v. Rayford, 12 S. & M. 369.

[4] Rogers v. Hall, 4 Watts, 359; Wright v. Hancock, 3 Munf. 521; Fougeres v. Zacharie, 5 J. J. Marsh, 504; Kittering v. Parker, 8 Ind. 44; Danjean v. Blacketer, 13 La. An. 595.

[5] Harney v. Pack, 4 S. & M. 229.

[6] Dalton v. Mitchell, 4 J. J. Marsh, 372; Fougeres v. Zacharie, 5 J. J. Marsh. 504; Marshall v. Green, 24 Ark. 410; vide Kane v. Drake, 27 Ind. 29.

[7] Bumpas v. Dotson, 7 Humph. 310.

[8] McLean v. Lafayette Bank, 3 McLean, 587.

[9] Ward v. Wehman, 27 Iowa, 279.

[10] Forsyth v. Matthews, 14 Penn. 100; McQuinnay v. Hitchcock, 8 Tex. 33; Kane v. Drake, 27 Ind. 29.

[11] Hartshorne v. Eames, 31 Me. 93.

[12] Goldsbury v. May, 1 Litt. 254.

[13] Adams v. Davidson, 10 N. Y. 309.

transaction is fair,[1] a parade of payment in the presence of witnesses,[2] are signs of fraud, for when a part is over-acted the delusion is broken and the fiction appears. The facility with which a fictitious payment may be fabricated renders it necessary for the grantee to produce all the proof which may reasonably be supposed to be in his power of the reality and fairness of the transaction,[3] and the want of clear proof is evidence of fraud.[4] Such proof is vital to uphold a transfer in other respects surrounded with suspicion,[5] and this require-ment is not met by the mere production of notes and receipts,[6] or the mere proof of payment without any at-tempt to show where the money came from,[7] how it was obtained or whose it was,[8] or what was done with it.[9]

ABSENCE OF EVIDENCE.—The omission of the grantee to testify or to produce the debtor or any other impor-tant witness, is the ground for an unfavorable presump-tion, and frequently exercises an important influence

---

[1] Comstock v. Rayford, 12 S. & M. 369.

[2] King v. Moon, 42 Mo. 551.

[3] Hunt v. Blodgett, 17 Ill. 583 ; Vandall v. Vandall, 13 Iowa, 247 ; Godfrey v. Germain, 24 Wis. 410.

[4] Duvall v. Waters, 1 Bl. 567 ; s. c. 11 G. & J. 37 ; Dorn v. Bayer, 16 Md. 144 ; Schaferman v. O'Brien, 28 Md. 565 ; Callan v. Statham, 23 How. 477 ; Robbins v. Parker, 3 Met. 117 ; Sands v. Hildreth, 14 Johns. 493 ; s. c. 2 Johns. Ch. 35 ; Brady v. Briscoe, 2 J. J. Marsh, 212 ; Harrison v. Campbell, 6 Dana, 263 ; Purkitt v. Polack, 17 Cal. 327 ; Allen v. Bonnett, L. R. 5 Ch. 577 ; Enders v. Swayne, 8 Dana, 103 ; Venable v. Bank, 2 Pet. 107 ; Jones v. Read, 3 Dana, 540.

[5] Callan v. Statham, 23 How. 477 ; Gibbs v. Thompson, 7 Humph. 179 ; King v. Moon, 42 Mo. 551.

[6] Fulmore v. Burrows, 2 Rich. Eq. 95.

[7] King v. Moon, 42 Mo. 551.

[8] Jackson v. Mather, 7 Cow. 301 ; King v. Moon, 42 Mo. 551.

[9] King v. Moon, 42 Mo. 551.

upon the final determination of the question of fraud.[1]
Want of preciseness as to dates, time and amount in their
testimony when produced excites suspicion, for the facts
occurring in a suspicious transaction would naturally
make an impression which would not be effaced from
the memory very soon and the testimony, if the transfer is recent, should be clear, accurate and specific.[2]

RELATIONSHIP.—Relationship is not a badge of fraud.[3]
Fraud, however, is generally accompanied with a secret
trust, and hence the debtor must usually select a
person in whom he can repose a secret confidence.
The sentiments of affection commonly generate this
confidence, and often prompt relatives to provide for
each other at the expense of just creditors. They are
the persons with whom a secret trust is likely to exist.
The same principle applies to all persons with whom the
debtor has a confidential relation. Any relation which
gives rise to confidence, though not a badge of fraud
strengthens the presumption that may arise from other
circumstances, and serves to elucidate, explain, or give
color to the transaction.[4] The doctrine applies to the

---

[1] Hale v. Saloon Omnibus Co. 4 Drew. 492; s. c. 28 L. J. Ch. 777;
Graham v. Furber, 78 E. C. L. 410; s. c. 14 C. B. 410; *in re* Hussman,
2 B. R. 140; Blaisdell v. Cowell, 14 Me. 370; Glenn v. Glenn, 17 Iowa,
498; Cox v. Shropshire, 25 Tex. 113; Newman v. Cordell, 43 Barb. 448;
Peebles v. Horton, 64 N. C. 374; *vide* Devries v. Phillips, 63 N. C. 53.

[2] Newman v. Cordell, 43 Barb. 448.

[3] Copis v. Middleton, 2 Madd. 410; Merrill v. Locke, 41 N. H. 486;
Sterling v. Ripley, 3 Chand. 166; Wrightman v. Hart, 37 Ill. 123; Dunlap
v. Bournonville, 26 Penn. 72; Bumpas v. Dotson, 7 Humph. 310; Wilson
v. Lott, 5 Fla. 305; Montgomery v. Kirksey, 26 Ala. 172; Kane v. Drake,
27 Ind. 29; Hempstead v. Johnston, 18 Ark. 123.

[4] Brady v. Briscoe, 2 J. J. Marsh, 212; Wilson v. Lott, 5 Fla. 305;
Montgomery v. Kirksey, 26 Ala. 172; Hanford v. Artcher, 4 Hill, 271;
s. c. 1 Hill, 347; Bumpas v. Dotson, 7 Humph. 310.

relationship of father,[1] mother,[2] father-in-law,[3] mother-in-law,[4] uncle,[5] brother,[6] sister,[7] brother-in-law,[8] sister-in-

[1] Hartshorn v. Eames, 31 Me. 93; McIntosh v. Bethune, 8 Ired. 139; Poague v. Boyce, 6 J. J. Marsh, 70; Wheelden v. Wilson, 44 Me. 1; Vandall v. Vandall, 13 Iowa, 247; Weaver v. Wright, 13 Rich. 9; Slattery v. Stewart, 45 Ill. 293; Forsyth v. Matthews, 14 Penn. 100; Scrivenor v. Scrivenor, 7 B. Mon. 374; Walter v. McNabb, 1 Heisk, 703.

[2] Lloyd v. Williams, 21 Penn. 327; Splawn v. Martin, 17 Ark. 146; Gardinier v. Otis, 13 Wis. 460; Coley v. Coley, 1 McCarter, 350; Sporrer v. Eifler, 1 Heisk, 633.

[3] Borland v. Walker, 7 Ala. 269; Railroad Co. v. Kyle, 5 Bosw. 587; Bozman v. Draughan, 3 Stew. 243; Seymour v. Lewis, 2 Beasley, 439; Wilson v. Horr, 15 Iowa, 489; Crawford v. Carper, 4 W. 'Va. 56; Planters' Bank v. Walker, 7 Ala. 926; Gordon v. Lowell, 21 Me. 251; Borland v. Mayo, 8 Ala. 104.

[4] Harrison v. Campbell, 6 Dana, 263; Watson v. Kennedy, 3 Strobh. Eq. 1; Wilson v. Lott, 3 Fla. 305.

[5] Felton v. White, 4 Jones (N. C.), 301; Wightman v. Hart, 37 Ill. 123; Demarest v. Terhune, 3 C. E. Green, 45; Waterman v. Donalson, 43 Ill. 29.

[6] Hudgins v. Kemp, 20 How. 45; Callan v. Statham, 23 How. 477; King v. Moon, 42 Mo. 551; Chappel v. Clapp, 29 Iowa, 161; Green v. Tantum, 4 C. E. Green, 105; Redfield Manf. Co. v. Dysart, 62; Penn. 62; Dewey v. Littlejohn, 2 Ired. Eq. 495; Hawkins v. Alston, 4 Ired. Eq. 137; Bredin v. Bredin, 3 Penn. 81; Millett v. Pottinger, 4 Met. (Ky.) 213; Smit v. People, 15 Mich. 497; Foster v. Grigsby, 1 Bush, 86; Pope v. Andrews, 1 S. & M. Ch. 135; Enders v. Swayne, 8 Dana, 103; How v. Camp, Walker Ch. 427; Nesbitt v. Digby, 13 Ill. 387; Wisner v. Farnham, 2 Mich. 472; Johnston v. Dick, 27 Miss. 277; Craver v. Miller, 65 Penn. 456; Reed v. Carl, 3 S. & M. 74; Steele v. Parsons, 9 Mo. 823; James v. Johnston, 22 La. An. 195.

[7] McRea v. Branch Bank, 19 How. 376; Kaine v. Weigley, 22 Penn. 179; Copenheaver v. Huffacker, 6 B. Mon. 18; Sayre v. Fredericks, 1 C. E. Green, 205; Sporrer v. Eifler, 1 Heisk, 633.

[8] Schaferman v. O'Brien, 28 Md. 565; Merrill v. Locke, 41 N. H. 485; Jackson v. Brush, 20 Johns. 5; Copenheaver v. Huffacker, 6 B. Mon. 18; Tubb v. Williams, 7 Humph. 367; Farmers' Bank v. Douglass, 11 S. & M. 469; Burtus v. Tisdall, 4 Barb. 571; Satterwhite v. Hicks, Busbee, 105; Planters' Bank v. Walker, 7 Ala. 926; Wilson v. Butler, 3 Munf. 559; Dalton v. Mitchell, 4 J. J. Marsh, 372; Venable v. Bank, 2 Pet. 107; Kaine v. Weigley, 22 Penn. 179; Steele v. Ward, 25 Iowa, 535; Steere v. Hoagland, 39 Ill. 264; Gibbs v. Thompson, 7 Humph. 179; Barrow v. Bailey, 5 Fla. 9; Bray v. Hussey, 24 Ind. 228; Burke v. Murphy, 27 Miss. 167; Bulkley v. Buffington, 5 McLean, 457; Hunt v. Knox, 34 Miss. 655; Sayre v. Fredericks, 1 C. E. Green, 205.

law,[1] son,[2] daughter,[3] son-in-law,[4] cousin,[5] nephew,[6] step-son,[7] grandson,[8] partner,[9] and confidential friend,[10] or agent.[11] Wherever this confidential relation is shown to exist, the parties are held to a fuller and stricter proof of the consideration,[12] and of the fairness of the transaction.[13]

---

[1] Smith v. Henry, 2 Bailey, 118; s. c. 1 Hill, 16; Young v. Stallings, 5 B. Mon. 307; Walcott v. Almy, 6 McLean, 23.

[2] Duvall v. Waters, 1 Bland, 567; s. c. 11 G. & J. 37; Farnsworth v. Bell, 5 Sneed, 531; Gibson v. Hill, 23 Tex. 77; Glenn v. Glenn, 17 Iowa, 498; Trimble v. Ratcliff, 9 B. Mon. 511; Ringgold v. Waggoner, 14 Ark. 69; Law v. Smith, 4 Ind. 56; Jones v. Read, 3 Dawa. 335; Shiveley v. Jones, 6 B. Mon. 274; Sheppard v. Iverson, 12 Ala. 97; Basey v. Daniel, 1 Smith, 252; Dick v. Grissom, 1 Freem. Ch. 428; Halbert v. Grant, 4 Mon. 580; Brady v. Briscoe, 2 J. J. Marsh, 212; Middleton v. Sinclair, 5 Cranch C. C. 409; Bean v. Smith, 2 Mason, 252; Sands v. Codwise, 4 Johns. 536; Jessup v. Johnston, 8 Jones (N. C.), 335; Carter v. Carpenter, 7 Bush, 257; Sheppard v. Iverson, 12 Ala. 97; Tripp v. Childs, 14 Barb. 85; Lewis v. Love, 2 B. Mon. 345; Jackson v. Spivey, 63 N. C. 261; Chappel v. Clapp, 29 Iowa, 161.

[3] Foster v. Woodfin, 11 Ired. 339; Haney v. Nugent, 13 Wis. 283; Marshall v. Green, 24 Ark. 410; Parsons v. McKnight, 8 N. H. 35; O'Connor v. Bernard, 2 Jo. 654; Clairborne v. Goss, 7 Leigh, 331.

[4] Duvall v. Waters, 1 Bland, 567; s. c. 11 G. & J. 37; Black v. Cadwell, 4 Jones (N. C.), 150; Rollins v. Mooers, 25 Me. 192; Garland v. Rives, 4 Rand, 282; Merry v. Bostwick, 13 Ill. 398; Hook v. Mowre, 17 Iowa, 195; Jackson v. Mather, 7 Cow. 301.

[5] Blodgett v. Chaplin, 48 Me. 322; Nelson v. Smith, 28 Ill. 495.

[6] Phettiplace v. Sayles, 4 Mason, 312; Copis v. Middleton, 2 Madd. 410; Langford v. Fly, 7 Humph. 585; Bibb v. Baker, 17 B. Mon. 292; Davis v. Gibbon, 24 Iowa, 257.

[7] Marlow v. Orgill, 8 Jur. (N. S.) 829.

[8] Smith v. Daniel, 1 Smith, 252; Bayze v. Daniel, 1 Ind. 378.

[9] Thompson v. Drake, 3 B. Mon. 565; Strong v. Hines, 35 Miss. 201.

[10] Gibbs v. Thompson, 7 Humph. 179; Yoder v. Standiford, 7 Mon. 478; Wells v. Thomas, 10 Mo. 237; Paxton v. Boyce, 1 Tex. 317.

[11] Clark v. French, 23 Me. 221; Cooke v. Smith, 3 Sandf. Ch. 333; Smead v. Williamson, 16 B. Mon. 492; Kinder v. Macy, 7 Cal. 206; Stanton v. Green, 34 Miss. 576; Bridge v. Loeschigk. 42 N. Y. 421.

[12] Dick v. Grissom, 1 Freem. Ch. (Miss.) 428; Hawkins v. Alston, 4 Ired. Eq. 137; Satterwhite v. Hicks, Busbee, 105; Brady v. Briscoe, 2 J. Marsh, 212; Brice v. Meyers, 5 Ohio, 121.

[13] Jenkins v. Pearce, 1 Jones (N. C.), 413; Black v. Cadwell, 4 Jones (N. C.), 150; Bowman v. Houdlette, 18 Me. 245; Lloyd v. Williams, 21 Penn. 327.

DELAY.—Mortgages and deeds of trust encumber the property which they cover, and thus in many instances embarrass the grantor's creditors in their efforts to subject it to the payment of their demands. If such instruments, however, are executed in good faith, the delay and hindrance that are merely incidental to the accomplishment of the object which the parties have in view or arise merely from a desire to have the property when sold bring the best price that can reasonably be obtained, under all the circumstances or result from a subsequent reluctance on the part of the mortgagee or trustee to embarrass, oppress or ruin the grantor, will not invalidate them or constitute a just ground of complaint on the part of creditors. A deed of trust or mortgage may for this reason contain a stipulation that the mortgagor or trustee shall retain or keep possession of the property until the *cestui que trust* or mortgagee, as the case may be, desires to take possession or requests that the property shall be sold.[1] The instrument may even contain a stipulation that the debtor may remain in possession for a certain period, unless an execution shall in the meantime be issued against him.[2] A deed of trust may also allow a liberal discretion to the trustee in the disposition of the property, both as to the time and as to the manner of making the sale.[3] Mere delay in enforcing a mortgage or deed of trust is simply a circumstance to be taken into consideration,[4]

---

[1] Dubose v. Dubose, 7 Ala. 235; Brock v. Headon, 13 Ala. 370; Marriott v. Givens, 8 Ala. 694.

[2] Alton v. Harrison, 4 L. R. Ch. 622; Lee v. Flannaghan, 7 Ir. 471; Prior v. White, 12 Ill. 261; Frost v. Mott, 34 N. Y. 253.

[3] Brock v. Headon, 13 Ala. 370; Burgin v. Burgin, 1 Ired. 453; Walthall v. Rives, 34 Ala. 91; Tarver v. Roffe, 7 Ala. 873.

[4] Galt v. Dibrell, 10 Yerg. 146; Davis v. Evans, 5 Ired. 525; Ely v. Carnley, 3 E. D. Smith, 489; Harshaw v. Woodfin, 64 N. C. 568; Lee v. Flannagan, 7 Ired. 471; Hardy v. Skinner, 9 Ired. Eq. 191; Burgin v. Burgin, 1 Ired. 453; Dewey v. Littlejohn, 2 Ired. Eq. 495.

for the creditors may proceed to collect their demands from the property if its value exceeds the amount secured by the mortgage or deed of trust without waiting for the party who holds such security, to cause a sale to be made. As the creditors are not materially injured by the delay, they have no legal grounds to complain on account of the compassion or humanity of the mortgagee or trustee, or on account of a desire, if such exists, to prevent a sacrifice of the property for the purpose of protecting the interests of the party who holds such security.

CHAPTER V.

POSSESSION.

PRELIMINARY REMARKS.—The history of the law respecting the rights of creditors in relation to the property of their debtor, sold, assigned or mortgaged by him, but remaining in his possession and under his control, is remarkable. It presents a perpetual struggle between a general rule of policy intended to cut off the possibility of fraudulent or collusive sales, prescribing that every sale, assignment or mortgage unaccompanied by change of possession, should be held fraudulent in the eye of the law and void against creditors, and, on the other side, the obvious hardship and injustice of numerous particular cases, where the innocent and even benevolent intention of the party was manifest, and the legal presumption of fraud appeared inequitable, oppressive, contrary to the truth of the case and the moral feelings of those who must apply and enforce the law. Thus it happened, that whilst the courts and the books laid down the rule broadly and often applied it strictly, that unless possession accompanies and follows the transfer it is fraudulent and void, yet, first case after case, and then class after class of exceptions was exempted from the rule, until there were numerous distinct grounds of exemption, such as the kind of sale, purchase under execution or distress for rent, necessity convenience, the customs of trade, the distance or situation of the place, the relation of the parties, motives of humanity or of friendship, and

special circumstances of various kinds more or less definitely defined.[1]

A point which has been so extensively litigated will
be best understood by an examination of the principles
that are involved, in the first place, and then of the authorities.

---

[1] Stoddard v. Butler, 20 Wend. 507, per Senator Verplanck. In a note
to Bissel v. Hopkins, 3 Cow. 166, the number of the exceptions are stated
to be twenty-four, the principal of which are as follows: 1. Where a
creditor is knowing and assenting to the sale (Steel v. Brown, 1 Taunt.
381). 2. Where the sale is conditional, (Per Coke, J. in Stone v. Grubbam, 2 Bulstr, 217; and per Buller, J. in Edwards v. Harben, 2 T. R. 587,)
i. e. in the last case a condition precedent to be performed by the vendee,
3. Where the goods remain with the vendor to be sold for the benefit of the
vendee, the vendor being a borrower on bottomry (*i. e.* a mortgagor), the
trust being declared by the deed (Bucknal v. Royston, Prec. Ch. 285).
4. Where A. purchases the goods on a *fi fa,* and leaves them with the
judgment debtor, to the intent that he pay for and redeem them (Cole v.
Davis. 1 Ld. Raym. 724). 5. Where the goods purchased in this *manner* are
left from benevolence or for a temporary and honest purpose (Kidd v.
Rawlinson, 2 B. & P. 59). 6. Where money is lent to buy furniture, and a
bill of sale honestly taken to secure the repayment of the money (Meggott
v. Mills, 1 Ld. Raym. 286). 7. Where the purchase was a fair one at public
sale, and the goods are left with a relation or friend (Per Shippen Ch. J. in
Walters, v. McLellan, 4 Dall. 208). 8. Where the vendor is an intended
husband, and sells to trustees to make a marriage settlement upon his future
wife (Hazelinton v. Gill, 3 T. R. 620, *in notis,* Cadogan v. Kennett, 2 Cowp.
432). 9. Where a bill of sale is a mortgage (Barrow v. Paxton, 5 Johns.
258; U. S. v. Hooe, 3 Cranch, 78). 10. Where the non-delivery arises from
the sickness of the vendor's depositary (Beals v. Guernsey, 8 Johns. 446). 11.
Where the assignment is of a cargo in a ship lying at the port where the assignment is executed, but bound to a foreign port, the assignment providing that remittances shall be made to liquidate the debt due to the vendee
in consideration of which debt the assignment is made, &c. (Dawes v. Cope,
4 Binn. 258). 12. Where the conveyance was late on Saturday night,
and the possessions remained unchanged till Monday (Wilt v. Franklin,
1 Binn, 502). 13. A purchase by a creditor in an execution (Watkins
v. Birch, 4 Taunt. 823). 14. A purchase under a landlord's warrant of distress (Guthrie v. Wood, 1 Starkie, N. P. 367). 15. A ship abroad may of
course be sold and possession retained by the vendor till her return
(Putnam v. Dutch, 8 Mass. 287). 16. A *bona fide* sale of bricks in a brick-
yard, accompanied with a lease of the yard to the vendee until the bricks
should be sold and removed, was held to be valid against the creditors of
the vendor without actual removal (Allen v. Smith, 10 Mass. 308).

DEPENDS UPON THE INTENT.—The question arises upon the construction of a positive statute, and a true solution cannot be attained without carefully considering
the terms of the act. The statute is directed, not against
an inconsistent possession, but a fraudulent design, not
against fair and honest contracts, but conveyances made
with the intent to delay, hinder or defraud creditors.[1]
The intent of the debtor is, therefore, by the very terms
of the act, the true and legitimate object of inquiry and
judicial investigation. If the fraudulent intent is present, the conveyance is void; if it is absent, the conveyance is valid. All the circumstances that accompany a
transaction are valuable only as they throw light upon
the debtor's intent.

VENDOR'S RIGHT TO LEAVE WITH VENDEE.—A full
and free power of disposal of chattels is an essential and
inherent incident of ownership, and the vendee has the
same right to leave them in the possession of the vendor
that he would have to take them into his own, or place
them in possession of a third person,[2] unless such act
necessarily and inevitably tends to deceive and defraud
creditors. The argument that the retention of possession is fraud *per se* cannot rest upon the incomplete-
ness of the purchaser's title, for in sales of personal
property actual delivery is not necessary to the transmission of the title.[3] By the contract of sale and present
payment of the price, or an agreement to pay it thereafter, the purchaser acquires the right of property and
may recover it by action. Thus, if A. sells property to
B. *in presenti*, and receives payment therefor, or B.'s note

---

[1] Davis v. Turner, 4 Gratt. 422 ; Hobbs v. Bibb, 2 Stew. 54; Bryant v.
Kelton, 1 Tex. 415.

[2] Hanford v. Artcher, 4 Hill, 271; s. c. 1 Hill, 374.

[3] Cole v. White, 26 Wend. 511; s. c. 24 Wend. 116.

or promise to pay at a future day, the title passes from A. and becomes vested in B., and is not affected by the failure of A. to deliver or of B. to demand the immediate possession. Now, as the dominion over a man's property belongs to him and not to his creditors, they ought to be allowed to subject to their demands only the right which remains in him and not that from which he has lawfully parted.[1]

POSSESSION IS BADGE OF FRAUD.—The want of possession, however, is a strong badge of fraud. The property is placed in the purchaser, the possession continues in the debtor, and by that means creditors, perceiving no visible diminution of the debtor's effects, rest satisfied and take no measures to secure their debts, until, perhaps, the whole estate of the debtor is exhausted whereas, should the vendee immediately take possession, creditors would thereby have notice that the debtor's estate was wearing away, and apply for the discharge of their demands in time. It has this further ill effect, that the debtor, still continuing in possession and being reputed owner, obtains credit upon a belief that he is the owner, and so by the fault of the vendee possesses the means of contracting debts without the means of paying them.[2] As it is out of the ordinary course of business for a person to buy goods and not to receive the possession, a sale without a change of possession enables the vendor to hold out false colors and obtain a false credit, by inducing others to trust him on account of his apparent property, and may be used to protect secret transfers. It, therefore, has a direct tendency to deceive and defraud creditors, and, as the law always holds that a person intends what-

---

[1] Davis v. Turner, 4 Gratt. 422.
[2] Ingles v. Donalson, 2 Hay. 57; Ludlow v. Hurd, 19 Johns. 218.

ever is the natural and probable consequence of his own acts, raises a presumption that the vendor intends to defraud his creditors.[1]

NOT CONCLUSIVE.—Although the retention of possession is for these reasons presumptive evidence of fraud, yet it is not conclusive, because possession is only *prima facie* evidence of title to personal property. How far it would have been wise to have determined originally that the actual possession should be considered as decisive evidence of all property is a question now too late to be discussed, because as far back as the year books,[2] a gradual was limited to A. for life, and afterwards to B. In modern times the courts, proceeding upon the same principle, have said that personal property may be carved out in the same manner and possession given to one for life and then over,[3] and it is now settled law that possession is only presumptive evidence of owner ship.[4] The frequent necessity of entrusting personal estate to others than the actual owner—to clerks, domestics, factors, mechanics and borrowers—forbids the adoption of the rule that possession shall always be deemed conclusive evidence of title.[5] But the line of distinction between presumptive and conclusive evidence of fraud is clearly drawn. If the inevitable consequence of an act is to defraud creditors, then that act is conclusive evidence of fraud. But if the tendency to defraud is only a natural and probable and not an inevitable consequence of an act, then that act is

---

[1] Griswold v. Sheldon, 4 N. Y. 580.

[2] 37 Hen. VI. 30.

[3] Jarman v. Woolloton, 3 T. R. 618; Haven v. Low, 2 N. H. 13.

[4] And there was no occasion otherwise for the statute of King James Stat. 21 Jac. 1, *re.* 19, S. 10 11; Arundell v. Phipps, 10 Ves. 139.

[5] Haven v. Low, 2 N. H. 13.

only presumptive evidence of fraud. As possession is only presumptive evidence of title, the retention of possession has only a probable tendency to deceive, and is, therefore, only presumptive evidence of an intent to defraud.

CAVEAT CREDITOR.—In purchases of personal property the rule *caveat emptor* applies, though the vendor may be in possession, and it is no harsher to apply a similar rule of *caveat* creditor.[1] Before giving credit he should diligently inquire as to the title of the property in the possession of the debtor. When he makes proper inquiry he may ascertain that the naked fact of possession after a sale is the only indication of fraud, and that even this indication is weakened by clear evidence of a full consideration, perfect publicity in the sale and little prior indebtedness on the part of the vendor. He may find that there was an express condition in the sale itself for a loan of the property to the vendor, and, considering the nature of the property and the character and situation of the parties, that this condition ought not to cast any suspicion on the transaction. Thus cases will occur to every one where property may be honestly loaned for a time to the vendor from mere charity; other cases for hire, and others still for the property to be repaired, freighted or manufactured. In others it may be left with the vendor from simple procrastination as to its removal, and in others because the property is of so ponderous a nature as to render a speedy removal inconvenient in the usual course of business. The length of time it is left or loaned, whether for hours, months

---

[1] Haven v. Low, 2 N. H. 13; Davis v. Turner, 4 Gratt. 422; Sydnor v. Gee, 4 Leigh, 535.

or years, would frequently much strengthen or weaken any presumption of fraud.[1] It is, morever, vain to attempt to so arrange the possession of personal property as altogether to prevent frauds upon creditors. Some circumspection and vigilance must be demanded of them. The most common transactions of life would be trammelled and embarrassed if the sole care were directed to the protection of creditors who ought to protect themselves.[2]

RULE OF EVIDENCE.—It cannot be denied that the retention of possession is a circumstance which does not lead necessarily to the giving of a delusive credit to the vendor, and sometimes happens not to be irreconcilable with a fair and honest contract free from all imagination of fraud. If, therefore, the object is to ascertain the merits of the case, it would seem that to hold the inference conclusive, and, in effect, an estoppel to all further investigation, would be against the plainest principles of presumptive evidence.[3] The rule that the retention of possession is a fraud *per se* is accordingly

---

[1] Haven v. Low, 2 N. H. 13. The rule that possession should be deemed conclusive evidence of title would not be any more effective to suppress fraud. If by the inquisitions of the judicial crucible a transaction, both honest and fair, may be alloyed until it is dishonest and fraudulent, by the inverse power of transmutation, a fraud may be refined until it is equivalent to honesty and truth. If truth may become constructive falsehood, by the same rule falsehood may become constructive truth. If the possession of personal chattels is or ought to be conclusive evidence of ownership, it is also, or ought to be, conclusive evidence that a person not in possession is not the owner. All then that remains for the fraudulent debtor to do, who would conclusively place his chattels beyond the reach of execution, is to place them in the possession of his friend, against whom no process has been issued. Stoddard v. Butler, 20 Wend. 507, *per* Senator Dickinson.

[2] Sydnor v. Gee, 4 Leigh, 535; Davis v. Turner, 4 Gratt. 422.

[3] Davis v. Turner, 4 Gratt. 422.

conceded to be one of policy and not of evidence, and it is admitted that upon no other ground can a court be justified in holding a sale fraudulent *per se* which to a jury is proved to be *bona fide*, and, in fact, free from the imputation of any fraud.[1] If the statute were ambiguous or doubtful, then the courts in construing it might be governed by motives of policy; but where the statute is so plain and explicit there is no room for such considerations. The courts can only look for the fraudulent intent. If that is present, the transaction is void; if that is absent, it is valid. Such are the imperative terms of the act. To disregard its terms and enter into a consideration of the requirements of public policy is to give no heed to the mandates of the statute and to usurp legislative functions. Questions of policy belong peculiarly to legislative bodies: questions of law are proper subjects for the determination of the courts.[2]

ENSNARES INNOCENT MEN.—The doctrine, however, has been supposed to have the advantage of simplicity, since it has been believed to afford a ready and easy solution to all questions coming within its range. But this supposed advantage is purchased at too dear a price. It is often obtained by a sacrifice of the justice of the case. How can it be otherwise when, in deciding a case, the correct decision of which depends on the

---

[1] Wilson v. Hooper, 12 Vt. 653; Kirtland v. Snow, 20 Conn. 23.

[2] Hanford v. Artcher, 4 Hill, 271. The difference between policy as laid down by a legislature and policy as enforced by courts is well illustrated by the difference in their mode of treating this subject. The latter prohibits all transactions where the vendor retains possession, while the former simply corrects the evil by requiring that there shall be an instrument in writing duly recorded, and obtains all the benefits that can be derived from the retention of possession.

good or evil intent of the parties, one single circumstance is arbitrarily seized on, and made conclusive evidence of evil intent, to the total exclusion of every circumstance which would prove good intent.[1] In seeking to catch rogues the law ought not to ensnare honest men. It may become so zealous against fraud as to restrain the free action of honesty, a result that would be most disastrous. Better is it that many frauds should go undetected than that the means of detection or prevention should treat honest men as guilty, or teach men to be always suspicious of their neighbors, and watchful that honest acts be precisely measured according to the standard of legal morality.[2]

SIMPLICITY NOT ATTAINED.—This supposed advantage of simplicity does not in fact exist. No one can glance at the confused mass of authorities upon this subject without perceiving that what was intended as a safe and easy guide to the detection and suppression of frauds has only led to an endless maze of disputation. There is scarcely a proposition in regard to the essence or the application of the doctrine upon which there may not be found a conflict of authorities. Those who doubt the truth of this will be best convinced by exploring the field of authority. The doctrine, though plausible, is extremely difficult in practice. It seeks to make a mere question of law of that which, in the

---

[1] "In my long experience, I have had occasion to observe the mischievous operation of the rule, for under its application I have found myself compelled as judge to pronounce transactions to be fraudulent and void as to creditors which were known to be perfectly fair and *bona fide*, and was not intended or calculated to delay, hinder or defraud creditors. (Davis v. Turner, 4 Gratt. 422, *per* Cabell, J.)"

[2] To be strict as to the tithe of mint, anise and cummin, and forgetful of the weightier matters of social duty. (Hugus v. Robinson, 24 Penn. 9.)

nature of things, is a mixed question of law and fact, and carries within itself the elements of perplexity and contrariety.[1]   The numerous exceptions which have been made to the operation of the rule are, moreover, attended with the practical inconvenience of multiplying collateral issues, both of law and of fact, without throwing any light upon the truth and justice of the cause.   They involve questions of practicability, disability, diligence and notice, upon which the case may be made to turn, irrespective of the fairness and good faith of the transaction.   It is, moreover, somewhat remarkable that a person should be convicted of a fraud upon a nice question whether he has used reasonable diligence or given due notice.[2]

LOOKS ONLY TO FORM.—There is also another grave objection to the rule.   It goes to the form rather than the substance of the transaction, and, consequently, may be readily evaded.   In simulated contracts it is easy to mold the conveyance so as to avoid the discrepancy. Nothing more is necessary than to give to the transaction the form of a sheriff's sale, or of any of the other

---

[1] Davis v. Turner, 4 Gratt. 422.   In those courts where the doctrine of fraud *per se* is held, it has accordingly been found that there are no more difficult and embarrassing questions than those which relate to the respective provinces of the court and of the jury to determine what is law and what is fact.   One of the questions upon which difficulty has arisen is fraud in the sale or transfer of chattels under 13 Eliz. c. 5. (McKibbin v. Martin, 64 Penn. 352.)

[2] Davis v. Turner, 4 Gratt. 422.   These exceptions must multiply as the exigency of circumstances may require, until ultimately they destroy the rule itself, or, what is the same thing, reduce it to one that is only *prima facie*.   Indeed, it seems impracticable to preserve unbroken any rule of inflexible rigor upon the subject, however inexorable in its terms, for the mind is apt to revolt against the despotism of a judicial dogma that oppresses the truth and justice of a cause, or to seek refuge in subtle distinctions as artificial as the rule itself.

admitted exceptions to the rule. The very notoriety which, in case of public sales, may be properly relied on as evidence to repel the imputation of fraud, is sometimes resorted to as a mere disguise; for example, goods may be purchased in at a sheriff's sale in the name of a confederate, with funds furtively furnished by or on the part of the embarrassed debtor.[1] The truth of the matter is that the doctrine has been prompted by a commendable wish to accomplish a desirable but impracticable object. If a short and easy mode could be found of cutting fraud up by the roots the discovery would be invaluable; but such an enterprise is beyond the limits of human wisdom. In human institutions, moreover, the question is not whether every evil contingency can be avoided, but what arrangements will be productive of the least inconvenience. But, even as the test of a fraudulent purpose, the rule in question has no claim to certainty; on the contrary, it concedes its own fallibility by crushing mercilessly the most convincing evidence of fairness and good faith.[2]

NOT GOOD POLICY.— Even on the simple ground of policy—the only ground on which it can by any possibility be sustained—the rule is open to grave objections. It restricts the free circulation of personal property, hampers the spirit of commerce, checks the generous impulses of the heart, and prohibits the charities of life. The farmer or mechanic finds it necessary

---

[1] Davis v. Turner, 4 Gratt. 422. It was accordingly found necessary in New York to hold that the retention of possession after a sheriff's sale is *prima facie* evidence of fraud. (Farrington v. Caswell, 15 Johns. 430; Taylor v. Mills, 2 Edw. Ch. 318; Gardenier v. Tubbs, 21 Wend. 169; Fonda v. Gross, 15 Wend. 628.)

[2] Davis v. Turner, 4 Gratt. 422; Stoddard v. Butler, 20 Wend. 507, *per* Senator Dickinson.

to sell his implements of husbandry or the tools of his trade, yet he cannot retain the possession, although they are the only means of support for himself and family.[1] A minister of the gospel cannot retain the horse that is essential to the performance of his duties.[2] Machinery must be removed from the manufactory.[3] The vendor cannot even be permitted to finish the articles which are in the process of manufacture.[4] A man cannot purchase chattels, and leave them with a feeble relative for the sake of comfort and assistance.[5] If the vendor and vendee live in the same house, there cannot be a valid sale of the furniture in it without a removal.[6]

COMMERCE PROMOTED.—Illustrations of the danger of false credit and fraudulent evasion of debt, whenever delivery and change of possession do not accompany and follow change of property, and of the modes in which such frauds can be effected, can be readily furnished, and their truth cannot be denied. Yet this is but one, and that the narrowest side of the question; whilst it is also that view of the matter which is most frequently, indeed, almost exclusively presented to the

---

[1] Doane v. Eddy, 16 Wend. 523.

[2] Doane v. Eddy, 16 Wend. 523.

[3] Swift v. Thompson, 9 Ct. 63; Tobias v. Francis, 3 Vt. 425.

[4] Carter v. Watkins, 14 Ct. 240.

[5] The law, which regards and scans with scrupulous vigilance every circumstance from which a legitimate inference of fraud or unfairness may be drawn, is, at the same time, not so wanting in humanity as to forbid the alleviation of distress and suffering by honest means. To hold such a transaction inconsistent with good faith or the rights of the creditors would be to stamp as a fraud what, by the law of God as well as by the common consent of mankind, is esteemed as a virtue. (Henderson v. Mabry 13 Ala. 713; Mauldin v. Mitchell, 14 Ala. 814.)

[6] Steelwagon v. Jeffries, 44 Penn. 407.

examination of courts. But a glance at the daily business of life out of court presents another aspect of the question. Transactions in which the goods are left in the possession of the vendor have grown out of the usages of modern society, the necessities of commerce, the conveniences of daily life, and the wants and usages of trade and industry. They have followed in the train of commerce, credit and enterprise. Like them, they have been largely productive of benefits to society. Yet those benefits, like the results of all other human actions, are not unmixed with evil. By such means, the adventure, capacity, acquirements and industry of the young or the needy have been aided and stimulated; large concerns of honorable but unfortunate merchants have been settled to the greatest advantage of the creditors and the least possible loss of the insolvent, and the kindness of parents or the generosity of friends has been enabled to preserve the comforts of a home to the wife and children of a bankrupt, without the slightest injury or fraud to creditors. Society reaps nothing but unquestioned benefit from nine-tenths of such transactions occurring in actual life. The other tenth may come before the courts. It is not then at all surprising that this different experience should give a different character to the whole in different minds. It is thus as to all the operations of commerce beyond mere barter and buying and selling for cash.[1]

RIGHTS OF OTHERS BESIDES CREDITORS.—Since the retention of possession may in a multitude of cases be beneficial and advantageous, there is another consideration that is entitled to great strength. Neither the legal nor the moral code should be administered for the

---

[1] Cole v. White, 26 Wend. 511, *per* Senator Verplanck.

sole benefit of creditors. They become creditors by their own volition, and have abundant means for their own protection. General creditors ought not to be placed upon a superior footing to him who furnishes his poor neighbor with a cow to nourish his children or a team to sow his crop or gather in his harvest. If the commercial interest cannot be sustained without trampling upon all others, and the ordinary charities of life besides, the sooner it finds its level the better. It is an idle dream to suppose that the cause of morals can be advanced by establishing a rule which ministers to the mercenary passions at the expense of the benevolent affections, or that the fountain of justice will send forth purer streams if they are forced to flow through artificial channels. The principles of law are but the enlightened and just conclusions of a moral people pronounced by their own tribunals. There ought not, therefore, to be two standards of morals, the one for courts of justice, and the other for the people in their ordinary intercourse, and when the law seeks to erect a standard of its own, it abandons its own fundamental principles and attempts an impossible task. Honesty cannot be divided into chapters, nor morality defined by sections.[1]

PRIMA FACIE EVIDENCE MAY BE EXPLAINED.—The doctrine that the retention of possession will under all circumstances render a transfer of personal property fraudulent and void has not been laid down by any court, nor adopted anywhere. There are admitted exceptions to the rule, varying in number and character according to the strictness with which the rule is administered. But evidence is either *prima facie* or con-

---

[1] Stoddard v. Butler, 20 Wend. 507, per Senator Dickinson.

clusive. If evidence is liable to be contradicted or explained it is only *prima facie*, but conclusive evidence cannot be contradicted. *Prima facie* evidence, although it admits the possibility of its falsity, yet is conclusive unless contradicted or explained. Conclusive evidence admits no such possibility of falsity. It is absolute verity. Any evidence which may be explained is not conclusive, but only *prima facie*. If, therefore, there are special cases in which special reasons may be given to show the fairness of the transaction notwithstanding the retention of possession, those reasons must be shown by evidence, and the nature of that evidence constitutes the case a special one within the rule. This evidence may be given in every case where it exists. It follows, then, that in every case the vendee may, if he can, show by evidence special reasons to take his case out of the general rule. The fact of possession in the vendor, as it may be explained, is not conclusive, but only *prima facie* evidence of fraud.[1]

EXPLANATORY EVIDENCE IS FOR JURY.—The real point of inquiry therefore is, not whether the retention of possession is presumptive or conclusive evidence of fraud, but whether the evidence in explanation of it is, in an action at law, for the consideration of the court or the jury. It is held in many cases that although the retention of possession is only presumptive evidence of fraud, the special reasons which are permitted to take a case out of the rule must be shown to and approved of by the court.[2]

---

[1] Hall v. Tuttle, 8 Wend. 375.

[2] Divver v. McLaughlin, 2 Wend. 596; Collins v. Brush, 9 Wend. 198; Coburn v. Pickering, 3 N. H. 415; Toby v. Reed. 9 Conn. 216; Carter v. Watkins, 14 Conn. 240; Planters' Bank v. Borland, 5 Ala. 531; Trask v. Bowers, 4 N. H. 309; Mauldin v. Mitchell, 14 Ala. 814.

In Connecticut the practice is slightly different. It is not according to

The presumption of fraud, however, arising from the retention of possession, is simply a presumption of an intent to hinder, delay and defraud creditors, and, consequently, is a presumption of a fact. It is true that the presumption is raised by the law, but only on the same principles on which presumptions are raised in other transactions. It is simply a presumption of a fact raised by the law, a legal evidence of fraud, conclusive in the absence of contradictory testimony, but open to refutation. It is only such a presumption that, unless contradicted or explained, the jury ought to believe it. The whole burden of proof is thrown upon the grantee and he must make it appear that he acted in good faith. It is strictly under the statute a question of fact, such as a jury may judge of, and must alone do so if the question comes before a court of common law.[1]

COURT CANNOT DETERMINE SUFFICIENCY OF EXPLANATORY EVIDENCE.—The statute has not given the court any power to determine what particular facts shall or shall not be sufficient evidence of honest intention, nor can it be derived from the acknowledged right to reject incompetent evidence, for this does not imply the right to exclude proof of such facts as by the ordinary laws of evidence and the common understanding of men go to prove honest intent, or to disprove deceit and collusion merely because in the view of the court such evidence is

---

the course of the court to call this a fraud *per se* and to direct the jury to find the sale void, but the question is submitted to the jury as a question of fact, with instruction that if they find none of the established exceptions, they will find the transaction fraudulent. Swift v. Thompson, 9 Conn. 63. But in Toby v. Reed. 9 Conn. 216, the term court was held to mean the jury acting under the direction of the court.

[1] Stoddard v. Butler, 20 Wend. 507, per Senator Verplanck.

not absolutely and in all cases demonstrative proof. It does not authorize the court to create a general rule of policy, declaring that certain facts which are not always of necessity incompatible with collusion shall never in any case be received as proof of good faith. This is in effect to declare that the question of intent shall be wholly a question of law. This intent to hinder, delay and defraud is a moral or intellectual fact, to be inferred by the jury from such external facts and circumstances as in the ordinary course of life would satisfy men of sound judgment. The courts have never presumed to lay down any arbitrary rule requiring some specific sort of evidence conclusive to the point and excluding all other testimony. Whatever fact can give probable indication of the moral fact to be ascertained is relevant and must go to the jury, unless excluded by some general law of evidence. Of its weight the jury are the judges. In every question of the fact of fraudulent intent, the intent is to be inferred from external facts or circumstances, and good faith may be established in the same way. What circumstances will amount to proof can never be matter of general definition. The legal test is the sufficiency of the evidence to satisfy the understanding and conscience of the jury. Absolute metaphysical and demonstrative certainty is not essential to proof by circumstances. It is sufficient if they produce moral certainty to the exclusion of reasonable doubts.[1]

---

[1] Cole v. White, 26 Wend. 511 ; s. c. 24 Wend. 116.

In this case Senator Verplanck cites the following words of Kent, Ch. J. : "The distribution of power, by which the court and jury mutually assist and check each other, seems to be the safest, and, consequently, the wisest. The constructions of the judges on the intention of the party may often be too speculative and refined, and not altogether just in their application to every case. Their rules may have too technical a cast, and

REVIEW OF AUTHORITIES.—The question, having thus far been considered on principle, will now be examined in the light of the authorities.

The earliest case under the statute is Twyne's case.[1] This was a criminal prosecution in the Star Chamber, where the court was the judge of both the law and the facts, and, consequently, there is not that discrimination between law and fact which is found in trials at law. This case arose as follows: Pierce was indebted to Twyne in £400, and was indebted also to Chamberlin in £200. Chamberlin brought an action of debt against Pierce, and, pending the writ, Pierce being possessed of goods and chattels of the value of £300, in secret made a general deed of gift of all his goods and chattels, real and personal whatsoever, to Twyne in satisfaction of his debt. Notwithstanding this, Pierce continued in pos-

---

become in operation too severe and oppressive. To judge accurately of motives and intentions does not require a master's skill in the science of the law. It depends more on the knowledge of the passions and of the springs of human action, and may be the lot of ordinary experience and sagacity." And then adds: "I cannot forbear adding, that among the many eminent public services and titles to lasting legal and literary honors of this venerable and distinguished jurist, his uniform and zealous guardianship of the trial by jury, even to the last hour of his judicial life, is conspicuous and remarkable. Eminent above his cotemporaries for profound and extensive legal science, bringing to the consideration of every important point at once the black-letter lore of our ancient common law, and the varied range of its subsequent changes, together with the legal reason of the Roman code, down to the application of its doctrines by the great continental jurists of our own days,—with all this rich store of scholarship and legal science, he, above all our judges, was the foremost to confess that there was still something that books cannot teach—that the knowledge of the motives and springs of human action can be gained from every-day experience better than from judicial rules—and that such rules are constantly liable to become harsh, technical, severe and oppressive, without the correcting aid of the every-day experience of men and life found in the jury-box."

[1] 3 Co. 80; s. c. Moore, 638 (1602).

session of the goods and some of them he sold, and he shore the sheep and marked them with his own mark. Afterwards Chamberlin obtained judgment against Pierce, and had a *fieri facias* directed to the sheriff of Southampton, who, by force of the writ, went to make execution of the goods, but divers persons, by the command of Twyne resisted him, claiming them to be the goods of Twyne, by virtue of the deed. Whether this conveyance was fraudulent and of no effect was the question.

Among other " signs and marks of fraud," the court said, "The donor continued in possession and used the goods as his own, and by reason thereof he traded and trafficked with others, and defrauded and deceived them." The court also resolved that "No gift shall be deemed *bona fide* which is accompanied with any trust, as if a man be indebted to five several persons in the several sums of £20, and hath goods of the value of £20, and makes a gift of all his goods to one of them, in satisfaction of his debt, but there is a trust between them that the donee shall deal favorably with him in regard of his poor estate, either to permit the donor, or some other for him, or for his benefit, to use or have possession of them, and is contented that he shall pay him his debt when he is able—this shall not be called *bona fide*." Thereupon Coke gives the following advice: "Immediately after the gift take the possession of the goods, for continuance of possession in the donor is a sign of trust." These remarks show that the retention of possession was at that time simply regarded as a mark of fraud, similar in its character and effect to secrecy, the pendency of a suit, unusual clauses, and the other signs of fraud enumerated by the court. The trust mentioned in the resolution was not simply a secret benefit, but a trust by which the title was held for the use of the debtor. Such a conveyance, by which the title is placed nominally in one person while it is beneficially in another, is unquestionably fraudulent, for it is merely colorable. Such trusts of chattels, when made in writing, are expressly made void by the statute of 3 H., 7, c. 4, and it was with reference to this that the court probably made the remark. It will also be noticed that Coke simply holds the retention of possession to be the sign of such a trust. Moreover, the possession retained in this case was not a mere naked possession, but a possession implying ownership and *jus disponendi*, with the knowledge and concurrence of the vendee. Pierce, the vendor, not only continued in possession of the goods, but he sold some of them. He shore the sheep, and marked them with his own mark. There was, therefore, a possession with an implication of ownership, and *jus disponendi;* but that is a very different species of possession from mere naked possession.[1]

In Bucknal et al. v. Roiston,[2] Brewer, a supercargo of a ship which was to go a voyage to the East Indies, having shipped on board several goods and commodities, borrowed of the plaintiffs £600, and gave a bottomry bond to pay £40 per cent. in case the ship should reign (as they called it) three years, and at the same time made a bill of sale to the plaintiffs of the goods and commodities he had on board, and of the produce and advantage that should be made thereof; and this was in the nature of a security or pledge for the re-payment of the £600 and £40 per cent. premium. The ship went her voyage, and the goods were sold, and with the money others bought, and those likewise invested in other goods, and

---

[1] Macdona v. Swiney, 8 Ir. Law (N. S.), 73.
[2] Prec. Ch. 285 (1709).

so there had been several barters and exchange of several sorts of goods. The ship, after three years, returned home, but it so happened that Brewer died upon the sea in his return home, and Roiston, who was a creditor of his by judgment for £1,500, obtained before the sale of those goods, got out letters of administration, and took possession of the goods and commodities returned home, and which belonged to Brewer. The plaintiffs thereupon brought their bill to have an account and discovery of the goods and satisfaction for the produce and advantage that was made thereof. Upon these facts the court said : "That the trust of these goods appeared upon the very face of the bill of sale ; that though they were sold to the plaintiffs, yet they trusted Brewer to negotiate and sell them for their advantage, and Brewer's keeping possession of them was not to give a false credit to him, but for a particular purpose agreed upon at the time of sale ; that here the plaintiffs are presently entitled to the trust of these goods, and to all the advantages consequential upon such trust, and may follow the goods for that purpose, and, therefore, decreed an account to be taken of the produce of those specific goods for the satisfaction of the plaintiff's claim."

It was in the course of the argument in this cause that Sir Edward Northey, the counsel for the defendant, said : "It has been ruled forty times, in my experience, at Guildhall, that if a man sells goods and still continues in possession as visible owner of them, that such sale is fraudulent and void as to creditors, and that the law has been always so held." Of this remark Savage, Ch. J.[1], justly observes : "If it was intended to say that such continuance in possession was conclusive evidence of fraud, and the fairness of the transaction might not be

---

[1] Hall v. Tuttle, 8 Wend. 375.

shewn by evidence, I can only say that not one of the forty cases thus decided is to be found reported." It will also be noticed that in this case the bill of sale was held to be valid, although the vendor remained in possession of the goods.

In Stone v. Grubbam,[1] which was an action of ejectment, Robert Cassey, who was possessed of a lease for years, made a gift of all his goods and chattels, including the lease, to Richard Saltingstone, but continued in possession after the transfer, and it was urged that for this reason the transfer was fraudulent. Coke, Ch. J., said: "If a man do mortgage his land and yet still continue his possession, no disseizin is wrought by this, and so is Winnington's case; if it was an absolute conveyance and a continuance in possession afterwards, this shall be adjudged in law to be fraudulent, for this hath the face of fraud; but otherwise it is, as it is here in this case, where the conveyance was only conditionally, as upon payment of money—there the interest doth not pass absolutely, but upon a future condition, for the gift was before upon the condition of the payment of such a sum by Sir Richard Saltingstone. As to the fraud, *dolus versatur in universalibus,* but when the conveyance is conditional, continuance in possession after this shall not, in the judgment of the law, be said to be fraudulent, and this is very clear; and, as to the value of the lease, this is not at all material. As to the matter of fraud, the same ought to be fraud at the beginning, for that subsequent fraud will not make this conveyance to be fraudulent clearly; the whole court agreed herein. If a man hath any intentions to evade out of the statute of Eliz., c. 5, whatsoever he shall say afterwards shall not amend the matter, but the same shall be fraud and

---

[1] 2 Buls. 217; s. c. 1 Rol. Rep. 3 (1615).

be within the statute, and that secrecy is a great badge
of fraud, but yet no concluding proof; the whole court
agreed herein. It was then demanded (by reason of an
objection made) in whose custody the lease was after
the gift. It was answered, and so proved, that the same
was always after (and until the assignment made to one
Weston) in the custody of Sir Richard Saltingstone, to
whom the gift was made. If the same had afterwards
continued in the custody of Cassey (who made the gift)
then the same would have been clearly fraudulent; but,
in regard that the contrary is here proved, it shall not
be adjudged to be a fraudulent conveyance within the
statute; the whole court agreed herein."

This case is obviously open to criticism. It is stated
that a tenant for years, having made a lease at will,
and the tenant at will having been ejected, brought the
action for this ejectment of his lessee at will. But from
the facts, it appears that Cassey originally owned the
lease and transferred it to Saltingstone, and that Saltingstone subsequently assigned it to Weston. None of
these persons, however, are parties to the suit. It is
not, therefore, clear how the question of fraud arose in
the case. In the next place, the question is not made to
turn upon the possession of the land, but upon the possession of the lease. From the remarks in regard to secrecy, it would appear that the inquiry as to the custody
of the title papers was made with reference to that
point. It is, moreover, conceded that the rule in regard
to the retention of possession is not applicable to leases
or other interests in land.[1] The report of this case in
Rolle's Reports is briefer, but gives what may be con-

---

[1] Cadogan v. Kennett, Cowp. 432; Ryall v. Rolle, 1 Ves. 348; s. c. 1
Atk. 165; Worsley v. De Mattos, 1 Burr, 467; Phettiplace v. Sayles, 4
Mason, 312.

sidered as the real point decided by the court. There the instruction to the jury is, that "If a man makes a gift, and the consideration is to be in the future, the continuance of the possession of the donor will not be fraudulent, unless it be expressly proved that it was made to defraud and to deceive creditors; as if a man mortgage lands to another upon a future condition, if the mortgagor continues in possession before the condition is broken, still he is not a disseizor, nor will it be fraudulent, for it is the custom in all such mortgages to suffer the mortgagor to continue in possession until condition broken, for he has the land for the security of his money, and before condition broken he is not to any detriment." It will also be observed that the transaction in this case was sustained.

The distinction between a mortgage and an absolute deed is also made in Lady Lambert's case.[1] There it is said that "If A., *bona fide* and for valuable consideration, mortgage his land whereof he hath a term of years to B., upon condition that if he repay the money to B. a year after that he shall re-enter, and B. doth covenant with A. that he shall take the profits of it until that time, &c., A. doth not pay the money, and B., hoping that he will pay it in time, doth suffer him to continue in possession and take the profit of it two or three years after, and in the interim judgment is had against A. upon a bond, and execution awarded; in this case, execution shall not be made of this lease, for this deed of mortgage shall not be said to be fraudulent as to the creditor, for when a conveyance is not fraudulent at the time of making of it, it shall never be said to be fraudulent for any matter *ex post facto*."

---

[1] Shep. Touch. 65.

In Meggot v. Mills,[1] it was proved that Wilson exercised the trade of a victualler, during which time Meggot furnished him with ale. Afterwards, he quit the trade of a victualler, and exercised the trade of an inn-keeper, and borrowed money of Mills (being Wilson's lessor) to buy goods to furnish his house, and for security of the money made a bill of sale of the goods to Mills, but kept the possession of them. After he became an inn-keeper, Meggot continued to sell him drink as before. He, however, paid Meggot several sums of money after he became an inn-keeper, amounting to as much as the debt was when he quit the trade of a victualler, but when he paid them he did not express upon what account. He was subsequently declared a bankrupt, and Meggot was appointed his assignee. Meggot brought an action in trover against Mills for the goods. Holt, Ch. J., said: " If these goods of Wilson's had been assigned to any other creditor, the keeping of the possession of them had made the bill of sale fraudulent as to the other creditors. But since the original agreement was thus, and that honestly, and really made for securing the money of the defendant Mills, which he had lent to Wilson for this purpose, the agreement was good and honest."

In Cole v. Davies,[2] it was resolved by Holt, Ch. J., " that if goods of A. are seized upon a *fieri facias*, and sold to B. *bona fide*, upon valuable consideration, though B. permits A. to have the goods in his possession upon condition that A. shall pay to B. the money as he shall raise it by the sale of the goods, this will not make the execution fraudulent."

---

[1] 1 Ld. Raym. 286; s. c. 12 Mod. 159 (1697).
[2] 1 Ld. Raym. 724 (1698.)

The case of Ryall v. Rowles [1] arose under the statute of 21 James I, c. 19, but the general doctrine of the retention of possession by the vendor was considered, Burnet, J., said: "The next consideration is, in what condition the creditors stood in relation to conditional sales or mortgages by their debtors to their prejudice, where the mortgagor continued in possession of the goods mortgaged, and the statute governing this matter is 13 Eliz., in which there is no distinction between conditional and absolute sales, provided they are fraudulent. This statute being made to protect creditors against all conveyances to defraud them, it was incumbent on a court of equity, or a jury at common law, upon considering the whole circumstances, to pronounce whether the conveyance was made with such intent or not. Where the neglect naturally tended to deceive creditors, it has been held a badge of fraud where left in his hands. But if, by concurrent circumstances it appeared the title deeds were not left to defraud creditors, but upon reasonable and honest purposes, or left with the vendor not so as to deceive touching his substance, that, being accompanied with other circumstances, could not be pronounced a badge of fraud. Therefore, it lay open upon this to determine whether fraudulent or not. The leading case on this is Twyne's case, where it is held that it was upon a valuable consideration, but not *bona fide*, from the continuing in possession and trading therewith. It is difficult, unless in very special cases, to assign a reason why an absolute or conditional vendee of goods should leave them with the vendor unless to procure a collusive credit, and it is the same whether in absolute or conditional sales, neither the statute nor the reason of the thing making any difference. But it is in-

---

[1] 1 Ves. 348; s. c. 1 Atk. 165 (1749).

sisted there are several cases where there is a distinction
as to this possession after sale between conditional and
absolute conveyances of lands or goods. That of lands
is not applicable to a case of goods: the case cited for
this was Stone v. Grubbam, 2 Buls. 226, and 1 Rol.
Rep. 3, but no argument from thence, unless the possession of lands and goods after a conveyance was on the
same footing. Possession is not otherwise a badge of fraud
unless as calculated to deceive creditors. There is no way
of coming at the knowledge of who is owner of goods
but by seeing in whose possession they are; the possession of land is of a different nature—there may be a
possession as tenant at will, as every mortgagor is of a
mortgage before the condition is broken. Every one
desiring credit entitles to an inquiry into his substance,
and, therefore, because the possession of land is of an
ambiguous nature, as it may be in the hands of the tenant as well as the owner, the title deeds, &c., may be required, but never at what market goods were bought,
the possession and usure of them being all. Lord Chief
Justice Holt takes up the case of Meggot v. Mills upon
the fraud, and gives it as his opinion that it was not
fraudulent, and it is very clear that it was not the distinction betwixt a conditional and absolute sale which
weighed with him at all. He distinguishes betwixt a
bill of sale to a landlord and to any other creditor, so
that it was his opinion that it was not fraudulent in case
of a landlord. But, though from all these cases it does
appear that in the construction of the 13 Eliz. there is
no distinction between conditional and absolute sales of
goods, if made with intent to defraud creditors, yet a
court of equity or a jury are left at large to construe
whether it was made with such intent or not." These
remarks admit of but one construction—the retention

of possession is not regarded as decisive, but the question of fraud is to be left to the jury to determine from all the circumstances of the case.

The case of Worseley v. De Mattos [1] arose under the statute of 21 Jac. c. 19, but the doctrine of possession was discussed. Lord Mansfield, in delivering the opinion of the court, said: " Every equivocal fact may be explained by circumstances. Hardly any deed is fraudulent upon the mere face of it. It is a good sale if the consideration be true; fraudulent if false; good if possession immediately follows; bad if it do not; nay, the not taking possession, being only evidence of fraud, may be explained."

Martin v. Podger et al. [2] was an action for trespass. Verdict was given in favor of the plaintiff, and the question arose upon a motion for a new trial. William Martin, being the owner of the goods in controversy, made a bill of sale of them to the plaintiff, who was his father, but remained in possession. The defendants seized the goods in the execution of a writ against the son. Lord Mansfield said: " As the goods were in the possession of the son, I think the judge should have left it to the jury whether, under these circumstances, the father had any right to recover. Therefore, I incline that a new trial should be granted." A rule was accordingly entered for a new trial, unless cause to the contrary were shown. Afterwards, upon an attempt to show cause, the court, finding the " circumstances of the bill of sale to have been extremely suspicious, were unanimous that the judge ought to have left it to the jury upon the ground of fraud."

From the report of this case in Burrows' Reports, it

[1] 1 Burr. 467 (1753).
[2] 2 W. Bl. 701 ; s. c. 5 Burr, 2631 (1770).

appears that the bill of sale was considered fraudulent in fact. It is there stated, that, for want of proof of the judgment, a verdict was found for the plaintiff, subject to the opinion of the court upon the question whether it was necessary for the defendants to produce a copy of the judgment upon which the writ of *fieri facias* issued. The court decided that it was necessary to produce a copy of the judgment. "But the whole court were likewise of opinion that this recovery in this action, brought by the father upon a fraudulent bill of sale, merely colorable, not a real, fair transaction, but leaving the possession in the son, and fraudulent even at common law, independent of the statute of 13 Eliz. c. 5, § 2, was shameful, unreasonable, and against justice, and that the verdict ought not to stand. It might have been left to the jury whether the plaintiff was in possession of the goods or not. It was a matter fit to be left to a jury. But it is a shameful thing to set up this fraudulent, colorable bill of sale as a real conveyance of the property." Upon the motion for a new trial Lord Mansfield said: "The verdict arises from a slip and inadvertence; it is against law and justice. The plaintiff has no merits. The bill of sale was fraudulent; the son remained in possession. The recovery is manifestly contrary to reason and justice."

Cadogan *et al.* v. Kennett *et al.*[1] was an action of trover, brought by the plaintiffs who were trustees under the marriage settlement of Lord Montfort against Kennett who was a judgment creditor of Lord Montfort's, and the other defendants who were sheriff's officers, to recover certain goods taken by them in execution under a *fi fa.* At the trial the marriage settlement was

---

[1] 2 Cowp. 432 (1776).

9

proved, by which it appeared that the goods in question,
which were the household goods belonging to Lord
Montfort, at his lordship's house in town, were conveyed
to plaintiffs, as trustees for the use of Lord Montfort for
life, remainder to Lady Montfort for her life, remainder
to the first and other sons of the marriage in strict
settlement. At the time of making the settlement it
was known that Lord Montfort was in debt, but he
thought the fortune of the lady he was to marry was
amply sufficient to pay all the debts he owed at that
time, and had no idea of disappointing any creditor.
Kennett was a creditor of Lord Montfort's at the time of
the settlement. At the trial Lord Mansfield thought the
possession of Lord Montfort was not fraudulent, because it was in pursuance, and in execution of the trust,
and the jury found a verdict for the plaintiffs. Upon a
motion for a new trial Lord Mansfield said : "Such a
construction is not to be made in support of creditors as
will make third persons sufferers. Therefore the statute
does not militate against any transaction *bona fide*, and
where there is no imagination of fraud, and so is the
common law. But if the transaction be not *bona fide*,
the circumstances of its being done for a valuable consideration will not alone take it out of the statute. I
have known several cases where persons have given a
fair and full price for goods, and where the possession
was actually changed, yet being done for the purpose of
defeating creditors, the transaction has been held fraudulent, and therefore void. There are many things which
are considered as circumstances of fraud. The statute
says not a word about possession. But the law says, if
after a sale of goods the vendor continue in possession,
and appear as the visible owner, it is evidence of fraud,
because goods pass by delivery, but it is not so in the

case of a lease, for that does not pass by delivery. The question therefore in every case is whether the act done is a *bona fide* transaction, or whether it is a trick and contrivance to defeat creditors. An argument, however, is drawn from the possession as a strong circumstance of fraud; but it does not hold in this case. It is a part of the trust that the goods shall continue in the house."

From this review of the authorities it will be seen that down to the time of Edwards v. Harben there was not a single case in which a transaction was held to be fraudulent on the ground of possession alone, and that the *obiter dicta* of Coke, in Stone v. Grubbam, and of Holt, in Meggot v. Mills, and the remarks of Sir Edward Northey, in Bucknal v. Roiston, are all that can be found to support the doctrine that the retention of possession is conclusive evidence of fraud.

Edwards v. Harben,[1] was an action of assumpsit for goods sold to the defendant's testator. It was proved that Mercer in his lifetime was indebted to the plaintiff in the sum of £22 18s. 6d. for goods sold and delivered and to the defendant in the sum of £191 for money lent. Mercer offered to the defendant a bill of sale of his goods, household furniture, and stock in trade in his house at Lewes, by way of security for the debt. The defendant refused to accept the same, unless he should be at liberty to enter upon the effects and sell them immediately after the expiration of fourteen days from the execution thereof, in case the money should not be sooner paid, to which Mercer agreed, and accordingly executed a bill of sale. All the effects described in the bill of sale remained in the possesion of Mercer until the time of his death. After the death of Mercer and before the

---

[1] 2 T. R. 587, (1788).

expiration of fourteen days from the execution of the bill of sale, the defendant entered the house of the deceased, and took possession of the effects contained in the bill of sale and afterwards sold them. The plaintiff sued him as executor *de son tort*. At the trial a verdict was found for the plaintiffs, subject to the opinion of the court, upon these facts. Buller J. in delivering the opinion of the court said: "On this case the question arises whether the bill of sale be void or not. This question came before the court in the last term, in the case of Bamford v. Baron, on a motion for a new trial from the Northern circuit, and after hearing that case argued, we thought it right to take the opinion of all the judges upon it. Accordingly we consulted with all the judges, who are unanimously of opinion that unless possession accompanies and follows the deed, it is fraudulent and void. I lay stress upon the words 'accompanies and follows' because I shall mention some cases where, though possession was not delivered at the time, the conveyance was not held to be fraudulent. There are many cases upon this subject from which it appears to me that the principle which I have stated never admitted of any serious doubt; so long ago as in the case in Bulstrode, the court held that an absolute conveyance, or gift of a lease for years, unattended with possession was fraudulent, but, if the deed is conditional, there the vendor's continuing in possession does not avoid it, because by the terms of the conveyance the vendee is not to have the possession till he has performed the condition. Now here the bill of sale was on the face of it absolute, and to take place immediately and the possession was not delivered, and that case makes the distinction between deeds or bills of sale which are to take place immediately and those which are to take place at some future time. For, in the latter case the possession continuing in the vendor till that future time, or till that condition is performed, is consistent with the deed, and such possession comes within the rule as accompanying and following the deed. That case has been universally followed by all the cases since. The Chancellor in the case of Bucknal v. Roiston, proceeded on the distinction which I have taken; he supported the deed because the want of possession was consistent with it. This has been argued by the defendant's counsel as being a case in which the want of possession is only evidence of fraud, and that it was not such a circumstance *per se* as makes the transaction fraudulent in point of law; that is the point which we have considered, and we are all of opinion that if there be nothing but the absolute conveyance, that, in point of law, is fraudulent. On the other hand there are cases where the vendor has continued in possession and the bill of sale has not been adjudged fraudulent if the want of immediate possession be consistent with the deed."

It is important to see upon what grounds the counsel, who impugned the validity of the bill of sale in this case, based his argument. He says: "This bill of sale is void, under 13 Eliz. c. 5, because it was not attended with any mark of possession, notorious to the rest of the world, but the vendor, by agreement with the vendee, which constitutes a part of the original transaction, continued in the possession and disposition of the goods mentioned in the bill of sale until his death. In considering this question, the two following principles may be supported: 1st. Whenever the vendor is found in the actual possession of goods which he has sold, such continuance in possession is *prima facie* evidence of an intent to delay, hinder, or defraud creditors, and throws it on the other party to rebut it by showing that the continuance in possession was with some other view. 2d. Whenever there is a positive agreement between the parties that the vendor shall be permitted, after the sale, to have for any space of time, not only the mere manual occupation, but also the disposition of the goods sold, to trade with them as his own, it is an actual fraud on the other creditors of the vendor. As to the first, every man is supposed to intend the natural and probable consequences of his own acts, unless it can be shown from circumstances that he acted upon some other motives. Now, in a case like the present, the natural and probable consequence of suffering another to continue in the possession of property not his own, is to hinder, delay, and defraud creditors of their just debts by giving him a false credit. Visible possession is the only criterion of personal property. Secondly, the bill of sale delivered under the circumstances of this case is an actual fraud upon the vendor's creditors. For here the false credit is not only the natural and probable, but the unavoidable, consequence of the deliberate act of the parties—an act incapable of explanation from any other motive than that of imposing on creditors—it is a stipulation from which neither party can draw a fair advantage. Either the vendor must be considered in the intermediate time as a trustee for the vendee, or that he is empowered to trade with the vendee's property for his own benefit. If the former, he receives no personal benefit from the stipulation; if the latter, it necessarily implies that the sale was not real, or that the consideration was not adequate; otherwise the vendee would not risk his property and give up part of his purchase for nothing. Apparent personal property is the principal foundation of general credit. It is material, therefore, when a person is reduced to part with this kind of property, especially such as is considered either as objects of personal accommodation, or as instruments of trade, that his creditors should be aware of his situation."

From these remarks it will be seen that possession alone was simply considered *prima facie* evidence of fraud. But the possession in this case was a possession implying ownership and *jus disponendi*. There was an actual, positive agreement that the vendor was not only to keep possession of the goods, but to deal with them as his own. It was the case of a trader who was daily selling goods, and whose business it was to sell, and the bill of sale covered his stock in trade.[1] The other cases in England, where the transaction has been considered fraudulent on account of the retention of possession, are of the same character. In Paget v. Perchard[2] the vendor kept a public house. The bill of sale was of all his effects, including all the liquors in the house as well as the furniture. After the execution of the bill of sale the vendor sold liquors in the usual way of his trade, received the money and did not account for it. Lord Kenyon held that, allowing the vendor to execute acts of ownership after parting with all his property by the bill of sale, was sufficient evidence of fraud. In Wordall v. Smith[3] the vendor made a bill of sale of all his effects, consisting of his household furniture and his stock in trade as a publican, but continued to carry on the business as usual for several weeks. The money received for sales was placed in a till to which he had

---

[1] Macdona v. Swiney, 8 Ir. Law (N. S.), 73.
[2] 1 Esp. 205, (1795).
[3] 1 Camp. 332, (1808).

access. Ryall v. Rowles,[1] and Worsely v. De Mattos
were also cases where traders mortgaged their stock in
trade, and after the execution of the mortgages continued to carry on their trade and sell the property
for their own benefit.[2] On the other hand, in none of the
cases where the transaction has been sustained, notwithstanding the retention of possession, was the vendor allowed to sell the goods for his own benefit.[3]

As the other cases in England simply constituted exceptions to the doctrine laid down in Edwards v.

---

[1] 1 Ves. 348.

[2] The only exception to these remarks is Bamford v. Baron, 2 T. R. 594.
That was an assignment for the benefit of creditors, and the debtor was
permitted to carry on the trade for a certain period, and account to the
trustee for all the profits of the trade from the date of the assignment. If
this case should be considered good law in England now, it would be
placed on a different ground.

In Edwards v. Harben, the ground chiefly relied on in argument, is
that by allowing the vendor to retain possession after the sale as apparent
owner, the vendee enables him to obtain a false credit. This would only
apply to subsequent creditors who trusted him on the faith of the property
It would not do to say that this of itself constitutes fraud, for then every
one who lends or hires property to another, a merchant who furnishes a
shop keeper with goods on credit, and thus enable him to hold himself
out as owner and thus obtain credit, would be guilty of the same sort of
fraud. Then it was argued, with respect to antecedent creditors, that it
tends to delay and hinder them—that relying on the appearance of
property in the debtor, they are prevented from taking proper means to enforce their demands. But in that case the debtor conveyed the whole of
his property, and whether immediate possession had been taken by the
vendee or not, antecedent creditors would have been equally defeated. In
such cases, then, it cannot be the failure to take possession by the vendee
which operates the fraud on such creditors. (Smith v. Henry, 1 Hill, 16.)
Doubts as to what was really decided in Edwards v. Harben are raised
by the remarks of Buller, J., in Buller's N. P. 258, and Hazelinton v. Gill,
3 T. R. 620, note. Weaver v. Joule, 91 E. C. L. 309; s. c. 3 C. B. (N. S.)
309; Reed v. Blades, 5 Taunt. 212, supports the distinction stated in the
text.

[3] Eastwood v. Brown, Ry. & Mood. 312; Hoffman v. Pitt, 5 Esp. 22
Eveleigh v. Purrsford, 2 Mood & Rob. 539. The only exception is Bento;
v. Thornhill, 2 Marsh, 427; s. c. 7 Taunt, 149.

Harben, until it was finally settled that the retention c
possession was only presumptive evidence of fraud, it i
not necessary, in this connection, to trace them any
further. For the purpose of understanding the course
of the decisions upon this subject, it should be borne in
mind that the rule laid down by the court in that case
was that the possession must be consistent with the
deed. As this principle was addressed merely to the
form of the transaction, it was readily complied with by
the insertion of a stipulation providing that the vendor
might retain the possession, and several deeds have been
held valid simply on the ground of the presence of such
a clause.[1] A rule that could be thus easily evaded was
of course practically worthless, and a modification was
found to be necessary.

In Vredenbergh v. White,[2] Barrow v. Paxton[3] and
Beals v. Guernsey,[4] it was held that possession was only
prima facie evidence of fraud, and open to explanation.
In Sturtevant v. Ballard,[5] the bill of sale contained a
stipulation that the vendor should have the use and
occupation of the articles for three months. Kent, Ch.
J. said: "The question arising upon this case is whether the sale is valid in law as against the judgment
creditor. The great point is whether the fact of
permitting the vendor to retain possession of the goods
did not render this sale fraudulent in law, notwithstanding such permission was inserted in the deed
as a condition of the contract. If there had been no

---

[1] Wooderman v. Baldock, 8 Taunt. 676; Martindale v. Booth, 3 B. &
A. 498.

[2] 1 Johns. Cas. 156 (1799).

[3] 5 Johns. 258 (1810).

[4] 8 Johns. 446 (1811).

[5] 9 Johns. 337 (1812).

such insertion, but the sale had been absolute on the face of it, and possession had not immediately accompanied and followed the sale, it would have been fraudulent as against creditors, and the fraud in such case would have been an inference or conclusion of law which the Court would have been bound to pronounce. But it by no means follows that such a sale, with such an agreement attached to it and appearing on the face of the deed is necessarily valid. There must be some sufficient motive, and of which the Court is to judge, for the non-delivery of the goods, or the law will still presume the sale to have been made with a view to 'delay, hinder or defraud creditors.' Delivery of possession is so much of the essence of the sale of chattels that an agreement to permit the vendor to keep possession is an exception to the usual course of dealing, and requires a satisfactory explanation. We may therefore safely conclude that a voluntary sale of chattels, with an agreement either in or out of the deed that the vendor may keep possession is, except in special cases to be shown to and approved of by the Court, fraudulent and void as against creditors. This is clearly not one of those cases." Hamilton v. Russell[1] preceded this case in point of time, but this case is the leading one in America[2] upon this subject.

In Wickham v. Miller,[3] Gates, J., held that the non-delivery of the goods is no more than *prima facie* evidence, and might be explained by circumstances, but the decision did not rest upon that point. In Butts v.

---

[1] 1 Cranch, 309.

[2] Clow v. Woods, 5 S. & R. 275; Coburn v. Pickering, 3 N. H. 415; Patten v. Smith, 5 Ct. 196; Gibson v. Love, 4 Fla. 217; Hundley v. Webb, 3 J. J. Marsh, 643; Planters' Bank v. Borland, 5 Ala. 531.

[3] 12 Johns. 320 (1815).

Swartout,[1] the plaintiff made a contract with the vendor, who was a cabinet-maker, for a bureau. When nearly completed, it was formally delivered but left with the vendor to be trimmed. The proof also showed that the vendor had other goods which he offered to the defendant, who was a constable, to satisfy the execution in his hands. Sutherland, J., said: "The question of fraud depends upon the motive. The non-delivery of the bureau is only one circumstance in proof of fraud, and it is accounted for."

The question arose again in Bissell v. Hopkins,[2] and Savage, Ch. J., said: "The question in every case is whether the act done is a *bona fide* transaction or whether it is a trick and contrivance to defeat creditors. The possession by the vendor of personal chattels after the sale is not conclusive evidence of fraud. The vendee may, notwithstanding, upon proof that the sale was *bona fide* and for a valuable consideration, and that the possession of the vendor after such sale was in pursuance of some agreement not inconsistent with honesty in the transaction, hold under his purchase against creditors. A good reason is given, in my judgment, why the vendor was not at once stripped of his property, as thereby his power of acquiring the means to pay his debts would have been taken from him."

After this decision there were six decisions in New York holding possession to be only presumptive evidence of fraud, and one declaring that the explanation must be satisfactory to the Court. Strict logic required that Bissell v. Hopkins should be considered as overruling Sturtevant v. Ballard. But the genius of the law

---

[1] 2 Cow. 431 (1823).
[2] 3 Cow. 166 (1824).

demands that conflicting cases shall be reconciled wherever reconciliation is possible. Accordingly, in Divver v. McLaughlin,[1] Savage, Ch. J., held that "The possession of personal property by the vendor or mortgagor inconsistent with the face of the deed is *prima facie* evidence of fraud, but subject to explanation. In other words, such possession is, except in special cases and for special reasons to be shown to and approved of by the Court, fraudulent and void as against creditors. The mortgage in this case, after forfeiture without explanation, must be held fraudulent and void as against creditors. The only real question, therefore, is whether the reasons shown why the possession was not changed are such as can be approved of by the Court under the special circumstances. The counsel for the defendant in error contends that this is a question for the jury. Upon a conceded state of facts fraud is a question of law. There is in this case no dispute about the facts; it is a question for the Court, therefore, to decide whether the mortgage was valid or void as against creditors."

The same principle was asserted in Jennings v. Carter[2] and in Archer v. Hubbell.[3]

This was the condition of the question at the time of the adoption of the Revised Code.[4] In the revision of the statute law it was attempted to settle all doubts and discrepancies by positive legislation and strict definition. Accordingly, the revisers recommended that " all sales or mortgages not accompanied by an immediate delivery and followed by an actual and continued change of possession should be void against the cred-

---

[1] 2 Wend. 596 (1829).   [2] 4 Wend. 514 (1830)
[3] 2 Wend. 446 (1829).   [4] 1830.

itors of the vendor," and this without any exception
and excluding all explanation.   But the same considerations of natural equity which had so often induced
courts to break in upon the judicial rule of legal policy,
had again equal weight with the legislature, so that, in
adopting the section recommended by the revisers, they
added a clause of exception, enabling the person claiming under the sale or assignment to rebut the legal presumption of fraudulent intention by positive evidence
of the good faith of the transaction. It was accordingly,
enacted first nearly in the strong and comprehensive
language of the revisers that every sale of goods and
chattels and every assignment by way of mortgage or
security " unless the same be accompanied by an immediate delivery, and be followed by an actual and continued change of possession, shall be pronounced to be
fraudulent and void as against creditors or subsequent
purchasers, and shall be conclusive evidence of fraud;"
then the legislature, of its own motion, added the ex-
cepting and qualifying clause " unless it shall be made
to appear on the part of the person claiming under such
sale or assignment that the same was made in good faith
and without any intent to defraud such creditors or
purchasers." This question of fraudulent intent a subsequent section enacted should be a question of fact and
not of law.[1]   These enactments were thought to have
settled the law conclusively, but they merely afforded a
new and remarkable proof of the imperfection of human
language and the impossibility of definitely settling any
great rule of law for the complicated affairs of human

---

[1] Rev. Stat. 13 6, § 5.

life merely by the general language of a statute or the provisions of a code.[1]

Hall v. Tuttle[2] arose before the adoption of the revised statutes, but was decided afterwards, and the court held that they were simply declaratory of what was understood to have been the law ever since the 13th Eliz., ch. 5, and what the common law was before that statute was enacted. But in Collins v. Brush[3] the court said: "It is incumbent upon the vendee to repel the presumption of fraud by showing some satisfactory reason for his omission to take the property into his possession. It is not sufficient to show a valuable consideration; some reason must be shown which the court can approve for leaving the goods in the possession of the vendor." The same doctrine was held in other cases.[4] It was also held that the distinction between conditional and absolute sales was abolished,[5] and that the mere accommodation of the parties was not a satisfactory explanation, so that the only effect of the enactments seemed to be to make the rule more rigorous.

The question arose again in Stoddard v. Butler.[6]

---

[1] Stoddard v. Butler, 20 Wend. 507; Smith v. Acker, 23 Wend. 653, per Senator Verplanck. The ground of all the errors of the decisions upon this subject would seem to be the desire of the court to establish a code of morals which shall put it out of the power of persons to commit fraud, rather than to carry out the intention of the legislature to provide means of detecting fraud when committed. Smith v. Acker, 23 Wend. 653, per Senator Hopkins.

[2] 8 Wend. 375 (1832).

[3] 9 Wend. 198 (1832).

[4] Gardner v. Adams, 12 Wend. 297 (1834); Doane v. Eddy, 16 Wend. 523 (1837); Randall v. Cook, 17 Wend. 53 (1837); Stevens v. Fisher, 19 Wend. 181 (1838); Beekman v. Bond, 19 Wend. 444 (1838).

[5] Gardner v. Adams, 12 Wend. 297; Doane v. Eddy, 16 Wend. 523; Randall v. Cook, 17 Wend. 53.

[6] 20 Wend. 507; s. c. 7 Paige, 163 (1838).

Butler, who was a creditor of Stoddard, instituted suit
and obtained judgment; but between the commencement of the suit and the recovery of the judgment
Stoddard executed an absolute assignment of his stock
of goods and of certain notes and accounts to Thurber
& Townsend, for and towards the payment and satisfaction of a debt due to them. The goods and notes and
accounts were left in the possession of Stoddard, who
was authorized, as the agent of the vendees, to sell the
goods and collect the notes and accounts, and they agreed
to give him a fair compensation for his services. The
complainants filed a bill in equity to set aside the conveyance as fraudulent. The vice-chancellor dismissed
the bill. The complainants appealed to the chancellor,
who reversed the decree of the vice-chancellor, and adjudged the assignment to be fraudulent. From this
decree the respondents appealed to the Court of Errors,
and thus for the first time was the question raised in
that court, the other decisions having been rendered in
the Supreme Court. The decree of the chancellor was
affirmed by a divided court: twelve for affirmance and
twelve for reversal. Two questions were raised: first,
whether possession alone rendered the transfer void, and
secondly, whether the property was disproportioned in
value to the amount of the debt intended to be satisfied,
thus making the assignment fraudulent in fact; and
upon both the court was divided, but three members of
the court—the President and Senators Tallmadge and
Edwards, who voted for affirmance—subsequently
adopted the opinion that the weight of the evidence to
repel the presumption was for the determination of the
jury, and two stated that their votes in this case were
given upon the ground of fraud in fact.[1] The important

---

[1] Smith v. Acker, 23 Wend. 653.

features of the case, however, were the opinions of Senator Dickinson and Senator Verplanck. That of Senator
Dickinson has been styled the ablest argument ever
delivered upon the subject, but his attempt to reconcile
all the conflicting decisions shows the condition of the
question at that time. The decision of the court left
the matter as unsettled as ever except that an impression prevailed that if a case should be brought before it
free from other questions, the doctrine of the Supreme
Court would be overruled.

The question came before it again in Smith v. Acker,[1]
and was the only point in the case. Bell made a mortgage to Smith & Hoe, and remained in possession.
The Sheriff seized the property on an execution against
Bell. Smith & Hoe brought an action of replevin.
The defendant moved for a non-suit. The plaintiff
insisted that the question of fraudulent intent should
be submitted as a question of fact to the jury. This
the judge refused to do, and ordered a nonsuit, and the
judgment was subsequently affirmed by the Supreme
Court. The plaintiffs thereupon sued out a writ of error, and removed the case into the Court of Errors.
The judgment was there reversed, on the ground that
the judge erred in assuming to decide upon the matters
of fact which belonged to the jury.

The question now took another aspect. Possession
was on all sides admitted to raise a presumption of
fraud, and the only point in dispute was in regard to
the mode of rebutting it, one party holding that the
explanation must be satisfactory to the court, and the
other party that the whole matter must be left to the

---

[1] 23 Wend. 653 (1840).

jury. In Stevens v. Fisher,[1] Cowen, J., had endeavored
to support the former by placing the doctrine upon the
right of the court to reject incompetent and irrelevant
testimony. This proposition was argued more at length
in White v. Cole.[2] He said: "The *quo animo* is a
question of fact for the jury when an explanation is
offered; that is, as I understand the phrase, not any and
everything which may be called an explanation, but
evidence pertinent to the question of fact. It stands on
the footing of any other question of fact to be determined by the jury. If the testimony offered be pertinent in the opinion of the judge, it is his duty to receive
it; if not, he is bound to reject it. This is a universal
rule in relation to trying all questions of fact, which
separates the province of the judge from the jury. The
question arises upon the competency of the evidence,
not the sufficiency. The statute gives the court no
power to determine what particular facts shall or shall
not be sufficient evidence of honest intention. The
statute says nothing one way or the other as to what
facts shall persuade or what shall be pertinent. For all
this the judge is left to the common law. The whole,
then, comes down to the question of what testimony is
admissible. The principle has, therefore, obtained an
almost universal footing, that the mere proof of a debt,
to whatever amount, shall not be allowed to excuse the
continuance of possession; and that it cannot be so
regarded by a jury, however necessary the use of the
property may be for the debtor. These two circumstances prove nothing of themselves. They do not make
an explanation, nor can the jury regard them as suffi-

---

[1] 19 Wend. 181.
[2] 24 Wend. 116 (1840).

cient to overturn the presumption of fraud derivable from the possession of the debtor. They are not pertinent evidence."

The case was carried up for review to the Court of Errors,[1] and this new position was fairly met and overruled. It was held that all facts or circumstances which to the common understanding and conscience of men may prove, or on their face may tend to prove, good faith are within the rightful privilege of the jury to hear and weigh; and the judgment was reversed because relevant testimony on a question of the fact of fraudulent intent was excluded from the consideration of the jury, whose right it was to pass upon its weight and sufficiency.

The controversy, however, was not yet terminated. Up to this time it had been carried on in a spirit of candid discussion, but now it took a partially personal tone. In Randall v. Cook, Bronson, J., observed: "Had it been declared fifty years ago that if a man conveyed his personal chattels and still kept them himself, under any pretence whatever, the transaction should be deemed absolutely fraudulent and void as against creditors, it would have saved an incalculable amount of time and money which has been expended in the litigation of questions of this kind, and it would, moreover, have rendered a most important service in the cause of good morals by removing all temptations to the numberless frauds which have been committed for the purpose of placing property beyond the reach of legal process." Commenting upon these remarks, Senator Dickinson[2] said: "If, at the same time, the law had laid its interdiction upon all human intercourse as to exchanges or

---

[1] Cole v. White, 26 Wend. 511 (1841).
[2] Stoddard v. Butler, 20 Wend. 507.

purchases of property, the same result would have been produced, and with about equal justice and propriety." Senator Hopkins also said :[1] " The same reasoning would be applicable to almost all the business transactions of life. If everything capable of being perverted in the hands of the dishonest to fraudulent purposes is to be done away, the honest portions of the community will have little left of all they deem most valuable. The reasoning would be equally applicable to all sales upon credit. Had all credits been prohibited fifty years ago it would no doubt have saved an incalculable amount of time and money."

In Butler v. Van Wyck,[2] Bronson, J., delivered a dissenting opinion, and, observing that his remarks had been made the text for spirited and witty commentary, and styling the opinion of Senator Hopkins the prevailing opinion, held that the decision of the Court of Errors should be disregarded.

In Hanford v. Artcher,[3] the Court of Errors, adhering to its previous decisions, felt called upon to notice and comment upon this opinion, and vindicate its course. In this case there was still another point. The question was submitted to the jury, but the judge instructed them that it was for them to decide whether there was any good reason shown, which they could approve, why there had not been an immediate delivery and an actual and continued change of possession. The Court of Errors, considering that the instruction restricted them to the consideration of good reasons to excuse a want of delivery and prevented them from considering the whole *bona fides* of the case, reversed the judgment. President

---

[1] Smith v. Acker, 23 Wend. 653.

[2] 1 Hill, 438.

[3] 4 Hill, 271; s. c. 1 Hill, 347 (1842).

Bradish said : "Instead of directing them to the only inquiry expressly prescribed by the statute, the judge led their minds to one not in terms embraced in its provisions and calculated to present to them a false issue. This was error. Instead of the inquiry thus directed he should have charged the jury to inquire whether it had been made to appear on the part of the vendee that the sale was made in good faith and without any intention to defraud creditors. This would have been in the language and spirit of the statute. But the direction gave an artificial, restricted and erroneous interpretation to the statute." It will thus be seen that the difference between the Court of Errors and the Supreme Court was in regard to what the question was to be tried and who should try it. The latter insisted that the issue was whether there was any satisfactory explanation and that the court should try it. The former said that the issue was a question of intent and that the jury should try it.

It would seem as though the questions were clearly and unmistakably settled, but it was subsequently asserted in Randall v. Parker[1] that all the cases upon this subject were reconcilable. This attempt at a reaction, however, was only temporary, and the point is now considered as finally and conclusively determined.[2] Thus terminated one of the most remarkable controversies in the whole annals of jurisprudence, a controversy extending over a period of more than two centuries and engaging the attention of the most eminent jurists of the times.

As this question may be considered to have turned

---

[1] 3 Sandf. 69.

[2] Thompson v. Blanchard, 4 N. Y. 303; Miller v. Lockwood, 32 N. Y. 293; Van Buskirk v. Warren, 39 N. Y. 119.

partly upon the peculiar statute of New York, it may be well to glance briefly at the course of the decisions in one other State. The doctrine that possession is conclusive evidence of fraud was held for a long time in Virginia.[1] In Land v. Jeffries,[2] Cabell, J., said: "The question does not by any means involve any doubt as to the effect of the mere circumstance of actual possession not passing from the grantor contemporaneously with the execution of the conveyance, nor as to the effect of the mere circumstance of such possession being found in his hands afterwards. Nobody ever pretended that either of these was such a circumstance *per se* as makes the transaction fraudulent in law. Everybody admits that the mere possession of personal property after an absolute conveyance is only evidence of fraud to be submitted to the jury, and that it is only *prima facie* evidence. Being only *prima facie* evidence of fraud, it must, from its very nature, be liable to be rebutted by other testimony, and, consequently, the possession of the vendor is susceptible of explanation as to its character, for the purpose of freeing it from the imputation of fraud.

Many cases might be stated as examples for showing the operation of this principle, but a single one will suffice. A man purchases the chattel of another for full consideration and *bona fide*. The chattel at the time of the sale is on the farm of the vendor. It is the expectation and intention of both parties that it shall be removed with all reasonable dispatch, and it remains, in the meantime, in the possession of the vendor, without

---

[1] Alexander v. Deneale, 2 Munf. 341; Williamson v. Farley, Gilmer, 15; Robertson v. Ewell, 3 Munf. 1 ; Glasscock v. Batton, 6 Rand, 78; Lewis v. Adams, 6 Leigh, 320; Mason v. Bond, 9 Leigh, 181; Tavenner v. Robinson, 2 Rob. 280.

[2] 5 Rand, 211; s. c. 599.

any regard to his convenience, but solely to await the reasonable convenience of the vendee in removing it. But before the vendee can thus remove it an execution comes out against the goods and chattels of the vendor, and the sheriff, finding the chattel in his possession, levies the execution upon it and sells it. In an action of trespass brought by the vendee against the sheriff, if the vendee exhibits nothing but his absolute bill of sale, the sheriff may show that notwithstanding the bill of sale the chattel was found by him in the vendor's possession. Now, as the possession of personal chattels is *prima facie* evidence of property in or of trust for the person possessing, the possession of the vendor thus exhibited would be, *prima facie*, inconsistent with the avowed object of the absolute conveyance to the vendee, and would therefore be *prima facie* evidence of a trust for the vendor, and that the absolute conveyance was intended as a cover to disguise and conceal that trust, and thereby to delay, hinder and defraud creditors. But still, this would be *prima facie* evidence only, liable to be rebutted by other testimony.

If, therefore, the vendee shall prove that the possession of the vendor was connected with no motive of benefit or advantage to the vendor, but was for the reasonable convenience of the vendee only, and was intended to continue no longer than such reasonable convenience required, all presumption of property in the vendor, or of trust for him is done away, and, consequently, the possession of the vendor is shown not to be inconsistent with the purpose of the absolute deed, and thus the whole foundation for the inference of fraud would be removed. But suppose that the sheriff should not only prove that the chattel was found in the actual possessison of the vendor, but that it was agreed between the vendor and vendee at the time of the convey-

ance that the chattel should remain in the possession of
the vendor for a long or a short time, to be used by him
during that time as if he were the owner. Such a possession by the vendor would be manifestly inconsistent
with the deed, for the deed purports to be for the sole
and exclusive benefit of the vendee, whereas the possession as explained by the agreement shows a trust for
the benefit of the vendor."

The doctrine was still further relaxed in the cases of
Sydnor v. Gee[1] and Lewis v. Adams.[2] The confidence
of the profession in the former decisions was thus shaken,
and doubts and uncertainty were produced. It was
therefore deemed best that the whole subject should be
reviewed, and the law finally settled, so as to preclude
future controversy. In Davis v. Turner,[3] it was determined that possession simply raised a presumption of
fraud, and that the weight and sufficiency of the evidence to rebut it was for the consideration of the jury.

THE AUTHORITIES.—The preponderance of the authorities are, at the present time, in favor of this
doctrine.[4]

---

[1] 4 Leigh, 535.   [2] 6 Leigh, 320.   [3] 4 Gratt. 422, 1848.

[4] England—Arundel v. Phipps, 10 Ves. 139; Martindale v. Booth, 3 B.
& A. 498; Eastwood v. Brown, Ry. & Mood, 312; Orlabar v. Harwar,
Comb, 348; Hoffman v. Pitt, 5 Esp. 22; Latimer v. Batson, 4 B. & C. 652;
Benton v. Thornhill, 2 Marsh, 427; s. c. 7 Taunt. 149; Martin v. Podger,
2 W. Bl. 701; s. c. 5 Burr. 2631; Carr v. Burdiss, 5 Tyrw. 309; Eveleigh
v. Purrsford, 2 Mood. & Rob. 539; Lindon v. Sharp, 6 M. & G. 895; Macdona v. Swiney, 8 Ir. Law (N. S.), 73. *Contra*, Edwards v. Harben, 2 T.
R., 587; Wordall v. Smith, 1 Camp. 332; Paget v. Perchard, 1 Esp. 205;
Legard v. Linley, Clayt. 38. Maine—Haskell v. Greely, 3 Me. 425; Reed
v. Jewett, 5 Me. 96; Ulmer v. Hills, 8 Me. 326; Bartlett v. Blake, 37 Me.
124; Googins v. Gilmore, 47 Me. 9. Massachusetts—Brooks v. Powers,
15 Mass., 244; Shumway v. Rutter, 7 Pick. 56; s. c. 8 Pick. 443; Macomber v. Parker, 14 Pick. 497; Fletcher v. Willard, 14 Pick. 464; Allen v.
Wheeler, 4 Gray, 123. New York—Smith v. Acker, 23 Wend. 653; Cole
v. White, 26 Wend 511; s. c. 24 Wend. 116; Hanford v. Artcher, 4 Hill,

ACTUAL, NOT MERELY CONSTRUCTIVE, CHANGE OF POS-
SESSION.—The change of possession required by the rule
is an actual, and not a merely constructive change.　An
actual change, as distinguished from that which by the

---

271 ; s. c. 1 Hill, 347 ; Beals v. Guernsey, 8 Johns. 446 ; Bissell v. Hopkins,
3 Cow. 166 ; Stewart v. Slater, 6 Duer, 83 ; Swift v. Hart, 12 Barb. 530 ;
Butts v. Swartout, 2 Cow. 431 ; Hall v. Tuttle, 8 Wend. 375 ; Prentiss v.
Slack, 1 Hill, 467 ; Fuller v. Acker, 1 Hill, 473 ; Lewis v. Stevenson, 2
Hall, 63 ; Groat v. Rees, 20 Barb. 26 ; Butler v. Miller, 1 N. Y. 496 ;
Thompson v. Blanchard, 4 N. Y. 303 ; Van Buskirk v. Warren, 39 N. Y.
119 ; s. c. 34 Barb. 457 ; Miller v. Lockwood, 32 N. Y. 293.　Contra,
Sturtevant v. Ballard, 9 Johns. 337 ; Williams v. Lowndes, 1 Hall, 579 ;
Divver v. McLaughlin, 2 Wend, 596 ; Doane v. Eddy, 16 Wend. 523 ; Col-
lins v. Brush, 9 Wend. 198 ; Randall v. Cook, 17 Wend. 53 ; Stevens v.
Fisher, 19 Wend. 181 ; Walker v. Snediker, Hoff. 145 ; Gardner v. Adams,
12 Wend. 297.　New Jersey—Miller v. Pancoast, 5 Dutch, 250.　Contra,
Chumar v. Wood, 1 Halst. 155.　Virginia—Davis v. Turner, 4 Gratt. 422 ;
Forkner v. Stewart, 6 Gratt. 197.　Contra, Williamson v. Farley. Gilmer,
15 ; Alexander v. Deneale, 2 Munf. 341 ; Robertson v. Ewell, 3 Munf. 1 ;
Land v. Jeffries, 5 Rand. 211, 599 ; Claytor v. Anthony, 6 Rand. 285 ;
Hardaway v. Manson, 2 Munf. 230 ; Lewis v. Adams, 6 Leigh. 320 ; Ma-
son v. Bond, 9 Leigh. 181 ; Tavenner v. Robinson, 2 Rob. 280 ; Glasscock
v. Batton, 6 Rand. 78.　North Carolina—Cox v. Jackson, 1 Hayw. 423 ;
Vick v. Keyes, 2 Hayw. 126 ; Falkner v. Perkins, 2 Hayw. 224 ; Trotter v.
Howard, 1 Hawk. 320 ; Smith v. Niel, 1 Hawk. 341 ; Rea v. Alexander, 5
Ired. 644.　Contra, Gaither v. Mumford, 1 N. C. T. R. 167.　South Carolina—Terry v. Belcher, 1 Bailey, 568 ; Smith v. Henry, 2 Bailey, 118.　Contra, Kennedy v. Ross, 2 Mills, 125 ; De Bardleben v. Beekman, 1 Dessau,
346.　The only exception to the rule in this　State is that of a sale to a
creditor in consideration of an existing debt.　In case of such a preference
there must be a change of the possession. Smith v. Henry, 1 Hill (S. C.), 16 ;
Anderson v. Fuller, 1 McMullan, Ch. 27 ; Fulmore v. Burrows, 2 Rich.
Eq. 96 ; Jones v. Blake, 2 Hill, Ch. 629.　Georgia—Butler v. Roll, Geo.
Decis, Part I, 37 ; Peck v. Land, 2 Kelly, 1 ; Carter v. Stanfield, 8 Geo. 49.
Alabama—Hobbs v. Bibb, 2 Stew. 54 ; Ayres v. Moore, 2 Stew. 336 ; Mar-
tin v. White, 2 Stew. 162 ; Blocker v. Burness, 2 Ala. 354 ; Killough v.
Steele, 1 Stew. & Port. 262 ; Borland v. Walker, 7 Ala. 269 ; Mayer v.
Clark, 40 Ala. 259.　Contra, Planters' Bank v. Borland, 5 Ala. 531 ; Bor-
land v. Mayo, 8 Ala. 104 ; Mauldin V. Mitchell, 14 Ala. 814 ; Millard v.
Hall, 24 Ala. 209.　Mississippi—Carter v. Graves, 6 How. (Miss.) 9 ; Bo-
gard v. Gardley, 4 S. & M. 302 ; Rankin v. Holloway, 3 S. & M. 614 ;
Comstock v. Rayford, 1 S. & M. 423 ; s. c. 12 S. & M. 369 ; Summers v.
Roos, 43 Miss. 749 ; Jayne v. Dillon, 27 Miss. 283.　Louisiana—Keller v.

mere intendment of the law follows the transfer of the
title, is an open, visible, public change, manifested by
such outward signs as render it evident that the posses-

Blanchard, 19 La. An. 53; Louisiana v. Ballio, 15 La. An. 555; Guice v.
Sanders, 21 La. An. 463; Haile v. Brewster, 13 La. An. 155; Sullice v.
Gradenigo, 15 La. An. 582. *Contra*, Jorda v. Lewis, 1 La. An. 59; Zach-
arie v. Kirk, 14 La. An. 433. Texas—Bryant v. Kelton, 1 Tex. 415; Mor-
gan v. Republic, 2 Tex. 279; McQuinnay v. Hitchcock, 8 Tex. 33; Con-
verse v. McKee, 14 Tex. 20; Earle v. Thomas, 14 Tex. 583; Gibson v.
Hill, 21 Tex. 225. Arkansas—Field v. Simco, 2 Eng. 269; Cocke v. Chap-
man, 2 Eng. 197; Stone v. Waggoner, 3 Eng. 204; George v. Norris, 23
Ark. 121. Tennessee—Callen v. Thompson, 3 Yerg. 475; Darwin v.
Handley, 3 Yerg. 502; Young v. Pate, 4 Yerg. 164; Grubbs v. Greer, 5
Cold. 160. *Contra*, Ragan v. Kennedy, 1 Tenn. 91. Ohio—Rogers v.
Dare, Wright, 136; Burbridge v. Seely, Wright, 359; Hombeck v. Van-
metre, 9 Ohio, 153. Indiana—Foley v. Knight, 4 Blackf. 420; Watson v.
Williams, 4 Blackf. 26; Hankins v. Ingolls, 4 Blackf. 35; Jones v. Gott, 9
Ind. 240; Nutter v. Harris, 9 Ind. 88; Kane v. Drake, 27 Ind. 29. Wis-
consin—Whitney v. Brunette, 3 Wis. 621; Smith v. Welch, 10 Wis. 91;
Bullis v. Borden, 21 Wis. 135; Bond v. Seymour, 1 Chand. 40; Sterling
v. Ripley, 3 Chand. 166. Michigan—Jackson v. Dean, 1 Doug. (Mich.)
519. United States—Warner v. Norton, 20 How. 448. *Contra*, Hamilton
v. Russell, 1 Cranch. 309. Canada—Hunter v. Corbett, 7 U. C. (Q. B.) 75.
Contra—Vermont—Mott v. McNiel, 1 Aik. 162; Weeks v. Wead, 2
Aik. 64; Fuller v. Sears, 5 Vt. 527; Durkee v. Mahoney, 1 Aik. 116;
Beattie v. Robins, 2 Vt. 181. New Hampshire—Coburn v. Pickering, 3 N.
H. 415; Page v. Carpenter, 10 N. H. 77; Paul v. Crooker, 8 N. H. 288;
Shaw v. Thompson, 43 N H. 130. *Contra*, Haven v. Low, 2 N. H. 13.
The doctrine in this State rests upon the theory of a secret trust: Co-
burn v. Pickering, 3 N. H. 415. Secrecy establishes it: Trask v. Bowers,
4 N. H. 309. Notoriety has a tendency to repel it: Paul v. Crooker, 8 N.
H. 288. Connecticut—Patten v. Smith, 4 Conn. 450; s. c. 5 Conn. 196;
Swift v. Thompson, 9 Conn. 63; Crouch v. Carrier, 16 Conn. 505; Osborne
v. Tuller, 14 Conn. 529. Pennsylvania—Babb v. Clemson, 10 S. & R. 419;
Clow v. Woods, 5 S. & R. 275; Hoofsmith v. Cope, 6 Whart, 53; Milne v.
Henry, 40 Penn. 352; Eagle v. Eichelberger, 6 Watts, 29. Delaware—Bow-
man v. Herring, 4 Harrington, 458. Florida—Gibson v. Love, 4 Fla. 217;
Sanders v. Pepoon, 4 Fla. 465. Kentucky—Goldsbury v. May, 1 Litt. 254;
Dale v. Arnold, 2 Bibb, 605; Grimes v. Davis, 1 Litt. 241; Middleton v.
Carroll, 4 J. J. Marsh, 143; Waller v. Todd, 3 Dana, 503; Wash v. Med-
ley, 1 Dana, 269. Illinois—Rhimes v. Phelps, 3 Gilman, 455; Thornton v.
Davenport, 1 Scam 296; Dexter v. Parkins, 22 Ill. 143; Ketchum v. Wat-
son, 24 Ill. 591; Bay v. Cook, 31 Ill. 336; Corgan v. Frew, 39 Ill. 31.
Missouri—Claflin v. Rosenberg, 42 Mo. 439; s. c. 43 Mo. 593; Sibly

sion of the owner, as such, 'has wholly ceased.[1]   The
possession of the vendor is always constructively the
possession of the vendee; the possession of an agent is
constructively the possession of his principal.   If the
change is merely constructive, the presumption of fraud
arises.[2]   If there is no change a purchaser from the
vendee will stand in the same condition as his vendor,
the intermediate purchaser, and the presumption will be
that both sales were fraudulent, as against the creditors of the first vendor.[3]   But if his vendor was never
the ostensible owner then his omission to take possession
raises no presumption of fraud.[4]   If there is a change
of possession prior to a levy, there is no presumption
of fraud.[5]

BURDEN OF PROOF.—The presumption is not merely
a presumption of a fraudulent intent on the part of the
vendor, but also of a concurrence in that intent on the
part of the vendee.   The possession in the vendor, therefore, is all that need be shown, in the first instance, by
the creditor contesting the validity of the transaction,
and, that being shown, the statute presumes it to be

---

v. Hood, 3 Mo. 206 ; Foster v. Wallace, 2 Mo. 231 ; King v. Bailey 6 Mo.
575.   *Contra*, s. c. 8 Mo. 332; Shepherd v. Trigg, 7 Mo. 151; Ross v.
Crutsinger, 7 Mo. 245 ; Kuykendall v. McDonald, 15 Mo. 416; State v.
Smith, 31 Mo. 566 ; State v. Evans, 38 Mo. 150; Middleton v. Hoff, 15
Mo. 415; Howell v. Bell, 29 Mo. 135.   California Code—Fitzgerald v.
Gorham, 4 Cal. 289; Whitney v. Stark, 8 Cal. 514.   Nevada—Doack v.
Brubacker, 1 Nev. 218.   Oregon—Monroe v. Hussey, 1 Oregon, 188.   This
subject is regulated by statute in Delaware, California, Nevada, and Mis-
souri.

[1] Cutter v. Copeland, 18 Me. 127.

[2] Hanford v. Artcher, 4 Hill, 271; Randall v. Parker, 3 Sandf. 69;
Otis v. Sill, 8 Barb. 102; Grant v. Lewis, 14 Wis. 487; Lesem v. Herriford,
44 Mo. 323.

[3] Lesem v. Herriford, 44 Mo. 323.

[4] Burling v. Patterson, 9 C. &. P. 570.

[5] Allen v. Cowan, 23 N. Y. 502.

fraudulent.[1]   The burden is then thrown upon the vendee to show, from all the circumstances surrounding the transaction, its true character, in order to repel the presumption of fraud,[2] and the evidence in explanation ought to be so clear as to leave no room to doubt the fairness of the sale.[3] If no evidence is given, the presumption becomes conclusive.[4]

POINT OF INQUIRY.—The presumption is a presumption of a fraudulent intent on the part of the vendor and of participation in it on the part of the vendee.   An inquiry, therefore, into the motives, reasons and causes for not changing the possession is irrelevant so far as it is designed to raise any distinct question for the determination of either the court or the jury. The true and sole inquiry is, whether the presumption of fraud is repelled by the evidence.[5] The court has no power to say what particular facts shall or shall not be sufficient evidence of honest intention.   Its only power is to determine what facts are admissible and relevant to determine the issue.   Any facts which impress the mind with a conviction that the sale was honest and *bona fide*, and was not designed as a mere trick to cover the property, should be submitted to the jury.[6] No explanation can be more satisfactory than that the possession was retain-

---

[1] Kuykendall v. Hitchcock, 15 Mo. 416.

[2] Kuykendall v. Hitchcock, 15 Mo. 416; Davis v. Turner, 4 Gratt. 422; Comstock v. Rayford, 12 S. & M. 369; Mills v. Walton, 19 Tex. 271; Grant v. Lewis, 14 Wis. 487.

[3] Smith v. Henry, 2 Bailey, 118; Davis v. Turner, 4 Gratt. 422; Jones v. Blake, 2 Hill Ch. 629.

[4] Carter v. Graves, 6 How. (Miss.) 9; Carter v. Stanfield, 8 Geo. 49; Beers v. Dawson, 8 Geo. 556; Allen v. Cowan, 28 Barb. 99; Mayer v. Webster, 18 Wis. 393; State v. Smith, 31 Mo. 566; State v. Rosenfield, 35 Mo. 472.   [5] Stewart v. Slater, 6 Duer, 83.

[6] Stoddard v. Butler, 20 Wend. 507, per Senator Dickinson.

ed for a fair and honest purpose.[1] There is no more satisfactory mode of disproving bad motives than by
proving such facts as indicate the existence of other motives, innocent at least or even laudable.[2] The intention
of the parties and the circumstances attending the transaction, may always be shown in order to repel the presumption.[3] All facts or circumstances which to the
common understanding and conscience of men may prove,
or on their face tend to prove, good faith, are accordingly within the rightful privilege of the jury to hear and
weigh. All facts such as commonly accompany and indicate good faith ought to be permitted to go to them.
The fact of a valid and adequate consideration, the notoriety of the transaction, the attending circumstances,
the relation of the parties, all the facts indicating a fair
intent,[4] such circumstances of publicity, reasonableness
as to amount, time, value and quantity of property, difficulty or inconvenience of removal, advantages of allowing it to remain or other circumstances agreeable with the
ordinary course of business and fair dealing as may tend
to rebut the presumption and satisfy the jury that there
was not any intent to hinder, delay or defraud creditors,
reasons of family kindness, reasons of prudence, or, in
short, any such reasons as ordinarily influence the conduct of honest men are admissible.[5] All such proof of facts
are subject to the general rules of the law of evidence.[6]

CONSIDERATION.—Whether proof of a consideration
is essential will depend upon circumstances. Title once
acquired by gift is not divested by the mere fact that

---

[1] Davis v. Turner, 4 Gratt. 422.
[2] Smith v. Acker, 23 Wend. 653.   [3] Homes v. Crane, 2 Pick. 607.
[4] Cole v. White, 26 Wend. 511.
[5] Smith v. Acker, 23 Wend. 653; Callen v. Thompson, 3 Yerg. 475.
[6] Cole v. White, 26 Wend. 511.

the donee does not immediately take the property into
his exclusive possession and appropriate it to his exclusive use.[1]   But if the condition of the debtor is such
at the time the transaction takes place that a gift would
not be valid, then proof of a consideration is indispensable.   It is only on the proof of a good consideration
that the case can go to the jury on the question of
fraud.[2]   The proof must go beyond a mere paper acknowledgment of it.   There must be evidence *dehors*
the instrument.   An acknowledgment in the deed is of
no force whatever in establishing the consideration as
against creditors[3]   If the consideration is nothing more
than what in law is considered a valuable consideration,
it will not be sufficient, because a disproportion between
the price paid and the value, when unreasonable, is evidence of a secret trust and creates a presumption of
fraud.[4]   Cases in which the question of inadequacy of
consideration arises between the grantor and grantee of
a deed where suit is instituted for the purpose of setting
aside the grant on the ground of imposition are not applicable in determining a question of the fairness of a
consideration between a vendee and creditor under the
statute concerning fraudulent conveyances.   What inadequacy of consideration would induce a court to set
aside a conveyance at the instance of the grantor on the
ground of imposition, is an entirely different question
from that degree of inadequacy, which would avoid a
sale on the ground of fraud in a suit by a creditor
against the vendee.   Courts will not weigh the value of

---

[1] Danley v. Rector, 5 Eng. 211.

[2] Tift v. Barton, 4 Denio. 171 ; Curd v. Lewis, 7 Gratt. 185.

[3] Allen v. Cowan, 28 Barb. 99; s. c. 23 N. Y. 502; Hanford v. Artcher,
4 Hill, 271.

[4] Bryant v. Kelton, 1 Tex. 415; Kuykendall v. Hitchcock, 15 Mo. 416;
contra, Keller v. Blanchard, 19 L. a An. 53.

the goods sold and the price received in very nice scales, but, all circumstances considered, there must be a reasonable and fair proportion between the one and the other.[1] The payment of an adequate price for the property, affords a strong indication of good faith, and is a circumstance to weaken, but still this alone may not be inconsistent with the existence of a collusive design to impose upon others.[2] Any intention to give the debtor a false credit will vitiate the transaction, for transfers made for the purpose of deceiving creditors are fraudulent.[3]

PROVINCE OF A JURY.—The whole circumstances should be submitted to the jury, and from all parts of the transaction taken together, it should be determined whether the transaction was or was not fraudulent in the concoction of it.[4] If there is no proof to rebut the presumption, there is nothing to be left to the jury to pass upon.[5] If there is any evidence of good faith, the court in submitting the question should instruct the jury that, because the possession is not changed, the law presumes the transfer to be fraudulent and void as against creditors, and casts the burthen of disproving fraud upon the person claiming under it.[6] If he fails in his evidence to show that the transfer was made in good faith without any intent to defraud creditors, the presumption of fraud first raised by the law becomes

---

[1] Kuykendall v. Hitchcock, 15 Mo. 416 ; State v. Evans, 38 Mo. 150.

[2] Smith v. Acker, 23 Wend. 653 ; Bryant v. Kelton, 1 Tex. 415.

[3] Homes v. Crane, 2 Pick. 607 ; D'Wolf v. Harris, 4 Mason, 534 ; Ross v. Crutsinger, 7 Mo. 245.

[4] Haven v. Low, 2 N. H. 13 ; Homes v. Crane, 2 Pick. 607.

[5] Tift v. Barton, 4 Denio, 171 ; Curd v. Lewis, 7 Gratt. 185.

[6] Griswold v. Sheldon, 4 N. Y. 580 ; Smith v. Welch, 10 Wis. 91 ; Smith v. Henry, 2 Bailey, 118 ; Gibson v. Hill, 21 Tex. 225 ; Hartman v. Vogel, 41 Mo. 570.

conclusive.[1] If the verdict is clearly erroneous, the court may grant a new trial.[2]

To what transactions the rule applies.—The reason why the retention of possession raises a presumption of fraud is because it tends to deceive creditors by giving the debtor a false credit, and because it is out of the ordinary course of business, and therefore indicates a secret trust. It is manifest that these reasons apply equally to all transactions, no matter what may be the form of the transfer. The manner in which the parties deal is merely evidence to show good faith. The rule is one in regard to the burden of proof, and the character of the instrument of transfer and the mode of making it are matters having more or less weight to show the fairness of the transaction. It applies to a concurrent possession,[3] mortgages,[4] especially after

---

[1] Kuykendall v. Hitchcock, 15 Mo. 416. The vendor may remain in possession until performance of condition by vendee. Scott v. Winship 20 Geo. 429. A partner may buy out the firm goods, employ his copartner and continue to use the firm name. Hamill v. Willett, 6 Bosw. 533. The law does not require that the vendor, acting as agent, should make known his agency to others to make his acts effectual in behalf of his principal. His failing to do so is mere evidence of fraud. Cutter v. Copeland, 18 Mo. 127. A sleigh purchased in the summer may be left with the vendor till winter. Clute v. Fitch, 25 Barb. 428.

[2] Vance v. Phillips, 6 Hill, 433; Dodd v. McCraw, 3 Eng. 83; Potter v. Payne, 21 Ct. 361; Randall v. Parker, 3 Sandf. 69. It is carrying a distrust of juries too far to suppose them incapable, with the aid of a wholesome *prima facie* presumption, to administer justice on this subject in the true spirit of the statute. It is better to confine the interposition of the court to guiding instead of driving them by instructions and to the power of granting new trials in cases of plain deviation. Davis v. Turner, 4 Gratt. 422.   [3] Stadtler v. Wood, 24 Tex. 622.

[4] Hombeck v. Vanmetre, 9 Ohio, 153; Ryall v. Rowles, 1 Ves. 348; s. c. 1 Atk. 165; Miller v. Pancoast, 5 Dutch. 250; Runyon v. Groshon, 1 Beasley, 86; Eveleigh v. Pursford, 2 Mood. & Rob. 539; Merrill v. Dawson, 1 Hemp. 563; Killough v. Steele, 1 Stew. & Port. 262. *Contra*, Mitchell v. Beal, 8 Yerg. 134; Maney v. Killough, 7 Yerg. 440; Gist v. Pressley, 2 Hill, Ch. 318; Desha v. Scales, 6 Ala. 356; Cutter v. Copeland, 18 Me. 127; Snyder v. Hitt, 2 Dana, 204.

default,[1] deeds containing a stipulation for the possession,[2] and sales under legal process,[3] whether the purchase is by the plaintiff[4] or a third person.[5] In all
transactions of this kind, when a valuable consideration
is proved, the only question that remains is one of good
or bad faith.[6] The rule in regard to the retention of
possession applies to *choses in action* as well as to personal property,[7] especially if they are negotiable.[8]

POSSESSION OF LAND.—The rule that possession is
presumptive evidence of fraud does not apply to conveyances of land. The reason for the distinction is
manifest. In the case of chattels, possession is *prima
facie* evidence of ownership. Upon this evidence of
ownership creditors have a right to rely : otherwise there
would be no protection against secret or collusive trans-

---

[1] Maney v. Killough, 7 Yerg. 440 ; Bank v. Gourdon, Speers Ch. 439;
Shurtleff v. Willard, 19 Pick. 202; Bogard v. Gardley, 6 S. & M. 302
Hankins v. Ingols, 4 Blackf. 35 ; Wiswall v. Ticknor, 6 Ala. 178; Ravisies
v. Alston, 5 Ala. 297 ; North v. Crowell, 11 N. H. 251. *Contra*, Fishburne
v. Kunhardt, 2 Speers, 556.   [2] Sommerville v. Horton, 4 Yerg. 541.

[3] Gardenier v. Tubbs, 21 Wend. 169; Floyd v. Goodwin, 8 Yerg. 484;
Creagh v. Savage, 14 Ala. 454 ; Williams v. Kelsey, 6 Geo. 365; Stovall
v. Farmers' Bank, 8 S. & M. 305. *Contra*, Garland v. Chambers, 11 S. &
M. 337; Foster v. Pugh, 12 S. & M. 416 ; Ewing v. Cargill, 13 S. & M. 79 ;
Wyatt v. Stewart, 34 Ala. 716 ; Montgomery v. Kirksey, 26 Ala. 172;
Guignard v. Aldrich, 10 Rich. Eq. 253.

[4] Farrington v. Caswell, 15 Johns. 430 ; Gardenier v. Tubbs, 21 Wend.
169 ; Taylor v. Mills, 2 Edw. Ch. 318.

[5] Fonda v. Gross, 15 Wend. 628; Breckenridge v. Anderson, 3 J. J.
Marsh, 710; Kilby v. Haggin, 3 J. J. Marsh, 208.

[6] Latimer v. Batson, 4 B. & C. 652 ; Eveleigh v. Purrsford, 2 Mood. &
Rob. 539. The reason for the conflict among the cases upon the points
just considered is historical rather than logical. The mode of conveyance
was first used to constitute an exception to the doctrine of fraud *per se*,
and then some of the courts, losing sight of this fact, considered it as constituting an exception to the rule of presumptive evidence.

[7] Welsh v. Bekey, 1 Penn. 57; Woodbridge v. Perkins, 3 Day, 364 ;
Hall v. Redding, 13 Cal. 214; Currie v. Hart, 2 Sandf. Ch. 353; *vide* Browning v. Hart, 6 Barb. 91; Livingston v. Littell, 15 Wis. 218.

[8] Mead v. Phillips, 1 Sandf. Ch. 83.

fers. But while possession of lands may be treated for some purposes and is regarded as the lowest evidence of title, yet the public look not to the possession, but to the title deeds or the proper records, to obtain proofs of title to such property. Creditors do this, and so does every person instituting an inquiry as to the condition of the title to a particular tract of land. The possession may with perfect consistency be in one person and the title in another. No one need be deceived unless he will. To hold that possession of realty by the vendor after sale is *per se* presumptive evidence of fraud would be in effect to abolish the distinction known and acknowledged between personal and real property, and to lose sight of the different methods for evidencing the title to the two kinds of property.[1] But the possession of the grantor is proper to be submitted to the jury. It must be taken, however, in connection with all the circumstances of the case.[2] Acts of ownership[3] or possession for a long time[4] may raise a presumption of fraud.

POSSESSION WITH JUS DISPONENDI.—The mere retention of possession of personal property is altogether different from the retention of possession accompanied with a power to dispose of it for the grantor's own benefit. Such a power in a mortgage is inconsistent with the nature

---

[1] Ryall v. Rowles, 1 Ves. 348; s. c. 1 Atk. 165; Cadogan v. Kennett, 2 Cowp. 432; Suiter v. Turner, 10 Iowa, 517; Steward v. Thomas, 35 Mo. 202; Hempstead v. Johnston, 18 Ark. 123; Wooten v. Clark, 23 Miss. 75; Noble v. Coleman, 16 Ala. 77; Barr v. H..tch, 3 Ohio, 527; Smith v. Lowell, 6 N. H. 67. *Contra*, Peck v. Land, 2 Kelly, 1; Belk v. Massey, 11 Rich 614; Bachemin v. Chaperon, 15 La. An. 4. When several lots are conveyed by one deed, the possession of a part of the property conveyed is *prima facie* evidence of the whole transaction, and not the transfer of the particular lot retained, is fraudulent. Perkins v. Patten, 10 Geo. 241.

[2] Steward v. Thomas, 35 Mo. 202; Barr v. Hatch, 3 Ohio, 527.

[3] Smith v. Lowell, 6 N. H. 67; Hancock v. Horan, 15 Tex. 507.

[4] Wooten v. Clark, 23 Miss. 75; Noble v. Coleman, 16 Ala. 77.

11

and character of the instrument, and is tantamount to a power of revocation. The object of a mortgage is to obtain a security beyond a simple reliance upon the honesty and ability of the debtor to pay, and to guard against the risk of all the property of the debtor being swept off by other creditors by fastening a special lien upon that covered by the mortgage. But a mortgage, with possession and power of disposition in the mortgagor for his own benefit, is nothing at last but a reliance upon the honesty of the mortgagor, and, in fact, is no security, as it is in the power of the mortgagor at any moment to defeat the mortgage lien by an entire disposition of the whole property. Such a mortgage is no certain security upon specific property. It depends entirely upon the honesty and good faith of the debtor. As he may dispose of it to creditors at will to satisfy his debts, there is no reason why creditors may not seize it against his will for the same object.

In such case the whole right to dispose of the property to pay a debt depends upon the will of the debtor, unaffected by the rights of the mortgagee, and there is no reason in permitting the will of the debtor to determine whether property shall legally go to pay his debts or not. If it is the will of the debtor to appropriate the mortgaged property to pay his debts, it is binding as against the mortgagee; but if it is not the will of the debtor, and the property is seized upon execution, the rights of the mortgagee, if the mortgage is valid, fasten upon the property and take it away from the execution creditor. The property, therefore, is not held by the mortgage, but the will of the debtor, because, if the debtor sees proper to dispose of it, he has the power under the mortgage. He may dispose of the property, defeat the mortgage, and put the money in his own pocket, but if he refuses to pay his debts and the property is taken on execution, the mortgagee steps in and restores it to the debtor. Such a mortgagee is not an operative instrument between the parties. It is no security so far as the debtor is concerned, and its only operation and effect is to ward off creditors. It is, therefore, fraudulent and void.[1] The terms of the instrument, however, must plainly express the right of the mortgagor to dispose of the property or the implication must be a necessary one.[2] A mere stipulation that property subsequently acquired shall be subject to the mortgage does not render it void.[3]

---

[1] Collins v. Myers, 16 Ohio, 547; Griswold v. Sheldon, 4 N. Y. 580; Spies v. Boyd, 1 E. D. Smith, 445; s. c. 11 Leg. Obs. 54; Armstrong v. Tuttle, 34 Mo. 432; Harman v. Abbey, 7 Ohio St. R. 218; Billingsley v. Bunce, 28 Mo. 547; King v. Kenan, 38 Ala. 63; Read v. Wilson, 22 Ill. 377; Stanley v. Bunce, 27 Mo. 269; Constantine v. Twelves, 29 Ala. 607; Addington v. Etheredge, 12 Gratt. 436; Walter v. Wimer, 24 Mo. 63; Brooks v. Wimer, 20 Mo. 503; Ranlett v. Blodgett, 17 N. H. 298; McLachlan v. Wright, 3 Wend. 348; Bishop v. Warner, 19 Conn. 460; Johnson v. Thweatt, 18 Ala. 741; Price v. Mazange, 21 Ala. 701; Carpenter v. Simmons, 1 Robt. 360; Ticknor v. Wiswall, 9 Ala. 305; Bowen v. Clark, 5 A. L. Reg. 203; Lang v. Lee, 3 Rand. 410; Farmers' Bank v. Douglass, 11 S. & M. 469; Martin v. Maddox, 24 Mo. 575; Martin v. Rice, 24 Mo. 581; Shaw v. Lowry, Wright, 190; Edgell v. Hart, 13 Barb. 380; s. c. 9 N. Y. 213; Russell v. Winne, 37 N. Y. 591; s. c. 4 Abb. Pr. (N. S.) 384; Welsh v. Beckey, 1 Penn. 57; Doyle v. Smith, 1 Cold. 15; Reed v. Blades, 5 Taunt. 212; Divver v. McLaughlin, 2 Wend. 596; Wood v. Lowry, 17 Wend. 492; Simpson v. Mitchell, 8 Yerg. 417; Place v. Longworthy, 13 Wis. 629; Jordan v. Turner, 3 Blackf. 309; Milburn v. Waugh, 11 Mo. 369; Hickman v. Perrin, 6 Cold. 135; vide Jones v. Huggeford, 3 Met. 515; Briggs v. Parkman, 2 Met. 258; Codman v. Freeman, 3 Cush. 306; Googins v. Gilmore, 47 Me. 9; Hughes v. Corey, 20 Iowa, 399; Jessup v. Bridge, 11 Iowa, 572; Wilhelmi v. Leonard, 13 Iowa, 330; Torbert v. Hayden, 11 Iowa, 435; Levy v. Welsh, 2 Edw. Ch. 438; Stedman v. Vickery, 42 Me. 132; Gay v. Bidwell, 7 Mich. 519; Mitchell v. Winslow, 2 Story, 630; Barnard v. Eaton, 2 Cush. 294; Oliver v. Eaton, 7 Mich. 108; Campbell v. Leonard, 11 Iowa, 489; Benton v. Thornhill, 7 Taunt. 149; Brinley v. Spring, 7 Me. 241; Abbott v. Goodwin, 20 Me. 408; Macomber v. Parker. 14 Pick. 497.

[2] Voorhis v. Langsdorf, 31 Mo. 451.

[3] Codman v. Freeman, 3 Cush. 306; Gardner v. McEwen, 19 N. Y. 123;

PAROL POWER TO SELL.—It is immaterial whether the power to sell the property is contained in the mortgage or is conferred by a parol agreement made at the time of its execution. If the mortgage is made and delivered under such an arrangement and with such a purpose, it is alike fraudulent and void, although the instrument does not on its face express that intent. It is because the instrument is made and delivered with intent that it shall operate in a manner which hinders, delays and defrauds creditors that it is void, and this intent may be proved by evidence *dehors* the instrument. The arrangement makes the instrument necessarily fraudulent, because it operates of necessity to hinder, delay and defraud creditors, by securing to the debtor the use and benefit of his property and its proceeds while it protects it from levy and sale for the payment of his debts.[1]   It must be shown, however, that sales made by the mortgagor were made with the knowledge or consent of the mortgagee.[2] A sale by a mortgagor or vendor, when made contrary to the purpose for which the property is left in his possession, will not vitiate the transfer.[3]

Brinley v. Spring, 7 Me. 241 ; State v. Tasker, 31 Mo. 445; Voorhis v. Langsdorf, 31 Mo. 451; State v. Byrne, 35 Mo. 147; Hickman v. Perrin, 6 Cold. 135.

[1] Collins v Myers, 16 Ohio, 547; Griswold v. Sheldon, 4 N. Y. 580; Delaware v. Ensign, 21 Barb. 85 ; Freeman v. Rawson, 5 Ohio, St. R. 1; Russell v. Winne, 37 N. Y. 591 ; s. c. 4 Abb. Pr. (N. S.) 384; Robbins v. Parker, 3 Met. 117; Gardner v. McEwen, 19 N. Y. 123 ; Marston v. Vultee, 12 Abb. Pr. 143 ; New Alb. Ins. Co. v. Wilcoxson, 21 Ind. 355 ; Howerton v. Holt, 23 Tex. 60 ; *in re* Kahley *et al.* 4 B. R. 124; Harvey v. Crane, 5 B. R. 218; *in re* Manly, 3 B.R. 75; s. c. 2 L. T. B. 89; Barnet v. Fergus, 51 Ill. 352 ; Steinart v. Deuster, 23 Wis. 136; Ross v. Wilson, 7 Bush. 29.

[2] Frost v. Warren, 42 N. Y. 204; Williston v. Jones, 6 Duer, 504 ; Summers v. Roos, 43 Miss. 749; Burgin v. Burgin, 1 Ired. 453.

[3] Macdona v. Swiney, 8 Ir. Law, 73; Allen v. Smith, 10 Mass. 308;

Power to sell as agent.—A mortgage containing stipulation that the mortgagor shall remain in possession and sell the mortgaged property as agent of the mortgagee, and account for the proceeds until the mortgage debt is paid, is not necessarily void. If carried out in good faith it does not delay, hinder or defraud creditors. Such a stipulation is merely a badge of fraud.[1]

Perishable articles.—Articles in their nature subject to be consumed in their use may be mortgaged without any imputation of fraud, provided they are not to be used and may be kept without damage until the mortgage debt shall become payable.[2] If the articles, however, are perishable, and cannot be so kept, or if there is an understanding that they may be used and consumed by the mortgagor, the mortgage is fraudulent and void.[3] Such perishable articles may, however, be

---

Archer v. Hubbell, 4 Wend. 514 ; Hankins v. Ingolls, 4 Blackf. 35 ; Saunders v. Turbeville, 2 Humph. 272.

[1] Hawkins v. Nat'l Bank, 1 Dillon, 462 ; s. c. 2 B. R. 108 ; Miller v. Lockwood, 32 N. Y. 293 ; Ford v. Williams, 13 N. Y. 577 ; s. c. 24 N. Y. 359 ; Abbott v. Goodwin, 20 Me. 408 ; Melody v. Chandler, 12 Me. 282 ; Constantine v. Twelves, 29 Ala. 607 ; Chophard v. Bayard, 4 Minn. 533 ; Weaver v. Joule, 91 E. C. L. 309 ; s. c. 3 C. B. (N. S.) 309 ; Allen v. Smith, 10 Mass. 308 ; Barker v. Hall, 13 N. H. 293 ; Conkling v. Shelley, 28 N. Y. 360 ; Hickman v. Perrin, 6 Cold. 135 ; Pope v. Wilson, 7 Ala. 690 ; Brinley v. Spring, 7 Me. 241 ; Spence v. Bagwell, 6 Gratt 444 ; Davis v. Ransom, 18 Ill. 396 ; Johnson v. Curtis, 42 Barb. 588 ; Summers v. Roos, 42 Miss. 749 ; Adler v. Claflin, 17 Iowa, 89 ; Wiswall v. Ticknor, 6 Ala. 178 ; vide Saunders v. Turbeville, 2 Humph. 272 ; Trabue v. Willis, Meigs, 583, note ; Bamford v. Baron, 2 T. R. 594, note.

[2] Robbins v. Parker, 3 Met. 117 ; Dewey v. Littlejohn, 2 Ired. Eq. 495 ; Charlton v. Lay, 5 Humph. 496 ; Cochran v. Paris, 11 Gratt. 348.

[3] Sommerville v. Horton, 4 Yerg. 541 ; Trabue v. Willis, Meigs, 583, note ; Wiley v. Knight, 27 Ala. 336 ; Farmers' Bank v. Douglass, 11 S. & M. 469 ; Johnson v. Thweatt, 18 Ala. 741 ; Ravisies v. Alston, 5 Ala. 297 ; vide Elmes v. Sutherland, 7 Ala. 262.

consumed when it is for the benefit of the mortgagee
than a favor rather to the debtor, as, for instance, in the
improvement, support or sustenance, of other property
enumerated in the mortgage.[1] The amount in number
and value of such articles may be so inconsiderable as
compared with the main subjects of the mortgage as to
justify the conclusion that they were embraced through
the inattention of the parties, and will not then vitiate
the transaction.[2] The rule in regard to perishable objects
is limited to chattels that are transient in their existence,
or of such a nature that their only use consists in their
consumption.[3]

WHAT TRANSFERS VALID.—It has been held that the
doctrine in regard to the retention of possession, accompanied with a power to sell for the debtor's benefit, applies only to conditional, and not to absolute sales,[4] but
this is questionable, for such a transfer is merely colorable.[5] If the goods are delivered to the mortgagor
before any creditor questions the validity of the mortgage, the transaction will be rendered valid.[6]

---

[1] Cochran v. Paris, 11 Gratt. 348; Dewey v. Littlejohn, 2 Ired. Eq. 495;
Ravisies v. Alston, 5 Ala. 297; Planters' Bank v. Clarke, 7 Ala. 765.

[2] Cochran v. Paris, 11 Gratt. 348; Dewey v. Littlejohn, 2 Ired. Eq. 495.

[3] Shurtleff v. Willard, 19 Pick. 202.

[4] Grubbs v. Greer, 5 Cold. 160.

[5] Paget v. Perchard, 1 Esp. 205.

[6] Brown v. Platt, 8 Bosw. 324; Read v. Wilson, 22 Ill. 377; Summers
v. Roos, 43 Miss. 749; Williston v. Jones, 6 Duer, 504.

The doctrine in the text is laid down according to the principles of
the common law, but these of course are liable to modification by the
statutes of the various States. It is no part of the scope of this work to
discuss these various acts, for it is to be presumed that every attorney is
more familiar with the statutes of his own State, and the decisions under
them, than a stranger. The work, however, would not be complete without a slight notice of them, and of the manner in which they affect the
doctrine relating to the retention of possession. These acts commonly
relate to bills of sale and mortgages of personal property, and are designed
to prevent the mischiefs that may arise from secret sales, and hence require

that such transfers shall be recorded in all cases where the grantor retains the possession. Such acts are in force in England, Maine, Connecticut, New York, Maryland, Virginia, West Virginia, North Carolina, Georgia, Indiana, Kentucky, Missouri, Michigan, Wisconsin, Minnesota, Iowa, Oregon and Ohio. The statutes of each State vary, but in general the recording of the transfer is equivalent to a change of possession. Bruce v. Smith, 3 H. & J. 499; Hambleton v. Hayward, 4 H. & J. 443 ; Bogard v. Gardley, 4 S. & M. 302; Harrington v. Brittain, 23 Wis. 541; Fister v. Beall, 1 H. & J. 31; Smith v. McLean, 24 Iowa, 322; Hughes v. Cory, 20 Iowa, 399; Kuhn v. Graves, 9 Iowa, 303.   When there is a change of possession (Minister v. Price, 1 F. & F. 686; Gough v. Everard, 2 H. & C. 1; s. c. 32; L. J. Ex. 210; s. c. 8 L. T. (N.S.) 363; Smith v. Wall, 18 L. T. (N.S.) 182); or when the property at the time of the transfer is not in the possession of the grantor (Thomas v. Hillhouse, 17 Iowa, 68) the instrument by which the transfer is made need not be recorded.   But if the grantor retains the possession, and the instrument is not recorded within the time required by the registration acts, the transfer is void.   Miller v. Bryan, 3 Iowa, 58; Prather v. Barker, 24 Iowa, 26.   Mere recording, however, will not give validity to an instrument that is tainted with actual fraud.   Garrett v. Hughlett, 1 H. & J. 3.

CHAPTER VI.

WHEN POSSESSION IS FRAUD PER SE.

The retention of possession has thus far been considered as simply affording a presumption of fraud, but as it is held to be conclusive in several States, a survey of this branch of the law is necessary to complete the examination of this subject.

NATURE OF THE RULE THAT POSSESSION IS FRAUD PER SE.—The rule that the retention of possession is conclusive evidence of fraud is one of policy,[1] and rests upon the doctrine that fraud is in all cases a question of law.[2] Although a valuable consideration may be paid, and the real intent of the parties may be to transfer the property, yet the possession continuing with the vendor is regarded as giving him a collusive credit, and as operating as a deceit and fraud upon creditors. The conveyance, therefore, is held void as to creditors, though there may be no fraud, in fact, in the transaction.[3] The rule excludes all regard to the actual intentions of the parties in every transaction that comes within its range.[4] The inference arising from the possession cannot be rebutted or repelled even by the strongest testimony of the actual fairness of the

---

[1] Wilson v. Hooper, 12 Vt. 653; Mills v. Camp, 14 Ct. 219; Kirtland v. Snow, 20 Ct. 23.

[2] Weeks v. Wead, 2 Aik. 64; Milne v. Henry, 40 Penn. 352; Sturtevant v. Ballard, 9 Johns. 337; Planters' Bank v. Borland, 5 Ala. 531.

[3] Weeks v. Wead, 2 Aik. 64; Milne v. Henry, 40 Penn. 352.

[4] Wilson v. Hooper, 12 Vt. 653.

intention of the parties.[1] Hence, it is immaterial whether the vendee was party or privy to any fraudulent intention of the vendor or not.[2]

CHARACTER OF DELIVERY.—The vendor must deliver to the vendee possession of the property in order to consummate the sale and render it valid as against creditors. The delivery must be actual, and such as the nature of the property and the circumstances of the sale will reasonably admit, and such as the vendor is capable of making. A mere symbolical or constructive delivery, where a real one is reasonably practicable, is of no avail; there must be an an actual separation of the property from the possession of the vendor at the time of the sale, or within a reasonable time afterwards, according to the nature of the property.[3] Symbolical delivery is necessary only where peculiar circumstances preclude the possibility of actual possession, and there it is equivalent to actual possession, because the transaction is susceptible of no act of greater notoriety. But where possession may be permanently changed by actual delivery of the thing, symbolical delivery is of itself a fraud, because it appears on the face of the transaction that the delivery was merely colorable.[4] Actual possession is used in contradistinction to constructive possession, which is incident of, and dependent on, right and title.[5] The possession of every vendor, after a sale, is constructively the possession of the vendee; the possession of

---

[1] Land v. Jeffries, 3 Rand. 211; s. c. 599; Hundley v. Webb 3 J. J. Marsh, 643.

[2] King v. Bailey, 6 Mo. 575.

[3] Billingsley v. White, 59 Penn. 464.

[4] Cunningham v. Neville. 10 S. & R. 201; Brawn v. Keller, 43 Penn. 104.

[5] Woods v. Bugbey, 29 Cal. 466.

an agent is constructively the possession of the principal. Such a change, however, is not sufficient. The
vendee cannot make the vendor his agent and then
rely upon his constructive possession.[1]

CHANGE MUST BE CONTINUOUS.—The word actual
also excludes the idea of a mere formal change of
the possession.[2] It is not sufficient that the vendor
gives to the vendee a delivery, which may be symbolical or a temporary delivery, and then takes the articles
back into his own possession and keeps and uses them
just the same as he did before. This is not the possession which the rule requires. There must be not only
a delivery, but a continuing possession.[3] The possession and beneficial use of the property by the vendor,
after the sale, is conclusive evidence against it. It is
the policy and very foundation of the rule to prevent
what it is the object of fraudulent conveyances to
secure—the beneficial use of the property to the
debtor.[4] The delivery must be made of the property;
the vendee must take the actual possession; the possession must be open and unequivocal, carrying with it
the usual marks and indications of ownership by the
vendee. It must be accompanied with such unmistak-
able acts of control and ownership as a prudent *bona
fide* purchaser would do in the exercise of his rights
over the property so that all persons may have notice

---

[1] Stoddard v. Butler, 20 Wend. 507; Trask v. Bowers, 4 N. H. 309;
Stephens v. Barnett, 7 Dana, 257; Fitzgerald v. Gorham, 4 Cal. 289;
Stewart v. Scannell, 8 Cal. 80; Stanford v. Scannell, 10 Cal, 7.

[2] Stevens v. Irwin, 15 Cal. 503.

[3] Young v. McClure, 2 W. & S. 147; Streeper v. Eckart, 2 Whart. 302;
Goldsbury v. May, 1 Litt. 254; Breckenridge v. Anderson, 3 J. J. Marsh,
714; McBride, v. McClelland, 6 W. & S. 94.

[4] Pierce v. Chipman, 23 Vt. 87.

that he owns and has possession of the property.[1] It must be such as to give evidence to the world of the claims of the new owner. This possession must be continuous—not taken to be surrendered back again—not formal, but substantial.[2] It is not necessary that a change of possession should at all times accompany the transfer. If it follows within a reasonable time thereafter, that is, as soon as the nature of the property and the circumstances attending the transfer will admit, it is sufficient.[3] A delay of four or six days is not material, if the property has not in the meantime been seized on legal process.[4]

QUESTION OF LAW.—The rule does not determine what acts shall constitute a delivery and continued change of possession.[5] Change of possession is mainly a fact-like possession or seizin, but of course the facts being conceded, or found, all these matters then resolve themselves into a mere judgment of law.[6] The question of change of possession is purely one of law, and as such is to be decided by the court. The court must

---

[1] Lay v. Neville, 25 Cal. 543.

[2] Stevens v. Irwin, 15 Cal. 503 ; Engles v. Marshall, 19 Cal. 320. Mere accidental words grow sometimes into undue importance. A learned judge of the Common Pleas happened, improperly, but without prejudice to any one, to apply the terms which qualify a possession under the statute of limitations to a case of this sort, and declared that the possession must be "actual, visible, notorious," and the reporter put this into his syllabus, though this court used only the word actual. Next comes another expression derived from the same source—" clear, unequivocal and conclusive." The expressions "visible and open," and "open and manifest," would seem to be more accurate. Hugus v. Robinson, 24 Penn. 9.

[3] Carpenter v. Mayer, 5 Watts, 483; Smith v. Stern, 17 Penn. 360 ; State v. King, 44 Mo. 238; McVicker v. May, 3 Penn. 224; Barr v. Reitz, 53 Penn. 256.

[4] McVicker v. May, 3 Penn. 224 ; Barr v. Reitz, 53 Penn. 256.

[5] Godchaux v. Mulford, 26 Cal. 314.

[6] Burrows v. Stebbins, 26 Vt. 659.

judge of those acts which are sufficient evidence of delivery.[1] Possession being a fraud in law, without regard to the intent of the parties, becomes a question for the court and not for the jury to decide.[2] When there is no proof to show that possession accompanied and followed the transfer, the court instructs the jury that the sale is fraudulent.[3] When, however, there is any evidence tending to prove a change of possession, the question must be submitted to the jury.[4] The evidence must be such as would justify the jury in inferring, under instructions from the court, that there has been an actual and exclusive change of possession.[5] When there is a conflict of testimony in regard to the change of possession, the question must necessarily be referred to the jury. Should the court in such a case attempt to assert authoritatively the presence of a legal fraud, it would be a usurpation of the rights of the jury.[6] The question is to be submitted to the jury to find the facts, and the court is to say what facts, if found by the jury, will constitute a sufficient change of possession.[7] The rule is no reason for excluding the evidence of the transfer. It is

---

[1] Cadbury v. Nolen, 5 Penn. 320; Burrows v. Stebbins, Vt. 659; Contra Lake v. Morris, 30 Ct. 201.

[2] Young v. McClure, 2 W. & S. 147; Carpenter v. Mayer, 5 Watts, 483; Milne v Henry, 40 Penn. 352.

[3] Young v. McClure, 2 W. & S., 147; Dewart v. Clement, 48 Penn. 413. In Connecticut, the question is submitted to the jury as a question of fact, with instruction that if they find none of the established exceptions, they will find the transaction fraudulent. Swift v. Thompson, 9 Conn. 63; Howe v. Keeler, 27 Conn. 538.

[4] Warner v. Carlton, 22 Ill. 415; Stephenson v. Clark, 20 Vt. 624.

[5] McKibbin v. Martin, 64 Penn. 352.

[6] Forsyth v. Matthews, 14 Penn. 100; Wilson v. Hooper, 12 Vt. 653; Hodgkins v. Hook, 23 Cal. 581.

[7] Burrows v. Stebbins, 26 Vt. 759; Stephenson v. Clark, 20 Vt. 624.

the judgment of the law upon the evidence, and not a ground to exclude evidence.[1]

JOINT POSSESSION.—Possession is the visible control of, and dominion over the goods.[2] If the vendee has such a possession it is sufficient. A concurrent possession of the vendor with the vendee,[3] or with an agent of the vendee,[4] is not such a substantial change as the rule requires. Such a possession is merely colorable. The reason why possession must be changed is to announce a change of ownership, and prevent the former owner from gaining a credit by his possession. Consequently the possession and use of the vendor to be within the rule, must be of the same description as that of a joint-owner in using, occupying, and disposing of the property. Nothing short of this would furnish any evidence that he yet remained the owner.[5] What given state of facts constitutes a concurrent possession is a question of law.[6] If the possession does not amount to a joint-possession the transfer is valid. Thus, if a lease of the goods to a third party is real and *bona fide* and not colorable, and he actually takes possession, then his possession in connection with that of the vendor will not be fraudulent.[7] It is important, therefore, to ascertain what facts are essential to prevent the possession from being joint.

---

[1] Sherron v. Humphreys, 2 Green, 217.

[2] Ludlow v. Hurd, 19 Johns. 218.

[3] Wordall v. Smith, 1 Campb. 332; Babb v. Clemson, 10 S. & R. 419; Boyd v. Dunlap, 1 Johns. Ch. 478; Stiles v. Shumway, 16 Vt. 435; Waller v. Cralle, 8 B. Mon. 11.

[4] Neate v. Latimer, 2 Y. & C. 257; Wordall v. Smith, 1 Campb. 332; Babb v. Clemson, 10 S. & R. 419.

[5] Allen v. Edgerton, 3 Vt. 442; Hall v. Parsons, 15 Vt. 358; s. c. 17 Vt. 271; Wilson v. Scott, 5 Fla. 305.

[6] Hall v. Parsons, 15 Vt. 358; s. c. 17 Vt. 276.

[7] Archer v. Hubbell, 4 Wend. 514.

CHARACTER OF THE CHANGE.—Separation of the property from the possession of the vendor implies nothing more than a change of the vendor's relation to it as owner, and consists in the surrender and transfer of his power and control over it to the vendee, but in order to prevent fraud, the rule requires that this shall be done by such appropriate significant acts as shall clearly show the vendor's intention to part with the possession of the property, and transfer it to the vendee.[1] There must be a complete change of the dominion and control over the property, and some act which will operate as a divestiture of title and possession from the vendor, and a transfer to the vendee. There must be some open, notorious or visible act clearly and unequivocally indicative of delivery and possession, such as putting up a new sign, or any other reasonable means which would impart notice to a prudent man that a change has taken place.[2] The act must be so open and manifest as to make the change of possession apparent and visible.[3]

MUST BE OBSERVABLE.—The change of possession must be such as is observable without inquiry. On the one hand, the purchaser must see to it that he so conducts with the property as to indicate by the appearances to an observer a change in the possession; and, on the other hand, the creditors of the vendor are bound to see what others can see and judge and act upon it with the prudence that is required of men in business affairs. The change of possession must be obvious or observable, or, as sometimes expressed, visible, or such that the appearances would indicate to an observer that there had been

---

[1] Billingsley v. White, 59 Penn. 464; State v. Schulein, 45 Mo. 521.
[2] Claflin v. Rosenberg, 42 Mo. 439.
[3] Billingsley v. White, 59 Penn. 464.

a change.[1] The appearances must indicate such a divesting of the possession of the vendor as any man knowing the facts which are ascertainable, would be bound to know and understand as the result of change of ownership. They must be such as he could not reasonably misapprehend.[2] When such a change is apparent creditors are put on the inquiry. The rule does not say that it is the duty of creditors to inquire or to presume a change when it is reasonably doubtful, but that the possession in such a case is joint and the sale void. This is in entire consistency with the settled rule that there must be a substantial and visible change of possession. If there is such a change, a careful observer will not be at a loss to determine who owns and has possession of the property. If it is doubtful, the law resolves the doubt against the party who should make the change of possession open and visible to the world. Creditors are not bound to inquire. It is sufficient if they carefully observe.[3]

CONCURRENT POSSESSION.—If there are such palpable tokens and proofs of the vendor's surrender of his dominion over the property as owner, and of the transfer of his possession to the vendee, the sale will not be declared fraudulent in law, although the vendor may act as the agent or servant of the vendee in the management and disposal of the property, provided that his acts are professedly and apparently done, not as owner, but as the agent or servant of the vendee, and are so understood by those with whom he deals. Such employment of the vendor in a subordinate capacity is colorable only, and not conclusive upon the question as to

---

[1] Stanley v. Robbins, 36 Vt. 422.
[2] Stephenson v. Clark, 20 Vt. 624 ; Parker v. Kendricks, 29 Vt. 388.
[3] Flanagan v. Wood, 33 Vt. 332.

whether there has been any immediate delivery and an actual change of the possession. He can not be allowed to remain with apparently sole and exclusive possession of the goods after the sale, for that would be inconsistent with such an open and notorious delivery and actual change as the rule exacts, in order to exclude from the transaction the idea of fraud. But if it is apparent to all the world that he has ceased to be the owner, and another has acquired and openly occupied that position; that he has ceased to be the principal in the charge and management of the property, and become only a subordinate or clerk, the reason of the rule is satisfied.

The immediate delivery and actual and continued change of possession are the ultimate facts, the employment of the vendor by the vendee in a subordinate capacity is only a probative fact.[1] If the change of possession is otherwise sufficiently shown, the mere fact of such agency is not, and never has been held to render the sale invalid.[2] The omission to change the sign on a store is not conclusive.[3] Nor is a mere change of the sign sufficient.[4] It is not necessary that the vendor shall be at all times in the store.[5] The same clerks may

---

[1] Godchaux v. Mulford, 26 Cal. 314.

[2] Billingsley v. White, 59 Penn. 464; State v. Schulein, 45 Mo. 521; Claflin v. Rosenberg, 42 Mo. 439; McKibbin v. Martin, 64 Penn. 352; Hugus v. Robinson, 24 Penn. 9; Dunlap v. Bournonville, 26 Penn. 72; England v. Ins. Co. 6 La. An. 5; Weil v. Paul, 22 Cal. 492; Godchaux v. Mulford, 26 Cal. 316; Warner v. Carlton, 22 Ill. 415; Powers v. Green, 14 Ill. 386; Stevens v. Irwin, 15 Cal. 503; Hall v. Parsons, 15 Vt. 358; s. c. 17 Vt. 271; Wilson v. Lott, 5 Fla. 305; Talcott v. Wilcox, 9 Conn. 134.

[3] Seavy v. Dearborn, 19 N. H. 351; Hugus v. Robinson, 24 Penn. 9; Read v. Wilson, 22 Ill. 377.

[4] Potter v. Payne, 21 Conn. 361.

[5] Billingsley v. White, 59 Penn. 464.

be employed, and it is immaterial where they board,[1]
but they can not be employed and paid by the vendor,
although he does it at the request of the vendee,[2] for
the possession is then in the vendor and not the vendee.
The rule requires that all such agency and control of
the vendor shall be excluded. If the transfer is kept
secret, the employment of the vendor as agent will
vitiate it.[3] The important inquiry is, who is at the
head controlling the property? If a careful observer
would be at a loss to know which of the two were at
the head, having the chief control of the property, it
must be deemed a joint possession.[4]

WHEN CONCURRENT IS FRAUDULENT.—In such cases of
concurrent possession it is a question for the jury whether
the change of possession has been actual and *bona fide*,
not pretended, deceptive, and collusive. If there are facts
tending to show that the grantor has a beneficial interest
in the business, or that the proceeds go to him beyond
a reasonable compensation for his services, or that he has
an unlimited power to draw upon the till, or that with
the knowledge of the vendee he takes money to pay his
own debts, these are facts for the jury.[5] The vendor
may, however, become a member of the firm which purchases the property,[6] or act as agent for the owner of
an undivided half of the property.[7] The vendee can

---

[1] Hall v. Parsons, 15 Vt. 358; s. c. 17 Vt. 271.

[2] Parker v. Kendricks, 29 Vt. 388.

[3] Trask v. Bowers, 4 N. H. 309; Allen v. Edgerton, 3 Vt. 442; Eck-
feldt v. Frick, 17 Leg. Int. 332.

[4] Allen v. Edgerton, 3 Vt. 442; Hall v. Parsons, 15 Vt. 358; s. c.
17 Vt. 271.

[5] McKibbin v. Martin, 64 Penn. 352.

[6] Utley v. Smith, 24 Conn. 290.

[7] Pier v. Duff, 63 Penn. 59.

not employ the former agent of the vendor, and then hire the property to the vendee,[1] but the vendor may be employed to use the property in the business of the vendee.[2] If A., being in possession of goods, sells them to B., and B. sells them to C., it is not fraudulent for C., after he has completely received the possession, to employ A. and allow him to have possession of the goods.[3]

POSSESSION OF LAND.—When the vendee relies upon a constructive possession of land to make out his possession of the property which remains upon the land, he must have such a deed as will vest in him a legal seizin, and it may be essential that the deed shall be recorded.[4] The deed, however, simply conveys the legal right of possession, but does not necessarily change the possession from the grantor to the grantee. Where the land sold remains in the actual possession of the vendor, there no constructive possession of the property on it can be raised, for the aid of the vendee, against such actual possession, for this would make the constructive possession more potential than the actual and apparent one.[5] Consequently, a mere surrender of a lease, which the vendor holds as tenant, to the vendee is not sufficient.[6] Where the vendor and vendee remain in the joint possession of the land, if the possession of

---

[1] Hurlburd v. Bogardus, 10 Cal. 518.

[2] Brown v. Riley, 22 Ill. 45.

[3] Cameron v. Montgomery, 13 S. &. R. 128.

[4] Stephenson v. Clark, 20 Vt. 624.

[5] Flanagan v. Wood, 33 Vt. 332 ; Rockwood v. Collamer, 14 Vt. 141; Lawrence v. Burnham, 4 Nev. 361 ; Cahoon v. Marshall, 25 Cal. 197.

[6] Steelwagon v. Jeffries, 44 Penn. 407; Kirtland v. Snow, 20 Conn. 23; Stiles v. Shumway, 16 Vt. 435.

the vendee is apparently that of a joint owner, and there is no actual and exclusive possession of the personal property by the vendee, the personal property on the land will be deemed to be in their joint possession.[1] But where the vendee has a visible and notorious possession, a surrender of a lease will enable him to obtain a valid title, although the vendor remains on the land.[2] Taking a lease is some evidence of a change of possession,[3] but not sufficient.[4] Upon a sale of wheat in the ground, the vendee may, however, lease the farm and employ the vendor as his agent.[5] Possession need not be taken of a windmill attached to the land, when both the land and the windmill are conveyed by a mortgage.[6] The constructive possession of the land is sufficient possession of the mill. A principal may make a purchase from an agent who manages his farm, if the transaction is open, and not calculated to give the vendor a false credit, and leave the goods upon the farm under the management of the vendor,[7] but secrecy will vitiate such a transaction.[8] When an agent sells goods to his principal which are already upon the principal's land, there need be no other change of possession, for the law will refer the possession to the principal in whom the property now is, and in whom the possession apparently was before.[9] Where the vendee

---

[1] Flanagan v. Wood, 33 Vt. 332.

[2] Talcott v. Wilcox, 9 Conn. 134.

[3] Conway v. Edwards, 6 Nev. 190.

[4] Flanagan v. Woods, 33 Vt. 332.

[5] Herron v. Fry, 2 Penn. 263. .

[6] Steward v. Lombe, 1 Brod. & B. 506.

[7] Lewis v. Whittemore, 5 N. H. 364 ; Wright v. Grover, 27 Ill. 426 ; Visher v. Webster, 13 Cal. 58.

[8] Trask v. Bowers, 4 N. H. 309; Stephens v. Barnett, 7 Dana, 257.

[9] Manton v. Moore, 7 T. R. 67.

owns a farm, and goes to live with the vendor upon it, and the vendor works it upon shares, and has the sole conduct of the business, the change is not sufficient;[1] but the vendee may purchase land, and the personal property upon it, and employ the vendor as overseer,[2] or as agent,[3] if he assumes an exclusive control of the property. So, also, if the vendor absconds, the fact that the vendor's family remains in the house is immaterial when the vendee exercises acts of dominion over the personal property.[4] If the vendee owns the house in which the goods are, and has the control and management of the household, without any intermeddling on the part of the vendor, the fact that the vendor lives with the vendee will not make the transfer void.[5] A steam-engine may be left on the premises, in the charge of an agent, and used by the vendee.[6] A man may have the exclusive possession of personal property which is upon land occupied by him and the vendor in common.[7] If the vendee owns the land,[8] or leases the house[9] where the property is placed, it is sufficient if the vendor removes from it. Wherever the constructive possession of land has been considered of any importance, there have been both delivery and acts of dominion over the property upon it.

---

[1] Mills v. Warner, 19 Vt. 609.

[2] Wilson v. Lott, 5 Fla. 305.

[3] Wilson v. Hooper, 12 Vt. 653.

[4] Burrows v. Stebbins, 26 Vt. 659.

[5] Ludlow v. Hurd, 19 Johns. 218; Wilson v. Lott, 5 Fla. 305.

[6] Funk v. Staats, 24 Ill. 632.

[7] Potter v. Mather, 24 Conn. 551; vide Hoffner v. Clark, 5 Whart. 545; Brawn v. Keller, 43 Penn. 104.

[8] Pacheco v. Hunsacker, 14 Cal. 120; Sharon v. Shaw, 2 Nev, 289.

[9] Barr v. Reitz, 53 Penn. 256.

WHERE THE RULE DOES NOT APPLY.—The rule does not apply to sales of property which is exempt from execution,[1] or to sales of partnership property, as against the creditors of one of the partners, because they can not levy upon the partnership property.[2] Upon the purchase of the equity of redemption, only so much of the right as was absolute can be deemed fraudulent, and upon declaring it alone void, the mortgagee is remitted to his pre-existent rights under his mortgage.[3] When an exchange is made by the vendor, without the concurrence of or consultation with the vendee, no distinction can be allowed between the article received and the one for which it is substituted.[4] If the property is converted into money, and the money is actually received by the vendee, this ends the question in regard to the delivery. The vendee may then take the money and purchase other property, and leave that with the first vendor. There is then no connection between this property and any other property which the vendor may have had, and creditors are put at once upon inquiry as to the origin of the title.[5] The rule does, however, apply to the chattel's offspring.[6]

POSSESSION BY FEME COVERT.—The possession of the wife is the possession of the husband,[7] but there is no case where the possession of the husband after marriage

---

[1] Anthony v. Wade, 1 Bush. 110; Morton v. Ragan, 5 Bush. 334; Foster v. McGregor, 11 Vt. 595; Patten v. Smith, 5 Conn. 196; s.c. 4 Conn. 450.

[2] Page v. Carpenter, 10 N. H. 77.

[3] Daniel v. Morrison, 6 Dana, 182; s. c. 6 J. J. Marsh, 398. *Contra,* Clayborn v. Hill, 1 Wash. (Va.) 177.

[4] Mills v. Warner, 19 Vt. 609.

[5] Ridout v. Burton, 27 Vt. 383.

[6] Mott v. McNiel, 1 Ark. 162.

[7] King v. Bailey, 6 Mo. 575.

of property conveyed by the wife before marriage has
been held inconsistent with the deed of the wife, where
that deed was absolute on its face, and without any
special stipulation, limitation, or reservation.[1]   The
possession to be conclusive evidence of fraud must
be ostensibly either actual or usufructuary, that
is, it must be a possession in fact by the debtor or
under him, or apparently to his use, such a possession
as would be a badge of property, and might therefore
give a delusive credit.   Although, after a separation,
a mensa, the possession by the wife *de jure* of her own
property or that of her husband may be his possession
for many legal purposes, nevertheless, her actual or
beneficial possession of the property of a benevolent
stranger or friend is not, either in fact or in law, the possession of her husband in any sense or for any purpose.
The constructive possession follows the title, and the
law presumes the possession to be in the owner, and not
in the absent husband, whose only right even to the
use is founded on the technical fiction of the identity
in law of husband and wife, or on the mere legal
power, still conceded to him by the common law, over
his wife and over the use of property in her possession.[2]   When there is no proof that property in the
possession of the husband is an acquisition from the
wife's own money or property, it belongs to the husband.[3]

SUFFICIENCY OF CHANGE VARIES WITH EACH CASE.—
What constitutes a sufficient change of possession must
be a question which will vary with circumstances, and
what may have been said by the courts on this subject

---

[1] Land v. Jeffries, 5 Rand. 599, 211; Prior v. Kinney, 6 Munf. 510.
[2] Chiles v. Bernard, 3 Dana, 95; Leonard v. Baker, 1 M. & S. 251.
[3] Milne v. Henry, 40 Penn. 352.

should be taken with reference to the case then before them, in relation to the character and situation of the property at the time of the sale.[1] When the goods are in the possession of the vendee, there need be no formal delivery of the possession.[2] It makes no difference whether the property is removed from the owner, or tho owner from the property. It is not the mere place the property occupies which gives color of possession to the former owner, but it is the connection the place itself has with the former owner indicating his apparent control over it.[3] An immediate delivery, and an actual and continued change of possession, are consistent with the retention of the property on the same premises. Removal is an evidence, and a strong one, of that change, but not the indispensable evidence. The exercise of ownership, and control by the vendee, and, above all, the absence of any such control by the vendor, are the true test by which to decide the validity of the transfer. The change must be notorious, and the possession and control of the vendee indisputable. The goods may be left on the premises, in the exclusive charge of an agent.[4] Even a removal is not sufficient, when the vendor accompanies the goods.[5]

PREVIOUS OWNERSHIP.—It is no excuse that the mortgagee sold the goods to the mortgagor, and took a mortgage as a security for the purchase money.[6]

---

[1] Hutchins v. Gilchrist, 23 Vt. 82.

[2] Lake v. Morris, 30 Conn. 201 ; Manton v. Moore, 7 T. R. 67.

[3] Barr v. Reitz, 53 Penn. 256 ; Craver v. Miller, 65 Penn. 456 ; Pacheco v. Hunsacker, 14 Cal. 120.

[4] Hutchins v. Gilchrist, 23 Vt. 82 ; Cartwright v. Phœnix, 7 Cal. 281 ; Lee v. Huntoon, 1 Hoffm. 447 ; Funk v. Staats, 24 Ill. 632.

[5] Weil v. Paul, 22 Cal. 492.

[6] Woodward v. Gates, 9 Vt. 358. In Meggott v. Mills, 1 Ld. Raym.

The period of the debtor's previous ownership is not permitted to qualify the rule; whether for a longer or shorter time it induces the same legal consequences. But the case of bailment to one who has never been owner is not within the rule, although he may, prior to the bailment, have made a contract to purchase, upon his failure to comply with which the bailor purchased.[1]

NOTICE.—If a creditor consents that the vendor shall remain in possession, he can not claim that the sale is fraudulent on this account alone,[2] but mere notice is not sufficient;[3] nor can a sheriff be prejudiced by any knowledge of the judgment creditor.[4] Knowledge that there is a separate defeasance to an absolute deed makes no difference, for what is void may be taken advantage of by all creditors.[5]

NOMINAL PARTY.—If the vendor is a mere trustee or nominal party, holding the title for the use of another, and sells absolutely the thing thus held, while it is in the possession of the beneficiary, the sale will be fraudulent, unless the possession is changed and conforms to the contract.[6] Where a sale is made by a

---

286, money was loaned to purchase goods, and a bill of sale taken as security, and the transfer was held valid. The same doctrine is laid down in Buller's N. P. 258. But it is said not to be law in Clow v. Woods, 5 S. & R. 275.

[1] Spring v. Chipman, 6 Vt. 662.

[2] Steel v. Brown, 1 Taunt. 381.

[3] Hower v. Geesaman, 17 S. & R. 251; Stark v. Ward, 3 Penn. 328; King v. Bailey, 6 Mo. 575; Lassiter v. Bussy, 14 La An. 699; Lawrence v. Burnham, 4 Nev. 361; Swift v. Thompson, 9 Conn. 63. *Contra*, Wooderman v. Baldoe, 8 Taunt. 676; Ludwig v. Fuller, 17 Me. 162.

[4] Meeker v. Wilson, 1 Gallis, 419; Hower v. Geesaman, 17 S. & R. 251. *Contra*, Ludwig v. Fuller, 17 Me. 162.

[5] Gaither v. Mumford, 1 N. C. T. R. 167.

[6] Breckinridge v. Anderson, 3 J. J. Marsh, 710.

person who has no title to the goods, with the assent and for the benefit of the real owner, the same principles will be applied as if the beneficiary were the nominal vendor. The rule would be of no avail if its application could be evaded by the introduction of a third person as nominal vendor, while the possession remains with the beneficial owner.[1]

BY OWNER TO DEBTOR.—It has never yet been held that a person may not give the possession of his goods to another. Putting a man into possession of goods, when they were not originally his, does not make them a fund for the payment of his debts.[2] The rule is limited to transfers by debtors. It has no application to transfer to debtors. There are certain necessary and lawful contracts, by which the owner parts with the possession, and yet fraud can not be presumed. Such are the contracts of lending and hiring, both very useful, and without which society could not well exist. It is of the essence of these that the owner should give up the possession for a time. Such, too, are contracts by which an artizan or manufacturer has the possession of materials belonging to another, for the purpose of making them up or repairing them for the owner. No suspicion of fraud can fairly arise where the transaction is in the usual course of business.[3]

CONDITIONAL SALE.—A stipulation that the title shall not pass to the vendee is not fraudulent, whether

---

[1] Laughlin v. Ferguson, 6 Dana, 111.

[2] Dawson v. Wood, 3 Taunt. 256; Craig v. Ward, 9 Johns. 197; Howard v. Sheldon, 11 Paige, 558; Clinn v. Russell, 2 Blackf. 772.

[3] Martin v. Mathiot, 14 S. & R. 214; Ayer v. Bartlett, 6 Pick. 71; Peters v. Smith, 42 Ill. 417.

verbal[1] or in writing,[2] and the vendee's creditors can
not seize the property until the condition precedent is
performed.[3] A third person may purchase the interests
of the vendor and conditional vendee, and leave the
property in the possession of such conditional vendee.[4]
Goods may also be placed in the hands of an insolvent
debtor, to sell in his own name and account for the proceeds, with a condition that the title shall not vest in
him until they are paid for.[5] In this mode creditors
are put to a great disadvantage, there being no title in
the debtor of which they can avail themselves at law,
even if the greater part of the consideration has been
paid. This renders such contracts objects of jealousy,
and they certainly ought to be critically scrutinized,
for they afford a most convenient screen for fraud between the parties to the bargain. But they are not
per se fraudulent. It is not sufficient merely for the
vendor to deliver the goods to the vendee, and permit
him to have them in such a manner as to induce others
to give him a false credit. If the vendor does this
with a fraudulent design to obtain credit for the
vendee, without doubt the creditors would hold the
property; but if he does nothing more than endeavor
to keep the security in his own hands, he will not be
prejudiced, although creditors may have been deceived

---

[1] Reeves v. Harris, 1 Bailey, 563; Baylor v. Smithers, 1 Litt. 105;
Hussey v. Thornton, 4 Mass. 405; Armington v. Houston, 38 Vt. 448; Bigelow v. Huntley, 8 Vt. 151; Myers v. Harvey, 2 Penn. 478. *Contra*, Ketchum
v. Watson, 24 Ill. 592; Martin v. Mathiot, 14 S. & R. 214.

[2] Dupree v. Harrington, Harp. 391; Ayer v. Bartlett, 6 Pick. 71;
Bradley v. Arnold, 16 Vt. 382; Paris v. Vail, 18 Vt. 277.

[3] Barrett v. Pritchard, 2 Pick. 512; Marston v. Baldwin, 17 Mass. 606;
Bigelow v. Huntley, 8 Vt. 151; Buckmaster v. Smith, 22 Vt. 203.

[4] Smith v. Foster, 18 Vt. 182.

[5] Merrill v. Rinker, 1 Bald. 528; Blood v. Palmer, 11 Me. 414; Chaffee
v. Sherman, 26 Vt. 237.

by the circumstances. The true question is, whether the transaction is *bona fide* or fraudulent. If the transaction is fraudulent, the vendor setting up a condition to the sale, yet suffering the vendee to be in possession but exercising full rights over the property, with the intent and purpose of enabling him to obtain credit on the strength of the property, he will not be able to avail himself of such condition, but the sale will be held to be absolute in regard to the creditors. But if *bona fide*, and the object of the condition is merely security to the vendor, he will not lose his property merely because some creditor of the vendee supposed it belonged to the vendee.[1]

QUESTION OF LAW.—There are some instances in which no change of possession is necessary, but they are special cases, and for special reasons to be shown to and approved of by the court.[2] Delivery of possession is deemed to be so much of the essence of the sale of chattels, that an agreement to permit the vendor to keep possession is an extraordinary exception to the usual course of dealing, and requires a satisfactory explanation. There must be

---

[1] Ayer v. Bartlett, 6 Pick. 71 ; Merrill v. Rinker, 1 Bald. 528.

[2] Sturtevant v. Ballard, 9 Johns. 337 ; Clow v. Woods, 5 S. & R. 275 ; Williams v. Lowndes, 1 Hall, 579 ; Divver v. McLaughlin, 2 Wend. 596 ; Doane v. Eddy, 16 Wend. 523 ; Collins v. Brush, 9 Wend. 198 ; Randall v. Cook, 17 Wend, 53 ; Coburn v. Pickering, 3 N. H. 415 ; Wooderman v. Baldock, 8 Taunt. 676 ; Patten v. Smith, 5 Conn. 196 ; s. c. 4 Conn. 450 ; Beekman v. Bond, 19 Wend. 444 ; Randall v. Parker, 3 Sandf. 69 ; Swift v. Thompson, 9 Conn. 63 ; Osborne v. Fuller, 14 Conn. 529 ; Carter v. Watkins, 14 Conn. 240 ; Stevens v. Fisher, 19 Wend. 181 ; Hundley v. Webb, 3 J. J. Marsh, 643 ; Gibson v. Love, 4 Fla. 217 ; Mauldin v. Mitchell, 14 Ala 814 ; Millard v. Hall, 24 Ala. 209. The practice in Connecticut differs slightly from that of the other States. Swift v. Thompson, 9 Conn. 63.

some sufficient motive, of which the court is to judge, for the non-delivery of the goods, or the rule presumes it to be made with a view to delay, hinder or defraud creditors.[1] It is necessary that the retention of the possession shall appear to be for a purpose fair, honest and absolutely necessary, or at least essentially conducive to some fair object the parties have in view, and which constitutes the motive for entering into the contract. It is necessary not only that appearances shall agree with the real state of things, but also that the real state of things shall be honest and consistent with public policy, and that it shall afford no unnecessary facility to deception.[2]

WHEN VENDOR AND VENDEE RESIDE TOGETHER.—The fact that the vendor and vendee reside together,[3] or board together in the same house,[4] or live together in the house upon the lot where the stable is which they use in common,[5] does not take the case out of the operation of the rule. Even occasional acts of ownership will not constitute a legal possession in the vendee if the goods are in the same situation as before.[6] There is a distinction, however, to be made between cases where the donor and donee live apart, and those where they necessarily live together. In the case of a father and child who, from their connexion, must live together at least until the child comes of age, it would have the effect of destroying all gifts to say that the possession

---

[1] Sturtevant v. Ballard, 9 Johns. 337.
[2] Clow v. Woods, 5 S. & R. 275.
[3] Jarvis v. Davis, 14 B. Mon. 529; Waller v. Cralle, 8 B. Mon. 11; Steelwagon v. Jeffries, 44 Penn. 407; Stiles v. Shumway, 16 Vt. 435.
[4] Hoffner v. Clark, 5 Whart. 545.
[5] Brawn v. Keller, 43 Penn. 104.
[6] Mott v. McNiel, 1 Aik. 162 ; Stiles v. Shumway, 16 Vt. 435.

must be considered that of the father.[1] A sister-in-law
is not within this exception.[2] If a son's possession and
use of the goods are exclusive, a sale will be valid
although his father may live with him. If mere cohabitation were a badge of fraud, a father's sale to his
unmarried son would seldom be sustained.[3]

MERE CONVENIENCE.—Where possession has been
withheld pursuant to the terms of an agreement, some
good reason for the arrangement beyond the mere convenience of the parties must appear.[4] Goods cannot
be retained for the purpose of being manufactured,[5] or
to complete a process of manufacture in progress at the
time of the sale,[6] or under a covenant to keep and
deliver at a future day,[7] or upon a conditional sale,[8] or
from motives of benevolence on the part of the
vendee.[9] An agreement on the part of the vendor
to pay for the use of the goods will not repel the
imputation of fraud.[10]

---

[1] Curry v. Ellerbe, 1 Bailey, 578; Kid v. Mitchell, 1 N. & M. 334;
Jacks v. Tunno, 3 Dessau, 1 ; Smith v. Littlejohn, 2 McCord, 362 ; Howard
v. Williams, 1 Bailey, 575; Braxton v. Gaines, 4 H. & M. 151; Wash v.
Medley, 1 Dana, 269 ; Enders v. Williams, 1 Met. (Ky.) 346; Dodd v.
McCraw, 3 Eng. 83 ; Humphries v. McCraw, 9 Ark. 91; Danley v. Rector,
5 Eng. 211; Clayton v. Brown, 17 Geo. 217; Goodwyn v. Goodwyn, 20
Geo. 600. *Contra*, Stiles v. Shumway, 16 Vt. 435.

[2] Smith v. Henry, 2 Bailey, 118.

[3] McVicker v. May, 3 Penn. 224; Braxton v. Gaines, 4 H. & M. 151.

[4] Clow v. Woods, 5 S. & R. 275; Jennings v. Carter, 2 Wend. 446;
Crouch v. Carrier, 16 Ct. 505; Gardner v. Adams, 12 Wend. 297; Doane v.
Eddy, 16 Wend. 523; Randall v. Cook, 17 Wend. 53.

[5] Carter v. Watkins, 14 Conn. 240; Pritchett v. Jones, 4 Rawle, 260.
Contra, Clow v. Woods, 5 S. & R. 275.

[6] Pritchett v. Jones, Rawle, 260.

[7] Brummel v. Stockton, 3 Dana. 134; Hundley v. Webb, 3 J. J. Marsh,
643; Grimes v. Davis, 1 Litt. 241 ; Millard v. Hall, 24 Ala. 209.

[8] Laughlin v. Ferguson, 6 Dana. 111.

[9] Mauldin v. Mitchell, 14 Ala. 814.

[10] Coburn v. Pickering, 3 N. H. 415 ; Streeper v. Eckart, 2 Whart. 302;

CONSISTENT WITH TITLE, NOT TERMS OF DEED.—The possession must be compatible with the title and not the terms of the instrument by which the transfer is made. Unless the contract of sale is conditional, or in trust, the possession should correspond with the title; and if the sale is unconditional and pass the absolute right of property from the vendor to the vendee, no reservation of the possession to the vendor in the written evidence of the sale will exempt the transaction from the imputation of fraud, in law, upon the rights of the creditors of the vendor.[1] But there is an essential difference between the effect of a possession retained by the maker of an absolute bill of sale and the possession retained by the maker of a mortgage. The object of the one is to pass the absolute right of property, and the object of the other is to give a security defeasible upon a particular contingency; the possession in the former case is utterly incompatible with the deed, whereas in the latter case there exists no such incompatibility.[2] Where by the terms of the conveyance the vendee is not to have possession until the performance or non-performance of a certain condition, there the vendor's continuing in possession is no evidence of fraud, because it is consistent with the trust appearing on the face of the deed, and is not to be presumed to give a false credit to the vendor.[3] In case of mortgages, the possession of the mortgagor is not inconsistent with the terms of the

Norton v. Doolittle, 32 Conn. 405; Goldsbury v. May, 1 Litt. 254; Laughlin v. Ferguson, 6 Dana. 111; Webster v. Peck, 31 Conn. 495; Paul v. Crooker, 8 N. H. 288; *contra*, Sydnor v. Gee, 4 Leigh, 535; Powers v. Green, 14 Ill. 386; Cunningham v. Hamilton, 25 Ill. 228; Pringle v. Rhame, 10 Rich. 72; Jones v. Blake, 2 Hill Ch. 629; Upson v. Raiford, 29 Ala. 188; Wheeler v. Train, 3 Pick. 254.

[1] Hundley v. Webb, 3 J. J. Marsh, 643.
[2] Merrill v. Dawson, 1 Hemp. 563.   [3] Badlam v. Tucker, 1 Pick. 389.

contract and the nature of the transaction, for before condition broken it is uncertain whether the property will vest absolutely in the mortgagee or not, and nothing is more common than to suffer the mortgagor to retain possession until this may be ascertained. Stipulations to this effect are often inserted in mortgage deeds.[1] It is for this reason that the retention of possession under a mortgage is not deemed in the judgment of the law to be fraudulent.[2] The condition, however, must be in the title, and not simply in the contract. The title must depend on condition, and be such as the court may consider legal and reasonable.[3] When the deed stipulates that the debtor may remain in possession until default in payment of any or all of the instalments, possession until default in payment of all the instalments is consistent with the deed.[4]

---

[1] Homes v. Crane, 2 Pick. 607.

[2] Stone v. Grubbam, 2 Bulst. 217; s. c. 1 Rol. Rep. 3; Martindale v. Booth, 3 B. & A. 498; Reed v. Wilmot, 7 Bing. 577; s. c. 5 M. & P. 553; Conrad v. Atlantic Ins. Co. 1 Pet. 385; Barrow v. Paxton, 5 Johns. 258; Adams v. Wheeler, 10 Pick. 199; Marsh v. Lawrence, 4 Cow. 461; Ash v. Savage, 5 N. H 545; Holbrook v. Baker, 5 Me. 309; Ward v. Sumner, 5 Pick. 59; D. Wolfe v. Harris, 4 Mason, 534; Brinley v. Spring, 7 Me. 241; Clayborn v. Hill, 1 Wash. (Va.) 177; Hundley v. Webb, 3 J. J. Marsh, 643; McGowen v. Hoy, 5 Litt. 239; Watson v. Williams, 4 Blackf. 26; Thornton v. Davenport, 1 Scam. 296; Rose v. Burgess, 10 Leigh, 186; U. S. v. Hooe, 3 Cranch. 73; Snyder v. Hitt, 2 Dana. 204; Merrill v. Dawson, 1 Hemp. 563; Fairbanks v. Bloomfield, 5 Duer, 434; Runyon v. Groshon, 1 Beasley, 86; Wilson v. Russell, 13 Md. 494. *Contra*, Doak v. Brubaker, 1 Nev. 218; Meyer v. Gorham, 5 Cal. 322; The Romp, Olcott, 196; Sibly v. Hood, 3 Mo. 206; Tobias v. Francis, 3 Vt. 425; Woodward v. Gates 9 Vt. 358; Clow v. Woods, 5 S. & R. 275; Welsh v. Bekey, 1 Penn. 57; Doane v. Eddy, 16 Wend. 523; Randall v. Cook, 17 Wend. 53; Swift v. Thompson, 9 Conn. 63; Case v. Winship, 4 Blackf. 425; King v. Bailey, 6 Mo. 575; Gist v. Pressley, 2 Hill Ch. 318; Reeves v. Harris, 1 Bailey, 563; Gaylor v. Harding, 37 Conn. 508. When the stipulation is that the mortgagor shall have possession, it is void though the possession is with the mortgagee; Meyer v. Gorham, 5 Cal. 322.

[3] Hundley v. Webb, 3 J. J. Marsh, 643

[4] Martindale v. Booth, 3 B. & A. 498; Magee v. Carpenter, 4 Ala. 469.

STIPULATION IN MORTGAGE.—Anciently it was usual to insert a clause in the mortgage that the mortgagor should retain possession until default, but the understanding and practice now is that the mortgagor remains in possession until default is made unless there is a contract to the contrary.[1] When a stipulation is inserted in the deed the possession must be consistent with it. If the deed stipulates that the mortgagee shall have the possession, the possession of the mortgagor is fraudulent.[2] The deed may contain a stipulation that the grantor shall receive the rents and profits until the grantee shall become entitled to demand the money which the deed is intended to secure.[3] A separate defeasance, instead of making the vendor's possession consistent with his deed, and thereby fair, evinces his guilt by making it more difficult to detect the fraud. It is a cover to a foul transaction, and not the evidence of a fair one. Even if the parties intend to make a mortgage, the form of the deed tells a falsehood to the world, the truth only remaining to themselves. It is too late to disclose the truth after the injury arising from the secrecy has been sustained.[4]

FRAUD IN FACT.—The rule does not declare that in conditional sales the retention of possession by the vendor may not be fraudulent, but that, as a general rule, it is not necessarily so.[5] Deeds of trust are subject to the same principles as mortgages.[6]

---

[1] Watson v. Williams, 4 Blackf. 26 ; Gist v. Pressley, 2 Hill Ch. 318 ; Maney v. Killough, 7 Yerg, 440.

[2] Jordan v. Turner, 3 Blackf. 309 ; Kitchell v. Bratton, 1 Scam. 300.

[3] U. S. v. Hooe, 3 Cranch. 73.

[4] Gaither v. Mumford, 1 N. C. T. R. 167 ; Laughlin v. Ferguson, 6 Dana. 111. *Contra*, Homes v. Crane, 2 Pick. 607 ; Bartlett v. Williams, 1 Pick. 288 ; Sydnor v. Gee, 4 Leigh, 535.

[5] Hundley v. Webb, 6 J. J. Marsh, 643.

[6] Head v. Ward, 1 J. J. Marsh, 280 ; Ravisies v. Alston, 5 Ala. 297 ;.

CONDITION BROKEN.—Possession after the condition is broken is not fraudulent, for when a conveyance is not fraudulent at the time of the making of it, it cannot be made fraudulent by any subsequent matter.[1] If the mortgagee fails to take possession immediately upon default, it cannot be assumed as a conclusion of law that the mortgage is fraudulent. If the transaction is fair in its inception, it cannot be denounced because the mortgagee does not avail himself of his rights *stricti juris*. The retention of possession by the mortgagor for an unreasonable length of time may warrant the inference that the mortgage is held up as a protection for his property against the demands of his creditors. But this is a conclusion which may be repelled by proof that the indulgence of the mortgagee is compatible with fair dealing, and induced by no intention to favor the mortgagor to the prejudice of creditors. It must, from the very nature of the case, be a question of fact for the solution of the jury.[2] Upon the extinguishment of the mortgage by the purchase of the equity of redemption, the possession should be changed, but the

---

Johnson v. Cunningham, 1 Ala. 249; Malone v. Hamilton, Minor, 286; Hopkins v. Scott, 20 Ala. 179.

[1] Lambert's Case, Shep. Touch. 65; Weaver v. Joule, 91 E. C. L. 309; s. c. 3 C. B. (N. S.) 309; De Wolf v. Harris, 4 Mason, 534; Head v. Ward, 1 J. J. Marsh, 280; Maples v. Maples, Rice Ch. 300; Gist v. Pressley, 2 Hill Ch. 318; Simerson v. Bank, 12 Ala. 205; Planters' Bank v. Willis, 5 Ala. 770; Dearing v. Watkins, 16 Ala. 20; Merrill v. Dawson, 1 Hemp. 563. *Contra*, Armstrong v. Baldock, Gow. 33; Reed v. Eames, 19 Ill. 594; Cass v. Perkins, 23 Ill. 382; Hanford v. Obrecht, 49 Ill. 146; Rhines v. Phelps, 3 Gilman, 455. No general rule can be established, but the mortgagee must act with promptness, and must use every reasonable effort to reduce the property into his immediate possession after a default of payment or other condition broken by which he becomes entitled to possession (Cass v. Perkins, 23 Ill. 382.)

[2] Planters' Bank v. Willis, 5 Ala. 770.

retention will make only the purchase of the equity of
redemption void, and the mortgage will be valid.[1]

MARRIAGE SETTLEMENTS.—The retention of possession under a marriage settlement, whether antenuptial[2]
or postnuptial,[3] and whether of the husband's property[4]
or the wife's,[5] is consistent with the deed, and does not
render the settlement void. The wife's possession is
considered as the possession of the trustee, and not of
the husband.[6] The fact that goods held by a trustee as
the separate property of the wife have been in the possession of her husband for a considerable time makes no
difference as to the right of the trustee to dispose of
them, or to recover the value if tortiously taken by or
in behalf of a creditor of the husband. It is difficult to
see how the wife could enjoy the avails of the property
without his participation, so long as they reside together.
Indeed, she may expressly authorize him to use or
enjoy her property without giving it to him, and his
creditors can not complain, as they will lose nothing
by the transaction. The possession of the property by
the husband, if not inconsistent with the nature of the
trust, is not considered as fraudulent.[7]

PURCHASES.—The interest is as much separate property as the principal, and purchases made with it are

---

[1] Laughlin v. Ferguson, 6 Dana, 111. *Contra*, Clayborn v. Hill, 1 Wash.
(Va.) 177 ; Glasscock v. Batton, 6 Rand. 78.

[2] Cadogan v. Kennett, Cowp. 432.

[3] Arundell v. Phipps, 10 Ves. 139 ; Charlton v. Gardner, 11 Leigh. 281 ;
Waller v. Todd, 3 Dana, 503 ; Larkin v. McMullin, 49 Penn. 29.

[4] Cadogan v. Kennett, Cowp. 432.

[5] Jarman v. Woolloton, 3 T. R. 618 ; Hazelinton v. Gill, 3 T. R. 620,
note.

[6] Jarman v. Woolloton, 3 T. R. 618.

[7] Merritt v. Lyon, 3 Barb. 110.

hers and subject to the same rules as the principal fund,[1] and her possession is the possession of the trustee, and not the possession of her husband.[2] By the common law the husband owns his wife's property. Consequently, if the income from the separate estate is delivered to her, either with the intent that it shall belong to her or without any agreement that it shall still continue to be a part of the separate estate, purchases made with it will be liable to the husband's creditors.[3] There may be facts which might warrant the inference that the goods have been purchased by the husband with his own funds, and that he has resorted to the pretext that they are a part of his wife's separate estate to protect them from the search of his creditors. These are subjects proper for the consideration of the jury.[4] The trustee for the wife may purchase the husband's goods at a sale under an execution, and leave them in the possession of the wife, although she resides with her husband.[5]

Public sale.—The notoriety of the change of possession will, in some instances, repel the presumption of fraud.[6] The mere seizure of goods on an execution is not sufficient. A person cannot, then, pay the judgment, take a bill of sale as security, and leave the goods in the possession of the debtor.[7] But, after a sale at public

---

[1] Merritt v. Lyon 3 Barb. 110.

[2] Danforth v. Woods, 11 Paige, 9.

[3] Shirley v. Shirley, 9 Paige, 363; Carne v. Brice, 7 M. and W. 183.

[4] Merritt v. Lyon, 3 Barb. 110.

[5] Quick v. Garrison, 10 Wend. 335; Cross v. Glode, 2 Esp. 574.

[6] Ryall v. Rowles, 1 Ves. 348; s. c. 1 Atk. 165; Armstrong v. Baldock, Gow. 33.

[7] Weil v. Paul, 22 Cal. 492; Laughlin v. Ferguson, 6 Dana, 111; Leech v. Shantz, 2 Phila. 310; s. c. 5 A. L. Reg. 620; Weeks v. Wead, 2 Aik. 64. *Contra*, Jezeph v. Ingram, 8 Taunt. 838.

auction under a deed of trust, the purchaser may permit
the debtor to keep the goods.[1] After a sale under a
distress for rent, the goods may be left in the possession
of the tenant.[2] The same principle applies to a sale
upon the foreclosure of a mortgage.[3]

SALE UNDER EXECUTION.—The retention of possession
after a sale under an execution rests upon even stronger
grounds. A distinction is established between a sale
made by the vendor or his individual agent, which, in
the absence of a physical coercion, is properly a voluntary as well as a private sale, and one made under a
legal mandate and by an officer of the law, and which
is therefore properly a coercive sale. And it is because
a sale of the latter class is made under command of the
law, and not under the mere will of the owner—by the
act of the law through its officer, and not by the individual act of the party or his agent, and with that fairness and publicity which the law requires and expects
from its officer, and not merely before such witnesses as
the owner may provide, that the law so far confides in
it as not to pronounce it conclusively void upon the mere
fact that the possession remains with the former owner.[4]

---

[1] Leonard v. Baker, 1 M. & S. 251; Fitler v. Maitland, 5 W. & S. 307;
Dallam v. Fitler, 6 W. & S. 323; Woodham v. Baldock, Gow. 35, note;
Gutzweiler v. Lachman, 28 Mo. 434; Ravisies v. Alston, 5 Ala 297; Bank
v. McDade, 4 Port. 252. *Contra*, Rogers v. Vail, 16 Vt. 327; Thompson v.
Yeck, 21 Ill. 73.

[2] Guthrie v. Wood, 1 Stark, 367; Waters v. McClellan, 4 Dall. 208;
Greathouse v Brown, 5 Mon. 280.

[3] Hanford v. Obrecht, 49 Ill. 146; Claytor v. Anthony, 6 Rand. 285;
Simerson v. Bank, 12 Ala. 205.

[4] Laughlin v. Ferguson, 6 Dana, 111; Gates v. Gaines, 10 Vt. 346;
Cole v. Davies, 1 Ld. Raym. 724; Myers v. Harvey, 2 Penn. 478; Perry v.
Foster, 3 Harring. 293; Allentown Bank v. Beck, 49 Penn. 394; McInstry
v. Tanner, 9 Johns. 135; Floyd v. Goodwin, 8 Yerg. 484; Bates v. Carter,
5 Vt. 602; Brandon v. Cunningham, 2 Stew. 249; Anderson v. Brooks, 11

The principle applies to sales by commissioners[1] as well as constables.[2] It is immaterial whether the purchase is made by a stranger,[3] or the execution creditor.[4] The advertisements may be given to the debtor to post, and the purchase may be for a low price.[5] The payment of rent for the use of the goods makes a stronger case than if the purchaser permits them to remain in the debtor's custody without any consideration.[6] The goods may be left in the possession of the debtor upon condition that he shall pay the money to the purchaser as he shall raise it by a sale of them.[7] Goods sold under an execution may be conveyed to a trustee for the sole and separate use of the debtor's wife.[8] It is not sufficient that the sale is made at auction by the sheriff. The sale by the sheriff must be upon legal process, and not under an agreement where any other person might as well have been agreed upon as he.[9]

MERE AGREEMENT.—If the sale is in fact made by the private agreement or understanding of the parties, and not by the coercion of the law, as under an execu-

---

Ala. 953; Coleman v. Bank, 2 Strobh. Eq. 285; Pennington v. Chandler, 5 Harring. 394; Dick v. Lindsay, 2 Grant, 431; Miles v. Edelen, 1 Duvall, 270.

[1] Miles v. Edelen, 1 Duvall, 270.

[2] Pennington v. Chandler, 5 Harring. 394; Perry v. Foster, 3 Harring. 293.

[3] Kidd v. Rawlinson, 2 B. & P. 59; Watkins v. Birch, 4 Taunt. 823; Latimer v. Batson, 4 B. & C. 652; Garrett v. Rhame, 9 Rich. 407; Boardman v. Keeler, 1 Aik. 158.

[4] Simerson v. Bank, 12 Ala. 205; Watkins v. Birch, 4 Taunt. 823; Boardman v. Keeler, 1 Aik. 158; Allentown Bank v. Beck, 49 Penn. 394; Gates v. Gaines, 10 Vt. 346.

[5] Allentown Bank v. Beck, 49 Penn. 394.

[6] Watkins v. Birch, 4 Taunt. 823; Myers v. Harvey, 2 Penn. 478.

[7] Cole v. Davies, 1 Ld. Raym. 724.

[8] Anderson v. Brooks, 11 Ala. 953.

[9] Batchelder v. Carter, 2 Vt. 168.

tion which has been satisfied, it partakes of the character of a private sale, and is subject to those rules of
law in relation to possession which are applied to private sales. The intervention and abuse of the process
of the court cannot change the aspect of the case.[1] So
also, although a sale under a trust deed has been adver-
tised, yet if the trustee is away on the day of sale, and
the debtor and *cestui que trust* enter into an arrangement
by which the latter sells the property at public auction,
it will be regarded as substantially a sale by the debtor
with the concurrence of the trust creditor.[2] This doctrine
in regard to the publicity of the transfer does not make
every public sale, with or without delivery, good. The
question of fraud is always open, and fraud vitiates
every sale.[3]

WHEN CHANGE IS IMPOSSIBLE.—The acts that will
constitute a delivery vary in the different classes of
cases, and depend very much upon the character and
quantity of the property sold, as well as the circumstances of each particular case. Such possession only
need be taken as the nature of the case will permit.[4]
Whenever the property is not so in the power of the
vendor as that he can give, or so in the reach of the
vendee as that he can receive possession, the want of
delivery does not constitute fraud, provided the vendee
takes possession as soon as it can reasonably be had.
The same acts are not necessary to make a good delivery
of ponderous articles, like a block of granite or a stack

---

[1] Stephens v. Barnett, 7 Dana, 257 ; Tavenner v. Robinson, 2 Rob. 280.

[2] Tavenner v. Robinson, 2 Rob. 280.

[3] Pennington v. Chandler, 5 Harring. 394 ; Taylor v. Mills, 2 Edw.
Ch. 318; Dickenson v. Cook, 17 Johns. 332; Farrington v. Caswell, 15
Johns. 430.

[4] Manton v. Moore, 7 T. R. 67.

of hay, as is required in case of an article of small bulk, as a parcel of bullion.[1] There must be a manual delivery of a single sack of grain at the moment of its sale, but upon the sale of two thousand sacks this cannot be done without incurring great and unnecessary expense and departing from the usual course of business.[2] Upon the sale of furniture in a dwelling-house, the property may be removed to another house, or the vendor may leave the house and the vendee take possession with all the ordinary *indicia* of ownership;[3] but in case of a sale of a large hotel, with many hundred lodging rooms, parlors and sitting-rooms, besides the culinary department, with its necessary offices all duly furnished, the furniture cannot be removed without great deterioration and expense. It is valuable mainly for the purpose for which it is used, and in the place where it is situated.[4] Upon the sale of a single board, or of a cart-load of boards, it would not do to set up a constructive delivery by marking and letting it remain where it is until it is convenient to remove it. The court would be bound to hold, as matter of law, that such articles are capable of actual delivery; but it would be different with a board-yard filled with many piles of lumber. There the circumstances are such as to render an actual delivery and removal impracticable, or at least injurious and expensive. The vendee must assume the control and do all that an honest man would reasonably be expected to do to advertise the public of the sale.[5] In such instances the

---

[1] Samuels v. Gorham, 5 Cal. 226 ; Doane v. Eddy, 16 Wend. 523; Randall v. Cook, 17 Wend. 53.

[2] Lay v. Neville, 25 Cal. 545.

[3] Steelwagon v. Jeffries, 44 Penn. 407.

[4] McKibbin v. Martin, 64 Penn. 352.

[5] McKibbin v. Martin, 64 Penn. 352; Long v. Knapp, 54 Penn. 514; Haynes v. Hunsicker, 26 Penn. 58.

rule is not impaired, but the case does not come with'n it.[1]

PONDEROUS ARTICLES.—Bricks in the kiln,[2] mown hay in the field,[3] unbaled hay,[4] cattle roaming over unenclosed plains,[5] growing crops,[6] trees in the woods[7] and a safe,[8] are instances of articles not susceptible of immediate change of possession. Machinery which may be separated from the building and removed without injury to it or the building, must be delivered at the time of the sale.[9] If a person buys a store of goods, he may continue the business in the same place.[10]

WHAT CHANGE NECESSARY.—In the case of ponderous articles, it is not necessary that there should be an actual removal of the goods and change of possession from hand to hand.[11] Every species of divestiture

---

[1] Sydnor v. Gee, 4 Leigh, 535; Land v. Jeffries, 5 Rand. 211.

[2] Allen v. Smith, 10 Mass. 308.

[3] Chaffin v. Doub, 14 Cal. 384.

[4] Conway v. Edwards, 6 Nev. 190.

[5] Walden v. Murdock, 23 Cal. 540.

[6] Bernal v. Hovious, 17 Cal. 541; Robbins v. Oldham, 1 Duvall, 28; Herron v. Fry, 2 Penn. 263; Bellows v. Wells, 36 Vt. 593; Morton v. Ragan, 5 Bush. 334; Visher v. Webster, 13 Cal. 58; Cummins v. Griggs, 2 Duvall, 87. By statute in California, a mortgage of growing crops must be recorded, and possession taken as soon as they are harvested. (Quiriaque v. Dennis, 24 Cal. 154.)

[7] Fitch v. Burk, 38 Vt. 683.

[8] Benford v. Schell, 55 Penn. 393.

[9] Swift v. Thompson, 9 Conn. 63; Tobias v. Francis, 3 Vt. 425; Gaylor v. Harding, 37 Conn. 508. By statute, in Vermont, there need be no change of possession of machinery when the mortgage is recorded. (Walworth v. Readsboro, 24 Vt. 252.)

[10] Hugus v. Robinson, 24 Penn. 9; Warner v. Norton, 20 How. 448; Hall v. Parsons, 15 Vt. 358; s. c. 17 Vt. 271; Dunlap v. Bournonville, 26 Penn. 72; Ford v. Chambers, 28 Cal. 13.

[11] Cartwright v. Phoenix, 7 Cal. 281; Luckenbach v. Brickenstein, 5 W. & S. 145; Allen v. Smith, 10 Mass. 308.

which can give the world notice should however be resorted to.[1] Each case must in a great manner depend upon
its own circumstances in regard to the acts that may be
requisite to manifest the actual and continued change
of possession.[2] It is sufficient that the vendee assumes
the direction and control, and in such an open, notorious manner as usually accompanies an honest transaction. Whether all is done that ought to be done,
and whether the change of possession is real and *bona
fide*, not merely colorable and deceptive, are questions
of fact that ought to be submitted to the jury.[3] If a
kiln of bricks is left in the exclusive possession of the
vendor, the sale will be fraudulent.[4] But setting up
stakes in the yard and marking the bricks, if notorious,
is sufficient. Merely telling the hands and others that
a raft belongs to the vendee is not a sufficient delivery.
The vendor can leave the raft after making a public
declaration in the presence of witnesses that he de-
livers it up to the vendee.[6] A formal delivery of
timber, accompanied with marking and counting, is
sufficient without any measurement.[7] It is not necessary that the marking of lumber in piles should be
done immediately at the time of the delivery. It is
sufficient if it is done within a reasonable time, that is,
as soon as it conveniently can be done.[8] The delivery
of the key where goods are locked up is a delivery of

---

[1] Chase v. Ralston, 30 Penn. 539; Hutchins v. Gilchrist, 23 Vt. 82.

[2] Lay v. Neville, 25 Cal. 545.

[3] McKibbin v. Martin, 64 Penn. 352; Chase v. Ralston, 30 Penn. 539;
Lay v. Neville, 25 Cal. 545.

[4] Woods v. Bugbey, 29 Cal. 466; Richards v. Schroeder, 10 Cal. 431.

[5] Allen v. Smith, 10 Mass. 308.

[6] Cadbury v. Nolen, 5 Penn. 320.

[7] Chase v. Ralston, 30 Penn. 539; Sanborn v. Kittredge, 20 Vt. 632 ;
Hutchins v. Gilchrist, 23 Vt. 82 ; Haynes v. Hunsicker, 26 Penn. 58.

[8] Long v. Knapp, 54 Penn. 514.

the goods themselves.[1] It will be symbolical only when the vendor remains in apparent connection with the goods, but is valid in other cases.[2] The vendor may be employed to cut and cure growing crops.[3] The vendee is entitled to a reasonable time in which to complete the delivery, by reducing the goods into his actual possession.[4]

DISTANCE.—When the chattels sold are so situated in regard to distance that there can be no delivery at the time of the sale, the case forms an exception to the general rule, and it is sufficient if the vendee without any gross *laches* takes possession and asserts his title in a reasonable time after he has an opportunity to take possession.[5] It is not in the power of the parties under such circumstances to deliver the possession, and consequently a delivery is not required. A familiar example of this doctrine is in the case of a sale of a ship,[6] or of goods at sea,[7] where possession is dispensed with upon the plain ground of its impossibility, and it is sufficient if the vendee takes possession of the property within a reasonable time after its return. The exception extends to protect contracts relating to ships which are at home, but in a port distant from the place where the contract is made. The distance between the place of

---

[1] Barr v. Reitz, 53 Penn. 256; Benford v. Schell, 55 Penn. 393.

[2] Barr v. Reitz, 53 Penn. 256.

[3] Cummins v. Griggs, 2 Duvall, 87; Fitch v. Burk, 38 Vt. 683. *Contra*, Welsh v. Bekey, 1 Penn. 57.

[4] Haynes v. Hunsicker, 26 Penn. 28; Walden v. Murdock, 23 Cal. 540.

[5] Ricker v. Cross, 5 N. H. 570; Meade v. Smith, 16 Conn. 366.

[6] Atkinson v. Maling, 2 T. R. 462; Badlam v. Tucker, 1 Pick. 389; Morgan v. Biddle, 1 Yeates, 3.

[7] Conrad v. Atlantic Ins. Co. 1 Pet. 385; Portland Bank v. Stacey, 4 Mass. 661; Dawes v. Cope, 4 Binn. 258; Gardner v. Howland, 2 Pick. 599.

sale and the port is immaterial.[1]   The transfer of ships
is commonly made by a bill of sale, and the title passes
upon the execution of the instrument.[2]   The delivery of
the bill of lading and policy of insurance is sufficient in
sales of goods.[3]

The vendee is not bound to follow the vessel from
port to port, but may reasonably wait her return to the
port where she belongs, and where the bill of sale is
executed.[4]   If the vendee appears chargeable with neglect in not taking possession seasonably, it is only
evidence of fraud, and may be explained.[5]   But
where the delay and negligence are gross, they will of
themselves defeat the conveyance against any subsequent attacking creditor.   Whether they exist or not
depends upon the situation and circumstances of the
vessel, and of the vendee.[6]   What precise period is embraced under the term reasonable time, and when that
degree of negligence is imputable by which a transfer
is vacated, has not been distinctly settled to a day or
an hour.[7]   A delay for one year has been held to
amount to an abandonment of all right under the conveyance.[8]   A return and stay for eleven days, if unknown to the vendee, and departure upon another

---

[1] Putnam v. Dutch, 8 Mass. 287.

[2] Putnam v. Dutch, 8 Mass. 287;   Portland Bank v. Stacey, 4 Mass.
661. In England, the delivery is made by delivering the grand bill of
sale. In Portland v. Stacey, 4 Mass. 661, it is said that there is no distinction
between what is commonly called the grand bill of sale in England, which
is necessary to pass ships at sea, and the bills of sale for vessels used in
America.

[3] Dawes v. Cope, 4 Binn. 258.

[4] Badlam v. Tucker, 1 Pick. 389.

[5] Badlam v. Tucker, 1 Pick. 389.

[6] Joy v. Sears, 9 Pick. 4 ; Mair v. Glennie, 4 M. & S. 240.

[7] Brinley v. Spring, 7 Me. 241.

[8] Meeker v. Wilson, 1 Gallis, 419.

voyage does not vitiate the sale.[1] It is not necessary
to have an agent in the home port when the vessel is
expected in another port.[2] Seizure on legal process before the expiration of a reasonable time is sufficient
excuse.[3] Notice to the captain of the transfer of the
ship is equivalent to the taking of possession.[4]

CONSTRUCTIVE POSSESSION.—The rule has its origin
in the doctrine that the retention of possession after a
sale gives the vendor a false credit, and deceives
creditors. This can only occur in the case of an
actual possession by the vendor, for wherever there
is merely a constructive possession, all persons are
put upon the inquiry. Such a possession does not
give a false credit. It is therefore a general principle
that a constructive possession will pass by a constructive
delivery.[5] A bill of sale is sufficient, for it places the
property at the disposal of the vendee, and gives him
not only the title, but a constructive possession with
power to reduce it to an actual possession at his own
pleasure.[6] When goods are in a warehouse, the delivery
is complete by an order on the warehouseman, and the
fact that the goods stand on the books of the warehouseman in the name of the vendor, who also sells some of
them afterwards, will not make the sale fraudulent.[7] In
case of a bailment, the property passes when the sale is
completed, and no formal delivery is necessary. The
sale is the only change of which the property is suscep-

---

[1] Turner v. Coolidge, 2 Met. 350.
[2] Joy v. Sears, 9 Pick. 4.
[3] Conrad v. Atlantic Ins. Co. 1 Pet. 385; Putnam v. Dutch, 8 Mass.
287.
[4] Brinley v. Spring, 7 Me. 241.
[5] Hutchins v. Gilchrist, 23 Vt. 82.
[6] Hutchins v. Gilchrist, 23 Vt. 82.
[7] Jones v. Dwyer, 15 East, 21.

tible.[1] After the execution of the bill of sale, the
vendee is entitled to a reasonable time either to give
notice of the fact to the bailee, or to take possession of
the property. Whether he uses this diligence, or is so
remiss that fraud ought to be inferred, is a question for
the jury.[2]

BAILEE.—If the vendor of goods in the care and
keeping of a third person, directs him to deliver them
to the vendee, and the party holding the goods on
notice and application of the vendee consents to retain
the goods for him, it is a sufficient delivery and transfer,
for the actual possession is then in such third person.[3]
This is upon the ground that the vendor after
such notice has neither the actual nor constructive
possession, and is divested of all control over the property.[4] The mere pendency of an attachment does not
prevent the transfer, for the garnishee has the power to
waive his right to hold possession of the property in
favor of a purchaser.[5] The principle does not apply
when the bailee is simply to pay over a part of the pro-

---

[1] Linton v. Butz, 7 Penn. 89; Goodwin v. Kelly, 42 Barb. 194; Nash
v. Ely, 19 Wend. 523; Butt v. Caldwell, 4 Bibb. 458.

[2] Ingraham v. Wheeler, 6 Ct. 277.

[3] Barney v. Brown, 2 Vt. 374; Spaulding v. Austin, 2 Vt. 555; Linton v. Butz, 7 Penn. 89; Whigham's Appeal, 63 Penn. 194; Kroesen v.
Seevers, 5 Leigh, 434; Warner v. Norton, 20 How. 448; Harding v. Janes,
4 Vt. 462; Pierce v. Chipman, 8 Vt. 334; Kendall v. Fitts, 22 N. H. 1;
Morse v. Powers, 17 N. H. 286; Hodgkins v. Hook, 23 Cal. 581; Mont-
gomery v. Hunt, 5 Cal. 366; Walcott v. Keith, 22 N. H. 196; Potter v.
Washburn, 13 Vt. 558; Cartwright v. Phoenix, 7 Cal. 281. In Vermont
the transfer is not valid without notice to the bailee. Moore v. Kelley, 5
Vt. 34. Notice by the vendor alone is not sufficient. Judd v. Langdon, 5
Vt. 231.

[4] Harding v. Janes, 4 Vt. 462.

[5] Walcott v. Keith, 22 N. H. 196.

ceeds to the vendee.[1] The vendor may subsequently
interfere temporarily to remove the property from one
place to another as the agent of the vendee,[2] or may
be employed to rent or sell the property.[3]

SERVANT.—This principle is not applicable to a
mere servant.[4] The possession of a mere servant or
hired man is but the possession of the master, and
does not, like the possession of other third persons,
put creditors upon inquiry. To give it that effect
there must be some change in the labor, or something external, to show to the world the new relation. Mere contract resting between the parties has
no such effect.[5]

SUBJECT TO INTEREST OF A THIRD PARTY.—Although
the property has been hired out, the owner may transfer the right, subject to the terms upon which it has
been hired. The subsequent holding by the person
who hired it should not be treated as the possession of
the vendor, opposed to the transfer of right. The possession does not continue to be the possession of the
vendor. It is not in its nature incompatible with the
right transferred, and ought not, therefore, to stamp the
contract as fraudulent in itself. With the transfer of
right in the property, the right of possession, subject to
the qualified interest held by another, is also transferred. The possession of such third person is a possession

---

[1] Richards v. Schroeder, 10 Cal. 431.

[2] Kendall v. Fitts, 22 N. H. 1.

[3] Harding v. Janes, 4 Vt. 462.

[4] Doak v. Brubacker, 1 Nev. 218; Hurlburd v. Bogardus, 10 Cal.
518.

[5] Flanagan v. Wood, 33 Vt. 332; Sharon v. Shaw, 2 Nev. 289; Sleeper
v. Pollard, 28 Vt. 709.

connected with the right of property, and ought, therefore, rather to be regarded, in the hands of the person hiring, as following the transfer of the right of property in the hands of the purchaser.[1] Mere notice, without any consent to hold for the vendee, will make the transfer unimpeachable.[2]

UPON ANOTHER'S LAND.—The same principle applies when the chattels are upon the land of another. Such goods are not in the actual possession or beneficial use of the debtor. All that he has is a constructive possession, flowing from his general right of property, and this possession will follow the right of property under a bill of sale. After the execution of the bill of sale, the goods cannot be considered as remaining even in his constructive possession. Much less has he any beneficial use and possession.[3] It is not necessary that there should be a change in the local situation of the property, for there may be a change in the possession, while the site of the property remains the same.[4] It is sufficient if the former owner is divested of the legal and ostensible control. When his connection with the article has ceased, it will not be presumed that he is in the visible, ostensible occupancy of the land.[5] The vendee is entitled to a reasonable time to take possession of the goods.[6]

---

[1] Butt v. Caldwell, 4 Bibb. 458; Kroesen v. Seevers, 5 Leigh, 434; Lynde v. Melvin, 11 Vt. 683; Roberts v. Guernsey, 3 Grant, 237; Thomas v. Hillhouse, 17 Iowa, 67.

[2] Wooley v. Edson, 35 Vt. 214.

[3] Hutchins v. Gilchrist, 23 Vt. 82.

[4] Hutchins v. Gilchrist, 23 Vt. 82; Cartwright v. Phoenix, 7 Cal. 281; Merritt v. Miller, 13 Vt. 416.

[5] Merritt v. Miller, 13 Vt. 416.

[6] Walden v. Murdock, 23 Cal. 540; Morse v. Powers, 17 N. H. 286.

PRIOR TO EXECUTION.—When there is no change of
possession at the time of the sale, it will be sufficient if
the vendee takes possession before the right of a creditor attaches, by levy under an execution or other legal
process.[1] If the change does not immediately follow
the sale, it is proper matter to go to the jury, on the
question of a fraudulent sale in fact.[2] When the possession has been with the vendee for a long period, the
transfer is valid, although the property remained with
the vendor for a considerable time after the sale.[3] It is
not sufficient to take possession after the vendor's
death.[4]

CHANGE AS TO PART.—Leaving a part of the goods
in the possession of the vendor, does not affect the part
of which the vendee has the possession. Though it is,
in point of law, conclusive of the voidness of the sale,
to the extent of the property thus remaining in the
possession of the vendor, it cannot determine conclusively, and as to other property, the question of fact
whether the vendee, in making the purchase, intended
to defraud the creditors of the vendor, or to aid him in
the accomplishment of that object. Such a fact is not
of itself, and without regard to the other facts of the

---

[1] Bartlett v. Williams, 1 Pick. 288; Hall v. Parsons, 15 Vt. 358; Kendall
v. Samson, 12 Vt. 515; Read v. Wilson, 22 Ill. 377; Calkins v. Lockwood,
16 Conn 276; Blake v. Graves, 18 Iowa, 312; Cruikshanks v. Cogswell, 26
Ill 366; Sydnor v. Gee, 4 Leigh, 535; Clute v. Steele, 6 Nev. 335; Smith
v. Stern, 17 Penn. 360. *Contra*, Carpenter v. Mayer, 5 Watts, 483; Gibson
v. Love, 4 Fla. 217; Chenery v. Palmer, 6 Cal. 119; Hackett v. Manlove,
14 Cal. 85; Ragan v. Kennedy, 1 Tenn. 91; Gardenier v. Tubbs, 21 Wend.
169; Claytor v. Anthony, 6 Rand. 285.

[2] Kendall v. Samson, 12 Vt. 515; Cruikshanks v. Cogswell, 26 Ill.
366.

[3] Henderson v. Mabry, 13 Ala. 713; Mauldin v. Mitchell, 14 Ala.
814.

[4] Shields v. Anderson, 3 Leigh, 729; Edwards v. Harben, 2 T. R. 587.

case, sufficient to require the conclusion that the whole sale is fraudulent and void.[1] The transfer is good and operative as to the articles delivered, and void and inoperative as to the residue.[2] But the possession and use of a part of the goods by the vendor is evidence to be weighed by the jury, in determining upon the honesty and validity of the transaction.[3]

CONTINUED.—The change of possession must not only be actual, but it must be continued in order to render a sale valid as against the vendor's creditors;[4] but one or more acts of intermeddling with the property by the vendor, after the sale, do not amount to a retention of possession.[5] A few and fitful instances of use by the vendor,[6] or temporary acts of ownership, without the consent of the vendee, will not vitiate the sale.[7] Temporary lendings or hirings,[8] or a temporary interference by the vendor, to remove the property from one place to another,[9] will not render the transaction void. But a mere temporary change, if the property revert immediately into the possession of the vendor, is not sufficient.[10] As the change of possession

---

[1] Brown v. Foree, 7 B. Mon. 357.

[2] Weller v. Wayland, 17 Johns. 102; D'Wolf v. Harris, 4 Mason, 515; Lee v. Huntoon, 1 Hoffm. 447; Spaulding v. Austin, 2 Vt. 555; Brown v. Foree, 7 B. Mon. 357; De Bardleben v. Beekman, 1 Dessau. 346; Hessing v. McCloskey, 37 Ill. 341.

[3] Spaulding v. Austin, 2 Vt. 555; Brown v. Foree, 7 B. Mon. 357; Contra, Foster v. Pugh, 12 S. & M. 416.

[4] Miller v. Garman, 28 Leg. Int. 405; Leech v. Shantz, 2 Phila. 310; s. c. 5 A. L. Reg. 620; Norton v. Doolittle, 32 Conn. 405.

[5] Lake v. Morris, 30 Conn. 201.

[6] Farnsworth v. Shepard, 6 Vt. 521; Lyndon v. Belden, 14 Vt. 423.

[7] Hodgkins v. Hook, 23 Cal. 581.

[8] Farnsworth v. Shepard, 6 Vt. 521; Lyndon v. Belden, 14 Vt. 423.

[9] Kendall v. Fitts, 22 N. H. 1.

[10] Morris v. Hyde, 8 Vt. 352; Norton v. Doolittle, 32 Conn. 405; Weeks v. Wead, 2 Aik. 64; Goldsbury v. May, 1 Litt. 254.

14

is necessary to consummate or perfect the vendee's right or title, if it is omitted through the neglect or disobedience of an agent, and the property thus finds its way back into the possession of the vendor, the vendee must bear the consequences.[1] But when the property at the time of the sale is in the hands of a bailee for a time limited, and the vendee has no right to immediate possession, and can not select an agent to take or keep possession for him, the fact that the bailee permits the property to go back into the possession of the vendor before the determination of his right, will not avoid the sale.[2]

SUBSEQUENT RETURN.—The rule is not an absolute prohibition of any subsequent return of the property into the possession of the vendor. After the sale has become perfected by such visible, notorious, and continued change of possession, that the creditors of the vendor may be presumed to have notice of it, a return of the property to the vendor will not, by its own mere operation, render the transaction fraudulent.[3] Before the return there must be such a change of possession as indicates to the world at large a change of ownership. It must be open, visible, and substantial, and such an one as indicates a change of possession, or a sufficient explanation should exist to show why the possession was not changed. It should be such as

---

[1] Morris v. Hyde, 8 Vt. 352.

[2] Lynde v. Melvin, 11 Vt. 683.

[3] Brady v. Haines, 18 Penn. 113 ; Graham v. McCreary, 40 Penn. 515 ; Clark v. Morse, 10 N. H. 236 ; French v. Hall, 9 N. H. 137 ; Prosser v. Henderson, 11 Ala. 484 ; Sutton v. Shearer, 1 Grant, 207 ; Carpenter v. Clark, 2 Nev. 243 ; Johnson v. Willey, 46 N. H. 75 ; Stevens v. Irwin, 15 Cal. 503 ; Waldie v. Doll, 29 Cal. 555 ; Lewis v. Wilcox, 6 Nev. 215 ; Brown v. Riley, 22 Ill. 45 ; Neece v. Haley, 23 Ill. 416. *Contra*, Van Pelt v. Littler, 10 Cal. 394 ; Bacon v. Scannell, 9 Cal. 271.

may fairly lead those around, if they have any interest in the matter, to a reasonable belief that there has been a sale and change of property.[1] The ostensible nature and purpose of the vendee's possession, as well as its duration, will be considered in determining whether it is so manifest and substantial as to be unprejudiced by allowing the property to return to the vendor's control.[2] If the property has been attached, this will assist in giving notoriety to the transfer.[3] The change of possession must also continue for such a length of time as will be likely to operate as a general advertisement of the change of title.[4] It is impossible to lay down a fixed rule applicable to all cases establishing the length of time a vendee of personal property should continue in the exclusive possession. Each case must necessarily be governed and determined by its own peculiar circumstances.[5] Eight or ten days[6] has been deemed insufficient. Five weeks has been considered sufficient.[7] The vendee after such an open change of the possession, may lend or let the goods to the vendor or employ him to sell or perform any other service about them with the same safety as he may a stranger.[8] But the return can only be for a temporary purpose. The vendor can not have the permanent possession and use of them in his own business.[9] A minor son may, how-

---

[1] Clark v. Morse, 10 N. H. 236.   [2] Houston v. Howard, 39 Vt. 54.

[3] Clark v. Morse, 10 N. H. 236.

[4] Carpenter v. Clark, 2 Nev. 243.

[5] Weil v. Paul, 22 Cal. 492.

[6] Weeks v. Wead, 2 Aik. 64; Rogers v. Vail, 16 Vt. 327; Mills v. Warner, 19 Vt. 609; Miller v. Garman, 28 Leg. Int. 405; Look v. Comstock, 15 Wend. 244. *Contra*, Cunningham v. Hamilton, 25 Ill. 228; Wright v. Grover, 27 Ill. 426.

[7] Brady v. Haines, 18 Penn. 113.

[8] Dewey v. Thrall, 13 Vt. 281; Harding v. Janes, 4 Vt. 462; Brady v. Haines, 18 Penn. 113.

[9] Mills v. Warner, 19 Vt. 609.

ever, purchase them in good faith, and bring them home to his father's, where he resides.[1]

An assignment of a chose in action, is subject to the rule which requires a change of possession.[2] In the case of things in action, the usual muniments of title should be conferred upon the grantee. In the case of stocks, the natural and appropriate indication of owner-ship is the entry upon the stock record.[3] There is no distinction between prior and subsequent creditors.[4]

LAND.—Possession of real estate is not without weight, and in a doubtful case would incline the court not to yield to any just suspicions arising from other causes. But it does not *per se* raise a presumption of fraud as it does in the case of personal estate. Posses-sion is *prima facie* evidence of ownership. The same rule does not apply to real estate. Possession is not there deemed evidence of ownership. The laws of most nations require solemn instruments to pass the title to real property. The public look not so much to pos-session as to the public records, as proofs of the title to such property. The possession must therefore be in-consistent with the sale and repugnant to it in terms or operation, before it raises a just presumption of fraud.[5]

---

[1] Jordan v. Frink, 3 Penn. 442.

[2] Welch v. Beekey, 1 Penna. 57 ; Woodbridge v. Perkins, 3 Day, 364; Hall v. Redding, 13 Cal. 214.   [3] Pinkerton v. Railroad, 42 N. H. 424.

[4] Clow v. Woods, 5 S. & R., 275 ; Young v. Pate, 4 Yerg. 164; Smith v. Lowell, 6 N. H. 67; Paul v. Crooker, 8 N. H. 288; Woodrow v. Davis, 2 B. Mon. 296 ; Rankin v. Holloway, 3 S. & M. 614; Smith v. McDonald, 25 Geo. 377.

[5] Phettiplace v. Sayles, 4 Mason, 312 ; Every v. Edgerton, 7 Wend. 259; Waller v. Todd, 3 Dana. 503; Avery v. Street, 6 Watts, 247; Bank of U. S. v. Houseman, 6 Paige, 526 ; Paulling v. Sturgus, 3 Stew. 95; Barr v. Hatch, 3 Ohio, 527; Short v. Tinsley, 1 Met. (Ky.) 397; Tibbals v. Jacobs, 31 Conn. 428; Merrill v. Locke, 41 N. H. 486; Lyne v. Bank, 5 J. J. Marsh, 545; Allentown Bank v. Beek, 49 Penn. 394; Ludwig v. Highley, 5 Penn, 132.

CHAPTER VII.

PREFERENCES.

REASONS WHY A PREFERENCE IS NOT FRAUDULENT.—
Where creditors take no specific security from their
debtor, they trust him upon the general credit of his
property and a confidence that it will not be dimin-
ished to their prejudice. They have, therefore, an
equitable interest in it which the law, under certain
circumstances, recognizes and enforces. The statute is
founded upon the principle of protecting this equitable
right. When a transfer, however, is made to a creditor,
his equity is the same as that of the others, and he is entitled to the benefit of the universal rule, that where
the equities are equal the legal title must prevail. An
existing indebtedness is, therefore, a good consideration
within the proviso which saves the rights of *bona fide*
purchasers. There being no equity prior to that of the
vendee, the necessity which calls for a new consideration in other cases does not exist.[1]

RIGHT TO PREFER IS A CONSEQUENCE OF OWNERSHIP.
—The abstract principles of natural justice dictate that
the property of an insolvent debtor should be applied
for the equal benefit of all creditors, but they have
been found impracticable without the aid of some arti-

---

[1] Seymour v. Wilson, 19 N. Y. 417; Adams v. Wheeler, 10 Pick. 199;
Gibson v. Seymour, 4 Vt. 518; Gleason v. Day, 9 Wis. 498; Seymour v.
Briggs, 11 Wis. 196 ; McMahan v. Morrison, 16 Ind. 172; Wilson v. Ayer,
7 Me. 207 ; Towsley v. McDonald, 32 Barb. 604; *vide* Harney v. Pack, 4
S. & M. 229 ; Pope v. Pope, 40 Miss. 516.

ficial system. The right of the debtor to use, control, and dispose of his property, is, in the absence of any statute, absolute, and he is in no manner rightfully subject to the dictation of his creditors, for they have no legal right in his property by reason of being creditors.[1] The principles of the common law could not be shaped to general ends in any other way. To make a different general rule would be to take away a man's right over his own property, and involve the necessity of vesting an inquisitorial power somewhere.[2] This is the only ground on which the right to prefer can be placed. So long as the property of a debtor remains in his hands unshackled by liens or incumbrances, his power over it is absolute, and he can, in the absence of any statute, dispose of it by way of satisfaction to his creditors as well as by sale.[3] If the right of giving a preference were to be denied while the debtor retains his property in his own hands, he would so far lose dominion over his own that he could not pay anybody, because whoever he paid would receive a preference.[4] It is therefore necessary to leave a discretion to the debtor within the limits of fraud. Society has to depend for its indemnity upon the teachings of the debtors' heart and conscience; upon those moral lights which all men possess, and upon the native sense of justice.[5]

THE LAW KNOWS NO DISTINCTION BETWEEN DEBTS. —The right of preference has been advocated by many

---

[1] Lampson v. Arnold, 19 Iowa, 479.

[2] Wilson v. Forsyth, 24 Barb. 105.

[3] Grover v. Wakeman, 11 Wend. 187; Danee v. Seaman, 11 Gratt. 778; Wilson v. Forsyth, 24 Barb. 105; Lupton v. Cutter, 8 Pick. 298; Robinson v. Rapelye, 2 Stew. 86; Tillou v. Britton, 4 Halst. 120.

[4] Lampson v. Arnold, 17 Iowa, 479.

[5] Niolon v. Douglass, 2 Hill Ch. 443.

enlightened jurists, on the ground that the debtor, possessing an intimate knowledge of the relative equities of his creditors, could make a more just distribution than the law. It has been said that there are some debts which a person honestly may, and even ought to prefer.[1] The notion however, of honorary debts in contradistinction to other debts founded on a fair and adequate consideration, is a dangerous distinction, and calculated to injure and mislead the moral sense. The law does not recognize such a principle of honor, and the courts have no means by which they can test its purity, or separate it from arbitrary, selfish, or vindictive motives of preference. The principle is too uncertain, flexible, and capricious in the application.[2] The law, moreover, can not recognize any distinction between legal obligations, nor defer its own wisdom and honesty to the wisdom and honesty of a delinquent debtor.[3]

A PREFERENCE NOT ALWAYS GIVEN TO MERITORIOUS DEBTS.—Experience also shows that a preference is sometimes given to the very creditor who is the least entitled to it, because he lent to the debtor a delusive credit, and that too no doubt under assurances of a well grounded confidence of priority of payment, and perfect indemnity in case of failure. It often happens that the creditor who has been the means of decoying others is secured, while the real business creditor, who parts with his property on liberal terms, and in manly confidence, is made the victim.[4] It is true that the debts preferred are usually considered and termed by the

---

[1] Murray v. Riggs, 15 Johns. 571; Dana v. Bank of U. S. 5 W. & S. 223.

[2] Riggs v. Murray, 2 Johns. Ch. 565.

[3] Grover v. Wakeman, 11 Wend. 187.

[4] Riggs v. Murray, 2 Johns. Ch. 565; s. c. 15 Johns. 571.

parties honorable and confidential, and these deceptive terms doubtless conceal from many the mischiefs and immorality of the system. But whether the terms are justly applied is a different question. There is, indeed, a mutual confidence and understanding when the debts are contracted. The friendly creditor lends his money or credit to furnish the capital which the borrower needs in the confidence, express or implied, that he shall incur no risk from the insolvency of the debtor, but that, in all events, whatever may be the losses and sufferings of others, he shall be protected. But a secret confidence by which the public is deceived, and creditors, excluded from its knowledge and benefits, made the victims of their credulity and ignorance—a confidence which in respect to third persons is a source of delusion and an instrument of fraud, assuredly deserves any other name than that of honorable. It is not an agreement that it implies, but a conspiracy.[1] Such an exercise of the right to prefer simply constitutes the debtor an agent to obtain money from one man and bestow it upon another at his will and pleasure.[2]

PREFERENCE NOT FAVORABLE TO COMMERCE.—It is thought by some that the right of preference favors commercial enterprise by affording to those destitute of capital a credit founded on the power of securing confidential at the expense of business creditors. If this is so, it is at best but a poor argument in its favor, for it is founded obviously in wrong. The facility of obtaining credit under such circumstances is, in theory nothing more than a facility for committing fraud, and, in practice, has proved nothing less. The experience of all commercial communities leads to the conclusion

---

[1] Nicholson v. Leavitt, 4 Sandf. 252.
[2] Boardman v. Halliday, 10 Paige, 223.

that this power of preferring creditors is a fruitful source of fraud, and in every respect mischievous and unwholesome.[1] The right moreover is not always exercised in favor of so-called meritorious debts. An influential creditor is often preferred while those who are poor, or are minors, or are absent, or want the means or spirit to engage in litigation, are abandoned.[2] The principle is also frequently perverted, and made subservient to the gratification of vindictive feelings, and to the perpetration of the foulest injustice, as well as ingratitude towards honest and confiding creditors.[3]

PREFERENCES NOT FRAUDULENT.—By virtue of his absolute dominion over his property, a debtor, however, may either give or allow a preference. It is no part of the policy of the statute to prohibit its application to the payment of one debt rather than another. The maxim *vigilantibus non dormientibus leges subserviunt* applies. Hence it is that a creditor who can secure a sufficiency, according to law, to satisfy his claim, is entitled to hold it against other creditors.[4] This right

---

[1] Grover v. Wakeman, 11 Wend. 187 ; Lupton v. Cutter, 8 Pick. 298 ; Atkinson v. Jordan, 5 Ohio, 295.

[2] Riggs v. Murray, 2 Johns. Ch. 565 ; s. c. 15 Johns. 571 ; Grover v. Wakeman, 11 Wend. 187.

[3] Cunningham v. Freeborn, 11 Wend. 241.

[4] Benton v. Thornhill, 2 Marsh. 427; s. c. 7 Taunt. 149 ; Eveleigh v. Purrsford, 2 Mood. & Rob. 539 ; Cameron v. Montgomery, 13 S. & R. 128 ; Ragan v. Kennedy, 1 Tenn. 91 ; Waterbury v. Sturtevant, 18 Wend. 853 ; McMenomy v. Roosevelt, 3 Johns. Ch. 446 ; Lewis v. Whittemore, 5 N. H. 364 ; Terry v. Belcher, 1 Bailey, 568 ; Phettiplace v. Sayles, 4 Mason, 312 ; Sommerville v. Horton, 4 Yerg. 541 ; Hoofsmith v. Cope, 6 Whart. 53 ; Maples v. Maples, Rice Ch. 300 ; Floyd v. Goodwin, 8 Yerg. 484; Wiley v. Lashlee, 8 Humph. 717; McQuinnay v. Hitchcock, 8 Tex. 33; Fromme v. Jones, 13 Iowa, 474 ; Parnell v. Howard, 26 Iowa, 38 ; Cowles v. Rickett, 1 Iowa, 582 ; Bruce v. Smith, 3 H. & J. 499 ; Cole v. Albers, 1 Gill, 412; Glenn v. Grover, 3 Md. 212; Anderson v. Tydings, 3 Md. Ch. 167; Mayfield v. Kilgour, 31 Md. 240; Grogan v. Cooke, 2 Ball. & B. 233; Holbird v.

moreover, is not affected by the debtor's insolvency,[1] or the preferred creditor's knowledge of such insolveney.[2]

ALTHOUGH OTHERS LOSE THEIR DEBTS.—The fact that a suit is pending,[3] or that the transfer includes all the debtor's property,[4] or that other creditors lose their debts by reason of the debtor's inability to meet all the demands against him,[5] does not necessarily affect

---

Anderson, 5 P. R. 235 ; Green v. Tanner, 8 Met. 411; Harrison v. Philips Academy, 12 Mass. 456; Guild v. Leonard, 18 Pick. 511 ; Buffum v. Green, 5 N. H. 71; Hendricks v. Robinson, 2 Johns. 283 ; s. c. 17 Johns. 438; Lewkner v. Freeman, Prec. Ch. 105; 1 Eq. Cas. Abr. 149; 2 Freem. 236; Williams v. Brown, 4 Johns. Ch. 682; M'Broom v. Rives, 1 Stew. 72; Eaton v. Patterson, 2 Stew. & Port. 9; Stover v. Herrington, 7 Ala. 142; Gary v. Colgin, 11 Ala. 514; Lowrie v. Stewart, 8 Ala. 163 ; Hinde v. Vattier, 1 McLean, 110 ; s. c. 7 Pet. 252 ; Coolidge v. Curtis, 7 A. L. Reg. 334; Blakey's Appeal, 7 Penn. 449; Worman v. Wolfersberger, 19 Penn. 59; Hutchinson v. McClure, 20 Penn. 63; Hickman v. Quinn, 6 Yerg. 96; Young v. Stallings, 5 B. Mon. 307; Bullock v. Irvine, 4 Munf. 450 ; Bates v. Cole, 10 Conn. 280; Kemp v. Walker, 16 Ohio, 118; Choteau v. Sherman, 11 Mo. 385; Moseley v. Gainer, 10 Tex. 393 ; Hubbard v. Taylor, 5 Mich. 155 ; Bull v. Harris, 18 B. Mon. 195.

[1] Glenn v. Grover, 3 Md. 212 ; Waite v. Hudson, 1 Dane Ab. 635 ; Green v. Tanner, 8 Met. 411; Auburn Bank v. Fitch, 48 Barb. 344; Williams v. Jones, 2 Ala. 314; Covanhovan v. Hart, 21 Penn. 495; Lloyd v. Williams, 21 Penn. 327; Ford v. Williams, 3 B. Mon. 550; Johnson v. McGrew, 11 Iowa, 151.

[2] Terry v. Belcher, 1 Bailey, 568; Sibly v. Hood, 3 Mo. 206; Hindman v. Dill, 11 Ala. 689; Fromme v. Jones, 13 Iowa, 474; Hessing v. McCloskey, 37 Ill. 341 ; Green v. Tanner, 8 Met. 411; Walsh v. Kelly, 42 Barb. 98; s. c. 27 How. Pr. 359; Johnson v. McGrew, 11 Iowa, 151;

[3] Kuykendall v. Hitchcock, 15 Mo. 416; Waterbury v. Sturtevant, 18 Wend. 353.

[4] Alton v. Harrison, L. R. 4 Ch. 622; Sibly v. Hood, 3 Mo. 206.

[5] Ocoee Bank v. Nelson, 1 Cold. 186; Ferguson v. Kumler, 11 Minn. 104; Lee v. Flannagan, 7 Ired. 471; Hopkins v. Beebe, 26 Penn. 85; Keen v. Kleckner, 42 Penn. 528; Lord v. Fisher, 19 Ind. 7; McGregor v. Chase, 35 Vt. 225; Prior v. White, 12 Ill. 261; Cason v. Murray, 15 Mo. 378; Hall v. Arnold, 15 Barb. 599; Ewing v. Runkle, 20 Ill. 448; Waddams v. Humphrey, 22 Ill. 661; Wheaton v. Neville, 19 Cal. 41; Brewster v. Bours, 8 Cal. 501; National Bank v. Sprague, 5 C. E. Green, 13; Guignard v. Aldrich, 10 Rich. Eq. 253; Central R. R. Co. v. Claghorn, Speer's Ch. 545; Williams v. Jones, 2 Ala. 314.

the validity of the preference. There is a distinction to be observed between the effect of a transfer by a debtor in failing circumstances made to pay one or more of his debts, and that intent to hinder, delay, or defraud his other creditors, against which the statute is aimed. The effect of the preference may be to delay them, or even to prevent them from obtaining payment at all, but if the motive is to pay the preferred debt, the transaction is not invalidated. The statute is aimed only at intended fraud, but the payment of a debt to one creditor is no fraud upon other creditors—no legal injury to them.[1]

PREFERENCE NOT AFFECTED BY PERSON OR MODE.— The preference may be given to any lawful demand against the debtor, whether due or not,[2] and whether held by his wife,[3] or his attorney,[4] or any other person. A corporation may prefer a director.[5] The preference may be given in any mode which the law recognizes as legal for effecting a transfer whether by a mortgage,[6] or a deed,[7] or judgment,[8] or the transfer of a note,[9] or of any

---

[1] York County Bank v. Carter, 38 Penn. 446; Meade v. Smith, 16 Conn. 356; Kirtland v. Snow, 20 Conn. 23; Hessing v. McCloskey, 37 Ill. 341.

[2] Carpenter v. Muren, 42 Barb. 300; Hill v. Northrop, 9 How. Pr. 525.

[3] Mayfield v. Kilgour, 31 Md. 240.

[4] Hill v. Rogers, Rice Ch. 7.

[5] Central R. R. Co. v. Claghorn, Speers Ch. 545.

[6] Kennaird v. Adams, 11 B. Mon. 102; Jones v. Naughright, 2 Stockt. 298; Carnall v. Duvall, 22 Ark. 136; Wiley v. Lashlee, 8 Humph. 717.

[7] Waterbury v. Sturtevant, 18 Wend. 353; Barr v. Hatch, 3 Ohio, 527; Buffum v. Green, 5 N. H. 71; Covanhovan v. Hart, 21 Penn. 495; Kemp v. Walker, 16 Ohio, 118; Morse v. Slason, 13 Vt. 296; Leadman v. Harris, 3 Dev. 144; Harrison v. Phillips Academy, 12 Mass. 456.

[8] Wilder v. Winne, 6 Cow. 284; Hill v. Northrop, 9 How. Pr. 525; Davis v. Charles, 8 Penn. 82; Lowry v. Coulter, 9 Penn. 349; Siegel v. Chidsey, 28 Penn. 279; Greenwalt v. Austin, 1 Grant, 169; Meeker v. Harris, 19 Cal. 278; Shedd v. Bank, 32 Vt. 709.

[9] Savings Bank v. Bates, 8 Conn. 505; Tillon v. Britton, 4 Halst. 120.

other property. A large debt may be split up into small sums, so as to bring it within a magistrate's jurisdiction, and judgments may be confessed thereon, and the property of the debtor taken on executions.[1] An attachment may be issued without the knowledge of the creditor.[2] The debtor may also apply his labor to increase the value of property which has been mortgaged.[3] A mere representation that the creditor wishes to protect the property from executions, will not of itself render the preference fraudulent.[4] The preference may be made to take effect at the death of the debtor.[5] The fact that the debtor at the time of giving the preference is about to abscond,[6] does not render it void.

INTENT TO DEFEAT AN EXECUTION.—A preference may be given and received for the express purpose of defeating an execution,[7] for the mere intent to defeat an execution does not of itself constitute fraud. The payment of a just debt is what the law admits to be rightful, and is not, therefore, fraudulent, either in law or in fact. The preferred creditor can not be affected injuriously with notice of the debtor's intent to prefer, and

---

[1] Floyd v. Goodwin, 8 Yerg. 484; Newdigate v. Lee, 9 Dana, 17; L'Avender v. Thomas, 18 Geo. 668; Bank v. Planter's Bank, 22 Geo. 466; Alexander v. Young, 28 Geo. 616.

[2] Baird v. Williams, 19 Pick. 381; *vide* Ryan v. Daly, 6 Cal. 238.

[3] Perry v. Pettingall, 33 N. H. 433. [4] Reynolds v. Wilkins, 14 Me. 104.

[5] Morse v. Slason, 13 Vt. 296; Exton v. Scott, 6 Sim. 31.

[6] Garr v. Hill, 1 Stockt. 210.

[7] Holbird v. Anderson, 5 T. R. 235; Wood v. Dixie, 53 E. C. L. 892; s. c. 7 Q. B. 892; Funk v. Staats, 24 Ill. 632; Darville v. Terry, 6 H. & N. 807; Hall v. Arnold, 15 Barb. 599; Hartshorne v. Eames, 31 Me. 93; Gassett v. Wilson, 3 Fla. 235; Wheaton v. Neville, 19 Cal. 41; Kuykendall v. Hitchcock, 15 Mo. 416; Rich v. Levy, 16 Md. 74; Weller v. Wayland, 17 Johns. 102; Waterbury v. Sturtevant, 18 Wend. 353; Wilder v. Winne, 6 Cow. 284; Barr v. Hatch, 3 Ohio, 527; Hendricks v. Mount, 2 South, 738; Walden v. Murdock, 23 Cal. 540.

thereby defeat an execution, because the purpose is honest and such as the law sanctions. This is not delaying or hindering within the meaning of the statute. It does not deprive other creditors of any legal right, for they have no right to a priority.[1]

One creditor of a failing debtor is not, under the statute, bound to take care of another. In such case, if the assets are not sufficient to pay all, somebody must suffer. It is a race in which it is impossible for every one to be foremost. He who has the advantage, whether he gets it by the preference of the debtor or by his own superior vigilance, or by both causes combined, is entitled, under the statute, to what he wins, provided he takes no more than his honest due. He is not obliged to look out for other creditors, or to consider whether they will or will not get their debts.[2] He does not violate any principle of the statute when he takes payment or security for his demand, though others are thereby deprived of all means of obtaining satisfaction of their own equally meritorious claims, and though he may be aware of the intent of the debtor to defeat the collection of them.[3] Fraud, in its legal sense, cannot be predicated of such a transaction.[4] Wherever there is a true debt and a real transfer, there is no collusion.[5]

---

[1] Uhler v. Maulfair, 23 Penn. 481; Bird v. Sitken, Rice Ch. 73.

[2] Covanhovan v. Hart, 21 Penn. 495; Auburn Bank v. Fitch, 48 Barb. 344.

[3] Dana v. Stanfords, 10 Cal. 269; Waterbury v. Sturtevant, 18 Wend. 353; Thornton v. Davenport, 1 Scam. 296; Ford v. Williams, 3 B. Mon. 550; Worland v. Kimberlin, 6 B. Mon. 608; Jones v. Naughright, 2 Stockt. 298; Young v. Dumas, 39 Ala. 60; Gray v. St. John, 36 Ill. 222; Banfield v. Whipple, 14 Allen, 13; Kennaird v. Adams, 11 B. Mon. 102; *vide*, Ashmead v. Hean, 13 Penn. 584.

[4] Chase v. Walters, 28 Iowa, 460; Auburn Bank v. Fitch, 48 Barb. 344; Kennaird v. Adams, 11 B. Mon. 102.

[5] Clemens v. Davis, 7 Penn. 263.

SECRET MOTIVES IMMATERIAL.—All that the law requires in the case of a preference is good faith.[1] Where creditors are equally honest, they are equally favored by the law, and their rights are determined according to their respective priorities.[2] The secret motives which prompt the preference are immaterial. The law can take no cognizance of feelings and intentions which are not manifested by external conduct. It cannot assign a bad motive to an act which is not wrong either in itself or in its necessary consequences. When the act is right, no secret feeling can change its character. In contemplation of law, the motive which results in proper action is not a bad one.[3] The desire to avoid a sacrifice,[4] or to prevent an expected criminal prosecution,[5] or an expectation to receive future employment,[6] or that the property will be settled upon the debtor's wife or family,[7] or mere caprice, or favoritism, or the gratification of secret ill-will,[8] does not affect the validity of the transfer, for such secret motives are not the subject of legal inquiry. Where there is merely a preference, even a jury is not at liberty to deduce fraud from that which the law pronounces honest.[9] The mere fact that the transfer includes all the property which is not exempt from execution, is not material.[10]

PREFERENCE MUST BE IN GOOD FAITH AND REAL.—A

---

[1] Phettiplace v. Sayles, 4 Mason, 312; Ford v. Williams, 3 B. Mon. 550.
[2] Lloyd v. Williams, 21 Penn. 327.
[3] Bunn v. Ahl, 21 Penn. 387.
[4] Barr v. Hatch, 3 Ohio, 527; Wheaton v. Neville, 19 Cal. 41.
[5] Marbury v. Brooks, 7 Wheat. 556; s. c. 11 Wheat. 78.
[6] Crawford v. Austin, 34 Md. 49.
[7] Young v. Stallings, 5 B. Mon. 307; Cureton v. Doby, 10 Rich. Eq. 411.
[8] Spaulding v. Strang, 37 N. Y. 135; s. c. 38 N. Y. 9.
[9] York County Bank v. Carter, 38 Penn. 446.
[10] Young v. Dumas, 39 Ala. 60.

transfer, however, may be fraudulent although it is made in consideration of an honest debt, for an honest claim may be used as a cover to a covinous transaction.[1] The distinction is between a transfer made solely by way of preference of one creditor over others, and a similar transfer made with a design to secure some benefit or advantage therefrom to the debtor,[2] or to delay creditors in the collection of their debts.[3] While the law permits an insolvent debtor to make choice of the persons he will pay, it denies him the right in doing it to contrive that other creditors shall never be paid,[4] or to use the debt of the preferred creditor as a colorable consideration to screen and protect his property from their claims,[5] or to delay, hinder, and embarrass them in the enforcement of their demands.[6] The amount of the property transferred compared with the debt intended to be secured or paid, and the number, amount, and character of the other debts are proper subjects for consideration in determining the good faith of the transactions towards other creditors.[7] The property

---

[1] Welcome v. Balchelder, 23 Me. 85.

[2] Banfield v. Whipple, 14 Allen, 13; Barr v. Hatch, 3 Ohio, 527 ; Bartels v. Harris, 4 Me. 146; Bullock v. Irvine, 4 Munf. 450.

[3] Johnson v. Whitwell, 7 Pick. 71.

[4] Drury v. Cross, 7 Wall. 299 ; James v. Railroad Company, 6 Wall. 752.

[5] Twyne's Case, 3 Co. 80; Benton v. Thornhill, 2 Marsh. 427; Graham v. Furber, 78 E. C. L. 410; Devries v. Phillips, 63 N. C. 53; Pulliam v. Newberry, 41 Ala. 168; Hartshorne v. Eames, 31 Me. 93; Passmore v. Eldridge, 12 S. & R. 198; Gans v. Renshaw, 2 Penn. 34; Goodhue v. Berrien, 2 Sandf. Ch. 630; Choteau v. Sherman, 11 Mo. 385; Johnson v. Sullivan, 23 Mo. 474; Clarkson v. White, 8 Dana, 11; Foster v. Grigsby, 1 Bush. 86; Kirtland v. Snow, 20 Ct. 23; Kuykendall v. McDonald, 15 Mo. 416; Constantine v. Twelves, 29 Ala. 607.

[6] Stoddard v. Butler, 20 Wend. 507; Kilby v. Haggin, 3 J. J. Marsh. 208; Cleveland v. Railroad Co. 7 A. L. Reg. 537; Edrington v. Rogers, 15 Tex. 188; Crowninshield v. Kittredge, 7 Met. 520; Bunn v. Ahl, 29 Penn. 387; Hancock v. Horan, 15 Tex. 507.

[7] Glenn v. Grover, 3 Md. 212; Adams v. Wheeler, 10 Pick. 199; Kuy-

must bear a reasonable proportion to the preferred debt.[1]

PREFERENCE TAINTED BY SECRET TRUST.—The right to prefer must be exercised in perfectly good faith. If the preference is merely a temporary arrangement to prevent a sacrifice of the property and preserve the rights of all to an equal distribution, with an understanding that the property shall constitute a part of an assignment to be subsequently executed, it is fraudulent. Such an arrangement is against the policy of the law and the plain legal rights of other creditors.[2] Creditors also are not allowed to gain a preference by means of a secret undertaking to hold a part of the property for the benefit of the debtor. *Quod alias justum et bonum est, si per fraudem petatur, malum et injustum efficitur.* The law looks with great jealousy upon the manner of giving preferences, and denounces all departures from good faith, and requires that the parties shall not secure any covert advantage to the debtor in prejudice of his creditors.[3] The law, however, does not interdict every species of favor to an unfortunate debtor under the penalty of vacating all securities taken on those terms. On the contrary, a creditor may be as indulgent, and show as much favor as he pleases as the price of obtaining security. Care must only be taken that there is no secret understand-

---

kendall v. Hitchcock, 15 Mo. 416; Edrington v. Rogers, 15 Tex. 188; Robinson v. Stewart, 10 N. Y. 189; Rahn v. McElrath, 6 Watts, 151; Hale v. Allnutt, 86 E. C. L. 505; s. c. 18 C. B. 505.

[1] Rahn v. McElrath, 6 Watts, 151; Robinson v. Stewart, 10 N. Y. 189.

[2] Johnson v. Whitwell, 7 Pick. 71; Low v. Graydon, 50 Barb. 414; Dalton v. Currier, 40 N. H. 237.

[3] White v. Graves, 7 J. J. Marsh. 523; Garland v. Rives, 4 Rand. 282; Pettibone v. Stevens, 15 Conn. 19; Kissam v. Edmondson, 1 Ired. Eq. 180.

ing constituting a trust in the creditor in derogation or contravention of the ostensible alienation or the transfer, will be deemed a cover, and consequently void.[1]

CREDITOR'S BOUNTY.—The preferred creditor may give a portion of his debt, or the property received in payment of it, as a bounty to the family of the debtor, for the generosity is not at the expense of other creditors. In every case the inquiry is as to the rights of the creditors, and if they are not deprived of any right there is no ground to set aside the transfer. An act of spontaneous kindness and indulgence on the part of the creditor should not be confounded with fraud in the debtor, and the best feelings should not be chilled and stifled by an overweening tendency to detect collusion.[2] The gift, however, must be the act of the creditor, independent of any arrangement between the debtor and creditor at the time, or as a part of the contract to convey property either as a security or in apparent payment of the debt. The law looks to the substance and not the form of transactions. If a gift is forced from the creditor by making a transfer of a part of the debt or property to the debtor's family the condition and price for obtaining security or payment for the balance, the transaction is fraudulent. Whatever benefit is secured, either openly or covertly, to the debtor out of the effects conveyed by him is inconsistent with the professed purpose of conveying to satisfy or secure the debt to the creditor, and for that reason is *mala fide* and void.[3]

---

[1] Jackson v. Brownell, 3 Caines, 222; Meeker v. Harris, 19 Cal. 278.

[2] Cureton v. Doby, 10 Rich. Eq. 411; Webb v. Roff, 9 Ohio st. R. 430; Young v. Dumas, 39 Ala. 60; Young v. Stallings, 5 B. Mon. 307.

[3] Kissam v. Edmondson, 1 Ired. Eq. 180; Garland v. Rives, 4 Rand. 282; Marshall v. Hutchinson, 5 B. Mon. 298.

15

BURDEN OF PROOF.—The burden of proof rests upon the creditors who impeach the preference,[1] and the fraudulent intent must be clearly shown.[2]

WHEN CREDITOR MAY PURCHASE.—Although the purchase exceeds the amount of the indebtedness, still if the excess is reasonably necessary for attaining the lawful purpose of satisfying the actual debt, the purchase to the whole extent may be attributed to the same motive of self interest, and therefore the mere fact of the excess does not of itself invalidate the transaction unless there are other circumstances tending to show a fraudulent intent on the part of the purchaser.[3]

---

[1] Glenn v. Grover, 3 Md. 212 ; Johnson v. McGrew, 11 Iowa, 151.

[2] Barr v. Hatch, 3 Ohio, 527 ; Jones v. Naughright, 2 Stockt. 298.

[3] Young v. Stallings, 5 B. Mon. 307 ; Ford v. Williams, 3 B. Mon. 550 ; Little v. Eddy, 14 Mo. 160 ; Bear's Estate, 60 Penn. 430.

CHAPTER VIII.

THE BONA FIDES OF THE TRANSFER.

INSOLVENT DEBTOR MAY SELL.—The statute does not deprive a man of the power to sell or otherwise dispose of his property, although he may be insolvent,[1] and the mere fact that the transfer may tend to delay or hinder his creditors will not alone render it fraudulent. Many sales made in the ordinary course of business may and do defeat creditors who could have levied upon the property if it had been retained for a while longer, yet these are valid.[2] The power of a debtor to sell implies the corresponding right of another to purchase. Mere insolvency alone does not vitiate any transfer. In addition to the indebtedness there must be an intent on the part of the debtor to delay, hinder, or defraud his creditors.

WHY INNOCENT VENDEE IS PROTECTED.—When the transfer is made for a valuable consideration, there must be not only a fraudulent intent, on the part of the debtor but also a participation in that intent on the part of the grantee, for the statute excepts from its operation all estates or interests which are upon good consideration and *bona fide*, lawfully conveyed, or assured to any person not having at the time of such conveyance or assu-

---

[1] Churchill v. Wells, 7 Cold. 364; Copis v. Middleton, 2 Madd. 410; Phettiplace v. Sayles, 4 Mason, 312; Pecot v. Amelin, 21 La. An. 667; Hardey v. Green, 12 Beav. 182; Smith v. Henry, 2 Bailey, 118.

[2] Atwood v. Impson, 5 C. E. Green. 150.

rance to him made any manner of notice or knowledge of such covin, fraud, or collusion. Creditors have an equitable interest in the property of the debtor which the law under certain circumstances recognizes and enforces, but when a valuable consideration is paid in good faith for a transfer, the interest of the creditor is superseded. The purchaser in such case, having parted with value upon the faith of the vendor's possession and ownership of the property, acquires not only the legal title, but an equity which is paramount to that of the creditors. It is obviously this equity alone arising out of the consideration paid, which protects the right of the purchaser, because the mere legal title is transferred by a gift as completely as by sale. The statute is based upon these principles. It is because both law and justice recognize the equitable interest of creditors in the property of the debtor that a transfer of such property to defeat their demands is declared to to be void, and the right of a *bona fide* purchaser for a valuable consideration is protected by the statute, because the equity of such purchaser is superior to that of a mere general creditor, for the obvious reason that the purchaser has not like the creditors trusted to the personal responsibility of the debtor, but has paid the consideration upon the faith of the debtor's actual title to the specific property transferred.[1] A man paying a full and valuable consideration in good faith for the property, may moreover justly suppose that the purchase, so far from diminishing the means of the vendor, for paying his debts, will afford him a facility for doing so.[2] It is upon these grounds that the rights of a grantee who acts in good faith, and gives a valuable con-

---

[1] Seymour v. Wilson, 19 N. Y. 417.
[2] Pierson v. Tom, 1 Tex. 577.

sideration, are protected although there may have been a fraudulent intent on the part of the debtor.[1]   The same principle is asserted in the civil law, *Hoc edictum eum coercit qui sciens eum in fraudem creditorum hoc facere, suscepit quod in fraudem fiebat.   Quare si quid in fraudem creditorum factum sit, si tamen is qui cepit, ignoravit, cessare videntur verba edicti.*[2]

GRANTEE WITHOUT CONSIDERATION NOT PROTECTED.— An inquiry into the good faith of the grantee is only necessary, however, when there is a valuable consideration for the transfer.[3]   The mere acceptance of a transfer,

---

[1] Heroy v. Kerr, 21 How. Pr. 409 ; Carpenter v. Muren, 42 Barb. 300; Waterbury v. Sturtevant, 18 Wend. 353; Borland v. Mayo, 8 Ala. 104; Waters v. Riggin, 19 Md. 536 ; Troxall v. Dunnock, 24 Md. 163 ; Hessing v. McCloskey, 37 Ill. 341 ; Smith v. Henry, 2 Bailey, 118; s. c. 1 Hill, 16 ; Sibly v. Hood, 3 Mo. 206; Wilson v. Lott, 5 Fla. 305; Swinerton v. Swinerton, 1 Dane Ab. 628; Kittredge v. Sumner, 11 Pick. 50 ; Green v. Tanner, 8 Met. 411; King v. Marissal, 3 Atk. 192; Badger v. Story, 16 N. H. 168; Johnson v. Johnson, 3 Met. 63; Currier v. Taylor, 19 N. H. 189; Sands v. Hildreth, 14 Johns. 493; Waterbury v. Sturtevant, 18 Wend. 353; Hall v. Arnold, 15 Barb. 599; Anderson v. Hooks, 9 Ala. 704 ; Davis v. Tibbetts, 39 Me. 279; McLaren v. Thompson, 40 Me. 284; Union Bank v. Toomer, 2 Hill Ch. 27; Blair v. Bass, 4 Blackf. 539; Thompson v. Saunders, 6 J. J. Marsh, 94; Violett v. Violett, 2 Dana, 323; Hutchinson v. Horn, 1 Smith, 242; Ratcliffe v. Trimble, 12 B. Mon. 32 ; Sterling v. Ripley, 3 Chand. 166 ; Splawn v. Martin, 17 Ark. 146; Ewing v. Runkle, 20 Ill. 448; Frank v. Peters, 9 Ind. 344; Dart v. Farmer's Bank, 27 Barb. 337; Fifield v. Gaston, 12 Iowa, 218 ; Miller v. Byran, 3 Iowa, 58 ; Palmer v. Henderson, 20 Ind. 297 ; Sisson v. Roath ; 30 Conn. 15 ; Hutchinson v. Watkins, 17 Iowa, 475 ; Meixsell v. Williamson, 35 Ill. 529 ; Apperson v. Ford, 23 Ark. 746; Mills v. Haines, 3 Head, 332; Hamilton v. Staples, 34 Conn. 316; Leach v. Francis, 41 Vt. 670; Byrne v. Becker, 42 Mo. 264; Webster v. Folsom, 58 Me. 230; Lassiter v. Davis, 64 N. C. 498; Rose v. Coble, 1 Phil. 517; McCormick v. Hyatt, 33 Ind. 546; Durfee v. Pavitt, 14 Minn. 424; Merchants' Bank v. Newton, 7 C. E. Green, 58.

[2] Dig. lib. 42 tit. 9, § 8, 1 Domat. B. 2 tit. 10.

[3] Newman v. Cordell, 43 Barb. 448; Wood v. Hunt, 38 Barb. 302; Peck v. Carmichael, 9 Yerg. 325 ; Gamble v. Johnson, 9 Mo. 605; Swartz v. Hazlett, 8 Cal. 118; Wise v. Moore, 31 Geo. 148; Clark v. Chamberlain, 13 Allen, 257; Hicks v. Stone, 13 Minn. 434 ; Lee v. Figg, 37 Cal. 328.

without a valuable consideration, is of itself sufficient evidence of a participation in the debtor's fraudulent intent.[1] *Simili modo dicimus et si cui donatum est non esse quaerendum an sciente ei cui donatum gestum sit, sed hoc tantum an fraudentur creditores. Nec videtur injuria, affici is qui ignoravit cum lucrum extorqueatur, non damnum infligatur. In hos tamen qui ignorantes ab eo qui solvendo non sit, liberalitatem acceperunt, hactenus actio erit danda, quatenus locupletiores facti sunt; ultra non.*[2]

GOOD FAITH AS WELL AS A VALUABLE CONSIDERATION. —A transfer, however, made on a good consideration, if it is not also *bona fide* is not within the proviso. The words of the proviso are " on a good consideration and *bona fide*." A transfer must therefore not only be on a good consideration, but also *bona fide*.[3] If a transfer is for a valuable consideration, the only question is whether it is *bona fide*.[4] And on that point every case stands on its own merits. If it is not in good faith, it is void, although the grantee pays a full consideration, for the law never allows one man to assist in cheating another.[5]

---

[1] Belt v. Raguet, 27 Tex. 471.

[2] Dig lib. 42 tit. 9, § 11; 1 Domat. B. 2 tit. 10.

[3] Twyne's Case, 3 Co. 80; Copis v. Middleton, 2 Madd. 410; Harrison v. Kramer, 3 Iowa, 543; Glenn v. Randall, 2 Md. Ch. 220; Wood v. Chambers, 20 Tex. 247.

[4] Hale v. Saloon Omnibus Co. 4 Drew, 492; s. c. 28 L. J. Ch. 777; Harman v. Richards, 10 Hare, 81; Holmes v. Penney, 3 K. & J. 90.

[5] Cadogan v. Kennett, Cowp. 432; Worsley v. DeMattos, 1 Burr. 467; Devon v. Watts, Doug. 86; Wickham v. Miller, 12 Johns. 320; Stein v. Hermann, 23 Wis. 132; Pulliam v. Newberry, 41 Ala. 168; Chappel v. Clapp, 29 Iowa, 161; Harrison v. Jaquess, 29 Ind. 208; Sayre v. Fredericks, 1 C. E. Green, 205; Carny v. Palmer, 2 Cold. 35; Weisiger v. Chisholm, 22 Tex. 670; Castro v. Illies, 22 Tex. 479; Gardinier v. Otis, 13 Wis. 460; Smith v. Culbertson, 9 Rich. 106; Barrow v. Bailey, 5 Fla. 9; Clark v. Wentworth, 6 Me. 259; Edrington v. Rogers, 15 Tex. 188; Robinson v. Holt, 39 N. H. 557; Duelly v. Van Houghton, 4 N. Y. Leg. Obs. 101; Johnston v. Dick, 27.

The reason is manifest. Fraud may as readily be effected when a full and fair price is paid as when nothing is paid. A person may resolve not to pay his debts, and another knowing this may treat with him and purchase his whole estate at a fair and full price, and thus enable him to defeat the claims of his creditors. Although the purchaser gains no advantage, he enables the debtor to evade the payment of his debts, and the effect upon the creditors is precisely the same as if nothing were paid.[1] As it is the intent to withdraw the debtor's property from the reach of his creditors that generally makes a transfer for full value fraudulent, a real exchange of a debtor's land for other land in the same neighbourhood of equal value and equally secure in point of title, can not be deemed fraudulent and void as to the grantor's creditors, except under exceptional circumstances.[2]

NOTICE TO GRANTEE.—Notice makes a man a *mala fide* purchaser. It is *per se* evidence of *mala fides*.[3] The words " without notice," in the proviso, however, are not applicable to the debt of the party making the transfer but to " covin fraud or collusion.[4]" *Quod ait praetor sciente, sic accipimus te conscio et fraudem participante ; non enim, si simpliciter scio illum creditores habere,*

Miss. 277; Johnson v. Sullivan, 23 Mo. 474 ; Rogers v. Evans, 3 Ind. 574 ; Borland v. Mayo, 8 Ala. 105 ; Shannon v. Commonwealth, 8 S. and R. 444; Johnson v. Brandis, 1 Smith, 263 ; Pettus v. Smith, 4 Rich. Eq. 197; Walcott v. Brander, 10 Tex. 419 ; Lowry v. Pinson, 2 Bailey, 324 ; Farmers' Bank v. Douglas, 11 S. & M. 469; Watson v. Dickens, 12 S. & M. 608; Moseley v. Gainer, 10 Tex. 393 ; Clements v. Moore, 6 Wall. 299 ; Peck v. Land, 2 Kelly, 1 ; Cadbury v. Nolen, 5 Penn. 320 ; Ayres v. Moore, 2 Stew, 336 ; Zerbe v. Miller, 16 Penn. 488.

[1] Rea v. Alexander, 5 Ired. 644 ; Lowry v. Pinson, 2 Bailey, 324 ; Brown v. Foree, 7 B. Mon. 357 ; Kaine v. Weigley, 22 Penn. 179; Clements v. Moore, 6 Wall. 299.

[2] Ford v. Williams, 3 B. Mon. 550.

[3] Humphries v. Freeman, 22 Tex. 45. [4] Jones v. Boulter, 1 Cox, 288.

*hoc sufficit ad contendendum teneri in factum actione,
sed si particeps fraudis est.*[1]   Mere knowledge of the
debtors insolvency,[2] or of a judgment,[3] or of a threatened
attachment,[4] is not sufficient, unless the object of the
debtor is to delay, hinder, or defraud his creditors, and
this purpose is known to the grantee.   Up to the day
of the delivery of the writ to the sheriff, the debtor may
transfer his personal property provided it is not a mere
trick to evade an execution.   But notice of a fraudulent
intent on the part of the debtor, will vitiate the transfer.

Actual knowledge is not necessary.   A knowledge
of facts sufficient to excite the suspicions of a prudent
man and to put him on inquiry,[5] or to lead a person of ordinary perception to infer fraud,[6] and the means of knowing by the use of ordinary diligence,[7] amount to notice
and are equivalent to actual knowledge in contemplation
of law.   The nature and circumstances of the transaction
may sometimes be such as must apprise the grantee of
its character and object.   *Res ipse loquitur.*[8]   If the
grantee is the debtor's wife, it will not require much

---

[1] Dig. lib. 42, tit. 9.

[2] Atwood v. Impson, 5 C. E. Green, 150 ; Hughes v. Monty, 24 Iowa,
499; Loeschigk v. Bridge, 42 N. Y. 421; Sisson v. Roath, 30 Conn. 15 ;
Merchants' Bank v. Newton, 7 C. E. Green, 58.

[3] Beals v. Guernsey, 8 Johns. 446 ; Waterbury v. Sturtevant, 18 Wend.
353 ; Bunyard v. Seabrook, 1 F. & F. 321.

[4] Lyon v. Rood, 12 Vt. 233 ; *vide* Reinheimer v. Hemingway, 35 Penn,
432.

[5] Mills v. Howeth, 19 Tex. 257 ; Green v. Tantum, 4 C. E. Green, 105 ;
s. c. 6 C. E. Green, 364; Atwood v. Impson, 5 C. E. Green, 150; Jackson
v. Mather, 7 Cow. 301 ; Smith v. Henry, 2 Bailey, 118.

[6] Johnson v. Brandis, 1 Smith, 263; Wright v. Brandis, 1 Ind. 336.

[7] Humphries v. Freeman, 22 Tex. 45 ; Farmer's Bank v. Douglas, 11 S.
& M. 469; Foster v. Grigsby, 1 Bush, 86 ; Garrahay v. Bayley, 25 Tex.
(Supp.) 294 ; *Contra*, Seavy v. Dearborn, 19 N. H. 351 ; Brown v. Foree,
7 B. Mon. 357 ; Sterling v. Ripley, 3 Chand. 166.

[8] Smead v. Williamson, 16 B. Mon. 492.

evidence to prove that his intentions are known to her.[1] Notice before the payment of the purchase-money is sufficient.[2] If the intent is known it is not material that the grantee is not apprised of the full extent of the debtor's fraudulent designs.[3] *Illud certe sufficit etsi unum scit creditorem fraudari, caeteros ignoravit, fore locum actioni.*[4]

MOTIVES OF DEBTOR AND GRANTEE NEED NOT BE THE SAME.—It is not necessary that the debtor and the grantee shall be actuated by like motives to cheat and defraud the grantor's creditors. The motives and intentions of the debtor and grantee may be different. If the grantee has notice at the time that the debtor is transferring his property to delay, hinder, or defraud his creditors, it will make the transfer void although he has no wish to defraud them. If, for instance, he purchases because he considers the property cheap and this is the only motive that induces him to purchase, the transfer is nevertheless fraudulent.[5] It has, however, been held that if the grantee has a connection with the property, and has reasons and motives for making the purchase entirely independent of the debtor's motives and purposes in wishing to sell, and which are both honest and adequate to every intent, and in exclusion of any intent or willingness to lend himself in aid of the debtor, the mere knowledge of the debtor's intent and purpose will not affect him as being a participant in the debtor's contemplated fraud, when he purchases for the preservation and promotion of his own business interest.

---

[1] Castro v. Illies, 22 Tex. 479.

[2] Parkinson v. Hanna, 7 Blackf. 400 ; *vide* Parker v. Crittenden, 37 Conn. 148.   [3] Ruffing v. Tilton, 12 Ind. 259.

[4] Dig. lib. 42, tit. 9.

[5] Edgell v. Lowell, 4 Vt. 405 ; Fuller v. Sears, 5 Vt. 527.

The decision is placed upon the ground that such a purchaser is not a mere volunteer.[1]   It must be considered, however, as going to the extreme verge of the law, and nothing but the most pressing exigencies could bring a case within this exception.

CO-OPERATION.—It is not necessary that the grantee shall be one of the originators of the fraudulent scheme. Fraud may be imputed to a party either by co-operation in the original design or by constructive co-operation from notice of it and from carrying the design into operation with such notice.   There is no difference between those who form the design and those who afterwards enter into it with a knowledge of its character and aid in carrying it out.[2]   The grantee is also bound by the acts of his agent which he adopts and confirms,[3] and if they are fraudulent his own innocence will not suffice to protect the transfer.

SALE TO PAY DEBTS.—The notice to the grantee must be a notice of an intent on the part of the debtor to delay, hinder, or defraud in the legal sense of those terms as used in the statute.   The law, however, does not deprive even an insolvent man of the right to sell his property to pay his debts.[4]   Where the necessary effect of a transfer is to secure the application of the full value of the property to the discharge of certain debts of the grantor in a manner satisfactory to the holders of those debts, the case is not distinguishable from that of a conveyance to the creditors themselves in discharge of real

---

[1] Root v. Reynolds, 32 Vt. 139.

[2] Stovall v. Farmer's Bank, 8 S. & M. 305.

[3] White v. Graves, 7 J. J. Marsh, 523; Wiley v. Knight, 27 Ala. 336 ; Pope v. Pope, 40 Miss. 516.

[4] Wood v. Shaw, 29 Ill. 444.

debts and at a fair price.[1] The right to prefer involves
the right to sell with the intent to give a preference.
Fraud does not consist in transferring property with a
view to prefer one creditor to another, but in the intent
to prefer one's self to all creditors.[2] Although a transfer is made with the intent to prevent the effect of a
suit, it is not necessarily fraudulent and void if made
also with intent to pay other creditors. A sale intended
to supply the means of paying just debts is not fraudulent and void merely because it may also have been
intended as a means of preventing one creditor from
sacrificing the debtor's property and thus defeating the
collection or payment of other debts. The intent to
delay certain creditors from the collection of their debts
by the due course of law will not necessarily vitiate the
sale, though known and so far concurred in by the vendee. If it is made also with the intent and as the means
of paying other creditors or all creditors, and upon
terms reasonably calculated to answer that purpose in
a satisfactory manner and to the extent of the value of
the property, it can not be condemned merely because
it may have been intended by the vendor to obstruct
some of the creditors in the legal coercion of their debts,
although this intention may have been known to the
vendee.[3]

KNOWLEDGE OF INTENT TO DEFEAT AN EXECUTION.
—If the grantee has reasonable grounds for supposing
that the debtor intends the transfer as a means to pay

---

[1] Ford v. Williams, 3 B. Mon. 550 ; Gregory v. Harrington, 33 Vt.
241; Brown v. Foree, 7 B. Mon. 357 ; Ocoee Bank v. Nelson, 1 Cold.
186 ; vide Cook v. White, 20 Cal. 598.

[2] Gregory v. Harrington, 33 Vt. 241 ; Bedell v. Chase, 34 N. Y.
386.

[3] Brown v. Smith, 7 B. Mon. 361 ; Wood v. Shaw, 29 Ill. 444.

some of his creditors, the mere knowledge that the
debtor also intends to baffle and defeat others does not
establish any notice of a fraudulent intent against him.[1]
His knowledge of the debtor's intent to defeat some of
his creditors affords, however, a presumption of a participation in an intent to hinder, delay, or defraud them,
and will authorize the conclusion that he did so participate unless the inference is repelled by the circumstances of the transaction.[2] The question is as to his own
actual participation in a fraudulent scheme, and this is
a question of fact. Although it may be inferred from
his knowledge of the debtor's intent to defeat some of
his creditors, yet as there may be and generally are
other and in different cases varying facts bearing upon
the question of participation, it is inconsistent with the
principles which regulate the investigation of mere
facts and the free inquiry after truth to make the grantee's knowledge of such intent on the part of the debtor
conclusive evidence of his participation in a fraudulent
intent. This would be to stop in the inquiry before its
real end is attained, to make a probable conclusion absolutely decisive of the question. His knowledge of an
intent to defeat some creditors is a fact tending more or
less strongly to prove a fraudulent participation on his
part, but must be considered in connection with other
facts in the determination of his actual motive and the
true character of the transaction.[3]

VALIDITY AFFECTED BY DISPOSITION OF PROCEEDS.—
The payment of a full consideration and the appropriation of it to the payment of creditors repel the pre-

---

[1] Brown v. Foree, 7 B. Mon. 357.

[2] Kendall v. Hughes, 7 B. Mon. 368; Brown v. Foree, 7 B. Mon.
357.

[3] Brown v. Foree, 7 B. Mon. 357 ; Brown v. Smith, 7 B. Mon. 361.

sumption.[1] Where a part only is so appropriated a difficult point is presented,[2] but if it can be fairly assumed upon all the circumstances that, instead of expecting and intending that the price paid by him should be withheld from creditors, the vendee expected it to be paid to them, and did not make the purchase in order to defraud them, he cannot be implicated in the fraud on the ground that he knew of the vendor's intent to thwart some of his creditors, and made the purchase without sufficiently guarding against a misapplication of the price. It would be too great a restriction upon the common business and traffic of men if every purchase from a debtor were to be conclusively invalidated because the proceeds are subsequently misapplied.[3] When a cloud, however, rests upon the disposition made by the debtor of the money, the *bona fides* of the vendee must be clearly shown.[4] A deed may be fraudulent even though it provides upon its face for the payment of all the debts due by the grantor,[5] or the grantee applies the purchase money to pay creditors.[6]

GOOD FAITH AFFECTED BY AMOUNT OF CONSIDERATION. —It has been truly said that those who undertake to impeach for *mala fides* a transfer which has been made for a valuable consideration, have a task of great difficulty to discharge,[7] for the presumption is that it is fair

---

[1] Kendall v. Hughes, 7 B. Mon. 368; Brown v. Foree, 7 B. Mon. 357; Johnson v. McGrew, 11 Iowa, 151 ; Uhler v. Maulfair, 23 Penn. 481; York County Bank v. Carter, 38 Penn. 446; *vide* Ashmead v. Hean, 13 Penn. 584 ; Lowry v. Pinson, 2 Bailey, 324.

[2] Ford v. Williams, 3 B. Mon. 550.

[3] Brown v. Foree, 7 B. Mon. 357; Brown v. Smith, 7 B. Mon. 361; *vide* Clements v. Moore, 6 Wall, 299.

[4] Stanton v. Green, 34 Miss. 576; Bastein v. Dougherty, 3 Phila. 30; Alexander v. Todd, Bond, 175.   [5] Drum v. Painter, 27 Penn. 148.

[6] Farmer's Bank v. Douglass, 11 S. & M. 469.

[7] Harman v. Richards, 10 Hare, 81.

and honest until the contrary is shown by evidence[1] sufficient for that purpose.[2] The participation in the fraud may be shown by circumstances, without the production of direct evidence,[3] but the proof must be clear and convincing.[4] The amount of the consideration paid is material when the good faith of the transfer is put in controversy. A small advance, merely to give color to the transaction, is not sufficient;[5] and, on the other hand, the property may sell below what might have been obtained by a careful sale.[6] An inadequate consideration, however, is a badge of fraud, and is not sufficient to support a transfer whose good faith is otherwise impeached.[7] If the transfer is in other respects fair and legal, time may be allowed for the payment of the purchase money,[8] but in such case it is the duty of the vendee to show that it is afterwards paid, and that the stipulation for credit was made in good faith.[9]

CONVEYANCE TO USE OF GRANTOR.—It is enacted by 3 H. VII, c. 4, that all deeds of gift of goods and chattels,

---

[1] Sibly v. Hood, 3 Mo. 206; Wilson v. Lott, 5 Fla. 305.

[2] Glenn v. Grover, 3 Md. 212; s. c. 3 Md. Ch. 29.

[3] Anderson v. Tydings, 3 Md. Ch. 167.

[4] Terrell v. Green, 11 Ala. 207.

[5] Michael v. Gay, 1 F. & F. 409; Monell v. Scherrick, 54 Ill. 269.

[6] Hale v. Saloon Omnibus Co. 4 Drew, 492; s. c. 28 L. J. Ch. 777; Stovall v. Farmer's Bank, 8 S. & M. 305.

[7] Kaine v. Weigley, 22 Penn. 179; Trimble v. Ratcliff, 9 B. Mon. 511; Robinson v. Robards, 15 Mo. 459; Lee v. Hunter, 1 Paige, 519; Barrow v. Bailey, 5 Fla. 9; Arnold v. Bell, 1 Hay. (N. C.) 396; Seaman v. White, 8 Ala. 656; State v. Evans, 38 Mo· 150; Durkee v. Mahoney, 1 Aik. 116; Kuykendall v. Hitchcock, 15 Mo. 416; Bryant v. Kelton, 1 Tex. 415; Bozman v. Draughan, 3 Stew. 243; vide, Union Bank v. Toomer, 2 Hill Ch. 27; Nunn v. Wilsmore, 8 T. R. 521; Grogan v. Cooke, 2 Ball. & B. 233; Middlecome v. Marlow, 2 Atk. 519; Penhall v. Elwin, 1 Sm. & Gif. 258; Blount v. Doughty, 3 Atk. 481; Thompson v. Webster, 7 Jur. (N. S.) 531; Copis v. Middleton, 2 Madd. 410; Wright v. Stannard, 2 Brock. 311.

[8] O'Neil v. Orr, 4 Scam. 1.

[9] Kaine v. Weigley, 22 Penn. 179.

made or to be made, of trust, to the use of that person
or persons that made the same deed of gift, be void
and of none effect. This statute is analogous to that of
27 H. VIII, c. 10, in its purpose; but it goes further,
and makes the whole transfer void. It is not directed
against trusts made with a fraudulent intent, but against
trusts themselves. There is not one word about intent
or object, or purpose, or excluding, injuring or delaying
creditors. The effect of the trust is not a subject for
consideration. Its mere existence avoids the transfer
and destroys the title as against creditors existing or subsequent. A conveyance by the owner of property to
another, in trust for himself, is, in effect, a conveyance
to himself, and such a measure can never be necessary
for any legal or honest purpose. He who, having the
full title, desires to retain the control and use of his
property and yet transfer it to another, can, in the
general course of human actions, have but one motive
for that measure, and that motive must be to defeat or
elude the claims of others. Hence all conveyances to
the use of the grantor are fraudulent and null against
creditors and others having just claims upon the grantor
or upon the property conveyed. In all the refinements
of uses and trusts, in the midst of multiplied distinctions between legal and equitable interests which have
abounded in the progress of Anglican jurisprudence,
this principle has never been doubted, and the mockery
of a transfer by a debtor of his property, to be held for
the use of the debtor, has never been allowed to defeat
the rights or remedies of creditors.[1]

OBJECT OF THE STATUTE.—The true name of this
statute is, a statute of personal uses. Its object is to

---

[1] Curtis v. Leavitt, 15 N. Y. 9.

render simply ineffectual purely nominal transfers of personal estate where the entire use and control are, by a declaration of trust in or out of the instrument, left in him who makes the transfer. It is founded upon the self-evident principle that a man's property should pay his debts, although he has vested a nominal title in some other person. For that purpose the statute declares the title to be in the debtor, and no transfer which is merely nominal can stand in the way. It has no reference to intentions, whether fraudulent or honest. There may be, in fact, no creditors until long after the transaction, but if the debtor has property they are entitled to be paid. The simple inquiry is, whether the property belongs to the debtor, not upon a theory of fraud and against his conveyance, but upon a theory of equitable title reserved to himself by the very conveyance which transfers the legal and nominal title to another.[1]

RESULTING TRUSTS.—The statute, however, has no application to cases of real and actual alienation upon a valuable consideration and for active and real purposes, although incidental benefits are reserved to the grantor. It is the transfer to the use of the grantor that is void, and not a transfer to other uses and for other purposes. The distinction is between mere passive trusts for the grantor's benefit, and those trusts which result from alienation for real active purposes in the course of business. Reservations for the benefit of the grantor, in and of themselves, are perfectly innocuous. A man proposing to create a security upon his estate, or to assign it upon any trust, has a plain right in general to reserve to himself just such interests and benefits as he and those with whom he is dealing can agree

---

[1] Curtis v. Leavitt, 15 N. Y. 9; Sturdivant v. Davis, 9 Ired. 365.

upon. The law upon this subject is entirely adapted
to the dealings of mankind. In the business of every
trader exigencies will arise requiring a pledge, mortgage, or some other assurance less than an absolute sale,
founded upon some actual dealing the very nature of
which implies that some residuary or partial interest
remains. Such instruments must, in the very necessity
of things, take effect according to their terms, and the
law therefore gives them effect. If the only object of
the conveyance or assignment is to secure the payment
of a loan of money, or of an existing debt, and the
express reservation or resulting of the residuary beneficial interest in the property is a necessary incident
of the conveyance in trust, and not one of its objects,
the rule does not apply. In all cases of a mortgage,
whether created in the form of a trust or otherwise,
the mortgagee acquires only a specific lien on the
property transferred, and the whole residuary interest
therein remains in or results, by implication of law,
to the grantor, and an express reservation of such
residuary interest being nothing more than what results
to the party by operation of law, will not vitiate the
assignment, for the mere expression of a trust where
the law implies one, if not expressed, cannot of itself
avoid a conveyance otherwise good. *Expressio eorum
quae tacite insunt nihil operatur.* It cannot be unlawful
to stipulate for that which the law provides. The expression of a trust, therefore, to restore the thing mortgaged or pledged to the mortgagor or pledgor, or to
return the surplus after the payment of the debt, is not
obnoxious to the statute unless it also appears that the
trust will operate to the prejudice and injury of creditors.[1] As the grantor may expressly provide for the

---

[1] Curtis v. Leavitt, 15 N. Y. 9; Ravisies v. Alston, 5 Ala. 297; Eaton v.

16

trust which would result by operation of law, it follows that he may in good faith direct that it shall be given to another.[1]

WHAT BENEFITS MAY BE RESERVED.—There are open trusts which may be reserved upon the face of the deed,[2] as, for instance, a life interest,[3] or a purchase in the joint names of the grantor and grantee.[4]   In the case of mortgages it is customary to stipulate that the mortgagor shall have the control and benefit of the estate until forfeiture.[5]   A stipulation may also be inserted that the mortgagor may retain possession until the mortgagee requires a sale.[6]   A stipulation that the grantee shall employ the debtor's apprentices is merely collateral, and does not vitiate the transaction.[7]   No

---

Perry, 29 Mo. 96; Leavitt v. Blatchford, 17 N. Y. 521; Dunham v. Whitehead, 21 N. Y. 131; Kneeland v. Cowles, 4 Chand. 46; McClelland v. Remsen, 16 Barb. 622; s. c. 14 Abb. Pr. 331 ; s. c. 23 How. Pr. 175; Phillips v. Zerbe Run Co. 25 Penn. 56; Johnson v. Cunningham, 1 Ala. 249; Pope v. Wilson, 7 Ala. 690; Malone v. Hamilton, Minor, 286; Howell v. Bell, 29 Mo. 135; Brinley v. Spring, 7 Me. 241; Rahn v. McElrath, 6 Watts, 151; Burgin v. Burgin, 1 Ired. 453; Austin v. Johnson, 7 Humph. 191; Tunnell v. Jefferson, 5 Harring. 206; Stanley v. Robins, 36 Vt. 422; Godchaux v. Mulford, 26 Cal. 316; Bartels v. Harris, 4 Me. 146; Hindman v. Dill, 11 Ala. 689; Leitch v. Hollister, 4 N. Y. 211; Van Buskirk v. Warren, 39 N. Y. 119; s. c. 34 Barb. 457; s. c. 13 Abb. Pr. 145; Stevens v. Bell, 6 Mass. 339; Smyth v. Ripley, 33 Conn. 306; Valance v. Miners' Ins. Co. 42 Penn. 441; *vide* Wilson v. Cheshire, 1 McCord Ch. 233.

[1] Green v. Tanner, 8 Met. 411.

[2] Low v. Carter, 21 N. H. 433.

[3] Lott v. De Graffenried, 10 Rich. Eq. 346; Adams v. Broughton, 13 Ala. 731.

[4] Christ's Hospital v. Budgin, 2 Vern. 683; Kingdom v. Bridges, 2 Vern. 67.

[5] Graham v. Lockhart, 8 Ala. 9; Wilson v. Russell, 13 Md. 494.

[6] Dubose v. Dubose, 7 Ala. 235; Brock v. Headen, 13 Ala. 370; Marriott v. Givens, 8 Ala. 694.

[7] Faunce v. Lesley, 6 Penn. 121.

man, however, is allowed to make a conveyance reserving the profits and income to himself for life, with a power to direct what disposition shall be made of the property after his death. He cannot be the equitable owner of property and still have it exempt from his debts.[1]

SECRET TRUSTS.—No conveyance is deemed *bona fide* within the proviso which is accompanied with any secret trust.[2] For instance, if a man is indebted to five several persons in the several sum of £20, and has goods of the value of £20, and makes a conveyance of all his goods to one of them, in satisfaction of his debt, but there is a trust that he shall deal favorably with him in regard to his poor estate, either to permit the grantor or some other for him, or for his benefit, to use or have possession of them, and is contented that he shall pay him his debt when he is able, this is not *bona fide* within the proviso.[3] The secret trust which is illustrated by this example, is manifestly a trust which makes the transfer merely colorable. If the transfer is intended in good faith to have operation in favor of the grantee, and to confer upon him a right to be exercised at his pleasure over the property, it will be valid; but if it is a mere sham, executed colorably, and only for the purpose of protecting the debtor, and without any real intention to convey the property to the grantee, it is void.[4]

---

[1] Mackarson's Appeal, 42 Penn. 330 ; Coolidge v. Melvin, 42 N. H. 510; Brinton v. Hook, 3 Md. Ch. 477; Ford v. Caldwell, 3 Hill, (S. C.) 248 ; Hunters v. Waite, 3 Gratt. 26 ; Watts v. Thomas, 2 P. Wms. 364.

[2] Twyne's Case, 3 Co. 80.

[3] Twyne's Case, 3 Co. 80.

[4] Eveleigh v. Purrsford, 2 Mood. & Rob. 539 ; Sydnor v. Gee, 4 Leigh, 535; Coburn v. Pickering, 3 N. H. 415; Beers v. Botsford, 13 Conn. 146; Michael v. Gay, 1 F. & F. 409; Claytor v. Anthony, 6 Rand. 285; New Eng. Ins. Co. v. Chandler, 16 Mass. 275 ; Rea v. Alexander, 5 Ired. 644.

COLLUSION.—Where it is made to appear that, notwithstanding the transfer, the debtor is to have the real use and beneficial ownership of the property, it is deemed that the transfer is not real, but is intended as a cover for the property to the ease and favor of the debtor, either generally or for some definite time.[1] So, also, if there is any collusion for the benefit of the debtor the transfer is void.   A note given as a fictitious consideration,[2] or secretly as a part of the consideration, so that the debtor may control it for his own use,[3] is a fraud upon the creditors, and renders the transaction covinous.

PURCHASER's BOUNTY.—It is not, however, every benefit conferred upon a debtor that renders a transfer fraudulent, but only such as are given in prejudice of the legal rights of creditors.   Strict and inexorable as the law is upon the subject of frauds, it does not require that a purchaser shall either ignore or abrogate the impulses of natural affection, or of sympathy towards the unfortunate.   If the transfer is valid, and in good faith, there is no principle of the common law, or construction of the statute, which prevents the grantee from aiding the debtor or his family,[4] or disposing of his own as he pleases.

TRANSFER MUST BE UNCONDITIONAL.—The contract by

---

[1] Leadman v. Harris, 3 Dev. 144; Sturdivant v. Davis, 9 Ired. 365; Grant v. Lewis, 14 Wis. 487.

[2] Rea v. Alexander, 5 Ired. 644.

[3] Platt v. Brown, 16 Pick. 553; Pettibone v. Stevens, 15 Conn. 19.

[4] Dallam v. Renshaw, 26 Mo. 533; Pinkston v. McLemore, 31 Ala. 308; Compton v. Perry, 23 Tex. 414; Ocoee Bank v. Nelson, 1 Cold. 186; Bumpas v. Dotson, 7 Humph. 310; Stuck v. Mackey, 4 W. & S. 196; Cureton v. Doby, 10 Rich. Eq. 411; Webb v. Roff, 9 Ohio St. R. 430; Young v. Dumas, 39 Ala. 60; Kilby v. Haggin, 3 J. J. Marsh. 208; Young v. Stallings, 5 B. Mon. 307.

which an insolvent debtor parts with his property must be
absolute and unconditional. Consequently, if he retains
the right to revoke the contract, and resume the ownership of the property, the power is inconsistent with a
fair, honest, and absolute transfer, and renders it fraudulent and void.[1] A stipulation that the vendee may
return the property whenever he chooses, and annul the
contract before the purchase money is paid, is, for the
same reason, fraudulent. It is not an unconditional
sale, and does not vest the title absolutely in any one
for a good consideration.[2] A mere parol agreement
that the debtor may repurchase the property whenever
he becomes able will not, however, vitiate the transfer,
if no substantial interest is thereby reserved.[3]

RIGHT OF POSSESSION AS A CONSIDERATION.—A full
consideration may be given in such a form as to defeat
creditors, and thus render a transfer void.[4] The law,
for instance, will not permit a debtor in failing circumstances to sell his property, convey it by deed without
any reservation, and yet secretly reserve to himself the
right to possess and occupy it for a limited time for his
own benefit. Such a transfer lacks the element of good
faith, for, while it professes to be an absolute conveyance
upon its face, there is a concealed agreement between
the parties to it inconsistent with its terms, securing a

---

[1] West v. Snodgrass, 17 Ala. 549; Bethel v. Stanhope, Cro. Eliz. 810;
Anon. Dyer, 295, a; Rex v. Nottingham, Lane, 42; Tarback v. Marbury,
2 Vern. 510; Peacock v. Monk, 1 Ves. Sr. 127; Jenkyn v. Vaughan, 3
Drew, 419; Rock v. Dade, May on Fraud, 519; vide, Sagitary v. Hide, 2
Vern. 44.

[2] Shannon v. Commonwealth, 8 S. & R. 444; West v. Snodgrass, 17
Ala. 549.

[3] Towle v. Hoit, 14 N. H. 61; Albee v. Webster, 16 N. H. 362; Newsom v. Roles, 1 Ired. 179; Glenn v. Randall; 2 Md. Ch. 220; Anderson
v. Fuller, 1 McMullan Ch. 27; Barr v. Hatch, 3 Ohio, 527.

[4] Bott v. Smith, 21 Beav. 511.

benefit to the grantor at the expense of those he owes. A trust thus secretly created, whether so intended or not, is a fraud on creditors, because it places beyond their reach a valuable right, and gives to the debtor the beneficial enjoyment of what rightfully belongs to his creditors.[1] So, also, in the reservation of a right to repurchase by parol, if there is a reservation of a substantial interest, it will defeat the transfer.[2]

SUPPORT OF DEBTOR.—An agreement to support the debtor or his family is a valuable consideration, but is not sufficient to uphold a transfer when the grantor is insolvent.[3] The transaction is equally fraudulent if enough is not left for the payment of the grantor's debts.[4] It is, in effect, a transfer to the use of the grantor, which is always void.[5] The gist of the objection consists, not in the amount to be paid in future support, but in the fact that the promise of future support forms part of the consideration as an inducement to the transfer. When it is shown that the present

---

[1] Lukins v. Aird, 6 Wall. 78; *vide* Oriental Bank v. Haskins, 3 Met. 332; St. John v. Camp, 17 Conn. 222.

[2] Towle v. Hoitt, 14 N. H. 61; Albee v. Webster, 16 N. H. 362.

[3] Albee v. Webster, 16 N. H. 362; Church v. Chapin, 35 Vt. 223; Gunn v. Butler, 18 Pick. 248; Geiger v. Welsh, 1 Rawle, 349; Jackson v. Parker, 9 Cow. 73; Robinson v. Stewart, 10 N. Y. 189; Smith v. Smith; 11 N. H. 459; Russell v. Hammond, 1 Atk. 13; Stokes v. Jones, 18 Ala. 734; Sturdivant v. Davis, 9 Ired. 365; Crane v. Stickles, 15 Vt. 253; Bott v. Smith, 21 Beav. 511; Morrison v. Morrison, 49 N. H. 69 ; Rollins v. Mooers, 25 Me. 192; Webster v. Withey, 25 Me. 326; Johnston. v. Harvey, 2 Penn. 82; Stanley v. Robbins, 36 Vt. 422 ; Miner v. Warner, 2 Phila. 124; s. c. 2 Grant, 448 ; Hawkins v. Moffatt, 10 B. Mon. 81; Henderson v. Downing, 24 Miss. 106; Robinson v. Robards, 15 Mo. 459; Knox v. Hunt, 34 Miss. 655; McLean v. Button, 19 Barb. 450; Coolidge v. Melvin, 42 N. H. 510.

[4] Crane v. Stickles, 15 Vt. 252; Jones v. Spear, 21 Vt. 426; Tyner v. Sommerville, 1 Smith, 149.

[5] Cadogan v. Kennett, Cowp. 432; Anon. Dyer, 295, a; Adams v. Adams, 1 Dane Ab. 636.

consideration is inadequate to satisfy his debts, whatever may be the amount secured to the debtor, the law, instead of entering upon the task of determining what part of the consideration is in money or other property, and what part is agreed to be paid in future support of the grantor, and holding the grantee responsible to creditors for the latter sum treats the conveyance as a nullity as between the grantee and the creditors, and holds the property liable for their claims.[1] Evidence may, however, be given to show that the grantee paid the full value for the property, and that the reservation of a right to future support is of no value to creditors, for they cannot complain if the grantee assumes burdens which are not to their prejudice.[2] An agreement under the same circumstances may also be made to employ the grantor.[3]

SUPPORT BY SOLVENT PERSON.—If the grantor is free from debt,[4] or retains property amply sufficient for the payment of all his debts,[5] he has a right to contract for his future support for a longer or shorter period, accordingly as he may deem best, for the owner of property can dispose of it as he thinks proper, if he does no wrong to his creditors.

---

[1] Sidensparker v. Sidensparker, 52 Me. 481.

[2] Slater v. Dudley, 18 Pick. 373; Albee v. Webster, 16 N. H. 362.

[3] Griffin v. Cranston, 10 Bosw. 1; s. c. 1 Bosw. 281.

[4] Buchanan v. Clark, 28 Vt. 799; Mills v. Mills, 3 Head, 705; Mahony v. Hunter, 30 Ind. 246; Usher v. Hazeltine, 5 Me. 471; Tibbals v. Jacobs, 31 Conn. 428.

[5] Hapgood v. Fisher, 34 Me. 407; Drum v. Painter, 27 Penn. 148; Johnston v. Zane, 11 Gratt. 552; Eaton v. Perry, 29 Mo. 96; Barrow v. Bailey, 5 Fla. 9; Wooten v. Clark, 23 Miss. 75; Parker v. Nichols, 7 Pick. 111; Johnson v. Johnson, 3 Met. 63.

CHAPTER IX.

CONSIDERATION

WHAT IS A GOOD CONSIDERATION.—An inquiry into
the consideration upon which a transfer is founded sometimes becomes important because there are circumstances
under which a debtor is not permitted to give away his
property, and, also, because only those who give a good
consideration are protected when there is a fraudulent
intent on the part of the grantor. The statute protects
all estates and interests which are conveyed on a good
consideration, and *bona fide*, but inasmuch as others may
lose their debts, which are things of value, the intent of
the act is that the consideration shall be valuable, for
equity requires that a transfer which defeats others shall
be made on as high and good consideration as the things
which are thereby defeated are Good consideration,
therefore, is construed to mean a valuable consideration,
as between creditors and others claiming under the
debtor.[1]

WHEN A TRANSFER IS VOLUNTARY.—A voluntary
conveyance is a transfer without any valuable consideration. In determining whether a transfer is voluntary,
the adequacy of the consideration does not enter into
the question. The character of purchase or voluntary

---

[1] Twyne's Case, 3 Co. 80; Cunningham v. Dwyer, 23 Md. 219; Killough v. Steele, 1 Stew. & Port. 262; Taylor v. Jones, 2 Atk. 600; Partridge v. Gopp, 1 Eden, 163; s. c. Ambl. 596; Thomson v. Dougherty, 12
S. & R. 448.

is determined by the fact whether anything valuable passes between the parties.[1] As a general rule a transfer is voluntary when it is founded upon a consideration which the law does not recognize as valuable, or is made in pursuance of an agreement which cannot be enforced, for where there is no remedy there is no right.[2] An illegal consideration is, in contemplation of law, no consideration, and is not therefore sufficient to support a transfer as against creditors.[3] A parol agreement to make a gift does not vest any right in the donee, either legal or equitable, for it cannot be enforced; consequently a transfer in pursuance of such an agreement only takes effect, as against creditors, from the time when the transfer is actually made.[4] But if a voluntary deed is executed at a time when the grantor has no interest, and he subsequently acquires an interest, the transfer takes effect from the date of the deed.[5] A transfer which the law would compel a party to make is not voluntary.[6]

STATUTORY DEFENCE MAY BE WAIVED.—To the proposition that a conveyance in pursuance or in consideration of an agreement which cannot be enforced is voluntary there is one exception. Wherever there is a moral obligation, which cannot be enforced on account of the provisions of a statute, there the party may waive the benefit of the statute, and the transfer will be valid as

---

[1] Jackson v. Peek, 4 Wend. 300; Shontz v. Brown, 27 Penn. 123; Washband v. Washband, 27 Conn. 424.

[2] Spurgeon v. Collier, 1 Eden. 55; Planck v. Schermerhorn, 3 Barb. Ch. 644; Penhall v. Elwin, 1 Sm. & Gif. 258; Goldsmith v. Russell, 5 D. M. & G. 547.

[3] Weeks v. Hill, 38 N. H. 199; Jose v. Hewitt, 50 Me. 248; Weeden v. Bright, 3 W. Va. 548.

[4] Rucker v. Abell, 8 B. Mon. 566; Davis v. McKinney, 5 Ala. 719; Hoye v. Penn, 1 Bland, 28; Worthington v. Bullitt, 6 Md. 172.

[5] Bonny v. Griffith, Hayes, 115.   [6] Buie v. Kelly, 5 Ired. 169.

against creditors. Thus a debt which is barred by the statute of limitations,[1] or a discharge in bankruptcy,[2] is a good consideration for a conveyance. The statute of frauds is a defence which the debtor may waive, and if he does so by executing the conveyance, it will be valid.[3] When a parol partition has been made of land, and each party has carried it out by taking possession of the part allotted to him, a deed may subsequently be made in pursuance of it.[4] The moral obligation resting upon the grantee holding under a fraudulent transfer is sufficient to support a reconveyance against his creditors.[5] Property which has been conveyed to a party, to give him the necessary qualification to hold an office, may be reconveyed.[6] A transfer in consideration of a parol ante-nuptial contract is not within the foregoing exception, and is merely voluntary.[7] A debt which has been discharged by the voluntary release of the creditor is not a good consideration as against other creditors.[8] The law thus makes a distinction between a release by a statute and a release by the voluntary act of the party.

---

[1] Sayre v. Fredericks, 1 C. E. Green, 205 ; Keen v. Kleckner, 42 Penn. 529; Updike v. Titus, 2 Beasley, 151; *vide* Crawford v. Carper, 4 W. Va. 56.

[2] Wilson v. Russell, 13 Md. 494.

[3] Livermore v. Northrop, 44 N. Y. 107 ; Dygert v. Remerschnider, 32 N. Y. 629; s. c. 39 Barb. 417; Sackett v. Spencer, 65 Penn. 89 ; Gibson v. Walker, 11 Ired. 327 ; *vide* Smith v. Lane, 3 Pick. 205.

[4] Bilsborrow v. Titus, 15 How. Pr. 95.

[5] Clark v. Rucker, 7 B. Mon. 583; Davis v. Graves, 29 Barb. 480; *contra*, Chapin v. Pease, 10 Conn. 69.

[6] Jackson v. Ham, 15 Johns. 261; Roberts v. Gibson, 6 H. & J. 116.

[7] Warden v. Jones, 2 D. G. & J. 76; s. c. 17 L. J. (Ch.) 190; Dundas v. Dutens, 2 Cox. 235; s. c. 1 Ves. Jr. 196 ; Spurgeon v. Collier, 1 Eden. 55; Murphy v. Abraham, 15 Ir. Eq. (N. S.) 371; Reade v. Livingston, 3 Johns. Ch. 481; Randall v. Morgan, 12 Ves. 67; Smith v. Greer, 3 Humph. 118; Hayes v. Jones, 2 Pat. & H. 583; Andrews v. Jones, 10 Ala. 400; Wood v. Savage, 2 Doug. (Mich.) 316.

[8] King v. Moore, 18 Pick. 376; Nightingale v. Harris, 6 R. I. 321.

An objection to receiving parol evidence can not arise when the party bound by the agreement has acted on it in good faith.[1]

WHEN CONSIDERATION MAY BE PAID.—The consideration must arise at the time of the transfer.[2] It is not, however, necessary that an actual payment shall be made. A promise to pay, or the giving of securities will constitute a party a purchaser.[3] A check given in good faith on a banker having funds to pay it is *prima facie* payment if accepted as cash, although its payment is subsequently suspended on account of a controversy concerning the property.[4] A transfer may be made for an annuity as well as for money in hand.[5] An existing debt[6] or liability, either as indorser[7] or surety[8] is suffi-

---

[1] Jones v. Ruffin, 3 Dev. 404.

[2] Starr v. Starr, 1 Ohio, 321.

[3] Seward v. Jackson, 8 Cow. 406; Shontz v. Brown, 27 Penn. 123; Pattison v. Stewart, 6 W. & S. 74; Stafford v. Stafford, 27 Penn. 144; Starr v. Strong, 2 Sandf. Ch. 139.

[4] Woodville v. Reed, 26 Md. 179.

[5] Union Bank v. Toomer, 2 Hill. Ch. 27.

[6] Holbird v. Anderson, 5 T. R. 235; Loeschigk v. Hatfield, 5 Robt. 26; Gleason v. Day, 9 Wis. 498; Seymour v. Wilson, 19 N. Y. 417; Adams v. Wheeler, 10 Pick. 199; Gibson v. Seymour, 4 Vt. 518; Seymour v. Briggs, 11 Wis. 196; McMahan v. Morrison, 16 Ind. 172; Towsley v. McDonald, 32 Barb. 604; Wilson v. Ayer, 7 Me. 207; *vide* Harney v. Pack, 4 S. & M. 229; Pope v. Pope, 40 Miss. 516.

[7] Jewett v. Warren, 12 Mass. 300; Newman v. Bagley, 16 Pick. 570; Buffum v. Green, 5 N. H. 71; Bartels v. Harris, 4 Me. 146; Prescott v. Hayes, 43 N. H. 593; Hendricks v. Robinson, 2 Johns. 283; s. c. 17 Wend. 438; Griffith v. Bank, 6 G. & J. 424; Bank v. McDade, 4 Port. 252; McLaren v. Thompson, 40 Me. 284; Stevens v. Hinckley, 43 Me. 440; Boswell v. Green, 1 Dutch. 390; Lindle v. Neville, 13 S. & R. 227; St. John v. Camp, 17 Conn. 222.

[8] Fling v. Goodall, 40 N. H. 208; Ferguson v. Furnace Co. 9 Wend. 345; Gorham v. Herrick, 2 Me. 87; Stedman v. Vickery, 42 Me. 132; Hopkins v. Scott, 20 Ala. 179; Leggett v. Humphreys, 21 How. 63; Miller v. Howry, 3 Penn. 374; Gibson v. Seymour, 4 Vt. 518; Pennington v. Woodall, 17 Ala. 685; Tunnell v. Jefferson, 5 Harring. 206.

cient. The debt may also be unliquidated.[1] If a father takes a note at the time of making an advance to his son, he retains the control of the money, and a transfer in consideration of it is valid, although he may not have intended under certain circumstances to enforce payment.[2] A person who is entering into a bond as surety, for the faithful performance by an officer of his public duties, may provide for his counter security; for there is a contract at the time to repay to the surety any money the latter may be compelled to pay for the principal, and the performance of this may be ensured by security taken either before or after default.[3]

NOT MERELY GOOD BETWEEN THE PARTIES.—The consideration must be valuable, and not such as is merely good between the parties,[4] but a mortgage to secure the debt of another is not voluntary.[5] A voluntary bond is not a good consideration as against creditors,[6] but if it is due, or the instalments payable thereon are in arrear, then the sum so due can be enforced at law, and is a good consideration for a conveyance made in good faith.[7] Interest which cannot be collected at law is not

---

[1] Dewey v. Littlejohn, 2 Ired. Eq. 495; *vide* Adams v. Adams, 1 Dane Ab. 636.

[2] Arnold v. Arnold, 8 B. Mon. 202.

[3] Dewey v. Littlejohn, 2 Ired. Eq. 495.

[4] Seymour v. Wilson, 19 N. Y. 417; *vide* Garretson v. Kane, 3 Dutch. 208.

[5] Marden v. Babcock, 2 Met. 99.

[6] Hawkins v. Allston, 4 Ired. Eq. 137; McGill v. Harman, 2 Jones Eq. 179; Stiles v. Att.-Gen. 2 Atk. 152; Gilham v. Locke, 9 Ves. 612; Stephens v. Harris, 6 Ired. Eq. 57; Craig v. Root, Cas temp, Talb. 153; Jones v. Powell, 1 Eq. Cas. Abr. 84; Lechnere v. Earl, 3 P. Wms. 211.

[7] Stiles v. Att.-Gen. 2 Atk. 152; Gilham v. Locke, 9 Ves. 612; Tanner v. Byne, 1 Sim. 160; Berry, *Ex parte*, 19 Ves. 218; Hopkirk v. Randolph, 2 Brock. 132; Welles v. Cole, 6 Gratt. 645; *Contra*, Bank v. Mitchell, Rice. Ch. 389.

a good consideration,[1] but there are many transactions in which interest is habitually charged and paid when it could not be claimed on the ground of strict legal right, and, as they are considered as fair and just between the parties, they are good as to others.[2]

VALUABLE CONSIDERATIONS.—The note of a minor is a good consideration, for there is no legal bar to his right to purchase property upon credit, and neither the vendor nor his creditors can avoid or impeach the transfer or question its validity upon the ground of his minority.[3] A second judgment may be taken for a prior judgment without releasing or satisfying the latter,[4] for a creditor may take as many successive judgments for his first as the debtor is willing to give, and each will be good and available until the debt, interest, and costs are paid. An absolute deed intended as a mortgage may be changed by the parties into a mortgage, and a judgment confessed for the debt.[5] A promise to pay specific debts whether by parol or in writing is a valuable consideration,[6] but when the debts are also incumbrances on the property the purchaser must agree to protect the debtor and the rest of his property from them, and not merely take the property subject to the incumbrances.[7]

---

[1] Whittacre v. Fuller, 5 Minn. 508; McKenty v. Gladwin, 10 Cal. 227; Scales v. Scott, 13 Cal. 76.

[2] Spencer v. Ayrault, 10 N. Y. 202.

[3] Matthews v. Rice, 31 N. Y. 457; Washband v. Washband, 27 Conn. 424; vide McCorkle v. Hammond, 2 Jones, (N. C.) 444; Winchester v. Reid, 8 Jones, (N. C.) 377.

[4] Smith's Appeal, 2 Penn. 331.   [5] Cox v. McBee, 1 Spears, 195.

[6] Shontz v. Brown, 27 Penn. 123; Jenkins v. Peace, 1 Jones, (N. C.) 413; Stevens v. Hinckley, 43 Me. 440; Gunn v. Butler, 18 Pick. 248; Pattison v. Stewart, 6 W. & S. 72; Meade v. Smith, 16 Conn. 356; Anderson v. Smith, 5 Blackf. 395; Seaman v. Hasbrouck, 35 Barb. 151; Keen v. Kleckner, 42 Penn. 529; Bell v. Greenwood, 21 Ark. 249; Preston v. Jones, 50 Penn. 54; Vanmeter v. Vanmeter, 3 Gratt. 148.

[7] U. S. v. Mertz, 2 Watts, 406.

RELEASE OF EQUITY OF REDEMPTION.—A conveyance of the equity of redemption by a mortgagor to a mortgagee without the payment of any new consideration is not a voluntary conveyance, and void as against creditors, when the amount due on the note or other obligation the payment of which is secured by the mortgage is equal to the whole value of the mortgaged premises. By operation of law and without any special agreement of the parties on the subject, it effects a discharge of the mortgage debt, either wholly if the estate is sufficient, or *pro rata* if of less value than the amount due. To make such a transaction a voluntary conveyance as against creditors, the estate must be of greater value than the debt.[1]

DAMAGES FOR UNLAWFUL MARRIAGE.—If a woman in contemplation of marriage conveys property to her intended husband and the marriage is void, the failure of the consideration constitutes a sufficient consideration for a re-conveyance.[2] As she can also maintain an action at law for the deceit by which she was led into such a marriage, the damages inflicted upon her constitute a valuable consideration for a transfer of his property to her.[3] Indemnity to a woman against the consequences of an illicit intercourse is also a good consideration within the statute,[4] but a transfer which looks to future cohabitation is illegal and void as against creditors.[5]

---

[1] Williams v. Robbins, 15 Gray, 590; Credle v. Carrawan, 64 N. C. 422.

[2] Forbush v. Willard, 16 Pick. 42.

[3] Fellows v. Emperor, 13 Barb. 92; Hutchinson v. Horn, 1 Smith, 242; Lady Cox's case, 3 P. Wms. 389; *vide* Gilham v. Locke, 9 Ves. 612.

[4] Wait v. Day, 4 Denio, 439; Gray v. Mathias, 5 Ves. 286.

[5] Wait v. Day, 4 Denio. 439; Sherman v. Barrett, 1 McMullen, 147; Hargroves v. Meray, 2 Hill Ch. 222; Lady Cox's case, 3 P. Wms. 389; Gray v. Mathias, 5 Ves. 286.

If a transfer, however, is made for a valuable consideration at the time it can not be vitiated by a subsequent cohabitation with the debtor any more than by cohabitation with any other person, unless such subsequent cohabitation entered into the consideration of the transfer.[1] A transfer as a mere gratuity to a paramour or for her to hold for the benefit of the grantor, or a purchase made in her name for the purpose of facilitating future illicit intercourse is not founded upon a good consideration within the meaning of the statute.[2] A claim of damages for seduction is a valuable consideration.[3]

FIRM PROPERTY TO PAY INDIVIDUAL DEBTS.—A firm is in law distinct from the members who compose it, and a transfer of the firm property to pay the separate debts of one of the partners is a voluntary conveyance.[4] A previous division of the property when the firm is insolvent will not make any difference, for there is then nothing to divide.[5] A debt contracted in the name of one of the partners may, however, be shown to have been for the benefit of the firm, and will then constitute a good consideration.[6] If the firm is insolvent, a separate creditor can not be injured by a transfer of one partner's interest in the partnership property to his co-

---

[1] Fellows v. Emperor, 13 Barb. 92.

[2] Wait v. Day, 4 Denio, 439.

[3] Carlisle v. Gaskill, 4 Ind. 219.

[4] Burtus v. Tisdall, 4 Barb. 571; Anderson v. Maltby, 2 Ves. Jr. 244; Elliot v. Stevens, 38 N. H. 311; Ferson v. Monroe, 21 N. H. 462; Geortner v. Canajoharie, 2 Barb. 625; Dart v. Farmer's Bank, 27 Barb. 337; Walsh v. Kelly, 42 Barb. 98; s. c. 27 How Pr. 359; Wilson v. Robertson, 21 N. Y. 587; Contra, Sigler v. Bank, 8 Ohio St. R. 511; National Bank v. Sprague, 5 C. E. Green, 13; Schaeffer v. Fithian, 17 Ind. 463; Armstrong v. Fahnestock, 19 Md. 58.

[5] Burtus v. Tisdall, 4 Barb. 571.

[6] Siegel v. Chidsey, 28 Penn. 279; Gwin v. Selby, 5 Ohio St. R. 96.

partner in consideration of the grantee's assuming the liabilities of the firm.[1] As each partner is personally liable for the payment of the partnership liabilities, a transfer of his separate property in consideration of a debt due by the firm is founded upon a good consideration.[2] Money loaned to a stockholder may be shown to have been used for the benefit of the corporation, and is a good consideration for a transfer made by the latter to the creditor.[3]

FUTURE ADVANCES.—A transfer may be made in good faith to secure indorsements[4] or future advances.[5] The mere fact that such transfer may afford an oppor-

---

[1] Griffin v. Cranston, 10 Bosw. 1; s. c. 1 Bosw. 281.

[2] Stewart v. Slater, 6 Duer, 83.

[3] Head v. Horn, 18 Cal. 211.

[4] Gardner v. Webber, 17 Pick. 407 ; Calkins v. Lockwood, 16 Conn. 276 ; U. S. v. Hooe, 3 Cranch, 73 ; Goddard v. Sawyer, 9 Allen, 78 ; Worseley v. De Mattos, 1 Burr, 467.

[5] Doyle v. Smith, 1 Cold. 15 ; Cole v. Albers, 1 Gill, 412 ; Hendricks v. Robinson, 2 Johns. 283 ; s. c. 17 Johns. 438; Craig v. Tappin, 2 Sandf. Ch. 78; Townsend v. Empire Co. 6 Duer. 208 ; Lansing v. Woodworth, 1 Sandf. Ch. 43; Bank of Utica v. Finch, 3 Barb. Ch. 293; Carpenter v. Blote, 1 E. D. Smith, 491 ; U. S. v. Hooe, 3 Cranch, 73 ; Shirras v. Craig, 7 Cranch, 34; Lawrence v. Tucker, 23 How. 14; Foster v. Reynolds, 38 Mo. 553; Allen v. Montgomery, R. R. Co. 11 Ala. 437; Coles v. Sellers, 1 Phila. 533; Crane v. Deming, 7 Conn. 387; Hubbard v. Savage, 8 Conn. 215; Commercial Bank v. Cunningham, 24 Pick. 270; Wescott v. Gunn, 4 Duer, 107; McDaniels v. Colvin, 16 Vt. 300; Collins v. Carlisle, 13 Ill. 254 ; Seaman v. Fleming, 7 Rich. Eq. 283 ; Bell v. Fleming, 1 Beasley. 13, 496; Griffin v. N. J. Co. 3 Stock. 49; Barnard v. Moore, 8 Allen, 273; Speer v. Skinner, 35 Ill. 282; Adams v. Wheeler, 10 Pick. 199; Badlam v. Tucker, 1 Pick. 398 ; Wilder v. Winne, 6 Cow. 284; Smyth v. Ripley, 33 Conn. 306; McGavock v. Deery, 1 Cold. 265; U. S. v. Lennox, 2 Paine, 180; Wilson v. Russell, 13 Md. 494; Irwin v. Wilson, 3 Jones Eq. 210; D'Wolf v. Harris, 4 Mason, 515; Blood v. Palmer, 11 Me. 414; Miller v. Lockwood, 32 N. Y. 293; Atkinson v. Maling, 2 T. R. 462; Googins v. Gilmore, 47 Me. 9 ; Holbrook v. Baker, 5 Me. 309; Griffin v. Stoddard, 12 Ala. 783 ; vide Bank v. Willard. 10 N. H. 210.

tunity for a fraudulent collusion is not a valid objection[1], for its validity depends upon the attending circumstances. A mortgage to secure future advances should indicate the extent of the lien with certainty,[2] but no certain sum need be named.[3] It may be taken for an absolute sum.[4] A judgment may also be taken to secure future advances.[5]

SERVICES BETWEEN MEMBERS OF THE SAME FAMILY.— The law implies no promise to pay for services rendered by members of a family to each other, whether by children, parents, grandparents, brothers, stepchildren, or other relations. The rule rests upon the simple reason that such services are not performed in the expectation or upon the faith of receiving pecuniary compensation. The services rendered in such cases are mutual, and it may often be difficult to decide upon which party the principal benefit is conferred. Services so rendered do not, therefore, constitute a valuable consideration for a transfer.[6] A claim for board when a child resides with his parents after his majority, rests upon the same principle.[7] As a parent is entitled to the earn-

---

[1] Wilson v. Russell, 13 Md. 494; U. S. v. Hooe, 3 Cranch, 73.

[2] Truscott v. King, 6 N. Y. 147; Younge v. Wilson, 24 Barb. 510; Craig v. Tappin, 2 Sandf. Ch. 78; Divver v. McLaughlin, 2 Wend. 596.

[3] Robinson v. Williams, 22 N. Y. 380.

[4] Miller v. Lockwood, 32 N. Y. 293; Shirras v. Craig, 7 Cranch, 34; Bevins v. Dunham, 1 Spears, 39; Tully v. Harloe, 35 Cal. 302; Summers v. Roos, 42 Miss. 749; *Contra*, Peacock v. Tompkins, Meigs, 317; Neuffer v. Pardue, 3 Sneed. 191.

[5] Brinkerhoff v. Marvin, 5 John's Ch. 320; Lansing v. Woodworth, 1 Sandf. Ch. 43; Livingston v. McInlay, 16 Johns. 165; Walker v. Snedeker, Hoff. 145; Truscott v. King, 6 N. Y. 147; *Contra*, Clapp v. Ely, 2 Stockt. 178; s. c. 3 Dutch. 555.

[6] Updike v. Titus, 2 Beasley, 151; Hack v. Stewart, 8 Penn. 213; Sanders v. Wagonseller, 19 Penn. 248; Van Wyck v. Seward, 18 Wend. 375; Zerbe v. Miller, 16 Penn. 488.

[7] Coley v. Coley, 1 McCarter, 350.

17

ings of his minor child,[1] and a husband to the earnings of his wife,[2] a transfer in consideration of such earnings by a person to his wife or child is voluntary. A contract by a minor for his emancipation constitutes a moral obligation, and is a sufficient consideration for a promise made by him when he is of age.[3]

---

[1] Swartz v. Hazlett, 8 Cal. 118; Brown v. McDonald, 1 Hill Ch. 297; Dick v. Gressim, 1 Freem. Ch. (Miss.) 428; Danley v. Rector, 10 Ark. 211.

[2] Skillman v. Skillman, 2 Beasley, 403; Belford v. Crane, 1 C. E. Green, 265 ; Cramer v. Reford, 2 C. E. Green, 367 ; Beach v. Baldwin, 14 Mo. 597 ; Pinkston v. McLemore, 31 Ala. 308.

[3] Geist v. Geist, 2 Penn. 441.

CHAPTER X.

COMPREHENSIVENESS OF THE STATUTE.—The statute invalidates all and every fraudulent feoffment, gift, grant, alienation, bargain and conveyance of land, tenements, hereditaments, goods and chattels, or any of them, or of any lease, rent, common, or other profit or charge out of the same lands, tenements, hereditaments, goods and chattels, or any of them, by writing or otherwise, and all and every bond, suit, judgment, and execution, and, as it is merely declaratory of the common law, the common law in its abhorrence of fraud is able to reach every other fraudulent device not included in it. *Ait prætor: Quæ fraudationis causa gesta erunt cum eo qui fraudem non ignoraverit de his curatori bonorum vel ei cui de ea re actionem dare opportebit infra annum, quo experiundi potestas fuerit, actionem dabo; idque etiam adversus ipsum qui fraudem fecit, servabo. Necessario prætor hoc edictum proposuit; quo edicto consulit creditoribus, revocando ea quaecunque in fraudem eorum alienata sunt. Ait ergo prætor, quæ fraudationis causa gesta erunt. Haec verba generalia sunt et continent in se omnem omnino in fraudem factam, vel alienationem vel quemcunque contractum. Quodcunque igitur fraudis causa factum est, videtur his verbis revocari, qualecunque fuerit, nam late ista verba patent. Sive ergo rem alienavit sive acceptilatione vel pacto aliquem liberavit, idem erit probandum. Et si pignora liberet vel quem alium in fraudem creditorum præponat vel ei præbuit exceptionem sive se obligavit fraudandorum creditorum causa sive numeravit pecuniam vel quodcunque aliud fecit in fraudem creditorum, palam est edictum locum habere. Gesta fraudationis causa accipere debemus non solum ea quæ contrahens gesserit aliquis, verumetiam si forte data opera ad judicium non adfuit vel litem mori patiatur vel a debitore non petit ut tempore liberatur aut usum fructum vel servitutem amittit et qui aliquid facit ut desinat habere quod habet, ad hoc edictum pertinet. In fraudem facere videri etiam eum qui non facit quod debet facere intelligendum est, id est si non utatur servitutibus; sed etsi rem suam pro derelicto habuerit ut quis eam suam faciat.*[1]

NOT TRANSFERS TO DEBTORS.—In order to be within the prohibition of the statute, the transfer must be one that is made by a debtor and not to a debtor. Although a person is insolvent, others may make any contract with him which is not otherwise prohibited by law. They may place goods in his hands to sell,[2] or leave them in his possession,[3] or allow him the profits arising from sales made by him,[4] even though he is to sell in his own name,[5] or deliver articles to him upon condition that the title shall not vest in him until he shall have paid all the purchase-money,[6] or advance money to a

---

[1] Dig. Lib. 42 tit. 9; 1 Domat. B. 2 tit. 10.

[2] Howard v. Sheldon, 11 Paige, 558; Blood v. Palmer, 11 Me. 414; Robinson v. Chapline, 8 Iowa, 91.

[3] Hill v. Hill, 1 Dev. & Bat. 336; Anderson v. Biddle, 10 Mo. 23; Norris v. Bradford, 4 Ala. 203.

[4] Patten v. Clark, 5 Pick. 4 ; McCullough v. Porter, 4 W. & S. 177.

[5] Blood v. Palmer, 11 Me. 414 ; Merrill v. Rinker, 1 Bald. 528.

[6] Esty v. Aldrich, 46 N. H. 127; Forbes v. Marsh, 15 Conn. 384; McFarland v. Farmer, 42 N. H. 386 ; Strong v. Taylor, 2 Hill, 326; Hill v. Freeman, 3 Cush. 257 ; Bailey v. Harris, 8 Iowa, 331 ; Reeves v. Harris, 1

mechanic under a stipulation for an interest in the article to be manufactured by him,[1] or purchase articles to be subsequently manufactured,[2] or employ a mechanic with wages varying according to the profits.[3]   Whenever property is thus placed in the hands of an insolvent debtor, it is always a question whether or not the form of the transaction is not merely colorable.   If there is in fact a sale,[4] or a gift,[5] the property will be liable to his debts.   The title will generally be considered to be vested in him when the property is delivered to him for consumption or to be dealt with in any way inconsistent with the ownership of the grantor, or in a manner that would necessarily destroy the grantor's lien or right of property.[6]   A devise with a secret trust to hold for the debtor is not within the statute.[7]

PAYMENTS TO A DEBTOR.—A payment of money to a debtor is not within the statute, even though it is made for the purpose of avoiding an attachment.[8]   *Apud*

Bailey, 563 ; Baylor v. Smithers, 1 Litt. 105 ; Bickerstaff v. Doub, 19 Cal. 109 ; Chaffee v. Sherman, 26 Vt. 237 ; Paris v. Vail, 18 Vt. 277 ; Ayer v. Bartlett, 6 Pick. 71 ; *Contra*, Rose v. Story, 1 Penn. 190 ; Haak v. Linderman, 64 Penn. 499; Becker v. Smith, 59 Penn. 69; Waldron v. Haupt. 32 Penn. 408; Leigh Co. v. Field, 8 W. & S. 232; Ketchum v. Watson, 24 Ill. 592.

[1] Beaumont v. Crane, 14 Mass. 400 ; Frost v. Willard, 9 Barb. 440 ; Glover v. Allen, 6 Pick, 209 ; Calkins v. Lockwood, 16 Conn. 276 ; Macomber v. Parker, 13 Pick. 175 ; Becker v. Smith, 59 Penn. 469 ; King v. Humphreys, 10 Penn. 217.

[2] Veazie v. Holmes, 40 Me. 69 ; Bartlett v. Blake, 37 Me. 124 ; *vide* Jenkins v. Erchelberger, 4 Watts, 121.

[3] Faulkner v. Waters, 11 Pick. 473.

[4] Merrill v. Rinker, 1 Bald. 528 ; Strong v. Taylor, 2 Hill, 326.

[5] Norris v. Bradford, 4 Ala. 203; Fitzhugh v. Anderson, 2 H. & M. 289 ; Ford v. Aikin, 4 Rich. 121 ; McDermott v. Barnum, 16 Mo. 114 ; 19 Mo. 204; *vide* Hollowell v. Skinner, 4 Ired. 165.

[6] Ludden v. Hazen, 31 Barb. 650 ; Dick v. Cooper, 24 Penn. 217; Heitzman v. Divil, 11 Penn. 264.

[7] M'Kee v. Jones, 6 Penn. 425.

[8] Simpson v. Dall, 3 Wall. 460 ; Fletcher v. Pillsbury, 35 Vt. 16.

Labeonem scriptum est eum qui suum recipiat, nullam videre fraudem facere, hoc est, eum qui quod sibi debetur receperat. Eum enim quem prœses invitum solvere cogat, impune non solvere, iniquum esse. Totum enim hoc edictum ad contractus pertinere, in quibus se prœtor non interponit, ut puta pignora, venditionesque.[1] When an agent exceeds his authority and purchases goods in the name of his principal as a means of covering them from his creditors, they are liable to execution and sale for his debts.[2]

ONLY THE CREDITORS OWN DEBTOR.—The statute, moreover, intends simply to guard a creditor from the fraudulent attempts of his debtor to delay, hinder, or defraud him of the recovery of his debt by disposing of the property, which he would have a right to seize as soon as he obtains a judgment. The very term creditor implies this. There can be no creditor but where there is a debtor, and no party is a creditor of any one save the person who owes him the money. The creditors of A. can not, therefore, derive any assistance from the act in respect to the fraudulent transfers of B. C. and D., for it is of no consequence to them what B. C. and D. may do with their property. Such transfers can not delay, hinder, or defraud them. Consequently a transfer by a *feme sole* on the eve of marriage for the purpose of protecting the property against the claims of the creditors of her intended husband is not fraudulent as against them.[3] A term of years which belongs to the debtor's wife as administratrix is not liable for his debts, and a

---

[1] Dig. lib. 42 tit. 9; see 61 Domat. B. 2 tit. 10.
[2] White v. Cooper, 3 Penn. 130.
[3] Land v. Jeffries, 5 Rand. 211, 599; Andrews v. Jones, 10 Ala. 400; Prior v. Kinney, 6 Munf. 510.

transfer of it is not within the statute as against his creditors.[1] But if a *feme sole*, being in debt, conveys her property in trust for her benefit and then marries a person who becomes a bankrupt, her property, so far as she takes a separate estate under the trust, is liable to satisfy her debts. Although the discharge of her husband releases her personally at law, yet her property is not discharged, for the failure to make a provision for her creditors renders the transfer fraudulent as against them.[2]

KIND OF PROPERTY.—In respect to the kind of property which may be the subject of a fraudulent transfer, the statute extends to lands, tenements, hereditaments, goods and chattels, and any lease rent, common or other profit or charge out of lands, tenements, hereditaments, goods or chattels. It is important, however, to bear in mind that the common law has not been repealed, and consequently will reach every species of property not included in this enumeration. The source from which the debtor derived the property is wholly immaterial.[3] If a transfer is fraudulent, the grantee can not retain the property on the ground that it is of no value.[4]

CHOSES IN ACTION.—The terms " goods and chattels " embrace things in action as well as in possession,[5] but as stock,[6] *choses in action*[7] and money[8] could not be taken

---

[1] Ridler v. Punter, Cro. Eliz. 291.

[2] Chubb v. Stretch, 9 L. R. Eq. 555; Briscoe v. Kennedy, 1 Bro. C. C. 17 note; Miles v. Williams, 1 P. Wms. 249; Hamlin v. Bridge, 24 Me. 145.

[3] Bank v. Ballard, 12 Rich. 259.

[4] Garrison v. Monaghan, 33 Penn. 232.

[5] Pinkerton v. Railroad Co. 42 N. H. 424.

[6] Horn v. Horn, Amb. 79; Dundas v. Dutens, 1 Ves. Jr. 196; Rider v. Kidder, 10 Ves. 360.

[7] Sims v. Thomas, 12 A. & E. 536; Grogan v. Cooke, 2 Ball. & B. 233; Norcut v. Dodd, 1 Cr. & Ph. 100.

[8] Duffin v. Furness, Sel. Cas. Ch. 77.

on execution at common law, it has been doubted whether a transfer of such property could be fraudu-lent. The question is one that relates merely to the remedy as affected by the character of the property, and, whenever a statute enables a creditor to reach such property, either by attachment or execution, a transfer of it becomes liable to investigation on the ground of fraud.[1] Even independently of such statutory provisions the better doctrine is that a court of equity in aid of an execution at law, may, for the purpose of suppressing fraud and enforcing justice, reach property which is not liable to legal process at law. Equity fol-lows out the law in this respect by adopting its maxims and carrying them out according to the principles of justice and right. Where the law fails equity, there-fore, affords relief for the purpose of enforcing the pay-ment of just debts.[2]

---

[1] Pinkerton v. Railroad, 42 N. H. 424; Gaylard v. Couch, 5 Day, 223; Warden v. Jones, 2 D. & J. 76; s. c. 27 L. J. Ch. 190; Sims v. Thomas, 12 A. & E. 536; Stokoe v. Cowan, 29 Beav. 637; Barrack v. Mc-Cullock, 3 K. & J. 110; Magawley's Trust, 5 D. & S. 1; Freeman v. Pope, 5 L. R. Ch. 538.

[2] Taylor v. Jones, 2 Atk. 600; Partridge v. Gopp, 1 Eden, 163; s. c. Ambl. 596; Bayard v. Hoffman, 4 Johns. Ch. 450; Horn v. Horn, Ambl. 79; Smithier v. Lewis, 1 Vern. 398; Hopkirk v. Randolph, 2 Brock. 132; Doughten v. Gray, 2 Stockt. 323; Law v. Payson, 32 Me. 521; Bean v. Smith, 2 Mason, 252; Catchings v. Manlove, 39 Miss. 655; Pringle v. Hodg-son, 3 Ves. 617; Planter's Bank v. Henderson, 4 Humph. 75; Abbott v. Tenney, 18 N. H. 109; Wright v. Petrie, 1 S. & M. Ch. 282; Green v. Tantum, 4 C. E. Green, 105; Hadden v. Spader, 20 Johns. 554; s. c. 5 Johns. Ch. 280; Tappan v. Evans, 11 N. H. 311; Chase v. Searles, 45 N. H. 511; Weed v. Pierce, 9 Cow. 722; West v. Saunders, 1 A. K. Marsh, 108; Greer v. Wright, 6 Gratt. 154; Harlan v. Barnes, 5 Dana. 219; Sargent v. Salmond, 27 Me. 539; *Contra*, Dundas v. Dutens, 1 Ves. Jr. 196; Rider v. Kidder, 10 Ves. 360; Matthews v. Feaver, 1 Cox, 278; Cosby v. Ross, 3 J. J. Marsh, 290; Winnibrinner v. Weisiger, 3 Mon. 32; Crozier v. Young, 3 Mon. 157; Grogan v. Cooke, 2 Ball. & B. 233; Buford v. Buford, 1 Bibb. 305; Sims v. Thomas, 12 A. & E. 536; Norcutt v. Dodd, 1 Cr. & Ph. 100; Bickley v. Norris, 2 Brev. 252; Duffin v. Furness, Sel. Cas. Ch. 77; Caillaud v. Estwick, 1 Anst. 381.

PURCHASES IN NAME OF ANOTHER.—At one time there was some question whether creditors could reach property which was paid for by the debtor when the title was fraudulently conveyed by the vendor to another.[1] The statute makes all fraudulent conveyances void, but if such a transfer were void, the title would remain in the grantor, and consequently the creditors could not seize the property. Such a contrivance is manifestly not within the provisions of the statute.[2] It is, however, within the principles of the common law which will not permit a debtor to convert his funds, which ought to be applied to pay his debts, to the purchase of property conveyed to another to the prejudice of his creditors.[3] Justice is attained by holding the grantee as a trustee for the benefit of the creditors upon the principle that a person acquiring a title by fraud shall be held as a trustee for the injured person, although he did not intend to acquire the property in that character.[4] It may be considered as settled that property so purchased in the name of another is liable to the demands of creditors.[5] As the theory of the law is that the

---

[1] Fletcher v. Sidley, 2 Vern. 490 ; Glaister v. Hewer, 8 Ves. 196 ; Proctor v. Warren, Sel. Cas. Ch. 78.

[2] Gowing v. Rich, 1 Ired. 553 ; Gardiner Bank v. Wheaton, 8 Me. 373 ; Gray v. Faris, 7 Yerg. 155.

[3] Taylor v. Heriot, 4 Dessau. 227.

[4] Coleman v. Cocke, 6 Rand. 618 ; Brown v. McDonald, 1 Hill. Ch. 297 ; Godding v. Brackett, 34 Me. 27 ; Gray v. Faris, 7 Yerg. 155 ; Bean v. Smith, 2 Mason, 252.

[5] Peacock v. Monk, 1 Ves. Sr. 127 ; Christy v. Courtenay, 13 Beav. 96 ; Farrow v. Teackle, 4 H. & J. 271 ; Wright v. Douglass, 3 Barb. 554 ; Taylor v. Heriot, 4 Dessau. 227 ; Proseus v. McIntyre, 5 Barb. 424 ; Coleman v. Cocke, 6 Rand. 618 ; Christ's Hospital v. Budgin, 2 Vern. 683 ; Doyle v. Sleeper, 1 Dana, 531 ; Bay v. Cook, 31 Ill. 336 ; Houghton v. Tate, 3 Y. & J. 486 ; Whittlesey v. McMahon, 10 Conn. 137 ; Tappan v. Bulter, 7 Bosw. 480 ; Wood v. Savage, 2 Doug. (Mich.) 316 ; Miller v. Wilson, 15 Ohio, 108 ; Carpenter v. Roe, 10 N. Y. 227 ; Mead v. Gregg, 12 Barb. 653 ; Croft v. Arthur, 3 Dessau. 223 ; National Bank v. Sprague, 5 C. E. Green, 13 ;

grantee holds the property as a trustee, the trust may always be enforced in equity.[1] Whether the property is also liable to an execution at law is a point upon which the decisions vary.[2] When the fraudulent grantee takes an assignment of an outstanding mortgage, pur-

---

Dewey v. Long, 25 Vt. 564; Gough v. Henderson, 2 Head, 628; Faringer v. Ramsay, 2 Md. 365; Stewart v. Cohn, 21 La. An. 349; North v. Bradway, 9 Minn. 183; Brown v. McDonald, 1 Hill Ch. 297; Cutter v. Griswold, Walk. Ch. 437; Brewster v. Power, 10 Paige, 562; Jackson v. Forrest, 2 Barb. Ch. 576; Neale v. Day, 28 L. J. Ch. 45; Barrack v. McCulloch, 3 K. & J. 110; DeChyrton's Case, Dyer, 295 a; Jencks v. Alexander, 11 Paige, 619; Sumner v. Sawtelle, 8 Minn. 309; Huggins v. Perine, 30 Ala. 396; Smith v. Parker, 4 Me. 452; Halbert v. Grant, 4 Mon. 580; Whittlesey v. McMahon, 10 Conn. 137; Whitney v. Stearns, 11 Met. 319; Baldwin v. Johnson, 8 Ark. 260; Doolittle v. Bridgman, 1 Greene, 265; *Contra* Fletcher v. Sidley, 2 Vern. 490; Glaister v. Hewer, 8 Ves. 196; Procter v. Warren, Sel. Cas. Ch. 78; Crozier v. Young, 3 Mon. 157.

[1] Patterson v. Campbell, 9 Ala. 933; Gardiner Bank v. Wheaton, 8 Me. 373; State Bank v. Harrow, 26 Iowa, 426; Smith v. Parker, 41 Me. 452; Brown v. McDonald, 1 Hill Ch. 297; Bertrand v. Elder, 23 Ark. 494; Corey v. Greene, 51 Me. 114; Marshall v. Marshall, 2 Bush. 415; Halbert v. Grant, 4 Mon. 580; Peay v. Sublet, 1 Mo. 449; Newell v. Morgan. 2 Harring. 225; Dockray v. Mason, 48 Me. 178; Bay v. Cook, 31 Ill. 336; Belford v. Crane, 1 C. E. Green, 265; Demaree v. Dreskell, 3 Blackf. 115; Rucker v. Abell, 8 B. Mon. 566; Gordon v. Lowell, 21 Me. 251; McDowell v. Cochran, 11 Ill. 31; Walcott v. Almy, 6 McLean. 23; Gentry v. Harper, 2 Jones. Eq. 177.

[2] Guthrie v. Gardner, 9 Wend. 414; Bodine v. Edwards, 10 Paige, 504; Arnot v. Beadle, 1 Hill. & D. 181; Tevis v. Doe, 3 Ind. 129; Pennington v. Clifton, 11 Ind. 162; Webster v. Withey, 25 Me. 326; Kimmel v. McRight, 2 Penn. 38; Cutter v. Griswold, Walk. Ch. 437; Roe v. Irwin, 32 Geo. 39; Coleman v. Cocke, 6 Rand. 618; Cecil Bank v. Snively, 23 Md. 253; Godding v. Brackett, 34 Me. 27; Clark v. Chamberlain, 13 Allen, 257; Wait v. Day, 4 Denio, 439; Hunt v. Blodgett, 17 Ill. 583. In the follow-cases it has been held not liable: Howe v. Bishop, 3 Met. 26; Garfield v. Hatmaker, 15 N. Y. 475; Brewster v. Power, 10 Paige, 562; Page v. Goodman, 8 Ired. Eq. 16; Worth v. York, 13 Ired. 206; Davis v. McKinney, 5 Ala. 719; Davis v. Tibbetts, 39 Me. 279; Gray v. Faris, 7 Yerg. 155; Dewey v. Long, 25 Vt. 564; Gowing v. Rich, 1 Ired. 553; Garrett v. Rhame, 9 Rich, 407; Jimmerson v. Duncan, 3 Jones, (N.C.) 537; Low v. Marco, 53 Me. 45; Webster v. Folsom, 58 Me. 230; Hamilton v. Cone, 99 Mass. 478; *vide* Goodwin v. Hubbard, 15 Mass. 210.

chased with debtor's money, the legal title is in the debtor.[1]

EXPENDITURES UPON ANOTHER'S LAND.—If a debtor uses his personal property upon the real estate of another, with the knowledge and consent of the owner, so that it becomes a part of such realty, for the purpose of defrauding his creditors, and preventing them from obtaining satisfaction of their demands, they may still follow the property into the hands of the owner of the premises thus benefited, and fasten their claims upon such premises to the extent of the debtor's property so appropriated.[2]   If a debt, however, has been created between the parties, the creditors can only have the debt appropriated to the satisfaction of their demands, but if no debt has been created, the appropriate remedy is to fasten their claim upon the real estate to the extent of the debtor's property thus made part of the realty.

POWER OF APPOINTMENT.—If a debtor has a general power of appointment, and executes it voluntarily without consideration for the benefit of a third person, the property so given under the power is liable to the demands of his creditors.[3]   A power is general within the meaning of the rule according to the persons or uses to which the property may be appointed under it, and

---

[1] Stephens v. Sinclair, 1 Hill, 143.

[2] Isham v. Schaffer, 60 Barb. 317; Lynde v. McGregor, 13 Allen, 182; Athey v. Knotts, 6 B. Mon. 24; *Contra*, Campion v. Cotton, 17 Ves. 264; Ewing v. Cantrell, Meigs. 364.

[3] Mackason's Appeal, 42 Penn. 330; Smith v. Garey, 2 Dev. & Bat. Eq. 42; Stillwell v. Mellersh, 20 L. J. Ch. 356; Townsend v. Windham, 2 Ves. Sr. 1; Lassels v. Cornwallis, 2 Vern. 465; s. c. Prec. Ch. 232; George v. Milbanke, 9 Ves. 189; Whittington v. Jennings, 6 Sim. 493; Thompson v. Towne, Prec. Ch. 52; Bainton v. Ward, 2 Atk. 172; Pack v. Bathurst, 3 Atk. 269; Thompson v. Towne, 2 Vern. 319; s. c. Prec. Ch. 52; Tallmadge v. Sill, 21 Barb. 34.

not according to the time when its exercise takes effect, or the instrument by which its exercise is to be manifested.[1] A general power is a power to appoint to whomsoever the donee pleases.[2] If there is only a power to appoint among certain persons, who are definitely described, so that the debtor cannot make the appointment for himself, his creditors cannot claim the benefit of it.[3] If the power is general, it makes no difference whether the appointment is by will or by deed.[4] It also makes no difference whether it is a power to charge a sum of money on land or to create a chattel interest out of land.[5] It has also been said that a general power makes the donee equitable owner of the estate, and gives him such a dominion over it as subjects it to his debts.[6]

EXEMPT PROPERTY.—Property which is exempt by a positive statute from liability for the owner's debts, is not susceptible of a fraudulent alienation, and consequently is not within the statute.[7] But if a transfer of land is merely colorable upon a secret trust, that the grantee will hold it for the debtor's benefit, after he has abandoned the use of it as a homestead, it is fraudulent.[8] Partners who own land in common, will

---

[1] Johnson v. Cushing, 15 N. H. 298; Tallmadge v. Sill, 21 Barb. 34.

[2] Tallmadge v. Sill, 21 Barb. 34.

[3] Townsend v. Windham, 2 Ves. Sr. 1.

[4] Townsend v. Windham, 2 Ves. Sr. 1.

[5] Townsend v. Windham, 2 Ves. Sr. 1.

[6] Bainton v. Ward, 2 Atk. 172; Ashfield v. Ashfield, 2 Vern. 287; Troughton v. Troughton, 3 Atk. 656; vide White v. Sansom, 3 Atk. 411.

[7] Bond v. Seymour, 1 Chand. 40; Legro v. Lord, 10 Me. 161; Vaughan v. Thompson, 17 Ill. 78; Wood v. Chambers, 20 Tex. 247; Cox v. Shropshire, 25 Tex. 113; Smith v. Allen, 39 Miss. 469; Martel v. Somers, 26 Tex. 551; Lishy v. Perry, 6 Bush. 515; Pike v. Miles, 23 Wis. 164; Dreutzer v. Bell, 11 Wis. 114; Anthony v. Wade, 1 Bush. 110; Morton v. Ragan, 5 Bush. 334; Foster v. McGregor, 11 Vt. 595; Patten v. Smith, 5 Conn. 196; s. c. 4 Conn. 450.

[8] Cox v. Shropshire, 25 Tex. 113.

not be allowed to divide it in fraud of creditors, so that each may claim a homestead.[1] It is also a fraud for a debtor to convert his assets into property, which is exempt from execution,[2] or to sell his property for the purpose of paying off a mortgage upon his homestead.[3] It has been held however, that if he has money on hand he may pay off such a mortgage.[4]

DEBTOR'S LABOR.—*Quod autem cum possit aliquid quaerere, non id agit ut adquirat, ad hoc edictum non pertinet. Pertinet enim edictum ad deminuentes patrimonium suum, non ad eos qui id agunt, ne locupletentur. Unde si quis ideo conditioni non paret ne committatur stipulatio in ea conditione est, ne faciat huic edicto locum.*[5] Such were the principles of the civil law, and such are the principles of law which have been recognized in the construction of the statute. Creditors have no power to compel a debtor to labor, and earn the means to pay their demands. He may resign himself to hopeless and endless want, or he may limit his exertions to just such an extent as may be adequate to furnish him the means of a scanty subsistence, and in all this he violates no legal right of his creditors. The law allows even more than this. His first and most imperative duty is to support and maintain himself and family, from the proceeds of his labor. He is under no legal or moral obligation to appropriate these to the benefit of his creditors, and leave himself and his family to suffer hunger and want.[6] Consequently he

---

[1] Bishop v. Hubbard, 23 Cal. 514.

[2] *In re* Henkel, 2 B. R. 167.

[3] Riddell v. Shirley, 5 Cal. 488.

[4] Randall v. Buffington, 10 Cal. 491.

[5] Dig. lib. 42 tit. 9, Sec. 1; 1 Domat. B. 2 tit. 10.

[6] Leslie v. Joyner, 2 Head, 514; Griffin v. Cranston, 1 Bosw. 281; Holdship v. Patterson, 7 Watts, 547; Teeter v. Williams, 3 B. Mon. 562; Abbey v. Deyo, 43 N. Y. 343; s. c. 44 Barb. 374.

has the right to enter into a contract to labor for another in consideration of the support and maintenance of himself and family.[1] If an attachment is laid in the hands of his employer, after a contract has been partially performed, he may refuse to complete it, and a new arrangement may be made for the purpose of protecting his subsequent earnings from the effect of such attachment.[2] He is not permitted, however, to make an assignment of his future earnings with the intent to delay, hinder or defraud his creditors.[3]

NOT APPLY LABOR TO ACCUMULATION OF PROPERTY.—Although the law will not compel a debtor to labor and earn money to pay his debts, yet there is a strong moral obligation resting upon him to use the strength, skill and talents with which he is endowed for that purpose, and this obligation is one which the law to a certain extent recognizes and enforces. He has an election to labor or not as he may please with which the law will not interfere. He is also countenanced by the law in the proper discharge of his duty to provide a maintenance and support for himself and his family. But beyond the necessary wants of himself and his family, there is a limit which the law does not allow him to transcend. He is not permitted to treasure up a fund accruing from his labor or vocation whatever it may be, and claim that it shall be protected for the benefit of himself or his family, against the demands of creditors.[4] Every agreement or contrivance entered into with a view to deprive his creditors of his future

---

[1] Leslie v. Joyner, 2 Head. 514; Tripp v. Childs, 14 Barb. 85; Holdship v. Patterson, 7 Watts, 547.

[2] Teeter v. Williams, 3 B. Mon. 562.

[3] Gragg v. Martin, 12 Allen, 498.

[4] Hamilton v. Zimmerman, 5 Sneed. 39.

earnings, and enable him to retain and use them for his own benefit and advantage, or to make a permanent provision for his family, is fraudulent and void. Although his creditors can not compel him to labor for the purpose of satisfying their demands, yet they have a just claim in law upon the fruits of his labor performed.[1]

BUSINESS IN WIFE'S NAME.—The law does not permit him to carry on a business in the name of his wife, so as to invest the proceeds of his skill and labor in her name.[2] If she has a separate estate she may employ him and compensate him for his services.[3] Such employment however must be in good faith, and not merely colorable.[4] If the character of an agent is assumed in an improper case, the law disregards it. An arrangement by which the husband acts as his wife's agent without any compensation, or for a compensation that is insufficient is in effect, an attempt to make a voluntary conveyance of the products of his skill and labor in her favor, and is void as against his creditors. She is entitled to her money with interest, and the balance will be appropriated to the payment of his debts.[5]

---

[1] Tripp v. Childs, 14 Barb. 85; Patterson v. Campbell, 9 Ala. 933; Waddingham v. Loker, 44 Mo. 132; vide Isham v. Schaffer, 60 Barb. 817.

[2] National Bank v. Sprague, 5 C. E. Green, 13; Quidort v. Pergeaux, 3 C. E. Green, 472; Keeney v. Good, 21 Penn. 349; Pauley v. Vogel, 42 Mo. 291.

[3] Knapp v. Smith, 27 N. Y. 277; Voorhis v. Bonesteel, 7 Blatch. 495; Gage v. Dauchy, 34 N. Y. 293; Feller v. Alden, 23 Wis. 301; Savage v. O'Neil, 43 N. Y. 298; Buckley v. Wells, 33 N. Y. 518; Abbey v. Deyo, 43 N. Y. 343.

[4] Kapp v. Smith, 27 N. Y. 277; Gage v. Dauchy, 34 N. Y. 293; Savage v. O'Neil, 43 N. Y. 298.

[5] Glidden v. Taylor, 16 Ohio St. R. 509; Feller v. Alden, 23 Wis. 301; Shackleford v. Collier, 6 Bush. 149; vide Ashurst v. Given, 5 W. & S. 323.

WIFE'S EARNINGS.—At common law, a husband is entitled to all the property which the wife acquires by her skill or labor during coverture. His right to her services and her earnings is absolute.[1] A transfer in consideration of services already performed or a renunciation of her future earnings stands on the same grounds as a voluntary conveyance.[2]

CHILD'S EARNINGS.—A parent by law is entitled to the earnings of his minor child. This right arises out of his obligation to support and educate the child, and this responsibility is one from which he can not absolve himself. As his power over the child's earnings arises from his duty to support and educate the child, it is commensurate with it. As long as the responsibility continues, the power over the child continues also. A promise by the parent to compensate the child for his services is therefore purely voluntary, and its validity depends upon the principles which regulate voluntary conveyances.[3] If the child works for another, the proceeds belong to the parent, and are not a valuable consideration for a transfer from the parent to the child.[4]

EMANCIPATION OF CHILD.—As the right of the parent, however, arises out of his obligation to support and educate the child, such earnings are subject in the

---

[1] Skillman v. Skillman, 2 Bearley, 403; Belford v. Crane, 1 C. E. Green, 265 ; Cramer v. Reford, 2 C. E. Green, 367 ; Shackelford v. Collier, 6 Bush. 149; Cropsey v. McKinney, 30 Barb. 47; Beach v. Baldwin, 14 Mo. 597 ; Pinkston v. McLemore, 31 Ala. 308.

[2] Pinkston v. McLemore, 31 Ala. 308; McLemore v. Knuckolls, 37 Ala. 662 ; Hinman v. Parkis, 33 Conn. 188; Ewing v. Gray, 12 Ind. 64.

[3] Swartz v. Hazlett, 8 Cal. 118 ; Brown v. McDonald, 1 Hill Ch. 297 ; Dick v. Grissom, 1 Freem. Ch. Miss. 428; Danley v. Rector, 10 Ark. 211.

[4] Winchester v. Reid, 8 Jones, (N. C.) 377; Worth v. York, 13 Ired. 206; U. S. v. Mertz, 2 Watts, 406.

first instance to a charge for that purpose, and no creditor has a right to have them applied to the payment
of his debt to the exclusion of a proper education and
maintenance.[1] If therefore the father emancipates the
child and allows him to provide for his own support and
education by his own labor, he does not withdraw from
his creditors any property or fund to which they are
legally or justly entitled for the payment of their demands.[2] It must, however, distinctly appear that there
has been a mutual abandonment of the rights and duties
of parent and child, and a relinquishment of all property in the child's earnings or they can not be protected
from the parent's creditors.[3] Marriage is of itself a
legal emancipation and entitles the child to the proceeds
of his labor independent of any act of emancipation on
the part of the parent, and if the parent then contracts
to pay him for his services, he is bound to do so and
creditors can not complain.[4]

CHARACTER OF CONVEYANCE.—The withering influence of the statute extends to all feofments, gifts, grants,
alienations, bargains, and conveyances, and all bonds,
suits, judgments, and executions, and the principles of
the common law will embrace every device not enumerated in the statute. Every description of contract, and
every transfer or conveyance of property, by what means
soever it is done, is vitiated by fraud. Whether the contract is oral or in writing; whether executed by the
parties with all the solemnities of deeds by seal[5] and
acknowledgment; whether in the form of the judgment

---

[1] Lord v. Poor, 23 Me. 569; Leslie v. Joyner, 2 Head, 514.
[2] Lord v. Poor, 23 Me. 569; Manchester v. Smith, 12 Pick. 113; Jenison v. Graves, 2 Blackf. 440; U. S. v. Mertz, 2 Watts, 406.
[3] U. S. v. Mertz, 2 Watts, 406.
[4] Dick v. Grissom, 1 Freem. Ch. (Miss.) 428.
[5] Garretson v. Kane, 3 Dutch. 208.

18

of a court, stamped with judicial sanction,[1] or carried out by the device of a corporation organized with all the forms and requirements demanded by any statute, if it is contaminated with fraud, the law declares it to be a nullity. Deeds, obligations, contracts, judgments, and even corporate bodies may be the instruments through which parties may obtain the most unrighteous advantages. All such devices and instruments have been resorted to for the purpose of covering up fraud, but whenever the law is invoked all such instruments are declared nullities. They are a perfect dead letter. The law looks upon them as if they had never been executed. They can never be justified or sanctified by any new shape or course, by forms or recitals, by cove-nants or sanctions, which the ingenuity or skill or genius of the rogue may devise.[2] The transfer must, however, be capable in point of law of executing or aiding in the execution of an illegal purpose.[3]

MODE IMMATERIAL.—If a tenant commits a forfeiture to the end that the reversioner may enter for the pur-pose of defrauding his creditors, it is a fraudulent con-veyance.[4] Where a judgment is given against a party and he suffers himself to be outlawed in felony with the intent to defraud his creditors and afterwards pur-chases a pardon and has restitution, his goods are still liable to execution on account of the fraud.[5] A fraudu-lent cancellation of an indebtedness will not discharge the debt.[6] A note for a debt taken in the name of

---

[1] Wilhelmi v. Leonard, 13 Iowa, 330 ; Hackett v. Manlove, 14 Cal. 85.

[2] Booth v. Bunce, 33 N. Y. 139; s. c. 24 N. Y. 592 ; Curtis v. Leavitt, 15 N. Y. 9.

[3] Heydock v. Stanhope, 1 Curt. 471.   [4] Anon Vent. 257.

[5] Beverly's Case, 2 Dyer, 245, c.; note Verney's Case, 2 Dyer, 245 c.

[6] Martin v. Root, 17 Mass. 222 ; Everett v. Read, 3 N. H. 55 ; McGay v. Keilback, 14 Abb. Pr. 142 ; Wise v. Tripp, 13 Me. 9 ; Wright v. Pe-trie, 1 S. & M. Ch. 282.

another is, as far as creditors are concerned, an assignment of the debt.[1]   A liability, however, which is still
in fieri and a mere contingent obligation may be cancelled, rescinded, or discharged.[2]   A remission of a
portion of rent that is due in an unfavorable year in
good faith is merely yielding up that which an enlarged
sense of justice requires shall not be exacted.[3]   A tenant in tail may disentail the property and re-settle it,
leaving the same estate to himself as he had before,
and the deed will not be fraudulent, for the creditors
have the same remedies, as far as he is concerned, which
they had before, namely, the power of going against
his life estate.[4]

CONTRACTS RELATING TO LAND.—A written contract
for the purchase of land upon which nothing has been
paid may be cancelled, and the property conveyed by
the owner to another for a valuable consideration.[5]
An oral contract in which there has been a part payment does not vest any interest in the debtor, which
is liable to an execution at law, and if he surrenders
or transfers his bargain, the property will not be liable.[6]
But if a surrender is fraudulently made, the creditors
may recover the money so paid.[7]   An assignment of a
mortgage in consideration of money paid by the debtor,
if made in fraud, is equivalent to a payment and cancellation of it.[8]

---

[1] Reppy v. Reppy, 46 Mo. 571; Freeman v. Burnham, 36 Conn. 469;
Camp v. Scott, 14 Vt. 387 ; Marsh v. Davis, 24 Vt. 363.

[2] McGay v. Keilback, 14 Abb. Pr. 142.

[3] Andrews v. Jones, 10 Ala. 400.

[4] Clements v. Eccles, 11 Ir. Eq. 229.

[5] Raffensberger v. Cullison, 28 Penn. 426.

[6] Miller v. Specht, 11 Penn. 449 ; Jackson v. Scott, 18 Johns. 94;
Botts v. Cozine, Hoff. 79 ; *vide* Bean v. Brackett, 34 N. H. 102.

[7] Alexander v. Tams, 13 Ill. 221 ; Botts v. Cozine, Hoff. 79.

[8] Stephens v. Sinclair, 1 Hill. 143.

FRAUDULENT JUDGMENT.—The forms of the law do not constitute a protection against fraud, or give validity to a transfer when good faith is absent. The statute was designed to leave property open to the free course of the law and to keep impediments out of the way of creditors. It was foreseen that a debtor knowing that the cause of a creditor and the means afforded him for the recovery of his debt are held sacred, might, and probably would, endeavor to take protection under it and surround himself with the formalities of the law and the rights of the creditor. To guard against this and to prevent the law from becoming the shield of fraud, the statute was extended to every mode of transfer which is not *bona fide*.[1] A fraudulent judgment, execution, and sale thereunder pass no title to the fraudulent vendee.[2] If a judgment or execution is kept on foot, after it has been satisfied, for fraudulent purposes, it comes within the statute as effectually as if originally contrived to delay, hinder or defraud creditors.[3]

FRAUDULENT SALES UNDER EXECUTIONS.—A valid judgment•and execution may be so used as to render a sale thereunder fraudulent.[4] A sale so conducted by fraud or improper contrivances as to enable a purchaser to buy more property than is necessary for the satisfaction of an execution is fraudulent,[5] for an execu-

---

[1] Yoder v. Standiford, 7 Mon. 478.

[2] Burnell v. Johnson, 9 Johns. 243; Christopherson v. Burton, 3 Exch. 160 ; s. c. 18 L. J. Exch. 60 ; Boardman v. Keeler, 1 Aik. 158; Metropolitan Bank v. Durant, 7 C. E. Green, 35.

[3] Gibbs v. Neely, 7 Watts, 305; Serfoss v. Fisher, 10 Penn. 184 ; Floyd v. Goodwin, 8 Yerg. 484.

[4] Crary v. Sprague, 12 Wend. 41; Yoder v. Standiford, 7 Mon. 478 ; Ward v. Lamberth, 31 Geo. 150.

[5] Kilby v. Haggin, 3 J. J. Marsh. 208.

tion can not be so used as to injure others and cover the title to a larger amount of property than is necessary to satisfy it.[1] The fraudulent vendee gains no title to the property, although an innocent creditor may by the sale obtain a good title to the money. It is a good sale, as to the creditor, to entitle him to receive the money, and yet no sale as to the fraudulent vendee to enable him to shelter the land from pursuit.[2] A sale under a mortgage so conducted as to enable a purchaser to buy the property at a price far below its value, as a mode by which, under the form of a public sale, the property may become vested in him without an adequate valuable consideration upon some secret confidence for the mortgagor is also fraudulent and void.[3]

PURCHASE UNDER EXECUTION WITH DEBTOR'S MONEY. —The intervention of the process of the law at the instance of a creditor who is innocent of the guilty scheme, and ignorant that he is made subservient to its execution, cannot protect the intent with which other parties act from investigation or confirm those parts of the transaction by which they would acquire or reserve valuable interests. The innocence of the judgment creditor cannot purge their bad faith. If the debtor advances the purchase-money at a sale under an execution, there is as against creditors no sale. There is no distinction between a conveyance directly from the

---

[1] Morris v. Allen, 10 Ired. 203 ; Brodie v. Seagrave, Taylor, 144 ; Hammock v. McBride, 6 Geo. 178; Stephens v. Barnett, 7 Dana, 257 ; Pennington v. Chandler, 5 Harring. 394; White v. Trotter, 14 S. & M. 30; Stovall v. Farmers' Bank, 8 S. & M. 305 ; Duncan v. Forsyth, 3 Dana, 229; Forrest v. Camp, 16 Ala. 642 ; Dick v. Cooper, 24 Penn. 217.

[2] Foulk v. M'Farlane, 1 W. & S. 297.

[3] Hawkins v. Alston, 4 Ired. Eq. 137 ; Overton v. Morris, 3 Port. 249 ; Beeler v. Bullett, 3 A. K. Marsh. 280; Garland v. Rives, 4 Rand. 282 ; Ansley v. Carlos, 9 Ala. 973; s. c. 8 Ala. 900 ; Roach v. Deering, 9 S. & M. 316; Bickley v. Norris, 2 Brev. 252; Compton v. Perry, 23 Tex. 414.

debtor and one from the sheriff. In reality the conveyance is from the debtor through the sheriff. It gives to the dealing the semblance of fairness but nothing more than the semblance. It does not make it fair though it increases the difficulty of detecting its unfairness, but when detected, that avoids this as well as other transfers however solemn. It is substantially as much a sale *inter partes* as if there were no intervention of the sheriff.[1] If the money is not paid at the time but is furnished afterwards, the same principle applies, as, for instance, if the plaintiff in the execution is the purchaser at the sale and gives no credit for the proceeds, but afterwards receives full satisfaction of his debt in another way.[2] Although the purchaser may advance a portion of the money, yet if he takes a deed with the intent to claim the estate absolutely as against other creditors, his own advances cannot rescue it from the legal consequences of the corrupt combination.[3] A redemption of land sold under an execution by virtue of a transfer of the right to redeem, and a deed in the name of the grantee leaves the title in the debtor if it is made fraudulently with his money.[4]

---

[1] Morris v. Allen, 10 Ired. 203; Abney v. Kingsland, 10 Ala. 355; Payne v. Craft, 7 W. & S. 458; Hays v. Heidelberg, 9 Penn. 203; Griffin v. Wardlaw, 1 Harper, 481; Dobson v. Erwin, 1 Dev. & Bat. 569; Miller v. Fraley, 21 Ark. 22; Rankin v. Arndt, 44 Barb. 251; Stovall v. Farmers' Bank, 8 S. & M. 305; Duncan v. Forsyth, 3 Dana, 229; Gutzwiller v. Lackman, 23 Mo. 168; Brown v. M'Donald, 1 Hill Ch. 297; Cumming v. Fryer, Dudley, 182; Ewing v. Gray, 12 Ind. 64; Marriott v. Givens, 8 Ala. 694; McBride v. Thompson, 8 Ala. 650.

[2] Schott v. Chancellor, 20 Penn. 195; s. c. 23 Penn. 68.

[3] Dobson v. Erwin, 1 Dev. & Bat. 569; Burke v. Murphy, 27 Miss. 167; Ewing v. Gray, 12 Ind. 64.

[4] Legro v. Lord, 10 Me. 161.

CHAPTER XI.

VOLUNTARY CONVEYANCES.

DEFINITION OF VOLUNTARY CONVEYANCE—A voluntary conveyance is a conveyance without any valuable consideration. The adequacy of the consideration does not enter into the question. The character of purchase or voluntary is determined by the fact whether anything valuable passes between the debtor and the grantee as a consideration for the transfer. If there is a valuable consideration, no matter how trivial or inadequate, the conveyance is not voluntary.[1] The doctrine of voluntary conveyances, moreover, applies only to transfers that are made with actual good faith. If there is an actual intent to hinder, delay, or defraud creditors, on the part of the grantor, then the law relating to fraudulent conveyances[2] as distinguished from mere voluntary conveyances is applicable.

INTENT OF DONOR ALONE.—It follows from the definition of a voluntary conveyance that the question in regard to its validity or invalidity depends upon the intent of the party making it, and not on the motive with which it is received. The proviso at the end of the statute only extends to transfers made upon a good consideration, and it has long been settled that the only consideration which is good within the mean-

---

[1] Jackson v. Peek, 4 Wend. 300; Shontz v. Brown, 27 Penn. 123; Washband v. Washband, 27 Conn. 424; Seward v. Jackson, 8 Cow. 406; Dygert v. Remerschnider, 32 N. Y. 629; s. c. 39 Barb. 417.

[2] Gruber v. Boyles, 1 Brev. 266.

ing of the statute is a valuable consideration.[1]   It is the innocent purchaser and not the innocent donee that is protected. The only question, therefore, is *quo animo* the gift or grant is made. It is the motive of the giver and not the knowledge of the acceptor that is to deter. mine the validity of the transfer.[2] If any evidence of the grantee's participation in the fraudulent intent of the grantor were necessary, the mere acceptance of the transfer would be sufficient, for the law would presume such participation from this fact alone.[3] A donee, who sets up a voluntary conveyance when it would, if estab- lished, defeat creditors, participates in and carries out the intent of the donor.

THERE MUST BE A FRAUDULENT INTENT.—The word " voluntary" is not to be found in the statute, and it is perfectly clear from the preamble that its provisions were pointed not at voluntary conveyances as such, but against transfers concocted in fraud, and devised by a debtor for the purpose of delaying and defrauding his creditors.[4] It comprehends such conveyances as are made of malice, fraud, covin, collusion, or guile, with

---

[1] Twyne's Case, 3 Co. 80 ;   Taylor v. Jones, 2 Atk. 600 ;   Thomson v. Dougherty, 12 S. & R. 448.

[2] Partridge v. Gopp, 1 Eden, 163 ; s. c. 1 Ambl. 596 ; Thomson v. Dougherty, 12 S. & R. 448 ; Mohawk Bank v. Atwater, 2 Paige, 54; Van Wyck v. Seward, 18 Wend. 375 ; Swartz v. Hazlett, 8 Cal. 118 ; Trimble v. Ratcliffe, 9 B. Mon. 511 ; Wood v. Hunt, 38 Barb. 302 ; Holmes v. Clark, 48 Barb. 237 ; Bennett v. McGuire, 58 Barb. 625 ;   Wise v. Moore, 31 Geo. 148 ;   Newman v. Cordell, 43 Barb. 448 ;   M'Meekins v. Edmonds, 1 Hill Ch. 288 ; Clark v. Chamberlain, 13 Allen, 257 ; Hicks v. Stone, 13 Minn. 434 ; Peck v. Carmichael, 9 Yerg. 325 ; Gamble v. Johnson, 9 Mo. 605.

[3] Belt v. Raguet, 27 Tex. 471.

[4] Jones v. Boulter, 1 Cox, 288 ; Worthington v. Shipley, 5 Gill, 449 ; Holloway v. Millard, 1 Madd. 414 ; Doe v. Routledge, Cowp. 705 ; Cado- gan v. Kennett, Cowp. 432 ; Gale v. Williamson, 8 M. & W. 405 ; O'Con- nor v. Bernard, 2 Jo. 654 ; Hamilton v. Greenwood, 1 Bay, 173 ; Thomson v. Dougherty, 12 S. & R. 448 ; Clayton v. Brown, 17 Geo. 217.

intent or purpose to delay, hinder, or defraud creditors. This intent or purpose constitutes the contaminating principle which will infect and vitiate the gift or conveyance and is required to bring a case within the act. The inquiry in case of a voluntary conveyance must, therefore, be in regard to the intent of the donor. If there is no intent on his part to delay, hinder, or defraud creditors, the conveyance is not within the statute; if, on the other hand, there is such an intent in the making of the transfer, then it is void as against creditors. In other words it is the intent and purpose with which the grantor acts, that characterizes the conveyance and renders it fraudulent under the statute. It is not conveyances, when a man owes, that are prohibited, but conveyances with the intent or purpose to delay, hinder, or defraud creditors.[1] The statute itself does not say that mere indebtedness shall be conclusive evidence or even any evidence of the intent to defraud. The statute is simply silent, both as to the kind of facts which shall be admissible on this question, and as to the degree of weight to which any facts which may be admissible shall be entitled.[2]

MODE OF ESTABLISHING FRAUDULENT INTENT.—It is not necessary, however, to prove an actual intent to delay, hinder, or defraud creditors.[3] Intent is an emotion or operation of the mind, and can usually be shown only by acts or declarations.[4] The motives which

---

[1] Lyne v. Bank, 5 J. J. Marsh. 545; Clayton v. Brown, 17 Geo. 217; Taylor v. Eubanks, 3 A. K. Marsh. 239; Mateer v. Hissim, 3 Penn. 160; Hunters v. Waite, 3 Gratt. 26; Weed v. Davis, 25 Geo. 684.

[2] Weed v. Davis, 25 Geo. 684.

[3] Carlisle v. Rich, 8 N. H. 44; Freeman v. Pope, 5 L. R. Ch. 538; Norton v. Norton, 5 Cush. 524; Potter v. McDowell, 31 Mo. 62; Jenkyn v. Vaughan, 3 Drew. 419; s. c. 25 L. J. (Ch.) 338; Smith v. Cherrill, 4 L. R. Eq. 390.

[4] Babcock v. Eckler, 24 N. Y. 623.

actuate men in the affairs of life can in general be ascertained only by an examination of their acts and all the concomitant circumstances, and a deduction of the motive from them in accordance with those principles which are shown by observation and experience to rule human conduct.[1] The intent to defraud need not, therefore, be made out by any direct proof of that particular fact. In this as well as in other cases where the intention with which an act is done is to be ascertained, it may be and usually is inferred or presumed from the knowledge of other facts. Men do not often declare their purpose when they are about to do an act injurious to others, and there is no means of arriving at a knowledge of the internal resolve or determination of the actor, but by reasoning or drawing inferences from his external conduct. To this kind of presumption resort is commonly had, not only in civil but in criminal cases. It is not a mere rule of law or of evidence in courts of justice, but all men are in the habit of acting upon this kind of presumption.[2]

INTENT A CONCLUSION OF LAW.—Every man is held to know the law and the facts regarding his own affairs.[3] The law also presumes that every man intends the necessary consequences of his act, and if the act necessarily delay, hinders, or defrauds his creditors, then the law presumes that it is done with a fraudulent intent.[4]

---

[1] Filley v. Register, 4 Minn. 391.

[2] Van Wyck v. Seward, 18 Wend. 375.

[3] Swartz v. Hazlett, 8 Cal. 118; Christy v. Courtenay, 13 Beav. 96; Hunters v. Waite, 3 Gratt. 26.

[4] Potter v. McDowell, 31 Mo. 62; O'Connor v. Bernard, 2 Jo. 654; Freeman v. Pope, 5 L. R. Ch. 538; Norton v. Norton, 5 Cush. 524; Smith v. Cherrill, 4 L. R. Eq. 390; French v. French, 6 D. M. & G. 95; s. c. 25 L. J. (Ch.) 612; Strong v. Strong, 18 Beav. 408; Freeman v. Burnham, 36 Conn. 469; Corlett v. Radcliffe, 14 Moore, P. C. 121; Reese River Mining Co. v. Atwell, 7 L. R. Eq. 347; Van Wyck v. Seward, 18 Wend. 375; Thompson v. Webster, 7 Jur. (N. S.) 531.

The intent is to be assumed from the act.[1] The circumstances of the act, or rather the act itself, is conclusive
evidence of fraud, for no man is permitted to say that
he does not intend the necessary consequences of his
own voluntary act.[2]

No INQUIRY INTO SECRET MOTIVES.—The law will not
speculate about what is actually passing in the donor's
mind,[3] for the act need not be immoral or corrupt. The
law does not concern itself about the private or secret
motives which may influence the debtor. It does not
deal with his conscience. He may make a conveyance
with the most upright intentions, really believing that
he has a right to do so, and that it is his right and
duty to do it, and yet, if the transfer is voluntary and hinders, delays, or defrauds his creditors, it is fraudulent.[4]
His actual motives may be considerations of generosity and kindness,[5] or an insufficient consideration of
the amount of his indebtedness or the extent of his
assets,[6] or ignorance, or mistake, or misconception.[7]
Apologies and excuses may be found to absolve him
from moral turpitude, but to these the law cannot
listen. It is vain to speculate upon his motives, or
adduce evidence of a fair purpose. The presumption
in such a case is conclusive, and against it all other
evidence is unavailing.[8] The debtor may have some

---

[1] Freeman v. Pope, 5 L. R. Ch. 538.

[2] Babcock v. Eckler, 24 N. Y. 623.

[3] Freeman v. Pope, 5 L. R. Ch. 538.

[4] Potter v. McDowell, 31 Mo. 62.

[5] Freeman v. Pope, 5 L. R. Ch. 538; Reese River Mining Co. v. Atwell,
7 L. R. Eq. 347.

[6] Norton v. Norton, 5 Cush. 524; Black v. Sanders, 1 Jones (N. C.), 67;
Van Wyck v. Seward, 18 Wend. 375.

[7] Hunters v. Waite, 3 Gratt. 26.

[8] Hunters v. Waite, 3 Gratt. 26.

other purpose in view, but the intent to defraud is a part and parcel of his act.[1]

PRINCIPLES OF THE LAW RELATING TO VOLUNTARY CONVEYANCES.—It is upon these principles that the law relating to voluntary conveyances rests. In the construction of the statute, they are deemed within its operation when they necessarily tend to defeat the just rights of creditors, even though they are made *bona fide* and with the intention of conferring a gratuitous benefit upon some meritorious object. The law stamps a man's generosity with the name of fraud when it prevents him from acting fairly towards his creditors, and presumes fraud if he disables himself from paying his debts. In such cases, the presumption of fraud arises and may exist without the imputation of moral turpitude.[2] The principle is that persons must be just be fore they can be generous, and that debts must be paid before gifts can be made.[3] This maxim finds as ready a response in the breast of the moralist as in that of the enlightened jurist, for it is based upon and has its sanction in the purest morality, the fountain of all law.[4]

VOLUNTARY CONVEYANCE IS A BADGE OF FRAUD. — A voluntary conveyance by a person who is indebted, is a well-recognized badge of fraud,[5] for its natural and probable tendency is to delay, hinder and defraud credit-

---

[1] Van Wyck v. Seward, 18 Wend. 375.

[2] O'Connor v. Bernard, 2 Jo. 654.

[3] Partridge v. Gopp, 1 Eden, 163; s. c. 1 Ambl. 596; Freeman v. Pope, 5 L. R. Ch. 538.

[4] Craig v. Gamble, 5 Fla. 430.

[5] Goodson v. Jones, Styles, 446; Doe v. Routledge, Cowp. 705; Hoye v. Penn, 1 Bland, 28; Jones v. Boulter, 1 Cox, 288; Woodson v. Pool, 19 Mo. 340; Russell v. Hammond, 1 Atk. 14; George v. Milbanke, 9 Ves. 189.

ors. The end in view must be to make the thing con·
veyed cease to be the ·property of him who conveys,
and become the property of him to whom it is conveyed, and consequently to withdraw it from the
creditors. There cannot be a conveyance, even one for
value, into which this intent does not enter. Hence,
the statute, after enacting that all conveyances made
with the intent to delay, hinder or defraud creditors,
shall be void, by the proviso excepts from the opera·
tion of that enactment conveyances made *bona fide* and
upon good, that is, valuable consideration. In such
case the price is substituted for the thing conveyed,
and the intent to withdraw the particular property,
although actually existing, is not *prima facie* injurious
to creditors. But a voluntary conveyance must be
founded upon a design to exempt the estate from the
claims of creditors, for the act of making the conveyance
can arise from no other intent, and inasmuch as no
other fund replaces the property so intended to be
exempted, that intent is injurious to the unsatisfied
creditors, and may amount to fraud within the statute.
To set up the transfer against creditors, if it is effectual,
may hinder and defeat them. To make title under it and
to set it up against all the world must be the very pur·
pose of the transfer. If the title of the donee would defeat
creditors, the intention of making the transfer must be to
hinder, delay and defraud them.[1] A voluntary con·
veyance is therefore considered as *prima facie* evidence
of an intent to delay, hinder or defraud creditors.[2]

---

[1] O'Daniel v. Crawford, 4 Dev. 197.

[2] Worthington v. Shipley, 5 Gill, 449; Holloway v. Millard, 1 Madd.
414; Gale v. Williamson, 8 M. & W. 405; Thompson v. Webster, 7 Jur.
(N. S.) 531; s. c. 4 D. & J. 600; s. c. 4 Drew 628; Jackson v. Tim-
merman, 7 Wend. 436; Jackson v. Town, 4 Cow. 599; Thompson v. Hammond, 1 Edw. Ch. 497; Lerow v. Wilmarth, 9 Allen, 382; Bortrand v.

. BURDEN OF PROOF.—The burden is thrown upon the donee to establish the circumstances which will repel the presumption of a fraudulent intent. The transfer stands condemned as fraudulent unless the facts which may give it validity are proved by him.[1] This presumption is not, however, conclusive, but may be met and rebutted by proof that the donor was, at the time of the conveyance, in prosperous circumstances and possessed of ample means to discharge all his pecuniary obligations.[2] If no evidence is given to show that the

---

Elder, 23 Ark. 494; Winchester v. Charter, 12 Allen, 606; s. c. 97 Mass. 140; s. c. 102 Mass. 272; Doyle v. Sleeper, 1 Dana, 531; Taylor v. Eubanks, 3 A. K. Marsh. 239; Wilson v. Buchanan, 7 Gratt. 334.

[1] Baxter v. Sewell, 3 Md. 334; s. c. 2 Md. Ch. 447; Spindler v. Atkinson, 3 Md. 409; s. c. 1 Md. Ch. 507; Ellinger v. Crowl, 17 Md. 361; Hunters v. Waite, 3 Gratt. 26; Crossley v. Elworthy, L. R. 12 Eq. 158; Wilson v. Buchanan, 7 Gratt. 334; Woolston's Appeal, 51 Penn. 452; Crumbaugh v. Kugler, 2 Ohio St. R. 373; Reynolds v. Lansford, 16 Tex. 286; Raymond v. Cook, 31 Tex. 373.

[2] Hinde's Lessee v. Longworth, 11 Wheat. 199; Salmon v. Bennett, 1 Ct. 525; Jacks v. Tunno, 3 Dessau. 1; Bennett v. Bedford Bank, 11 Mass. 421; Parker v. Proctor, 9 Mass. 390; Hamilton v. Greenwood, 1 Bay. 173; Seward v. Jackson, 8 Cow. 406; s. c. 5 Cow. 67; Teasdale v. Reaborne, 2 Bay. 546; Taylor v. Heriot, 4 Dessau. 227; Taylor v. Eubanks, 3 A. K. Marsh. 239; Hudnal v. Wilder, 4 McCord, 294; s. c. 1 McCord, 227; Jackson v. Post, 15 Wend. 588; Jackson v. Town, 4 Cow. 599; Planck v. Schermerhorn, 3 Barb. Ch. 644; Babcock v. Eckler, 24 N. Y. 623; Holmes v. Clark, 48 Barb. 237; Fulton v. Fulton, 48 Barb. 581; Mayberry v. Neely, 5 Hump. 337; Norton v. Norton, 5 Cush. 524; Clayton v. Brown, 17 Geo. 217; Bird v. Bolduc, 1 Mo. 701; Cutter v. Griswold, Walk. Ch. 437; Brackett v. Waite, 4 Vt. 389; Chambers v. Spencer, 5 Watts, 404; Brice v. Myers, 5 Ohio, 121; Hunters v. Waite, 3 Gratt. 26; Filley v. Register, 4 Minn. 391; Pomeroy v. Bailey, 43 N. H. 118; Bay v. Cook, 31 Ill. 336; Arnett v. Wanett, 6 Ired. 41; Jones v. Young, 1 Dev. & Bat. 352; Dodd v. McCraw, 3 Eng. 83; Hall v. Edrington, 8 B. Mon. 47; Lane v. Kingsberry, 11 Mo. 402; Trimble v. Ratcliff, 9 B. Mon. 511; Young v. White, 25 Miss. 146; Swartz v. Haslett, 8 Cal. 118; Weed v. Davis, 25 Geo. 684; Parrish v. Murphree, 13 How. 92; Wilson v. Buchanan, 7 Gratt. 334; Picquet v. Swan, 4 Mason, 443; Grimes v. Russell, 45 Mo. 431; Gridley v. Watson, 53 Ill. 186; Pike v. Miles, 23 Wis. 164; Place v. Rhem, 7 Bush, 585; Frank v. Kessler, 30 Ind. 8; Worthington v. Shipley, 5 Gill. 449;

donor had ample means to meet his liabilities, then the
transfer must be deemed void as against creditors.[1]

VOLUNTARY CONVEYANCE BY ONE FREE FROM DEBT.
—By virtue of the absolute dominion which a man has
over his own property, he may make any disposition of
it which does not interfere with the existing rights of
others, and such disposition, if it is fair and real, will be
valid.   To allow a man less than this would be to deny
him the power of disposing of his own according to his
good will and pleasure.[2]   There is no more objection to
a man's giving away his property, if he is able to do it,
than there is to his selling it.[3]   If a man is entirely free
from debt, he may therefore make a voluntary conveyance in good faith.[4]   He may, if he pleases, give away

---

Brown v. Austin, 35 Barb. 341; s. c. 22 How. Pr. 394; Peck v. Brum-
magim, 31 Cal. 440; Leavitt v. Leavitt, 47 N. H. 329; Duhme v. Young,
3 Bush. 343; King v. Thompson, 9 Pet. 204; Dick v. Hamilton, Deady,
322; Wilder v. Brooks, 10 Minn. 50; Hinman v. Parkis, 33 Conn.
188; Greenfield's Estate, 14 Penn. 489; Woolston's Appeal, 51 Penn. 452;
Townsend v. Maynard, 45 Penn. 198; Moritz v. Hoffman, 35 Ill. 553;
Carson v. Foley, 1 Iowa, 52; Whittier v. Prescott, 48 Me. 367; Hopkirk
v. Randolph, 2 Brock. 132; Howard v. Williams, 1 Bailey, 575; Skarf v.
Soulby, 1 H. & Tw. 426; s. c. 1 Me & G. 364; s. c. 16 Sim. 344; s. c. 19
L. J. (Ch.) 30; Bucklin v. Bucklin, 1 Keyes, 141; Borst v. Spelman, 4
N. Y. 284; Ellinger v. Crowl, 17 Md. 361.

[1] Ellinger v. Crowl, 17 Md. 361.

[2] Sexton v. Wheaton, 8 Wheat. 229; Thompson v. Dougherty, 12 S. &
R. 448.

[3] Creed v. Lancaster Bank, 1 Ohio St. R. 1.

[4] Sexton v. Wheaton, 8 Wheat. 229; Goodson v. Jones, Styles, 446;
Middlecome v. Marlow, 2 Atk. 519; Faringer v. Ramsay, 4 Md. Ch. 33;
Townsend v. Windham, 2 Ves. 1; Russell v. Hammond, 1 Atk. 14; Battersbee v. Farrington, 1 Swanst. 106; Bonny v. Griffith, 1 Hayes, 115; Benton
v. Jones, 8 Conn. 186; Stevens v. Olive, 2 Bro. C. C. 90; Glaister v.
Hewer, 8 Ves. 196; Sweeney v. Damron, 47 Ill. 450; Winebrinner v.
Weisiger, 3 Mon. 32; Baker v. Welch, 4 Mo. 484; Charlton v. Gardner,
11 Leigh, 281; Haskell v. Bakewell, 10 B. Mon. 106; Sagitary v. Hide, 2
Vern. 44; Walker v. Burrows, 1 Atk. 93; Holmes v. Penney, 3 K. & G.
90; Roberts v. Gibson, 6 H. & J. 116; Phillips v. Wooster, 36 N. Y. 412;
s. c. 3 Abb. Pr. (N. S.) 475.

all his property, if he does it fairly and openly. The magnitude of the estate conveyed may awaken suspicion, and strengthen other circumstances if they exist, but taken alone it can not be considered as proof of fraud. A man who makes such a conveyance necessarily impairs his credit, and, if openly done, warns those with whom he deals not to trust him too far.[1]

VOLUNTARY CONVEYANCE BY ONE IN DEBT.—It is only where a man is indebted that his power of voluntary alienation is restricted, for no man has such an absolute power over his own property as that he can alienate the same, when such alienation directly and necessarily tends to delay, hinder or defraud his creditors, unless it is made on good consideration, and *bona fide*.[2] Where a creditor takes no specific security from his debtor, he trusts him upon the general credit of his property, and a confidence that he will not diminish it to his prejudice.[3] A man is generally trusted, or obtains credit, in proportion to the property he appears to own. When creditors trust him, they look to his possessions as evidence of his ability to pay, and as a fund from which, if other resources of the debtor fail, they are to receive their demands. After credit is obtained, for the debtor to divest himself of property by giving it away, and thereby rendering himself unable to pay his debts, or to perform his contracts, is unjust, and a fraud upon his creditors. It is a violation of the confidence which they reposed in him.[4] It is true that they frequently look

---

[1] Sexton v. Wheaton, 8 Wheat. 229; Martin v. Olliver, 9 Humph. 561; Kid v. Mitchell, 1 N. & M. 334; Stevens v. Olive, 2 Bro. C. C. 90; Dick v. Hamilton, Deady, 322.

[2] Partridge v. Gopp, 1 Eden, 163; s. c. 1 Ambl. 596.

[3] Eppes v. Randolph, 2 Call. 103.

[4] Brice v. Myers, 5 Ohio, 121.

to the debtor's honesty, industry and skill in business,[1] but the law cannot take these into account, for they do not afford any means by which the payment of debts can be enforced.

MERE INDEBTEDNESS.—It is not any and every indebtedness, however, that will amount to a prohibition of the debtor's power to make a gift. When there is no actual intent to defraud, there can be no inference of such an intent from the mere fact of a voluntary conveyance, unless the natural and inevitable consequence of the act is to delay, hinder, or defraud the creditors of the donor. The real and just construction of the statute does not, therefore, warrant the proposition that the existence of any debts at the time of the making of the gift would be such evidence of a fraudulent intention as to induce and oblige a court to set aside a voluntary conveyance, because there is scarcely any man who can avoid being indebted to some amount. He may intend to pay every debt as soon as it is contracted, and constantly use his best endeavors and have ample means to do so, and yet may be frequently, if not always, indebted in some small sum. There may be a withholding of claims contrary to his intention by which he is kept indebted in spite of himself.[2] To say that the mere circumstance of a person's being indebted at the time, without reference to the comparative state of his debts and of his means of paying them, is conclusive evidence of a fraudulent intention with respect to his creditors, would be asserting that which is contrary to every day's experience, and would be giving an operation to the statute not to be warranted upon the

---

[1] Toulmin v. Buchanan, 1 Stew. 67.
[2] Townsend v. Westacott, 2 Beav. 340.

19

most liberal rules of construction in the suppression of fraud.[1] It is accordingly settled that mere indebtedness alone is not sufficient to render a voluntary conveyance void.[2]

---

[1] Taylor v. Eubanks, 3 A. K. Marsh. 239.

[2] Manders v. Manders, 4 Ir. Eq. 434; Skarf v. Soulby, 1 H. & Tw. 426; s. c. 1 Mc. & G. 364; s. c. 16 Sim. 344; s. c. 19 L. J. (Ch.) 30; Martyn v. McNamara, 4 Dr. & War. 411; Wilson v. Howser, 12 Penn. 109; Posten v. Posten, 4 Whart. 27; Izzard v. Izzard, 1 Bailey Ch. 228; Lyne v. Bank, 5 J. J. Marsh. 545; Dietus v. Fuss, 8 Md. 148; Lush v. Wilkinson, 5 Ves. 384; Burkey v. Self, 4 Sneed, 121; Dillard v. Dillard, 3 Humph. 41; Smith v. Littlejohn, 2 Me. C. 362; Thacher v. Phinney, 7 Allen, 146; Brackett v. Waite, 4 Vt. 389; Arnett v. Wanett, 6 Ired. 41; Smith v. Reavis, 7 Ired. 341; Martin v. Evans, 2 Rich. Eq. 368; Dewey v. Long, 25 Vt. 564; Miller v. Pearce, 7 W. & S. 97; Mateer v. Hissim, 3 Penna. 160; Hudnal v. Wilder, 4 McCord, 294; s. c. 1 McCord, 227; Simpson v. Graves, 1 Riley, Ch. 219; Kipp v. Hanna, 1 Bland, 26; *Contra*, Reade v. Livingston, 3 Johns. Ch. 481; Bayard v. Hoffman, 4 Johns. Ch. 450; McLemore v. Knuckolls, 37 Ala. 662; Miller v. Desha, 3 Bush, 212; Stiles v. Lightfoot, 26 Ala. 443; Spencer v. Godwin, 30 Ala. 355; Pinkston v. McLemore, 31 Ala. 308; Lowry v. Fisher, 2 Bush, 70; Davis v. McKinney, 5 Ala. 719; Miller v. Thompson, 3 Port. 196; Cato v. Easley, 2 Stew. 214; Gilmore v. N. A. Land Co., 1 Pet. C. C. 460; Cook v. Johnson, 1 Beasley, 51; Moore v. Spence, 6 Ala. 506; Costillo v. Thompson, 9 Ala. 937; Lockyer v. De Hart, 1 Halst. 450; Houston v. Boyle, 10 Ired. 496; Enders v. Williams, 1 Met. (Ky.) 346; Hansen v. Buckner, 4 Dana. 251; Laurence v. Lippincott, 1 Halst. 473; Mitchell v. Berry, 1 Met. (Ky.) 602; Todd v. Hartley, 2 Met. (Ky.) 206; Bogard v. Gardley, 4 S. & M. 302; Foote v. Cobb, 18 Ala. 585; High v. Nelms, 14 Ala. 350; Gannard v. Eslava, 20 Ala. 732; Swayze v. McCrossin, 13 S. & M. 317; Spencer v. Godwin, 30 Ala. 355; Thomas v. De Graffinreid, 17 Ala. 602; *vide* Johnson v. West, 43 Ala. 689. In Russell v. Hammond, (1 Atk. 14) Lord Hardwicke said, " I have hardly known one case where the person conveying was indebted at the time of the conveyance that has not been deemed fraudulent." and in Townsend v. Windham, (2 Ves. 1) he said, " I know of no case where a man indebted at the time makes a mere voluntary conveyance to a child without consideration and dies indebted, but that it shall be considered as part of his estate for the benefit of his creditors." These remarks have given rise to considerable controversy, but they may be explained by the fact that in his time the main controversy was whether voluntary conveyances were within the statute. By some the doctrine was called artificial. Jones v. Boulter, 1 Cox, 288. The main point was to establish the principle, and his language should be construed with a view

INDEBTEDNESS MUST BE CONSIDERED IN CONNECTION WITH DONOR'S ESTATE.—Indebtedness is only one circumstance from which an inference of an intent to defraud may be drawn,[1] and must be considered in connection with the donor's estate.[2] If the debts are fully secured,[3] or are fully provided for in the conveyance,[4] the gift is in the same condition as if the donor were entirely free from debt.

COMPARATIVE INDEBTEDNESS.—The true rule by which the fraudulency or fairness of a voluntary conveyance is to be ascertained, in this respect, is founded on a comparative indebtedness, or in other words on the pecuniary ability of the donor at the time to withdraw the amount of the donation from his estate without the least hazard to his creditors, or in any material degree lessening their then prospects of payment.[5] In other words the fraudulent intent is to be collected from the comparative value and magnitude of

---

to the facts of the case and the controversy of the times. It must be remembered that all the cases in which Lord Hardwicke holds this language are cases where there was no other property out of which the existing debts could be satisfied. These were all cases in equity where bills had been filed to have satisfaction out of the estate voluntarily settled. Howard v. Williams, 1 Bailey, 575; Kipp v. Hanna, 2 Bland, 26; Hopkirk v. Randolph, 2 Brock. 132.

[1] Richardson v. Smallwood, Jac. 552; Cadogan v. Kennett, 2 Cowp. 432; Lyne v. Bank of Ky. 5 J. J. Marsh. 545; Skarf v. Soulby, 1 H. & Tw. 426; s. c. 1 Mc. & G. 364.

[2] Dietus v. Fuss, 8 Md. 148.

[3] Stephens v. Olive, 2 Bro. C. C. 90; Manders v. Manders, 4 Ir. Eq. 434; Pell v. Tredwell, 5 Wend. 661; Johnson v. Zane, 11 Gratt. 552; Hester v. Wilkinson, 6 Humph. 218.

[4] George v. Millbank, 9 Ves. 189; Kid v. Mitchell, 1 N. & M. 334; Hester v. Wilkinson, 6 Humph. 215; Vance v. Smith, 2 Heisk, 343.

[5] Kipp v. Hanna, 2 Bland. 26; Bonny v. Griffith, Hayes, 115; Taylor v. Heriot, 4 Dessau. 227; Babcock v. Eckler, 24 N. Y. 623; Taylor v. Eubanks, 3 A. K. Marsh. 239.

the gift.[1] It must be determined from all the circumstances in each particular case, whether there was an
intent on the part of the donor in making the conveyance to delay, hinder, or defraud his creditors.[2] A
gift of such inconsiderable value as to come under the
denomination of a present, made under circumstances
entirely free from suspicion, has never been hunted up
by a creditor and claimed as a part of the donor's estate. A riding horse, wedding clothes, jewels, an instrument of music, or any other gift which is usual in the
particular locality, come strictly, when made by a man
of unquestionable solidity, within that class of dona-
tions which are denominated presents.[3]

INSOLVENCY.—If the donor at the time is indebted to
the extent of insolvency, the conveyance is void. A
gift by a person unable to pay his debts, so directly and
inevitably tends to delay and hinder creditors, and so
plainly violates the moral duty of honesty that the least
regard to fair dealing and integrity renders it necessary to pronounce it void. Such a transaction is not to
be looked on only as a means by which the intent to defraud may be inferred. The act is altogether incompatible and irreconcilable with a contrary intent. It is
an act of fraud in itself. If the donor is insolvent, the
only question is whether or not a conveyance is voluntary, and if it is voluntary it is void as against creditors.[4]

---

[1] Partridge v. Gopp, 1 Eden, 163; s. c. Ambl. 596; Jacks v. Tunno, 3
Dessau. 1.

[2] Thompson v. Webster, 7 Jur. (N. S.) 531; s. c. 4 Drew. 628; Clements
v. Eccles, 11 Ir. Eq. 229.

[3] Hopkirk v. Randolph, 2 Brock. 132.

[4] Morgan v. M'Lelland, 3 Dev. 82; Wellington v. Fuller, 38 Me. 61;
Kimmel v. McRight, 2 Penn. 38; Stickney v. Borman, 2 Penn. 67;
Shontz v. Brown, 27 Penn. 123; Carl v. Smith, 28 Leg. Int. 366; Burck-
myer v. Mairs, Riley, 208; Dulany v. Green, 4 Harring. 285; Walcott v.

A conveyance which leaves the grantor insolvent stands on the same footing as a gift by a person who is insolvent at the time of making it.[1] If for instance, a person having 10,000*l.*, and owing that amount, gives away 5,000*l.*, it is clearly a fraud. If the effect is to withdraw any portion of the property so that there does not remain sufficient to enable creditors to pay themselves, the conveyance is clearly within the statute.[2] A transfer of all the donor's property is for this reason fraudulent.[3] A universal donee is bound to pay the debts of the donor existing at the time of the donation, or to abandon the property thus given to him.[4]

DEBTOR NEED NOT BE INSOLVENT.—It is not necessary, however, that insolvency should either be proved

---

Almy, 6 McLean, 23; Doughty v. King, 2 Stockt. 396; Barnard v. Ford, L. R. 4 Ch. 247; Peat v. Powell, Ambl. 387; Sargent v. Chubbuck, 19 Iowa, 37; Harvey v. Steptoe, 17 Gratt. 289; Caswell v. Hill, 47 N. H. 407; Reppy v. Reppy, 46 Mo. 571; Gardner v. Baker, 25 Iowa, 343; Bennett v. McGuire, 58 Barb. 625; Raymond v. Cook, 31 Tex. 373; Worthington v. Shipley, 5 Gill, 449; Manhattan Co. v. Osgood, 15 Johns. 162; Buist v. Smyth, 2 Dessau. 214; Lyne v. Bank, 5 J. J. Marsh. 545; Beckham v. Secrest, 2 Rich. Eq. 54; Arnold v. Bell, Hayw. 396; Caston v. Cunningham, 3 Strobh. 59; Godell v. Taylor, Wright, 82; Fones v. Rice, 9 Gratt. 568; Doughty v. King, 3 Stock. 396; Craig v. Gamble, 5 Fla. 430; Gray v. Tappan, Wright, 117; O'Brien v. Coulter, 2 Blackf. 421; Rundle v. Murgatroyd, 4 Dall. 304; Reynolds v. Lansford, 16 Tex. 286; Burpee v. Bunn, 22 Cal. 194; Catchings v. Manlove, 39 Miss. 655; Everett v. Read, 3 N. H. 55; Humbert v. Methodist Church, Wright, 213; Welcome v. Batchelder, 23 Me. 85; Carlisle v. Rich, 8 N. H. 44; *vide* Clements v. Eccles, 11 Ir. Eq. 229; Bond v. Swearingen, 1 Ohio, 182; Gale v. Williamson, 8 M. & W. 405; Alexander v. Todd, Bond, 175.

[1] Shears v. Rogers, 3 B. & A. 362; Smith v. Cherrill, L. R. 4 Eq. 390; Jackson v. Bouley, Car. & M. 97; Freeman v. Burnham, 36 Conn. 469; Coates v. Gerlach, 44 Penn. 43; Ammon's Appeal, 63 Penn. 284; Clayton v. Brown, 30 Geo. 490; Stewart v. Rogers, 25 Iowa, 395.

[2] French v. French, 6 D. M. & G. 95; s. c. 25 L. J. (Ch.) 612; Taylor v. Heriot, 4 Dessau. 227; Chambers v. Spencer, 5 Watts. 404.

[3] Harlan v. Barnes, 5 Dana, 219.

[4] Porche v. Moore, 14 La. An. 241.

or presumed in order to render a voluntary conveyance void.[1] If the indebtedness is so large that the effect of the transfer is to defraud creditors, the conveyance will be void.[2] If insolvency takes place shortly after the making of the conveyance, that is enough.[3] Solvency is generally to be judged of by the event. If the debtor continues embarrassed, and, becoming more and more involved, ends in total and acknowledged insolvency, this is sufficient evidence of his insolvency, as to the existing creditors whose debts remain unpaid.[4] The only exception to this rule is where a man is perfectly solvent at the time of the transfer and is afterward rendered insolvent through some unexpected loss, or something which could not have been reasonably reckoned on at the time of the conveyance.[5] Insolvency at the time of the rendition of a judgment, always raises a presumption of insolvency at the time of the gift.[6]

BURDEN OF PROOF.—If the debts are ultimately paid,[7] or the donor accumulates other property sufficient to

---

[1] Parrish v. Murphree, 13 How. 92; Thompson v. Webster, 7 Jur. (N. S.) 531; s. c. 4 Drew. 628; Jones v. Slubey, 5 H. & J. 372; Jacks v. Tunno, 3 Dessau. 1; Parkman v. Welch, 19 Pick. 231; Simpson v. Graves, 1 Riley Ch. 219; Swartz v. Hazlett, 8 Cal. 118; Denison v. Tatersall, 18 L. T. (N. S.) 303; Townsend v. Westacott, 2 Beav. 340; Potter v. Mc-Dowell, 31 Mo. 62; Richardson v. Smallwood, Jac. 552; Wilson v. Buchanan, 7 Gratt. 334; Worthington v. Bullett, 6 Md. 172; s. c. 2 Md. Ch. 99; vide Lush v. Wilkinson, 5 Ves. 384; Norcutt v. Dodd, Cr. & Ph. 100; Martyn v. M'Namara, 4 Dr. & War. 411.

[2] Holmes v. Penney, 3 K. & J. 90.

[3] Crossley v. Elworthy, L. R. 12 Eq. 158; Townsend v. Westacott, 2 Beav. 340; Wilson v. Buchanan, 7 Gratt. 334.

[4] Izzard v. Izzard, 1 Bailey Ch. 228; Richardson v. Rhodus, 14 Rich. 95; Caston v. Cunningham, 3 Strobh. 59.

[5] Crossley v. Elworthy, 12 L. R. Eq. 158; Howard v. Williams, 1 Bailey Ch. 575.

[6] Carlisle v. Rich, 8 N. H. 44.

[7] Davis v. Herrick, 37 Me. 397; Smith v. Reavis, 7 Ired. 341.

meet them when judgments are obtained upon them,[1] the conveyance will generally be valid. It is only when debts, either prior or subsequent, remain unpaid that any question can arise concerning its validity. The party who sets up a voluntary conveyance in opposition to the claims of pre-existing creditors, is required to show that the means of the donor, independent of the property conveyed, were abundantly ample to satisfy all his creditors.[2] The inquiry is limited to the circumstances of the donor at the time of the conveyance.[3] The proof must show not merely a sufficiency of other property to pay the demand of the creditor who assails the transfer, but a sufficiency to pay all the debts then owing by the grantor.[4] Liabilities,[5] demands arising from a tort,[6] and judgments rendered in another State,[7] must be taken into consideration. Debts which are secured by the promise of a co-partner, who subsequently pays them,[8] and liabilities as an indorser when there is no proof that the persons for whom he was liable were unable to pay the respective sums for which he was responsible,[9] can not be taken into account. The price bid at a sheriff's sale a long time subsequent is not conclusive evidence of the value of the property.[10]

PROOF MUST BE CLEAR.—To rebut the presumption

---

[1] Smith v. Reavis, 7 Ired. 341.

[2] Jones v. Taylor, 2 Atk. 600.

[3] King v. Thompson, 9 Pet. 204 ; Posten v. Posten, 4 Whart. 27.

[4] Birely v. Staley, 5 G. &. J. 432.

[5] Hanet v. Dundass, 4 Penn. 178 ; Manhattan Co. v. Osgood, 15 Johns. 162 ; Trimble v. Ratcliff, 9 B. Mon. 511 ; vide Black v. Sanders, 1 Jones (N. C.), 67 ; Houston v. Boyle, 10 Ired. 496.

[6] Crossley v. Elworthy, 12 L. R. Eq. 158.

[7] Clark v. Depew, 25 Penn. 509.   [8] Hitt v. Ormsbee, 12 Ill. 166.

[9] King v. Thompson, 9 Pet. 204 ; vide Van Wyck v. Seward, 18 Wend. 375.

[10] Posten v. Posten, 4 Whart. 27.

of fraud, the proof must be clear, full, and satisfactory.[1] If there is a reasonable doubt of the adequacy of the grantor's means, then the voluntary conveyance must fall, for the effect of it is to delay and hinder his creditors.[2] It is incumbent on the donee to show a case not only without taint, but free from suspicion.[3] The condition of the donor must be shown to be such that a prudent man with an honest purpose and a due regard to the rights of his creditors could have made the gift.[4] This is to be ascertained not merely by taking an account of the grantor's debts and credits, and striking a balance between them, but by an examination of the general state of his affairs.[5]

ORDINARY COURSE OF EVENTS.—If, in the ordinary course of events, the donor's property turns out to be inadequate to the discharge of his debts, the presumption of fraud remains, although the property reserved may have been deemed originally adequate to that purpose.[6] If he is unable to meet his debts in the ordinary course prescribed by law for their collection, or is reduced to that situation where an execution against him would be unavailing, the conveyance is void,[7] for a solvency which the law cannot employ in the payment of the debt of an unwilling debtor, is not

---

[1] Henderson v. Dodd, 1 Bailey Ch. 138; Miller v. Wilson, 15 Ohio, 108; Young v. White, 25 Miss. 146.

[2] Worthington v. Bullett, 6 Md. 172; s. c. 3 Md. Ch. 99; Williams v. Banks, 11 Md. 198; Seward v. Jackson, 8 Cow. 406; Henderson v. Dodd, 1 Bailey Ch. 138; Howard v. Williams, 1 Bailey, 575; Swartz v. Hazlett, 8 Cal. 118; Richardson v. Smallwood, Jac. 552.

[3] Hopkirk v. Randolph, 2 Brock. 132.

[4] Parrish v. Murphree, 23 How. 92.

[5] Shears v. Rogers, 3 B. & A. 362; Hunters v. Waite, 3 Gratt. 26.

[6] Blakeney v. Kirkeley, 2 N. & M. 544; Madden v. Day, 1 Bailey, 337; Howard v. Williams, 1 Bailey Ch. 575; McClenachan's Case, 2 Yeates, 503.

[7] Potter v. McDowell, 31 Mo. 62.

distinguishable by any valuable difference from insolvency. The term solvency, in cases of this kind, implies
as well the present ability of the debtor to pay out of
his estate all his debts, as also such attitude of his
property as that it may be reached and subjected by
process of law to the payment of such debts.[1] The
probable necessary and reasonable demands for the support of the donor and his family must therefore be
taken into account and deducted.[2] The question of solvency, moreover, depends not upon the nominal value
of unsalable goods, but upon whether enough can be
realized from the property to pay his liabilities.

HAZARDS OF BUSINESS.—Although the property reserved is equal in nominal value to the donor's existing
indebtedness, that does not constitute such sufficient
security for his debts as his creditors are entitled to
require. They have the right to expect satisfaction of
their debts out of his property, and he has no right, in
law or morals, to throw upon them the loss which must
necessarily occur in converting it into money.[3] A
scanty provision for the payment of debts will not, for
this reason, render the conveyance valid.[4] Property
worth $7,250 has been deemed insufficient to meet debts
amounting to $6,848,[5] and property worth $48,000 has
been held not to be ample to meet debts to the amount
of $42,000.[6] The mere production of deeds of convey-
ance, unaccompanied by any proof of the existence of
the property conveyed, and the title of the grantor

---

[1] Eddy v. Baldwin, 32 Mo. 369.
[2] Meyer v. Mohr, 19 Abb. Pr. 299.
[3] Churchill v. Wells, 7 Cold. 364 ; Parrish v. Murphree, 13 How. 92.
[4] Salmon v. Bennett, 1 Conn. 525.
[5] Black v. Sanders, 1 Jones (N. C.) 67.
[6] Crumbaugh v. Kugler, 2 Ohio St. R. 373; Miller v. Wilson, 15 Ohio, 108.

thereto, or his possession thereof, 'or the possession thereof by the grantee, is wholly insufficient to estab-lish the solvency of the donor.[1]

PROPERTY MUST BE ACCESSIBLE.—Whether the prop-erty reserved is what will be deemed ample, does not depend entirely on the amount and value, as the real end to be accomplished is that the conveyance shall not deprive creditors of the means of collecting their debts. Hence, the nature and situation of the property is to be regarded as well as the amount and value, in view of the facilities that the creditors may have for the collection of their debts.[2] The property must be so circumstanced that neither delay nor difficulty, nor expense, need be encountered before it can be made available to creditors. The donor must not only have ample means remaining to discharge all his obligations, but these means must be readily and conveniently accessible to his creditors.[3] If the remaining property is heavily incumbered,[4] or consists of the life-estate of a person advanced in years,[5] or in feeble health,[6] or of property that cannot be taken on execution,[7] or of property which is in its nature very unstable and cannot be easily traced,[8] or of depreciating commercial paper,[9] it is not sufficient. The property must also be in the State where the donor resides. If

---

[1] Birely v. Staley, 5 G. & J. 432.

[2] Church v. Chapin, 35 Vt. 223.

[3] Worthington v. Bullett, 6 Md. 172; s. c. 3 Md. Ch. 99; Mohawk Bank v. Atwater, 2 Paige, 54.

[4] Worthington v. Bullett, 6 Md. 172; s. c. 3 Md. Ch. 99; Hunters v. Waite, 3 Gratt. 26.

[5] Williams v. Banks, 11 Md. 198.

[6] Strong v. Strong, 18 Beav. 408.

[7] Van Wyck v. Seward, 18 Wend. 375; Henderson v. Lloyd, 3 F. & F. 7; Hunters v. Waite, 3 Gratt. 26; Church v. Chapin, 35 Vt. 223.

[8] Blakeney v. Kirkeley, 2 N. & M. 544.

[9] McClenachan's Case, 2 Yeates, 503.

it is in some other country where creditors can not reach it, the gift may be set aside.[1]

DIFFERENCE BETWEEN THAT GIVEN AND THAT RE-SERVED.—If a party possessed of real estate and also of other assets consisting of *choses in action* gives away the former and leaves his creditors to resort to the latter, where their remedy may be precarious and diffi-cult, and the property at all events less readily and conveniently accessible, the conveyance of necessity operates to hinder and delay creditors in the collection of their debts.[2] When the donor's assets, however, con-sist only of debts and book accounts, and he takes a small sum to buy land, which he causes to be conveyed as a gift to another, the *bona fides* of the transaction and the sufficiency of his remaining assets to satisfy existing creditors must be judged by the character and nature of the property which he had at the time of making the gift.[3] When the property is not conven-iently accessible to creditors, the conveyance is liable to be set aside, although the donor at the time of the gift is not only not insolvent, but may have enough prop-erty left in some form or another to satisfy all his debts.[4]

SOLVENCY DETERMINED BY RESULT.—The voluntary conveyance must be such as a prudent and just man would make with a proper regard to his condition and circumstances, and a due consideration of all future

---

[1] Heath v. Page, 63 Penn. 280; Thompson v. Webster, 7 Jur. (N. S.) 531; French v. French, 6 D. M. & G. 95; s. c. 25 L. J. (Ch.) 612; Church v. Chapin, 35 Vt. 223.

[2] Worthington v. Bullett, 3 Md. Ch. 99; Warner v. Dove, 33 Md. 579.

[3] Warner v. Dove, 33 Md. 579.

[4] Thompson v. Webster, 7 Jur. (N. S.) 531; French v. French, 6 D. M. & G. 95; s. c. 25 L. J. (Ch.) 612.

events which prudence and integrity can foresee.[1] Existing creditors have no ground for complaint if they stand by and suffer subsequent creditors to sweep away the reserved property by obtaining judgments and executions before them,[2] and on the other hand the donor's solvency must not depend upon success in the business in which he is engaged,[3] or the skillful management of his affairs.[4] The risk and hazard of his speculations or of his financial arrangements can not either legally or honestly be thrown upon his creditors.

ACCIDENTS.—The law, however, provides against fraud and the intention to defraud, and not accidents or calamities. The gift, therefore, will be valid although the property may ultimately turn out to be inadequate, if this is occasioned by some accident which human foresight could not guard against,[5] as by losses in trade,[6] or by fire,[7] or by storms.[8] The ordinary fluctuations in the value of property, however, occasioned by the condition of mercantile affairs can not be ranked among casualties. These fluctuations are constantly taking place, and men must calculate upon and be pre-

---

[1] Swartz v. Hazlett, 8 Cal. 118.

[2] Eigleberger v. Kibler, 1 Hill Ch. 113; Howard v. Williams, 1 Bailey, 575; Richardson v. Rhodus, 14 Rich. 95.

[3] Carpenter v. Roe, 10 N. Y. 227; Crossley v. Elworthy, 12 L. R. Eq. 158.

[4] Bertrand v. Elder, 23 Ark. 494; Young v. White, 25 Miss. 146.

[5] Jacks v. Tunno, 3 Dessau. 1; Brackett v. Waite, 4 Vt. 389; Chambers v. Spencer, 5 Watts, 404; Mateer v. Hissim, 3 Penna. 160; Smith v. Yell, 8 Ark. 470; Pepper v. Carter, 11 Mo. 540; Howard v. Williams, 1 Bailey Ch. 575; vide O'Daniel v. Crawford, 4 Dev. 197.

[6] Howard v. Williams, 1 Bailey Ch. 575.

[7] Pepper v. Carter, 11 Mo. 540.

[8] Brackett v. Waite, 4 Vt. 389; vide Chamberlayne v. Temple, 2 Rand. 384.

pared for them.[1] The same principle applies to losses that occur from the wastefulness and improvidence of the donor. These are matters that prudence and sagacity can foresee, and the risk can not therefore be thrown upon the creditors.[2]

THERE NEED BE NO SECRET TRUST.—It has been said that when a person who is in debt makes a gift the law intends a trust between them, as that the donee will in consideration of such voluntary conveyance relieve the donor and not see him suffer want,[3] and that this presumed trust affords the evidence of an intent to defraud.[4] It is well settled, however, that it is not necessary to establish any secret trust.[5] The conveyance will be invalid, although there is a real transfer between the parties, if the circumstances are such as to raise a conclusive presumption of an intent to defraud.

---

[1] Izzard v. Izzard, 1 Bailey Ch. 228; Wilson v. Buchanan, 7 Gratt. 334. In Clements v. Eccles (11 Ir. Eq. 229), a case was put by way of illustration of a loss of the reserved property by defect of title, and it was intimated that such loss would fall on the creditors, but on principle this can not be so. The donor ought to be held to know the character of his title to his land.

[2] Hunters v. Waite, 3 Gratt. 26; Spirett v. Willows, 3 D. J. & S. 293; s. c. 34 L. J. (Ch.) 365; s. c. 11 Jur. (N. S.) 70. The case of Spirett v. Willows has been treated as one of actual fraud (vide Freeman v. Pope, 5 L. R. Ch. 538), but the reported facts of the case do not sustain the statement, nor did the court so consider it. Moreover it can well stand as a case of constructive fraud. The indebtedness was £370. The amount reserved was £720. The donor's discharge in bankruptcy was suspended for three years on account of unjustifiable extravagance. It was a case of sheer improvidence and not distinguishable in principle from Hunters v. Waite, and there is not a single case in the whole reports that would support a voluntary conveyance under such circumstances.

[3] Twyne's Case, 3 Co. 80.

[4] Kipp v. Hanna, 2 Bland, 26.

[5] Partridge v. Gopp, 1 Eden, 163; s. c. Ambl. 596; Emery v. Vinall, 26 Me. 295.

WHEN VOLUNTARY CONVEYANCE IS VALID.—If the debtor's circumstances are such that he may lawfully make a gift, he may give his property to a stranger,[1] as well as to those to whom he is bound by ties of kinship or natural affection, and on the other hand the mere fact that the donor is under a moral obligation to the donee, such as what is called the debt of nature from a parent to his child, will not render the conveyance valid, for his obligations to his creditors are paramount. When a man's circumstances, however, are such as to enable him to discharge both, it is his duty to do so.[2] A man of wealth feels himself bound to advance his children, when they leave him to act for themselves and to perform their own parts on the great theatre of the world. His own feelings and public opinion would equally reproach him should he withhold from them those aids which his circumstances and their education and station in life may seem to require. A reasonable advancement under such circumstances would obviously be a provision required by justice and the common sense of mankind.[3] A person engaged in hazardous pursuits often regards it also as a sacred duty to his wife and children to set apart, by conveyance for their use, a certain and reasonable portion of his estate when he is free from the shackles of debt, and thereby keep them somewhat secure from the ills of poverty to which those engaged in the traffic of buying and selling are peculiarly liable.[4] The statute was not intended to interfere with such transfers or to disturb the ordinary and safe transactions in society made in good faith,

---

[1] Holloway v. Millard, 1 Madd. 414; Speise v. M'Coy, 6 W. & S. 485.

[2] Brice v. Myers, 5 Ohio, 121.

[3] Hopkirk v. Randolph, 2 Brock. 132.

[4] Haskell v. Bakewell, 10 B. Mon. 106.

and which at the time subjected creditors to no hazard. No fraudulent intent, no intent to delay, or in any manner to injure creditors, can be inferred from such conveyances. The consequence can not be apprehended from the acts, and therefore the acts can not be considered as constructively fraudulent. They must be regarded as fair dispositions of property, a fair exercise of the power of ownership, and not within the statute.

PARTIALLY VOLUNTARY.—It is manifest that conveyances may be partially as well as entirely voluntary. When there is no actual intent to defraud, a valuable consideration though inadequate will sustain the transfer in a court of law.[1] The rule in equity, however, is different. A court of equity can do full justice to all parties by allowing the deed to stand as security for the consideration actually paid, and appropriating the balance to the payment of the vendor's debts. If there is any difference between the price paid and the actual value of the property, courts of equity will therefore regard the conveyance to the extent of the difference as voluntary.[2] As between the vendor and the vendee the courts will not weigh the consideration in golden scales, but the rule is different where creditors

---

[1] Jackson v. Peek, 4 Wend. 300.

[2] Worthington v. Bullett, 6 Md. 172; s. c. 3 Md. Ch. 99; Matthews v. Feaver, 1 Cox, 278; Wright v. Stannard, 2 Brock. 311; Corlett v. Radcliffe, 14 Moore, P. C. 121; Van Wyck v. Seward, 18 Wend. 375; Robinson v. Stewart, 10 N. Y. 189; M'Meekins, v. Edmonds, 1 Hill Ch. 288; Norton v. Norton, 5 Cush. 524; Trimble v. Ratcliffe, 9 B. Mon. 511; Crumbaugh v. Kugler, 2 Ohio St. R. 373; Herschfeldt v. George, 6 Mich. 456; Church v. Chapin, 35 Vt. 223; Hopkirk v. Randolph, 2 Brock. 132; vide, Union Bank v. Toomer, 2 Hill Ch. 27; Turnley v. Hooper, 2 Jur. (N. S.) 108.

are concerned.[1] It is difficult to say what will amount
to an inadequate consideration, and no general rule has
been or can be laid down. Each case must depend
upon its own circumstances. The consideration, however, must be palpably less than the real value of the
property or what it would bring at public sale in the
market,[2] or what it might reasonably be supposed that
the vendor would have taken from any other person.[3]

---

[1] Matthews v. Feaver, 1 Cox, 278; *vide* Nunn v. Wilsmore, 8 T. R.
521; Grogan v. Cooke, 2 Ball & B. 233; Middlecome v. Marlow, 2 Atk.
519; Penhall v. Elwin, 1 Sm. & Gif. 258; Thompson v. Webster, 7 Jur.
(N. S.) 531; Blount v. Doughty, 3 Atk. 481; Taylor v. Heriot, 4 Dessau.
227; Copis v. Middleton, 2 Madd. 410; Wright v. Stannard, 2 Brock.
311.

[2] Worthington v. Bullett, 6 Md. 172; s. c. 3 Md. Ch. 99.

[3] Black v. Cadwell, 4 Jones, (N. C.) 150; Arnold v. Bell, 1 Hay.
(N. C.) 396.

CHAPTER XII.

NUPTIAL SETTLEMENTS.

ANTE-NUPTIAL SETTLEMENT.—In the absence of all fraud, a party, before marriage, has the right to insist on such terms as may be deemed proper, as a consideration and inducement for the marriage,[1] and a contract so made is, in contemplation of law founded upon a valuable consideration. The indissoluble nature of the marriage contract, the alteration which it effects in the personal condition of the parties, and the nature of the rights, duties and disabilities which arise from it, render the consideration of marriage important and valuable, and constitute the parties purchasers for a valuable consideration.[2] Consequently if it is made in good faith, and without notice of fraud to the parties who take under it, it is unimpeachable by creditors.[3] Both parties must concur in or have cognizance of any intended fraud, in order to render the settlement void. If the settlor alone intends a fraud, and the other party has no notice of it, the settlement will be valid.

---

[1] Hardey v. Green, 12 Beav. 182.

[2] Magniac v. Thompson, 7 Pet. 348; Frazer v. Thompson, 1 Giff. 49.

[3] Magniac v. Thompson, 7 Pet. 348; Partridge v. Gopp, 1 Eden, 163; s. c. Ambl. 596; Campion v. Cotton, 17 Ves. 264; Cadogan v. Kennett, 2 Cowp. 432; ex parte McBurnie, 1 D. M. & G. 441; Andrews v. Jones, 10 Ala. 400; Eppes v. Randolph, 2 Call. 103; Coutts v. Greenhow, 2 Munf. 363; s. c. 4 H. & M. 485; Hazelinton v. Gill, 3 T. R. 620; Bunnel v. Witherow, 29 Ind. 123; Tunno v. Trezevant, 2 Dessau. 264; Frank's Appeal, 59 Penn. 190; Jones' Appeal, 63 Penn. 324; Croft v. Arthur, 3 Dessau. 223; Bank v. Marchand, T. U. P. Charlt. 247.

SPECIFIC MARRIAGE.—The contract, however, must be made with reference to a specific marriage, and not a mere future possible state or condition of matrimony; as where a father promises a daughter that if, at any after period of life, she shall choose to enter into wedlock, he will in that event, and upon its occurrence, give, convey or pay to her specified money or property. In such a case there is no mutuality, either of promise or consideration. The agreement of the father is founded upon no undertaking or promise of the daughter, and upon no valuable consideration, but is merely for a future contingent advancement of the daughter. It is not, in the eye of the law, in consideration of marriage.[1] If, however, there is a specific marriage in contemplation, a mere legal contract, and promise made in good faith, to marry another, is a valuable consideration. In reference to the question of the sufficiency and value of the consideration, and consequently of the validity of the title, there is no real and substantial difference between a marriage formally solemnized and a binding and obligatory agreement which has been fairly and truly, and above all suspicion of collusion, made to form such connection, and enter into that relation.[2]

CONTEMPORANEOUS GIFT.—A reasonable gift, made contemporaneously with a marriage, and accompanied with a delivery of possession, has strong claims to be considered as a gift in consideration of the marriage, for it is not usual to convey property by deed which passes by delivery, nor to use the solemnity of delivery expressly in consideration of marriage, although that may be the real consideration.[3] The gift, however,

---

[1] Willes v. Cole, 6 Gratt. 645.

[2] Smith v. Allen, 5 Allen, 454.

[3] Hopkirk v. Randolph, 2 Brock. 132; Toulmin v. Buchanan, 1 Stew. 67; Andrews v. Jones, 10 Ala. 400.

must be contemporaneous with the marriage.[1] A deed made prior to the marriage cannot be connected with the marriage articles, when there is no reference in the deed to them.[2]

STATEMENTS IN ARTICLES.—It is not necessary that the marriage articles should contain an enumeration of the property which is subject to the settlement.[3] Chattels, stocks, books, plate, jewelry, and merchandise may be settled as well as land.[4] The articles may stipulate that all the property to which either of the parties may become subsequently entitled shall also be subject to the settlement.[5] A stipulation that the husband and wife shall take the profits jointly will not render the property liable to his creditors.[6]

To WHOM EXTENDS.—The consideration of marriage extends to the wife's children by a former marriage,[7] the husband's children by a former marriage,[8] and children of the parties born before the marriage.[9] When the articles go beyond the immediate objects of the marriage, and provide for collateral relatives, the settlement as to them, not being supported by the marriage,

---

[1] Hayes v. Jones, 2 Pat. & H. 583; *vide* Toulmin v. Buchanan, 1 Stew. 67.

[2] Croft v. Arthur, 3 Dessau. 223.

[3] Jarman v. Woolloton, 3 T. R. 618; Arundell v. Phipps, 10 Ves. 139.

[4] Campion v. Cotton, 17 Ves. 264; Cadogan v. Kennett, 2 Cowp. 432; Bank v. Marchand, U. P. Charlt. 247.

[5] Hardey v. Green, 12 Beav. 182.

[6] Scott v. Gibbon, 5 Munf. 86.

[7] Newstead v. Searles, 1 Atk. 165; Ithell v. Bean, 1 Ves. Sr. 215; Ball v. Burnford, Prec. Ch. 113.

[8] Doe v. Routledge, 2 Cowp. 705; *vide* Bank v. Marchand, T. U. Charlt. 247.

[9] Coutts v. Greenhow, 2 Munf. 363; s. c. 4 H. & M. 485.

is purely voluntary.[1] The consideration of marriage runs through the whole settlement, and supports all its provisions, those which relate to the husband as well as those which relate to the wife. If, therefore, the settlement is valid when it is made, no event afterwards can alter it. If a settlement is made by a father upon the marriage of his son, on the husband and wife for their lives, and afterwards upon the children, and the wife dies without any issue, the settlement will be valid against the father's creditors. The law is the same in the case of a stranger.[2]

GOOD FAITH.—A man who is indebted may, on his marriage, make a settlement of his property, provided the settlement is made honestly and in good faith,[3] and the wife's knowledge of his indebtedness will not alone render it void.[4] It is, however, clearly established that marriage cannot be made the means of committing fraud. If there is an intent to delay, hinder or defraud creditors, and to make the celebration of a marriage a part of a scheme to protect property against the rights of creditors, the consideration of marriage cannot support the settlement.[5] The question in every case is whether the settlement is a *bona fide* transaction or whether it is a trick and contrivance to defeat creditors.[6]

---

[1] Smith v. Cherrill, L. R. 4 Eq. 390.

[2] Nairn v. Prowse, 6 Ves. 752.

[3] Bulmer v. Hunter, L. R. 8 Eq. 46; s. c. 38 L. J. (Ch.) 543; s. c. 20 L. T. (N. S.) 942; *ex parte* McBurnie, 1 D. M. & G. 441; Betts v. Union Bank, 1 H. & G. 175.

[4] Campion v. Cotton, 17 Ves. 264; Frazer v. Thompson, 1 Giff. 49; Richardson v. Horton, 7 Beav. 112.

[5] Colombine v. Penhall, 1 Sm. & Gif. 228; *ex parte* Mayor Mont. 292; Bulmer v. Hunter, L. R. 8 Eq. 46; s. c. 38 L. J. (Ch.) 543; s. c. 20 L. T. (N. S.) 942.

[6] Cadogan v. Kennett, 2 Cowp. 432.

WIFE'S PARTICIPATION.—The wife, however, must be connected with the fraud to make the settlement invalid.[1] Fraud may be imputed to her either from direct co-operation in the original design at the time of its concoction, or from constructive co-operation by carrying the design into execution after she has received notice of it. The execution of the settlement after she has received notice of a fraudulent design renders her a participator and party to the fraud. It necessarily involves combination and participation.[2] Notice of the fraud may be inferred from the facts and circumstances of the settlement.[3] If the amount of property settled is extravagant, or grossly out of proportion to the station and circumstances of the husband, this of itself is sufficient notice of the fraud.[4]

How FAR VALUABLE.—Marriage is sometimes put on the footing of a pecuniary consideration, and it is said that if a person sells his property for a full consideration, and squanders the money, his creditors have no redress. From this it is inferred that marriage will afford the same protection. But in the case of a *bona fide* sale, the seller parts with his property, the purchaser parts with his money, and the law will presume that the object is the payment of his debts. But the purchaser is not answerable for the misapplication of the money. It is not so with a marriage settlement. The seller does not, in fact, part with his property. It is still intended for his own enjoyment.

---

[1] Campion v. Cotton, 17 Ves. 264; Bulmer v. Hunter, L. R. 8 Eq. 46; s. c. 38 L. J. (Ch.) 543; s. c. 20 L. T. (N. S.) 942.

[2] Magniac v. Thompson, 7 Pet. 348.

[3] Colombine v. Penhall, 1 Sm. & Gif. 228; Bulmer v. Hunter, L. R. 8 Eq. 46; s. c. 38 L. J. (Ch.) 543.

[4] *Ex parte* McBurnie, 1 D. M. & G. 441; Croft v. Arthur, 3 Dessau. 223.

Neither does he receive in return anything that will satisfy his creditors. His wife will not be received in payment of his debts. It is not to be understood that, because marriage is equivalent to a pecuniary consideration, it is to be considered in the nature of an actual purchase. A settlement is not intended as the price of the wife, but as a provision for the family. It must, therefore, be reasonable, and with a due regard to the rights of others. Although a marriage contract cannot be estimated in dollars and cents, yet some idea can be formed of what would constitute a comfortable provision for a family at the commencement of married life. And in forming a judgment of the *bona fides* of the transaction, an inquiry will be made as to the value of a man's property, the amount of his debts, the general state of his property, and the value of that belonging to his wife; and if the provision is found greatly disproportionate to his means, having regard to all these circumstances, it cannot fail to excite a suspicion of fraud. Although marriage is a good consideration, and a settlement founded thereon may prevail even against creditors, it is not necessarily so under all circumstances, and to any extent. The reasonableness of it may as well be inquired into as the adequacy of price in a case of pecuniary consideration.[1]

In pursuance of ante-nuptial agreement.—A post-nuptial settlement, made in good faith, in pursuance of written marriage articles, is valid. The wife becomes a creditor of her husband by virtue of the marriage article, and if the settlement is made in part performance of the articles, *bona fide* and without fraud, it is

---

[1] Simpson v. Graves, 1 Riley Ch. 232; *ex parte* McBurnie, 1 D. M. & G. 441; Croft v. Arthur, 3 Dessau. 223; *vide* Bank v. Marchand, T. U. Charlt. 247.

simply a discharge of a legal obligation, and stands on the same footing as a preference to any other creditor.[1] Such a settlement may be made on the eve of the rendition of a judgment against the husband, but it must be real, and not merely colorable.[2]

NOT IN CONFORMITY WITH ARTICLES.—A settlement which goes beyond the marriage articles[3] or does not correspond with any precision to them[4] is a voluntary settlement. When the articles stipulate that the husband shall furnish a house in a suitable manner, as he shall judge fit and proper, he has a discretion which he may exercise in a reasonable manner, according to his station and associations in life. If he furnishes it extravagantly, or at a useless and wanton expense, he does not act within the true spirit and meaning of the articles, and commits a fraud on his creditors as to the excess.[5] The mere recital of the existence of articles in the settlement is not binding upon the creditors, and they may show that no such articles were made at the time of the marriage.[6]

PAROL ANTE-NUPTUAL AGREEMENT.—The statute of frauds[7] enacts that no action shall be brought to charge any person upon any agreement made upon consideration of marriage, unless the agreement upon which such action shall be brought, or some memorandum or note

---

[1] Magniac v. Thompson, 7 Pet. 348; Lockwood v. Nelson, 16 Ala. 294; Brunsden v. Stratton, Prec. Ch. 520.

[2] Magniac v. Thompson, 7 Pet. 348.

[3] Saunders v. Ferrill, 1 Ired. 97; Shaw v. Jakeman, 4 East. 207.

[4] Reade v. Livingston, 3 Johns. Ch. 481; Blow v. Maynard, 2 Leigh, 29; Simpson v. Graves, 1 Riley Ch. 232; Shaw v. Jakeman, 4 East. 207.

[5] Magniac v. Thompson, 7 Pet. 348.

[6] Battersbee v. Farrington, 1 Swanst. 106; Reade v. Livingston, 3 Johns. Ch. 481; Simpson v. Graves, 1 Riley Ch. 219.

[7] 29 Car. II, c. 3, s. 4.

thereof shall be in writing, and signed by the party to be charged therewith, or some other person thereunto by him lawfully authorized. A parol agreement in consideration of marriage constitutes a demand that cannot be enforced, because it is within the prohibition of this act, and consequently a settlement made in consideration of such an agreement is without any legal consideration and voluntary.[1] Neither marriage,[2] nor a written acknowledgment after marriage,[3] nor a representation at the time of the marriage, that a post-nuptial settlement will be valid,[4] can give validity to the settlement when otherwise void, or exempt it from the operation of the statute. Representations which are not inserted in the marriage contract, and to which no reference is made in the settlement cannot be enforced and will not uphold a subsequent settlement.[5] A settlement in consideration of a previous marriage, without the recital of any articles is a voluntary settlement.[6]

---

[1] Dygert v. Remerschnider, 32 N. Y. 629; s. c. 39 Barb. 417; Warden v. Jones, 2 D. & J. 76; s. c. 27 L. J. (Ch.) 190; Dundas v. Dutens, 2 Cox, 235; s. c. 1 Ves. Jr. 196; Spurgeon v. Collier, 1 Eden, 55; Murphy v. Abraham, 15 Ir. Eq. (N. S.) 371; Reade v. Livingston, 3 Johns. Ch. 481; Smith v. Greer, 3 Humph. 118; Randall v. Morgan, 12 Ves. 67; Hayes v. Jones, 2 Pat. & H. 583; Andrews v. Jones, 10 Ala. 400; Wood v. Savage, 2 Doug. (Mich.) 316; Borst v. Corey, 16 Barb. 136; Izzard v. Izzard, 1 Baily Ch. 228; Simpson v. Graves, Riley Ch. 219; vide Loeffes v. Lewen, Prec. Ch. 370; Hall v. Light, 2 Duvall, 358.

[2] Warden v. Jones, 2 D. G. & J. 76; s. c. 27 L. J. (Ch.) 190.

[3] Randall v. Morgan, 12 Ves. 67; Reade v. Livingston, 3 Johns. Ch. 481; Jones v. Henry, 3 Litt. 427.

[4] Warden v. Jones, 2 D. G. & J. 76; s. c. 27 L. J. (Ch.) 190; Simpson v. Graves, 1 Riley Ch. 219.

[5] Murphy v. Abrahams, 15 Ir. Eq. (N. S.) 371; Saunders v. Ferrell, 1 Ired. 97.

[6] Beaumont v. Thorp, 1 Ves. 27; Reade v. Livingston, 3 Johns. Ch. 481; Deubell v. Fisher, R. M. Charlt. 36.

IN CONSIDERATION OF PORTION.—If after marriage a settlement is made by the husband upon his wife in consideration of a portion or a sum of money advanced by another person, such settlement will be good, and for a valuable consideration.[1] Whether the money is paid before or after the settlement is not material if the settlement is made in consideration of the payment or the promise to pay.[2] If a father secures the portion which his daughter is entitled to under her mother's marriage settlement upon his own estate, and the portion so secured is subsequently paid to the husband, it is a valuable consideration for a settlement.[3]

DEED OF SEPARATION.—If a *feme covert* is entitled, on account of the misconduct of her husband, to obtain a divorce, and to have a proper allowance from him, she may, instead of strictly prosecuting that right, accept a maintenance from him, and the settlement will be upheld against creditors.[4] On account of the disability which at common law prohibited the husband and his wife from making a valid contract between each other, a deed of separation is always made through the intervention of a trustee.[5] A covenant by the trustee to indemnify the husband against any claim for alimony[6] or the debts which the wife may contract after the separation is a valuable consideration for the settlement.[7] If the

---

[1] Wheeler v. Caryl, Amb. 121 ; Nunn v. Wilsmore, 8 T. R. 521; Stileman v. Ashdown, 2 Atk. 477; Jones v. Marsh, Cas. temp. Talb. 64; Anon. Prec. Ch. 101; Russell v. Hammond, 1 Atk. 13; Ramsden v. Hylton, 2 Ves. Sr. 304; Gardner v. Painter, Cas. temp. King, 65 ; Brown v. Jones, 1 Atk. 188.

[2] Brown v. Jones, 1 Atk. 188.

[3] Wheeler v. Caryl, Amb. 121.

[4] Hobbs v. Hull, 1 Cox, 445.

[5] Legard v. Johnson, 3 Ves. 352.

[6] Worrall v. Jacob, 3 Mer. 256.

[7] Stephens v. Olive, 2 Bro. C. C. 90; Worrall v. Jacob, 3 Mer. 256; Wells v. Stout, 9 Cal. 479 ; King v. Brewen, 2 Bro. C. C. 93 *note*; Hargroves v. Meray, 2 Hill Ch. 222.

trustee does not execute the deed of separation,[1] or omits to indemnify the husband against any claim for alimony or the debts of the wife,[2] the settlement is without a valuable consideration to support it.

CONTRACT BETWEEN HUSBAND AND WIFE.—A husband may, either with[3] or without[4] the intervention of a trustee, enter into a contract with his wife for a valuable consideration, and a settlement made in pursuance of such an agreement will be good against prior as well as subsequent creditors. Such settlements, however, are always watched with considerable jealousy, on account of the relative situation of the parties, and the convenient cover they afford to a debtor to protect his property and impose upon his creditors.[5]

WIFE'S PROPERTY.—Whether the consideration is valuable will depend upon its character. By the common law the husband by marriage became the purchaser and owner of his wife's personal property, and obtained the right to reduce her *choses in action* to possession, and appropriate them for his own benefit. Her personal property and money, therefore, do not at common law constitute a valuable consideration for a promise made by him to her.[6] If her *choses in action* have been re-

---

[1] Legard v. Johnson, 3 Ves. 352 ; Wells v. Stout, 9 Cal. 479.

[2] Cropsey v. McKinney, 30 Barb. 47 ; Fitzer v. Fitzer, 2 Atk. 511 ; Nunn v. Wilsmore, 8 T. R. 521 ; Clough v. Lambert, 10 Sim. 174.

[3] Bank v. Lee, 13 Pet. 107 ; Arundell v. Phipps, 10 Ves. 139.

[4] Schaffner v. Reuter, 37 Barb. 44; Wickes v. Clarke, 8 Paige, 161; Babcock v. Eckler, 24 N. Y. 623 ; Stockett v. Holliday, 9 Md. 480 ; Dygert v. Remerschnider, 32 N. Y. 629 ; s. c. 39 Barb. 417; Bullard v. Briggs, 7 Pick. 533; Bank v. Brown, Riley Ch. 131 ; s. c. 2 Hill Ch. 558 ; Miller v. Tolleson, Harp. Ch. 145.

[5] Blow v. Maynard, 2 Leigh. 29.

[6] Harvey v. Alexander, 1 Rand. 219; Farmers' Bank v. Long, 7 Bush, 337 ; Lewis v. Caperton, 8 Gratt. 148 ; Coates v. Gerlach, 44 Penn. 43; Lyne v. Bank, 5 J. J. Marsh. 545 ; Bank v. Mitchell, Rice Eq. 389 ; Beach v. White, Walk. Ch. 495; Briggs v. Mitchell, 60 Barb. 288.

duced to possession, they belong absolutely to him, and do not constitute a valuable consideration any more than her personal property.[1]

A WIFE'S CHOSES IN ACTION.—A *chose in action* which is not reduced to possession remains the property of the wife, and does not vest in the husband by the marriage. The marital right does not extend to the property while a *chose in action*, but enables the husband to reduce it to possession, and thereby acquire it. The property becomes his not upon the marriage, but upon the fact of his obtaining possession. Her *choses in action* therefore, may be settled upon her, and will also constitute a valuable consideration for a contract with her.[2] So, also, if her money is in the hands of another who withholds it, until the husband makes a provision for her, it will support the settlement.[3]

RIGHT TO SETTLEMENT.—If her property is only recoverable in equity,[4] or has come to her during coverture

---

[1] Wylie v. Basil, 4 Md. Ch. 327; Whittlesey v. McMahon, 10 Conn. 137; Pierce v. Thompson, 17 Pick. 391; Hurdt v. Courtenay, 4 Met. (Ky.) 139; Briggs v. Mitchell, 60 Barb. 288; Lewis v. Caperton, 8 Gratt. 148; Barker v. Woods, 1 Sandf. Ch. 129; Hatch v. Gray, 21 Iowa, 29.

[2] Blake v. Jones, 1 Bailey Ch. 141; Gallego v. Gallego, 2 Brock. 285; Pierce v. Thompson, 17 Pick. 391; Athey v. Knotts, 6 B. Mon. 24; Gore v. Waters, 2 Bailey, 477; Nims v. Bigelow, 45 N. H. 343; Wheeler v. Emerson, 44 N. H. 182; Ready v. Bragg, 1 Head. 511; Gasset v. Grout, 4 Met. 486; McCauley v. Rodes, 7 B. Mon. 462; Mechanic Bank v. Taylor, 2 Cranch, C. C. 507; Ryan v. Bull, 3 Strobh. Eq. 86.

[3] Brown v. Jones, 1 Atk. 188; Middlecome v. Marlow, 2 Atk. 519; Pott v. Todhunter, 2 Coll. 76; Gassett v. Grout, 4 Met. 486; Bank v. Brown, Riley Ch. 131; Wickes v. Clarke, 8 Paige, 161; Ryan v. Bull, 3 Strobh. Eq. 86; Poindexter v. Jeffries, 15 Gratt. 363; Kennedy v. Head, 32 Geo. 629; *vide* Robinett's Appeal, 36 Penn. 174.

[4] Wheeler v. Caryl, Amb. 121; Legard v. Johnson, 3 Ves. 352; Moore v. Rycault, Prec. Ch 22; Bank v. Brown, Riley Ch. 131; Poindexter v. Jeffries, 15 Gratt. 363; Marshall v. McDaniel, 8 B. Mon. 175; Spirett v. Willows, 3 D. J. & S. 293; Barnard v. Ford, L. R. 4 Ch. 247.

by gift or inheritance,[1] she is entitled to a settlement which a court of equity will invariably enforce in favor of the wife, and even the children of the marriage, against the husband and all claiming under him, such as assignees or creditors. The same circumstances which would induce a court of equity to compel a settlement by the husband or those claiming under him, or in his right will operate to uphold a settlement already made to the same extent that would be required if one should be directed to be made under the view of the court, for the parties may do voluntarily what the law would compel them to do. The settlement should be reasonable and adequate, and may be of a part or the whole of the property according to the circumstances.[2] If it is reasonable at the time it is made, it will not be impaired by subsequent acquisitions.[3]

WIFE'S SEPARATE ESTATE.—Her land[4] or separate estate[5] constitutes a valuable consideration for a settlement. If the husband's creditors levy upon his life estate in her lands, she may convey a portion of the ground to them as a consideration to induce them to unite with her

---

[1] Wickes v. Clarke, 8 Paige, 161; Hinton v. Scott, Moseley, 336; Smith v. Greer, 3 Humph. 118; Bank v. Brown, 2 Hill Ch. 558; McCauley v. Rodes, 7 B. Mon. 462.

[2] Poindexter v. Jeffries, 15 Gratt. 363.

[3] Marshall v. McDaniel, 8 B. Mon. 175.

[4] College v. Powell, 12 Gratt. 372 ; Clerk v. Nettlestrip, 2 Levinz, 148; Latimer v. Glenn, 2 Bush. 535; Wilson v. Ayer, 7 Me. 207.

[5] Savage v. O'Neil, 43 N. Y. 298; Stockett v. Holliday, 9 Md. 480; Bank v. Lee, 13 Pet. 107; Cottle v. Tripp, 2 Vern. 220; Taylor v. Heriot, 4 Dessau. 227; Ward v. Shallet, 2 Ves. Sr. 16; Bank v. Brown, Riley Ch. 131; Acraman v. Corbett, J. & H. 410; Butler v. Ricketts, 11 Iowa, 107 ; Woodworth v. Sweet, 44 Barb. 268; Kendrick v. Taylor, 27 Tex. 695; Lormore v. Campbell, 60 Barb. 62; Butterfield v. Stanton, 44 Miss. 15; Sweeney v. Damron, 47 Ill. 450; McLaurie v. Partlow, 53 Ill. 340; White v. Sansom, 3 Atk. 410.

in a transfer of the residue to a trustee for her benefit.[1] If her father makes a mistake as to the effect of a gift of land to her and her husband, they may unite in a surrender, and the property may then be given to her.[2] If her husband converts her separate property to his own use without her consent, this will be a good consideration for a transfer by him.[3] So also in case he purchases property with her separate funds, and takes the title in his own name, he may subsequently convey it to her, for this is only what the law would compel him to do.[4]

CONTINGENT RIGHT OF DOWER.—The release of a contingent right of dower is a valuable consideration.[5] A release without any promise,[6] or upon a mere expectation[7] of a recompense, or a mere promise to release, is not a valuable consideration, but if the relinquishment is made on the faith of a promise, the transfer may be subsequent.[8]

NOT WITHOUT CONTRACT.—An estate previously received by the husband in the right of his wife is not a good

---

[1] Hubbard v. Remick, 10 Me. 140.

[2] Barncord v. Kuhn, 36 Penn. 383.

[3] Wiley v. Gray, 36 Miss. 510.

[4] Wilson v. Sheppard, 28 Ala. 623.

[5] Marshall v. Hutchinson, 5 B. Mon. 298; Jones v. Boulter, 1 Cox, 288; Unger v. Price, 9 Md. 552; Ellinger v. Crowl, 17 Md. 361; Wright v. Stannard, 2 Brock. 311; Bullard v. Briggs, 7 Pick. 533; Quarles v. Lacy, 4 Munf. 251; Harrison v. Carroll, 11 Leigh, 476; Bank v. Brown, Riley Ch. 131; Harvey v. Alexander, 1 Rand. 219; College v. Powell, 12 Gratt. 372; Hollowell v. Simonson, 21 Ind. 398; Cottle v. Tripp, 2 Vern. 220; Ward v. Crotty, 4 Met. (Ky.) 59; Low v. Carter, 21 N. H. 433; Nims v. Bigelow, 45 N. H. 343.

[6] Woodson v. Pool, 19 Mo. 340; Taylor v. Moore, 2 Rand. 563.

[7] Lewis v. Caperton, 8 Gratt. 148.

[8] College v. Powell, 12 Gratt. 372.

consideration for a subsequent conveyance to her.[1] Even
the appropriation of her separate estate with her knowledge and consent will not constitute a good consideration unless there is an agreement by him to repay the
money so appropriated.[2] If a settlement can not
be made without her aid, her joining in it will constitute a good consideration for a settlement in her
favor.[3]

How FAR VALID.—When a settlement is valid, the
increase[4] and property purchased with the proceeds
of the estate settled are within its protection.[5] A defective settlement which is otherwise valid is good in
equity against the creditors.[6]

PURCHASES BY FEME COVERT.—The possession of the
wife is *prima facie* the possession of the husband, and
consequently raises a presumption of ownership in him.
In case of a purchase by a wife during coverture, the
burden is upon her to prove distinctly that she paid
for the thing purchased with funds that were not
furnished by the husband. Evidence that she purchased amounts to nothing unless it is accompanied by
clear and full proof that she paid for it with her own
separate funds—not that she has the means of paying—
but that she in fact paid. In the absence of such proof

---

[1] Lyne v. Bank, 5 J. J. Marsh. 545 ; Hurdt. v. Courtenay, 4 Met. (Ky.)
139; Farmers' Bank v. Long, 7 Bush, 337.

[2] Kuhn v. Stansfield, 28 Md. 210; Blow v. Maynard, 2 Leigh, 29;
Wickes v. Clarke, 8 Paige, 161.

[3] Harman v. Richards, 10 Hare, 81; Acraman v. Corbett, 1 J. & H.
410; Russell v. Hammond, 1 Atk. 13.

[4] Hazelinton v. Gill, 3 T. R. 620.

[5] Jarman v. Woolloton, 3 T. R. 618; Blanchard v. Ingersoll, 4 Dall.
305.

[6] Brown v. Jones, 1 Atk. 188.

the presumption is that her husband furnished the means of payment. This rule applies to purchases of real as well as personal estate.[1]

---

[1] Winter v. Walter, 37 Penn. 155 ; Gamber v. Gamber, 18 Penn. 363 ; Keeney v. Good, 21 Penn. 349; Walker v. Reamy, 36 Penn. 410; Black v. Nease, 37 Penn. 433; Mercer v. Miller, 5 Fla. 277; Parvin v. Capewell, 45 Penn, 89.

CHAPTER XIII.

SUBSEQUENT CREDITORS.

RIGHTS AT COMMON LAW.—In Twyne's Case[1] it is said that by the common law an estate made by fraud can be avoided only by him who has a former right, title, interest, debt or demand, as a sale in open market by covin will not bar a right which is more ancient, and a covinous gift will not defeat an execution in respect of a former debt, but he who hath right, title, interest, debt, or demand more puisne can not avoid a gift or estate precedent by the common law. It will be observed, however, that these remarks, as far as they affect subsequent creditors, are mere dicta and not supported by any decided case. It is, moreover, difficult to perceive upon what ground they rest. Even at the common law fraud vitiates every transaction into which it enters, and fraud accompanied with damage always gives a right of action. These well recognized principles are sufficient to protect even subsequent creditors. The better doctrine, therefore, even in this respect, is that the principles and rules of the common law as now known and understood would have attained every end proposed by the statute.[2] The principles, however, had not been previously recognized and applied, and the statute thus had the effect of introducing new principles.

---

[1] 3 Co. 80.
[2] Cadogan v. Kennett, 2 Cowp. 432.

WITHIN STATUTE.—The statute embraces not merely conveyances made with intent to delay, hinder or defraud creditors, but conveyances made with the intent to delay, hinder or defraud others. The word "others" is inserted to take in all manner of persons as well creditors, after as before the conveyance whose debts should be defrauded. The enacting clause is still stronger because the word "creditors" is not mentioned, but general words "person or persons." The words of the statute seem to be so general in order to take in all persons who shall be any ways hindered.[1] It is accordingly well settled, that if a party makes a conveyance of his property with the express intent to become indebted to another, and to defraud him of his debt by means of this artifice, such subsequent creditor may contest and by proof defeat the transfer, although he was not a creditor of the grantor at the time of the conveyance.[2]

KIND OF INTENT.—The intent which will in general make such a transfer void, is an actual intent to defraud and must be proved,[3] and the burden of proof rests upon the subsequent creditor.[4] It is not necessary, however, to prove such intent by direct and express

---

[1] Taylor v. Jones, 2 Atk. 600.

[2] Littleton v. Littleton, 1 Dev. & Bat. 327; Ridgeway v. Underwood, 4 Wash. C. C. 129; Howe v. Ward, 4 Me. 195; Shontz v. Brown, 27 Penn. 123; Black v. Nease, 37 Penn. 433; Russell v. Stinson, 3 Hey. 1; New Haven St. Co. v. Vanderbilt, 16 Conn. 420; Cook v. Johnson, 1 Beasley, 51; National Bank v. Sprague, 5 C. E. Green, 13; Barling v. Bishopp, 29 Beav. 417; Stileman v. Ashdown, 2 Atk. 477; Rol. Abr. 34; Murphy v. Abraham, 15 Ir. Eq. (N. S.), 371; Miller v. Wilson, 15 Ohio, 108; Anon. 1 Wall. Jr. 107; Lyman v. Cessford, 15 Iowa, 229; Bogard v. Gardley, 4 S. & M. 402; Williams v. Banks, 11 Md. 198.

[3] Reid v. Gray, 37 Penn. 508; Horn v. Ross, 20 Geo. 210; Cole v. Varner, 31 Ala. 244; Lynch v. Raleigh, 3 Ind. 273; Nicholas v. Ward, 1 Head, 323; Blake v. Jones, 1 Bailey Ch. 141.

[4] Loeschigk v. Hatfield, 5 Robt. 26; Nicholas v. Ward, 1 Head, 323.

evidence, for this would be impracticable in many instances where the conveyance ought not to be established. The intent may be collected from the circumstances of the case, and such badges of fraud as the transaction wears.[1] Some of the usual badges are the recording,[2] or omission to record the conveyance,[3] possession of the property and obtaining a false credit thereby,[4] the subsequent erection of improvements,[5] the magnitude of the conveyance compared with the grantor's means,[6] the existence of prior debts at the time of the transfer,[7] the concealment,[8] or notoriety of the transfer,[9] the immediate engagement in a hazardous business,[10] and the contracting of debts immediately after the transfer.[11]

---

[1] Hutchinson v. Kelly, 1 Rob. 123; Larkin v. McMullen, 49 Penn. 29; Thomson v. Dougherty, 12 S. & R. 448; Bogard v. Gardley, 4 S. & M. 302; Wright v. Henderson, 7 How. (Miss.) 539; Johnston v. Zane, 11 Gratt. 552.

[2] Sexton v. Wheaton, 8 Wheat. 229; Bank v. Patton, 1 Rob. 499; Dick v. Hamilton, Deady, 322,

[3] Lyman v. Cessford, 15 Iowa, 229; Naylor v. Baldwin, Rep. Ch. 69; Beeckman v. Montgomery, 1 McCarter, 106; Case v. Phelps, 39 N. Y. 164; *in re* Rainsford, 5 B. R. 381; Keating v. Keefer, 5 B. R. 133; s. c. 4 A. L. T. 162.

[4] Pell v. Tredwell, 5 Wend. 661; Bradley v. Buford, Kentuck Decis. 19; Farmers' Bank v. Long, 7 Bush. 337; Ayer v. Bartlett, 6 Pick. 71; Merrill v. Rinker, 1 Bald. 528.

[5] Tappan v. Butler, 7 Bosw. 480; Dick v. Hamilton, Deady, 322.

[6] Belford v. Crane, 1 C. E. Green, 265.

[7] Richardson v. Rhodus, 14 Rich. 95; Huggins v. Perrine, 30 Ala. 396; Redfield v. Buck, 35 Conn. 328; Pawley v. Vogel, 42 Mo. 291.

[8] Hungerford v. Earle, 2 Vern. 261; Sands v. Hildreth, 2 Johns. Ch. 35; s. c. 14 Johns. 493; Lewkner v. Freeman, 2 Freem. 236.

[9] Madden v. Day, 1 Bailey, 337; Snyder v. Christ, 39 Penn. 503; Mixell v. Lutz, 34 Ill. 382; Roberts v. Gibson, 6 H. & J. 116.

[10] Mullen v. Wilson, 44 Penn. 413; Thomson v. Dougherty, 12 S. & R. 448; Beeckman v. Montgomery, 1 McCarter, 106; Cramer v. Reford, 2 C. E. Green, 367; Carpenter v. Roe, 10 N. Y. 227; Case v. Phelps, 39 N. Y. 164; Lyne v. Bank, J. J. Marsh. 545; Mackay v. Douglass, 26 L. T. (N. S.) 721.

[11] Barling v. Bishopp, 29 Beav. 417; Case v. Phelps, 39 N. Y. 164;

MERE SUBSEQUENT INDEBTEDNESS.—The simple fact
of a subsequent indebtedness is not sufficient to make
a transfer fraudulent. There must exist at the time on
the part of the grantor a fraudulent view, and until
this fraudulent purpose is established, either by positive proof or the exhibition of such facts as justify
the inference of its actual existence, the conveyance
cannot be set aside.[1] Even a mere expectation of indebtedness, or an intent to contract debts if there is
only an intent not coupled with a fraudulent purpose,
to convey the property in order to keep it from being
reached by creditors, will not render the transfer invalid.[2]
The mere intent to keep the property from subsequent
creditors is not alone sufficient. No conveyance can be
made which may not in certain contingencies tend to
put property beyond the reach of the creditors of the
grantor, and the happening of such contingencies may
be reasonably supposed to be within the contemplation
of every person, who does not intend to withdraw
himself from the active pursuits of life. But such a
conveyance is not for that reason void, as against
subsequent creditors, unless it is also made with a
design to defraud them. The conveyance must be
made with an intent to put the property out of
the reach of debts, which the grantor at the time
of the conveyance intends to contract, and which he
does not intend to pay, or has reasonable grounds to
believe, that he may not be able to pay. There need
not be an intent to contract any particular debt or

Bullitt v. Taylor, 34 Miss. 708; Lyman v. Cessford, 15 Iowa, 229; Snyder
v. Christ, 39 Penn. 499; Mason v. Rogers, 1 Root, 324; Thomson v.
Dougherty, 12 S. & R. 448; Herschfeldt v. George, 6 Mich. 456; Church-
hill v. Wells, 7 Cold. 364; Ware v. Gardner, L. R. 7 Eq. 317; Mackay v.
Douglas, 26 L. T. (N. S.) 721.

[1] Lyman v. Cessford, 15 Iowa, 229.

[2] Snyder v. Christ, 39 Penn. 499.

debts. It is sufficient if there is an intent to contract debts, and a design to avoid the payment of such debts by the conveyance.[1]

ACTUAL INTENT.—If a conveyance is made with direct reference to immediate future indebtedness, and with the actual intent to deprive the future creditor of a security, upon which he has a right to rely such intent, is actually fraudulent. Persons to whom a debt accrues, have a right to expect that their debtor will deal fairly and in good faith with them, and if upon the eve of an indebtedness about to be incurred and with a view thereto, and without the knowledge of the party extending the credit, the debtor makes a voluntary conveyance of property upon which he knows that his contemplated creditor relies or has a right to rely, this is an actual fraud, upon such subsequent creditor.[2] Such an act will not be relieved of its fraudulent character, by the mere fact that the conveyance is placed upon record if the creditor has no actual notice, and the conveyance without his negligence operates as a surprise upon him[3]

NOT MERE VOLUNTARY CONVEYANCE.—A voluntary conveyance made in good faith, and valid against creditors whose debts exist at the time of its execution, is also valid against subsequent creditors.[4] In

---

[1] Winchester v. Charter, 12 Allen, 606 ; s. c. 97 Mass. 140; s. c. 102 Mass. 272.

[2] Churchill v. Wells, 7 Cold. 364 ; Beeckman v. Montgomery, 1 Mc-Carter, 106 ; Barling v. Bishopp, 29 Beav. 417 ; Case v. Phelps, 39 N. Y. 164; Bullitt v. Taylor, 34 Miss. 708.

[3] Churchill v. Wells, 7 Cold. 364; Moore v. Blondheim, 19 Md. 172.

[4] Shaw v. Standish, 2 Vern. 326; Kipp v. Hanna, 2 Bland, 26 ; Kidney v. Coussmaker, 12 Ves. 136; Sagitary v. Hide, 2 Vern. 44; Walker v. Burrows, 1 Atk. 93; Townsend v. Windham, 2 Ves. Sr. 1; Roberts v. Gibson, 6 H. & J. 116; Holmes v. Penney, 3 K. & J. 90; Mattingly v.

such a case, the character or amount of the consideration is immaterial, and not the subject of inquiry. If there is no evidence of fraud in fact, in the execution of a deed or any subsequent acts from which fraud can be legally inferred, subsequent creditors can not be permitted to inquire into the fact, whether the consideration expressed is the true consideration. In other words they

Nye, 8 Wall. 370; Pike v. Miles, 23 Wis. 164; Lormore v. Campbell, 60 Barb. 62; Place v. Rhem, 7 Bush, 585; Tappan v. Butler, 7 Bosw. 480; Pierson v. Heisey, 19 Iowa, 114; Vance v. Smith, 2 Heisk. 343; Horn v. Volcano Co. 13 Cal. 62; Whitescarver v. Bonny, 9 Iowa, 480; Hamilton v. Thomas, 3 Hey. 127; Hanson v. Power, 8 Dana, 91; Winn v. Barnett, 31 Miss. 653; Johnston v. Zane, 11 Gratt. 552; Smith v. Littlejohn, 2 McCord, 362; Pepper v. Carter, 11 Mo. 540; Haskell v. Bakewell, 10 B. Mon. 106; Crumbaugh v. Kugler, 2 Ohio St. R. 373; Gugen v. Sampson, 4 F. & F. 974; Abbott v. Hurd, 7 Blackf. 510; Anon. 1 Wall. Jr. 107; Ingram v. Phillips, 3 Strobh. 565; Holloway v. Millard, 1 Madd. 414; Wells v. Stout, 9 Cal. 479; Niller v. Johnson, 27 Md. 6; Charlton v. Gardner, 11 Leigh, 281; Thomas v. DeGraffenreid, 17 Ala. 602; Cole v. Varner, 31 Ala. 244; Waterson v. Wilson, 1 Grant, 74; Kid v. Mitchell, 1 N. & M. 334; Usher v. Hazeltine, 5 Me. 471; Stiles v. Lightfoot, 26 Ala. 443; Richardson v. Rhodus, 14 Rich. 95; Paige v. Kendrick, 10 Mich. 300; Converse v. Hartley, 31 Conn. 372; Benton v. Jones, 8 Conn. 186; Hurdt v. Courtenay, 4 Met. (Ky.), 139; Lyman v. Cessford, 15 Iowa. 229; Mixell v. Lutz, 34 Ill. 382; Bohn v. Headley, 7 H. & J. 257; Reade v. Livingston, 3 Johns. Ch. 481; Bennett v. Bedford Bank, 11 Mass. 421; Lyne v. Bank, 5 J. J. Marsh. 545; Botts v. Cozine, Hoff. Ch. 79; Iley v. Niswanger, 1 McCord Ch. 518; Howard v. Williams, 1 Bailey, 575; Adams v. Adams, 1 Dane Ab. 628; Loeschigk v. Hatfield, 5 Robt. 26; Wilbur v. Fradenburgh, 52 Barb. 474; Holmes v. Clark, 48 Barb. 237; Howe v. Ward, 4 Me. 195; Bank v. Patton, 1 Rob. 499; Nicholas v. Ward, 1 Head, 323; Martin v. Oliver, 9 Humph. 561; Jones v. Marsh, Cas. temp. Talb. 64; Todd v. Hartley, 2 Met. (Ky.), 206; Eigleberger v. Kibler, 1 Hill Ch. 113; Sexton v. Wheaton, 8 Wheat. 228; Bank v. Housman, 6 Paige, 526; Cosby v. Ross, 3 J. J. Marsh. 290; Winebrenner v. Weisiger, 3 Mon. 32; Smith v. Greer, 3 Humph. 318; Ridgeway v. Underwood, 4 Wash. C. C. 129; Brewster v. Power, 10 Paige, 562; Baker v. Gilman, 52 Barb. 26; Reed v. Woodman, 4 Me. 400; Miller v. Miller, 23 Me. 22; Bangor v. Warren, 34 Me. 324; Bank v. Ennis, Wright, 605; Henderson v. [Dodd, 1 Bailey Ch. 138; *vide* Witherdon v. Jumper, May on Fraud, 519; Peterson v. Williamson, 2 Dev. 326.

are in no better situation than the grantor himself, through whom they claim who is estopped to deny that the consideration stated in the deed was actually received and paid. The extent and sufficiency of the consideration in reference to the value of the property is only material, where the grantor is indebted at the time of the conveyance, and creditors are seeking to set aside the deed on the ground of fraud. But for the mere purpose of conveying the property by an instrument, which is to operate under the statute of uses, it is sufficient, if any consideration appears upon the face of the conveyance, sufficient to raise the use, and neither the grantor nor his heirs are permitted to aver or prove that the consideration stated therein, did not in fact exist. If such consideration is expressed so as to make a valid deed as against the grantor, it will also be valid against subsequent creditors.[1]

VOID AGAINST PRIOR CREDITORS.—Subsequent creditors may, however, impeach a voluntary conveyance by showing antecedent debts sufficient in amount to afford a reasonable evidence of a fraudulent intent.[2] The intent to defraud antecedent creditors is *prima facie* evidence of an intent to defraud subsequent creditors.[3] The true principle is, that a fraudulent intent against one or more creditors is fraudulent against all, and the statute justifies no other distinction between prior and subsequent creditors than that which arises from the necessity of showing a fraudulent intent against some

---

[1] Bank of U. S. v. Housman, 6 Paige, 526.

[2] Mead v. Gregg, 12 Barb. 653; Richardson v. Rhodus, 14 Rich. 95; Huggins v. Perrine, 30 Ala. 396; Charlton v. Gardner, 11 Leigh, 281; Doyle v. Sleeper, 1 Dana, 531; Redfield v. Buck, 35 Conn. 328; Pawley v. Vogel, 42 Mo. 291.

[3] Horn v. Volcano Co. 13 Cal. 62.

creditor, which cannot be done in behalf of creditors whose demands were not in existence at the time of the conveyance, but by proving either a prior indebtedness or a prospective fraud against them only.[1] It is accordingly settled, that if the donor is insolvent at the time of the transfer, the conveyance is void as against subsequent creditors.[2] The general rule in regard to voluntary conveyances undoubtedly is that they are void only so far as may be necessary to satisfy prior creditors, and that if they are paid the conveyance will stand.[3]

CONTINUOUS INDEBTEDNESS.—The mere fact, however that the prior debts have been paid off will not alone render the transaction valid, though it is entitled to great weight. A great deal will depend upon the mode in which such debts are paid. Paying off one debt by contracting another is not getting out of debt. Proving therefore, that the prior debts have been paid off is doing nothing if in so doing the donor has contracted others to an equal amount,[4] and is not sufficient. *Ita demum revocatur quod fraudandorum causa factum est, si eventum fraus habuit; scilicet si hi creditores*

---

[1] Hutchinson v. Kelly, 1 Rob. 123; Thomson v. Dougherty, 12 S. & R. 448.

[2] Vertner v. Humphreys, 14 S. & M. 130; Iley v. Niswanger, 1 McCord Ch. 518; Carpenter v. Roe, 10 N. Y. 227; Madden v. Day, 1 Bailey, 337; Parish v. Murphree, 13 How. 92; Beach v. White, Walk. Ch. 495; Hurdt v. Courtenay, 4 Met. (Ky.) 139; Lowry v. Fisher, 2 Bush, 70; Ridgway v. Underwood, 4 Wash. C. C. 129.

[3] Ingrem v. Phillips, 3 Strobh. 565; O'Connor v. Bernard, 2 Jo. 654; Lyne v. Bank, 5 J. J. Marsh. 545; Sweny v. Ferguson, 2 Blackf. 129; Freeman v. Burnham, 36 Conn. 469; Abbott v. Tenney, 18 N. H. 109; Marsh v. Fuller, 18 N. H. 360; King v. Tharp, 26 Iowa, 283; Curtis v. Price, 12 Ves. 89; Pell v. Tredwell, 5 Wend. 661; Hudnal v. Wilder, 4 McCord, 294; Wilbur v. Fradenburgh, 52 Barb. 474; Webb v. Roff, 9 Ohio St. R. 430; Todd v. Hartley, 2 Met. (Ky.) 206; Converse v. Hartley, 31 Conn. 372.

[4] Madden v. Day, 1 Bailey, 337; Mills v. Morris, Hoff. Ch. 419.

*quorum fraudandorum causa fecit, bona ipsius vendi-
derunt, Cœterum si illos dimisit quorum fraudandorum
causa fecit, et alios sortitus est, si quidem simpliciter
dimissis prioribus quos fraudare voluit, alios postea
sortitus est, cessat revocatio: si autem horum pecunia
quos fraudare noluit, priores dimisit quos fraudare
voluit; Marcellus dicit revocationi locum fore. Secundum
hanc distinctionem et ab imperatore, Severo et Antonino
rescriptum est eoque jure utimur.*[1] Such a continuous indebtedness has been justly compared to a stone
descending a mountain covered with snow. Its bulk
is increased every time it rolls over, but still, every
added particle is referable to the stone originally
put in motion as the cause of its adhesion to the aggre-
gate mass.[2] In such instances the subsequent creditors
are subrogated to the rights of the creditors whose
debts their means have been used to pay.[3] Any other
rule would simply permit the debtor to take the property of subsequent creditors and give it to his donee.
The doctrine in regard to change of creditors, with a
continuation of indebtedness, only applies, however,
when the donor is insolvent at the time of the gift.[4]
There must be something more than an extensive business
whose balances are daily changing sides on his ledger.[5]
The proof of prior debts must be specific,[6] and this

---

[1] Dig. Lib. 42, tit. 9.

[2] Brown v. McDonald, 1 Hill Ch. 297.

[3] Richardson v. Smallwood, Jac. 552; Holmes v. Penney, 3 K. & J.
90; O'Connor v. Bernard, 2 Jo. 654; Mills v. Morris, 1 Hoffm. 419;
Savage v. Murphy, 34 N. Y. 508; s. c. 8 Bosw. 75; McElwee v. Sutton,
2 Bailey, 128; Churchill v. Wells, 7 Cold. 364; Madden v. Day, 1 Bailey,
337; Brown v. M'Donald, 1 Hill Ch. 297; Wilson v. Buchanan, 7
Gratt. 334; Beach v. White, Walk. Ch. 495; Mills. v. Morris, Hoff. Ch.
419; Whittington v. Jennings, 6 Sim. 493; Newlin v. Garwood, 1 Whart.
Dig. 572; Caston v. Cunningham, 3 Strobh. 59.

[4] Anon. 1 Wall. Jr. 107; Creed v. Lancaster Bank, 1 Ohio St. R. 1.

[5] Moritz v. Hoffman, 35 Ill. 553.

[6] Smith v. Greer, 3 Humph. 113; White v. Sansom, 3 Atk. 410.

proof must also be accompanied by evidence of the donor's inability to pay those debts.[1]

REMEDIES.—As there is no right without a remedy, it follows from the foregoing principles that subsequent creditors may institute proceedings to set aside a voluntary conveyance.[2] Whenever their rights depend upon the existence of prior debts, they must, however, show that there are such.[3] As a general rule, when a voluntary conveyance is set aside at the instance of prior creditors, subsequent creditors will participate in the fund.[4]

CONVEYANCE TO USE OF DEBTOR.—The statutes which make property conveyed to the use of the grantor liable to his debts are founded upon the principle that a man's property should pay his debts, although he has vested a nominal title in some one else. For that purpose they declare the title to be in the grantor, and no trans-

---

[1] Loeschigk v. Hatfield, 5 Robt. 26; Wilbur v. Fradenburgh, 52 Barb. 474; Hutchinson v. Kelly, 1 Rob. 123; Bank v. Patton, 1 Rob. 499.

[2] Thomson v. Dougherty, 12 S. & R. 448; Beach v. White, Walk. Ch. 495 ; Hurdt v. Courtenay, 4 Met. (Ky.) 139; Jenkyn v. Vaughan, 3 Drew, 419; Freeman v. Pope, 5 L. R. Ch. 538; Skarf v. Soulby, 1 Me. & G. 364; s. c. 1 H. & Tw. 426; Pratt v. Curtis, 6 B. R. 139; Chamley v. Dunsany, 2 Sch. & Lef. 689 ; vide Ede v. Knowles, 2 Y. & C. (N. S.) 172; Tripp v. Vincent, 3 Barb. Ch. 613.

[3] Lush v. Wilkinson, 5 Ves. 384; Holloway v. Millard, 1 Madd. 414; Manders v. Manders, 4 Ir. Eq. 434; Tripp v. Vincent, 3 Barb. Ch. 613, Kidney v. Coussmaker, 12 Ves. 136.

[4] Ammons' Appeal, 63 Penn. 284; Trimble v. Turner, 13 S. & M. 348; Beach v. White, Walk. Ch. 495; Norton v. Norton, 5 Cush. 524; Botts v. Cozine, Hoff. Ch. 79; Churchill v. Wells, 7 Cold. 364; Kidney v. Coussmaker, 12 Ves. 136, note; Iley v. Niswanger, 1 McCord Ch. 518; Hargroves v. Meray, 2 Hill Ch. 222; Kipp v. Hanna, 2 Bland, 26 : Thomson v. Dougherty, 12 S. & R. 448; Richardson v. Smallwood, Jac. 552; St. Amand v. Barbara, Com. 255; O'Connor v. Bernard, 2 Jo. 654; Contra, Williams v. Banks, 11 Md. 198; Ward v. Hollins, 14 Md. 158 ; vide Converse v. Hartley, 31 Conn. 372 ; Todd v. Hartley, 2 Met. (Ky.) 206.

fer which is entirely nominal can stand in the way. The simple inquiry is whether the property belongs to the debtor, not upon any theory of fraud and against the terms of the conveyance, but upon a theory of equitable title reserved to the grantor by the very terms of the conveyance, which transfers the legal and nominal title to another. Property so held in trust for the grantor is liable to subsequent as well as prior creditors.[1] A conveyance to the use of the grantor during his life with power to dispose of it by will or direct its course after his death, is a conveyance to his use, and the property so conveyed is liable to those who deal with him after its execution. A man can not be the equitable owner of property and still have it exempt from his debts.[2] A power of revocation inserted in a deed will also render the property liable to subsequent creditors.[3]

DISCRETION OF TRUSTEE.—A deed, however, is not fraudulent against subsequent creditors from the fact that it contains a trust to apply the interest of the property in such manner as the trustee in his discretion may think fit towards the benefit of the grantor, or his wife or his children. If the grantor parts *bona fide* by the deed with all control over the property and vests it in the trustee in order to give him the absolute power to deal with it as he pleases for the benefit of himself or his wife or his children, it is not fraudulent against subsequent creditors any more than if it were a conveyance simply for the benefit of the wife and children of

---

[1] Curtis v. Leavitt, 15 N. Y. 9.
[2] Mackason's Appeal, 42 Penn. 330; Brinton v. Hook, 3 Md. Ch. 477; Ford v. Caldwell, 3 Hill, (S. C.) 248; Coolidge v. Melvin, 42 N. H. 510; Hunters v. Waite, 3 Gratt. 26; Watts v. Thomas, 2 P. Wms. 364.
[3] Tarback v. Marbury, 2 Vern. 510.

the grantor. The mere fact that the grantor may possibly derive some benefit under it will not render it
fraudulent. If, however, there is any secret trust for
the benefit of the grantor, the deed will be fraudulent
under the statute.[1]

COLORABLE TRANSFERS.—If a deed is merely colorable, and a secret trust and confidence exist for the
benefit of the grantor, it is void not only against precedent but subsequent creditors, for it is in such a case
a continuing fraud, and may actually operate as such as
well in reference to debts contracted after as before the
conveyance. Property conveyed in trust is still the
property of the grantor for every beneficial purpose, and
the secret trust in a conveyance tainted with actual
fraud, renders the property liable to subsequent
creditors.[2] A discrimination, however, must be made
between the different kinds of fraudulent conveyances
and the different degrees and shades of fraud in each.
For some a valuable and adequate consideration is paid
yet they are made with a view to aid the debtor to

---

[1] Holmes v. Penney, 3 K. & J. 90.

[2] Clark v. French, 23 Me. 221; Whitmore v. Woodward, 28 Me. 392;
Damon v. Bryant, 2 Pick. 411; McLane v. Johnson, 43 Vt. 48; King v.
Wilcox, 11 Paige, 589; Henry v. Fullerton, 13 S. & M. 631; Hargroves v.
Meray, 2 Hill Ch. 222; Marston v. Marston, 54 Me. 476; Parkman v.
Welch, 19 Pick. 231; McConihe v. Sawyer, 12 N. H. 396; Ladd v.
Wiggin, 35 N. H. 421; Gove v. Lawrence, 26 N. H. 484; Wadsworth v.
Havens, 3 Wend. 411; Smith v. Espy, 1 Stockt. 160; Flynn v. Williams.
7 Ired. 32; Smith v. Lowell, 6 N. H. 67; Smyth v. Carlisle, 17 N. H. 417;
Dart v. Stewart, 17 Ind 221; Livermore v. Boutell, 11 Gray, 217; Hook
v. Mowre, 17 Iowa, 195; Ruffing v. Tilton, 12 Ind. 259; Ward v. Enders,
29 Ill. 519; Davis v. Stern, 15 La. An. 177; King v. Wilcox, 11 Paige,
589; Pennington v. Clifton, 11 Ind. 162; Herschfeldt v. George, 6 Mich,
456; Merrill v. Meachum, 5 Day, 341; Lewis v. Love, 2 B. Mon. 345;
Carlton v. King, 1 Stew. & Port. 472; Williams v. Avery, 38 Ala. 115;
vide Stone v. Myers, 9 Minn. 303; Lynch v. Raleigh, 3 Ind. 273; Summers v. Roos, 43 Miss. 749.

convert his property into that which can not be attached or levied upon, and so to aid him in placing it beyond the reach of creditors. Such conveyances will in general be good against subsequent creditors, for there is no secret trust for the benefit of the vendor.[1] The purpose or effect of a deed must in general be to injure subsequent creditors in order to render it void as to them. The question is generally one of fact. The conveyance can only be valid as to them when they are not intended or liable to be delayed, hindered, or defrauded by it.[2] When a transfer is rendered fraudulent by the retention of possession, it is also void as to them, for they are deceived by the false appearance of wealth and thereby induced to give the vendor credit.[3]

---

[1] Clark v. French, 23 Me. 221 ; O'Connor v. Bernard, 2 Jo. 654; Hall v. Sands, 52 Me. 355.

[2] Hall v. Sands, 52 Me. 355.

[3] Clow v. Woods, 5 S. & R. 275 ; Young v. Pate, 4 Yerg. 164; Smith v. Lowell, 6 N. H. 67; Paul v. Crooker, 8 N. H. 288; Woodrow v. Davis, 2 B. Mon. 298; Rankin v. Holloway, 3 S. & M. 614; Smith v. McDonald, 25 Geo. 377.

CHAPTER XIV.

ASSIGNMENTS FOR THE BENEFIT OF CREDITORS.

MODERN DEVICE.—Assignments for the benefit of creditors are for the most part an American device, and are of a comparatively modern origin.[1] It is true that deeds of composition have been used for a long time, but there is a manifest distinction between the two instruments. An assignment is a transfer by a debtor of the whole or a part of his effects to some person in trust to pay his creditors. A composition is a contract between a debtor and one or more of his creditors, by which it is agreed that the debtor shall be discharged on his transfer to such creditor or creditors of certain stipulated effects to be held by them absolutely. A mere glance at these definitions will show an essential distinction between the two transactions. An assignment is the voluntary act of the debtor. The creditors need not be consulted, nor need they be parties to it. A composition is necessarily the result of a treaty with the creditors severally, however many may join in the same writing and the creditors are parties to it.[2]

DEEDS OF TRUST.—There is also a distinction be-

---

[1] In Grover v. Wakeman, 11 Wend. 187, Senator Tracy says, that he can find no trace of their distinct recognition in the English courts prior to 1805; but Bamford v. Baron 2 T. R. 594, note is before that date.

[2] Wiener v. Davis, 18 Penn. 331; Grover v. Wakeman, 11 Wend. 187, per Senator Tracy.

tween an assignment and a deed of trust in the nature
of a mortgage. The former conveys the property absolutely to a trustee to be sold for the payment of the
debts named in it, and the latter purports to be a security for a debt with power to sell if the debt is not
paid.[1] The former is an absolute and indefeasible conveyance of the subject matter thereof for the purpose
expressed, whereas the latter is conditional and defeasible. A deed of trust in the nature of a mortgage
is a conveyance in trust by way of security, subject to
a condition of defeasance or redeemable at any time
before the sale of the property. A deed conveying
property to a trustee as mere collateral security for the
payment of a debt, with the condition that it shall become void on the payment of the debt when due and
with power to the trustee to sell the property and pay
the debt in case of default on the part of the debtor is
a deed of trust in the nature of a mortgage. By an absolute deed of trust the grantor parts absolutely with
the title, which vests in the grantee unconditionally for
the purpose of the trust. The latter is a conveyance to
a trustee for the purpose of raising a fund to pay debts,
while the former is a conveyance in trust for the purpose of securing a debt subject to a condition of defeasance.[2] The former the law presumes to be executed
with reference to the benefit of the creditors and not to
the advantage of the debtor. In one class the object is
to gain time for the debtor by agreement with the
creditor; in the other the debtor offers his property to
his creditors for distribution with such priorities as he
may prescribe.[3]

---

[1] State v. Benoist, 37 Mo. 500.
[2] Hoffman v. Mackall, 5 Ohio St. R. 124.
[3] Green v. Trieber, 3 Md. 11; Fouke v. Fleming, 13 Md. 392.

SOLVENT DEBTOR.—A voluntary deed of trust by a solvent debtor must not, moreover, be confounded with an assignment by an insolvent debtor, for the benefit of all or particular creditors.[1] It differs from a mortgage executed concurrently with the creation or extension of a debt because it is voluntary, and from an assignment by an insolvent debtor in view of his insolvency because it is the act of a solvent man. Such a deed of trust does not differ materially from a mortgage.[2] When it does not appear from the face of the deed that the grantor owes any debts besides those which he provides for, no inference can arise that it is made with the intent to delay, hinder, or defraud creditors, for where there are no creditors there can be no intention to defraud them.[3] But when the deed on its face purports to be made by a solvent debtor, proof may be given of his insolvency, and, if that is established, it will then be governed by the same principles as if the insolvency appeared on its face.[4] The avowed object of an assignment is to place the property conveyed by it beyond the legal pursuit of creditors, and by the instrument itself to provide another mode for the payment of their debts,[5] and it must not therefore contain any provisions to defeat or hinder this purpose beyond such reasonable delay as may be incidental and necessary to the proper execution of the trust.[6]

---

[1] Hodge v. Wyatt, 10 Ala. 271 ; Elmes v. Sutherland, 7 Ala. 262; Pope v. Wilson, 7 Ala. 690 ; Dubose v. Dubose, 7 Ala. 235 ; Graham v. Lockhart, 8 Ala. 9 ; Frow v. Smith, 10 Ala. 571 ; Fouke v. Fleming, 13 Md. 392 ; Hardy v. Skinner, 9 Ired. 191.

[2] Elmes v. Sutherland, 7 Ala. 262 ; Green v. Banks, 24 Tex. 508.

[3] Pope v. Wilson, 7 Ala. 690.

[4] Hardy v. Skinner, 9 Ired. 191; Hardy v. Simpson, 13 Ired. 132 ; Green v. Banks, 24 Tex. 508.

[5] Pope v. Wilson, 7 Ala. 690.

[6] Green v. Trieber, 3 Md. 11.

GENERAL AND PARTIAL.—Assignments for the benefit of creditors are commonly called voluntary assignments, to distinguish them from such as are made by the compulsion of the law.[1] There are two kinds of assignments, styled respectively general and partial. An assignment which conveys all the property of the debtor is a general assignment. One which conveys only a part of the property of the debtor is a partial assignment.[2] One of the primary and essential elements of an assignment is the transfer of the title and interest of the debtor in the property assigned.[3] The property must also be conveyed to an assignee, to be held by him in trust for creditors.[4] If either of these essentials is wanting, the transaction is not an assignment for the benefit of creditors.[5]

CREDITORS NOT PARTIES.—To the creation of a trust by deed in favor of any person, it is not necessary that the *cestui que trust* should either be a party or assent to it. It is clear that trusts may lawfully be created where there can be no present assent, for they may be in favor of persons not in existence. It is sufficient in general that in such cases there is a competent grantor to convey and a competent grantee to take the property. As to trusts created for the benefit of creditors, and to which they are not, technically speaking, parties, if *bona fide* made, they are unquestionably valid, and pass a legal estate to the trustee. The sole question that can arise, independent of the bankrupt law, is whether

---

[1] Manny v. Logan, 27 Mo. 528.

[2] Stetson v. Miller, 36 Ala. 642; Mussey v. Noyes, 26 Vt. 462; Noyes v. Hickok, 27 Vt. 36; Shapleigh v. Baird, 26 Mo. 322; Manny v. Logan, 31 Mo. 91; Lampson v. Arnold, 17 Iowa, 479.

[3] Banning v. Sibley, 3 Minn. 389.

[4] Peck v. Merrill, 26 Vt. 686; Mussey v. Noyes, 26 Vt. 462.

[5] Beans v. Bullitt, 57 Penn. 221.

the conveyance is *bona fide* or fraudulent.[1] It is not necessary that the deed shall be executed by the *cestuis que trust*, in order to give validity to its provisions. The instant the legal title becomes vested in the assignee a trust arises in behalf of those in whose favor it is declared, provided there is a sufficient consideration to sustain it.[2]

---

[1] Halsey v. Whitney, 4 Mason, 206; Nicoll v. Mumford, 4 Johns. Ch. 522; Houston v. Nowland, 7 G. & J. 480; Cunningham v. Freeborn, 11 Wend. 241; s. c. 3 Paige, 537; s. c. 1 Edw. 256; Marbury v. Brooks, 7 Wheat. 556; s. c. 11 Wheat. 78; Pope v. Brandon, 2 Stew. 401; Hempstead v. Johnston, 18 Ark. 123; Layson v. Rowan, 7 Rob. (La.) 1; Reinhard v. Bank of Kentucky, 6 B. Mon. 252; Jones v. Dougherty, 10 Geo. 273; Robinson v. Rapelye, 2 Stew. 86; Brown v. Minturn, 2 Gallis. 557; Wheeler v. Sumner, 4 Mason, 183; Duvall v. Raisin, 7 Mo. 449; Skipwith v. Cunningham, 8 Leigh, 271; U. S. Bank v. Huth, 4 B. Mon. 423; Repplier v. Buck, 5 B. Mon. 96; Hall v. Denison, 17 Vt. 310.

[2] Skipwith v. Cunningham, 8 Leigh, 271. The common law doctrine , in Maine, Massachusetts and New Hampshire, was different. An assignment was not valid without the assent of the creditors. An attachment made before such assent was given was entitled to priority. Widgery v. Haskell, 5 Mass. 144; Hooper v. Hills, 9 Pick. 435; Marston v. Coburn, 17 Mass. 454; Russell v. Woodword, 10 Pick. 408; Viall v. Bliss, 9 Pick. 18; Edwards v. Mitchell, 1 Gray, 239; Wiley v. Collins, 11 Me. 193; Carr v. Dole, 17 Me. 358; Leeds v. Sayward, 6 N. H. 83. With the assent of the creditors an assignment could be made. Stevens v. Bell, 6 Mass. 339; Collins v. Wiley, 11 Me. 193; Boyden v. Moore, 11 Pick. 162. When made without the assent of the creditors, it was valid as to those that did assent subsequently. Hastings v. Baldwin, 17 Mass. 552; Harris v. Sumner, 2 Pick. 129; Foster v. Saco Manuf. Co. 12 Pick. 451; Lupton v. Cutter, 8 Pick. 298; Nostrand v. Atwood, 19 Pick. 281; Everett v. Walcott, 15 Pick. 94; Beach v. Viles, 2 Pet. 675; Gore v. Clisby, 8 Pick. 555. An attachment was entitled to priority over creditors who subsequently assented. Ward v. Lamson, 6 Pick. 358; Bradford v. Tappan, 11 Pick. 76; Leeds v. Sayward, 6 N. H. 83; Denie v. Hart, 2 Pick. 204; Copeland v. Wells, 8 Me. 411. The burden of proof was on the assignee to show the existence of the debts, Russell v. Woodward, 10 Pick. 408, and that the property was needed to satisfy the demands of those who had assented. Borden v. Sumner, 4 Pick. 265; Widgery v. Haskell, 5 Mass. 144. It was not necessary that the assent should be in writing Wiley v. Collins, 11 Me. 193. An assignment could not be made by a deed poll. Boyden v. Moore, 11 Pick. 162; Brewer v. Pitkin, 11 Pick. 298. The law did not

22

CONSIDERATION.—A nominal consideration is sufficient to support the use.[1] If a consideration of money
is expressed in the assignment, no averment or evidence
can be received to the contrary.[2] The relation of debtor
and creditor between the assignor and assignee,[3] and
the undertaking on the part of the assignee to pay the
proceeds of the estate to the creditors of the assignor,[4]
are a sufficient valuable consideration. The real consideration is the debts due to the creditors, and these
constitute a valuable consideration in the highest sense
of the term,[5] and relieve the assignment from the imputation of fraud that would result from a naked gift.[6]

PRESUMPTION OF ASSENT.—The creditors may reject

---

give any preference to an attachment or an assignment, and would not
marshal the assets to aid either. Gore v. Clisby, 8 Pick. 555; Lupton v.
Cutter, 8 Pick. 295; Copeland v. Weld, 8 Me. 411. Under the present
statutes of Maine and New Hampshire, an assignment is valid against a
subsequent attachment, although the creditors have not assented. Fisk v.
Carr, 20 Me. 301; Fellows v. Greenleaf, 43 N. H. 421. The same rule
prevailed under the statute of Massachusetts, Shattuck v. Freeman, 1 Met.
10, but assignments are now void under the insolvent laws of that State.
Stanfield v. Simmons, 12 Gray, 442; Contra, Adams v. Blodgett, 2 Woodb.
& Min. 233.

[1] Cunningham v. Freeborn, 11 Wend. 241; U. S. Bank v. Huth, 4 B.
Mon. 423; Repplier v. Buck, 5 B. Mon. 96; Hall v. Denison, 17 Vt. 310;
Jones v. Dougherty, 10 Geo. 273; Contra, M'Kinley v. Combs, 1 Mon. 105.

[2] Wilt v. Franklin, 1 Binn. 502.

[3] Cunningham v. Freeborn, 11 Wend. 241; Ward v. Trotter, 3 Mon. 1;
Jones v. Dougherty, 10 Geo. 273.

[4] Wilt v. Franklin, 1 Birns. 502; Halsey v. Whitney, 4 Mason, 206;
Haven v. Richardson, 5 N. H. 113; U. S. Bank v. Huth, 4 B. Mon. 423;
Hall v. Denison, 17 Vt. 310; Petrikin v. Davis, Morris, 296; Fermester v.
McRorie, 12 Ired. 287; Gates v. Labeaume, 19 Mo. 17.

[5] Halsey v. Whitney, 4 Mason, 206; U. S. Bank v. Huth, 4 B. Mon.
423; Hudson v. Maze, 3 Scam. 578; Hall v. Denison, 17 Vt. 310; Lawrence v. Davis, 3 McLean, 177; Meeker v. Saunders, 6 Iowa, 61; Stephenson v. Hayward, Prec. Ch. 310; Hollister v. Loud, 2 Mich. 309; Gates v.
Labeaume, 19 Mo. 17.

[6] U. S. Bank v. Huth, 4 B. Mon. 423; Hollister v. Loud, 2 Mich. 309.

the beneficiary interest given to them by the assignment, and, if they do, it falls to the ground, and becomes
a resulting trust for the debtor. But if the trust is for
their benefit, the law presumes their assent to it until
the contrary is shown.[1] Whether the beneficiaries in
the trust deed are apprised of the conveyance or not is
not material. When it comes to their knowledge they
are entitled to accept or reject its provisions.[2] An express avowal of that assent is not necessary to the
operation of the assignment,[3] for the deed is complete
when executed by the parties to it.[4] If an assent is expressly given, it operates retroactively to confirm the
conveyance *ab initio*.[5] Even without such assent the
assignment will prevail over a subsequent execution or
attachment.[6] If one *cestui que trust* renounces the trust,
then it either enures solely to the benefit of the rest, or if
there are no others, it results to the debtor. But until
the renunciation is made, or implied from circumstances,
the trust continues. It arises without any act on the
part of the *cestuis que trust*, and in many instances they
may know nothing of it until sometime after the date

---

[1] Halsey v. Whitney, 4 Mason, 206; Wheeler v. Sumner, 4 Mason, 183;
Abercrombie v. Bradford, 16 Ala. 560; Farquharson v. McDonald, 2 Heisk,
404; England v. Reynolds, 38 Ala. 370; Hyde v. Olds, 12 Ohio St. R. 591;
Price v. Parker, 11 Iowa, 144; Fellows v. Greenleaf, 43 N. H. 421; Brown
v. Lyon, 17 Ala. 659; Rankin v. Lodor, 21 Ala. 380; Lanier v. Driver, 24
Ala. 149; Gale v. Mensing, 20 Mo. 461; Sadlier v. Fallon, 4 R. I. 490; U.
S. v. Bank of U. S., 8 Rob. (La.) 262; Forbes v. Scannell, 13 Cal. 242;
Tompkins v. Wheeler, 16 Pet. 106; *Contra*, Naylor v. Fosdick, 4 Day, 146;
Brown v. Burrill, 1 Root, 252; Widgery v. Haskell, 5 Mass. 144; Leeds v.
Sayward, 6 N. H. 83; Edwards v. Mitchell, 1 Gray, 239; Waters v. Cornly,
3 Harring. 117. In England each case is governed by its own circum-
stances. Smith v. Hurst, 10 Hare, 30; s. c. 15 E. L. & Eq. 520.

[2] Furman v. Fisher, 4 Cold. 626.

[3] Nicoll v. Mumford, 4 Johns. Ch. 522.

[4] Brooks v. Marbury, 11 Wheat. 78.

[5] Halsey v. Whitney, 4 Mason, 206.

[6] Rankin v. Lodor, 21 Ala. 380.

of its creation. The deed, however, is good and available on the instant of its execution, and can only be avoided by the dissent, express or implied, of the *cestuis que trust*.[1] The doctrine of implied assent is limited to those cases where there is a reasonable presumption of such assent, and does not apply to any deed which does not appear to be for the benefit of the creditors.[2] This presumption is not founded on the face of the instrument, but in the nature and circumstances of the entire case.[3]

The assignment, not only need not, but should not contain any provision for the creditors to sign it or become parties to it.[4] When it expressly excludes all implied assent, by requiring that the creditors shall manifest their consent in a prescribed mode,[5] or by stipulating for the sanction of a majority of the creditors, before it can take effect,[6] there can be no presumption of assent. When the provision is for those who execute it within a certain time, the creditors can only claim a benefit under it by executing it within that time.[7] The mere omission to sign the deed will not make the deed void unless there is some express requirement to that effect.[8] The assent will not be presumed unless the assignment devotes the property absolutely and under all circumstances to the payment of debts.[9]

---

[1] Skipwith v. Cunningham, 80 Leigh, 271.

[2] Smith v. Leavitts, 10 Ala. 92 ; Lockhart v. Wyatt, 10 Ala. 231.

[3] Stewart v. Spencer, 1 Curt. 157.

[4] Fellows v. Greenleaf, 43 N. H. 421.

[5] Todd v. Bucknam, 11 Me. 41; Swearinger v. Slicer, 5 Mo. 241; Moore v. M'Duffy, 3 Hawks, 578.

[6] Lawrence v. Davis, 3 McLean, 177; Shearer v. Loftin, 26 Ala. 703.

[7] Brown v. Lyon, 17 Ala. 653.

[8] Fellows v. Greenleaf, 43 N. H. 421 ; Gale v. Mensing, 20 Mo. 461.

[9] Kalkman v. McElderry, 16 Md. 56.

CONDITION.—Where there are conditions in the assignment as for instance that the creditors shall release their debts, the presumption of assent does not arise because it involves a question of discretion upon which different minds may draw different conclusions. If therefore an assent on the part of creditors is necessary to give full effect to such an assignment, it is not complete until such assent is expressly given.[1] This presumption of assent only arises when the deed is for the benefit of the creditors; consequently if it is fraudulent either in fact or in law, there is no such presumption.[2] No assent can he presumed when the assignment requires that the creditors shall give to the debtor a credit for the balance that remains due after the proceeds are distributed,[3] or where the majority of the creditors are to have the power to fix the time for the sale of the property,[4] or where the assignee is disqualified,[5] or where the liability of the assignee is limited to actual receipts or wilful defaults,[6] or where the assignees are not to be responsible for the neglect of each other.[7] There is also a distinction between an assignment by an insolvent debtor, and a deed of trust by a solvent debtor.[8] If the latter

---

[1] Halsey v. Whitney, 4 Mason, 206; Drake v. Rogers, 6 Mo. 317; Hurd v. Silsbee, 10 N. H. 108; *vide* Skipwith v. Cunningham, 8 Leigh, 271; Hall v. Dennison, 17 Vt. 310; Sadlier v. Fallon, 4 R. I. 490. Upon this subject the law varies with each State according to whether it upholds or avoids assignments exacting releases.

[2] Townsend v. Harwell, 18 Ala. 301; Stewart v. Spencer, 1 Curt. 157; Ashley v. Robinson, 29 Ala. 112; Benning v. Nelson, 23 Ala. 801; Baldwin v. Peet, 22 Tex. 708.

[3] Todd v. Bucknam, 11 Me. 41; Elmes v. Sutherland, 7 Ala. 262.

[4] Shearer v. Loftin, 26 Ala. 703.

[5] Spinney v. Portsmouth Co. 25 N. H. 9.

[6] Brown v. Warren, 43 N. H. 430; Spinney v. Portsmouth Co. 25 N. H. 9.

[7] Spinney v. Portsmouth Co. 25 N. H. 9.

[8] Elmes v. Sutherland, 7 Ala. 262; Hodge v. Wyatt, 10 Ala. 271;

postpones the time for payment beyond the time when the debts become due or involves any risk of the destruction or deterioration of the property, no presumption of assent will arise.[1]

Dissent.—The doctrine of implied assent is for the benefit of the ·creditors, and they may, if they think proper, decline to avail themselves of it.[2] And this may be done by any distinct and unequivocal act of renunciation.[3] Those who assail the assignment must repel the presumption of assent by proof of disclaimer or abandonment on the part of the creditors provided for.[4]

Effect of refusal.—The refusal of one or more creditors to accept, does not render the deed invalid as to other creditors who desire to claim a benefit under it. If valid in other respects the assignment is a security for them, notwithstanding, the refusal of one or more of the creditors to accept it. The effect of a refusal by a creditor to take under the deed, is the same as if he had been omitted.[5] The distinction is between a deed which contemplates or needs the assent of all the creditors before it can become complete or valid, and a deed which does not require the consent of all. In the latter case the assent of a part only

---

Pope v. Wilson, 7 Ala. 690; Dubose v. Dubose, 7 Ala. 235; Graham v. Lockhart, 8 Ala. 9.

[1] Hodge v. Wyatt, 10 Ala. 271; Elmes v. Sutherland, 7 Ala. 262 ; Evans v. Lamar, 21 Ala. 333; Kemp v. Porter, 7 Ala. 138; Graham v. Lockhart, 8 Ala. 9 ; Shearer v. Loftin, 26 Ala. 703.

[2] Smith v. Leavitts, 10 Ala. 92.

[3] Farquharson v. McDonald, 2 Heisk, 404.

[4] U. S. Bank v. Huth, 4 B. Mon. 423 ; Moffat v. Ingham, 7 Dana, 495.

[5] Smith v. Leavitts, 10 Ala. 92; Halsey v. Whitney, 4 Mason, 206 ; Hastings v. Baldwin, 17 Mass. 552; Gordon v. Coolidge, 1 Sumner, 537 ; Pitrikin v. Davis, Morris, 296; Kinnard v. Thompson, 12 Ala. 487.

will make it valid as far as it respects them.[1] In
the former case, inasmuch as there can be no presumption of assent, the deed is within the general rule of
mandates, that until the persons for whose benefit they
are made, signify their assent, they are revocable
by the grantor. In such case the levy of an execution
prior to the consent of all, is equivalent, so far as the
execution creditor is concerned, to a revocation by the
debtor.[2] This doctrine applies to all cases where the
presumption of assent does not arise.

IRREVOCABLE.—The debtor can not revoke the
assignment nor can he even extinguish it by getting a
reconveyance, for no act of the assignee can affect the
rights of the *cestuis que trust.*[3] The assignment, how-

---

[1] Mauldin v. Armitstead, 14 Ala. 702; Brown v. Lyon, 17 Ala. 659.

[2] Lockhart v. Wyatt, 10 Ala. 231; Hodge v. Wyatt, 10 Ala. 271;
Elmes v. Sutherland, 7 Ala. 262 ; Shearer v. Loftin, 26 Ala. 703.

[3] Furman v. Fisher, 4 Cold 626; Hyde v. Olds, 12 Ohio St. R. 591 ;
Ingram v. Kirkpatrick, 6 Ired. Eq. 462; Forbes v. Scannell, 13 Cal. 242;
Brown v. Chamberlain, 9 Fla. 464; Hall v. Denison, 17 Vt. 310; Stewart
v. Hall, 3 B. Mon. 218; *ex parte* Conway, 12 Ark. 302; Skipwith v. Cun-
nigham, 8 Leigh, 271; Sheldon v. Smith, 28 Barb. 593; *Contra,* Pitts v.
Viley, 4 Bibb. 446 ; M'Kinley v. Combs, 1 Mon. 105; Langton v. Tracey,
1 Nels. 126 ; Galt v. Dibrell, 10 Yerg. 146; Brevard v. Neely, 2 Sneed,
164.   The doctrine in England is that an assignment is revocable, Ger-
rard v. Lauderdale, 3 Sim. 1 ; Page v. Broom, 4 Russ. 6; Acton v. Woodgate, 2 M. & K. 492; Griffith v. Ricketts, 7 Hare, 299; Smith v. Hurst,
10 Hare, 30 ; Law v. Bagwell, 4 Dr. & War. 398; Brown v. Cavendish, 1
J. & L. 606 ; Gibbs v. Glamis, 11 Sim. 584; Ravenshaw v. Collier, 7 Sim.
3; Simmonds v. Palles, 2 J. & L. 489 ; Walwyn v. Coutts, 3 Sim. 14; s.
c. 3 Mer. 707; the deed is not revocable after such communications as
will give the creditors an interest in it; Griffith v. Ricketts, 7 Hare, 299 ;
Acton v. Woodgate, 2 M. & K. 492; Harland v. Binks, 69 E. C. L. 713;
nor when there is a covenant not to revoke ; Griffith v. Ricketts, 7 Hare,
299 ; nor after the payment of an instalment; Kirwan v. Daniel, 5 Hare,
493 ; the trustee upon revocation may retain for his own debt ; Wilding
v. Richards, 1 Coll. 655 ; Griffith v. Ricketts, 7 Hare, 299; Siggers v.
Evans, 32 E. L. & Eq. 139.

ever, is revocable when the creditors refuse to accept,[1] or when they delay for so long a time as to create a counter presumption to rebut the presumption of assent.[2]   In either of these cases it may be altered, cancelled, or changed by the parties to it.

PARTIES MAY ALTER.—An assignment which is fraudulent on its face is binding on those who assent to it,[3] and consequently the debtor alone can not change or modify the terms of the transfer in any respect.[4]   It is different, however, when the parties consent to a change.   The distinction between void and voidable must be regarded.   A deed or instrument utterly void is as one that never existed.   It passes nothing, confers no right or title upon the party named as grantee, and is of no effect as between the immediate parties to it.   An instrument or deed fraudulent as to creditors and voidable by them is nevertheless valid as between the parties to it, and the title is deemed to have passed and vested in the grantee.   A deed which is fraudulent under the statute, is voidable only and not absolutely void.[5]   A void deed is incapable of confirmation or of being made good by any subsequent act of the party, while one which is merely voidable may be confirmed and will then be effectual for all purposes unless the rights of third persons intervene and prevent it.

---

[1] Gibson v. Chedic, 1 Nev. 497; Gibson v. Rees, 50 Ill. 583.

[2] Gibson v. Rees, 50 Ill. 583.

[3] Hone v. Henriquez, 13 Wend. 240; s. c. 2 Edw. 120; Van Winkle v. McKee, 7 Mo. 435; Johns v. Bolton, 12 Penn. 339; Geisse v. Beall, 3 Wis. 367; Bellamy v. Bellamy, 6 Fla. 62.

[4] Porter v. Williams, 9 N. Y. 142; s. c. 12 How. Pr. 107; Sheldon v. Smith, 28 Barb. 593; Metcalf v. Van Brunt, 37 Barb. 621.

[5] Hone v. Woolsey, 2 Edw. 289.

MODE OF ALTERATION.—It is immaterial in what form the alteration may be made, whether by a reconveyance back to the debtor and a re-assignment by him or by another assignment without a reconveyance,[1] or by an instrument reiterating the trusts and dispensing with the provisions which make it void.[2] The court will look to the object and intent of the parties and give effect to their acts so as to carry such intention into effect wherever it is fair and honest. The only persons who need unite in such a reformation of the instrument are those who have in fact become parties to it. The title of the assignee is good in the first instance until creditors can take measures to impeach and avoid the instrument, and the creditors for whom no provision is made in the assignment can not complain of the modification, for no trust results in their favor.[3]

The validity of such a deed always depends upon the presumed assent of the creditors who are provided for by its terms, and when the deed is fraudulent there is no such presumption. The assignment then belongs to that class of instruments which is revocable until all the creditors have assented, and may be cancelled, abrogated, or modified at pleasure by those who are parties to it.[4] But one void deed can not be made good by another void deed, nor can the two be construed together as one instrument.[5] A deed of appointment under a power reserved in the assignment can not

---

[1] Brahe v. Eldridge 17 Wis. 184; Bridges v. Hindes, 16 Md. 101; Sumner v. Hicks, 2 Black, 532; Ingraham v. Wheeler, 6 Conn. 277; Mills v. Argall, 6 Paige, 577; Pierce v. Brewster, 32 Ill. 268.

[2] Hone v. Woolsey, 2 Edw. 289; Conkling v. Carson, 11 Ill. 503 ; Merrill v. Englesby, 28 Vt. 150; Murray v. Riggs, 15 Johns. 571; *vide* Porter v. Williams, 9 N. Y. 142; s. c. 12 How. Pr. 107 ; Smith v. Howard, 20 How. Pr. 121 ; Gates v. Andrews, 37 N. Y. 657.

[3] Hone v. Woolsey, 2 Edw. 289.

[4] Insurance Co. v. Wallis, 23 Md. 173.

[5] Bridges v. Hindes, 16 Md. 101.

have any more validity than the assignment itself, for
it can not be supported and carried into effect while
the assignment is set aside.[1]   There must in all cases be
an abandonment of the fraudulent deed.   The assignee
can not hold the good security and yet avail himself of
that which is vicious, much less can he make the new
security a means of sustaining that which is illegal.[2]
An alteration or revocation can not prejudice the rights
of a creditor who has obtained a valid lien upon the
property.[3]

FORM.—No particular form of words or instrument
is necessary to constitute a valid assignment of chattels
or *choses in action.*   Any valid transfer by which the
uses and trusts for which the property is assigned and
to which it is to be appropriated by the assignee, are
intelligibly indicated and declared, is an assignment.[4]
If the deed is intelligible, brevity is not a badge of
fraud.[5]   In general, it is not desirable to do more than
to direct, in general terms, a sale of the property and
collection of the debts assigned, and to designate to
what debts and in what order the proceeds shall be
applied.[6]   An assignment of personal property and
choses in action need not be under seal.[7]   It may be by
parol.   A mere delivery of the subject assigned is sufficient.[8]   The form of the assignment is immaterial.   An

---

[1] Lentilhon v. Moffat, 1 Edw. 451; Averill v. Loucks, 6 Barb. 470;
Mitchell v. Stiles, 13 Penn. 306; *vide* Murray v. Riggs, 15 Johns. 571;
s. c. 2 Johns. Ch. 565.

[2] Mackie v. Cairns, 5 Cow. 547; s. c. 1 Hopk. 373; D'Ivernois v.
Leavitt, 23 Barb. 63.

[3] Porter v. Williams, 9 N. Y. 142; s. c. 12 How. Pr. 107; Gates v.
Andrews, 37 N. Y. 657.

[4] Norton v. Kearney, 10 Wis. 443.

[5] Forbes v. Scannell, 13 Cal. 242; Meeker v. Saunders, 6 Iowa, 61.

[6] Dunham v. Waterman, 17 N. Y. 9; Jessup v. Halse, 21 N. Y. 168.

[7] Forbes v. Scannell, 13 Cal. 242.

[8] Brown v. Chamberlain, 9 Fla. 464.

assignment consisting of three parts is as valid as an assignment consisting of but one part.[1] *Choses in action* may be assigned as well as property susceptible of or actually reduced to possession.[2] When an assignment is made by a firm, and some of the partners constitute another firm, the assets of both firms may be assigned by one and the same deed instead of by different deeds.[3]

SCHEDULES.—No schedule either of the creditors or of the property need be annexed.[4] The fact that it transfers money and *choses in action* does not make any difference.[5] An enumeration in detail is not necessary to make a legal transfer. It is sufficient if there is reasonable certainty in the description of the property intended to be conveyed.[6] If there is no such certainty

---

[1] Page v. Weymouth, 47 Me. 238.

[2] U. S. v. Bank of U. S. 8 Rob. (La.) 262.

[3] Gordon v. Cannon, 18 Gratt. 387.

[4] Brashear v. West, 7 Pet. 608: Wilt v. Franklin, 1 Binn. 502; Hower v. Glasaman, 17 S. & R. 251; Wooster v. Stanfield, 11 Iowa, 128; Brown v. Chamberlain, 9 Fla. 464; Halsey v. Whitney, 4 Mason, 206; Pearpoint v. Graham, 4 Wash. C. C. 332; Keyes v. Brush, 2 Paige, 311; Cunningham v. Freeborn, 11 Wend. 241; Meeker v. Saunders, 6 Iowa, 61; Parker v. Price, 11 Iowa, 144; Gordon v. Cannon, 18 Gratt. 387; Forbes v. Scannell, 13 Cal. 242; Linn v. Wright, 18 Tex. 317; Haven v. Richardson, 5 N. H. 113; Deaver v. Savage, 3 Mo. 252; Duvall v. Raisin, 7 Mo. 449; Robins v. Embry, 1 S. & M. Ch. 207; *ex parte* Conway, 12 Ark. 302; U. S. Bank v. Huth, 4 B. Mon. 423; Dana v. Lull, 17 Vt. 390; Kevan v. Branch, 1 Gratt. 274; Brown v. Lyon, 17 Ala. 659; Shackelford v. Planters' Bank, 22 Ala. 238; Hollister v. Loud, 2 Mich. 309; Matthews v. Poultney, 33 Barb. 127; Robinson v. Rapelye, 2 Stew. 86; Strong v. Carrier, 13 Conn. 319; Pitrikin v. Davis, Morris, 296; Nye v. Van Husan, 6 Mich. 329.

[5] Brown v. Lyon, 17 Ala. 659.

[6] Halsey v. Whitney, 4 Mason, 206; Spring v. Strauss, 3 Bosw. 607; Emerson v. Knower, 8 Pick. 63; Woodward v. Marshall, 22 Pick. 468; Haven v. Richardson, 5 N. H. 113; Rundlett v. Dole, 10 N. H. 458; Clark v. Mix, 15 Conn. 152; Birchell v. Strauss, 28 Barb. 293.

in the description of the articles purported to be conveyed, no transfer is effected.[1]

STATEMENT OF DEBTS.—There need be no estimate of the value of the property. All the debtor wants and all the creditors can expect is that the fair value of the property shall be applied to the payment of the debts, and that value is best ascertained by a sale of the property.[2] But where a schedule is made a part of the conveyance, and is referred to as containing a specification of the property intended to be conveyed, it must be annexed not only as a description and specification of the property, but as necessary by the very terms of the instrument to complete the conveyance or transfer, and without it the deed is void.[3] The assignment need not name the creditors or the amount due to each. This must necessarily be the form of every general assignment for the benefit of all the creditors, for otherwise it would be special as to the persons named.[4] A description of the debts so as to identify them is all that is necessary, and this is important to the creditors. A debt may be described by the name of the creditor, and its amount may be left to be ascertained subsequently.[5] It is a direction to pay the sum due whatever that may be.[6] The fact that some of the creditors are workmen is immaterial.[7] There need be no schedule of the creditors, to whom no preference is given.[8] An

---

[1] Crow v. Ruby, 5 Mo. 484; Drakeley v. Deforest, 3 Conn. 272; Ryerson v. Eldred, 18 Mich. 12.

[2] Haven v. Richardson, 5 N. H. 113; England v. Reynolds, 38 Ala. 370.

[3] Moir v. Brown, 14 Barb. 39.

[4] England v. Reynolds, 38 Ala. 370; Brown v. Knox, 6 Mo. 302; U. S. Bank v. Huth, 4 B. Mon. 423; Barcroft v. Snodgrass, 1 Cold. 430; Van Hook v. Walton, 28 Tex. 59; *vide* Caton v. Moseley, 25 Tex. 374.

[5] Layson v. Rowan, 7 Rob. (La.) 1; Van Hook v. Walton, 28 Tex. 59.

[6] Butt v. Peck, 1 Daly, 83.

[7] Bank v. Talcott, 22 Barb. 550.

[8] Halsey v. Whitney, 4 Mason, 206.

omission of the schedule of preferred creditors will not make the assignment void when the other trusts are capable of execution.[1] Creditors may be required to cause the amount of their claims to be written on a schedule.[2] The parties may provide for a future enumeration and annex schedules subsequently.[3] They may allow additions to be made with the consent of the debtor, the assignee and any one of the creditors.[4] A clause which requires an oath to be made by the omitted creditors, at the option of the assignee, does not make the assignment void, for it merely reposes confidence in him in the discharge of his duties.[5]

OMISSION IS BADGE OF FRAUD.—The omission of schedules is, however, a badge of fraud.[6] This is but an application of the maxim that fraud lurks in loose generalities. It is, moreover, difficult to conceive of anything better calculated to delay creditors than a deed of assignment conveying all the property real and personal of the debtor, without any description or estimate of value for the benefit of creditors who are not consulted or named in the deed, or the amounts due them set forth or in any way made known.[7]

---

[1] Scott v. Guthrie, 10 Bosw. 408.

[2] Todd v. Bucknam, 11 Me. 41.

[3] Halsey v. Whitney, 4 Mason, 206 ; Bank v. Talcott, 22 Barb. 550; Ely v. Hair, 16 B. Mon. 230; Clap v. Smith, 16 Pick. 247.

[4] Halsey v. Whitney, 4 Mason, 206.

[5] Halsey v. Whitney, 4 Mason, 206.

[6] Brown v. Lyon, 17 Ala. 659; Pine v. Rikert, 21 Barb. 469; Kellogg v. Slauson, 15 Barb. 56 ; Van Nest v. Yoe, 1 Sandf. Ch. 4; Pearpoint v. Graham, 4 Wash. C. C. 232; Stevens v. Bell, 6 Mass. 339; Halsey v. Whitney, 4 Mason, 206 ; Wilt v. Franklin, 1 Binn. 502.

[7] Cummings v. McCullough, 5 Ala. 324. In Indiana, the schedule need not be recorded with the assignment. Black v. Weathers, 26 Ind. 242. In New York, by act of 1860, Ch. 348, § 2, the debtor is required within twenty days to make and deliver to the county judge an inventory, verified by affidavit. A failure to comply with the statute makes the assign-

DESIGNATION OF ASSIGNEE.—The assignee must be designated. When the assignment is made to partners, it is not material whether they are designated by the firm name or their individual names, if the language used is such as to indicate with certainty the persons who are nominated as assignees.[1] The insertion of the name of the assignee is essential to the validity of the instrument.[2] A delivery of the assignment to the assignee is sufficient.[3] A delivery in fact or in law to some person, or into some place beyond the debtor's control, is indispensable.[4] A delivery to the clerk to be recorded,[5] or to a third person,[6] or a deposit of it in the post office,[7] is sufficient. There must also be an acceptance of the trust. A delivery without an acceptance is nugatory.[8] The mere taking of the instrument and retaining it is nothing. An agreement to accept before the execution of the assignment is sufficient.[9] The acceptance will be presumed;[10] but this presumption is

---

ment void. Juliand v. Rathbone, 39 N. Y. 369; Fairchild v. Gwynne. 16 Ab. Pr. 23; s. c. 14 Abb. Pr. 121; De Camp v. Marshall, 2 Abb. Pr. (N. S.) 373; *Contra*, Evans v. Chapin, 12 Abb. Pr. 161; s. c. 20 How. Pr. 289; Van Vleet v. Slauson, 45 Barb. 317; Barbour v. Everson, 16 Abb. Pr. 366; Read v. Worthington, 9 Bosw. 617.

[1] Forbes v. Scannell, 13 Cal. 242.

[2] Reamer v. Lamberton, 59 Penn. 462.

[3] Ingraham v. Grigg, 13 S. & M. 22.

[4] Marston v. Coburn, 17 Mass. 454; M'Kinney v. Rhoades. 5 Watts, 343; Brevard v. Neely, 2 Sneed, 164; Caldwell v. Bruggerman, 4 Minn. 270; Van Hook v. Walton, 28 Tex. 59.

[5] Tompkins v. Wheeler, 16 Pet. 106; Major v. Hill, 13 Mo. 247; Hoffman v. Mackall, 5 Ohio St. R. 124.

[6] Moore v. Collins, 3 Dev. 126.

[7] M'Kinney v. Rhoades, 5 Watts, 343.

[8] Crosby v. Hillyer, 24 Wend. 280; Quincy v. Hall, 1 Pick. 357; Pierson v. Manning, 2 Mich. 445.

[9] Hoffman v. Mackall, 5 Ohio St. R. 124.

[10] Wilt v. Franklin, 1 Binn. 502; M'Kinney v. Rhoades, 5 Watts, 343; Siggers v. Evans, 32 Eng. L. & Eq. 139.

liable to be rebutted.[1]   An acceptance before any ad-
verse steps are taken by others is sufficient.[2]

It is not necessary for the assignee to sign the deed
to make it valid.   All that equity requires is his assent
and acceptance of the trust.   If he does any one act by
which his assent may be implied, equity holds him
bound for its performance, and will not release him from
his voluntary obligation.   There is no necessity for the
execution by the assignee.   Any act done in relation
to the property, showing that he claims it as assignee,
or desires to reduce it into possession, undeniably prove
his assent.[3]   Taking possession of the estate is an acceptance of the trust, and binds the assignee to execute it
in every particular as effectually as if he enters into an
express covenant to do so.[4]   When there are two
assignees, if one refuses to accept, the other assignee becomes vested with the trust in the same manner as if
the dissenting assignee had not been named in the instrument.[5]   The assignee cannot, without the consent of
the debtor, accept the assignment in part and reject it
in part.   If he adopts it all, he must adopt it *in toto*.
He cannot affirm it as to some debts and disaffirm it as
to others.[6]   The assignee's title to the goods is complete
by the execution of the assignment, subject to be defeated by his laches in not giving reasonable notice, or
in not following up his title to possession.[7]

---

[1] Wilt v. Franklin, 1 Binn. 502; Crosby v. Hillyer, 24 Wend. 280;
Pierson v. Manning, 2 Mich. 445; Spencer v. Ford, 2 Rob. (Va.) 648.

[2] Lampson v. Arnold, 19 Iowa, 479.

[3] *Ex parte* Conway, 12 Ark. 302; Flint v. Clinton Co. 12 N. H. 430;
State v. Benoist, 37 Mo. 500.

[4] Cunningham v. Freeborn, 11 Wend. 241; Price v. Parker, 11 Iowa, 144.

[5] Mead v. Phillips, 1 Sandf. Ch. 83; Moir v. Brown, 14 Barb. 39;
Metcalf v. Van Brunt, 37 Barb. 621; Gordon v. Coolidge, 1 Sumner, 537;
ex parte Conway, 12 Ark. 302; Forbes v. Scannell, 13 Cal. 242.

[6] Gordon v. Coolidge, 1 Sumner, 537.

[7] Bholen v. Cleveland, 5 Mason, 174; West v. Tupper, 1 Bailey, 193;

LEGAL EFFECT.—The assignment creates a trust. All
the legal interest vests nominally in the assignee, but
substantially in the *cestuis que trust* or creditors, and
the residuum, if any, after the payment of debts results
to the grantor. The assignee has not even a beneficiary
interest in the estate; he is seized for others, and not
for himself. The moment he is seized, that moment all
the substantial interests pass out of him into others.
He is merely the legal recipient or organ by which the
conveyance is rendered valid for higher and more beneficial purposes. In no possible event or contingency
can he take or retain any interest in his own hands for
himself without being called to account, and pay over
to those who are equitably entitled to take it. All the
parties to the deed have the right to go into a court of
equity and have the trust specifically executed.[1] The
recording of an assignment is, in the absence of fraud,
sufficient notice to creditors.[2]

INCIDENT OF OWNERSHIP.—The right to make an
assignment results from that absolute dominion which
every man has over that which is his own, and is not of
itself calculated to excite suspicion.[3] If a debtor can
make a valid assignment of his property to his creditors
to pay his debts, he can execute a like conveyance to
an assignee to discharge the demands of his creditors.
The assignee is the medium through which the payment
is directed to be made. He is seized of the legal estate
for the benefit of the creditors, all equity being in the

Frazier v. Fredericks, 1 Zab. 162; Wilt v. Franklin, 1 Bin. 502; *Contra*,
Caldwell v. Buggerman, 4 Minn. 270.

[1] *Ex parte* Conway, 12 Ark. 302; U. S. Bank v. Huth, 4 B. Mon. 423;
Hall v. Dennison, 17 Vt. 310; Houston v. Nowland, 7 G. & J. 480; Marbury
v. Brooks, 7 Wheat. 556; s. c. 11 Wheat. 78.

[2] Farquharson v. Eichelberger, 15 Md. 63.

[3] Brashear v. West, 7 Pet. 608; *ex parte* Conway, 12 Ark. 302.

cestuis que trust, and the assignment only constitutes the means and appointment by which debts are to be paid. If a debtor can pay his debts directly to his creditors himself, there is nothing to prevent him from directing a third person or assignee to pay them. If in one instance it is a moral as well as a legal duty to pay, in the other it is but the performance of the same act, and is supported by the same just consideration. Neither the amount of the indebtedness, nor the means by which debts are directed to be paid, can alter the right to make payment. It is the right, as well as the duty, of a debtor to devote his property to the satisfaction of his debts, and the exercise of this right by the honest performance of this duty can not be deemed a fraud. Such assignments are usually made to an assignee because the mode of distributing the fund is in general far more convenient than for the debtor to make payment directly to the creditors themselves. It is doing the same thing indirectly instead of directly.[1]

WHO MAY ASSIGN.—A corporation, unless restrained by some statute or express provision in its charter, may make an assignment as well as an individual.[2] An assignment may be made by an executor.[3]

PARTNERS.—It is not competent for one partner,

---

[1] *Ex parte* Conway, 12 Ark. 302.

[2] Hill v. Reed, 16 Barb. 280; McCallie v. Walton, 37 Geo. 611; State v. Bank, 6 G. & J. 205; Union Bank v. Ellicott, 6 G. & J. 363; De Ruyter v. St. Peter's Church, 3 N. Y. 238; Pope v. Brandon, 2 Stew. 401; Robins v. Embry, 1 S. & M. Ch. 207; *ex parte* Conway, 12 Ark. 302; Flint v. Clinton Co. 12 N. H. 430; Hopkins v. Gallatin Co. 4 Humph. 403; London v. Parsley, 7 Jones (N. C.), 313. Assignments by corporations, in contemplation of insolvency, are prohibited in New York by 1 Rev. Stat. 603, § 4; Sibell v. Remsen, 33 N. Y. 95; Smith v. Consolidated Stage Co. 18 Abb. Pr. 418; Robinson v. Bank, 21 N. Y. 406; Loring v. Vulcanized Gutta Percha Co. 36 Barb. 329; s. c. 30 Barb. 644; Harris v. Thompson, 15 Barb 62.

[3] Wolverhampton Bank v. Marston, 7 H. & N. 147.

23

without the assent or authority of the other partners, to make a general assignment of the partnership property to a trustee for the payment of debts. No such power can be implied from the partnership relation. Each partner possesses an equal and general power and authority in behalf of the firm to dispose of the partnership property and effects for any and all purposes within the scope of the partnership and in the course of its trade and business. But the authority of each of several partners as agent of the firm is necessarily limited to transactions within the scope and object of the partnership and in the course of its trade or affairs. A general assignment to a trustee of all the funds and effects of the partnership for the benefit of creditors is the exercise of a power without the scope of the partnership enterprise and amounts of itself to a suspension or dissolution of the partnership itself. It is no part of the ordinary business of the partnership but outside and subversive of it. No such authority as that can be implied from the partnership relation.[1] One partner may execute an assignment when he has previous authority.[2] The same reason applies where an ex-

---

[1] Welles v. March, 30 N. Y. 344 ; Coope v. Bowles, 42 Barb. 87 ; s. c. 18 Abb. Pr. 442; s. c. 28 How. Pr. 10 ; Robinson v. Gregory, Appeals Dec. 1863 ; s. c. 29 Barb. 560 ; Hughes v. Ellison, 5 Mo. 463 ; Dana v. Lull, 17 Vt. 390 ; Hook v. Stone, 34 Mo. 329 ; Gates v. Andrews, 37 N. Y. 657 ; Stein v. La Dow, 13 Minn. 412 ; Havens v. Hussey, 5 Paige, 30 ; Hitchcock v. St. John, 1 Hoff. 511 ; Kirby v. Ingersoll, Harring. Ch. 172 ; Sheldon v. Smith, 28 Barb. 593 ; McClelland v. Remsen, 36 Barb. 622 ; s. c. 14 Abb. Pr. 331; s. c. 23 How. Pr. 175 ; Bowen v. Clark, 5 A. L. Reg. 203 ; *Contra*, Deckard v. Case, 5 Watts, 22 ; Hennessey v. Western Bank, 6 W. & S. 300 ; Robinson v. Crowder, 4 McCord, 519 ; Gordon v. Cannon, 18 Gratt. 387.

[2] Welles v. March, 30 N. Y. 344 ; Baldwin v. Tynes, 19 Abb. Pr. 32 ; Kelly v. Baker, 2 Hilt. 531 ; Roberts v. Shephard, 2 Daly, 110 ; Harrison v. Sterry, 5 Cranch, 289 ; Kendall v. New Eng. Carpet Co. 13 Conn. 383 ; Pike v. Bacon, 21 Me. 280 ; Kemp v. Carnley, 3 Duer, 1 ; Forbes v. Scannell, 13 Cal. 242 ; Lassel v. Tucker, 5 Sneed. 1.

traordinary emergency occurs in the affairs of the partnership and the other partner can not be consulted on account of his absence under circumstances which furnish reasonable ground for inferring that he intended to confer upon the assigning partner authority to do any act for the firm which could be done with his concurrence if he were present. An assignment will be valid when the assignor is the sole manager and the other partner lives out of the State,[1] or in a foreign country.[2] One partner may also make an assignment when the other partner assents,[3] or absconds,[4] or has sold out his interest to the assignor.[5] A dormant partner need not execute the assignment.[6] Surviving partners may make an assignment.[7] Partners can not make an assignment when one is a minor, for the assignment must be absolute and irrevocable and not subject to any defeasance by the act of any of the parties, but the act of the infant is voidable and may be counteracted by him either before or at maturity.[8]

INCIDENTAL DELAY.—The necessary effect of every general assignment even where the creditors are to be paid *pari passu* is to hinder and delay them in the collection of their debts, by withdrawing the property from the reach of any legal process to which they may wish to resort. It interrupts and presents obstacles to their legal remedies, and thus tends to hinder those

---

[1] McCullough v. Summerville, 8 Leigh, 415.

[2] Forbes v. Scannell, 13 Cal. 242.

[3] Ely v. Hair, 16 B. Mon. 230 ; Mills v. Argall, 6 Paige, 577.

[4] Palmer v. Myers, 29 How. Pr. 8; s. c. 43 Barb. 509 ; National Bank v. Sackett, 2 Daly, 395.

[5] Clark v. McClelland, 2 Grant, 31.

[6] Drake v. Rogers, 6 Mo. 317.

[7] Egbert v. Woods, 3 Paige, 517; Hutchinson v. Smith, 7 Paige, 26; French v. Lovejoy, 12 N. H. 458 ; *Contra*, Barcroft v. Snodgrass, 1 Cold. 430.

[8] Fox v. Heath, 21 How. Pr. 384 ; Yates v. Lyon, 5 A. L. J. 122.

who are disposed to prosecute their suits.[1]   Not only is such its necessary effect, but the actual intent of the debtor generally is to place the property beyond the immediate power and action of his creditors by preventing them from obtaining any judgments by which it may be bound, or from issuing any execution or attachment under which it may be sold. He means to hinder the creditors from collecting their debts out of his property by any proceeding against himself as their debtor, and to delay them from receiving any portion of their debts until they shall become entitled to a dividend under the assignment. The intent thus to hinder and delay them is not only to be plainly deduced from the nature of the trust, but not unfrequently is confessed by its terms. In fact it was upon this very ground, the apparent and certain intent to hinder and delay the creditors, that originally the validity of a general assignment, although for the benefit of all the creditors without distinction, was not only seriously doubted but seriously contested.[2] But it is not every conveyance which will have the effect of delaying or hindering creditors in the collection of their debts that is fraudulent within the statute, for such is the effect *pro tanto* of every assignment that can be made by one who has creditors. Every assignment of a man's property, however good and honest the consideration, must diminish the fund out of which satisfaction is to be made to his creditors.

WHAT INTENT IS NECESSARY.—The object of the statute is to prevent deeds fraudulent in their inception and intention, and not merely such as in

---

[1] Dunham v. Waterman, 17 N. Y. 9 ; *vide* Burdick v. Post, 12 Barb. 168.

[2] Pickstock v. Lyster, 3 M. & S. 371; King v. Watson, 3 Pri. 6.

their effect may hinder or delay creditors. It is the corrupt and covinous motive, the fraudulent intention, the *mala mens*, with which the assignment or conveyance is made that constitutes the fraud against which the denunciations of the statute are directed, and without the existence, in fact, or presumed existence of an immoral or bad intention or motive, fraud can not be perpetrated either at common law or under the statute.[1] Fraud depends not upon the fact of delay but upon the character of the delay and the motive which actuates it.[2] The statute was never intended to restrict the debtor from paying or securing creditors whom moral duty and a sense of justice may dictate the propriety of paying or securing, or from doing equal and exact justice to all by placing his means in a condition to that end. So long as a debtor remains in contemplation of law the absolute owner of property, it can not be said of an appropriation of that property exclusively to the purpose of paying debts that it is a contrivance to delay, hinder, and defraud creditors. He merely exerts a power over property which the law gives him as owner for a purpose which is not in law wrongful.[3] Such an appropriation can not be deemed to be made with the fraudulent intent or purpose to hinder or delay, but with the higher and better intent and purpose of paying or securing all equally, or providing for those who are most meritorious.[4] All the law can reasonably demand is a faithful application of the debtor's property

---

[1] U. S. Bank v. Huth, 4 B. Mon. 423 ; Hollister v. Loud, 2 Mich. 309 ; Meux v. Howell, 4 East, 1 ; Hafner v. Irwin, 1 Ired. 490; U. S. v. Bank of U. S. 8 Rob. (La.) 262; True v. Congdon, 44 N. H. 48; Church v. Drummond, 7 Ind. 17; Gates v. Labeaume, 19 Mo. 17; Baldwin v. Peet, 22 Tex. 708.

[2] Christopher v. Covington, 2 B. Mon. 357.

[3] Hafner v. Irwin, 1 Ired. 490.

[4] U. S. Bank v. Huth, 4 B. Mon. 423.

to the payment of debts, and when this object is accomplished by an assignment or deed of trust for the benefit of his creditors, the hindrance and delay which may operate to the prejudice of particular creditors is simply an unavoidable incident to a just and lawful act. Such mere incident to a lawful act does not vitiate the transfer.[1]

INTENT TO DEFEAT EXECUTION.— Although the intent to deprive all or particular creditors of their lawful suits, and hinder and delay them in the recovery of their just demands, is confessed or proved, still the assignment, if by its terms all the property which it embraces must be applied ratably or otherwise to the payment of debts is upheld as valid and effectual. The mere intent to avoid an execution or other legal process does not in point of law make it void.[2] It may even be made on the same day that a verdict is rendered against the assignor,[3] and the claim of the creditor assailing it may be specially in the contemplation of the debtor.[4] It will not in such case be void, even as against the persons

---

[1] Hoffman v. Mackall, 5 Ohio St. R. 124 ; Townsend v. Stearns, 32 N. Y. 209; Guerin v. Hunt, 8 Minn. 477; in some of the cases it is said that the fraud depends upon the primary motive. If the primary motive is to delay, then the assignment is fraudulent, but if the primary motive is to make a distribution of the property it is valid. In one hindrance or delay is the main and primary purpose, in the other it is only an incidental effect. Eyre v. Beebe, 28 How. Pr. 333; Stickney v. Crane, 35 Vt. 89 ; Baldwin v. Peet, 22 Tex. 708.

[2] Riches v. Evans, 9 C. & P. 640; Johnson v. Osenton, L. R. 4 Ex. 107; Lee v. Green, 35 Eng. L. & Eq. 261; Bowen v. Bramridge, 6 C. & P. 140; Wolverhampton Bank v. Marston, 7 H. & N. 147; Wilt v. Franklin, 1 Binn. 502; Pickstock v. Lyster, 3 M. & S. 373; Jackson v. Cornell, 1 Sandf. Ch. 348; Heydock v. Stanhope, 1 Curt. 471 ; vide Dalton v. Currier, 40 N. H. 237.

[3] Jackson v. Cornell, 1 Sandf. Ch. 348.

[4] Horwitz v. Ellenger, 31 Md. 492.

who are in fact very materially hindered and delayed, and were meant to be so. It is valid even against the creditors whom it deprives and is intended to deprive of that full satisfaction of their debts which by their superior diligence in prosecuting their suits they would otherwise have certainly obtained. The explanation is that although in these cases the intent to hinder and delay the creditors is manifest, it is just as certain that there is no intent to cheat or defraud them, and the reasonable construction of the statute is that it is only such a hindrance or delay as is intended to operate, or, if permitted, could operate as a fraud upon the creditors, that was meant to be prohibited.[1]

All the law can reasonably demand of a debtor is the faithful application of his entire property to the satisfaction of his debts, and where, by the terms of the assignment, this is secured, the hindrance or delay which they create, however they may operate to the prejudice of particular creditors, are disregarded, since they are only the necessary means of accomplishing a justifiable and lawful end. They fall it is true within the words of the statute, but as they are free from the imputation of fraud, and produce no benefit to the debtor at the expense of the creditors, they are not embraced within its meaning, and are justly excluded from its operation.[2] It makes no difference, therefore, that the debtor is in failing circumstances, that suits are threatened, that judgments exist against him or that executions against him are momentarily expected. Under any or all of these contingencies he has the full and absolute right to dispose of his property for the payment of his debts.[3] The fact,

---

[1] Hoffman v. Mackall, 5 Ohio St. R. 124.

[2] Nicholson v. Leavitt, 4 Sandf. 252.

[3] Stewart v. English, 6 Ind. 176; Hollister v. Loud, 2 Mich. 309.

therefore, that the assignment is made for the purpose of avoiding the preference that might otherwise be obtained by legal process in a race of eager diligence by disappointed creditors, does not make the assignment invalid. Such is generally the motive to the making of such an assignment.[1]

SECRET MOTIVES.—The inducements which may have led to the assignment are not to be inquired into. It is with the act of the party, and not with the secret springs which prompted it that the courts have to deal.[2] If the assignment is such as the law authorizes and approves, the secret motives that prompted it are entirely immaterial.[3] Even a stratagem to prevent an execution till an assignment can be made will not render it void. This is due to the fact that creditors have no lien upon a debtor's property. The dominion over it is vested in the debtor, and so long as the property continues to belong to him unaffected by liens, his conduct for the purpose of imposing upon a creditor, and keeping him at bay, will not divest him of that dominion, or disqualify him from making an appropriation of it for the benefit of his creditors.[4] This moreover is not the kind of fraud that makes an assignment void. The only illegality which avoids it is that which makes or endeavors to make it the instrument of defeating or delaying the collection of debts. It is not, therefore, for the same reason competent for a creditor to vacate an assignment as to himself, while it may be good as to everyone else by showing that there was fraud or misrepresentation on the

---

[1] Horwitz v. Ellinger, 31 Md. 492.

[2] Pike v. Bacon, 21 Me. 280.

[3] Horwitz v. Ellinger, 31 Md. 492; Mackintosh v. Corner, 33 Md. 598.

[4] Pike v. Bacon, 21 Me. 280.

part of the debtor in the creation of the debt due to him.[1]

FRAUDULENT INTENT.—Although an assignment is made for the purpose of securing genuine debts, that may not be the only purpose. It may be one purpose and yet the assignment may be fraudulently made.[2] But the only intent which will vitiate the assignment is a fraudulent intent, that is, an intent which the law will not permit to be carried into effect, an intent to secure some benefit to the debtor, or to withhold some right from his creditors beyond what the law permits. If this intent is expressed in the deed, the court may declare it to be void; but if the fraudulent intent is not expressed in the deed, then it can only be invalidated by proof that the fraudulent intent existed at the time of the execution of the deed.[3] The assignment cannot be made the means of covering up and preserving the property for the debtor's use, or of withdrawing and protecting it from the lawful actions, remedies, and demands of his creditors. If it is devised and contrived as a scheme for keeping the property under the secret control of the debtor, or for keeping it out of the market for an indefinite period, or until there shall be a rise in the prices, or for locking it up in any way for the debtor's own use and benefit; if it is not designed in good faith for the payment of debts really owed, but the whole transaction is con-

---

[1] Horwitz v. Ellinger, 31 Md. 492; Mattison v. Demarest, 4 Robt. 161; Pierce v. Jackson, 2 R. I. 35; Reinhard v. Bank of Kentucky, 6 B. Mon. 252; vide Kennedy v. Thorp, 3 Abb. Pr. (N.S.) 131; Waverly Bank v. Halsey, 57 Barb. 249.

[2] State v. Benoist, 37 Mo. 500.

[3] Bailey v. Mills, 27 Tex. 434; Van Hook v. Walton, 28 Tex. 59.

ceived in collusion, malice, covin, and bad faith, and tainted with secret fraud, it is void.[1]

To PREVENT SACRIFICE.—But the mere intent on the part of the debtor to prevent a sacrifice of his property does not necessarily and of itself render an assignment void. This will depend upon the purpose with which the sacrifice is sought to be avoided. If the purpose is to prevent a race of diligence among creditors so that they may receive a larger dividend, it is lawful. But if the purpose is to prevent the sacrifice that would be caused by a forced sale so that the debtor may receive a larger surplus after the payment of his debts, it is unlawful and fraudulent.[2] A sale of all the debtor's property followed immediately by an assignment of the notes received in payment, is fraudulent, if it is made for the purpose of preventing a sacrifice and keeping the property for his benefit.[3] If the purchase, however, is in good faith, the giving of a note and the making of an assignment shortly afterwards is no fraud.[4]

FRAUD MUST BE IN THE BEGINNING.—The only fraud which will vitiate an assignment is fraud in its concoction. If there is no fraud in its inception, the property vests immediately in the assignee for the benefit of the creditors, and no subsequent fraudulent dealings can re-

---

[1] State v. Benoist, 37 Mo. 500; Work v. Ellis, 50 Barb. 512; Wilson v. Pearson, 20 Ill. 81; Byrd v. Bradley, 2 B. Mon. 239; Smith v. Leavitts, 10 Ala. 92; Caldwell v. Williams, 1 Ind. 405; Fuller v. Ives, 6 McLean, 478.

[2] Angell v. Rosenburg, 12 Mich. 241; Shackelford v. Planter's Bank, 22 Ala. 238; Hefner v. Metcalf, 1 Head, 577; Gere v. Murray, 6 Minn. 305; vide Ward v. Trotter, 3 Mon. 1.

[3] Litchfield v. Pelton, 6 Barb. 187; Cooke v. Smith, 3 Sandf. Ch. 333; Mills v. Carnley, 1 Bosw. 159.

[4] Loeschigk v. Baldwin, 38 N. Y. 326.

vest the property in the debtor, or have a retroactive effect so as to avoid the assignment itself.[1] An assignment honestly made for an honest purpose can not be defeated by proof that the assignee abused his trust, misappropriated the property, or acted however dishonestly in its disposal, or that he took unwise or even apparently dishonest means to preserve the property from litigation or levy by a creditor.[2]

ASSIGNEE'S PARTICIPATION.—An assignment is founded upon a valuable consideration. It is not like a mere gift, for it is supported by the debts due to the creditors. Although the conveyance is in terms to the assignee, it is in fact to the creditors, and they are the real beneficiaries. A fraudulent intent, therefore, on the part of the debtor alone is not sufficient to avoid the assignment.[3] The assignment is not void when neither the

---

[1] Klapp v. Shirk, 13 Penn. 589; Shattuck v. Freeman, 1 Met. 10; Petrekin v. Davis, Morris, 296; Wooster v. Stanfield, 11 Iowa, 128; Hotop v. Durant, 6 Abb. Pr. 371, *note;* Cox v. Platt, 32 Barb. 126; s. c. 19 How. Pr. 121; Matthews v. Poultney, 33 Barb. 127; Browning v. Hart, 6 Barb. 91; Wilson v. Forsyth, 24 Barb. 105; Pike v. Bacon, 21 Me. 280; Gates v. Labeaume, 19 Mo. 17; Hempstead v. Johnston, 18 Ark. 123; Cornish v. Dews, 18 Ark. 172; Beck v. Parker, 65 Penn. 262; Baldwin v. Buckland, 11 Mich. 389.

[2] Cuyler v. McCartney, 40 N. Y. 221; Hotop v. Durant, 6 Abb. Pr. 371, *note;* Matthews v. Poultney, 33 Barb. 127; U. S. Bank v. Huth, 4 B. Mon. 423; Meeker v. Saunders, 6 Iowa, 61; Savery v. Spaulding, 8 Iowa, 239; Cox v. Platt, 32 Barb. 126; s. c. 19 How. Pr. 121; Shattuck v. Freeman, 1 Met. 10; Petrekin v. Davis, Morris 96; Wooster v. Stanfield, 11 Iowa, 128.

[3] Myers v. Kinzie, 26 Ill. 36; Wise v. Wimer, 23 Mo. 237; Gates v. Labeaume, 19 Mo. 17; Wilson v. Eifler, 7 Cold. 31; Marbury v. Brooks, 7 Wheat. 556; s. c. 11 Wheat. 78; Bancroff v. Blizzard, 13 Ohio, 30; Cornish v. Dews, 18 Ark. 172; Mandel v. Peay, 20 Ark. 325; Hollister v. Loud, 2 Mich. 309; Governor v. Campbell, 17 Ala. 566; Abercrombie v. Bradford, 16 Ala. 560; Thomas v. Talmadge, 16 Ohio St. R. 434; *Contra,* Rathbun v. Platner, 18 Barb. 272; Foley v. Bitter, 34 Md. 646; Griffin v. Marquardt, 17 N. Y. 28; Mead v. Phillips, 1 Sandf. Ch. 83; Wilson v. Forsyth, 24 Barb. 105; Kayser v. Heavenrich, 5 Kansas, 324; Gere v. Murray, 6 Minn. 305;

creditors nor the assignee participate in the fraud.[1]
Notice of the fraud to the assignee, however, is sufficient.[2]
An acceptance of the deed with notice of such facts as
are sufficient to put him on the inquiry will invalidate
it.[3] When the assignee participates in the fraud, a presumption of assent on the part of the creditors would
also involve a presumption that they have notice of the
facts which make the assignment fraudulent, and are
thus parties and participators in the fraud.[4]

CONSTRUCTION OF DEED.—Fraud is always a question
of intent, for no man can justly be said to be guilty of
a fraud by accident or mistake.[5] The law, however,
presumes that every person intends the consequences
which necessarily flow from his acts,[6] and that he un-
derstands the legal import of every instrument which
he executes. The construction of an instrument is a
question of law. Its legal effect is a matter upon
which the court ought to pass.[7] Whenever the fraud

Stickney v. Crane, 35 Vt. 89; Lampson v. Arnold, 19 Iowa, 479; Irwin v.
Keen, 3 Whart. 347; Flanigan v. Lampman, 12 Mich. 58; Ruble v. Mc-
Donald, 18 Iowa, 493; Pierson v. Manning, 2 Mich. 445; Stone v. Marshall,
7 Jones, (N. C.) 300. In some cases it is said that the fraudulent intent of
the debtor will vitiate the assignment when none of the creditors have assented, because no assent can be presumed to support a fraudulent assignment. Townsend v. Harwell, 18 Ala 301; Stewart v. Spencer, 1 Curt.
157; Benning v. Nelson, 23 Ala. 801; Green v. Banks, 24 Tex. 508; Baldwin v. Peet, 22 Tex. 708.

[1] Bancroft v. Blizzard, 13 Ohio, 30.

[2] State v. Benoist, 37 Mo. 500; Caldwell v. Williams, 1 Ind. 405; Caldwell v. Rose, 1 Smith, 190; Stewart v. Spencer, 1 Curt. 157; *Contra*, Pinneo v. Hart, 30 Mo. 561.

[3] Stewart v. Spencer, 1 Curt. 157.

[4] Green v. Banks, 24 Tex. 508; State v. Benoist, 37 Mo. 500; *vide* Marbury v. Brooks, 7 Wheat. 556; s. c. 11 Wheat. 78.

[5] Grover v. Wakeman, 11 Wend. 187, per Senator Edmonds.

[6] Mackie v. Cairns, 5 Cow. 547.

[7] Sheldon v. Dodge, 4 Denio, 217.

is apparent upon the face of the instrument it is a ques·
tion of fraud in law. Evidence that the deed was designed to be beneficial is inadmissible. There is nothing
for a jury to pass upon when the court can see that the
instrument is fraudulent on its face. The validity of
the deed is determined by the character with which
the law stamps it, without reference to extrinsic facts
as to motive. If the law imputes to the grantor a de·
sign in making the deed, no evidence of intention can
change the presumption. If the law declares the deed
to be void, it is no matter how the question of fraud in
in fact may stand.[1] When an assignment is fraudulent
on its face, it is void without reference to the actual
knowledge of either the assignee or the creditors. The
fraudulent stipulation in the deed fixes the assignee and
all the creditors claiming under it with a concurrence in
the unlawful intent.[2] When the instrument, however,
appears to be fair, and its validity depends upon extrinsic evidence, the question must be submitted to
the proper tribunal to determine as a matter of fact
whether it is fraudulent or not.[3]

SEVERAL INSTRUMENTS MAY CONSTITUTE ONE TRANS-
ACTION.—All papers executed in pursuance of an original design contemplated and determined upon in the
beginning, are in law deemed to constitute one transaction and are construed together, whether made on the

---

[1] Green v. Trieber, 3 Md. 11; Malcolm v. Hodges, 8 Md. 418; Inloes
v. American Exchange Bank, 11 Md. 173; Goodrich v. Downs, 6 Hill,
438; Boardman v. Halliday, 10 Paige, 223; Abercrombie v. Bradford, 16
Ala. 560; Pierson v. Manning, 2 Mich. 445; Murray v. Riggs, 15 Johns.
571; Harris v. Sumner, 2 Pick. 129; Richards v. Hazard, 1 Stew. & Port.
139; Howell v. Edgar, 3 Scam. 417.

[2] Palmer v. Giles, 5 Jones Eq. 75.

[3] Johnson v. McAllister, 30 Mo. 327; Dunham v. Waterman, 17 N.
Y. 9.

same day,[1] or on different days.[2]   The mere fact that
two or more conveyances are made at the same time has
no necessary influences upon determining whether they
constitute one transaction.[3]   An individual may not only
execute on the same day but be preparing at the same
time a conveyance for the purpose of defrauding his
creditors, and another for the purpose of securing an
honest debt.   In such case the two acts could not properly be said to be one and the same transaction, the
object and the end of one being entirely different from
the object and end of the other.[4]   It has for this reason
been held that conveyances made at different dates for
the purpose of securing different sums can not be considered as one transaction.[5]   Whether the deeds constitute one transaction is a question for the jury.[6]   A
valid instrument, however, can never be impaired by a
subsequent attempt to aid it by an invalid instrument.[7]

ONE FRAUDULENT CLAUSE VITIATES THE WHOLE DEED.
—A fraudulent stipulation makes the whole instrument
void.   When a deed is void as to part, it is void altogether.   The taint as to part affects the entirety.
Where a conveyance is good in part and bad in part
as against the provisions of the statute, it is void *in toto*
and no interest passes to the grantee under the part

---

[1] Mussey v. Noyes, 26 Vt. 462.

[2] Berry v. Cutts, 42 Me. 445; Holt v. Bancroft, 30 Ala. 193; Burrows v. Lehndorf, 8 Iowa, 96; Spaulding v. Strang, 36 Barb. 310; M'Allister v. Marshall, 6 Binn. 338 ; Cummings v. McCullough, 5 Ala. 324.

[3] Lampson v. Arnold, 19 Iowa, 479 ; Mann v. Witbeck, 17 Barb. 388 ; Norton v. Kearney, 10 Wis. 443.

[4] Mower v. Hanford, 6 Minn. 535.

[5] Wynkoop v. Shardlow, 44 Barb. 84.

[6] Mower v. Hanford, 6 Minn. 535.

[7] Lansing v. Woodworth, 1 Sandf. Ch. 43.

which is good.[1] The parties to the assignment can not produce evidence, where the validity of the assignment is assailed, to show that the vicious clause apparent on its face was inserted or retained by inadvertence or mistake, and so give to the instrument an actual character altogether different from its apparent character. Undoubtedly if a clause is inserted or retained by inadvertence or mistake, and against the intention of the parties, it may be re-formed, and upon re-formation will be relieved of its vicious taint, and be valid as to the creditors assailing it. But without such rectification the instrument must stand or fall upon the character impressed upon its face by the parties, and by them sent out upon the world as expressing the contract and purposes of the parties to it.[2]

CONSTRUED STRICTLY.—Assignments are often made the means of fraud and are not regarded in the courts with special favor.[3] Courts, however, are under no obligation to be astute to destroy them.[4] The legal intendments are all in favor of their validity the same as of other instruments.[5] The same fair and reasonable rules of construction must be applied to them as are

---

[1] Albert v. Winn, 7 Gill. 446; Hyslop v. Clarke, 14 Johns. 458 ; Mackie v. Cairns, 5 Cow. 547; s. c. 1 Hopk. 373; Goodrich v. Downs, 6 Hill, 438 ; McClurg v. Lecky, 3 Penna. 83; Robins v. Embry, 1 S. & M. Ch. 207 ; Jacot v. Corbett, 1 Chev. Eq. 74; Howell v. Edgar, 3 Scam. 417; Dana v. Lull, 17 Vt. 390; Caldwell v. Williams, 1 Ind. 405 ; Pierson v. Manning, 2 Mich. 445; Green v. Branch Bank, 33 Ala. 643; Greenleaf v. Edes, 2 Minn. 264; Palmer v. Giles, 5 Jones Eq. 75 ; vide Bradway's Estate, 1 Ashm. 212.

[2] August v. Seeskind, 6 Cold. 166; Hooper v. Tuckerman, 3 Sandf. 311.

[3] Heacock v. Durand, 42 Ill. 230; Stewart v. English, 6 Ind. 176.

[4] Read v. Worthington, 9 Bosw. 617.

[5] Turner v. Jaycox, 40 Barb. 164; s. c. 40 N. Y. 470; Townsend v. Stearns, 32 N. Y. 209; Read v. Worthington, 9 Bosw. 617.

adopted in ascertaining the meaning of other instruments.[1]

ONUS PROBANDI.—The *onus* is upon the creditor who
assails an assignment to show that it is in plain violation of the law.[2] It is a universal rule in the construction of all deeds that fraud is never to be presumed.
The reason of the rule rests upon such plain principles
of justice and propriety, that it needs not the force of
argument or the weight of authority to support it.
The party that charges fraud is bound to prove it, and
that, too, by legal and competent evidence. This evidence may be found in the deed itself, or it may be
established by other affirmative proof. But still, in
both cases, fraud either actual or constructive must be
brought to light with reasonable certainty and shown
to be fairly applicable to the agreement sought to be
impeached. Mere conjecture or surmise, however probable or persuasive, is never allowed to establish fraud.[3]
Where an instrument is ambiguous in its terms and admits of two constructions, that interpretation should be
given to it which will render it legal and operative
rather than that which will render it illegal and void.[4]
If mere words are relied on as the sole evidence of
guilt, it is not enough that they admit of a construction
consistent with the imputed wrong unless they are inconsistent also with a lawful act and an honest purpose.[5]

---

[1] Whipple v. Pope, 33 Ill. 334.

[2] Townsend v. Stearns, 32 N. Y. 209.

[3] *Ex parte* Conway, 12 Ark. 302.

[4] Grover v. Wakeman, 11 Wend. 187 ; Bank v. Talcott, 22 Barb. 550;
Darling v. Rogers, 22 Wend. 483 ; Jewett v. Woodward, 1 Edw. 195 ;
Rapalee v. Stewart, 27 N. Y. 310; Whipple v. Pope, 33 Ill. 334 ; Booth v.
McNair, 14 Mich. 19; Townsend v. Stearns, 32 N. Y. 209; Shackelford v.
Planters' Bank, 22 Ala. 238.

[5] Townsend v. Stearns, 32 N. Y. 209.

It is not, moreover, by selecting isolated words, inadvertently used, and giving them their most unfavorable construction, that fraud is to be imputed. The whole tenor of the instrument is to be taken into view in pronouncing upon its general character.[1]

No INFERENCE THAT DEBTOR CONTEMPLATED A VIO-
LATION OF THE TRUST.—The trust, like all others confided to human hands, is liable to abuse, but this is no argument against its validity.[2] The law will not defeat an instrument by inferring that the debtor contemplated an illegal act on the part of the assignee.[3] It presumes that the assignee will apply a general power which can have a lawful operation to a lawful purpose. When the provision is susceptible of an honest application, it can not be said to have that necessary evil tendency which justifies the inference of a fraudulent intent.[4] The question, therefore, in construing an assignment is not whether a fraud may be committed by the assignee, but whether the provisions of the instrument are such that, when carried out according to their apparent and reasonable intent, they will be fraudulent in their operation. It is only when the authority is express to do an illegal act that the instrument will be held void.[5]

For the same reason the possibility of a mistake or misapprehension on the part of the assignee will not warrant the total abrogation of an instrument.[6] A

---

[1] Brigham v. Tillinghast, 15 Barb. 618; s. c. 13 N. Y. 215.

[2] *Ex parte* Conway, 12 Ark. 302; Ward v. Tingley, 4 Sandf. Ch. 476 ; Hoffman v. Mackall, 5 Ohio St. R. 124.

[3] Kellogg v. Slauson, 11 N. Y. 302.

[4] Watkins v. Wallace, 19 Mich. 57.

[5] Kellogg v. Slauson, 11 N. Y. 302; s. c. 15 Barb. 56 ; Brigham v. Tillinghast, 15 Barb. 618; s. c. 13 N. Y. 215; Ward v. Tingley, 4 Sandf. Ch. 476 ; Berry v. Hayden, 7 Iowa, 469; Norton v. Kearney, 10 Wis. 443.

[6] Eyre v. Beebe, 28 How. Pr. 333.

24

power will not be implied in order to overturn an instrument. The reservation of a supposed existing right
will not be construed into the grant of a power.[1] But
if there is a stipulation in the deed which makes it
fraudulent in law, the court will not look to the circumstances of the case to ascertain whether it can ever
become operative.[2] It is likewise immaterial that a
power is contingent, and that no occasion has arisen
for its operation. The question is what does it enable
the debtor to accomplish, and the law presumes that he
intends all that the instrument provides.[3] The mere
fact that two provisions independent in their nature are
found in the same instrument, can never avail to stamp
upon them, or either of them, the character of fraud
when the provisions separately construed are admitted
to be lawful.[4]

RULE OF CONSTRUCTION.—The safe rule of construction is to regard every assignment which operates to
delay creditors for any purpose whatever not distinctly
calculated to promote their interests as contrary to the
policy of the statute.[5]

LAW OF STATE WHERE MADE.—The fact that an instrument can not be enforced in another State is no
reason why it should not be enforced by the courts of
the State where it is made. To allow the laws of other
States to control the legality of the acts and contracts
of its own citizens in their domestic operations would

---

[1] Van Nest v. Yoe, 1 Sandf. Ch. 4.

[2] Boardman v. Halliday, 10 Paige, 223 ; Sheldon v. Dodge, 4 Den.
217.

[3] Grover v. Wakeman, 11 Wend. 187 ; s. c. 4 Paige, 23; Mead v. Phillips, 1 Sandf. Ch. 83.

[4] Nicholson v. Leavitt, 4 Sandf. 252; s. c. 6 N. Y. 510; s. c. 10 N. Y. 591.

[5] Grover v. Wakeman, 11 Wend. 187; s. c. 4 Paige, 23.

violate every principle of governmental independence. Lawful acts done within one State can not be made unlawful by provisions having no authority beyond the territory of the State adopting them. If no assignment were valid which would not be valid wherever the debtor had property, there would be few valid assignments. The only ground which a court can have for setting aside an assignment made in the State where the court sits is because it violates the laws of that State, and those laws can not be violated by a disregard of any but their own policy, and the court has no call or jurisdiction to enforce any external or foreign policy.[1]

CONTEMPORANEOUS CIRCUMSTANCES.—It is not sufficient to invalidate an assignment, that the debtor at the time of making it is embarrassed,[2] or executes it voluntarily,[3] or without the request or knowledge of the creditors.[4] It is not necessary that the creditors shall be consulted, or that the fact shall appear upon the face of the deed.[5] The assignment may convey all the debtor's property.[6] It need not convey all.[7] An assignment by a firm need not convey the separate estates of the partners.[8]

---

[1] Watkins v. Wallace, 19 Mich. 57 ; Frink v. Buss, 45 N. H. 325.

[2] Layson v. Rowan, 7 Rob. (La.) 1.

[3] Layson v. Rowan, 7 Rob. (La.) 1.

[4] Reinhard v. Bank of Kentucky, 6 B. Mon. 252.

[5] Brashear v. West, 7 Pet. 608; Danee v. Seaman, 11 Gratt. 78.

[6] Layson v. Rowan, 7 Rob. (La.) 1.

[7] Meeker v. Saunders, 6 Iowa, 61; Berry v. Matthews, 13 Md. 537 ; Price v. De Ford, 18 Md. 489; Doremus v. Lewis, 8 Barb. 124; Wilson v. Forsyth, 24 Barb. 105; vide Smith v. Woodruff, 1 Hilt. 462. When a statute requires that it shall convey all, it is sufficient if the deed by the terms of the law where it is made conveys all. Frink v. Buss, 45 N. H. 325 ; Watkins v. Wallace, 19 Mich. 57.

[8] Blake v. Faulkner, 18 Ind. 47; Garner v. Frederick, 18 Ind. 507 ; Guerin v. Hunt, 6 Minn. 375; s. c. 8 Minn. 477; Contra, Simmons v. Curtis, 41 Me. 373; Derry Bank v. Davis, 44 N. H. 548.

SOLVENT DEBTOR.—As assignments for the benefit of creditors are generally made by insolvent debtors, it is not unfrequently said that such dispositions of property can be made only by that class of persons. But this doctrine has no foundation in principle. These assignments are in their nature simple trusts for the payment of debts. The power to create such trusts is not peculiar to insolvent men. On the contrary, it is a power more unquestionably possessed by men who are entirely solvent. Persons of undoubted ability may dispose of their property as they please, so far as the question of power merely is concerned. This right of disposition on general principles of law and justice was never doubtful except in cases of a debtor's inability to meet his engagements. It was the insolvency rather than the solvency of the debtor which suggested the doubt in regard to the right of putting the whole or any part of his property in trust for the benefit of creditors. It is undoubtedly true that a solvent as well as an insolvent person may make a fraudulent assignment. In either condition the question is one of fact, depending mainly on other circumstances where the instrument is on its face free from obnoxious provisions. In either case, if the intention is to hinder or delay creditors, the transaction is fraudulent, but that intention can not be inferred from one condition of the debtor any more than from the other.[1]

LEGAL RIGHTS.—The validity of an assignment must in both cases be determined according to the respective legal rights of the debtor and the creditors. The law

---

[1] Ogden v. Peters, 21 N. Y. 23; s. c. 15 Barb. 560; Angell v. Rosenburg, 12 Mich. 241 ; *Contra*, Van Nest v. Yoe, 1 Sandf. Ch. 4 ; Planck v. Schermerhorn, 3 Barb. Ch. 644; Burt v. McKinstry, 4 Minn. 204 ; *in re* Randall and Sunderland, 3 B. R. 4 ; s. c. 2 L. T. B. 69 ; s. c. Deady, 557.

provides that the debtor shall fulfil his obligations and on his default gives to the creditors a remedy for the recovery of their demands and a sale of the property of the debtor for their payment. This is a strict legal right. The law gives to the creditors alone the right to determine whether the debtor shall have further indulgence, or whether they will pursue their remedy for the collection of their debts. If the real object of the debtor, therefore, is to gain time, to prevent the speedy sale and conversion which an execution would inevitably accomplish, and to protect his interests in the surplus by placing the property beyond the reach of the process of the law, then, in the very language of the statute, he hinders, delays, and ultimately defrauds his creditors, whatever may be the pretence under which he cloaks the act.[1]

To PREVENT A SACRIFICE.—Where the property of the debtor is insufficient to pay his debts, the desire to protect it from sacrifice, and have it realize as much as possible, is not inconsistent with fair dealing and honesty, and instead of violating the policy of the law or the rights of creditors is in harmony with both, and exempt from the charge of fraud.[2] But where the property at the time of the assignment is much more than sufficient to satisfy all demands, the accomplishment of this object can only be at the expense of the creditors and for the benefit of the debtor. The law, however, does not tolerate such a purpose on the part of the debtor. He has no right to protect his property from sacrifices at the expense of his creditors.

---

[1] Van Nest v. Yoe, 1 Sandf. Ch. 4; Planck v. Schermerhorn, 3 Barb. Ch. 644 ; Knight v. Packer, 1 Beasley, 214 ; London v. Parsley, 7 Jones (N. C.) 313; Burt v. McKinstry, 4 Minn. 204; Lehmer v. Herr, 1 Duvall, 360.

[2] Angell v. Rosenburg, 12 Mich. 241 ; Burt v. McKinstry, 4 Minn. 204; Ely v. Cook, 18 Barb. 612.

The latter have the right to demand their debts in full without delay where the assets of the debtor are sufficient for that purpose.[1] The true rule, therefore, is that the intent to avoid a sacrifice will invalidate an assignment when the sacrifice is sought to be prevented by the debtor himself so as to enable him to realize something by way of a surplus or otherwise,[2] but not where the sole or primary intent is to enable the creditors to realize their demands and prevent loss or injury to any one.[3]

BURDEN OF PROVING SOLVENCY.—The burden of proving the solvency of the debtor rests upon the creditor who assails the assignment.[4] A mere nominal difference between the assets and liabilities is not sufficient, especially where the former includes debts due to the assignor at their face without reference to the question whether they are collectible.[5] Where the excess of assets is so unreasonably large as to force the conclusion that the assignment is made in the interest of the debtor, and to protect him from the sacrifice attending a forced sale, rather than for the benefit of creditors, then the assignment may be fraudulent, but the question of reasonableness or unreasonableness of the excess must depend upon a variety of circumstances amongst which the convertibility of the assets into money is the most important.[6]

---

[1] Burt v. McKinstry, 4 Minn. 204.

[2] Rokenbaugh v. Hubbell, 5 Law Rep. (N. S.) 95 ; s. c. 15 Barb. 563, note ; Angell v. Rosenburg, 12 Mich. 241.

[3] Rokenbaugh v. Hubbell, 5 Law Rep. (N. S.) 95 ; s. c. 15 Barb. 563, note ; Angell v. Rosenburg, 12 Mich. 241.

[4] Kellogg v. Slauson, 11 N. Y. 302 ; s. c. 15 Barb. 56 ; Haven v. Richardson, 5 N. H. 113.

[5] Livermore v. Northrop, 44 N. Y. 107 ; Guerin v. Hunt, 8 Minn. 477 ; s. c. 6 Minn. 375.

[6] Guerin v. Hunt, 8 Minn. 477 ; s. c. 6 Minn. 375.

DEBTOR'S BELIEF.—The debtor's belief that he is solvent is only proper evidence to consider in determining the intent with which the assignment is made.[1] It is susceptible of an explanation consistent with honesty of purpose. So far as it relates to the charge of actual fraud, much must depend upon the strength of the belief. That might approach very near to a certainty and thus justify the inference,[2] but a belief that a surplus of only the most trifling character will remain, while without an assignment the property will be so sacrificed that a large portion of his debts will remain unpaid, furnishes very slight if any evidence of fraud.[3] The debtor may believe himself solvent, and yet have so much doubt upon the subject from the uncertain valuation of his property, and particularly of that part of it which consists of *choses in action* and the representations of his friends, that he may honestly suppose that an assignment will prove beneficial to his creditors.[4] He may also suppose that his property is sufficient for the payment of his debts, and yet that, before he can render it available, it will probably be so far reduced by hasty or forced sales, and his liabilities so far increased by the addition of costs created by anxious and competing creditors that it will become inadequate to satisfy all his debts. Under such a supposition, and in such circumstances, an assignment will be valid.[5] If, more-

---

[1] Bates v. Ableman, 13 Wis. 644 ; *Contra,* Van Nest v. Yoe, 1 Sandf. Ch. 4 ; Baldwin v. Buckland, 11 Mich. 389 ; Burt v. McKinstry, 4 Minn. 204.

[2] Ogden v. Peters, 21 N. Y. 23 ; s. c. 15 Barb. 560 ; Angell v. Rosenburg, 12 Mich. 241.

[3] Bates v. Ableman, 13 Wis. 644.

[4] Ogden v. Peters, 21 N. Y. 23 ; s. c. 15 Barb. 560 ; Angell v. Rosenburg, 12 Mich. 24 ; Ely v. Cook, 18 Barb. 612.

[5] Ogden v. Peters, 15 Barb. 560 ; s. c. 21 N. Y. 23 ; Rokenbaugh v. Hubbell, 5 Law Rep. (N. S.) 95 ; s. c. 15 Barb. 563, note ; Bates v. Ableman, 13 Wis. 644 ; Angell v. Rosenburg, 12 Mich. 241.

over, he is at the time unable to pay his debts according to the usage of trade, or is unable to proceed in his business without some general arrangement with his creditors by way of extension of time of payment, then he is insolvent and can rightfully make an assignment.[1] Even the belief that he is solvent when in fact he is not so, will not invalidate an assignment if it is made in good faith.[2]

SELECTION OF ASSIGNEE.—The debtor may select the assignee.[3] The assignee may be a creditor,[4] or a joint debtor.[5] He need not be a creditor.[6] He may be a relative.[7] An assignment from one partner to another of the partnership property to secure the payment of the partnership debts would be a palpable attempt on their part to keep the property under their own control, for, unless there is a surplus, the assignor would have no interest in the partnership effects which could pass by the assignment so as to give any greater interest to the assignee than he before possessed.[8] A corporation may select its president.[9] The reservation of the power to fill any vacancy that may occur is valid, for it is simply designed to keep the trust alive and

---

[1] Savery v. Spaulding, 8 Iowa, 239.

[2] Savery v. Spaulding, 8 Iowa, 239 ; *Contra*, Van Nest v. Yoe, 1 Sandf. Ch. 4 ; Burt v. McKinstry, 4 Minn. 204.

[3] Wilt v. Franklin, 1 Binn. 502; Nicholls v. McEwen, 17 N. Y. 22; s. c. 21 Barb. 65 ; *vide* Burd v. Smith, 4 Dall. 76.

[4] *Ex parte* Conway, 12 Ark. 302 ; Wooster v. Stanfield, 11 Iowa, 128 ; Frink v. Buss, 45 N. H. 325.

[5] Wooster v. Stanfield, 11 Iowa, 128.

[6] Wilt v. Franklin, 1 Binn, 502 ; U. S. Bank v. Huth, 4 B. Mon. 423 ; Repplier v. Buck, 5 B. Mon. 96.

[7] Winchester v. Crandall, 1 Clarke, 371; Baldwin v. Buckland, 11 Mich. 389.

[8] Sewall v. Russell, 2 Paige, 175.

[9] Pope v. Brandon, 2 Stew. 401.

in active operation,[1] but a power to remove the assignee gives a control over him and holds him in obedience to the debtor, and is equivalent to a power on the part of the debtor to control and direct the administration of the whole trust fund, and, therefore, renders the assignment void.[2] Although a failing debtor may select his own trustee, he has no right to vest his estate in improper or unworthy persons, and thus jeopardize the rights of creditors. It is his duty as an honest man to select such a person as will afford a reasonable assurance to the creditors that the fund will be safe in his hands.[3]

ASSIGNEE'S QUALIFICATIONS.—The assignee must be a man qualified and competent to discharge the duties of the trust which he is to assume, and of sufficient character and pecuniary ability to afford the assurance that the trust will be faithfully and honorably administered.[4] To prevent abuse of the right of selection and to avoid its being made a convenient engine of fraud, the utmost good faith is required of the debtor. The selection must be made with reference to the interests of the creditors rather than that of the debtor. Hence, if the assignee is so deficient in age, health,[5] business capacity,[6] or standing, pecuniary responsibility,[7] or character for integrity,[8] that a prudent man honestly looking to the interests of the creditors alone would not be likely to

---

[1] Robins v. Embry, 1 S. & M. Ch. 207; Vansands v. Miller, 24 Conn. 180 ; vide Planck v. Schermerhorn, 3 Barb. Ch. 644.

[2] Robins v. Embry, 1 S. & M. Ch. 207.

[3] Reed v. Emery, 8 Paige, 417.

[4] Cram v. Mitchell, 1 Sandf. Ch. 251.

[5] Currie v. Hart, 2 Sandf. Ch. 353; Cram v. Mitchell, 1 Sandf. Ch. 251.

[6] Cram v. Mitchell, 1 Sandf. Ch. 251 ; Guerin v. Hunt, 6 Minn. 375; s. c. 8 Minn. 477; Walker v. Adair, Bond, 158.

[7] Reed v. Emery, 8 Paige, 417 ; Haggarty v. Pittman, 1 Paige, 298 ; Connah v. Sedgwick, 1 Barb. 210 ; Angell v. Rosenburg, 12 Mich. 241.

[8] Clark v. Groom, 24 Ill. 316.

select him as a proper person for the performance of the
trust, then his selection will furnish an inference more
or less strong according to the circumstances that the
debtor in making the selection is actuated by some
other motive than the desire to promote the interests of
the creditors. This inference will be strengthened if
the assignee is a clerk or near relative,[1] or a person
likely to be easily influenced by the debtor, as this
will tend to raise a presumption that the assignment
is intended to be used for the debtor's benefit, or that
there is some secret trust in his behalf,[2] or that there is
an intention to place the property beyond the reach of
the creditors.[3]

Non-residence,[4] blindness,[5] want of learning,[6] conflicting interests,[7] and insolvency[8] are regarded as dis-
qualifications. In respect to the latter, the principle is
not confined to actual insolvency, but extends to any
case where the property or pecuniary means of the
assignee are clearly inadequate to afford a proper responsibility, or to any state of pecuniary embarrassment

---

[1] Lehmer v. Herr, 1 Duvall, 360.

[2] Angell v. Rosenburg, 12 Mich. 241.

[3] Reed v. Emery, 8 Paige, 417. Assignments are frequently made to the
confidential friends or connections of the assignor and the property kept
by the trustees for their own personal use, but more generally for the use
of the assignor, and hence it becomes a convenient way in which debtors
in failing circumstances are enabled to place their property out of the
reach of attaching creditors, and at the same time use it for their own
purposes. The difficulty of making even responsible trustees account to
creditors is so great as usually to prevent their attempting it, and it is of
course never attempted in the more common case where the trustee is not
responsible. Beers v. Lyon, 21 Conn. 604.

[4] Cram v. Mitchell, 1 Sandf. Ch. 251 ; Cox v. Platt, 32 Barb. 126 ; s. c.
19 How. Pr. 121.

[5] Cram v. Mitchell, 1 Sandf. Ch. 251.

[6] Cram v. Mitchell, 1 Sandf. Ch. 251 ; Gueron v. Hunt, 6 Minn. 375;
s. c. 8 Minn. 477.

[7] Hays v. Doane, 3 Stockt. 84.

[8] Angell v. Rosenburg, 12 Mich. 241.

likely to deprive the creditors of this security.[1] A subsequent insolvency is not sufficient, for it must be an
insolvency existing at the time of the execution of the
assignment.[2] The insolvency of the assignee must, however, be known to the debtor in order to invalidate the
assignment.[3] His general reputation in the neighborhood
where he resides, and among men whose dealings and
interests prompt them to observation and inquiry may
be shown for the purpose of proving such knowledge.[4]

MERELY A BADGE.—The existence of disqualifica-
cations is presumptive but not conclusive evidence of
fraud. The intent of the debtor is to be ascertained,
not by any one fact or circumstance, but by every fact
and circumstance that may throw light upon the transaction.[5] Thus, in the case of insolvency, the high character of the assignee for integrity and business capacity
may sometimes compensate in a great measure if not entirely for his want of pecuniary means, and afford nearly if not quite as strong assurance to creditors that the
funds will be safe in his hands, and that the trusts will
be faithfully executed.[6] An agreement after the execution of the deed not to put it on record for a few days
does not vitiate the assignment. The fact connected
with others may be some evidence of actual fraud, but
it does not establish a secret agreement under which
there is a reservation of any benefit to the grantor.[7]

---

[1] Angell v. Rosenburg, 12 Mich. 241.

[2] Jackson v. Cornell, 1 Sandf. Ch. 348.

[3] Browning v. Hart, 6 Barb. 91.

[4] Angell v. Rosenburg, 12 Mich. 241.

[5] Reed v. Emery, 8 Paige, 417 ; Wilson v. Ferguson, 10 How. Pr. 175;
Pearce v. Beach, 12 How. Pr. 404 ; Clark v. Groom, 24 Ill. 316; Guerin v.
Hunt, 6 Minn. 375 ; s. c. 8 Minn. 477; Angell v. Rosenburg, 12 Mich. 241.

[6] Angell v. Rosenburg, 12 Mich. 241 ; Pearce v. Beach, 12 How. Pr. 404;
Clark v. Groom, 24 Ill. 316.

[7] Hoopes v. Knell, 31 Md. 550 ; M'Kinney v. Rhoads, 5 Watts, 343;
vide Hafner v. Irwin, 1 Ired. 490.

CHANGE OF POSSESSION.—It is not necessary that a change of possession should accompany the transfer.[1] The assignee may, for his own accommodation, permit the debtor to remain in possession,[2] especially if the creditors consent.[3] The retention of possession is, however, a badge of fraud.[4] The assignee may also employ the debtor as his agent when such employment is not a condition of executing the assignment nor the result of a prior positive engagement.[5] Mere expectation on the part of the debtor that he will be employed is not sufficient to invalidate an

---

[1] Mitchell v. Willock, 2 W. & S. 253; Fitler v. Maitland, 5 W. &. S. 307; Dallam v. Fitler, 6 W. & S. 323; Cameron v. Montgomery, 13 S. & R. 128; Vernon v. Morton, 8 Dana, 247; Walters v. Whitlock, 9 Fla. 86; Strong v. Carrier, 13 Conn. 319; Osborne v. Fuller, 14 Conn. 529; Klapp v. Shirk, 13 Penn. 589 ; Caldwell v. Rose, 1 Smith, 190 ; Caldwell v. Williams, 1 Ind. 405; Moore v. Smith, 35 Vt. 644; State v. Benoist, 37 Mo. 500; *Contra*, Hower v. Geesaman, 17 S. & R. 251; Dewey v. Adams, 4 Edw. Ch. 21 ; Hart v. Gedney, 1 Law Rep. 69; Ingraham v. Wheeler, 6 Conn. 277.

[2] Vredenburgh v. White, 1 Johns. Cas. 156.

[3] Scott v. Ray, 18 Pick. 360.

[4] Van Nest v. Yoe, 1 Sandf. Ch. 4 ; Hitchcock v. St. John, 1 Hoff, 511; Forbes v. Logan, 4 Bosw. 475; Ball v. Loomis, 29 N. Y. 412; Jacobs v. Remsen, 36 N. Y. 668; Livermore v. Northrop, 44 N. Y. 107; Boyden v. Moore, 11 Pick. 162; Vernon v. Morton, 8 Dana, 247; Pitts v. Viley, 4 Bibb. 446 ; Cummings v. McCullough, 5 Ala. 324; Byrd v. Bradley, 2 B. Mon. 239; Strong v. Carrier, 13 Conn. 319; Wright v. Linn, 16 Tex. 34 ; Flanigan v. Lampman, 12 Mich. 58; Terry v. Butler, 43 Barb. 395; Van Hook v. Walton, 28 Tex. 59.

[5] Browning v. Hart, 6 Barb. 91 ; Nicholson v. Leavitt, 4 Sandf. 252 ; s. c. 6 N. Y. 510; s. c. 10 N. Y. 591; Ogden v. Peters, 15 Barb. 560 ; s. c. 21 N. Y. 23; Rokenbaugh v. Hubbell, 5 Law Rep. (N. S.) 95 ; s. c. 15 Barb. 563; Pearson v. Rockhill, 4 B. Mon. 296 ; Tompkins v. Wheeler, 16 Pet. 106 ; Casey v. Janes, 37 N. Y. 608; Gordon v. Cannon, 18 Gratt. 387; Beamish v. Conant, 24 How. Pr. 94; Wilbur v. Fradenburgh, 52 Barb. 474; Fitler v. Maitland, 3 W. & S. 307 ; Van Hook v. Walton, 28 Tex. 59; Blow v. Gage, 44 Ill. 208; Baldwin v. Buckland, 11 Mich. 389; Deckard v. Case, 5 Watts, 22; Vernon v. Morton, 8 Dana, 247; Shattock v. Freeman, 1 Met. 10; Forbes v. Scannell, 13 Cal. 242; Savery v. Spaulding, 8 Iowa, 239 ; Hubbard v. Winborne, 4 Dev. & Bat. 137 ; Hall v. Wheeler, 13 Ind. 371.

assignment.[1] Such employment is, however, a badge of fraud.[2] In all cases where the debtor is left in possession, it is imperative for the party supporting the validity of the transaction to prove that the assignment was executed in good faith, and without any intent to defraud.[3] If there is no change in the course of the business after the execution of the assignment it is a badge of fraud.[4]

DEBTOR'S ADVICE.—Every insolvent debtor has at least a moral interest in the advantageous disposition of the property in order that it may go as far as possible in the payment of his debts and the satisfaction of his creditors, and, therefore, any suggestion offered by him which may be useful to the assignee and beneficial to the creditors, so far from showing that he intended by the assignment to defraud his creditors, indicates that he was actuated by good motives from the beginning.[5]

POWER OF REVOCATION.—The debtor must part with the property free from any control over, or interference with it, and from any contingency on which he may or may not resume it at his pleasure.[6] A personal trust

---

[1] Ogden v. Peters, 15 Barb. 560; s. c. 21 N. Y. 23; Nicholson v. Leavitt, 4 Sandf. 252. In Connecticut the debtor can not be employed before the inventory is returned to the court of probate, Peck v. Whiting, 21 Conn. 206.

[2] Jackson v. Cornell, 1 Sandf. Ch. 348; Wilson v. Ferguson, 10 How. Pr. 175; Connah v. Sedgwick, 1 Barb. 210; Linn v. Wright, 18 Tex. 317; Guerin v. Hunt, 6 Minn. 375; s. c. 8 Minn. 477.

[3] Mead v. Phillips, 1 Sandf. Ch. 83; Cram v. Mitchell, 1 Sandf. Ch. 251.

[4] Wilson v. Ferguson, 10 How. Pr. 175; Connah v. Sedgwick, 1 Barb. 210; Cummings v. McCullough, 5 Ala. 324; Adams v. Davidson, 10 N. Y. 309; Pine v. Rikert, 21 Barb. 469; Moffat v. Ingham, 7 Dana, 495; Smith v. Leavitts, 10 Ala. 92.

[5] Eyre v. Beebe, 28 How. Pr. 333.

[6] Whallon v. Scott, 10 Watts, 237; vide Hafner v. Irwin, 1 Ired. 490; Dana v. Bank of U. S. 5 W. & S. 223; Planters' and Merchants' Bank v. Clarke, 7 Ala. 765; Janney v. Barnes, 11 Leigh, 100; Sheppards v. Turpin, 3 Gratt. 401.

to the assignee to terminate upon his death or resigna-
tion, with full power to resign, renders the assignment
fraudulent.[1] When a power of revocation is reserved
to the debtor, the necessary inference is that the assignment is made with the intent to delay, hinder, or
defraud creditors, for its only effect is to mask the
property,[2] even though it is only to be exercised in case
any creditor refuses to assent to the deed.[3] A power
to make loans on the security of the estate is equivalent
to a power of revocation.[4]

POWER TO SUBSEQUENTLY DECLARE THE USES.—Every
assignment is absolutely void if it does not appoint
and declare the uses for which the property is to be
held, and to which it is to be applied. A provision
that the uses shall be subsequently declared by the
debtor will not do. They must accompany the instrument and appear on its face, in order to rebut the
conclusive presumption of a fraudulent intent, which
would otherwise arise.[5] The reason is manifest. If
an assignment reserves to the debtor the right to
declare or change the uses at some subsequent time,
the creditors can never know what their rights are,
so as to render it safe for them to attempt to assert
those rights in any suit or proceeding either at law or
in equity. For if any one of such creditors should institute a suit to compel the assignee to account and
pay over the trust fund as directed by the assignment,
the debtor would unquestionably exercise the discretion

---

[1] Smith v. Hurst, 10 Hare, 30 ; s. c. 22 L. J. Ch. (N. S.) 289; s. c. 17
Jur. 30; s. c. 15 Eng. L. & Eq. 520.

[2] Riggs v. Murray, 2 Johns. Ch. 565; s. c. 15 Johns. 571; Cannon v.
Peebles, 4 Ired. 204; s. c. 2 Ired. 449.

[3] Hyslop v. Clarke, 14 Johns. 458.

[4] Sheppards v. Turpin, 3 Gratt. 373.

[5] Grover v. Wakeman, 11 Wend. 187; s. c. 4 Paige, 23; Harvey v.
Mix, 24 Conn. 406; Burbank v. Hammond, 3 Sumner, 429.

of preferring other creditors to him, and no prudent man would subject himself to the costs of a fruitless litigation under such an assignment for his pretended benefit.

The effect of such an assignment therefore is to place the creditors directly within the power of the debtor, and to compel them to acquiesce in such terms as he may think proper to prescribe, as the only condition upon which they can get any part of the proceeds of the property of their debtor. It furnishes the means for inducing them to relinquish a part of their claims or to refrain from enforcing them against the trust fund. It enables the debtor to set his creditors at defiance, and compel them to bid against each other for his favor. To place them in such a situation is clearly a fraud upon them, and must necessarily hinder and delay them in the collection of their debts.[1] So long, therefore, as the debtor is permitted to make an assignment of his property in trust for the payment of his debts without consulting his creditors on the subject, it is absolutely necessary for the protection of their rights that the equitable interests in the assigned property shall be fixed and determined by the assignment itself.[2]

SUBSEQUENT SCHEDULES.—The limitation of the right to declare the uses to a certain period does not obviate the objection. The law requires that the assignment must itself fix and determine the rights of the creditors in the assigned property. The principle is the same whether the debtor reserves the right to determine the preferences to be given within sixty days, six months, or three years.[3] The effect of a provision

[1] Boardman v. Halliday, 10 Paige, 223 ; Barnum v. Hempstead, 7 Paige, 568; Gazzam v. Poyntz, 4 Ala. 374.

[2] Averill v. Loucks, 6 Barb. 470 ; Mitchell v. Stiles, 13 Penn. 306.

[3] Averill v. Loucks, 6 Barb. 470.

that the debtor may at a future period prepare and annex schedules of the debts, giving preferences to the
creditors, is substantially to confer upon him the right
to give future preferences among his creditors, and consequently renders the deed fraudulent.[1] Even if the
schedules are prepared and annexed subsequently, the
assignment can not be considered valid even from the
time when such schedules are annexed. If the assignment is fraudulent and void when executed, it can not
be rendered valid and operative by any subsequent act
of the debtor performed in the execution of a fraudulent power.[2]

POWER TO GIVE SUBSEQUENT PREFERENCES CAN NOT
BE GIVEN TO ANOTHER.—As the debtor can not reserve
the power to himself of giving a preference, he can not
legally confer it on the assignee. The same objection
in principle exists in both cases. A discretionary
power, therefore, in the assignee to pay off or discharge
any of the claims in preference to other debts provided
for in the assignment, renders the instrument void.[3]
When the right depends upon a contingency, the fact
that the creditors who may be postponed will not be
injured is immaterial, for no future event can make a
conveyance valid which contains illegal provisions.[4] A
direction to the assignee to pay such other debts as the
debtor may thereafter specify out of any surplus which
may be left after paying all the debts named in the in-

---

[1] Averill v. Loucks, 6 Barb. 470.

[2] Averill v. Loucks, 6 Barb. 470 ; Mitchell v. Stiles, 13 Penn. 306 ; *vide*
Hotop v. Neidig, 17 Abb. Pr. 332.

[3] Barnum v. Hempstead, 7 Paige, 568; Boardman v. Halliday, 10
Paige, 223 ; Strong v. Skinner, 4 Barb. 546; Sheldon v. Dodge, 4 Den.
217 ; Gazzam v. Poyntz, 4 Ala. 374; Smith v. Hurst, 10 Hare, 30 ; s. c.
15 Eng. L. & Eq. 520 ; s. c. 17 Jur. 30; 22 L. J. Ch. (N. S.) 289.

[4] Sheldon v. Dodge, 4 Denio, 217.

strument does not vitiate it.[1] The principle does not apply to a clause constituting the creditors who may notify the assignee before a certain day a third class in order of payment.[2]

FICTITIOUS DEBTS.—An appropriation of the property to the payment of debts not owing by the assignor and not contracted on his account,[3] or for a larger sum than is due,[4] to the prejudice of his creditors, is evidence of fraud. This will not, however, make the assignment void unless the assignee participates in the fraud.[5] No creditor is concluded by taking under the assignment from impeaching any of the debts attempted to be secured by it, and showing fraud and collusion in such of them as may stand in his way, and the payment of which would operate to his prejudice.[6] The impeached

---

[1] Hall v. Wheeler, 13 Ind. 371.

[2] Ward v. Tingley, 4 Sandf. Ch. 476 ; it has been held that a provision that a certain sum under the direction of the debtor shall be paid to other creditors is good; Graham v. Lockhart, 8 Ala. 9; and that a provision that the debtor shall be at liberty to direct other creditors to be paid in like manner as those provided for in the assignment is good; Cannon v. Peebles, 2 Ired. 449; s. c. 4 Ired. 204.

[3] Henderson v. Haddon, 12 Rich. Eq. 393; Bank v. Talcott, 22 Barb. 550.

[4] Bank v. Fink, 7 Paige, 87; American Exchange Bank v. Webb, 15 How. Pr. 193 ; s. c. 36 Barb. 291; Angell v. Rosenburg, 12 Mich. 241; Kavanaugh v. Beckwith, 44 Barb. 192; Hastings v. Baldwin, 17 Mass. 552; Guerin v. Hunt, 6 Minn. 375; s. c. 8 Minn. 477.

[5] Mackintosh v. Corner, 33 Md. 598 ; Hempstead v. Johnston, 18 Ark. 123 ; Hardcastle v. Fisher, 24 Mo. 70; Harris v. De Graffenreid, 11 Ired. 89 ; Pinneo v. Hart, 30 Mo. 561; Nightingale v. Harris, 6 R. I. 321; Starr v. Dugan, 22 Md. 58; Woodward v. Marshall, 22 Pick. 468; *Contra* Fiedler v. Day, 2 Sandf. 594 ; Planck v. Schermerhorn, 3 Barb. Ch. 644; Webb v. Daggett, 2 Barb. 9; Irwin v. Keen, 3 Whart. 347; American Exchange Bank v. Webb, 15 How. Pr. 193; s. c. 36 Barb. 291; Mead v. Phillips, 1 Sandf. Ch. 83; Jacobs v. Remsen, 36 N. Y. 668; Livermore v. Northrop, 44 N. Y. 107; Terry v. Butler, 43 Barb. 395; Lehmer v. Herr, 1 Duvall, 360; Stone v. Marshall, 7 Jones (N. C.) 300.

[6] Mackintosh v. Corner, 33 Md. 598; Starr v. Dugan, 22 Md. 58; Hardcastle v. Fisher, 24 Mo. 70.

25

claim is extinguished by the fraud, and the share that would otherwise have been appropriated to its payment sinks into the residue for the benefit of those who are entitled to the residue by the terms of the deed.[1] The mere statement that notes are made by a third person does not justify the inference that the assignor is not under obligation to pay them,[2] nor is a court authorized to judicially know that the person named in the schedule is the assignor, although the names are identical.[3] Relationship does not authorize the conclusion that a debt is not a fair one in the absence of evidence that it is fraudulent.[4] A direction to the assignee to pay the debts of the assignor, though equivocal, means debts owing by him[5]

REAL DEBTS.—A provision may be made for the payment of a note given for an obligation to which the statute of frauds would have been a good defence, for it is optional with the debtor whether he will set up the defence or not,[6] but no provision can be made for a claim which has been discharged by a release from the creditor. The moral obligation is not sufficient in such a case to support the demand as against other creditors.[7]

DEBTOR'S WIFE.—Whenever the debtor has received or borrowed the property of his wife, under circumstances which, in a court of equity, would be regarded as creating a debt to her from him, and as entitling her

---

[1] Hardcastle v. Fisher, 24 Mo. 70.
[2] Bank v. Talcott, 22 Barb. 550.
[3] Blow v. Gage, 44 Ill. 208.
[4] Layson v. Rowan, 7 Rob. (La.) 1.
[5] Pine v. Rikert, 21 Barb. 469.
[6] Livermore v. Northrop, 44 N. Y. 107.
[7] Nightingale v. Harris, 6 R. I. 321.

to be considered and treated as his creditor therefor, he is allowed to pay such debt from his property, in the same manner and upon the same principles upon which he is allowed to pay any other debt to any other creditor. The temptation which may exist in such cases for the perpetration of frauds for the benefit of the debtor's family, makes it especially the duty of courts and juries to scrutinize very closely and carefully all transactions between the husband and wife to see that claims in favor of the wife are not trumped up on the eve of insolvency. The pre-existence of the debt must be very clearly proved, and its honesty most fully established, before it is allowed. But if honest, the debt of the wife is none the less sacred because it is due from her husband.[1] A provision may also be made for the payment of a mortgage for the purpose of restoring her inchoate right of dower in the mortgaged premises discharged of the mortgage. As between the creditors themselves the mortgaged property is the primary fund for paying the mortgage debt, but as against all creditors, except the mortgage creditor, the equity of the wife is entitled to as much consideration as their demands.[2]

SURETIES.—The debtor has the undoubted right to provide for the payment of any legal obligation. Hence, an assignment may provide for sureties and indorsers, as well as creditors.[3] The holders and owners of the

---

[1] McCartney v. Welch, 44 Barb. 271; Planck v. Schermerhorn, 3 Barb. Ch. 644.

[2] Dimon v. Delmonico, 35 Barb. 554.

[3] Ketiltas v. Wilson, 36 Barb. 298; s. c. 23 How. Pr. 69; Copeland v. Weld, 8 Me. 411; Duvall v. Raisin, 7 Mo. 449; Vaughan v. Evans, 1 Hill Ch. 414; Bank v. Talcott, 22 Barb. 550; Halsey v. Whitney, 4 Mason, 206; Stevens v. Bell, 6 Mass. 339; Bank v. Cox, 6 Me. 395; Cunningham v. Freeborn, 11 Wend. 241; s. c. 1 Edw. 256; s. c. 3 Paige, 537.

claims designed to be protected, may compel an appropriation of the assigned property to their payment, and consequently the provision has the same effect as if the holders were named the *cestuis que trust* in the instrument.[1] The fact that the liability is contingent, does not constitute a valid objection, for an assignment to protect a contingent liability no more hinders or delays creditors than one to pay a debt not yet due, even if the assignee is not authorized to pay such debt before its maturity, for the assignee has a right to retain sufficient funds in his hands to meet such liability, and distribute the residue, and after the liability is disposed of, distribute the balance.[2] A direction to the assignee to indemnify a surety, is a direction to pay the obligation as it becomes due, for in no other way can the guarantor be fully protected and saved harmless from the payment thereof.[3]

SECURED DEBTS.—A provision for the payment of a debt which has been previously secured by either a judgment or a mortgage, or otherwise, does not affect the validity of the assignment. If it is paid out of the assigned estate, the property upon which it is a lien will be left without hindrance to be resorted to by the other creditors for the payment of their debts. If the debt is imperfectly secured, it is not objectionable to provide for it in the assignment. If it is amply secured, a provision for its payment will not render the assignment void.[4] But such a provision should be considered as made subject to the equity, as between the creditors, to have the mortgage debt paid out of the mortgaged

---

[1] Griffin v. Marquardt, 21 N. Y. 121 ; s. c. 17 N. Y. 28.

[2] Read v. Worthington, 9 Bosw. 617; Loeschigk v. Jacobson, 26 How. Pr. 526 ; s. c. 2. Robt. 645.

[3] Loeschigk v. Jacobson, 26 How. Pr. 526 ; s. c. 2 Robt. 645.

[4] Strong v. Skinner, 4 Barb. 546 ; Hastings v. Palmer, 1 Clarke, 52.

property.[1] Provision may also be made for the pay·
ment of an attaching creditor, provided his attachment
is sustained. The fact that it is conditional and contingent is immaterial, for it could not be otherwise when
the validity of the attachment is questioned.[2] It is
proper for the assignment to set forth the securities
held by the secured creditor, but the omission of any
reference to them is not inconsistent with entire honesty
and good faith.[3] A debt fully secured by a mortgage
may also be excluded.[4]

VARIOUS DEBTS.—Provision may be made for the
payment of an unsettled account,[5] or of notes which
have been purchased at a discount,[6] or of a bequest to
the debtor, as executor, to employ in business and pay
the profits to others, even though it is so employed by
him.[7] A direction to the assignee to pay debts which
are, or may become due, means debts existing at the
date of the assignment, and to become due afterwards,
and includes debts already due. The phrase "may
become due," when applied to actual debts then owing
to creditors, means debts which shall become payable
thereafter; and when applied to persons under a contingent liability for the debtor, means sums of money
which shall thereafter become payable to them by reason of such contingent liability.[8] A provision for a
debt of a firm due to another firm in which all or some

---

[1] Dimon v. Delmonico, 35 Barb. 554.

[2] Grant v. Chapman, 38 N. Y. 293.

[3] Stern v. Fisher, 32 Barb. 198.

[4] Cross v. Bryant, 2 Scam. 36.

[5] Reinhard v. Bank of Kentucky, 6 B. Mon. 252.

[6] Powers v. Graydon, 10 Bosw. 630; s. c. 25 How. Pr. 512; Low v.
Graydon, 50 Barb. 414.

[7] Tilford's Case, 8 Watts, 531.

[8] Read v. Worthington, 9 Bosw. 617; Brainerd v. Dunning, 30 N. Y.
211; Benedict v. Huntington, 32 N. Y. 219; Butt v. Peck, 1 Daly, 83;
Van Hook v. Walton, 28 Tex. 59.

of the partners are interested, is valid, because partnerships are, in a modified sense, corporate bodies, and are not to be confounded with the individuals composing them. They are societies, and their assets are to be administered as the assets of an association.[1] A provision cannot be made for the debts which the separate partners may have against the firm before the firm creditors are paid.[2] A note given to a former partner, upon his withdrawal from the firm, may be provided for.[3]

By PARTNERS.—An appropriation of firm property to pay the individual debt of one of the partners, is, in effect a gift from the firm to the partner, and the attempt to assign partnership property to pay the private debts of one of the partners, before the firm debts are paid, when the firm is insolvent, affords a conclusive presumption of an actual fraudulent design on the part of the debtors.[4] It is a fraud upon the joint creditors, for one partner to authorize his share of the property of the firm to be applied to the payment of a debt for which neither he nor his property is liable at law or in equity. This right of the firm creditors to priority of payment out of the firm assets, can not be impaired by

---

[1] Fanshawe v. Lane, 16 Abb. Pr. 71; *vide* Kayser v. Heavenrich, 5 Kansas, 324.

[2] Goddard v. Hapgood, 25 Vt. 351.

[3] Mattison v. Demarest, 4 Robt. 161; Blow v. Gage, 44 Ill. 208; Smith v. Howard, 20 How. Pr. 121.

[4] Wilson v. Robertson, 21 N. Y. 587; s. c. 19 How. Pr. 350; Cox v. Platt, 32 Barb 126; s. c. 19 How. Pr. 121; Lester v. Abbott, 28 How. Pr. 488; s. c. 3 Robt. 691; Knauth v. Bassett, 34 Barb. 31; Henderson v. Haddon, 12 Rich. Eq. 393; Keith v. Fink, 47 Ill. 272; Ruhl v. Phillips, 2 Daly, 45; Heye v. Bolles, 33 How. Pr. 266; s. c. 2 Daly, 231; French v. Lovejoy, 12 N. H. 458; Kirby v. Schoonmaker, 3 Barb. Ch. 46. In some cases it is held that the appropriation is void but the assignment valid. Nicholson v. Leavitt, 4 Sandf. 252; s. c. 6 N. Y. 510; s. c. 10 N. Y. 591; McCollough v. Somerville, 8 Leigh, 415; Read v. Baylies, 18 Pick. 497; Kemp v. Carnley, 3 Duer, 1; Nye v. Van Husan, 6 Mich. 329; Lassel v. Tucker, 5 Sneed, 1; Gordon v. Cannon, 18 Gratt. 387.

any consideration having reference to the amount of capital contributed by each of the individual partners.[1]

When the separate property assigned by each partner exceeds the amount of his separate debts, a direction that separate debts shall be paid out of the partnership property, will not vitiate the assignment.[2] Evidence may also be given to show that there are no individual debts, but the burden of proof rests on the parties claiming under the instrument.[3] Debts contracted in the name of one of the partners, may be shown to be in reality partnership debts.[4] Partnership property may be applied to the payment of debts which are not partnership debts, but for which all the partners are bound.[5] A direction that the property shall be distributed among the creditors according to their respective equities, is good, for it contemplates a distribution according to law.[6] If a partnership is dissolved in good faith, and one partner takes the property and assumes the debts of the firm, he may subsequently assign the property for the payment of his individual creditors,[7] or of the creditors of any new firm of which he may become a creditor.[8] An appropriation of the firm property to the payment of individual debts, is

---

[1] Wilson v. Robertson, 21 N. Y. 587 ; s. c. 19 How. Pr. 350.

[2] Van Nest v. Yoe, 1 Sandf. Ch. 4 ; Knauth v. Bassett, 34 Barb. 31 ; Hollister v. Loud, 2 Mich. 309.

[3] Hurlbert v. Dean, 2 Keyes, 97 ; *Contra*, Lester v. Abbott, 28 How. Pr. 488 ; s. c. 3 Robt. 691.

[4] Cox v. Platt, 32 Barb. 126 ; s. c. 19 How. Pr. 121 ; Read v. Baylies, 18 Pick. 437 ; Marks v. Hill, 15 Gratt. 400 ; Barcroft v. Snodgrass, 1 Cold. 430.

[5] Smith v. Howard, 20 How. Pr. 121.

[6] Heckman v. Messinger, 49 Penn. 465 ; Maennel v. Murdock, 13 Md. 264.

[7] Robb v. Stevens, 1 Clarke, 192 ; Yearsley's Estate, 1 A. L. Reg. 636 ; Marsh v. Bennett, 5 McLean, 117 ; Price v. De Ford, 18 Md. 489 ; *vide* Heye v. Bolles, 2 Daly, 231 ; s. c. 33 How. Pr. 266.

[8] Smith v. Howard, 20 How. Pr. 121.

not, it seems, a ground for setting aside the assignment
at the instance of an individual creditor, as he cannot
in any manner be affected by it.[1]

SEPARATE PROPERTY TO FIRM DEBTS.—The rule that
the individual property must be first applied to the
payment of the separate debts does not limit or restrict
the partners in administering their own funds, for the
reason that there is no recognized lien or priority of
claim in favor of the several classes of creditors upon
the different funds and classes of assets belonging to the
debtors.   Each partner is liable for the firm debts, and
all the property, both partnership and individual, is
pledged to the payment of the partnership as well as
the individual debts and all that creditors can demand
is that the property shall be appropriated to the payment of debts, and it is no fraud to pay one class instead of another.   The debts provided for in an assignment of the individual property may be those for which
he is liable jointly with others, or severally and alone.
The only question is whether he is liable, and if so, the
appropriation can not be fraudulent.[2]   The only right
of the private creditor in such case is to compel the
partnership creditors to resort first to the partnership
funds until they exhaust them.

DISPOSITION OF SURPLUS BY PARTNERS.—When an
assignment devotes the individual and partnership
property to the payment of the partnership debts, and
provides for a distribution of the surplus among the

---

[1] Morrison v. Atwell, 9 Bosw. 503.

[2] O'Neil v. Salmon, 25 How. Pr. 246 ; Kirby v. Schoonmaker, 3 Barb.
Ch. 46; Van Rossum v. Walker, 11 Barb. 237; Eyre v. Beebe, 28 How.
Pr. 333; Fox v. Heath, 16 Abb. Pr. 163 ; s. c. 21 How. Pr. 384; Gadsden
v. Carson, 9 Rich. Eq. 252; Newman v. Bagley, 16 Pick. 570; French v.
Lovejoy, 12 N. H. 458; vide Jackson v. Cornell, 1 Sandf. Ch. 348.

separate creditors, it should direct a distribution to be made according to the respective rights of the separate creditors, for an appropriation without such discrimination will render the deed fraudulent, because it authorizes the property of an insolvent debtor to be applied in part to the payment of the debts of another person, for which neither he nor his property is in any wise bound before his own just debts are satisfied.[1] Evidence may, however, be given to show that there will be no surplus after the payment of the partnership debts.[2] A direction to the assignee after the payment of the partnership debts to pay all the private and individual debts of each partner is valid, for an illegal intent, is not to be implied in the absence of an express direction, and the assignee may pay the debts of each partner out of his individual property.[3]

EQUALITY.—Whenever a man becomes unable to pay his debts, the law regards his property as of right belonging to his creditors.[4] Morally he is then a trustee for all his creditors, and each is entitled to a ratable share of his property and estate. As his property in equity and justice belongs to his creditors, an assignment in favor of all his creditors equally is in conformity with the general policy of the law.[5] One of the favorite maxims of the law is that equality is equity; hence if there are no circumstances of fraud or *mala fides* attached to the transaction, the law favors rather than discourages such an act on the part of an unfortunate

---

[1] Smith v. Howard, 20 How. Pr. 121; O'Neil v. Salmon, 25 How. Pr. 246; Kitchen v. Reinsky, 42 Mo. 427.

[2] Turner v. Jaycox, 40 N. Y. 470; s. c. 40 Barb. 164; *Contra*, Smith v. Howard, 20 How. Pr. 121.

[3] Eyre v. Beebe, 28 How. Pr. 333.

[4] Gere v. Murray, 6 Minn. 305.

[5] Albert v. Winn, 7 Gill. 446; s. c. 5 Md. 66; s. c. 2 Md. Ch. 169; s. c. 2 Md. Ch. 42.

debtor.[1] By such a course he performs an honest act
and discharges a moral duty of which none can reasonably complain, and to which objection can seldom be
made, except by such as may seek to secure their own
claims at the expense of other creditors. In such case,
however, the debtor does not seek to evade or defeat
the rights of the creditors, but to protect their interests
according to the extent and character of their respective
claims, and those who assail the assignment seek to draw
to themselves more than their just proportion of the
debtor's effects to the prejudice of other creditors.
There is, therefore, no ground to impeach the legality or
fairness of the assignment when it is made in good faith.[2]

PREFERENCES.—By virtue of the absolute dominion
which a man has over his own property, he may, however, give preferences in an assignment, but preferential
assignments are not encouraged. The law rather tolerates than approves them. They are inconsistent with
an enlarged equity, and are, therefore, held to the
strictest conditions. Courts watch the exercise of the
right to prefer with jealousy, and are not required by
any reasons of expediency or justice to enlarge it or give
it dangerous facilities.[3]

---

[1] Malcolm v. Hall, 9 Gill. 177.

[2] State v. Bank, 6 G. & J. 205; Wilt v. Franklin, 1 Binn. 502; Meux v.
Howell, 4 East. 1; Ingliss v. Grant, 5 T. R. 530 ; Vredenbergh v. White, 1
Johns. Cas. 156 ; Pickstock v. Lyster, 3 M. & S. 371; King v. Watson, 3
Pri. 6; Nicoll v. Mumford, 4 Johns. Ch. 522; Vernon v. Morton, 8 Dana,
247 ; Robins v. Embry, 1 S. & M. Ch. 207; Adams v. Blodgett, 2 Wood
& Min. 233; Fisher v. Dinwiddie, 12 B. Mon. 208; Evans v. Jones, 11
Jur. (N. S.) 784; Halsy v. Whitney, 4 Mason, 206; Hall v. Denison, 17
Vt. 310.

[3] Riggs v. Murray, 2 Johns. Ch. 565; s. c. 15 Johns. 571 ; Cunning-
ham v. Freeborn, 11 Wend. 241; s. c. 1 Edw. 256 ; s. c. 3 Paige, 537;
American Exchange Bank v. Inloes, 7 Md. 380 ; Nichols v. McEwen, 17
N. Y. 22 ; s. c. 21 Barb. 65 ; Stone v. Marshall, 7 Jones (N. C.), 300 ;
Blow v. Gage, 44 Ill. 208.

The right to prefer, however, has never been considered immoral or fraudulent.[1] It was a privilege at common law, and has not been abridged by the statute. Apart from the provisions of a bankrupt law, a debtor may, in virtue of that absolute dominion which he holds over his estate make a *bona fide* assignment for the payment of debts with stipulations in favor of preferred creditors.[2] He may assign the whole of his property

---

[1] Estwick v. Caillaud, 5 T. R. 420; s. c. 2 Anst. 381; Cunningham v. Freeborn, 11 Wend. 241; s. c. 1 Edw. 256; s. c. 3 Paige, 537.

[2] Beatty v. Davis, 9 Gil. 211; McColgan v. Hopkins, 17 Md. 395; Tompkins v. Wheeler, 16 Pet. 106; Marbury v. Brooks, 7 Wheat. 556; s. c. 11 Wheat. 78; Wilkes v. Ferris, 5 Johns. 335; Wynne v. Glidewell, 17 Ind. 446; Layson v. Rowan, 7 Rob. (La.) 1; Murray v. Riggs, 15 Johns. 571, s. c. 2 Johns. Ch. 565; Hatch v. Smith, 5 Mass. 42; Embry v. Clapp, 38 Geo. 245; Stevens v. Bell, 6 Mass. 339; De Forrest v. Bacon, 2 Conn. 633; Jacobs v. Remsen, 36 N. Y. 668; Putnam v. Hubbell, 42 N. Y. 106; Cameron v. Montgomery, 13 S. & R. 128; Robinson v. Rapelye, 2 Stew. 86; Wiley v. Collins, 11 Me. 193; Deaver v. Savage, 3 Mo. 252; Stevenson v. Agry, 7 Ohio, 2d part, 247; Pearson v. Rockhill, 4 B. Mon. 296; Moffatt v. M'Dowell, 1 McCord Ch. 434; M'Collough v. Sommerville, 8 Leigh, 415; How v. Camp, Walk. Ch. 427; King v. Trice, 3 Ired. Eq. 568; *ex parte* Conway, 12 Ark. 302; U. S. Bank v. Huth, 4 B. Mon. 423; Merrick v. Henderson, Walk. 485; Cross v. Bryant, 2 Scam. 36; Smith v. Campbell, Rice, 352; Petrekin v. Davis, Morris, 296; Holbrook v. Baker, 4 Fla. 87; Hollister v. Loud, 2 Mich. 309; Kneeland v. Cowles, 4 Chand. 46; Cooper v. McClun, 16 Ill. 435; U. S. v. Bank of U. S. 8 Rob. (La.) 262; Hampton v. Morris, 2 Met. (Ky.) 336; Hempstead v. Starr, 3 Day, 340; Hower v. Geesaman, 17 S. & R. 251; M'Menomy v. Ferrers, 3 Johns. 71.

They are prohibited in the following States:—

Maine—Rev. Stat. Ch. 70; Berry v. Cutts, 40 Me. 445.

New Hampshire—True v. Congdon, 44 N. H. 48.

Vermont—Act of 1852, Passumpsic Bank v. Strong, 42 Vt. 295. General assignments were formerly prohibited. Mussey v. Noyes, 26 Vt. 462; Noyes v. Hickok, 27 Vt. 36; Merrill v. Englesby, 28 Vt. 150; Bishop v. Catlin, 28 Vt. 71; Farr v. Brackett, 30 Vt. 344.

Massachusetts—Wyles v. Beals, 1 Gray, 233; Edwards v. Mitchell, 1 Gray, 239; Bowles v. Graves, 4 Gray, 117; in that State no assignment is valid, Stanfield v. Simmons, 12 Gray, 442.

Connecticut—Rev. Stat. Title 14 Ch. 4; Richmondville Manuf. Co. v. Pratt, 9 Conn. 487; Godell v. Williams, 21 Conn. 419; Beers v. Lyons, 21 Conn. 604.

New Jersey—Act Apr. 16, 1846; 1 R. S. 316, Dixon's Dig. 27; Varnum

for the benefit of a single creditor in exclusion of all
others, or he may distribute it in unequal proportions,

---

v. Camp. 1 Green, 326; Fairchild v. Hunt, 1 McCarter, 367; Knight v.
Packer, 1 Beasley, 214; the statute does not apply to an assignment by a
fraudulent grantee as a compromise with the creditors who have assailed
the conveyance, Emerick v. Harlan, 1 Beasley, 229.

Pennsylvania—Purdon's Digest, 52; Law v. Mills, 18 Penn. 185;
Wiener v. Davis, 18 Penn. 331; Miners' National Bank's Appeal, 57 Penn.
193; Driesbach v. Becker, 34 Penn. 152.

Georgia—Preferences were formerly prohibited, but are not now. Lamb
v. Radcliff, 28 Geo. 520; Norton v. Cobb, 20 Geo. 44; Banks v. Clapp, 12
Geo. 514; Eastman v. McAlpin, 1 Kelly, 157; Cameron v. Scudder, 1
Kelly, 204; Watkins v. Jenks, 24 Geo. 431; Ezekiel v. Dixon, 3 Kelly,
146 ; Dawson v. Figuiero, 16 Geo. 610.

Alabama Code, secs. 1555, 1556—Holt v. Bancroft, 30 Ala. 193; Price
v. Mazange, 31 Ala. 701.

Kentucky Act, March 10, 1856—Rev. Stat. (Stanton) 553; Hampton
v. Morris, 2 Met. (Ky.) 336.

Ohio—Rev. Stat. (S. & C.) 709 ; Dickson v. Rawson, 5 Ohio St. R. 218;
Floyd v. Smith, 9 Ohio St. R. 546 ; Harkraker v. Leiby, 4 Ohio St. R. 602;
Hull v. Jeffrey, 8 Ohio, 390; Harshman v. Lowe, 9 Ohio, 92; Mitchell v.
Gazzam, 12 Ohio, 815; Doremus v. O'Hara, 1 Ohio St. R. 45.

Missouri—Rev. Stat. Ch. 8; partial assignments may give preferences,
Shapleigh v. Baird, 26 Mo. 322 ; Woods v. Timmernan, 27 Mo. 107;
Many v. Logan, 31 Mo. 91.

Wisconsin—Rev. Stat. Ch. 63; Page v. Smith, 24 Wis. 368.

Iowa—Wiiliams v. Gartrell, 4 Greene, 287 ; Cole v. Dealman, 13 Iowa,
551 ; Revision 1860, Ch. 77; Burrows v. Lehndorf, 8 Iowa, 96 ; Bebb v.
Preston, 1 Iowa, 460; partial assignments may prefer, Lampson v. Arnold,
19 Iowa, 479.

California—All assignments are prohibited by the insolvent law—Che-
ver v. Hays, 3 Cal. 471,—although a third person intervenes,—Groschen
v. Page, 6 Cal. 138,—or they are judicial,—Adams v. Woods, 8 Cal. 152.
But the insolvency of the debtor must be established. Morgentham v.
Harris, 12 Cal. 245. The prohibition does not extend to an assignment of
a bill of lading for the benefit of the vendor. Le Cacheux v. Cutter, 6 Cal.
514.

New York—Assignments by moneyed corporations when insolvent or in
contemplation of insolvency are prohibited, 1 Rev. Stat. 591; Hurlbut v.
Carter, 21 Barb. 221 ; Bowery Bank Case, 5 Abb. Pr. 415 ; the same pro-
hibitions also extend to limited partnerships 1 Rev. Stat. 766, §§ 20, 21;
Fanshawe v. Lane, 16 Abb. Pr. 71; Greene v. Breck, 28 Barb. 73 ; s. c.
10 Abb. Pr. 42. The general effect of the State statutes is not to invalidate the assignment but to make it operate for the benefit of all. Law v.

either among a part or the whole of them.[1] A surviving partner,[2] or a corporation,[3] may give a preference.

INCIDENTAL EFFECT TO DEFEAT OTHERS.—The mere fact that the preference defeats all other creditors does not affect the validity of the assignment.[4] A deliberate intention on the part of the debtor that certain creditors shall not be paid out of the property assigned until a preferred class shall be paid is not of itself a fraudulent intent.[5] There may even be an intent to defeat an execution.[6] There must be other ingredients in the case to make the transaction fraudulent. There must be a fraudulent intent. Every conveyance by which an insolvent debtor conveys his whole property to a few preferred creditors, not being more than sufficient to pay their debts, necessarily tends to delay and defeat all other creditors; but however strong the intention is thereby to defeat or delay the latter, still the conveyance is not void on that account.

The law allows a creditor to give a preference to

Mills, 18 Penn. 185 ; Shapleigh v. Baird, 26 Mo. 322 ; Floyd v. Smith, 9 Ohio St. R. 546 ; Dickson v. Rawson, 5 Ohio St. R. 218 ; Shouse v. Utterback, 2 Met. (Ky.) 55; Given v. Gordon, 3 Met. (Ky.) 538 ; Price v. Mazange, 31 Ala. 701. They do not generally apply to sale to a creditor to pay his own debt and account for the balance. Chaffees v. Risk, 24 Penn. 432 ; Pomeroy v. Manin, 2 Paine, 476 ; Carey v. Giles, 10 Geo. 9 ; Banks v. Clapp, 12 Geo. 514 ; *vide* Page v. Smith, 24 Wis. 368 ; Bebb v. Preston, 1 Iowa, 460.

[1] New Albany R. R. Co. v. Huff, 19 Ind. 444.

[2] Hutchinson v. Smith, 7 Paige, 26 ; *Contra*, Barcroft v. Snodgrass, 1 Cold. 430.

[3] Catlin v. Eagle Bank, 6 Conn. 233; Dana v. Bank of U. S. 5 W. & S. 223; Burr v. M'Donald, 3 Gratt. 215 ; Arthur v. Commercial Bank, 9 S. & M. 394 ; Town v. Bank, 2 Doug. (Mich.) 530 ; Hightower v. Mustian, 8 Geo. 506 ; U. S. v. Bank of U. S. 8 Rob. (La.) 262; Dundas v. Bowler, 3 McLean, 397.

[4] Marbury v. Brooks, 7 Wheat. 556 ; s. c. 11 Wheat. 78 ; Byrd v. Bradley, 2 B. Mon. 239.

[5] Wilson v. Eifler, 7 Cold. 31.

[6] Hollister v. Loud, 2 Mich. 309.

creditors by a *bona fide* conveyance. It allows any creditor also by an execution to acquire a preference *in invitum*. But which shall prevail depends entirely upon the priority of the acts by which the preference is legally acquired. Neither is, of itself, a fraud upon the other.[1] The suing creditors strive in a legal way to make their debts to the exclusion of others, and have no right to complain if they are surpassed and out-stripped in the race of diligence by another legal mode of obtaining satisfaction. It is only a fair contest be-tween creditors by legal means to secure themselves. Since in law they are equally meritorious, the strongest legal right must prevail.[2] The debtor may also select the time of making an assignment, so as to make the preference effectual.[3]

SECRET MOTIVES.—A previous threat is immaterial, for a thing which would be lawful without a threat can not become unlawful because it is done in pursuance of a threat. The declaration of an intention by a debtor to do what the law sanctions as right and proper, will not render an assignment fraudulent.[4] Neither law nor equity inquire into the reasons or mo-tives for the preference. The motive which prompted it, provided an honest debt is secured, is not the sub-ject of legal inquiry. If in selecting the objects of his

---

[1] Halsey v. Whitney, 4 Mason, 206; Bank v. Cox, 6 Me. 395; Tomp-kins v. Wheeler, 16 Pet. 106; Jaques v. Greenwood, 12 Abb. Pr. 232; Wynne v. Glidewell, 17 Ind. 446; New Albany R. R. Co. v. Huff, 19 Ind. 444; Chandler v. Caldwell, 17 Ind. 256; Bailey v. Mills, 27 Tex. 434.

[2] Hefner v. Metcalf, 1 Head. 577.

[3] Tompkins v. Wheeler, 16 Pet. 106.

[4] Spaulding v. Strang, 37 N. Y. 135; s. c. 38 N. Y. 9; s. c. 32 Barb. 235; s. c. 36 Barb. 310; Wilson v. Britton, 6 Abb. Pr. 84, 97; s. c. 20 Barb. 562; Place v. Miller, 6 Abb. Pr. (N. S.) 178; *vide* Gasherie v. Apple, 14 Abb. Pr. 64; Renard v. Graydon, 39 Barb. 548; s. c. 36 Barb. 310; s. c. 32 Barb. 235; s. c. 25 How. Pr. 78; Dickerson v. Benham, 20 How. Pr. 343.

preference he is guided by mere caprice or favoritism rather than by the superior claims of some of his creditors over others, it is not a subject of legal complaint.[1] He may even be influenced by an expectation to receive employment from the preferred creditors.[2] If the debtor's purpose is to prevent a sacrifice of his property and a race of diligence among his creditors by appropriating it to his preferred creditors, this will not be fraudulent, because it is just what he has a right to do.[3]

CONSEQUENCE OF RIGHT TO PREFER.—The right to prefer necessarily involves the right to postpone.[4] A claim may be postponed unless certain collaterals are accounted for.[5] The assignment may provide that no interest shall be paid upon any debt until the principal of all the debts is paid.[6] No principle of public policy or morality is infringed by an agreement among the common creditors of an insolvent debtor, who is about to make an assignment, that he shall prefer one and postpone another, and a promise by one creditor to pay another a certain sum upon condition that the latter, who is a surety for the debtor, will consent to the giving of a preference to him is valid when the surety is solvent.[7]

RESERVATIONS TO DEBTOR.—The fundamental principle of law and justice is that all the property of an insolvent debtor shall be applied to the discharge of his

---

[1] Spaulding v. Strang, 37 N. Y. 135; s. c. 38 N. Y. 9; s. c. 32 Barb. 235; s. c. 36 Barb. 310; Hollister v. Loud, 2 Mich. 309; ex parte Conway, 12 Ark. 302.

[2] Crawford v. Austin, 34 Md. 49.

[3] Rindskoff v. Guggenheim, 3 Cold. 284.

[4] Ex parte Conway, 12 Ark. 302.

[5] Bellows v. Partridge, 19 Barb. 176.

[6] Ingraham v. Grigg, 13 S. & M. 22.

[7] Halton v. Jordan, 29 Ala. 266.

debts. If the debtor may want sustenance, so also may the creditor, and if one of them must suffer the misfortune must, according to law and morals, fall on the debtor. An assignment must, therefore, be made in good faith for the purpose of paying debts and without any intent to lock up the property from creditors for the use of the debtor. When a person has the full title and desires to retain the control and use of his property and yet transfers it to another to be held for his use, he can, in the general course of human actions, have but one motive for the measure, and that motive must be to defeat or elude the claims of others.[1] This is in the reason why all stipulations for any benefit in favor of the debtor render an assignment null and void. The debtor can not retain the use and enjoyment of the property and turn creditors over for their debts to the rents and profits,[2] nor transfer his property and substitute his own bond in its place.[3] An express appropriation of a portion of the property to his use,[4] or for his support,[5] or any provision for his family,[6] renders the assignment void. The mere fact that the debts of the creditors who assent to it amount to more than the value of the property is immaterial.[7]

The debtor can not postpone creditors to a future

---

[1] Mackie v. Cairns, 5 Cow. 547 ; s. c. 1 Hopk. 373.

[2] Green v. Trieber, 3 Md. 11 ; Galt v. Dibrell, 10 Yerg. 146.

[3] Green v. Trieber, 3 Md. 11.

[4] Green v. Trieber, 3 Md. 11; Mackie v. Cairns, 5 Cow. 547; s. c. 1 Hopk. 373; Johnston v. Harvey, 2 Penna. 82; Richards v. Hazard, 1 Stew. & Port. 139; Coate v. Williams, 9 Eng. L. & Eq. 481 ; s. c. 7 Exch. 205; Contra, Murray v. Riggs, 15 Johns. 571 ; s. c. 2 Johns. Ch. 565; Austin v. Bell, 20 Johns. 442; Estwick v. Caillaud, 5 T. R. 420; s. c. 2 Anst. 381.

[5] Green v. Trieber, 3 Md. 11 ; Johnston v. Harvey, 2 Penna. 82.

[6] M'Allister v. Marshall, 6 Binn. 338 ; M'Clurg v. Lecky, 3 Penna. 83 ; Bradway's Estate, 1 Ashm. 212 ; Green v. Branch Bank, 33 Ala. 643; Contra, Young v. Booe, 11 Ired. 247.

[7] M'Allister v. Marshall, 6 Binn. 338.

day and have the funds in the meantime applied to the prosecution of his business.[1] An assignment which is to continue until the profits pay the debts when the property itself is to revert to the debtor is fraudulent, for it tends to lock up the estate indefinitely, thereby hindering and delaying creditors unreasonably, and securing an ultimate and permanent advantage to the debtor.[2] A debtor has no right, for the same reason, to subject his creditors to the alternative of agreeing that he shall have further time and pay by instalments prescribed by himself or lose all benefit of his property and chance of being paid in case it should require the whole to satisfy those who may assent to the deed. The effect is to gain time by coercing the creditors who may come in, and to hinder and delay those who may refuse the terms of the deed, as well as those not provided for. Indulgence cannot be demanded at the option of the debtor and on his own terms.[3]

No provision can be made for the payment of the expenses incurred by the assignee in obtaining a release for the debtor,[4] or for the payment of the expenses of the debtor in obtaining the benefit of the bankrupt law.[5] A preference can not be given for the purpose of securing to the debtor the future use of a dwelling house, without paying rent or being liable therefor.[6] A pro-

---

[1] Bodley v. Goodrich, 7 How. 276 ; Cleveland v. Railroad Co. 7 A. L. Reg. 537.

[2] Arthur v. Commercial Bank, 9 S. & M. 394; Fellows v. Commercial Bank, 6 Rob. (La.) 246 ; Contra, Robins v. Embry, 1 S. & M. Ch. 207 ; Balto. & Ohio R. R. Co. v. Glenn, 28 Md. 287.

[3] Green v. Trieber, 3 Md. 11.

[4] Austin v. Bell, 20 Johns. 442.

[5] Sewall v. Russell, 2 Paige, 175.

[6] Elias v. Farley, 40 N. Y. 398 ; s. c. 5 Abb. Pr. (N. S.) 39.

vision for future advances and future liabilities,[1] or a loan not received at the time of executing the assignment,[2] renders the transfer fraudulent. A stipulation that the debtor shall be permitted to transact business for a certain period, without any proceedings being taken against him, either at law or in equity,[3] or contemplating the resumption of business,[4] avoids the assignment. Any reservation in favor of any member of a firm is a trust in favor of the assignors as much as one in favor of all the assignors.[5] A stipulation may be inserted requiring a note given in an exchange of accommodation notes to be surrendered as a condition of a preference.[6]

RIGHT TO POSSESSION.—An express reservation of the right to remain in possession until the property is sold,[7] or for such a time as the assignee in his discretion may deem proper,[8] will not vitiate the transfer. A stipulation in the deed for possession by the debtor for a definite time is an express trust for him, and raises a presumption of fraud, unless the period is so short as to leave it indifferent whether it is for the convenience of the assignee and the benefit of the estate, or for

---

[1] Barnum v. Hempstead, 7 Paige, 568; Lansing v. Wordworth, 1 Sandf. Ch. 43; Currie v. Hart, 2 Sandf. Ch. 353; Peacock v. Tompkins, Meigs. 317.

[2] Sheldon v. Dodge, 4 Denio, 217.

[3] Berry v. Riley, 2 Barb. 307; Sheppards v. Turpin, 3 Gratt. 373.

[4] Fairchild v. Hunt, 1 McCarter, 367.

[5] Judson v. Gardner, 4 Leg. Obs. (N. Y.) 424.

[6] Oliver Lee & Co.'s Bank v. Talcott, 19 N. Y. 146; Bank v. Talcott, 22 Barb. 550.

[7] Baxter v. Wheeler, 9 Pick. 21; Dewey v. Littlejohn, 2 Ired. Eq. 495; Moore v. Collins, 3 Dev. 126; Lanier v. Driver, 24 Ala. 149; Contra, Knight v. Packer, 1 Beasley, 214.

[8] Planters' Bank v. Clarke, 7 Ala. 765; Abercrombie v. Bradford, 16 Ala. 560; Shackelford v. Planters' Bank, 22 Ala. 238.

the benefit of the debtor.[1] No express stipulation can be inserted requiring the employment of the debtor.[2]

When an assignment is void on account of a reservation in favor of the debtor, creditors may seize the property reserved,[3] or the property assigned.[4]

CONCEALMENT.—Concealment of a portion of the assets conveyed by the terms of the assignment does not necessarily invalidate the assignment,[5] but is merely a circumstance tending to prove fraud.[6] The same principle applies when the debtor absconds with a portion of the estate.[7] These acts are a fraud on the assignment rather than a fraud in it.[8] But if the debtor, through the agency of the assignee, retains more than he can hold under the exemption laws of the State, the assignment is fraudulent.[9]

---

[1] Hardy v. Skinner, 9 Ired. 191; Hardy v. Simpson, 13 Ired. 132. Six months—Kevan v. Branch 1 Gratt. 274; Janney v. Barnes, 11 Leigh, 100; Coate v. Williams, 9 Eng. L. & Eq. 481; s. c. 7 Exch. 205,—and eight months—Hempstead v. Johnston, 18 Ark. 123—have been deemed to be not unreasonable. In Virginia, two years, with the right to take the profits—Dance v. Seaman, 11 Gratt. 778,—and have all the debts over the receipts contracted during that time paid out of the trust fund—Balto. & Ohio R. R. Co. v. Glenn, 28 Md. 287—is good.

[2] McClurg v. Lecky, 3 Penna. 83; *Contra*, Young v. Booe, 11 Ired. 347; Janney v. Barnes, 11 Leigh, 100; Marks v. Hill, 15 Gratt. 400; Rindskoff v. Guggenheim, 3 Cold. 284.

[3] M'Allister v. Marshall, 6 Binn. 338; M'Clurg v. Lecky, 3 Penna. 83.

[4] M'Clurg v. Lecky, 3 Penna. 83.

[5] Reinhard v. Bank of Kentucky, 6 B. Mon. 252.

[6] Guerin v. Hunt, 6 Minn. 375; s. c. 8 Minn. 477; Smith v. Mitchell, 12 Mich. 180; Blackman v. Wheaton, 13 Minn. 326; Lehmer v. Herr, 1 Duvall, 360; Ruble v. McDonald, 18 Iowa, 493.

[7] Wilson v. Forsyth, 24 Barb. 105; American Exchange Bank v. Webb, 15 How. Pr. 193; s. c. 36 Barb. 291; Gates v. Labeaume, 19 Mo. 17; Miller v. Halsey, 4 Abb. Pr. (N. S.) 28; Thomas v. Tallmadge, 16 Ohio St. R. 434; Spencer v. Jackson, 2 R. I. 35; *vide* Waverley Bank v. Halsey, 57 Barb. 249; Foley v. Bitter, 34 Md. 646; Stewart v. Spencer, 1 Curt. 157; Nightingale v. Harris, 6 R. I. 321.

[8] Thomas v. Tallmadge, 16 Ohio St. R. 434.

[9] Carlton v. Baldwin, 22 Tex. 724; Stewart v. Spencer, 1 Curt. 157;

EXCEPTIONS FROM OPERATION OF DEED.—An exception whereby the property is retained by the debtor and not conveyed to the assignee is not a reservation of a benefit to the debtor and does not vitiate the assignment.[1] A declaration that certain notes were made for the accommodation of the debtor and directing their return to the makers simply excepts them from the operation of the deed , and does not justify an inference of fraud.[2] Whatever is exempt from execution may be reserved to the debtor.[3] The rule that there must be no provision for the benefit of the debtor does not apply to a sale. The debtor may take notes for a part of the purchase-money and provide that the balance shall be paid to his creditors. Such a stipulation simply relates to the manner in which the property shall be paid for by the purchaser.[4] A second assignment can not be made for the purpose of indemnifying the assignee for acts to be done by him in compromising with creditors and extinguishing a prior assignment.[5]

RESIDUARY INTERESTS.—There is a distinction between an express trust for the debtor and a benefit which is merely incidental to a trust created for another

---

Nightingale v. Harris, 6 R. I. 321 ; Farrin v. Crawford, 2 B. R. 181 ; *in re* Chamberlain et al. 3 B. R. 173.

[1] Bank v. Cox, 6 Me. 245 ; Carpenter v. Underwood, 19 N. Y. 520; Pearce v. Jackson, 2 R. I. 35 ; Knight v. Waterman, 36 Penn. 258 ; Bates v. Ableman, 13 Wis. 644; Baldwin v. Peet, 22 Tex. 708 ; Ingraham v. Grigg, 13 S. & M. 22 ; *vide* Foster v. Libby, 24 Me. 448 ; Moss v. Humphrey, 4 Greene (Iowa), 443.

[2] Price v. De Ford, 18 Md. 489.

[3] Dow v. Platner, 16 N. Y. 562 ; Mulford v. Shirk, 26 Penn. 473 ; Hollister v. Loud, 2 Mich. 309; Baldwin v. Peet, 22 Tex. 708 ; Garnor v. Frederick, 18 Ind. 507 ; Smith v. Mitchell, 12 Mich. 180 ; Heckman v. Messinger, 49 Penn. 465 ; Brooks v. Nichols, 17 Mich. 38 ; Farquharson v. McDonald, 2 Heisk, 404 ; Sugg v. Tilman, 2 Swan. 208.

[4] Beach v. Bestor, 47 Ill. 521.

[5] Fairchild v. Hunt, 1 McCarter, 367.

object.[1] A residuary interest necessarily arises in every
case where property is assigned in trust to pay debts,
for the surplus by operation of law results in trust for
the debtor, but unless the assignment is merely colorable and made for the sake of the resulting trust, it is
not void.[2] An express reservation of the surplus to the
debtor is a mere expression of that which the law would
provide without such a declaration, and does not therefore vitiate the transfer.[3]

---

[1] Curtis v. Leavitt, 15 N. Y. 9; s. c. 17 Barb. 309; Van Buskirk v.
Warren, 39 N. Y. 119; s. c. 34 Barb. 457; s. c. 13 Abb. Pr. 145.

[2] Wilkes v. Ferris, 5 Johns. 335.

[3] Hempstead v. Johnston, 18 Ark. 123; Ely v. Hair, 16 B. Mon. 230;
Brown v. Lyon, 17 Ala. 659; Dance v. Seaman, 11 Gratt. 778; Graham v.
Lockhart, 8 Ala. 9 ; Hindman v. Dill, 11 Ala. 689; Dana v. Bank of U. S.
5 W. & S. 223; Johnson v. McAllister, 30 Mo. 327; Miller v. Stetson, 32
Ala. 166; Moore v. Collins, 3 Dev. 126; Andrews v. Ludlow, 5 Pick. 28;
Vaughan v. Evans, 1 Hill Ch. 414; Floyd v. Smith, 9 Ohio St. R. 546 ;
Dickson v. Rawson, 5 Ohio St. R. 218 ; New Albany R. R. Co. v. Huff,
19 Ind. 444; McFarland v. Birdsall, 14 Ind. 126; Richards v. Levin, 16
Mo. 596 ; Conkling v. Carson, 11 Ill. 503 ; Beck v. Burdett, 1 Paige, 305 ;
Contra, Barney v. Griffin, 2 N. Y. 365; Goodrich v. Downs, 6 Hill, 438;
Lansing v. Woodworth, 1 Sandf. Ch. 43 ; Strong v. Skinner, 4 Barb. 546;
Collomb v. Caldwell, 16 N. Y. 484; Truitt v. Caldwell, 3 Minn. 364 ; Ban-
ning v. Sibley, 3 Minn. 389; Green v. Trieber, 3 Md. 11; Therasson v.
Hickok, 37 Vt. 454; Maberry v. Shisler, 1 Harring. 349 ; Berry v. Riley,
2 Barb. 307 ; Pierson v. Manning, 2 Mich. 445; Dana v. Lull, 17 Vt. 390.
The deed can not be made valid by proof that there will be no surplus,—
Barney v. Griffin, 2 N. Y. 365; Goodrich v. Downs, 6 Hill, 438; Dana v.
Lull, 17 Vt. 390,—or by proof that the omission was the effect of haste or
inadvertence; Hooper v. Tuckerman, 3 Sandf. 311.   The doctrine that the
reservation of the surplus renders the deed void is placed in those States
where it is adopted upon the ground that the effect is to lock up the property until the creditors, provided for in the assignment, are paid,—Dana
v. Lull, 27 Vt. 390,—because the other creditors can not sell the interest of
the debtor subject to the assignment, as they could if it were a mortgage.
Leitch v. Hollister, 4 N. Y. 211; Dunham v. Whitehead, 21 N. Y. 131;
McClelland v. Remsen, 36 Barb. 622; s. c. 14 Abb. Pr. 331; s. c. 23 How.
Pr. 175 ; Estwick v. Caillaud, 2 Anst. 381; s. c. 5 T. R. 420.   The oppo-
site doctrine is held in other cases; Murray v. Riggs, 15 Johns. 571 ; s. c.
2 Johns. Ch. 565; Austin v. Bell, 20 Johns. 442; Skipwith v. Cunning-

When no surplus is expected, an omission to provide for the distribution of any balance that may remain does not affect the transfer.[1] There may be a provision that the surplus shall be paid to the debtor or creditors in the discretion of the assignee.[2]

WHEN RESERVATION OF SURPLUS FRAUDULENT.—The reservation of the surplus may, however, be fraudulent. This will depend upon the proportion the value of the estate bears to the debts secured by the assignment. If the assignment covers a great deal of property as a security for a small amount of debts, so that the resulting interest of the debtor is really the valuable interest, the purpose professed is so obviously a mere pretence as not to conceal the true purpose from detection. In such a case the debtor is obviously providing for himself and not for his creditors.[3] Inadequacy of consideration is, however, merely indicative of fraud and not conclusive evidence.[4]

SURPLUS IN ASSIGNMENT BY PARTNERS.—The partnership effects are the primary and natural fund for the payment of the debts of the firm, and the individual property of each member of the firm is the natural fund for the discharge of his private debts. It is therefore perfectly proper for the partners, in making an assign-

---

ham, 8 Leigh, 271; Janney v. Barnes, 11 Leigh, 100; Marks v. Hill, 15 Gratt. 400; Ely v. Hair, 16 B. Mon. 230; Graham v. Lockhart, 8 Ala. 9.

[1] Doremus v. Lewis, 8 Barb. 124; Bishop v. Halsey, 3 Abb. Pr. 400; Spies v. Joel, 1 Duer, 669.

[2] Kneeland v. Cowles, 4 Chand. 46.

[3] Moore v. Collins, 3 Dev. 126; Beck v. Burdett, 1 Paige, 305; Hastings v. Baldwin, 17 Mass. 552.

[4] George v. Kimball, 24 Pick. 254.

ment of the property and effects of the firm for the purpose of discharging their joint debts, to direct the residue of the assigned property, if there should happen to
be any, to be returned to them, so that it may be divided between them according to their respective equitable interests therein, leaving each to pay his private
debts out of his own individual property.[1] Such an
assignment is not fraudulent, because the rights of the
separate creditors are subject to an equitable adjust-
ment of accounts between the partners themselves.[2]
The result will be the same if the assignment contains
no direction to pay the residue of the proceeds to the
debtors after paying the firm debts, for the law itself
creates a resulting trust in their favor as to such surplus.[3] Real estate held by the partners jointly may be
shown to be partnership property.[4]

When one partner, with the consent of his co-
partner, assigns his individual estate and the partnership assets to pay his private debts, there may be a
reservation in favor of such co-partner of a sum equal
to his interest.[5] An assignment of the individual estate
made after the execution of an assignment of the firm
property is not void, because there is no provision for

---

[1] Bogert v. Haight, 9 Paige, 297; Butt v. Peck, 1 Daly, 83 ; Hubler
v. Waterman, 33 Penn. 414; vide Goddard v. Hapgood, 25 Vt.
351.

[2] Collomb v. Caldwell, 16 N. Y. 484; Collumb v. Read, 24 N. Y.
505.

[3] Bogert v. Haight, 9 Paige, 297.

[4] Collumb v. Read, 24 N. Y. 505. When the assignment includes both
individual and partnership property, the surplus can not be reserved to
the debtors without providing for the individual creditors,—Collomb v.
Caldwell, 16 N. Y. 484,—but it has been held that proof must be given
that there are separate debts. Bogert v. Haight, 9 Paige, 297.

[5] Mandel v. Peay, 20 Ark. 325.

the payment of debts which are fully provided for in the firm assignment.[1]

SURPLUS AFTER PAYMENT OF ALL.—There is no objection to a reservation to the debtor of what may remain after the payment of all his debts. He may properly enough take to himself what in such case the law would grant as a resulting trust.[2] When the object of the trust is accomplished, what remains will belong to the debtor by operation of law.[3]

TIME FOR CLOSING TRUST.—Delay is necessarily incident to every assignment, but how far it may be necessary to accomplish the object of a distribution of the property must always depend upon the character and condition of the property, and of the debts to be paid. Any terms which vary from a plain, direct, and immediate application of the effects of the debtor to the payment of his creditors are badges of fraud.[4] It is not necessary that the assignment shall fix a time within which the execution of the trust shall be completed, for the trust is under the control of a court of equity, which will compel the assignee to exercise reasonable diligence.[5]

---

[1] Bogert v. Haight, 9 Paige, 297. It has been held that an assignment of the individual estate is void, if the surplus is reserved to the debtor without providing for the partnership debts. Goddard v. Hapgood, 25 Vt. 351.

[2] Sangston v. Gaither, 3 Md. 40; Beatty v. Davis, 9 Gill. 211; Wintringham v. Lafoy, 7 Cow. 735.

[3] Van Rossum v. Walker, 11 Barb. 237; Ely v. Cook, 18 Barb. 612; Robins v. Embry, 1 S. & M. Ch. 207; Cross v. Bryant, 2 Scam. 36; Hall v. Denison, 17 Vt. 310; Hollister v. Loud, 2 Mich. 309; Hoffman v. Mackall, 5 Ohio St. R. 124; Finlay v. Dickerson, 29 Ill. 9; Matter v. Potter, 54 Penn. 465; Van Hook v. Walton, 28 Tex. 59; Farquharson v. McDonald, 2 Heisk. 404; Gibson v. Walker, 11 Ired. 327.

[4] Carlton v. Baldwin, 22 Tex. 724.

[5] Wilt v. Franklin, 1 Binn. 502; Hower v. Geesaman, 17 S. & R. 251;

TIME MUST BE REASONABLE.—If, however, any time is prescribed it must be reasonable. What is a reasonable time depends upon the nature and circumstances of each particular case. What would be reasonable and proper in one case might be utterly unreasonable and improper in another. Too limited a period of action under the assignment may be as strong evidence of fraud as one which is too extended. The time must always be regulated by the nature and character of the property assigned, and the time necessary to collect and convert it into money. Regard must also be had to the number of creditors and the distance at which they may be placed. For instance, an assignment limiting the time for creditors to file their claims to thirty days would be clearly fraudulent against creditors residing at a great distance. On the other hand, an assignment extending the time to twelve months, where all the creditors reside in the neighbourhood, would be equally fraudulent, unless, from the nature of the property assigned, it could not be put in a shape for distribution at an earlier period.[1]

A postponement of the time of distribution for eight months,[2] and twelve months,[3] has been held good. A postponement for more than a year has been considered bad.[4] A requirement that the trust shall be closed within two years has been held valid.[5] The vesting of a power in a majority of the creditors to postpone the distribution indefinitely vitiates the assign-

Stevens v. Bell, 6 Mass. 339; Hollister v. Loud, 2 Mich. 309 ; Bellamy v. Bellamy, 6 Fla. 62; New Albany R. R. Co. v. Huth, 19 Ind. 444.

[1] Robins v. Embry, 1 S. & M. Ch. 207.
[2] Hempstead v. Johnston, 18 Ark. 123.
[3] Robins v. Embry, 1 S. & M. Ch. 207.
[4] Sheerer v. Lautzerheizer, 6 Watts, 543.
[5] Dana v. Bank of U. S. 5 W. & S. 223.

ment.[1] As the assignment may provide that a distribution shall only be made among those creditors who assent to it,[2] the time allowed for expressing their consent should be reasonable.[3]

DELAY IN SALE AND DISTRIBUTION.—In every assignment a certain amount of discretion is necessarily granted to the assignee. He must, necessarily, from the very nature of the trust conferred upon him, judge for himself, in the absence of express directions, when he can best convert the property into money. Some delay of creditors is the necessary consequence of all assignments, but that alone does not vitiate them. The delay must be shown to be the intent and object of the assignment, not an incidental consequence of it. The object and intent to devote the property to the payment of creditors being meritorious, the unavoidable delay in bringing the property to sale has never been considered as bringing such assignments within the statute.[4] It is the duty of the assignee to proceed without delay and in a proper manner to convert the property into money and pay the debts. He is not, however, bound to proceed to make forced sales after the manner of a sheriff holding property on an execution, unless the terms of the assignment or the manifest interests of the creditors require it. All that is required of the assignee is that he act in good faith, exercise a fair discretion, and do in the premises according to his instructions what a man

---

[1] Sheppards v. Turpin, 3 Gratt. 373; Shearer v. Loftin, 26 Ala. 703.

[2] Conkling v. Carson, 11 Ill. 503; Finlay v. Dickerson, 29 Ill. 9.

[3] One year has been considered reasonable. Vaughan v. Evans, 1 Hill. Ch. 414 ; Contra, Repplier v. Orrich, 7 Ohio, 2d part, 246; Knight v. Packer, 1 Beasley, 214. Twenty months is allowed in Tennessee. Mayer v. Pulliam, 2 Head. 346; Farquharson v. McDonald, 2 Heisk, 404.

[4] Sackett v. Mansfield, 26 Ill. 21 ; Wooster v. Stanfield, 11 Iowa, 128 ; McClung v. Bergfield, 4 Minn. 148.

of ordinary prudence and care would do in regard to his own business.[1] The assignment may by express terms confer upon him all that the law gives by implication.[2]

ILLEGAL POWER VITIATES.—No illegal power, however, should be conferred, for this will render the whole assignment void. The debtor being the absolute owner of the property and in no manner obliged to assign may annex such conditions and qualifications to the transfer as he pleases. If he annex an improper condition, the court must pronounce the assignment itself void. It can not hold the transfer good and disregard the condition, because that would be to take the property from the debtor against his will. He having consented to part with his title only upon certain conditions, the transfer and condition must stand or fall together. If, therefore, the court upholds the assignment, it must of necessity protect and enforce the terms and conditions upon which it is made. A discretion vested in the assignee, however, will always be construed to mean a reasonable and legal discretion, and will be under the control of a court of equity.[3]

LEGAL RIGHTS.—The validity of every power conferred upon an assignee must be determined according to the respective legal rights of the debtor and his creditors. Where an individual has incurred an obligation to pay money, the time of payment is an essential

---

[1] Hoffman v. Mackall, 5 Ohio St. R. 124.

[2] McClung v. Bergfield, 4 Minn. 148.

[3] Goddard v. Hapgood, 25 Vt. 531 ; Benedict v. Huntington, 32 N. Y. 219; *vide* Nicholson v. Leavitt, 6 N. Y. 510; s. c. 10 N. Y. 591; s. c. 4 Sand. 252; Dunham v. Waterman, 17 N. Y. 9; s. c. 6 Abb. Pr. 357; s. c. 3 Duer, 166; Jessup v. Hulse, 21 N. Y. 168; s. c. 29 Barb. 539; Billings v. Billings, 2 Cal. 107.

part of the contract. When it arrives the law demands an appropriation by the debtor of his property
in discharge of his liability, and, if he fails, will of itself
by its own process compel a performance of the duty.
The debtor by the creation of the trust may direct the
application of his property and devolve the duty of
making the appropriation upon a trustee. This the
law permits, and such delay as may be necessary for
that purpose.[1] But any delay beyond what may be
necessary for the proper execution of the trust involves
an illegal hindrance and thus renders the instrument
fraudulent and void.

DELAY OF SALE.—A direction to delay the sale of
the property for the purpose of obtaining higher prices
renders the assignment void, for the creditors are entitled
to have it sold at the best prices it will bring immediately after the execution of the deed.[2] If the interval
between the date of the assignment and the day appointed for the sale appears unreasonably long, it
is indicative of an intent to shield the property for
a time for the use of the debtor and vitiates
the transfer.[3] Forty days,[4] three months,[5] four
months,[6] nine months,[7] and eleven months[8] have been
considered good. One year,[9] eighteen months,[10] two

---

[1] Nicholson v. Leavitt, 6 N. Y. 510; s. c. 10 N. Y. 591; s. c. 4 Sandf.
252; Barney v. Griffin, 2 N. Y. 365.

[2] Hart v. Crane, 7 Paige, 37; Hart v. Gedney, 1 Law Rep. 69.

[3] Hafner v. Irwin, 1 Ired. 490.   [4] Hafner v. Irwin, 1 Ired. 490.

[5] Christopher v. Covington, 2 B. Mon. 357.

[6] Cannon v. Peebles, 2 Ired. 449; s. c. 4 Ired. 204.

[7] Gilmer v. Earnhardt, 1 Jones (N. C.), 559.

[8] Young v. Booe, 11 Ired. 347.

[9] Sheerer v. Lauterheizer, 6 Watts, 543; *Contra*, Graham v. Lockhart,
8 Ala. 9; Farquharson v. McDonald, 2 Heisk, 404; Rindskoff v. Guggenheim, 3 Cold. 284.

[10] Barcroft v. Snodgrass, 1 Cold. 430.

years,[1] three years,[2] and five years[3] have been held fatal. The fact that the assignment is made for the benefit of a part only of the creditors whose debts are equal to the fund assigned and who do not complain of the delay thereby imposed does not alter the case, for there is nothing to prevent them from pursuing their remedy against other assets of the debtor, and they might by superior vigilance exhaust those assets, leaving the fund set apart by the instrument tied up till the end of the prescribed period, when it would revert to the debtor.[4]

WITHOUT DELAY.—A direction to the assignee to sell without delay is good, for it means that he shall proceed to sell without unreasonable or unnecessary delay.[5] The assignee can not sell at once, but is bound to exercise reasonable care and prudence in regard to the time and circumstances of the sale. He may take time to advertise, and must therefore select the day when the sale is to take place. If no bidders should attend upon the day appointed, he would have the power, and it would be his duty, to postpone the sale to another day. He will be obliged also to determine whether the property shall be sold in separate parcels or all in one parcel, and to exercise in that and other similar respects some discretion as to the manner and circumstances of the sale. In all these arrangements he is bound to consult the interests of the creditors, and

---

[1] Quarles v. Kerr, 14 Gratt. 48; *vide* Dance v. Seaman, 11 Gratt. 778.

[2] Adlum v. Yard, 1 Rawle, 163.

[3] Storm v. Davenport, 1 Sandf. Ch. 135.

[4] Storm v. Davenport, 1 Sandf. Ch. 135. It has been held that the deed may direct that the property shall not be sold until judgment is obtained against the sureties Planters' and Merchants' Bank v. Clarke, 7 Ala. 765.

[5] Griffin v. Marquardt, 21 N. Y. 121 ; s. c. 17 N. Y. 28.

has no right to defer the sale any longer than these interests may be supposed imperatively to require.[1]

DISCRETION.—It is manifestly impracticable to sell in all cases alike within the same period after the execution of the assignment without discrimination. A discretion may therefore be left to the assignee to be regulated and controlled by the rules of law prohibiting all delay except such as may be necessary for a suitable preparation and a proper protection of the interests of the creditors.[2] A discretion of this character is one that results *ex necessitate* from the duty which he has to perform. The assignee may also be allowed to select the place for sale.[3] A provision which requires the assignee to regard the interests of the debtor rather than that of the creditors vitiates the transfer, but a direction to sell at such time as may be best for the interest of the parties concerned is legal, for he should consult the interests of the parties in the order and according to their lawful rights.[4] The price may be left to his discretion.[5] A direction to him to sell at fair and reasonable prices is valid, for whatever prices he can obtain upon a sale

---

[1] Jessup v. Hulse, 21 N. Y. 168; s. c. 29 Barb. 539.

[2] Jessup v. Hulse, 21 N. Y. 168; s. c. 29 Barb. 539; Bellows v. Patridge, 19 Barb. 176; Meeker v. Sanders, 6 Iowa, 61; Ogden v. Peters, 21 N. Y. 23; s. c. 15 Barb. 560; Townsend v. Stearns, 32 N. Y. 209; McClung v. Bergfield, 4 Minn. 148; Finlay v. Dickerson, 29 Ill. 9; McCallie v. Walton, 37 Geo. 611; Farquharson v. Eichelberger, 15 Md. 63; Maennel v. Murdock, 13 Md. 164; Mussey v. Noyes, 26 Vt. 462; Inloes v. American Exchange Bank, 11 Md. 173; Benedict v. Huntington, 32 N. Y. 219; Clapp v. Utley, 16 How. Pr. 384; Sackett v. Mansfield, 26 Ill. 21; *vide* Woodburn v. Mosher, 9 Barb. 255; Murphy v. Bell, 8 How. Pr. 468.

[3] Cannon v. Peebles, 2 Ired. 449; s. c. 4 Ired. 204.

[4] Booth v. McNair, 14 Mich. 19.

[5] Ashurst v. Martin, 9 Port. 566; Norton v. Kearney, 10 Wis. 443.

fairly made is in legal contemplation a fair and reason-able price.[1] A direction to him to sell as soon as it can be done without material sacrifice would be proper for the same reason.[2]

MODE OF SELLING.—The power may be given to him to sell at either public or private sale.[3] A direction to sell at public auction is a badge of fraud, because it in-dicates an intention to sacrifice the property.[4] A pro-vision that the assignee may sell gradually in the man-ner and on the terms in which the debtor would have sold the property in the course of his business makes the deed void. It simply seeks, through the instrumentality of an assignee, to provide for carrying on the business in the same manner in which it had been before con-ducted, and for an indefinite period free from all control or interference on the part of creditors. A debtor can not thus postpone his creditors for an indefi-nite period without their consent. A conveyance which thus attempts to deprive creditors of their just rights to enforce their claims against the property of their debtor by placing it beyond their control for an indefi-nite and uncertain period must be regarded in con-science and law as a fraud.[5] If a manufacturer has on hand a quantity of raw material at the time of the as-signment, the assignee may be permitted to continue the manufactory until this is worked up, and to pur-

---

[1] Ely v. Hair, 16 B. Mon. 230.

[2] Wooster v. Stanfield, 11 Iowa, 128.

[3] Halstead v. Gordon, 34 Barb. 422; Sackett v. Mansfield, 26 Ill. 21; Hoffman v. Mackall, 5 Ohio St. R. 124; Nye v. Van Husan, 6 Mich. 329; Marks v. Hill, 15 Gratt. 400.

[4] Work v. Ellis, 50 Barb. 512.

[5] American Exchange Bank, v. Inloes, 7 Md. 380; s. c. 11 Md. 173; Truitt v. Caldwell, 3 Minn. 364; Gere v. Murray, 6 Minn. 305; vide Rind-skoff v. Guggenheim, 3 Cold. 284.

chase any necessary article for that purpose.[1] The object of this power is to prevent the sacrifice that would
be occasioned by a sale of unmanufactured articles, and
thus more effectually promote the interests of the
creditors. It must therefore be made merely ancillary
to the winding up of the debtor's business. If it makes
the creditors partners, it will render the assignment
void.[2] It is always a badge of fraud,[3] and the circumstances which will justify it must appear upon the face
of the assignment, so that the court may determine
whether it is valid or void as a question of law.[4]

SALES ON CREDIT.—A prohibition of sales on credit
is valid, for the assignee in the exercise of a just discretion may postpone a sale so as to prevent a sacrifice.[5]
If, however, there are any circumstances which go to
show that a forced sale is intended to the injury of
the creditors, they should be taken into consideration as
an important item of evidence, and in connection with
other facts may justify the inference of an intent to defraud.[6] If the instrument is wholly silent as to the
manner or terms of sale, the authority of the assignee to
exercise a discretion in regard to a sale for cash, or on
a reasonable credit is unquestionable upon the ordinary

---

[1] De Forrest v. Bacon, 2 Conn. 633; Cunningham v. Freeborn, 11 Wend.
241; s. c. 3 Paige, 537; s. c. 1 Edw. 256; Foster v. Saco Manuf. Co. 12
Pick. 451; Woodward v. Marshall, 22 Pick. 468; Kendall v. New Eng.
Carpet Co. 13 Conn. 383; Janes v. Whitbread, 73 E. C. L. 406; s. c. 5 Eng.
L. & Eq. 431; Marks v. Hill, 15 Gratt. 400; Rindskoff v. Guggenheim, 3
Cold. 284; *Contra*, Renton v. Kelly, 49 Barb. 536; Dunham v. Waterman,
17 N. Y. 9; s. c. 3 Duer, 166; s. c. 6 Abb. Pr. 357.

[2] Owen v. Body, 5 A. & E. 28.

[3] De Forrest v. Bacon, 2 Conn. 633.

[4] Inloes v. American Exchange Bank, 11 Md. 173.

[5] Carpenter v. Underwood, 19 N. Y. 520; Grant v. Chapman, 38 N. Y.
293; Stern v. Fisher, 32 Barb. 198; Van Rossum v. Walker, 11 Barb.
237.

[6] Van Rossum v. Walker, 11 Barb. 237.

principles which govern the duties of trustees.[1] An express provision, therefore, for that which would be implied by law if it were absent, will not vitiate the assignment.[2]

A sale by an assignee upon credit may be an act of good faith and the proper exercise of discretion, according to circumstances. An inflexible rule that an assignee

---

[1] Hoffman v. Mackall, 5 Ohio St. R. 124.

[2] Hoffman v. Mackall, 5 Ohio St. R. 124; Conkling v. Conrad, 6 Ohio St. R. 611; Gates v. Labeaume, 19 Mo. 17; Billings v. Billings, 2 Cal. 107; Baldwin v. Peet, 22 Tex. 708; Christopher v. Covington, 2 B. Mon. 357; Shackelford v. Planters' Bank, 22 Ala. 238; Johnson v. McAllister, 30 Mo. 327; Abercrombie v. Bradford, 16 Ala. 560; Gimmell v. Adams, 11 Humph. 283; Petrekin v. Davis, Morris, 296; Smith v. Leavitts, 10 Ala. 92; Vaughan v. Evans, 1 Hill Ch. 414; England v. Reynolds, 38 Ala. 370; State v. Benoist, 37 Mo. 500; Gilmer v. Earnhardt, 1 Jones (N. C.) 559; Berry v. Matthews, 13 Md. 537; Farquharson v. Eichelberger, 15 Md. 63; Neally v. Ambrose, 21 Pick. 185; Rogers v. De Forest, 7 Paige, 272; Ashurst v. Martin, 9 Port. 566; *Contra*, Nicholson v. Leavitt, 6 N. Y. 510; s. c. 10 N. Y. 591; s. c. 4 Sandf. 252; D'Ivernois v. Leavitt, 23 Barb. 63; Burdick v. Post, 12 Barb. 168; s. c. 6 N. Y. 522; Houghton v. Westervelt, Seld. Notes, No. 1, 32; Porter v. Williams, 9 N. Y. 142; s. c. 12 How. Pr. 107; Lyons v. Platner, 11 N. Y. Leg. Obs. 87; Rapalee v. Stewart, 27 N. Y. 310; Gates v. Andrews, 37 N. Y. 657; Bowen v. Parkhurst, 24 Ill. 257; Greenleaf v. Edes, 2 Minn. 264; Truitt v. Caldwell, 3 Minn. 364; Pierce v. Brewster, 32 Ill. 268; Sutton v. Hanford, 11 Mich. 513; Hutchinson v. Lord, 1 Wis. 286; Keep v. Sanderson, 2 Wis. 42; s. c. 12 Wis. 352; Haines v. Campbell, 8 Wis. 187; Sumner v. Hicks, 2 Black, 532. The power to sell upon such terms and conditions as in the judgment of the assignee may appear best and most for the interest of the creditor is valid, for it does not permit a sale on credit; Kellogg v. Slauson, 11 N. Y. 302; s. c. 15 Barb. 56; Whitney v. Krows, 11 Barb. 198; Southworth v. Sheldon, 7 How. Pr. 414; Clark v. Fuller, 21 Barb. 128; Wilson v. Ferguson, 10 How. Pr. 175; Wilson v. Robertson, 21 N. Y. 587; s. c. 19 How. Pr. 350; Grant v. Chapman, 38 N. Y. 293; Hutchinson v. Lord, 1 Wis. 286; Keep v. Sanderson, 2 Wis. 42; s. c. 12 Wis. 352; Berry v. Hayden, 7 Iowa, 469; Whipple v. Pope, 33 Ill. 334; Booth v. McNair, 14 Mich. 19; McCallie v. Walton, 37 Geo. 611; *Contra*, Schufeldt v. Abernethy, 2 Duer, 533. The sale can not be for money or "available means;" Brigham v. Tillinghast, 13 N. Y. 215; s. c. 15 Barb. 618. The objection does not apply when the assignment is made to the creditors themselves; Van Buskirk v. Warren, 39 N. Y. 119; s. c. 34 Barb. 457; s. c. 13 Abb. Pr. 145; Goss v. Neale, 5 Moore, 19.

27

must, under all circumstances, sell for cash, may at times prove disastrous to the interests of the creditors. Credit may enter largely at times into business transactions, so that to realize anything like a fair value in the sale of property, it may be necessary, under some circumstances, that the assignee shall be allowed the discretion to sell upon credit.[1] If, however, the assignment requires a credit to be given beyond that authorized by law on sales by executors and administrators, it will in general be deemed conclusive evidence of fraud.[2] The power to sell on credit is always a badge of fraud.[3]

DELAY OF DISTRIBUTION.—A power to withhold the distribution of the assets for any length of time which the assignee, in his discretion, may think proper, would be invalid, for it would give him the power to constrain the creditors into a commutation or release of their claims.[4] If there is no authority to sell, a power to deliver the property to creditors who will take it at stipulated prices vitiates the deed.[5] A bank may authorize a sale of its own notes.[6] Real estate can not be reserved until all the personal property is exhausted.[7]

COMPROMISE.—The assignee may be allowed to compromise bad and doubtful debts due to the assignor.[8]

---

[1] Hoffman v. Mackall, 5 Ohio St. R. 124.

[2] Conkling v. Conrad, 6 Ohio St. R. 611. Six months has been held good; Gilmer v. Earnhardt, 1 Jones (N. C.) 559.

[3] Billings v. Billings, 2 Cal. 107 ; Baldwin v. Peet, 22 Tex. 708 ; Carlton v. Baldwin, 22 Tex. 704. In Cannon v. Peebles, 2 Ired. 449, the terms were left to the debtor.

[4] D'Ivernois v. Leavitt, 23 Barb. 63.

[5] Banning v. Sibley, 3 Minn. 389.

[6] Montgomery v. Galbraith, 11 S. &. M. 555.

[7] Pierson v. Manning, 2 Mich. 445.

[8] Dow v. Platner, 16 N. Y. 562; Brigham v. Tillinghast, 15 Barb. 618; s.c. 13 N. Y. 215; Robins v. Embry, 1 S. & M. Ch. 207; Murphy v. Bell, 8 How. Pr. 468; White v. Monsarrat, 18 B. Mon. 809; Berry v. Hayden, 7 Iowa, 469 ; Price v. De Ford, 18 Md. 489 ; Watkins v. Wallace, 19 Mich. 57.

Without such a power he may lose a favorable opportunity to unite with others in a composition with a failing debtor, thus losing the whole claim, when by a judicious and timely settlement he could have secured a large portion of it.[1] Compositions, moreover, instead of increasing, diminish the nominal assets; instead of nursing the estate by delay, so as to enhance the probability of a surplus for the debtor's benefit, tend to a more speedy realization at the expense of a possible sacrifice to some extent of his interests. The power of composition can, therefore, in no sense be called a reservation in favor of the debtor, except in the honest and lawful sense of paying his debts as far and as fast as possible.[2] Power may be given to the assignee to submit disputes that may arise about the property, or the debts owing to or by the assignor to arbitration.[3]

UNCOLLECTIBLE DEBTS.—When debts are uncollectible, it would be absurd to require suit to be brought.[4] A direction to collect the debts and demands, or so much thereof as may be found collectible, is good. The assignee may also sell such demands at public auction, when the interests of the estate require such a disposition.[5] Under peculiar circumstances the debtors to the estate were permitted to pay in eight annual instalments.[6]

POWER OVER PROPERTY.—It is manifest that the assignee ought to be vested with the means and discretion plainly essential to the proper execution of the trust.[7] He may, therefore, be vested with the power

---

[1] Bellows v. Patridge, 19 Barb. 176.
[2] Dow v. Platner, 16 N. Y. 562 ; Price v. De Ford, 18 Md. 489.
[3] Watkins v. Wallace, 19 Mich. 57.
[4] Watkins v. Wallace, 19 Mich 57.
[5] Casey v. Janes, 37 N. Y. 608.
[6] *Ex parte* Conway, 12 Ark. 302.
[7] Bellows v. Patridge, 19 Barb. 176.

to insure,[1] to relieve the property from incumbrances,[2] to release goods from an attachment by giving bond, and indemnifying himself from the estate,[3] to commence, maintain, continue, and prosecute, and also to defend, all suits at law or in equity, which he may deem necessary to the execution of the trust,[4] to employ suitable agents at a reasonable compensation to be paid out of the estate,[5] to pay rent and taxes until the estate is sold,[6] to advertise for creditors in one or more newspapers as soon as conveniently may be, and to select for this purpose such papers as he may deem best calculated to give information to the creditors,[7] and to adopt such measures generally in relation to the settlement of the estate, as will in his judgment promote the true interests thereof.[8]

POWER TO MORTGAGE.—A power to mortgage the property if he shall deem it necessary is beneficial, for it may enable him to guard against a forced and ruinous sale, and may thus be advantageously used for the interests of the creditors.[9] A power to manage and im-

---

[1] Whitney v. Krows, 11 Barb. 198.

[2] Whitney v. Krows, 11 Barb. 198.

[3] Vernon v. Morton, 8 Dana, 247.

[4] Van Nest v. Yoe, 1 Sandf. Ch. 4; Morton v. Vernon, 8 Dana, 247.

[5] Mann v. Whitbeck, 17 Barb. 388; Vernon v. Morton, 8 Dana, 247; Rankin v. Lodor, 21 Ala. 380; Coate v. Williams, 9 Eng. L. & Eq. 481; s. c. 7 Exch. 205; Gordon v. Cannon, 18 Gratt. 387; Maennel v. Murdock, 13 Md. 164; Van Dine v. Willett, 24 How. Pr. 206; s. c. 38 Barb. 319; Casey v. Janes, 37 N. Y. 608; Hennessey v. Western Bank, 6 W. & S. 300; Nye v. Van Husan, 6 Mich. 329.

[6] Van Dine v. Willett, 24 How. Pr. 206; s. c. 38 Barb. 319; Morrison v. Atwell, 9 Bosw. 503; Eyre v. Beebe, 28 How. Pr. 333.

[7] Ward v. Tingley, 4 Sandf. Ch. 476.

[8] Mann v. Whitbeck, 17 Barb. 388.

[9] Beatty v. Davis, 9 Gill, 211. This power is not allowed in New York; Darling v. Rogers, 22 Wend. 483; s. c. 7 Paige, 272; Van Nest v. Yoe, 1 Sandf. Ch. 4; Planck v. Schermerhorn, 3 Barb. Ch. 644.

prove the estate means that the estate is to be so managed and improved or ameliorated in respect to its condition as will be most beneficial for the creditors.[1]

EXEMPTING ASSIGNEE FROM LIABILITY.—While the assignee should be vested with such discretionary powers as are essential to the proper execution of the trust, he ought also to be held responsible for the faithful performance of his duties to the full extent of the liability that the law imposes. The diligence of a prudent man is the measure of his duty. He stands in the light of a paid agent and not in that of a gratuitous bailee. Such an agent is liable for ordinary negligence or the want of that degree of diligence which persons of common prudence are accustomed to use about their own business and affairs. A debtor is not permitted to put at hazard the trust fund which justly belongs to his creditors by authorizing the assignee to manage it without due prudence and caution.[2]

Every provision in an assignment, therefore, which exempts the assignee from any liability that he would by law be subjected to as assignee, is, of itself, a badge of fraud. The insertion of clauses which, in their operation, may lead to the waste and loss of the property, declares an intention on the part of the debtor to devote his property to some purpose other than that of the payment of his debts. The intent to hinder, delay, and defraud creditors is a necessary legal inference from the provision. As between bailor and bailee there is no objection to stipulating that the bailee shall not be liable for any mere negligence, for it affects the contracting parties alone. But in case of an assignment

---

[1] Hitchcock v. Cadmus, 2 Barb. 381; *vide* Schlussell v. Willett, 34 Barb. 615; s. c. 12 Abb. Pr. 397; s. c. 22 How. Pr. 15.

[2] Litchfield v. White, 7 N. Y. 438; s. c. 3 Sand. 545.

the rights of third parties are affected, and the debtor is bound to select an assignee that will do all that the law requires of a trustee in respect to the rights of those that have a beneficial interest in the property assigned.[1]

Good faith is not sufficient, for gross negligence may be entirely consistent with good faith and honesty of intention.[2] A provision that the assignee shall not be accountable for property which does not actually come to his possession renders the deed void, for he is bound to use due diligence to obtain possession.[3] The assignee is bound to use due diligence and good faith in the selection of fit agents and to hold them to a strict and prompt responsibility for their acts, and after the discharge of this obligation he may be exempt from liability for losses arising through their negligence, defalcation, or misfeasance.[4]

REASONABLE EXPENSES.—A provision may be made for the payment from the fund of the just and reasonable expenses, costs, charges, and commissions of executing and carrying the assignment into effect.[5] The

---

[1] Olmstead v. Herrick, 1 E. D. Smith, 310; Metcalf v. Van Brunt, 37 Barb. 621 ; McIntire v. Benson, 20 Ill. 500; Robinson v. Nye, 21 Ill. 592 ; Finlay v. Dickerson, 29 Ill. 9; True v. Congdon, 44 N. H. 48; August v. Seeskind, 6 Cold. 166 ; Jacobs v. Allen, 18 Barb. 549; Whipple v. Pope, 33 Ill. 334; Hennessey v. Western Bank, 6 W. & S. 300; vide Maennel v. Murdock, 13 Md. 164; Ashurst v. Martin, 9 Port. 566; Rankin v. Lodor, 21 Ala. 380.

[2] Hutchinson v. Lord, 1 Wis. 286.

[3] McIntire v. Benson, 20 Ill. 500; Finlay v. Dickerson, 29 Ill. 9 ; True v. Congdon, 44 N. H. 48; Pitts v. Viley, 4 Bibb. 446 ; vide Gordon v. Cannon, 18 Gratt. 387.

[4] Baldwin v. Peet, 22 Tex. 708; Gordon v. Cannon, 18 Gratt. 387 ; Van Nest v. Yoe, 1 Sandf. Ch. 4; Jacobs v. Allen, 18 Barb. 549 ; Hennessey v. Western Bank, 6 W. & S. 300; Ashurst v. Martin, 9 Port. 566; Rankin v. Lodor, 21 Ala. 380.

[5] Eyre v. Beebe, 28 How. Pr. 333 ; Butt v. Peck, 1 Daly, 83; Iselin v. Dalrymple, 27 How. Pr. 137; s. c. 2 Robt. 142; Halstead v. Gordon, 34 Barb. 422; Jacobs v. Remsen, 36 N. Y. 668.

estate may be charged with the expenses and commissions of the assignee.[1] The assignee may demand payment for his services before accepting the trust.[2] The compensation allowed by the assignment must be reasonable. An excessive allowance divests a portion of the property from those who ought to have it, and may induce the assignee to consult the interest of the debtor at the expense of the creditors.[3] A provision can not be made allowing the assignee both commissions and fees as an attorney. Such an allowance places him in two inconsistent positions, which he ought not to be permitted to occupy, for the same reason that a trustee ought not to be permitted to purchase at his own sale. If a third person were to be employed as counsel, the assignee would probably proceed to close up the assignment with as little litigation as possible. But where the assignee is to pay fees to himself as counsel, a direct pecuniary inducement is offered to him to engage in useless litigation and thereby impair the fund and delay the final settlement of the assignment. The assignee is also placed under a constant temptation to consult himself in his capacity of attorney in the transaction of every piece of business connected with the trust, to turn from himself as assignee to himself as attorney, and take advice and charge

---

[1] Bank v. Cox, 6 Me. 395; Keteltas v. Wilson, 36 Barb. 298; s. c. 23 How. Pr. 69; Halstead v. Gordon, 34 Barb. 422; Blow v. Gage, 44 Ill. 208 ; Lentilhon v. Moffatt, 1 Edw. 451; U. S. v. Huth, 4 B. Mon. 423; Vernon v. Morton, 8 Dana, 247; Flint v. Clinton Co. 12 N. H. 430. In New York the assignee's compensation is limited to the commissions allowed by law to executors, administrators, and guardians; Barney v. Griffin, 2 N. Y. 365; Campbell v. Woodworth, 24 N. Y. 304 ; s. c. 33 Barb. 425. In other States an excessive allowance is merely a badge of fraud; Arthur v. Commercial Bank, 9 S. & M. 394 ; Ingraham v. Grigg, 13 S. & M. 22.

[2] Myers v. Fenn, 5 Wall. 205.

[3] Barney v. Griffin, 2 N. Y. 365.

the fund with a fee. A failing debtor can not be permitted to confide a power of this character to a person
of his own selection, and thereby tempt him to constant
infidelity to his trust.[1]

ATTORNEY'S FEES.—All reasonable and proper charges
incurred by the assignee in the employment of attorneys
may be allowed. The protection of the estate may
often render it necessary to consult and to employ
counsel, and the sums paid in such cases should be
allowed to a reasonable extent in all cases where it appears that any necessity induced such consultation or
employment, or that circumstances existed which justified the expenditure. Such sums are properly embraced
in the item of expenses.[2] Even without such a provision the assignee has the power to enforce and defend
rights connected with and growing out of the trust, and
to pay the expenses so incurred.[3]

DEBTOR'S EXPENSES.—No allowance can be made for
the expenses incurred by the debtor in defending suits
which may be brought by creditors for the recovery of
their debts,[4] or in relation to the trust.[5] Such an allowance would secure a benefit from the fund to which
the debtor is not entitled, and if upheld would enable
him to drive his creditors into almost any terms of compromise. It is a standing notice to all creditors that
any effort which they may make to question the amount
due to them or to others, as stated in the assignment, or

---

[1] Heacock v. Durand, 42 Ill. 230; Nichols v. McEwen, 17 N. Y. 22;
s. c. 21 Barb. 65.

[2] Butt v. Peck, 1 Daly, 83.

[3] Iselin v. Dalrymple, 27 How. Pr. 137; s. c. 2 Robt. 132; Jacobs v.
Remsen, 36 N. Y. 668.

[4] Sewall v. Russell, 2 Paige, 175.

[5] Austin v. Bell, 20 Johns. 442.

to compel its execution, will be resisted by the debtor to the end of the law, and that he will then subtract the costs and expenses incurred by him, in so doing, from the fund to which they are looking for a dividend. It also postpones a distribution for an indefinite length of time. The assignee can not reasonably conjecture what amount of expenses will be incurred by the debtor in litigation, for the latter has the power to determine what suits shall be defended, and to what extremity of appeal such defence shall be carried. To avoid responsibility he would be compelled to defer the close of his trust until these should be ascertained. It would, therefore, place in the hands of the debtor a means, arising from the assigned property, to deter creditors from questioning his acts, and ultimately to coerce them into his own terms of settlement.[1] The assignment may name the attorney to be employed by the assignee.[2]

PAYMENT OF DIVIDENDS.—There may be a requirement that no dividend shall be paid unless the person entitled thereto, or his agent, or some credible person certify on oath that the demand is really due and founded on a lawful consideration,[3] or unless the debt is duly proved.[4] The amount of the demand may be limited to such as may be found to be due upon examination and settlement.[5] A prohibition of payment, unless the debtor pronounces the claim to be just, with

---

[1] Mead v. Phillips, 1 Sandf. Ch. 83.

[2] Baldwin v. Peet, 22 Tex. 708.

[3] Ashurst v. Martin, 9 Port. 566 ; U. S. Bank v. Huth, 4 B. Mon. 423.

[4] U. S. Bank v. Huth, 4 B. Mon. 423 ; Spencer v. Jackson, 2 R. I. 35 ; U. S. v. Bank of U. S. 8 Rob. (La.) 262.

[5] Mussey v. Noyes, 26 Vt. 462.

permission to the creditors to establish their demands by suit or arbitration, is good.[1] Costs that have accrued or may accrue may be excluded.[2] The assignee may be required to exhibit a statement of his accounts periodically to the debtor.[3]

COMPOSITION WITH CREDITORS.—The assignee can not be allowed to compound with the creditors.[4] A provision excluding or postponing all creditors who sue the debtor or bring the estate into litigation renders the assignment fraudulent. Such a condition is calculated and intended to deter creditors from attacking the deed lest they lose the benefits of its provisions. It is a hindrance to creditors in the recovery of their just demands. It not only imposes upon them the necessity of acquiescing in the operation of the deed, but it places them at the mercy of the assignee. They must take what he chooses to pay; or if they refuse and sue they get nothing.[5]

---

[1] *Ex parte* Conway, 12 Ark. 302; Robins v. Embry, 1 S. & M. Ch. 207.

[2] Gates v. Labeaume, 19 Mo. 17.

[3] *Ex parte* Conway, 12 Ark. 302; Robins v. Embry, 1 S. & M. Ch. 207.

[4] Grover v. Wakeman, 11 Wend. 187; s. c. 4 Paige, 23; Woodburn v. Mosher, 9 Barb. 255; Hudson v. Maze, 3 Scam. 578; Smith v. Leavitts, 10 Ala. 92; Smith v. Hurst, 10 Hare, 30; s. c. 15 Eng. L. & Eq. 520; *vide* White v. Monsarrat, 18 B. Mon. 809; State v. Benoist, 37 Mo. 500.

[5] Gimell v. Adams, 11 Humph. 283; Marsh v. Bennett, 5 McLean, 117; Riggs v. Murray, 2 Johns. Ch. 565; s. c. 15 Johns. 571; *vide* McFarland v. Birdsall, 14 Ind. 126.

CHAPTER XV.

NATURE OF QUESTION.—An assignment sometimes contains a stipulation that no creditor shall share in the estate until he shall execute a release discharging the debtor from all demands against him. The question in such case is whether an assignment for the benefit of creditors, upon condition that each shall execute a previous release of his whole debt, or be postponed until all other creditors signing a release shall be satisfied in full, is valid; in other words, whether a debtor in failing circumstances and unable to pay all his debts, may say to his creditors that they shall have none of his estate unless they will release the whole of their claim for a portion, and if they decline to surrender the whole for a part, they shall be deferred to the precarious balance which the assenting creditors may leave for the satisfaction of the claims of the recusant creditors.

PUBLIC POLICY.—Every restraint calculated to deter a debtor in failing circumstances from acting on the fears and apprehensions of his creditors ought to be sustained. It is sound policy in commercial affairs, and the best security for fair dealing, that the creditor should be assured that there is not with the debtor an option at any time to compel him to accept a portion of his debt, or incur the contingency of losing the whole. To sustain such an assignment is to enable the debtor to prescribe his own law. The debtor dictates the terms of the settlement. If the creditor refuses, his safest security for his debt, the property of his debtor, is transferred beyond his reach. Unlike deeds of composition, to which none are compelled and the assent of all is necessary, and without the assent of all nothing passes, in such an assignment the terms are absolute and irrevocable, and the creditor must take them as they stand or refuse at the risk of losing his debt. It is the will of the debtor which is law to the creditor. The debtor by this contrivance makes his own bankrupt law. He has, however, no right to dictate terms to his creditors, and to exclude a *bona fide* creditor from all benefit in his property who will not accede to those terms.[1]

COERCION.—Parties not under legal disabilities may make such contracts as they please, and if they are supported by a consideration, and there is no fraud in the case, they will not be disturbed. If a debtor, therefore, with his property in his own hands and open to the legal pursuit of his creditors, can satisfy them that it is for their interest to accept a compromise and give him an absolute discharge, there is no legal objection to it. They treat upon equal terms. The ordinary legal remedies of the creditor are not obstructed. But the case is materially changed when the debtor first places his property beyond the reach of his creditors and then proposes to them terms of accommodation. He obstructs their legal remedies, hinders and delays them in the prosecution of their suits by putting his property into the hands of an assignee, with the view of getting

---

[1] Brown v. Knox, 6 Mo. 302; Miller v. Conklin, 17 Geo. 430 ; Henderson v. Bliss, 8 Ind. 100.

an absolute discharge from his debts, and exempting his future acquisitions from all liability.[1] It is taking an undue advantage of creditors to impose this condition. *Volenti non fit injuria*, if the creditors accept, but it is making volunteers by compulsion. It is mockery to say that consent under such circumstances is optional or voluntary.

Upon principles of morality, law, and justice, a debtor is bound to apply his present property and his future earnings and acquirements to the payment of his just debts, and creditors upon the clearest principles of natural justice and of law have a right to pursue such property, earnings, and acquirements until their claims are fully satisfied and paid. Of this inherent right of the creditor, unless relinquished by his consent, the debtor has no right to deprive him. All unjust and indirect means used by a debtor to extort from his creditor a surrender of such rights; all physical or moral coercion resorted to by a debtor to effect such purpose, are fraudulent against creditors. The design of an assignment exacting releases is apparent upon the face of the deed, and can not leave a moment's doubt upon the subject in the mind of any one. Its object is by a species of moral duress, by indirect means, by a violation of the principles of natural justice and right, to place the creditors in a condition whereby they are compelled to relinquish all claim to any part of the present property of their debtor, or to surrender all right to seek payment out of his future earnings and acquirements. But the debtor has no right to insist on a release as the only condition upon which his property shall be distributed; consequently he has no right to make a provision designed and calculated to procure a release. The law

---

[1] Grover v. Wakeman, 11 Wend. 187 ; s. c. 4 Paige, 23.

will not allow a person to accomplish indirectly what
he is prohibited from doing directly. The injustice and
impropriety of such an effort on the part of the debtor
must, moreover, shock the moral sense, and its fraudulent design and effect upon the rights of those creditors
who refuse to release are obvious.[1]

DISTINCTION BETWEEN CONDITIONAL AND UNCONDI-
TIONAL PREFERENCES.—A debtor may, undoubtedly, by
a transfer of his property, prefer one creditor or class
of creditors to another, but the transfer must be *bona
fide* for the purpose of conferring a benefit on the
creditor, not of securing a benefit to the debtor. The
privilege can not be exerted as a device contrived for
the purpose of obtaining a benefit to the debtor, by
imposing on his creditors what in law can not be otherwise regarded than as a fraudulent moral coercion
practiced upon them to induce an unwilling surrender
to him of their just rights.[2] It does not, therefore, follow that, because a debtor may grant a preference absolutely that he may also do so conditionally. The
distinction is obvious. In the one case he proposes to
pay one or more creditors, still leaving his liability and
the balance of his property unaffected as regards the
others, while in the other case he designs to influence
or coerce all into the terms stipulated, or remove his
property out of their reach. He holds out to the
creditors this contingent preference to become absolute
only by an act of the creditor, beneficial to the debtor
himself by a release of the debt. Such a power would
enable the debtor at any time to nullify the statute and
lock up his property against his creditors until they ac-

---

[1] McCall v. Hinkley, 4 Gill, 128 ; The Watchman, Ware, 232.
[2] Brown v. Knox, 6 Mo. 302 ; McCall v. Hinkley, 4 Gill, 128.

cept the terms he chooses to dictate.[1]   If one assignment
fails through their refusal to accept, he may make
another assignment of the resulting trust and thus keep
them perpetually at bay.

The real object of the provision, moreover, is not so
much to afford a preference to particular creditors as to
secure a release from them.   And to this end it is ad-
mirably adapted.   It is contrived so as to create a
scramble among the creditors, and a scramble under
such circumstances that its natural result will be an unjust advantage to the debtor.   It takes away from
every creditor the power of acting in the premises according to his individual wishes and judgment, and
makes his final course dependent on the course adopted
by every other creditor.   The purpose of producing
this perplexity and embarrassment is, not to effect a
just distribution of the estate, but to secure an important advantage to the debtor by its skillful distribution.
This advantage, moreover, is not one to which he is in
equity and good conscience entitled.   The law does not
recognize any right on the part of an insolvent debtor
to an absolute discharge from his creditors on distributing his estate among them.

FUTURE EARNINGS.—One who contracts a debt agrees
not merely that he will pay it if his present property is
sufficient, but also if his future acquisitions shall give him
the power.   In fine he pledges both the property he possesses and his capacity to acquire property.   It is not true
that parties have in view only the property in possession
when the contract is formed, or that the obligation of indebtedness does not extend to future acquisitions.   The
prospect of an inheritance frequently forms a leading inducement to credit, and industry, talents, and integrity

---

[1] Grover v. Wakeman, 11 Wend. 187; s. c. 4 Paige, 23; Albert v. Winn,
7 Gill. 446; s. c. 5 Md. 66.

constitute a fund which is as confidently trusted to as property itself. There is not a country in the world where a debtor, by his own act, can compel his creditors to take his property and discharge him from his indebtedness. The *cessio bonorum* of the Roman law, which greatly mitigated the severity of the ancient law by releasing the debtor who delivered up his estate to his creditors from a degrading servitude, did not operate to extinguish the debt. His subsequent acquisitions, with some exceptions, were liable until his debts were fully paid.[1]

The right, either legal or moral, of a debtor, to provide in his assignment for a release from debts which he has not paid, stands on no better ground than a right to secure from his creditors a return of a certain per centage on the property distributed, or an engagement that his creditors shall give him a new credit.[2] In either case there is a reservation of a benefit to the debtor. When there is a reservation of the future earning and acquirement, it constitutes an attempt to obtain a full release by a partial payment.[3] Although the statute permits a debtor to prefer one creditor to another, it does not permit him to prefer himself to any creditor.

DISSENT OF JURISTS.—Wherever such an assignment has been sustained it has been against the sound conviction and judgment of the courts, and with a constant expression of regret that a doctrine at variance with equity and with morals must be maintained upon the prevailing understanding of the public. In deference to this opinion some among the purest and loftiest legal minds have yielded to their own convictions. Chief Justice Marshall

---

[1] Grover v. Wakeman, 11 Wend. 187.

[2] Grover v. Wakeman, 11 Wend. 187.

[3] McCall v. Hinkley, 4 Gill. 128 ; Albert v. Winn. 7 Gill. 446; s. c. 5 Md. 66; Grover v. Wakeman, 11 Wend. 187.

said : " We are far from being satisfied that upon general principles such a deed ought to be sustained." [1] Justice Story said: " I am free to say that if the question were entirely new, and many estates had not passed upon the faith of such assignments, the strong inclination of my mind would be against the validity of them." [2] Chief Justice Taney said : " The court was not prepared to affirm that preferences of this character are entirely consistent with the principle of the statute of 13 Eliz." [3] These eminent men yielded to what at the time was deemed the preponderance of opinion, but the judgment and conviction of these great ornaments and lights of the law may still be challenged to support the doctrine of the invalidity of such an assignment. The doctrine is also supported by the weight of authority.[4]

---

[1] Brashear v. West, 7 Pet. 608.

[2] Halsey v. Whitney, 4 Mason, 206.

[3] White v. Winn, 8 Gill. 499.

[4] Grover v. Wakeman, 11 Wend. 187; s. c. 4 Paige, 23; Albert v. Winn. 7 Gill. 446; s. c. 5 Md. 66; s. c. 2 Md. Ch. 169; Widgery v. Haskell, 5 Mass. 144; Ingraham v. Geyer, 13 Mass. 146; Harris v. Sumner, 2 Pick. 129; Ingraham v. Wheeler, 6 Conn. 277 ; Atkinson v. Jordan, 5 Ohio, 295; s. c. Wright, 247; The Watchman, Ware, 232; Armstrong v. Byrne, 1 Edw. 79; Mills v. Levy, 2 Edw. 183; Ames v. Blunt, 5 Paige, 13; Van Winkle v. McKee, 7 Mo. 435; Brown v. Knox, 6 Mo. 302; Drake v. Rogers, 6 Mo. 317; Barrett v. Reed, Wright, 700; Howell v. Edgar, 3 Scam. 417; Pearson v. Crosby, 23 Me. 261; Woolsey v. Urner, Wright, 606 ; Ramsdell v. Sigerson, 2 Gilman, 78; Conklin v. Carson, 11 Ill. 503; Vose v. Holcomb, 31 Me. 407; Jones v. Dougherty, 10 Geo. 273; Graves v. Roy, 13 La. 454; Miller v. Conklin, 17 Geo. 430; Henderson v. Bliss, 8 Ind. 100; Smith v. Woodruff, 1 Hilt. 462; Butler v. Jaffray, 12 Ind. 504; Wilde v. Rawlings, 1 Head, 34; Palmer v. Giles, 5 Jones Eq. 75; Hurd v. Silsbee, 10 N. H. 108; Wyles v. Beales, 1 Gray, 233; Edwards v. Mitchell, 1 Gray, 239; Bowles v. Graves, 4 Gray, 117; Contra, McCall v. Hinkley, 4 Gill. 128 ; Kettlewell v. Stewart,8 Gill, 472 ; White v. Winn, 8 Gill. 499; Green v. Trieber, 3 Md. 11; Brashear v. West, 7 Pet. 608; Lippincott v. Barker, 2 Binn. 174; King v. Watson, 3 Price, 6; Halsey v. Whitney, 4 Mason, 206; Pearpoint v. Graham, 4 Wash. C. C. 332; Bank v. Cox, 6 Me. 395; Doe v. Scribner, 41 Me. 277; Nostrand v. Attwood, 19 Pick. 281; Livingston v. Bell, 3 Watts, 198; Lea's Appeal, 9 Penn. 504; Robinson v. Rapelye, 2 Stew. 86; Haven v. Richardson, 5 N. H. 113;

RELEASE WHILE DEBTOR REMAINS OWNER.—A preference given in consequence of a release is valid. In no
sense can it be said that an agreement by a debtor with
a creditor, to prefer him for a part of his demand in an
assignment, on condition or in consideration that he shall
be released from the balance, is a fraud upon those who
refuse to become parties to such a contract. The parties treat upon equal terms. The property is open to
the pursuit of creditors, and their ordinary legal remedies are not in any degree obstructed. That being so,
and with the property still in the hands of the debtor,
there is no legal objection to any contract of compromise
between the two, even though the consideration for such
compromise moving to the creditors is the advantage of
a preference over others in a contemplated assignment.[1] The assignee may also covenant to obtain a
release.[2]

MUST CONVEY ALL.—As there are some States in
which an assignment exacting releases is held valid, the
law relating to them will now be considered.

Such an assignment must convey all the property of
the debtor.[3] The creditors are entitled to the benefit of

Todd v. Bucknam, 11 Me. 41; Niolon v. Douglass, 2 Hill Ch. 443; Skipwith v. Cunningham, 8 Leigh, 271; Ashurst v. Martin, 9 Port. 566; Hall
v. Denison, 17 Vt. 310; Phippen v. Durham, 8 Gratt. 457; Heydock v.
Stanhope, 1 Curt. 471; Spencer v. Jackson, 2 R. I. 35; Dockray v. Dockray, 2 R. I. 547; Nightingale v. Harris, 6 R. I. 321; Gordon v. Cannon,
18 Gratt. 387.

[1] Spaulding v. Strang, 37 N. Y. 135; s. c. 38 N. Y. 9; s. c. 32 Barb.
235; s. c. 36 Barb. 310; Low v. Graydon, 50 Barb. 414; Hatch v. Smith,
5 Mass. 42; Powers v. Graydon, 10 Bosw. 630; s. c. 25 How. Pr. 512; Renard v. Graydon, 39 Barb. 548; s. c. 25 How. Pr. 178; s. c. 36 Barb. 310;
s. c. 32 Barb. 235.

[2] Hastings v. Belknap, 1 Denio, 190.

[3] Green v. Trieber, 3 Md. 11; Sangston v. Gaither, 3 Md. 40; Seaving
v. Brinkerhof, 5 Johns. Ch. 329; Thomas v. Jenks, 5 Rawle, 221; Hennessey v. Western Bank, 6 W. & S. 300; *in re* Wilson, 4 Penn. 430; Johns

the whole estate, of which they can not be deprived by an arrangement which would impose upon them the necessity of resorting to a part of it in exclusion of the rest. The very imposition of a choice which might prove unfortunate would be an exposure of them to a peril which they are not bound to encounter. An assignment, therefore, that would present but a part of the effects to the creditors and refuse the rest is necessarily fraudulent, inasmuch as it might be a means to extort an unfair advantage.[1] When it is made by partners, it must convey all their property as well their individual estate as their partnership effects.[2]

NOT RESERVE SHARE OF DISSENTING CREDITORS.—If the assignment stipulates that the share which would otherwise belong to the creditor who should come in and accede to the terms and execute a release, shall, on his refusal or default, be paid back to the debtor, or placed at his disposal by the assignee, it is deemed oppressive and fraudulent and destroys the validity of the assignment. The effect is to lock up the surplus until the preferred creditors are paid off and the others are not only hindered and delayed in their remedies, but they are necessarily involved in controversy. The property passes to the assignee and cannot be touched, and the only remedy would be against him as assignee.[3]

---

v. Bolton, 12 Penn. 339; Graves v. Roy, 13 La. 454; Henderson v. Bliss, 8 Ind. 100; Gadsden v. Carson, 9 Rich. Eq. 252; Gordon v. Cannon, 18 Gratt. 387; *Contra*, Halsey v. Whitney, 4 Mason, 206; Bank v. Cox, 6 Me. 395; Spencer v. Jackson, 2 R. I. 35.

[1] Hennessey v. Western Bank, 6 W. & S. 300; *in re* Wilson, 4 Penn. 430; Weber v. Samuel, 7 Penn. 499.

[2] Insurance Co. v. Wallis, 23 Md. 173; Thomas v. Jenks, 5 Rawle, 221; Hennessey v. Western Bank, 6 W. & S. 300; Henderson v. Bliss, 8 Ind. 100; Gordon v. Cannon, 18 Gratt. 387.

[3] Reavis v. Garner, 12 Ala. 661; Sangston v. Gaither, 3 Md. 40; Trieber v. Green, 3 Md. 11; Hollins v. Mayer, 3 Md. Ch. 343; Burd v.

RESERVATION OF SURPLUS.—The surplus which remains after the payment in full of all the claims of the
creditors who assent to the deed, can not be reserved to
the debtor.[1] There must be no reservation to the
debtor, either express or implied. The court cannot
look outside of the assignment to ascertain whether
there will be a surplus or not. That would make the
efficacy of the instrument depend on extrinsic circumstances when the law requires that its intent shall be
gathered from its face. When the surplus is not disposed of in the assignment it belongs to the debtor as
a resulting trust. It is true the other creditors may
prosecute their claims against the assignee in respect of
this surplus, but they could arrest it only by process
of law, and the debtor has no right to compel them
to resort to this, for the fund would be claimed
not under the deed but as the property of the
debtor.[2]

No EXTRINSIC EVIDENCE.—It is the duty of the party
who sets up the assignment to show that the debtor has
done what the law requires to give it validity and
effect.[3] Extrinsic evidence can not be given to show
that in point of fact the assignment does convey all the
property which the debtor had at the time of its execu-

Smith, 4 Dall. 76; Austin v. Bell, 20 Johns. 442; Seaving v. Brinkerhoff,
5 Johns. Ch. 329; Lentilhon v. Moffat, 1 Edw. 451; *Contra*, Halsey v.
Whitney, 4 Mason, 206; Andrews v. Ludlow, 5 Pick. 28; Dockray v.
Dockray, 2 R. I. 547.

[1] Bridges v. Hindes, 16 Md. 101; Grimshaw v. Walker, 12 Ala. 101;
Contra, Andrews v. Ludlow, 5 Pick. 28; Livingston v. Bell, 3 Watts, 198;
Mechanics' Bank v. Gorman, 8 W. & S. 304; Haven v. Richardson, 5 N.
H. 113; Skipwith v. Cunningham, 8 Leigh, 271; Gordon v. Cannon, 18
Gratt. 387; Todd v. Bucknam, 11 Me. 41.

[2] Malcolm v. Hodges, 8 Md. 418; West v. Snodgrass, 17 Ala. 549.

[3] Sangston v. Gaither, 3 Md. 40; Keighler v. Nicholson, 4 Md. Ch.
86.

tion.[1] The deed on its face must show that it conveys
all the debtor's property, and its terms must be inconsistent with the retention of any property either real or
personal.[2] No particular words are necessary to be
used, but such must be employed as will convey all the
debtor's property. All that is required is, that the
words should comprehend all, and thereby negative
every presumption that there is other property. Any
apt words to this end will be sufficient.[3] The words
"estate of every kind and description" are sufficient.[4]
It is not necessary that there should be words of inheritance. In a deed of trust conveying property for
the payment of the debts of the grantor, the omission of
the words "and his heirs" does not have the effect of
confining the grant to personalty, but where the intent
to convey all the property of the debtor is manifest, a
fee simple in realty passes by implication under the
deed.[5]

All the partners must unite in the execution of such
an assignment.[6] The right of dower of the debtor's
wife need not be conveyed.[7] A creditor who holds a
claim against two debtors composing one firm, has no
right to complain because a person who is partner with
them in another firm does not join in the deed. All he

---

[1] Barnitz v. Rice, 14 Md. 24; *Contra*, Nightingale v. Harris, 6 R. I.
321; Gordon v. Cannon, 18 Gratt. 387.

[2] Rosenberg v. Moore, 11 Md. 376; Barnitz v. Rice, 14 Md. 24; Seaving v. Brinkerhoff, 5 Johns. Ch. 329.

[3] Barnitz v. Rice, 14 Md. 24.

[4] Farquharson v. Eichelberger, 15 Md. 63; Bridges v. Hindes, 16 Md.
101.

[5] Farquharson v. Eichelberger, 15 Md. 63; Spessard v. Rohrer, 9 Gill.
261; Angell v. Rosenburg, 12 Mich. 241.

[6] *In re* Wilson, 4 Penn. 430; Hennessey v. Western Bank, 6 W. & S.
300; *vide* Gordon v. Cannon, 18 Gratt. 387.

[7] Breitenbach v. Dungan, 1 A. L. Reg. 419.

has a right to ask is that the assets of his debtors, both individual and partnership, shall be made liable for the payment of his debt.[1]

A provision for the payment of forty per cent., with a stipulation for a return of the surplus, renders the deed void.[2] If the deed professes to convey all but assigns only a portion, it is fraudulent.[3] If the debtor absconds with a portion of the funds and executes an assignment of the balance, the deed is void, but it must be proved that he intends to defraud by the deed, and that it is actually the instrument to defraud.[4] A release will be void if the debtor has executed prior fraudulent conveyances.[5]

REASONABLE TIME.—The deed should give to the creditors all the information in the power of the debtor as to the nature and value of the property conveyed, and the amount of the debts intended to be provided for, and a reasonable time to obtain such information as the deed may not afford, and to make up their minds deliberately and understandingly whether they will accept or reject the offer made to them. If this is not done when it can conveniently be done the omission is

---

[1] Maennel v. Murdock, 13 Md. 164. It has been held that property encumbered beyond its value—Fassett v. Phillips, 4 Whart. 399,—or of small value—Phippen v. Durham, 8 Gratt. 457,—need not be included, and that a small sum might be reserved to pay small debts; Skipwith v. Cunningham, 8 Leigh, 271.

[2] Jacot v. Corbett, 1 Chev. Eq. 71. It has been held that a provision for the payment of only a certain per cent. is good when it appears that no benefit will result thereby to the debtor; Nightingale v. Harris, 6 R. I. 321.

[3] Le Prince v. Guillemot, 1 Rich. Eq. 187; Nightingale v. Harris, 6 R. I. 321.

[4] Stewart v. Spencer, 1 Curt. 157; Spencer v. Jackson, 2 R. I. 35; Nightingale v. Harris, 6 R. I. 321; Foley v. Bitter, 34 Md. 646.

[5] Doe v. Scribner, 41 Me. 277.

a badge of fraud.[1] What is a reasonable time is a matter dependent upon the particular circumstances of each case. A time may be so short or so long as justly to raise a presumption of fraud.[2] If no time is fixed within which the release must be executed the deed is void.[3] Two months,[4] and six months,[5] have been deemed sufficient. Nine months has been considered too long.[6] A different time may be allowed to resident and non-resident creditors.[7]

No doubt which may exist as to the construction of the deed, nor any difficulty which may arise in making an election can affect the case, if the meaning of the deed can be ascertained. The circumstances which create the doubt or difficulty may tend to prove, and even be in themselves sufficient to prove an intent to delay, hinder, and defraud creditors and make the deed void, but if no such intention exists the deed will be valid.[8]

PREFERENCES.—The deed need not convey the property for the benefit of all creditors equally, but may give preferences,[9] and confer a benefit upon some creditors absolutely and to others only upon condition.[10]

---

[1] Gordon v. Cannon, 18 Gratt. 387.

[2] Halsey v. Whitney, 4 Mason, 206; Pearpoint v. Graham, 4 Wash. C. C. 232; Ashurst v. Martin, 9 Port. 566.

[3] Henderson v. Bliss, 8 Ind. 100; Pearpoint v. Graham, 4 Wash. C. C. 232.

[4] Pearpoint v. Graham, 4 Wash. C. C. 232; Gordon v. Cannon, 18 Gratt. 387; Contra, Fox v. Adams, 5 Me. 245.

[5] Halsey v. Whitney, 4 Mason, 206; Ashurst v. Martin, 9 Port. 566.

[6] Burd v. Smith, 4 Dall. 76.

[7] Hennessey v. Western Bank, 6 W. &. S. 300.

[8] Gordon v. Cannon, 18 Gratt. 387.

[9] Maennel v. Murdock, 13 Md. 164; Gordon v Cannon, 18 Gratt. 387.

[10] Rankin v. Lodor, 21 Ala. 380.

The property may be delivered in specie to the cred-itors at prime cost, for when a common price is fixed as a measure of distribution, it is immaterial at what it is put, provided the actual value is not more than adequate to satisfaction in full,[1] and the question of prime cost may be left to be settled by the assignee.[2] No provision can be made in favor of creditors who have released under a prior assign-ment.[3]

THE RELEASE.—The form of the release may be pre-scribed, for the creditor is a purchaser of his preference and must take it on the debtor's terms.[4] The deed may provide for the release of sureties.[5] It is not neces-sary that the creditors should assent before the deed is recorded.[6] One partner is competent in his own name or in the name of the firm to release a debt, and for the same reason he may enter into a composition and exe-cute an assignment and it will release the debt. A sig-nature and sealing in the name of the firm with a single seal is good and valid to release the debt and bind the rights of the firm.[7]

When the taint which avoids the deed is apparent on the face of the instrument, a release is made with full knowledge of the fraud and does not give it valid-ity.[8] Such a deed, however, is not binding upon the creditors who execute releases until it is declared void by a competent court. As the deed is void, the con-

---

[1] Bayne v. Wylie, 10 Watts, 309.
[2] Bayne v. Wylie, 10 Watts, 309.
[3] Nightingale v. Harris, 6 R. I. 321.
[4] Bayne v. Wylie, 10 Watts, 309.
[5] Bank v. Cox, 6 Me. 395.
[6] Haven v. Richardson, 5 N. H. 113.
[7] Halsey v. Whitney, 4 Mason, 206.
[8] *In re* Wilson, 4 Penn. 430.

sideration upon which the releases are executed wholly fails, and the creditors who execute them may, with the consent of the debtor obtain judgment upon their original debts, lay an attachment in the hands of the assignee and hold the fund against a subsequent attachment laid by a creditor who does not execute a release.[1]

---

[1] Insurance Co. v. Wallis, 23 Md. 173.

CHAPTER XVI.

HOW FAR A FRAUDULENT TRANSFER IS VOID.

GOOD BETWEEN PARTIES.—The statute was designed solely to protect the rights of creditors, and, consequently, it renders a fraudulent transfer void only as against them, and makes no provision whatever in regard to its effect between the parties. This is the effect of the word "only." This word was inserted to restrict the broad provisions of the statute to the rights which the legislature designed to protect, and thus left the relative rights of the parties to the provisions of the common law.[1] A conspiracy to defraud creditors is an offence against good morals, common honesty, and sound public policy, for it is a let and hindrance to the due course and execution of law and justice, and tends to overthrow all true and plain dealing, bargaining and chevisance between man and man without which no commonwealth or civil society can be maintained or continued. It is, therefore, a proper case for the application of the maxim "*In pari delicto melior est conditio defendentis.*" *Porro autem si et dantis et excipientis turpis causa sit, possessorem potiorem esse et ideo repetitionem cessare.*[2]

The principle that a collusive contract binds the

---

[1] Nellis v. Clark, 4 Hill, 424; s. c. 20 Wend. 24.
[2] Dig. Lib. 12 Tit. 5 (C.) 8.

parties to it is a principle which commends itself no less to the moralist than to the jurist, for no dictate of duty calls on a judge to extricate a rogue from his own toils. On any other principle a knave might gain but could not lose by a dishonest expedient, and induce-ments would be furnished to unfair dealing if the courts were to repair the accidents of an unsuccessful trick. It is, therefore, in accordance with a wise and liberal policy which requires the consequences of a fraudulent experi-ment to be made as disastrous as possible, that a fraudu-lent grantee is allowed to retain the property, not for any merit of his own, but for the demerit of his con-federate.[1] The law endeavors to environ a debtor with all possible perils, and make it appear that honesty is the best policy.[2]

BINDS GRANTOR AND HIS REPRESENTATIVES.—A fraudu-lent transfer is good as against the grantor,[3] his heirs,[4]

---

[1] Stewart v. Kearney, 6 Watts, 453; Falconer v. Jones, 3 Dev. 334.

[2] Murphy v. Hubert, 16 Penn. 50.

[3] Stewart v. Iglehart, 7 G. & J. 132; Freeman v. Sedgwick, 6 Gill. 28; Phettiplace v. Sayles, 4 Mason, 312; Canton v. Dorchester, 8 Cush. 525; Terrell v. Imboden, 10 Leigh, 321; Simpson v. Graves, Riley Ch. 232; Gifford v. Ford, 3 Vt. 532; Hartley v. M'Annulty, 4 Yeates, 95; Stewart v. Dailey, 6 Litt. 212; Chessman v. Exall, 6 Exch. 341; Sumner v. Murphy, 2 Hill, (S. C.) 488; Leshey v. Gardner, 3 W. & S. 314; Newell v. Newell, 34 Miss. 385; Williams v. Avent, 5 Ired. Eq. 47; Tuesley v. Robinson, 103 Mass. 558; Dale v. Harrison, 4 Bibb. 65; Byrd v. Curlin, 1 Humph. 466; Noble v. Noble, 26 Ark. 317.

[4] Getzler v. Saroni, 18 Ill. 511; Cushwa v. Cushwa, 5 Md. 44; Dan-zey v. Smith, 4 Tex. 411; Kimball v. Eaton, 8 N. H. 391; Jewell v. Porter, 31 N. H. 34; Jackson v. Garnsey, 16 Johns. 189; Ober v. Howard, 11 Mo. 425; Stewart v. Ackley, 52 Barb. 283; Dearman v. Radcliffe, 5 Ala. 192; Reichart v. Castator, 5 Binn. 109; Jackson v. Dutton, 3 Har-ring. 98; Barton v. Morris, 15 Ohio, 408; Trempner v. Barton, 18 Ohio, 418; Church v. Church, 4 Yeates, 280; Laney v. Laney, 2 Ind. 196; McLaughlin v. McLaughlin, 16 Mo. 242; Lokerson v. Stillwell, 2 Beasley, 357; Anderson v. Rhodus, 12 Rich. Eq. 104; Gillespie v. Gillespie, 2 Bibb. 89; Horner v. Zimmerman, 45 Ill. 14.

executors,[1] administrators,[2] agents,[3] parties claiming under him,[4] and his vendees and grantees.[5] A fraudu-

[1] Dorsey v. Smithson, 6 H. & J. 61 ; Welsh v. Bekey, 1 Penna. 57 ;
Orlabar v. Harwar, Comb. 348 ; Odronaux v. Helie, 3 Sandf. Ch. 512;
Anderson v. Dunn, 19 Ark. 650 ; Eubanks v. Dobbs, 4 Ark. 173; Howell
v. Edmonds, 47 Ill. 79.

[2] Hawes v. Leader, Yelv. 196 ; s. c. Cro. Jac. 270 ; Thomas v. Soper, 5
Munf. 28 ; Kinnemon v. Miller, 2 Md. Ch. 407; King v. Clark, 2 Hill Ch.
611; Coltraine v. Causey, 3 Ired. Eq. 246 ; Thomas v. Soper, 5 Munf. 28;
Cocke v. Bromley, 6 Munf. 184 ; Martin v. Martin, 1 Vt. 91 ; Dunbar v.
McFall, 9 Humph. 505; Choteau v. Jones, 11 Ill. 300; Peaslee v. Barney, 1
Chip. 331 ; Bank v. Burke, 4 Blackf. 141; McLaughlin v. McLaughlin, 16
Mo. 242; Avery v. Avery, 12 Tex. 54; Connell v. Chandler, 13 Tex. 5; Crosby
v. De Graffenreid, 19 Geo. 290 ; Beale v. Hall, 22 Geo. 431 ; Winn v. Bar-
nett, 31 Miss. 653; Gully v. Hull, 31 Miss. 20; George v. Williamson, 26
Mo. 190 ; Brown v. Finley, 18 Mo. 375 ; Jordan v. Fenno, 13 Ark. 593 ;
Lassiter v. Cole, 8 Humph. 621 ; Adams v. Broughton, 13 Ala. 731;
Moore v. Minerva, 17 Tex. 20 ; Moody v. Fry, 3 Humph. 567 ; Dennison
v. Ely, 1 Barb. 610; Osborne v. Moss. 7 Johns. 161; *Contra*, Buehler v.
Gloninger, 2 Watts, 226 ; Stewart v. Kearney, 6 Watts, 453; Williams v.
Williams, 34 Penn. 312 ; Freeman v. Burnham, 36 Conn. 469 ; Everett v.
Read, 3 N. H. 55 ; Kingsbury v. Wild, 3 N. H. 30; Brownell v. Curtis, 10
Paige, 210; Babcock v. Booth, 2 Hill, 183; Caswell v. Caswell, 28 Me.
232 ; Morris v. Morris, 5 Mich. 171; Holland v. Cruft, 20 Pick. 321;
Drinkwater v. Drinkwater, 4 Mass. 354 ; Norton v. Norton, 5 Cush. 524;
Gibbons v. Peeler, 8 Pick. 254 ; Welsh v. Welsh, 105 Mass. 385; Sullice v.
Gradenigo, 15 La. An. 582 ; Hunt v. Butterworth, 21 Tex. 133; Allen v.
Allen, 18 Ohio St. R. 234; Allen v. Mower, 17 Vt. 61 ; Love v. Mickals, 11
Ind. 227; McLane v. Johnson, 43 Vt. 48; Abbott v. Tenney, 18 N. H. 109.
The right of executors and administrators to impeach a fraudulent convey-
ance when the estate is insolvent is conferred by statute in Massachusetts,
Vermont, New Jersey, North Carolina, Wisconsin, Michigan, Ohio, Indiana,
Louisiana, New York, and Texas, and several of the above cases are upon
those statutes.   It was held in the following cases that property fraudulently conveyed was assets in the hands of the executor ; Shears v. Rogers, 3 B.
& A. 362; Anon, 2 Rol. Rep. 173; Bethel v. Stanhope, Cro. Eliz. 810; Anon,
Cary, 25 ; Smith v. Pollard, 4 B. Mon. 66.   Where the personal representative proceed under a statute or otherwise, he can only impeach a transfer
when the estate is insolvent; Wall v. Prov. Inst. 3 Allen, 96; Hess v. Hess,
19 Ind. 238; Pringle v. Pringle, 59 Penn. 281.

[3] Newson v. Douglass, 7 H. & J. 417 ; Owen v. Dixon, 17 Conn. 492.

[4] Moseley v. Moseley, 15 N. Y. 334; Wright v. Wright, 2 Litt. 8;
Roane v. Vidal, 4 Munf. 187 ; Neeley v. Wood, 10 Yerg. 486 ; Douglas v.
Dunlop, 10 Ohio, 162; McClesky v. Leadbetter, 1 Kelly, 551; Ellis v.
McBride, 27 Miss. 155.

[5] Bull v. Harris, 18 B. Mon. 195 ; Doolittle v. Lyman, 44 N. H. 608;

lent receipt to a person who owes money to the debtor is as binding as any other transfer.[1] If the property is transferred by a deed with covenant of warranty, and the debtor subsequently purchases the property at a sale under an execution against him, the title thus obtained enures to the benefit of the fraudulent grantee, and the debtor[2] and parties purchasing from him with notice of the prior transfer,[3] are estopped by the covenant from denying or resisting the title of the fraudulent grantee. The debtor's executor, however, may purchase the property after a sale, and will obtain a good title.[4]

EXECUTORY CONTRACTS.—The same principles of policy which require that a fraudulent transfer shall be held valid as between the parties, also demand that no aid or relief shall be granted for the enforcement of any agreement arising out of a fraudulent transaction. The suppression of fraud is far more likely in general to be accomplished by leaving the parties without remedy against each other, and thus introducing a prevent-

Vanzant v. Davies, 6 Ohio St. R. 52; Marston v. Brackett, 9 N. H. 336; Foster v. Walton, 5 Watts, 378; Coppage v. Barnett, 34 Miss. 621 ; Long v. Wright, 3 Jones (N. C.), 290 ; Stevens v. Morse, 47 N. H. 532; Gregory v. Haworth, 25 Cal. 653; Bayless v. Elean, 1 Cold. 96; Lawton v. Gordon, 34 Cal. 36; Fowler v. Stoneum, 11 Tex. 478 ; Hubbs v. Brockwell, 3 Sneed, 574 ; Eddins v. Wilson, 1 Ala. 237; Douglas v. Dunlap, 10 Ohio, 162; Garrison v. Brice, 3 Jones (N. C.), 85; vide Lewis v. Castleman, 27 Tex. 407 ; Plummer v. Worley, 13 Ired. 423 ; Ingles v. Donalson, 2 Hay (N. C.), 57; Searcy v. Carter, 4 Sneed, 271 ; Mason v. Baker, 1 A. K. Marsh. 208; Lewis v. Love, 2 B. Mon. 345; Cox v. Jackson, 6 Allen, 108 ; Wyman v. Brown, 50 Me. 139; Newsom v. Lycan, 3 J. J. Marsh. 440; Elliott v. Horn, 10 Ala. 348 ; Lewis v. Caperton, 8 Gratt. 148 ; McGuire v. Miller, 15 Ala. 394 ; Beall v. Williamson, 14 Ala. 55.

[1] Sickman v. Lapsley, 13 S. & R. 224.

[2] Dunbar v. McFall, 9 Humph. 505; Trempner v. Barton, 18 Ohio, 418; Gibbs v. Thayer, 6 Cush. 30.

[3] Perry v. Calvert, 22 Mo. 361.

[4] Smith v. Pollard, 4 B. Mon. 66.

ive check naturally connected with a want of confidence and a sole reliance upon personal honor. Any other doctrine would, moreover, destroy the rule itself, for parties could evade it by means of an agreement made at the time of the transfer. It is upon these principles that the maxim *ex turpi causa non actio oritur* is found· ed. *Pacta quœ contra leges et constitutiones vel contra bonos mores sunt, nullam vim habere indubitati juris est.*[1]

EQUITY WILL NOT ENFORCE AGREEMENTS.—Whenever a party to a fraud applies to a court of equity, the reasons for witholding relief are much stronger, for he who seeks equity must have an honest and just claim. Equity, therefore, never decrees a specific performance of an agreement made by the fraudulent grantee to re-convey the property to the debtor. The violation of such an agreement is no fraud. *Fraus non est fallere fallentem.*[2] For the same reason the trusts in a fraudu-lent deed can not be enforced.[3]

---

[1] Dig. Lib. 2 Tit. 3, § 6.

[2] Anon, Cary, 18; Gaylord v. Couch, 3 Day, 223 ; Freeman v. Sedg-wick, 6 Gill. 28 ; Canton v. Dorchester, 8 Cush. 525 ; Sweet v. Tinslar, 52 Barb. 271 ; Stewart v. Iglehart, 7 G. & J. 132 ; Wright v. Wright, 2 Litt. 8; Mulford v. ———, 2 Hay, 244; James v. Bird, 8 Leigh, 510; Smith v. Elliott, 1 Pat. & H. 307; Hollis v. Morris, 2 Harring. 128; Payne v. Bru-ton, 10 Ark. 53 ; Jones v. Gorman, 7 Ired. Eq. 21; Peacock v. Terry, 9 Geo. 137; Galt v. Jackson, 9 Geo. 151; Ellington v. Currie, 5 Ired. Eq. 21; Britt v. Aylett, 11 Ark. 475 ; Lee v. Lee, 19 Mo. 420; Grider v. Graham, 4 Bibb. 70; Baldwin v. Cawthorne, 19 Ves. 166; Franklin v. Stagg, 22 Mo. 193; Martin v. Martin, 5 Bush. 47; Roane v. Vidal, 4 Munf. 187 ; Joyce v. Joyce, 5 Cal. 161; Jones v. Read, 3 Dana. 540; St. John v. Bene-dict, 6 Johns. Ch. 111; Baldwin v. Campfield, 4 Halst. Ch. 891; Marlatt v. Warwick, 4 C. E. Green, 443; Lokerson v. Stillwell, 2 Beasley, 357 ; Hershey v. Whiting, 50 Penn. 240; Holliday v. Holliday, 10 Iowa, 200; Eyre v. Eyre, 4 C. E. Green, 42 ; Stephens v. Harrow, 26 Iowa, 458; *vide* Taylor v. Weld, 5 Mass. 109 ; Barnard v. Sutton, 12 L. J. Ch. (N. S.) 312; Smith v. ———, 2 Hay (N. C.), 229.

[3] Stewart v. Ackley, 52 Barb. 283 ; Sweet v. Tinslar, 52 Barb. 271 ; Murphy v. Hubert, 16 Penn. 50.

. RELIEF WHEN THERE IS FRAUD ON DEBTOR.—This rule only applies, however, when the parties are in *pari delicto*. Both parties must be equally guilty. If the debtor does not enter into the transaction freely and with a fraudulent purpose, then the fraud is not such as merits the utter reprobation of a court of equity. Where the debtor is not the originator of the fraud, but is enticed into the transaction either through weakness of mind,[1] or the advice of his attorney,[2] or creditor,[3] to whom the transfer is made, equity will grant relief, not on account of any right in the debtor, but for the purpose of preventing the perpetration of a greater fraud by the grantee. The parties although *in delicto* are not in *pari delicto*, and a remedy is given on the ground of *mala fides* in the grantee and the necessity of preventing imposition. So also if a *feme covert* is induced by fraudulent practices to unite with her husband in the conveyance of her own estate for the purpose of defrauding his creditors by depriving them of a remedy against his interest in it, she may have the transfer set aside.[4]

CERTAIN AGREEMENTS VALID.—If there is no valid claim against the grantor, an agreement to reconvey may be enforced, although the transfer is made to defeat an anticipated recovery in an action against him. The statute only protects just and lawful actions, and if he is successful in his resistance to the demand the transfer can not be considered fraudulent, for he has a right to shield his property from all unlawful claims.[5]

---

[1] Prewett v. Coopwood, 30 Miss. 369; Freelove v. Cole, 41 Barb. 318; Beale v. Hall, 22 Geo. 431 ; *vide* Smith v. Elliott, 1 Pat. & H. 307.

[2] Ford v. Harrington, 16 N. Y. 285 ; Freelove v. Cole, 41 Barb. 318.

[3] Austin v. Winston, 1 H. & M. 33.

[4] Stewart v. Iglehart, 7 G. & J. 132.

[5] Dearman v. Dearman, 4 Ala. 521; Brady v. Ellison, 2 Hay (N. C.), 348 ; Smith v. Bowen, 2 Hay (N. C.), 296; Baker v. Gilman, 52 Barb. 26 ; *Contra*, Tantum v. Miller, 3 Stockt. 551.

An arrangement made in good faith, by which a party purchases the debtor's property at a sale under an execution with a promise to reconvey to the debtor upon the payment of the purchase money may be enforced.[1] If the parties voluntarily rescind the fraudulent conveyance a subsequent arrangement between them in regard to the same property will not be tainted by the previous fraud.[2] If the fraudulent transfer consists of a mortgage, the debtor may file a bill to redeem the property from its operation.[3]

RIGHTS OF GRANTEES.—If the transfer is made to two grantees, an agreement between them whereby one purchases the property under a judgment, with the understanding that the title shall remain in the other, can not be enforced when it is a part of the original fraudulent scheme.[4] An agreement for a division, however, which has been acted upon, and upon the faith of which expenditures have been made, may be enforced.[5] If the fraudulent grantee executes the secret fraudulent trust under which he received the transfer, one *cestui que trust* can not defeat the full execution of the trust nor appropriate the exclusive benefit to himself by relying upon the fraudulent intent with which the transfer was made.[6] Equity will not decree a sale at the instance of one tenant in common when the land is incapable of partition, for the hazards of an unsound title should remain with those who have taken it.[7]

---

[1] Fluharty v. Beatty, 4 W. Va. 514.
[2] Parker v. Tiffany, 52 Ill. 286 , Matthews v. Buck, 43 Me. 265.
[3] Smith v. Quartz Mining Co. 14 Cal. 242.
[4] Waller v. Mills, 3 Dev. 515.
[5] Proseus v. McIntyre, 5 Barb. 424.
[6] Turner v. Campbell, 3 Gratt. 77 ; s. c. 1 P. & H. 256.
[7] Haydon v. Denslow, 27 Conn. 335.

ACTIONS AT LAW UPON EXECUTORY CONTRACTS.—The principles upon which a specific performance of an agreement to reconvey is refused apply also to an action at law upon such an agreement, or upon a note given as the consideration for a fraudulent transfer. There is a marked and settled distinction between executory and executed contracts of a fraudulent character. Whatever the parties to an action have executed for fraudulent purposes, the law refuses to lend its aid to enable either party to disturb. Whatever the parties have fraudulently contracted to execute, the law refuses to compel the contractor to execute or pay damages for not executing. In both cases it leaves the parties where it finds them.[1] If a note constitutes the consideration for a fraudulent transfer, it will not be rendered valid by including an additional honest consideration, for the rule is that where one part of an entire contract is void the whole is void.[2] The maker may also show in an action upon such a note that the property has been taken away by the grantor's creditors,[3] but such a defence would not be good against a bona fide holder.[4] A third person who is innocent of the fraud may enforce a promise

---

[1] Nellis v. Clark, 4 Hill, 424; s. c. 20 Wend. 24: Smith v. Hubbs, 10 Me. 71 ; Johnson v. Morley, Hill & D. Sup. 29; Niver v. Best, 10 Barb. 369; Walker v. McConnico, 10 Yerg. 228 ; Norris v. Norris, 9 Dana, 317; Roden v. Murphy, 10 Ala. 804; Walton v. Bonham, 24 Ala. 513; Harvin v. Weeks, 11 Rich. 601; Welby v. Armstrong, 21 Ind. 489; Powell v. Inman, 8 Jones (N. C.), 436 ; Church v. Muir, 33 N. J. 318; *Contra*, Findley v. Cooley, 1 Blackf. 262; Sherk v. Endress, 3 W. & S. 255; Telford v. Adams, 6 Watts, 429; Moore v. Thompson, 6 Mo. 353 ; Dyer v. Homer, 22 Pick. 253 ; Conner v. Carpenter, 28 Vt. 237 ; Carpenter v. McClure, 39 Vt. 9; Harvey v. Varney, 98 Mass. 118; Springer v. Drosch, 32 Ind. 486.

[2] Niver v. Best, 10 Barb. 369.

[3] Dyer v. Homer, 22 Pick. 253 ; Bailey v. Foster, 9 Pick. 139.

[4] Gregory v. Harrington, 33 Vt. 241.

made to him for a valuable consideration, although it grew out of the fraudulent transaction.[1]

ACTIONS AT LAW BY GRANTEE.— A fraudulent grantee has a legal title which he may enforce in an action at law, for the debtor and those claiming under him can not set up the fraud to avoid the transfer.[2] If the debtor, after the property has once been delivered, recovers the possession, the grantee may have the aid of the law to regain it.[3] The grantee may not only recover the property, but if that has been converted by the debtor to his own use, he may recover the value.[4] When a mortgage is fraudulent, the mortgagee may enforce his legal right to the property by an action at law.[5] A fraudulent grantee,[6] or mortgagee,[7] however, can not enforce any claim to or against the property in a court of equity. The only remedy is at law. The only exception to this rule seems to be in a case where the grantee is deprived of his remedy at law by some subsequent act of the debtor.[8] If the grantee executes

---

[1] Moore v. Meek, 20 Ind. 484.

[2] Cushwa v. Cushwa, 5 Md. 44; Anderson v. Dunn, 19 Ark. 650; Ellis v. Higgins, 32 Me. 34; Murphy v. Hubert, 16 Penn. 50 ; Broughton v. Broughton, 4 Rich. 491; Jackson v. Garnsey, 16 Johns. 189 ; Gifford v. Ford, 5 Vt. 532; Starke v. Littlepage, 4 Rand, 368 ; Daniels v. Fitch, 8 Penn. 495; Epperson v. Young, 8 Tex. 135; McClenny v. Floyd, 10 Tex. 159; Gillespie v. Gillespie, 2 Bibb. 89.

[3] Rochelle v. Harrison, 8 Port. 351.

[4] Hoeser v. Kraeka, 29 Tex. 450.

[5] Fitzgerald v. Forristal, 48 Ill. 228 ; Stores v. Snow, 1 Root. 181; Gifford v. Ford, 5 Vt. 532; Williams v. Williams, 34 Penn. 312; Bibb v. Baker, 17 B. Mon. 292; Bowman v. McKleroy, 14 La. An. 587.

[6] Mason v. Baker, 1 A. K. Marsh. 208; Caston v. Ballard, 1 Hill, 406; vide Greenwood v. Coleman, 34 Ala. 150.

[7] Shiveley v. Jones, 6 B. Mon. 274; Wearse v. Peirce, 24 Pick. 141: Demerritt v. Miles, 22 N. H. 523 ; Westfall v. Jones, 23 Barb. 9 ; Jones v. Comer, 5 Leigh, 350 ; Miller v. Marckle, 21 Ill. 152; Brookover v. Hurst, 1 Met. (Ky.), 665.

[8] Baldwin v. Cawthorne, 19 Ves. 166.

the contract to reconvey he will be bound, for the law will not then lend its aid to him.[1] When the re-conveyance is in apparent execution of the fraudulent trust for the purpose of a sale, the fraudulent grantee can not claim the proceeds.[2] One grantee is not responsible to another for property which he has returned to the debtor.[3]

GRANTEE CAN NOT ENFORCE EXECUTORY CONTRACTS.—The principles of the law which prohibit any action upon a fraudulent executory contract apply equally to the grantee. A court of equity will not enforce an agreement to surrender a note, given as the consideration, upon a re-conveyance of the property.[4] No action at law can be maintained upon a note given with a fraudulent mortgage,[5] or upon a covenant of warranty to recover damages when the property has been taken by the grantor's creditors.[6]

GOOD AGAINST THIRD PARTIES.—The title of a fraudulent grantee is not only good against the debtor but it is also good against all parties except creditors and their representatives. It is voidable only at the suit of creditors, and if no creditor interposes and complains, the transfer is as binding and effectual to pass the title as if made with the best intents and for the most innocent and commendable purposes.[7] The estate passes *toties quoties* by every subsequent conveyance,

---

[1] Dearman v. Radcliffe, 5 Ala. 192 ; Fargo v. Ladd, 6 Wis. 106 ; White v. Brocaw, 14 Ohio St. R. 339.

[2] Fargo v. Ladd, 6 Wis. 106.

[3] Riddle v. Lewis, 7 Bush. 193.

[4] Bryant v. Mansfield, 22 Me. 360 ; Servis v. Nelson, 1 McCarter, 94.

[5] Brookover v. Hurst, 1 Met. (Ky.) 665.

[6] Surlott v. Beddow, 3 Mon. 109 ; Rea v. Smith, 19 Wend. 293.

[7] Hall v. Stryker, 9 Abb. Pr. 342 ; s. c. 29 Barb. 105.

and is good against all the world except creditors in the possession of every successive grantee, even with notice of the fraud. The title is good against the debtor's tenant,[1] a prior mortgagee,[2] third parties who are not creditors,[3] mere wrong doers,[4] the grantee's own tenant,[5] or bailee,[6] purchasers from the grantee so long as they refuse to surrender the property,[7] and stockholders when the transfer is made by a corporation.[8] A fraudulent assignee of a *chose in action* has a good title as against the party from whom the money is due and can enforce the payment.[9]

---

[1] Steadman v. Jones, 65 N. C. 388; Griffin v. Wardlaw, Harp. 481; Moseley v. Moseley, 15 N. Y. 334; Cushwa v. Cushwa, 5 Md. 44.

[2] Hodson v. Treat, 7 Wis. 263; Stone v. Locke, 46 Me. 445; Stone v. Bartlett, 46 Me. 438; Fetrow v. Merriwether, 53 Ill. 275.

[3] Kid v. Mitchell, 1 N. & M. 334; Wade v. Green, 3 Humph. 547; Fowler v. Lee, 4 Munf. 373; Shadbolt v. Bassett, 1 Lans. 121; McGuire v. Faber, 29 Penn. 436; Anderson v. Bradford, 5 J. J. Marsh. 69; Clute v. Fitch, 25 Barb. 428; Van Etten v. Hurst, 6 Hill, 311; Johnson v. Jeffries, 30 Mo. 423; Hatch v. Bates, 54 Me. 136; Damon v. Bryant, 2 Pick. 411; Glassner v. Wheaton, 2 E. D. Smith, 352; Puryear v. Beard, 14 Ala. 121; Bessey v. Wyndham, 6 A. &. E. (N. S.), 166; Schettler v. Brunette, 7 Wis. 197; Hall v. Snowhill, 2 Green, 8; Paige v. O'Neal, 12 Cal. 483; Boyd v. Brown, 17 Pick. 453; McGuire v. Faber, 25 Penn. 436; Hopkins v. Webb, 9 Humph. 519; Johnson v. Elliott, 26 N. H. 67; Burgett v. Burgett, 1 Ohio, 219; Randall v. Phillips, 3 Mason, 378; Lenox v. Notrebe, 1 Hemp. 251; Simon v. Gibson, 1 Yeates, 291; Woodman v. Bodfish, 25 Me. 317; Hill v. Pine River Bank, 45 N. H. 300.

[4] Worth v. Northam, 4 Ired. 102; Thompson v. Moore, 36 Me. 47; The Lion, 1 Sprague, 40; Costenbader v. Shuman, 3 W. & S. 504; Remington v. Bailey, 13 Wis. 332; Pierce v. Hasbrouck, 49 Ill. 26.

[5] Russell v. Fabyan, 27 N. H. 529; s. c. 34 N. H. 218.

[6] Hendricks v. Mount, 2 South. 738; Fairbanks v. Blackington, 9 Pick. 93.

[7] La Crosse R. R. Co. v. Seeger, 4 Wis. 268; Sharp v. Jones, 18 Ind. 314; Campbell v. Erie R. R. Co. 46 Barb. 540.

[8] Ashurst's Appeal, 60 Penn. 290.

[9] Pickens v. Hathaway, 100 Mass. 247; Ogden v. Prentice, 33 Barb. 160; Morey v. Forsyth, Walk. Ch. 465; Hamilton v. Gilbert, 2 Heisk, 680; Rohrer v. Turrill, 4 Minn. 407.

CREDITORS MUST HAVE LEGAL PROCESS.—It is commonly said that a fraudulent conveyance is void against creditors, but this must be taken in a limited sense. The law provides a mode for determining the rights of all parties, and does not permit even a creditor to act as a judge in his own case.[1] Any other course would jeopardize the order and harmony of society. A fraudulent conveyance, moreover, does not confer any additional rights upon creditors. They can not seize the property of their debtor without any legal process and appropriate it of their own accord to the satisfaction of their demands. Neither the general principles of law nor the particular laws which are enacted for the collection of debts confer any such rights upon them. They may cause it to be appropriated to the payment of their debts, but they can do this only in the mode which the law prescribes, and if they depart from that mode their proceedings are unauthorized by law and they thereby make themselves liable as wrong doers to the owner of the property. Prior to the transfer they are liable to the debtor himself. After the transfer they are liable to the grantee, because all the rights of the debtor in relation to the property pass to him.

Consequently the expression that a fraudulent transfer is void against creditors simply means that the rights of creditors as such are not, with respect to the property, affected by such transfer, but that they may, notwithstanding the transfer, avail themselves of all the remedies for collecting their debts out of the property or its avails which the law has provided in favor of creditors, and that in pursuing those remedies they may treat the property as though the transfer had not been made, that is, as the property of the debtor. The

---

[1] Williford v. Conner, 1 Dev. 379.

transfer is ineffectual to shield the property in the hands of the grantee from the just claims of the creditors of the grantor when those claims are prosecuted against it in the manner pointed out by the law. His title, however, is good against even creditors, unless they protect themselves against him by pursuing that pre- scribed course by which alone the property can be made available for the satisfaction of debts. A creditor at large, as it is termed, can not impeach the conveyance, but only a creditor having some process on which the property may be lawfully seized, and by which it is made liable, either immediately or ultimately, to be ap- propriated in satisfaction of his debt. Without such process he has no right to meddle with the property, and if he does so he is liable to all the consequences of an unlawful interference equally with any other person.[1]

If the creditor is in the possession of the property, he can not retain it on the ground of the indebtedness of the grantor to him,[2] or set up his judgment as an offset to the demand.[3] In an action against him upon a *chose in action,* he can not show that an assignment of it is fraudulent.[4] Before he can impeach the transfer, he must have an execution, attachment, or some other

---

[1] Williford v. Conner, 1 Dev. 37; Hilzeim v. Drane, 10 S. & M. 556; Owen v. Dixon, 17 Conn. 492; McGee v. Campbell, 7 Watts, 545; Dorsey v. Smithson, 6 H. & J. 61; Barton v. Vanheythuysen, 11 Hare, 126; s. c. 18 Jur. 344; Osborne v. Moss, 7 Johns. 161; Brown v. Gilmore, 16 How. Pr. 527; Carter v. Bennett, 4 Fla. 283; Pennington v. Woodall, 17 Ala. 685; Graser v. Stellwagon, 25 N. Y. 315; Eyrick v. Hetrick, 13 Penn. 488; Andrews v. Durant, 18 N. Y. 496; Whitfield v. Whitfield, 40 Miss. 352; Green v. Kornegay, 4 Jones (N. C.), 66.

[2] Dorsey v. Smithson, 6 H. & J. 61; Andrews v. Durant, 18 N. Y. 496; Barton v. Vanheythuysen, 11 Hare, 126; s. c. 18 Jur. 344.

[3] Lawrence v. Bank, 35 N. Y. 320; s. c. 3 Robt. 142.

[4] Ogden v. Prentice, 33 Barb. 160.

legal process which authorizes the seizure of the property.[1] This process may be a warrant of distress,[2] or
an attachment,[3] as well as an execution. The process,
however, must be valid, and all the steps subsequent to
the seizure which are prescribed by law for the disposition of the property must be pursued. The relation
between the creditor, at whose instance it is issued, and
the officer who serves it, must not be sundered by such
irregularities as render the proceeding void from the
beginning.[4] Consequently the title of the grantee is
good against a void attachment,[5] or a void levy,[6] or a
levy after the return day of the writ,[7] or out of the officer's bailiwick,[8] or a purchaser under a void judgment,[9]
or a landlord who distrains before the rent is due,[10] or a
fraudulent judgment,[11] or a judgment which has been
satisfied.[12]

---

[1] Andrews v. Durant, 18 N. Y. 496; Rinchey v. Stryker, 26 How. Pr.
75; Schlussell v. Willett, 32 Barb. 615; s. c. 12 Abb. Pr. 397; s. c. 22
How. Pr. 15; Tiffany v. Warren, 37 Barb. 571; s. c. 24 How. Pr.
293.

[2] Allen v. Camp, 1 Mon. 231; Frost v. Mott, 34 N. Y. 253; Rinchey v.
Stryker, 26 How. Pr. 75; *Contra*, Frisbie v. Thayer, 25 Wend. 396.

[3] Frost v. Mott, 34 N. Y. 253; Ward v. McKenzie, 33 Tex. 297.

[4] Owen v. Dixon, 17 Conn. 492; Andrews v. Marshall, 43 Me. 272;
s. c. 48 Me. 26; Eaton v. Cooper, 29 Vt. 444; Wooley v. Edson, 35 Vt.
214; *vide* Daggett v. Adams, 1 Me. 198; Johnston v. Harvey, 2 Penna. 82;
Howland v. Ralph, 3 Johns. 20.

[5] Halsey v. Christie, 21 Wend. 9; Zimmerman v. Lamb, 7 Minn. 421;
Wanamaker v. Bowes, 36 Md.

[6] Cleaveland v. Deming, 2 Vt. 534; Barley v. Tipton, 29 Mo. 206; Russell v. Dyer, 40 N. H. 173; Davis v. Ranson, 26 Ill. 100; Candler v. Fisher,
11 Md. 332.

[7] Sheerer v. Lautzerheizer, 6 Watts, 543.

[8] McGee v. Campbell, 7 Watts, 545.

[9] Warren v. Hall, 6 Dana, 450; Carter v. Bennett, 4 Fla. 283; Hemphill v. Hemphill, 34 Miss. 68.

[10] Evans v. Herring, 3 Dutch, 243.

[11] Wilhelmi v. Leonard, 13 Iowa, 330; Hackett v. Manlove, 14 Cal. 85.

[12] Chiles v. Bernard, 3 Dana, 95; Jackson v. Cadwell, 1 Cow. 622;
Shinkle v. Letcher, 47 Ill. 216.

PROOF OF JUDGMENT AS WELL AS EXECUTION.—
Whenever the validity of the seizure is put in controversy, the creditor or the officer, as the case may be, must
establish a right to seize the property by proof which
is adequate as against the grantee, and this in the case
of an execution can only be done by the production of
the judgment as well as the writ.[1] If the property is
taken upon an attachment, there must be proof not
only of the regularity of the attachment,[2] but of the
demand of the creditor at whose instance the attachment was issued.[3] This is necessary in order to establish a right to seize the property. It is not necessary
to prove the entire debt upon which the attachment
issued,[4] or do more than show a *prima facie* right to
issue the attachment without establishing the amount
due.[5] The parties will not be liable to the grantee if
the attachment is merely defeated by a plea of set-off.[6]
A collusive demand, created merely for the purpose of
attacking the transfer, can not prevail against it.[7]

DEED BY DEBTOR.—A deed from the debtor does not
give the creditor any right to seize the property or any
claim upon it. As the transfer binds the debtor he

---

[1] High v. Wilson, 2 Johns. 46; Wright v. Crockett, 7 Mo. 125; Dameron v. Williams, 7 Mo. 138; Eaton v. White, 2 Wis. 292; Paige v. O'Neal,
13 Cal. 483; Bickerstaff v. Doub. 19 Cal. 109; Martin v. Podger, 2 W. Bl.
701; s. c. 5 Burr, 2631; Hoffman v. Pitt, 5 Esp. 22; Reed v. Blades,
5 Taunt. 212; White v. Morris, 11 C. B. 1015; Glave v. Wentworth, 6 A. B. 173; Ogden v. Hesketh, 2 Car. & K. 772; Ackworth v.
Kempe, 1 Doug. 40; Luke v. Billers, 1 Ld. Raym. 733; M'Gowan v. Hoy,
5 Litt. 239.

[2] Noble v. Holmes, 5 Hill, 194; Thornburgh v. Hand, 7 Cal. 554; Keys
v. Grannis, 3 Nev. 548.

[3] Sanford v. Wiggin, 14 N. H. 441; Damon v. Bryant, 2 Pick. 411;
Clute v. Fitch, 25 Barb. 428; Maley v. Barrett, 2 Sneed, 501; Currier v.
Ford, 26 Ill, 488; Jones v. Lake, 2 Wis. 210.

[4] Walker v. Lovell, 28 N. H. 138.

[5] Fuller v. Sears, 5 Vt. 527.

[6] Gates v. Gates, 15 Mass. 310.

[7] Esty v. Long, 41 N. H. 103.

has no title that he can transmit. In the capacity of purchaser, the creditor obtains no rights, and in the capacity of creditor he can only appropriate the property towards the satisfaction of his demand by virtue of some legal process.[1] Without a lien upon the property by virtue of some process, a creditor has no right to intervene in a suit.[2]

RATIFICATION BY CREDITOR.—A fraudulent transfer is merely voidable, and, consequently, is capable of confirmation, either by assent at the time or by a subsequent ratification, for no one can predicate fraud of facts which have his assent upon a full knowledge of them. *Preterea illud sciendum est, eum qui consentientibus creditoribus a fraudatore vel emit vel stipulatus est vel quid aliud contraxit, non videri in fraudem creditorum fecisse, nemo enim videtur fraudare eos qui sciunt et consentiunt.*[3] Mere notice,[4] or acquiescence,[5] is not sufficient, nor can one creditor be affected or prejudiced by the assent of others.[6] Before there can be any binding ratification, the creditor must have notice or knowledge of the facts which constitute the fraud.[7] If he has, however, been guilty of negligence in availing himself of information within his reach, constructive notice may be imputed to

---

[1] Haines v. Campbell, 8 Iowa, 187; Fox v. Willis, 1 Mich. 321; s. c. Walk. Ch. 535; Grimsley v. Hooker, 3 Jones Eq. 41; Barton v. Vanheythuysen, 11 Hare, 126; s. c. 18 Jur. 344; Tate v. Liggatt, 2 Leigh, 84; *Contra*, Frost v. Goddard, 25 Me. 414; Woodward v. Solomon, 7 Geo. 246; Lee v. Brown, 7 Geo. 275.

[2] Horn v. Volcano Co. 13 Cal. 62; Graser v. Stulwagon, 25 N. Y. 315; Williams v. Bizzell, 11 Ark. 718; Cox v. Fraley, 26 Ark. 20; Rhodes v. Cousins, 6 Rand. 188.

[3] Dig. Lib. 42 Tit. 9, § 9.

[4] Derry Bank v. Davis, 44 N. H. 548.

[5] Knauth v. Bassett, 34 Barb. 31; Jenness v. Berry, 17 N. H. 549.

[6] M'Allister v. Marshall, 6 Binn. 338; Litchfield v. Pelton, 6 Barb. 187.

[7] Clark v. Rowling Hill & D. Sup. 105; Baldwin v. Tuttle, 23 Iowa, 66; Foulk v. M'Farlane, 1 W. & S. 297; Van Nest v. Yoe, 1 Sandf. Ch. 4.

him.[1] If, with notice of the fraud either actual or constructive, he makes any agreement upon consideration
confirming the transfer, or any statement or agreement
to that effect, upon the faith of which the grantee acts
as he would not otherwise do, or under such circumstances that his subsequent assertion of his rights as a
creditor, if permitted, would operate as a fraud, he will
be held to have confirmed the transfer.[2] In the case of
a fraudulent assignment, if a creditor enters into any
agreement with the other creditors,[3] or receives a dividend under the assignment,[4] with notice of its character
he can not afterwards impeach it. A trustee, who is
also a creditor, is estopped from assailing the deed under which he acts.[5] If the debtor's assignee in bankruptcy demands and receives the purchase money, this
act of positive affirmance ratifies the transfer.[6] The
grantor of a deed, by which property that is paid for
by the debtor is conveyed to another, can not impeach
it for fraud because he is a party to the transaction.[7]
A creditor under, and by whose advice the transfer is

---

[1] Scott v. Edes, 3 Minn. 377.

[2] Jenness v. Berry, 17 N. H. 549 ; Lane v. Lutz, 1 Keyes, 203; Johns
v. Bolton, 12 Penn. 339; Dingley v. Robinson, 5 Me. 127 ; Seymour v.
Lewis, 2 Beasley, 439 ; Tate v. Liggatt, 2 Leigh, 84 ; Okie v. Kelly, 12
Penn. 323 ; Irwin v. Longworth, 20 Ohio, 581 ; Renick v. Bank, 8 Ohio,
529 ; Myers v. Leinster, 7 Jr. Eq. 146.

[3] Rapalee v. Stewart, 27 N. Y. 310; Bull v. Loveland, 10 Pick. 9;
Fiske v. Carr, 20 Me. 301 ; Jones v. Dougherty, 10 Geo. 273 ; Burrows v.
Alter, 7 Mo. 424 ; vide Hurd v. Silsbee, 10 N. H. 108.

[4] Adlum v. Yard, 1 Rawle, 163; Lanahan v. Latrobe, 7 Md. 268; Scott
v. Edes, 3 Minn. 377 ; Geise v. Beall, 3 Wis. 367 ; Richards v. White, 7
Minn. 345 ; Whitney v. Freeland, 26 Miss. 481 ; Gutzwiller v. Lackman,
23 Mo. 168; vide Vose v. Holcomb, 31 Me. 407; Crutchfield v. Hudson, 23
Ala. 393.

[5] Strong v. Willis, 3 Fla. 124.

[6] Okie v. Kelly, 12 Penn. 323.

[7] Phillips v. Wooster, 36 N. Y. 412; s. c. 3 Abb. Pr. (N. S.) 475;
French v. Mehan, 56 Penn. 286.

made is, for the same reason, held to assent to, and to be bound by it,[1] especially when he is an active participant in the fraud.[2]

CREDITOR'S KNOWLEDGE OF THE FRAUD.—A creditor who receives a note given as a consideration of the transfer, with full knowledge of the facts, can not afterwards impeach it.[3] Although he did not have notice at the time of taking the note, yet if he retains or uses it after he has acquired such notice, he is bound the same as if he had acted on previous information.[4] A creditor who has trusted his debtor, after being fully informed by the latter that he has put his property out of his hands by a conveyance valid as between him and his grantee, though voidable as to existing creditors, can never claim that the conveyance is fraudulent and void as to him on account of such indebtedness.[5] If an assignment is assented to by all the creditors, it can not be attacked by subsequent creditors, for the former have the right to elect to take the provision made for them although the assignment is fraudulent and have a prior equity to be paid out of the property assigned.[6]

ESTOPPEL.—Before a creditor can be held to be estopped by any act of his from impeaching the transfer there must be a benefit conferred upon him, or a disadvantage suffered by the grantee such as can bind the conscience of the former or clothe his act with the char-

---

[1] Olliver v. King, 8 D. M. & G. 110 ; s. c. 55 Eng. L. & Eq. 312 ; s. c. 25 L. J. Ch. 427 ; s. c. 2 Jur. (N. S.) 312 ; s. c. 1 Jur. (N. S.) 1067 ; Pell v. Tredwell, 5 Wend. 661; *Contra*, Waterhouse v. Benton, 5 Day, 136.

[2] Smith v. Espey, 1 Stockt. 160.

[3] Butler v. O'Brien, 5 Ala. 316 ; Furness v. Ewing, 2 Penn. 479.

[4] Butler v. O'Brien, 5 Ala. 316.

[5] Baker v. Gilman, 52 Barb. 26.

[6] Ames v. Blunt, 5 Paige, 13; Therasson v. Hickok, 37 Vt. 454 ; Ogden v. Prentice, 33 Barb. 160.

acter of a contract.[1] A mere provision in an assignment
in favor of a creditor does not, of itself, prevent him
from assailing it, for an assignment, when executed, must
bind all or none of the creditors.[2] Merely laying an
attachment in the hands of the grantee does not confirm the transfer,[3] but a creditor can not seize the goods
and also garnish the grantee.[4] When the money raised
by a sale under a prior execution is appropriated by
law to a subsequent execution, a creditor who receives
it innocently and ignorantly is not thereby prevented from attacking the sale,[5] but if he accepts
the money with full knowledge of all the facts, he
thereby ratifies the sale and waives all objection to
it.[6]

To operate as an estoppel, the act of the creditor
must be intended to be a direct recognition and acknowl-
edgement of the validity of the transfer, and not the
result of a mere collateral arrangement.[7] If a debtor
sells his goods in consideration of an annuity payable
to his wife, and a policy of insurance, a creditor who
accepts of the policy as a security for his debt will not
be estopped from attempting to have the annuity appropriated to the satisfaction of his demand.[8] If other
creditors proceed to sell the property, the transfer is
nullified as to all, and a creditor who has assented to it
may become a purchaser at the sale, and as his title

---

[1] Hayes v. Heidelberg, 9 Penn. 203.

[2] Smith v. Howard, 20 How. Pr. 121; O'Neil v. Salmon, 25 How. Pr.
246.

[3] M'Kee v. Gilchrist, 3 Watts, 230; Craver v. Miller, 65 Penn.
456.

[4] Clapp v. Rogers, 38 N. H. 435.

[5] Foulk v. M'Farlane, 1 W. & S. 297.

[6] Kilby v. Haggin, 3 J. J. Marsh. 208.

[7] Hayes v. Heidelberg, 9 Penn. 203.

[8] French v. French, 6 D. M. & G. 95; s. c. 25 L. J. (Ch.) 612.

will be derived from a source superior to the transfer, he will take the property discharged from it.[1]

CREDITOR MUST RETURN BENEFIT.—A creditor who has received a benefit under a fraudulent transfer must return it before he can impeach the transaction. He may have his election either to confirm the transfer or attempt to avoid it, but he cannot do both. By receiving a benefit under the transfer claimed to be fraudulent, he thereby affirms it so as to be estopped from setting up the fraud. If he desires to rescind, he must rescind *in toto*. By receiving a benefit under the transfer he thereby becomes *pro tanto* a party to, and a participant in, the fraudulent transaction, from which he must show himself wholly clear before he is entitled to be heard to impeach it.[2] If a creditor accepts a part of the property which is subsequently taken from him, he may assail the transfer.[3] If a creditor is estopped, the estoppel will extend to a party who purchases under his judgment.[4]

TITLE IN DEBTOR IN CONTEMPLATION OF LAW.—The theory of the law is that a fraudulent transfer passes nothing as against creditors. For all purposes of appropriating the property to the satisfaction of their demands, the property is deemed to be still vested in the debtor.[5] The legal as well as the equitable title still

---

[1] Hayes v. Heidelberg, 9 Penn. 203; *vide* McWhorter v. Huling, 3 Dana, 348.

[2] Lemay v. Bibeau, 2 Minn. 291; Scott v. Edes, 3 Minn. 377; Butler v. O'Brien, 5 Ala. 316; *in re* Wilson, 4 Penn. 430; Wills v. Munro, cited 43 Barb. 584.

[3] Lee v. Hunter, 1 Paige, 519.

[4] Smith v. Espey, 1 Stockt. 160.

[5] Pratt v. Wheeler, 6 Gray, 520; Gooch's Case, 5 Co. 60; Austin v. Bell, 20 Johns. 442; Lowry v. Orr, 1 Gilman, 70; Marston v. Marston, 54 Me. 476; Angier v. Ash, 26 N. H. 99; Scully v. Kearns, 14 La. An. 436; Gleises v. McHatton, 14 La. An. 560.

remains in him, and creditors who obtain judgments against him afterwards acquire liens upon his property, wherever such are given by the law, according to the dates of their respective judgments in the same manner precisely as if no such transfer had ever been made.[1] The rights of the grantee's creditors are no higher than those of the grantee himself. They must claim through him and not above or beyond him. Consequently he has no interest upon which the lien of judgments against him can attach so as to be entitled to priority over the liens of judgments against his grantor.[2] The grantee's assignee in bankruptcy has merely a defeasible title, subject to be defeated by the creditors of the grantor.[3] But a sale under an execution against the grantee will pass a good title as against the debtor.[4] If the creditors of the grantor sell the property under execution, it is not afterwards liable to the creditors of the grantee.[5] It has, on the other hand, been held that after an actual seizure by the creditors of the grantee, the property can not be reclaimed by an officer acting under an execution against the grantor.[6] An assignee claiming under a fraudulent assignment made by a firm does not represent the partnership creditors, and can not interpose in their behalf to prevent the property

---

[1] M'Kee v. Gilchrist, 3 Watts, 230; Jacoby's Appeal, 67 Penn. 434; Hoffman's Appeal, 44 Penn. 95 ; Beekman's Appeal, 38 Penn. 385; Sanders v. Wagonseller, 19 Penn. 248; Minin v. Warner, 2 Phila. 124; Codwise v. Gelston, 10 Johns. 507 ; Manhattan Co. v. Evertson, 6 Paige, 457 ; Miner v. Warner, 2 Grant, 448; Eastman v. Schettler, 13 Wis. 324; Wooten v. Clarke, 23 Miss. 75 ; *Contra*, Miller v. Sherry, 2 Wall. 237.

[2] Haymaker's Appeal, 53 Penn. 306.

[3] Pratt v. Wheeler, 6 Gray, 520.

[4] Robinson v. Monjoy, 2 Halst. 173.

[5] Booth v. Bunce, 24 N. Y. 592; s. c. 33 N. Y. 139; s. c. 35 Barb. 496.

[6] Gibbs v. Chase, 10 Mass. 125.

from being taken upon a judgment against one of the partners for a separate debt.[1]

PURCHASER UNDER EXECUTION.—The purchaser at a sale under an execution acquires all the right, title, and interest in the property which the debtor had prior to the transfer, is vested with the rights of the creditor, entitled to the same relief, and can protect his title against the frauds of the judgment debtor, in the same manner and to the same extent that the judgment creditor might have done had he purchased. It is true that he holds as a purchaser and not as a judgment creditor, but as he represents a creditor he is entitled to the full benefit of the statute.[2] The inadequacy of the price does not affect the rights of the purchaser, for the parties to a fraudulent transaction have no cause to complain, because the cheapness of the purchase is due to the unwarrantable acts of the debtor himself in throwing a cloud over his title and thus causing a sacrifice of his property.[3]

PROOF OF TITLE.—In order to establish his title, a purchaser must produce the judgment as well as the

---

[1] Jacques v. Greenwood, 12 Abb. Pr. 232.

[2] Pepper v. Carter, 11 Mo. 540; Barr v. Hatch, 3 Ohio, 527; Fishburne v. Kunhardt, 2 Speers, 556; Jones v. Crawford, 1 McMullan, 376; Russell v. Dyer, 33 N. H. 186; Sands v. Hildreth, 14 Johns. 493; s. c. 2 Johns. Ch. 35; Eastman v. Schettler, 13 Wis. 324; Duvall v. Waters, 1 Bland. 567; s. c. 11 G. & J. 37; Cole v. White, 26 Wend. 511; s. c. 24 Wend. 116; Wadsworth v. Havens, 3 Wend. 411; Carpenter v. Simmons, 1 Robt. 360; Thomson v. Dougherty, 12 S. & R. 448; Carter v. Castleberry, 5 Ala. 277; Douglass v. Dunlap, 10 Ohio, 162; Middleton v. Sinclair, 5 Cranch C. C. 409; Laurence v. Lippincott, 1 Halst. 473; Miller v. Tolleson, Harp. Ch. 145; Croft v. Arthur, 3 Dessau. 223.

[3] Thomson v. Dougherty, 12 S. & R. 448; Hildreth v. Sands, 2 Johns. Ch. 35; s. c. 14 Johns. 493; Laurence v. Lippincott, 1 Halst. 473; Mullen v. Wilson, 44 Penn. 413.

writ under which the property has been sold,[1] and when land is sold he must also show a deed from the officer who made the sale.[2] The rights which he acquires are simply those which the debtor had at the time of the transfer. Prior liens are not affected by the transfer, and, as he takes merely the quantity of interest which the debtor had, his title is subject to such liens.[3] It has been held that, if the fraudulent transfer consists of a mortgage, and one creditor merely levies upon and sells the equity of redemption, another creditor may levy upon and sell the whole property, and the purchaser at the second sale will obtain a valid title to the whole property.[4] The grantee can not set up a defect in the debtor's title for the purpose of defeating a recovery by a purchaser and thus retaining the property.[5]

SALE SUBJECT TO TRANSFER.—Whether a purchaser represents the rights of creditors will in some instances depend upon the interest that is sold. If the fraudulent transfer consists of a mortgage, a creditor may elect to treat it as valid and subsisting, and sell only the equity of redemption. The purchaser will not then represent the creditor's right to inquire into the consideration of the mortgage debt, or to impeach it upon any grounds not open to the debtor himself, and will gain no advantage whatever from the fact that the sale was by a sheriff on execution for the satisfaction of a debt.[6] If

---

[1] M'Creery v. Pursley, 1 A. K. Marsh. 114 ; Wright v. Crockett, 7 Mo. 125 ; Dameron v. Williams, 7 Mo. 138; Delesdernier v. Mowry, 20 Me. 150; Hyman v. Bailey, 13 La. An. 450.

[2] Hiney v. Thomas, 36 Mo. 377.

[3] Byrod's Appeal, 31 Penn. 241 ; Fisher's Appeal, 33 Penn. 294.

[4] Bullard v. Hinkley, 6 Me. 289 ; McWhorter v. Huling, 3 Dana, 348.

[5] Zerbe v. Miller, 16 Penn. 488 ; vide Birge v. Nock, 34 Conn. 156.

[6] Flanders v. Jones, 30 N. H. 154 ; Russell v. Dudley, 3 Met. 147; McWhorter v. Huling, 3 Dana. 348.

the debtor has been declared a bankrupt, the right to elect whether to affirm or avoid the mortgage can only be exercised by his assignee. He may either treat it as valid and sell only the equity of redemption, or he may elect to avoid it and sell the whole title to the property. If he sells merely the equity of redemption, the purchaser can not impeach the mortgage.[1] If, however he elects to treat it as void he is not bound to incur the delay and expense necessarily incident to the prosecution to final judgment of legal proceedings to establish the invalidity of the mortgage, but may treat it as null and void, and sell and convey his whole interest in the mortgaged estate. The right to deny and contest the validity of the mortgage will in such case pass to the purchaser.[2]

No LEVY ON PROFITS OR PROCEEDS.—The grantee has a valid title until the creditors, by asserting their rights in due course of law, defeat it, and when defeated it is not rendered void *ab initio*, but only from the time of the levy of the execution under which the property is sold. Consequently he can not be made liable in an action at law for the mesne profits. For the same reason when land is fraudulently conveyed the creditors can not levy upon the crops,[3] or upon property which he has converted from realty into personalty, as, for instance, plaster dug from the ground or stone taken from a quarry,[4] unless they can show that his title to such personal property is merely colorable. If the property is sold, the proceeds or other property received in exchange is not liable to an attachment or ex-

---

[1] Tuite v. Stevens, 98 Mass. 305 ; Brewer v. Hyndman, 18 N. H. 9.

[2] Freeland v. Freeland, 102 Mass. 475 ; Dwinel v. Perley, 32 Me. 197; Gibbs v. Thayer, 6 Cush. 30.

[3] Jones v. Bryant, 33 N. H. 53.

[4] Garbutt v. Smith, 40 Barb. 22.

30

ecution at law, for the statute only operates upon property conveyed by the debtor, and that which the grantee
receives as a consideration for the sale never belonged to
the debtor and is not within the statute. The only
remedy in such a case is by a bill in equity.[1]

SUBSEQUENT EVENTS.—A creditor may treat a partition made by the grantee as legal on the ground that
it was made by the debtor through the agency of the
grantee by means of the deed, and at the same time insist that the deed is void so far forth as it is designed
to defraud creditors.[2] As the statute operates upon
the conveyance and not upon the estate transferred, the
creditors will take all the estate which the debtor has
at the time when they impeach the transfer and not
merely the interest transferred. If the debtor, at the
time of the transfer, has a defeasible estate, which subsequently becomes absolute, the whole estate is liable
to his creditors.[3]

RIGHTS OF GRANTEE.—The right to redeem property
sold under an execution belongs to the grantee and not
to the debtor,[4] but the redemption will not give him
a good title.[5] If the grantee gives a bond to dissolve
an attachment levied upon the property and thus re-
gains possession of it, his title is still liable to be impeached by other creditors.[6] It has also been held

---

[1] Lawrence v. Bank, 35 N. Y. 320; s. c. 3 Robt. 142; Tubb v. Williams,
7 Humph. 367 ; Campbell v. Erie R. R. Co. 46 Barb. 540; Childs v. Derrick, 1 Yerg. 79; Richards v. Ewing, 11 Humph. 327 ; Contra, Abney v.
Kingsland, 10 Ala. 355; Carville v. Stout, 10 Ala. 796; Lynch v. Welsh,
3 Penn. 294; Heath v. Page, 63 Penn. 280; French v. Breidelman, 2
Grant, 319.

[2] Staples v. Bradley, 23 Conn. 167.

[3] Flynn v. Williams, 7 Ired. 32 ; s. c. 1 Ired. 509.

[4] Russell v. Fabyan, 34 N. H. 218; s. c. 27 N. H. 529.

[5] Ricker v. Ham, 14 Mass. 137; Williams v. Thompson, 13 Pick. 298.

[6] Jacobi v. Schloss, 7 Cold. 385.

that the grantee does not get a good title even by a purchase at a sale under an execution.[1] The surplus that remains after satisfying an execution belongs to the grantee.[2]

DOWER. EXEMPTION.—If the debtor's wife unites in an absolute conveyance of land, her right to a dower is extinguished.[3] In the case of a fraudulent mortgage, she has a dower interest which may be assigned to her.[4] When property is fraudulently purchased in the name of another, there is no dower interest in it.[5] A homestead can not be claimed out of property fraudulently conveyed,[6] nor can any exemption be allowed out of such property.[7]

RESCISSION.—The law does not deprive parties of the power of repentance, but rather encourages them to abandon fraudulent conveyances and make honest bargains instead of them. The grantee will not be liable to creditors if he restores the property to the debtor,[8] or applies it to the payment of the grantor's

---

[1] Spindler v. Atkinson, 3 Md. 309; s. c. 1 Md. Ch. 507.

[2] Taylor v. Williams, 1 Ired. 249; Williams v. Avent, 5 Ired. Eq. 47; Shorman v. Farmers' Bank, 5 W. & S. 373; Glassner v. Wheaton, 2 E. D. Smith, 352; Waterbury v. Westervelt, 9 N. Y. 598; Bostwick v. Menck, 40 N. Y. 383.

[3] Meyer v. Mohr, 19 Abb. Pr. 299; Cox v. Wilder, 5 B. R. 443; Manhattan Co. v. Evertson, 6 Paige, 457; Stewart v. Johnson, 3 Harrison, 87; Coppage v. Barnett, 34 Miss. 621; vide Belford v. Crane, 1 C. E. Green, 265; Dugan v. Massey, 6 Bush. 81; Summers v. Babb, 13 Ill. 483; Robinson v. Bates, 3 Met. 40; Lowry v. Fisher, 2 Bush, 70; Wyman v. Fox, 59 Me. 100.

[4] Harrison v. Campbell, 6 Dana, 263.

[5] Miller v. Wilson, 15 Ohio, 108.

[6] Sumner v. Sawtelle, 8 Minn. 309; Cox v. Wilder, 5 B. R. 443; Stancell v. Branch, 1 Phillips, 306.

[7] Huey's Appeal, 29 Penn. 219; Carl v. Smith, 28 Leg. Int. 366; Stevenson v. White, 5 Allen, 148; vide Newman v. Willetts, 52 Ill. 98.

[8] Cramer v. Blood, 57 Barb. 155.

debts.[1] The parties may also rescind the fraudulent contract and enter into a new contract for a sale or other transfer of the property, and if the latter is made in good faith and for a valuable consideration it will not be contaminated by the fraud in the first.[2] If property is purchased in part with funds furnished by the debtor and in part by the grantee, it may be sold and the grantee's share invested in other property.[3] Although a mortgage is fraudulent, yet if the property is sold and the proceeds applied to pay the debt, other creditors can not afterwards raise any objections.[4] The grantor and the grantee may also unite in a transfer of the property to a *bona fide* purchaser, and he will acquire all the rights of both, and will not be necessarily affected by any illegality in the first transfer.[5]

THERE MUST BE RESTITUTION.—There is no valid repentance, however, without an entire restitution where this is possible. All the benefits of the fraudulent arrangement must be abandoned. A transfer can not be purified by merely abandoning the fraudulent purpose for which it was given and using it for an honest one.[6]

---

[1] Hutchins v. Sprague, 4 N. H. 469; Kaupe v. Bridge, 2 Robt. 459; Crowninshield v. Kittredge, 7 Met. 520.

[2] King v. Cantrel, 4 Ired. 251; Merrill v. Meachum, 5 Day, 341; Matthews v. Buck, 43 Me. 265; Borland v. Mayo, 8 Ala. 104; White v. White, 13 Ired. 265; Thrall v. Spencer, 16 Conn. 139; Waller v. Todd, 3 Dana, 503; Oriental Bank v. Haskins, 3 Met. 332; Harvey v. Mix, 24 Conn. 406; *vide* Halcombe v. Ray, 1 Ired. 340.

[3] Allen v. Holland, 3 Yerg. 343.

[4] Roane v. Bank, 1 Head, 526; Stoddard v. Butler, 7 Paige, 163; s. c. 20 Wend. 507; Peacock v. Tompkins, Meigs, 317.

[5] Eaton v. Campbell, 7 Pick. 10; Breckinridge v. Anderson, 3 J. J. Marsh. 710; Gridley v. Wynant, 23 How. 500; Brown v. Riley, 22 Ill. 45; Wall v. White, 3 Dev. 105; White v. White, 13 Ired. 265; Parker v. Crittenden, 37 Conn. 148.

[6] Bunn v. Ahl, 29 Penn. 387.

If a transfer is fraudulent, the subsequent payment in full of the purchase money will not render it valid.[1] So also if the transaction is merely colorable, it will not be purged by any subsequent payment or advances in part without rescinding the whole, whether made to the debtor or the creditors. If any part of the fraudulent purpose remains it vitiates the whole.[2] A consideration paid at the time when a party assents to a deed placed on record without his knowledge is not, however, a subsequent consideration.[3]

ADMINISTRATOR, ASSIGNEE.—If the grantee dies before a rescission of the transfer, the personal property will vest in his personal representatives, and no return can be made which will interfere with their rights.[4] When a judgment is confessed for certain articles in favor of an administrator, accompanied with a secret trust, the trust is void, and the distributees may require the enforcement of the judgment.[5] If the debtor subsequently makes an assignment, the creditors may still have the fraudulent transfer set aside, for he can not transfer any right to his assignee which he himself does not possess.[6]

---

[1] Borland v. Mayo, 8 Ala. 104; Chenery v. Palmer, 6 Cal. 119.

[2] Wood v. Hunt, 38 Barb. 302 ; Danjean v. Blacketer, 13 La. An. 595; Lynde v. McGregor, 13 Allen, 182 ; Stone v. Grubbam, 2 Bulst. 217; s. c. 1 Rol. Rep. 3; Law v. Payson, 32 Me. 521; Halcombe v. Ray, 1 Ired. 340.

[3] Smith v. Espy, 1 Stockt. 160.   [4] Dearman v. Radcliffe, 5 Ala. 192.

[5] Kavanaugh v. Thompson, 16 Ala. 817.

[6] Brownell v. Curtis, 10 Paige, 210; Browning v. Hart, 6 Barb. 91 ; Storm v. Davenport, 1 Sandf. Ch. 135; Thomson v. Dougherty, 12 S. & R. 448 ; Vandyke v. Christ, 7 W. & S. 373 ; Leach v. Kelsey, 7 Barb. 466 ; Estabrook v. Messersmith, 18 Wis. 545; Maiders v. Culver, 1 Duvall, 164; Van Keuren v. McLaughlin, 21 N. J. Eq. 163 ; Luckenbach v. Brickenstein, 5 W. & S. 145 ; vide Englebert v. Blanjot, 2 Whart. 240; Swift v. Thompson, 9 Conn. 63 ; Galt v. Dibrell, 10 Yerg. 146; Gaylor v. Harding, 37 Conn. 508 ; Rood v. Welch, 28 Conn. 157; Shipman v. Ætna Ins. Co. 29 Conn. 245.

MORTGAGE DEBT, EQUITY OF REDEMPTION.—A fraudulent mortgage does not extinguish the debt for which
it was given, and if the security fails the debt remains
in full force. As it did not arise *ex turpi causa*, it can
not be merged by anything merely collateral.[1] A
fraudulent release of an equity of redemption does not
destroy or extinguish the mortgage. When the creditors avoid the conveyance the law remits and restores
the mortgagee to his previously existing legal rights.
This gives the statute its proper and legitimate effect,
permits the purchaser to hold nothing by his fraudulent contract, and the creditors to take all their debtor
fraudulently conveyed and nothing more. The very
avoiding of the fraudulent conveyance revives and
renews the former valid lien and restores the parties
to their original position.[2]

VOID IN PART IS VOID IN TOTO.—If a part of the
consideration for a transfer is merely a nominal or colorable consideration, contrived to hinder, delay, or defraud creditors, the whole transfer is void.[3] If a man
who has goods but of the value of 30*l.* is indebted to
two men, viz., to one in 20*l.* and to another in 10*l.* and
the debtor transfers all his goods to him to whom he
owes 10*l.* to the intent that for the residue above the

---

[1] Haven v. Low, 2 N. H. 13.

[2] Ladd v. Wiggin, 35 N. H. 421; Mead v. Combs, 4 C. E. Green, 112;
Stokoe v. Cowan, 29 Beav. 637; Ripley v. Severance, 6 Pick. 474; Britt
v. Aylett, 11 Ark. 475; Towle v. Hoitt, 14 N. H. 61; Irish v. Clayes, 10
Vt. 81; Stedman v. Vickery, 42 Me. 132; Daniel v. Morrison, 6 Dana, 182;
s. c. 6 J. J. Marsh. 398; *vide* Clayborn v. Hill, 1 Wash. (Va.) 177.

[3] Floyd v. Goodwin, 8 Yerg. 484; Marriott v. Givens, 8 Ala. 694; Ta-
tum v. Hunter, 14 Ala. 557; Burke v. Murphy, 27 Miss. 167; McKenty
v. Gladwin, 10 Cal. 227; Scales v. Scott, 13 Cal. 76; Fiedler v. Day, 2
Sandf. 594; Mead v. Combs, 4 C. E. Green, 112; Hall v. Heydon, 41 Ala.
242; Albee v. Webster, 16 N. H. 362; Coolidge v. Melvin, 42 N. H. 510;
Johnson v. Murchison, 1 Winst. 292.

10l. he shall be favorable unto him, the sale is altogether void, for it is fraudulent in part.[1] So also if a creditor takes a judgment,[2] or issues an attachment,[3] for more than is due, the fraud corrupts and destroys the whole. There must, however, be fraud to bring a case within this principle. If there is no fraud or wrong done, or attempted, or intended to be done, the principle does not apply. If an attachment or judgment is taken for too much inadvertently, and the creditor has no purpose of obtaining any more than is due to him, it will be valid.[4]

FRAUDULENT AS TO PART OF THE PROPERTY.—If a mortgage is made with the intent to secure a part of the property to the mortgagee, and to cover the residue for the use of the debtor it is void as to the whole. To render an instrument valid it must be given in good faith and without any intent to hinder or defraud cred-itors. This can not be true when the object as to a part of the property is to defraud creditors. This un-lawful design vitiates the entire instrument. The unlaw-ful design can not be confined to one particular parcel of property. Entire honesty and good faith are neces-sary to render the instrument valid, and whenever it appears that one object was to defraud creditors, the en-tire deed is in judgment of law void.[5] When fraud,

---

[1] Wilson & Wormal's Case, Godbolt, 161.

[2] Pierce v. Partridge, 3 Met. 44; Whiting v. Johnson, 11 S. & R. 328; Fryer v. Bryan, 2 Hill Ch. 56; Bowie v. Free, 3 Rich. Eq. 403; Dickinson v. Way, 3 Rich. Eq. 412; Gates v. Johnson, 3 Penn. 52.

[3] Fairfield v. Baldwin, 12 Pick. 388; Taaffe v. Josephson, 7 Cal. 352; Hale v. Chandler, 3 Mich. 531; Harding v. Harding, 25 Vt. 487.

[4] Felton v. Wadsworth, 7 Cush. 587; Ayres v. Husted, 15 Conn. 504; Shedd v. Bank, 32 Vt. 709; Davenport v. Wright, 51 Penn. 294; Wilder v. Fondey, 4 Wend. 100; Harris v. Alcock, 10 G. & J. 226.

[5] Russell v. Winne, 37 N. Y. 591; s. c. 4 Abb. Pr. (N. S.) 384; Tick-nor v. Wiswall, 9 Ala. 305; Goodhue v. Berrien, 2 Sandf. Ch. 630; Darwin

however, is imputed from the mere omission to deliver the possession of the property to the grantee, the transfer will be good as to the articles which are delivered, although it may be void as to the residue.[1]

A FRAUDULENT STIPULATION.—A fraudulent stipulation in a written instrument vitiates the entire instrument. The taint as to a part makes the whole void. Wherever an instrument is good in part and fraudulent in part, it is void altogether, and no interest passes under the part which is good.[2]

SEVERAL GRANTEES.—The same instrument may be evidence of a gift, grant, or conveyance to different individuals and for different objects, and may be invalid as to one of the grantees without affecting the other. They may be so disconnected in respect to the consideration that the fraud of one can not implicate the other in any dishonest purpose. If, for instance, a deed is made to secure two distinct claims, one of which is real and the other fictitious, it will be void as to the fraudulent grantee and valid as a security for the claim of the

v. Handley, 3 Yerg. 502; Young v. Pate, 4 Yerg. 164; Sommerville v. Horton, 4 Yerg. 541 ; Swinford v. Rogers, 23 Cal. 233; *vide* Shurtleff v. Willard, 19 Pick. 202; Chase v. Walker, 26 Me. 555 ; Barnet v. Fergus, 51 Ill. 352 ; *in re* Kahley et al. 4 B. R. 124; Allen v. Brown, 43 Geo. 305.

[1] D'Wolf v. Harris, 4 Mason, 515 ; De Bardleben v. Beckman, 1 Dessau. 346; Brown v. Foree, 7 B. Mon. 357; Weller v. Wayland, 17 Johns. 102 ; Lee v. Huntoon, Hoff. 447 ; Spaulding v. Austin, 2 Vt. 555 ; Hessing v. McCloskey, 37 Ill. 341.

[2] Hyslop v. Clarke, 14 Johns. 458; Mackie v. Cairns, 5 Cow. 547; s. c. 1 Hopk. 373; Goodrich v. Downs, 6 Hill, 438; Albert v. Winn, 7 Gill, 446; McClurg v. Lecky, 3 Penna. 83 ; Robins v. Embry, 1 S. & M. Ch. 207; Jacot v. Corbett, 1 Chev. Eq. 71; Howell v. Edgar, 3 Scam. 417; Dana v. Lull, 17 Vt. 390; Caldwell v. Williams, 1 Ind. 405; Pierson v. Manning, 2 Mich. 445; Green v. Branch Bank, 33 Ala. 643; Greenleaf v. Edes, 2 Minn. 264; Palmer v. Giles, 5 Jones Eq. 75 ; Spies v. Boyd, 1 E. D. Smith, 445; s. c. 11 Leg. Obs. 54.

innocent grantee.[1] If, however, the grantee who has a
valid claim knows at the time of the execution of the
deed that the other claim is fictitious, the deed will be
void as to both grantees.[2]

A fraudulent recovery stands good to bar those in
remainder or reversion, as if there had been no fraud.
The deed declaring the uses is void. The recovery
stands as a recovery simply without any deed to lead or
declare the uses.[3] When the fraud consists in the creation of an annuity upon a consideration paid by the
debtor to the grantor, the instrument is not void so far
as it creates the annuity, but it is void so far as it directs who shall take the benefit.[4] Although a debtor
refuses to take a deed for land purchased by him for
the purpose of defrauding his creditors, the agreement
will be valid against the creditors of the vendor.[5] If a
note is taken in the name of another, the maker, when
innocent of the fraud, can not be held liable to creditors.[6]

---

[1] Prince v. Shepard, 9 Pick. 176; Anderson v. Hooks, 9 Ala. 704; Gary
v. Colgin, 11 Ala. 514; vide Pettibone v. Phelps, 13 Conn. 445 ; Estabrook
v. Messersmith, 18 Wis. 545.

[2] Lewis v. Caperton, 8 Gratt. 148; Swartz v. Hazlett, 8 Cal. 118.

[3] Tarleton v. Liddell, 17 Q. B. 390; s. c. 4 DeG. & Sim. 538.

[4] Shee v. French, 3 Drew. 716 ; Neale v. Day, 28 L. J. Ch. 45 ; French
v. French, 6 D. M. & G. 95 ; s. c. 25 L. J. Ch. 612; Wakefield v. Gibbon,
1 Giff. 401.

[5] Cutting v. Pike, 21 N. H. 347.

[6] Patterson v. Whittier, 19 N. H. 192.

CHAPTER XVII.

BONA FIDE PURCHASERS.

PURCHASER AS WELL AS GRANTEE PROTECTED.—*Is qui a debitore cujus bona possessa sunt sciens rem emit iterum alii bona fide ementi vendidit.   Quæsitum est an secundus emptor conveniri potest ; sed verior Sabini sententia bona fide emptorem non teneri ; quia dolus ei duntaxat nocere debeat qui eum admisit.*[1]   The principle that fraud is only prejudicial to him who participates in it is also recognized by the statute.   The proviso protects all interests and estates lawfully conveyed or assured upon good consideration, and *bona fide* to a person who, at the time of such conveyance or assurance, has no manner of notice or knowledge of the covin, fraud or collusion.   These terms are broad and extensive.   They apply to any conveyance, whether from the fraudulent grantor or fraudulent grantee.   They are meant to protect a *bona fide* purchaser for a valuable consideration, without notice of the fraud from the operation of the statute.   This is manifest as well from the internal evidence of the proviso as from the plainest maxims of equity and justice.   The proviso is general.   It exempts any conveyance upon good consideration and *bona fide* to any person not having notice of the fraud or collusion from the effect of the statute.   Its

---

[1] Dig. Lib. 42 Tit. 9 ; 3 Pothier Pand. Lib. 42, Tit. 8, Art. 3, § 25, p. 195.

benefits, therefore, extend to any *bona fide* purchaser for valuable consideration, whether he purchases from the fraudulent grantor or the fraudulent grantee.[1]

The great object of the law is to afford certainty and repose to titles honestly acquired. It is of no public utility to destroy titles so acquired on account of the taint of a prior secret fraud, which may be unsuspected and unknown, and which, probably, no diligence could detect. A purchaser who pays a fair price for an ostensibly fair title without notice of any latent fraud in any previous link of the title has a higher equity than the creditors. They may lose their debts; if they can recover the property from him, he may lose the money which he paid for it. The equities between them are equal, and he has the legal title, and consequently the prior right, for the law never divests one of a legal title in order to invest another with it where there are no equitable reasons for so doing. He will, therefore, hold the estate purged of the anterior fraud that infected the title.[2]

VOIDABLE ONLY.—The statute, it is true, declares a fraudulent transfer to be clearly and utterly void, frustrate and of none effect. There is a distinction, however, between a transfer which is an absolute nullity and one which is voidable only. No transfer can be pronounced in a legal sense utterly void which is valid as to some persons, but may be avoided at the election of others. A thing is void which is done against law at the very time of doing it, and where no person is

---

[1] Anderson v. Roberts, 18 Johns. 515 ; s. c. 2 Johns. Ch. 372 ; Mateer v. Hissim, 3 Penna. 160 ; Bean v. Smith, 2 Mason, 252 ; Martin v. Cowles, 1 Dev. & Bat. 29.

[2] Lee v. Abbe, 2 Root. 359 ; Bean v. Smith, 2 Mason, 252 ; Martin v. Cowles, 1 Dev. & Bat. 29.

bound by the act, but a thing is voidable which is done by a person who ought not to have done it, but who, nevertheless, can not avoid it himself after it is done. Whenever the act done takes effect as to some purposes, and is void as to persons who have an interest in impeaching it, the act is not a nullity, and, therefore, in a legal sense, is not utterly void, but merely voidable.[1] The transfer, however, is good between the parties. As against the debtor it is effectual, and the fraudulent grantee has a title and a right to alienate. The only infirmity in his title is its liability to be impeached by creditors. As to all others it is perfect, and when it has passed into the hands of an innocent holder even this infirmity is cured and the title becomes sound and indefeasible.[2] There is no distinction in this respect between actual and constructive fraud.[3]

---

[1] Anderson v. Roberts, 18 Johns. 515; s. c. 2 John. Ch. 372; Martin v. Cowles, 1 Dev. & Bat. 29.

[2] George v. Kimball, 24 Pick. 234; Gridley v. Wynant, 23 How. 500; Wilson & Wormal's Case, Godbolt, 161; Martin v. Cowles, 1 Dev. & Bat. 29; Thompson v. M'Kean, 1 Ashmead, 129; Hood v. Fahnestock, 8 Watts, 489; Mateer v. Hissim, 3 Penna. 160; Ewing v. Cargill, 13 S. & M. 79; Blake v. Williams, 36 N. H. 39; Paige v. O'Neal, 12 Cal. 483; Green v. Tanner, 8 Met. 411; Sutton v. Lord, 1 Dane. Ab. 631; Goodale v. Nichols, 1 Dane. Ab. 631; Gordon v. Haywood, 2 N. H. 402; Hawkins v. Sneed, 3 Hawks, 149; Hoy v. Wright, Brayt. 208; Neal v. Williams, 18 Me. 391; Trott v. Warren, 11 Me. 227; Erskine v. Decker, 39 Me. 467; Bean v. Smith, 2 Mason, 252; Jackson v. Terry, 13 Johns. 471; Lee v. Abbe, 2 Root, 359; Coleman v. Cocke, 6 Rand. 618; King v. Trice, 3 Ired. Eq. 568; Cummings v. McCullough, 5 Ala. 324; Sheldon v. Stryker, 42 Barb. 284; s. c. 27 How. Pr. 387; Wineland v. Coonce, 5 Mo. 296; Pine v. Rikert, 21 Barb. 469; Simpson v. Simpson, 7 Humph. 275; Ewing v. Cargill, 13 S. & M. 79; Choteau v. Jones, 11 Ill. 300; Commonwealth v. Richardson, 8 B. Mon. 81; Richards v. Ewing, 11 Humph. 327; Colquitt v. Thomas, 8 Geo. 258; Sinclair v. Healy, 40 Penn. 417; Curtis v. Riddle, 7 Allen, 185; Rankin v. Arndt, 44 Barb. 251; Parker v. Crittenden, 37 Conn. 148; *Contra*, Preston v. Crofut, 1 Conn. 527, note; Read v. Staton, 3 Hey. (Tenn.) 159.

[3] Thompson v. Lee, 3 W. &. S. 479.

MUST BE BONA FIDE.—An inquiry in regard to the rights of a purchaser only becomes material when he purchases for a valuable consideration without notice of the fraud. If he does not give a valuable consideration,[1] or if he has notice of the fraud,[2] he is in the same position towards the creditors as the fraudulent grantee, for he is, in the contemplation of the law, a participant in the fraud. If he takes a transfer in payment of a pre-existing debt due from the grantee, he is not entitled to protection against the creditors, for the avoidance of the conveyance places him in no worse situation than he was before, and the creditors have the stronger equity.[3] The relinquishment of a security is a good consideration.[4] The transaction between the fraudulent grantee and the purchaser must be completely closed by the payment of all the purchase money and the completion of the transfer before the notice, or the purchaser can not hold the property.[5] Notice before the payment of the purchase money,[6] or the completion of the transfer,[7] is sufficient to invalidate the transaction. Merely giving security for the purchase money is not enough to entitle a party to the character of a purchaser for a valuable consideration.[8] An innocent mortgagee as

---

[1] Forrest v. Camp, 16 Ala. 642.

[2] Parkman v. Welch, 19 Pick. 231; Wise v. Tripp, 13 Me. 9; Garland v. Rives, 4 Rand. 282; Knox v. Hunt, 18 Mo. 174; O'Connor v. Bernard, 2 Jo. 654; Dockray v. Mason, 48 Me. 178.

[3] Manhattan. Co. v. Evertson, 6 Paige, 457; Agricultural Bank v. Dorsey, 1 Freem. Ch. (Miss.) 338; Jessup v. Hulse, 29 Barb. 539; Contra, Knox v. Hunt, 18 Mo. 174; Thornton v. Hook, 36 Cal. 223; Okie v. Kelly, 12 Penn. 323.

[4] Agricultural Bank v. Dorsey, 1 Freem. Ch. 338.

[5] Dugan v. Vattier, 3 Blackf. 245; Colquitt v. Thomas, 8 Geo. 258.

[6] Dixon v. Hill, 5 Mich. 404; vide Newlin v. Osborne, 6 Jones (N. C.), 128.

[7] Farnsworth v. Bell, 5 Sneed, 531; Jones v. Read, 3 Dana, 540.

[8] Rogers v. Hall, 4 Watts, 359.

well as a *bona fide* purchaser is within the protection of the proviso.[1]

WHAT NOTICE SUFFICIENT.—The notice of the fraud need only be sufficient to put a man of ordinary prudence and experience in business transactions upon the inquiry.[2] It is sufficient if the information is so definite as to enable the purchaser to ascertain whether it is authentic, and sufficiently clear and authentic to put the purchaser on inquiry, and to enable him to conduct that inquiry to the ascertainment of the fact. It is not necessary that the notice should be in the shape of a formal communication. Whatever is sufficient to direct his attention to the prior rights and equities of creditors and to enable him to ascertain their nature by inquiry will operate as notice.[3]

When a purchaser has knowledge of any fact sufficient to put him on inquiry, he is presumed either to have made the inquiry and ascertained the extent of the rights that he may possibly prejudice or to have been guilty of a degree of negligence fatal to the claim to be considered a *bona fide* purchaser.[4] This notice may be derived from the statement of creditors or other parties.[5] The debtor's retention of the possession of land,[6] or personal property,[7] is not a sufficient notice of any fraud in the transaction. The purchaser is chargeable with notice of all the matters which ap-

---

[1] Stone v. Bartlett, 46 Me. 439.

[2] Ringgold v. Waggoner, 14 Ark. 69; Johnston v. Harvey, 2 Penna. 82; Baker v. Bliss, 39 N. Y. 70.

[3] Martel v. Somers, 26 Tex. 551.

[4] Baker v. Bliss, 39 N. Y. 70.

[5] Martel v. Somers, 26 Tex. 551.

[6] Suiter v. Turner, 10 Iowa, 517.

[7] Danzey v. Smith, 4 Tex. 411; Boyle v. Rankin, 22 Penn. 168.

pear to be within the knowledge and memory of his agent.[1]

APPARENT ON FACE OF THE INSTRUMENT.—The law sanctions a conveyance founded upon the consideration of blood or of marriage merely. The legal presumption, therefore, is that such a conveyance is valid and not a fraud upon the rights of any one. The mere fact that a purchaser from the holder of such a title has notice that it was not founded upon a pecuniary consideration is not sufficient to make it his duty at his peril to inquire whether the title of his grantor was not fraudulent. On the contrary he has a right to act upon the legal presumption that such a deed of gift or voluntary settlement was honestly made until some other fact is brought to his knowledge to raise a suspicion in his mind that the conveyance is fraudulent.[2] He is, however, bound to take notice of any fraud apparent upon the face of a deed under which he claims title.[3]

SUBSEQUENT JUDGMENT.—In the case of a fraudulent transfer of land, a subsequent judgment against the grantor is not constructive notice to a purchaser from the grantee, for upon searching the records and finding the transfer, the person who is about to purchase is not bound to go further and search the records for the purpose of ascertaining whether subsequent judgments may not have been recovered against the debtor.[4] The title even of a purchaser at a sale under an execution issued upon such

---

[1] Hook v. Mowre, 17 Iowa, 195; *vide* Hood v. Fahnestock, 8 Watts, 489.

[2] Frazer v. Western, 1 Barb. Ch. 220; s. c. 1 How. App. Cas. 448; Sparrow v. Chesley, 19 Me. 79.

[3] Farmers' Bank v. Douglass, 11 S. & M. 469; Johnson v. Thweatt, 18 Ala. 741; Spencer v. Godwin, 30 Ala. 355; Palmer v. Giles, 5 Jones Eq. 75; Ward v. Trotter, 3 Mon. 1; Johnston v. Harvey, 2 Penna. 82.

[4] Ledyard v. Butler, 9 Paige, 132; Jackson v. Terry, 13 Johns. 471.

judgment will not derive any strength from the lien of
the judgment, but in determining the rights of the parties will be deemèd to date only from the sale.[1] Although the purchaser from the grantee has not placed
his deed on record, he will have the better right as
against a party who purchases subsequently at a sheriff's
sale.[2] Although a judgment or an execution may be a
lien by force of the statute as against the parties to the
fraud, yet as against purchasers there is no lien upon
any property the title to which is not in the execution
debtor. Consequently a purchaser may acquire a good
title even after an execution has been issued.[3] If a party
purchases, however, after the levying of an execution or
an attachment[4] or during the pendency of a suit against
the grantee calling his title in question, he is a purchaser
pendente lite, and his rights are subordinate to those of
the creditors.[5] A sale under an execution will prevail
over a subsequent purchase from the grantee.[6] It has,
however, been held that a sale under an execution of
property fraudulently purchased in the name of another
and a record of the sheriff's deed would not prevail
against a subsequent *bona fide* purchaser from the
grantee on the ground that the registry of a deed is
only evidence of a notice to subsequent purchasers under
the same grantor.[7]

---

[1] Scott v. Purcell, 7 Blackf. 66.

[2] Coleman v. Cocke, 6 Rand. 618; *vide* Ledyard v. Butler, 9 Paige,
132; Jackson v. Terry, 13 Johns. 471.

[3] Williams v. Lowe, 4 Humph. 62; *Contra*, McCabe v. Snyder, 3 Phila.
192.

[4] Tuttle v. Turner, 28 Tex. 759.

[5] Jackson v. Andrews, 7 Wend. 152; Collumb v. Read, 24 N. Y. 505.

[6] M'Crcery v. Pursley, 1 A. K. Marsh. 114 ; Baxter v. Sewell, 3 Md.
334; s. c. 2 Md. Ch. 447 ; Reed v. Smith, 14 Ala. 380 ; Brown v. Niles, 16
Ill. 385; Read v. Staton, 3 Hey. (Tenn.) 159.

[7] Crockett v. Maguire, 10 Mo. 34.

MARRIAGE.—If the property fraudulently conveyed has been any inducement to a marriage, the marriage constitutes a valuable consideration, and the husband and wife are considered as purchasers.[1] The marriage, however, must take place before there is a lien upon the property.[2]

WHEN PURCHASE MAY BE MADE.—A *bona fide* purchaser at a sale under an execution obtains a good title although the judgment is fraudulent.[3] A purchaser with notice of the fraud will get a good title when no debts contracted prior to his purchase remain unpaid.[4] A purchaser without notice of the fraud may sell the property to a person who has notice, for the law does not know of an unencumbered estate which is forfeited by alienation or for which the owner can not pass a good title to a purchaser.[5]

TRANSFER TO CREDITOR.—Until there is a lien or seizure by virtue of some legal proceeding, the grantee can do all that the debtor could have done had he retained the property. He may, therefore, sell or mortgage it to the creditors of the grantor. As between the debtor and the grantee, the power of the grantee to convey needs no recognition or addition whatever, and his right to do so in favor of a creditor is as between

[1] Wood v. Jackson, 8 Wend. 9; Bentley v. Harris, 2 Gratt. 357; Huston v. Cantril, 11 Leigh, 136; East Ind. Co. v. Clavell, Gilb. 37; s. c. Prec. Ch. 377; s. c. 28 L. J. Ch. 719; George v. Milbanke, 9 Ves. 189; Martyn v. McNamara, 4 Dr. & War. 411; Hopkirk v. Randolph, 2 Brock. 132; *vide* Stokes v. Jones, 18 Ala. 734; s. c. 21 Ala. 731; Miller v. Thompson, 3 Port. 196; O'Brien v. Coulter, 2 Blackf. 421.

[2] Fones v. Rice, 9 Gratt. 568.

[3] Griffin v. Wardlaw, Harp. 481; Imray v. Magnay, 11 M. & W. 267.

[4] Toole v. Darden 6 Ired. Eq. 394.

[5] Mateer v. Hissim, 3 Penna. 160; Wilson v. Ayer, 7 Me. 207.

the parties to the transaction unquestionable. The assent of the debtor is not of the slightest value so far as power is concerned. By the transfer the debtor assents in fact to whatever the grantee may choose to do with the property, and he effectually assents in law to whatever the grantee may honestly do with it.[1] Whenever the grantee does that which the law would compel him to do, there is no reason for disturbing his act, and, therefore, if he applies it to pay the demand of a creditor the transfer will be good to that extent, because the property receives the same direction and application which the law would give it upon declaring the transfer void. The creditor, moreover, will receive a good title although he has full knowledge of the fraud.[2] The creditor, however, must act in good faith.[3] If he takes an absolute deed and pays the grantee the difference between the amount of his debt and the value of the property, he will not obtain a good title unless the sum so paid is so small that the desire to obtain satisfaction of his claim constitutes the real inducement to the transaction.[4] The transfer to the creditor must, moreover, be made in the consummation of an honest and laudable purpose on the part of the grantee. If it is made not for the purpose of payment or security, but in consideration of an assignment of the debt to him, it does not come under the protection of the principle that permits a creditor to obtain payment out of the property in whosesoever hands it may

---

[1] Webb v. Brown, 3 Ohio St. R. 246.

[2] Boyd v. Brown, 17 Pick. 453; Webb v. Brown, 3 Ohio St. R. 246; Stark v. Ward, 3 Penn. 328; Agricultural Bank v. Dorsey, 1 Freem. Ch. 338; vide Waggoner v. Cooley, 17 Ill. 239.

[3] Copenheaver v. Huffaker, 6 B. Mon. 18; Brown v. Webb, 20 Ohio, 389.

[4] Baker v. Bliss, 39 N. Y. 70.

be.[1] If a fraudulent mortgage is made by a debtor, the creditors to whom he transfers the mortgage notes will not have a prior claim upon the property.[2]

---

[1] Waggoner v. Cooley, 17 Ill. 239.

[2] Johnston v. Dick, 27 Miss. 277; *vide* Davis v. Gibbon, 24 Iowa, 257.

CHAPTER XVIII.

WHO ARE CREDITORS.

CLAIM MUST BE CAPABLE OF ENFORCEMENT.—The statute by express terms makes a fraudulent transfer void as against creditors and others who have just and lawful actions, suits, debts, accounts, damages, penalties, forfeitures, heriots, mortuaries, or reliefs. The sole object of the statute is to protect lawful debts, claims, or demands, and not those which are unlawful or pretended, and which have no foundation in law or justice. A pretended claim,[1] and a demand founded upon an illegal consideration,[2] or which can not for any other reason be enforced,[3] are not, therefore, within its protection. The law, however, does not permit a debtor to determine whether a claim is just or unjust. That question is one which must be settled by the judicial tribunal alone. It will not do to allow a man's preponderating self interest to decide which of his debts are just and which unjust, for under such a rule he might decide his debts to be unjust when he could no longer procrastinate payment.[4]

LIBERAL CONSTRUCTION.—The statute by the words "creditors and others" embraces others than those who

---

[1] Baker v. Gilman, 52 Barb. 26.

[2] Alexander v. Gould, 1 Mass. 165; Fuller v. Bean, 30 N. H. 181; Hanson v. Power, 8 Dana, 91; Bruggerman v. Hoerr, 7 Minn. 337.

[3] Hart v. Hart, 5 Watts, 106; Edwards v. M'Gee, 31 Miss. 143.

[4] Brady v. Briscoe, 2 J. J. Marsh. 212; Hook v. Mowre, 17 Iowa, 195.

are strictly and technically creditors.[1] Even the word
"creditor" does not receive a strict definition, for a
party who is not strictly speaking a creditor may stand
in the equity of a creditor and have an interest that may
be defrauded.[2] The statute protects all just and lawful
actions, suits, debts, accounts, damages, penalties, and
forfeitures, and consequently all persons having such
interests must be included in the phrase "creditors and
others."[3]

CHARACTER IMMATERIAL.—The character of the claim,
if it is just and lawful, is immaterial. It need not be
due, for although the holder can not maintain an action
until it is due, he, nevertheless, has an interest in the
property as a fund out of which the demand ought to
be paid.[4] A contingent claim is as fully protected
as one that is absolute.[5] A liability as surety is within
the statute as much as a liability as principal.[6] The
statute embraces all pecuniary damages incurred by
reason of the obligation of a contract, whether of an ascertained amount or only sounding in damages, and
whether actually asserted or only demandable.[7] It in-

---

[1] Feigley v. Feigley, 7 Md. 537 ; Shontz v. Brown, 27 Penn. 123.

[2] Shontz v. Brown, 27 Penn. 123; Hutchinson v. Kelly, 1 Rob. 123;
Walradt v. Brown, 1 Gilman, 397.

[3] Twyne's Case, 3 Co. 80 ; Walradt v. Brown, 1 Gilman, 397; Alston
v. Rowles, 13 Fla. 117.

[4] Howe v. Ward, 4 Me. 195; Cook v. Johnson, 1 Beasley, 51; Mott v.
Danforth, 6 Watts, 304.

[5] Seward v. Jackson, 8 Cow. 406 ; s. c. 5 Cow. 67; Van Wyck v. Se-
ward, 18 Wend. 375; s. c. 6 Paige, 62; s. c. 1 Edw. 327; Shontz v.
Brown, 27 Penn. 123; McLaughlin v. Bank of Potomac, 7 How. 220;
Woodley v. Abby, 5 Call. 336 ; Gannard v. Eslava, 20 Ala. 732; Bay v.
Cook, 31 Ill. 336; Cook v. Johnson, 1 Beasley, 51 ; Manhattan Co. v. Os-
good, 15 Johns. 162; s. c. 3 Cow. 612.

[6] Russell v. Stinson, 3 Hey, 1; Carl v. Smith, 28 Leg. Int. 366; Crane
v. Stickles, 15 Vt. 252 ; Hutchinson v. Kelly, 1 Rob. 123 ; Curd v. Lewis,
7 Gratt. 185; Gibson v. Love, 4 Fla. 217; Bay v. Cook, 31 Ill. 336.

[7] Hutchinson v. Kelly, 1 Rob. 123.

cludes voluntary bonds,[1] and claims which are payable after the decease of the debtor.[2] Its protection extends to an action for slander,[3] or a tort,[4] a breach of a promise to marry,[5] the support of a bastard child,[6] a false representation,[7] a demand or forfeiture due to the State for offences,[8] and a claim for usurious interest.[9]

FEME COVERT AND OTHERS.—The claim of a *feme covert* against her husband under a marriage settlement,[10] or in proceedings instituted to obtain a divorce and alimony,[11] is within the statute. A stockholder is not allowed to

---

[1] Adams v. Hallett, L. R. 6 Eq. 468; Hanson v. Buckner, 4 Dana, 251.

[2] Adams v. Hallett, L. R. 6 Eq. 468; Rider v. Kidder, 10 Ves. 360; 12 Ves. 202; s. c. 13 Ves. 123; *vide* Henderson v. Dodd, 1 Bailey Ch. 138.

[3] Jackson v. Myers, 18 Johns. 425; Lillard v. McGee, 4 Bibb. 165; Hord v. Rust, 4 Bibb. 231; Fowler v. Frisbie, 3 Conn. 320; Walradt v. Brown, 1 Gilman, 397; Hall v. Sands, 52 Me. 355; Langford v. Fly, 7 Humph. 585; Johnson v. Brandis, 1 Smith, 263; Wright v. Brandis, 1 Ind. 336; Farnsworth v. Bell, 5 Sneed, 531; Rogers v. Evans, 3 Ind. 574.

[4] Jackson v. Mather, 7 Cow. 301; Paul v. Crooker, 8 N. H. 288; McLean v. Morgan, 3 B. Mon. 282; Lewkner v. Freeman, 1 Eq. Cas. Abr. 149; s. c. 2 Freem. 236; s. c. Prec. Ch. 105; M'Erwin v. Benning, 1 Hawks. 474; Fox v. Hills, 1 Conn. 295; Greer v. Wright, 6 Gratt. 154; Wilcox v. Fitch, 20 Johns. 472; Foote v. Cobb, 18 Ala. 585; Patrick v. Ford, 5 Sneed, 532 note; Vance v. Smith, 2 Heisk. 343; Barling v. Bishopp, 29 Beav. 417.

[5] Lowry v. Pinson, 2 Bailey, 324; Smith v. Culbertson, 9 Rich. 106.

[6] Damon v. Bryant, 2 Pick. 411.

[7] Miner v. Warner, 2 Grant. 448; s. c. 2 Phila. 124.

[8] Rex v. Nottingham, Lane, 42; State v. Fife, 2 Bailey, 337; Jones v. Ashurst, Skin, 357; Morewood v. Wilkes, 6 C. & P. 144; Shaw v. Bran, 1 Stark. 319; Saunders v. Wharton, 32 L. J. (Ch.) 224; s. c. 1 N. R. 256; Perkins v. Bradley, 1 Hare, 219; s. c. 6 Jur. 254.

[9] Heath v. Page, 63 Penn. 280.

[10] Rider v. Kidder, 10 Ves. 360; s. c. 12 Ves. 202; s. c. 13 Ves. 123.

[11] Feigley v. Feigley, 7 Md. 537; Blenkinsopp v. Blenkinsopp, 1 D. M. & G. 495; s. c. 12 Beav. 568; s. c. 21 L. J. Ch. 404; Taylor v. Wyld, 8 Beav. 159; Claggett v. Gibson, 3 Cranch C. C. 359; Boils v. Boils, 1 Cold. 284; Brooks v. Caughran, 3 Head, 464; Ruffing v. Tilton, 12 Ind. 259; Livermore v. Boutelle, 11 Gray, 217; Turner v. Turner, 44 Ala. 437; Morrison v. Morrison, 49 N. H. 69; Frakes v. Brown, 2 Blackf. 295; Chase v. Chase, 105 Mass. 385; Boughslough v. Bouslough, 68 Penn. 495.

transfer his property so as to defeat a liability imposed upon him by statute for the debts of the corporation.[1] An heir can not fraudulently alien assets which have descended for the purpose of defeating his liability for the debts of his ancestor.[2] A transfer for the purpose of defeating a sequestration,[3] or an attachment,[4] is as fraudulent as a transfer to defeat an execution. The responsibility for the acts of a partner,[5] or of the principal to whom an accommodation indorser lends his name,[6] is a risk which the party who enters into such a contract assumes and has no right to evade. The word "forfeiture" in the statute is intended not only of a forfeiture of an obligation, recognizance, or such like, but to every thing which shall by law be forfeit to the king or subject. Therefore, if a man, to prevent a forfeiture for felony or by outlawry, makes a conveyance of all his goods, and afterwards is attainted, or outlawed, the goods are forfeited notwithstanding the conveyance.[7]

RIGHT NOT PERSONAL.—The right to hold the transfer void is not merely personal. A creditor can not treat it as void except as to his demand. If he transfers his claim, he can not impeach it any longer on the

---

[1] Marcy v. Clark, 17 Mass. 330.

[2] Gooch's Case, 5 Co. 60; Leonard v. Bacon, Cro. Eliz. 234; Apharry v. Bodingham, Cro. Eliz. 350; Richardson v. Horton, 7 Beav. 112; Hetfield v. Jacques, 5 Halst. 259.

[3] Hamblyn v. Ley, 3 Swanst. 301, n.; Coulston v. Gardinier, 3 Swanst. 279; Empringham v. Short, 3 Hare, 461.

[4] Pendleton and Gustin's Case, 1 Leon, 47; Getzler v. Saroni, 18 Ill. 511; Dixon v. Hill, 5 Mich. 404; Rinchey v. Stryker, 26 How. Pr. 75; Van Kirk v. Wilds, 11 Barb. 520; Thayer v. Willett, 9 Abb. Pr. 325; s. c. 5 Bosw. 344; Swanzy v. Hunt, 2 N. & M. 211; Contra, Hall v. Stryker, 9 Abb. Pr. 342; s. c. 29 Barb. 105; Bentley v. Goodwin, 15 Abb. Pr. 82.

[5] Thomson v. Dougherty, 12 S. & R. 448.

[6] Cook v. Johnson, 1 Beasley, 51.

[7] Twyne's Case, 3 Co. 80.

ground of fraud. But as to the demand or any suit thereon, until paid or discharged, such a transfer is utterly void. Whoever may become the owner of the debt can enforce it against the property.[1] The transfer is void not only against creditors, but against those who represent creditors. It is void as against sheriffs,[2] purchasers at a sale under an execution,[3] assignees in bankruptcy,[4] and receivers appointed in proceedings supplemental to an execution.[5]

AT WHAT TIME ACCRUES.—The distinction between prior and subsequent creditors makes it important at times to inquire into the date and origin of a demand. It may be laid down as a general rule that all claims which arise from contract, are in force from the date of the agreement. The liability dates from that time, although no demand accrues until a subsequent date.[6] A

---

[1] Warren v. Williams, 52 Me. 343.

[2] Turvill v. Tupper, Latch, 222; Schlussell v. Willets, 32 Barb. 615; s. c. 12 Abb. Pr. 397; s. c. 22 How. Pr. 15; Hozey v. Buchanan, 16 Pet. 215; Clute v. Fitch, 25 Barb. 428; Pierce v. Jackson, 6 Mass. 242; Imray v. Magnay, 11 M. & W. 267; Scarfe v. Halifax, 7 M. & W. 288.

[3] Cole v. White, 26 Wend. 511; s. c. 24 Wend. 116; Barr v. Hatch, 3 Ohio, 527; King v. Bailey, 6 Mo. 575; s. c. 8 Mo. 332.

[4] Badger v. Story, 16 N. H. 168; Anderson v. Maltbie, 2 Ves. Jr. 244; Carr v. Hilton, 1 Curt. 230; Ward v. Van Bokkelen, 2 Paige, 289; Giraud v. Mazier, 13 La. An. 147; Nouvet v. Bollinger, 15 La. An. 293; Shackleford v. Collier, 6 Bush. 149; Grimsby v. Ball, 11 M. & W. 531; Pott v. Todhunter, 2 Coll. 76; Butcher v. Harrison, 4 B. & A. 129; Jamison v. Chestnut, 8 Md. 34; Bradshaw v. Klein, 1 B. R. 146; s. c. 1 L. T. B. 72; in re Meyers, 1 B. R. 162; s. c. 2 Bt. 424; in re Metzger, 2 B. R. 114; Contra, Reavis v. Garner, 12 Ala. 661; Waters v. Dashiell, 1 Md. 455; Robinson v. McDonnell, 2 B. & Ald. 134.

[5] Bostwick v. Beizer, 10 Abb. Pr. 197; Porter v. Williams, 9 N. Y. 142; s. c. 12 How. Pr. 107; Contra, Seymour v. Wilson, 16 Barb. 294; Hayner v. Fowler, 16 Barb. 300.

[6] Seward v. Jackson, 8 Cow. 406; s. c. 5 Cow. 67; Van Wyck v. Seward, 18 Wend. 375; s. c. 6 Paige, 62; s. c. 1 Edw. 327; Gannard v. Eslava, 20 Ala. 732; Black v. Caldwell, 4 Jones (N. C.), 150; Stone v. Myers, 9 Minn. 303; vide White v. Sansom, 3 Atk. 411; East Ind. Co. v. Clavell,

covenant with a general warranty,[1] and a bond of conveyance,[2] take effect from the date of the instrument. A surety is subrogated to all the rights of the creditor whose claim he has paid.[3] An indorser has the same rights as the holder of a note.[4] The claim of a surety against either the principal,[5] or against his co-surety,[6] is referred to the date of the execution of the obligation. A demand arising from a tort is in force from the time of the commission of the wrong.[7] A trustee becomes a debtor as soon as he receives the trust fund.[8] An accommodation note dated anterior to the transfer, though discounted subsequently, is regarded as a prior claim.[9] A judgment for costs takes effect only from the rendition of the judgment.[10] A judgment for a prior and subsequent demand, is a subsequent debt, for it can not be apportioned.[11]

Gilb. 37; s. c. Prec. Ch. 377; s. c. 28 L. J. Ch. 719; Richardson v. Smallwood, Jac. 552; Mountford v. Ranie, 2 Keble, 499; Fales v. Thompson, 1 Mass. 134.

[1] Gannard v. Eslava, 20 Ala. 732; Seward v. Jackson, 8 Cow. 406; s. c. 5 Cow. 67; Van Wyck v. Seward, 18 Wend. 375; s. c. 6 Paige, 62; s. c. 1 Edw. 327; vide Bridgford v. Riddell, 55 Ill. 261.

[2] Stone v. Myers, 9 Minn. 303.

[3] Cato v. Easley, 2 Stew. 214; Sargent v. Salmond, 27 Me. 539; Choteau v. Jones, 11 Ill. 301; Greene v. Starnes, 1 Heisk, 582; Hurdt v. Courtenay, 4 Met. (Ky.) 139; Taylor v. Heriot, 4 Dessau. 227; Huston v. Cantril, 11 Leigh, 136; Swindersine v. Miscally, 1 Bailey Ch. 304; Heighe v. Farmers' Bank, 5 H. & J. 68.

[4] Cramer v. Reford, 2 C. E. Green, 367.

[5] Thompson v. Thompson, 19 Me. 244; Carlisle v. Rich, 8 N. H. 44.

[6] Howe v. Ward, 4 Me. 195; Sargent v. Salmond, 27 Me. 539; Raymond v. Cook, 31 Tex. 373.

[7] Walradt v. Brown, 1 Gilman, 397; Langford v. Fly, 7 Humph. 585; Farnsworth v. Bell, 5 Sneed, 531; vide Meserve v. Dyer, 4 Me. 52; Slater v. Sherman, 5 Bush, 206; Fowler v. Frisbie, 3 Conn. 320.

[8] McLemore v. Nuckolls, 37 Ala. 662.

[9] Williams v. Banks, 11 Md. 198; s. c. 19 Md. 22.

[10] Pelham v. Aldrich, 8 Gray, 515; Ogden v. Prentice, 33 Barb. 160.

[11] Baker v. Gilman, 52 Barb. 26; Reed v. Woodman, 4 Me. 400; Usher v. Hazeltine, 5 Me. 471; Miller v. Miller, 23 Me. 22; Moritz v. Hoffman, 35 Ill. 553; Quimly v. Dill, 40 Me. 528.

EVIDENCE TO ANTEDATE.—A judgment is *prima fa-cie* a claim only from the institution of the suit.[1] The legal presumption is that a note is executed by the maker at the date upon its face,[2] and that an indorsement was made before the maturity of the note.[3] In the absence of proof, the origin of a debt is referred to the date of the note.[4] The rights of a creditor, however, arise from the fact that a debt is due. Any change, therefore, of the evidence of the existence of the debt does not exert any influence upon these rights. Evidence may be introduced to show that a judgment is founded upon a prior claim.[5] A note may be shown to be given for a prior account,[6] or in renewal of a prior note.[7] A novation does not affect the rights under the debt.[8] A renewal by which a liability is created different from that created by the original debt is a new debt.[9]

---

[1] Niller v. Johnson, 27 Md. 6.

[2] Williams v. Banks, 11 Md. 198; s. c. 19 Md. 22; Emery v. Vinall, 26 Me. 295.

[3] McDowell v. Goldsmith, 6 Md. 319; s. c. 2 Md. Ch. 370; 25 Md. 214.

[4] Johnston v. Zane, 11 Gratt. 552.

[5] Hinds v. Longworth, 11 Wheat. 198; Harlan v. Barnes, 5 Dana, 219; Williams v. Jones, 2 Ala. 314; Chandler v. Van Roeder, 24 How. 224.

[6] Moore v. Spence, 6 Ala. 506; Blue v. Penniston, 27 Mo. 272; *vide* Bangor v. Warren, 34 Me. 324; Eigleberger v. Kibler, 1 Hill Ch. 113; Morsell v. Baden, 22 Md. 391.

[7] McLaughlin v. Bank of Potomac, 7 How. 220; Lowry v. Fisher, 2 Bush, 70.

[8] Gardner v. Baker, 25 Iowa, 343.

[9] Bank v. Marchand, 2 T. U. Charlt. 247.

CHAPTER XIX.

INTERNATIONAL LAW.

LEX LOCI.—The validity of an instrument conveying property is to be determined according to the laws of the place where it is made.[1] If it is invalid by those laws, it will not be valid anywhere.[2] Questions of evidence pertain to the remedy and are decided by the *lex fori*. Fraud may, therefore, be inferred from facts which would not be conclusive in the State where the instrument was executed.[3] A sale in an adjoining State to which the property has been removed for the purpose of evading an execution, will not purify the fraud.[4]

LAND.—The title and disposition of real estate is exclusively subject to the laws of the country where the land is located, and a conveyance of it must conform to those laws.[5] The courts of one State have no jurisdic-

---

[1] Martin v. Hill, 12 Barb. 631; Fairbanks v. Bloomfield, 5 Duer, 434; Balto. & Ohio R. R. Co. v. Glenn, 28 Md. 287; French v. Hall, 9 N. H. 137; Livermore v. Jenckes, 21 How. 126; Barton v. Bolton, 3 Phila. 369.

[2] Fellows v. Commercial Bank, 6 Rob. (La.) 246; Graves v. Roy, 13 La. 454; Maberry v. Shisler, 1 Harring. 349.

[3] Barton v. Bolton, 3 Phila. 369.

[4] Watts v. Kilburn, 7 Geo. 356.

[5] Osborn v. Adams, 18 Pick. 245, Bentley v. Whittemore, 3 C. E. Green, 366; Lamb v. Fries, 2 Penn. 83; Evans v. Dunkelberger, 3 Grant, 134.

tion or authority to set aside a fraudulent conveyance of land situate in another State.[1]

PERSONAL PROPERTY.—It is one of the maxims of international jurisprudence that personal property as a rule has no *situs*, but appertains to the person of the owner, and that as a consequence such owner can dispose of it by any instrument or in any method and to such uses as are authorized by the law of the place where the conveyance is executed. The rule is not so much a convenience as it is a necessity of trade, one of those fundamental things without which traffic would be in all its parts impeded. If the law of the locality of personalty were to be taken as the criterion of the legality of its transfer, it is evident the transmission would often be attended with serious perplexity, for it would on most occasions be quite impracticable for the owner of the goods, or the creditor to whom the debt was due, to ascertain with sufficient exactness the diversified requirements of the local laws of the different countries through which such goods might pass, or in which the person of the debtor might at any moment happen to be. The principle that personal effects have no locality arises out of the necessities of trade. It is, accordingly, held almost universally that an assignment or transfer valid by the laws of the State where it is made will be upheld everywhere.[2] A debt has no *situs*

---

[1] Fetter v. Cirode, 4 B. Mon. 482; Nicholson v. Leavitt, 4 Sandf. 252; *vide* D'Ivernois v. Leavitt, 23 Barb. 63.

[2] Noble v. Smith, 6 R. I. 446; Moore v. Willett, 35 Barb. 663; Van Buskirk v. Warren, 39 N. Y. 119; s. c. 34 Barb. 457; s. c. 13 Abb. Pr. 145; Cage v. Wells, 7 Humph. 195; Fairbanks v. Bloomfield, 5 Duer, 434; Ackerman v. Cross, 40 Barb. 465; Richardson v. Leavitt, 1 La. An. 430; Caskie v. Webster, 2 Wallace, Jr. 131; Law v. Mills, 18 Penn. 185; Speed v. May, 17 Penn. 91; Frazier v. Fredericks, 4 Zab. 162; Russell v. Tunno, 11 Rich. 303; Hanford v. Paine, 9 A. L. Reg. 553; Robinson v. Rapelye, 2

and is deemed in contemplation of law to be attached to and to follow the person of the creditor.[1]

STATE STATUTES.—There is an exception to the rule that a conveyance of personalty valid in the State where it is made will be upheld everywhere. Every State or nation possesses the power to pass laws for the protection and security of its own citizens, and being looked to for the protection of property within its territorial limits, has the unquestionable right to adopt such regulations for its transfer as may be deemed necessary to protect and secure its own citizens from impositions and fraud. And if such regulations are adopted in conflict with the general rule they will prevail.[2] But a construction should not be hastily given which would lead to a conflict if an interpretation can be fairly made to avoid it, or, in other words, there should be a clear and manifest repugnance between them to justify the

---

Stew. 86; U. S. v. Bank of U. S. 8 Rob. (La.) 262; Mowry v. Crocker, 6 Wis. 326; Newman v. Bagley, 16 Pick. 570; Bholen v. Cleveland, 5 Mason, 174; U. S. Bank v. Huth, 4 B. Mon. 423; Atwood v. Protection Ins. Co. 14 Conn. 555; Hanford v. Paine, 32 Vt. 442; Walters v. Whitlock, 9 Fla. 86; Dundas v. Bowler, 3 McLean, 397; Houston v. Nowland, 7 G. & J. 480; Means v. Hapgood, 19 Pick. 105; Greene v. Mowry, 2 Bailey, 163; West v. Tupper, 2 Bailey, 193; Ferguson v. Clifford, 37 N. H. 86; Livermore v. Jenckes, 21 How. 126; Born v. Shaw, 29 Penn. 288; Balto & Ohio R. R. Co. v. Hoge, 34 Penn. 214; *vide* Woodward v. Gates, 9 Vt. 358; Fishburne v. Kunhardt, 2 Spears, 556; Golden v. Cockril, 1 Kansas, 259; Ingraham v. Geyer, 13 Mass. 146; Fox v. Adams, 5 Me. 245; The Watchman, Ware, 232.

[1] Atwood v. Protection Ins. Co. 14 Conn. 555; Sanderson v. Bradford, 10 N. H. 260; Caskie v. Webster, 2 Wallace, Jr. 131; Walters v. Whitlock, 9 Fla. 86.

[2] Zipcey v. Thompson, 1 Gray, 243; Ingraham v. Geyer, 13 Mass. 146; Fall River Ironwork Co. v. Croade, 15 Pick. 11; Boyd v. Rockport Mills, 7 Gray, 406; Varnum v. Camp, 1 Green, 326; Richmondville Manuf. Co. 9 Conn. 487; Bryan v. Brisbin, 26 Mo. 423; Beirne v. Patton, 17 La. 589; Stricker v. Tinkham, 35 Geo. 176; Guillander v. Howell, 35 N. Y. 657; Hanford v. Paine, 32 Vt. 442.

courts to disregard the general rule which is respected and regarded by all civilized nations upon the principles of comity. The peace and harmony among States and nations, and the mutual protection, security, and safety of the rights of the citizens of each, demand that the law of nations should not, on slight grounds, be impaired or disregarded.[1] Even when a transfer is invalid by the laws of the State where the property is located, it will, if valid by the laws of the State where it is made, be binding upon the citizens of that State,[2] and all others except the citizens of the State for whose protection the laws were passed.[3] Citizens of such State who purchase claims after the transfer have only such rights as their vendor had.[4] If a transfer is valid by the laws of the State where it is made, and in which the property is located, it will be valid everywhere.[5]

NOTICE TO DEBTOR.—In the case of an assignment of a debt notice is necessary to charge the debtor with the duty of payment to the assignee, and if without notice, he pays the debt to the assignor or it is recovered by process against him, he will be discharged from the debt. Notice after attachment and prior to a recovery is sufficient.[6]

---

[1] U. S. Bank v. Huth, 4 B. Mon. 423; Hanford v. Paine, 32 Vt. 442.

[2] Benedict v. Parmenter, 13 Gray, 88; Whipple v. Thayer, 16 Pick. 25; Daniels v. Willard, 16 Pick. 36; Burlock v. Taylor, 16 Pick. 335; Moore v. Bonnell, 31 N. J. 90; Maberry v. Shisler, 1 Harring. 349.

[3] Todd v. Bucknam, 11 Me. 41; Sanderson v. Bradford, 10 N. H. 260; Forbes v. Scannell, 13 Cal. 242; vide Brown v. Knox, 6 Mo. 302.

[4] Richardson v. Forepaugh, 7 Gray, 546; Hunt v. Lathrop, 7 R. I. 58; Todd v. Bucknam, 11 Me. 41.

[5] Reid v. Gray, 37 Penn. 508; Newman v. Bagley, 16 Pick. 570; Wales v. Alden, 22 Pick. 245; Means v. Hapgood, 19 Pick. 105; Jones v. Taylor, 30 Vt. 42; Forbes v. Scannell, 13 Cal. 242; Goddard v. Winthrop, 8 Gray, 180; Benedict v. Parmenter, 13 Gray, 88; Varnum v. Camp, 1 Green, 326; vide Skiff v. Solace, 23 Vt. 279.

[6] Mowry v. Crocker, 6 Wis. 326; Noble v. Smith, 6 R. I. 446; Martin

When there is no evidence of what the foreign law is, it will be assumed to be the same as that which governs the tribunal where the question arises.[1]

---

v. Potter, 11 Gray, 37 ; Walters v. Whitlock, 9 Fla. 86 ; Bank v. Gettinger, 3 W. Va. 309; *vide* Martin v. Potter, 34 Vt. 87; Rice v. Courtis, 32 Vt. 460.

[1] Russell v. Tunno, 11 Rich. 303; Beirne v. Patton, 17 La. 589; Hurdt v. Courtenay, 4 Met. (Ky.) 139; Green v. Trieber, 3 Md. 11; Sangston v. Gaither, 3 Md. 40; Savage v. O'Neil, 43 N. Y. 298; Ferguson v. Clifford, 37 N. H. 86.

CHAPTER XX.

EXECUTIONS, JUDGMENTS, AND ATTACHMENTS.

DELAY IN EXECUTION.—The statute avoids all executions issued or kept on foot with intent to delay, hinder, or defraud creditors.[1] The intent may be inferred from circumstances, and if it is established the levy loses its preference. The end and object of an execution is to obtain satisfaction of the debt for which it issues, and, being delivered to the proper officer, it gives to the creditor a priority, because the law points out the officer's duty which is to execute it without delay. Any act of the creditor which diverts the execution from its legitimate purpose, renders it void against other creditors, and deprives him of his right to priority.[2] The delivery of an execution to a sheriff, with instructions to do nothing under it, is no delivery, and confers no privileges upon the creditor. If he instructs the sheriff to make no seizure or levy until he gives him further orders, or until a distant day, and in the mean time another execution comes to the sheriff with orders to proceed, the second writ will in law be deemed the first in order.[3] The fact that the prior execution was

---

[1] Snyder v. Kunkleman, 3 Penna. 487; Burnell v. Johnson, 9 Johns. 243; Howell v. Alkyn, 2 Rawle, 282.

[2] Berry v. Smith, 3 Wash. C. C. 60.

[3] Cook v. Wood, 1 Harrison, 254; Knower v. Barnard, 5 Hill, 377; Patton v. Hayter, 15 Ala. 18; Wood v. Gary, 5 Ala. 43; Branch Bank v. Robinson, 5 Ala. 623; Porter v. Cocke, Peck, 30; Freburger's Appeal, 40 Penn. 244; Wise v. Darby, 9 Mo. 131; Field v. Liverman, 17 Mo. 218; Kempland v. Macauley, Peake's N. P. C. 65; Bradley v. Wyndham, 1

intended to be enforced is immaterial.[1] A direction to the sheriff not to proceed to a sale unless urged on by younger executions will likewise render an execution void.[2] A direction after a levy has the same effect as a direction made before a levy.[3] If a countermand is given before the issuing of a second execution, the efficacy of the first execution will be restored.[4] When the direction is merely to delay for a stipulated time, the execution will be good after the expiration of that time.[5] A second execution will not be affected by the delay under a prior execution upon the same judgment.[6]

A creditor has the right to issue an execution for the purpose of being before other creditors, and thus securing or obtaining his debt. All that the law requires is that a man, without meaning to get payment himself, shall not hinder others from getting their money.[7] Consequently after he has sued out an execution, he is bound to be both prompt and honest in the steps he takes to enforce it. Delay always raises a suspicion that an execution is set on foot to protect the property from other creditors.[8]

Wils. 44 ; Hickman v. Caldwell, 4 Rawle, 376; Smallcomb v. Buckingham, 5 Mod. 375; s. c. 1 Salk. 320; s. c. 1 Ld. Raym. 251; Kellogg v. Griffin, 17 Johns. 274; Storm v. Woods, 11 Johns. 110; U. S. v. Conyngham, 4 Dall. 358; Colby v. Cressy, 5 N. H. 237; *vide* Stirling v. Van Cleve, 7 Halst. 285; Swigert v. Thomas, 7 Dana, 220.

[1] Hunt v. Hooper, 12 M. & W. 664.

[2] Pringle v. Isaacs, 11 Price, 445; Weir v. Hale, 3 W. & S. 285; Freeburger's Appeal, 40 Penn. 244; Kimball v. Munger, 2 Hill, 364; *vide* Cumberland Bank v. Hann, 4 Harrison, 166; Stirling v. Van Cleve, 7 Halst. 285.

[3] Branch Bank v. Broughton, 15 Ala. 127.

[4] Berry v. Smith, 3 Wash. C. C. 60.

[5] Benjamin v. Smith, 4 Wend. 332.

[6] Sterling v. Van Cleve, 7 Halst. 285.

[7] Smith's Appeal, 2 Penn. 331.

[8] Lovick v. Crowder, 2 Man. & Ry. 84; s. c. 8 B. & C. 132; West v. Skip, 1 Ves. Sr. 239.

DEBTOR'S POSSESSION AFTER LEVY.—The sheriff is not bound to remove the property after he has made a levy. He may leave it in the actual possession of the debtor until the day of sale, and in such case the law will consider the debtor as the sheriff's agent or bailiff.[1] If there is no intent to postpone the sale and the parties act in good faith, the creditor may also consent that the goods shall be left in the debtor's possession.[2] The debtor, however, can not be permitted to sell or consume the property for his own benefit after the levy.[3]

DELAY IN SELLING.—Delay on the part of the sheriff in enforcing an execution will not, of itself, postpone an execution unless it is so long as to raise a presumption of a consent on the part of the creditor.[4] But if the

---

[1] Cumberland Bank v. Hann, 4 Harrison, 166; Thompson v. Van Vechten, 5 Abb. Pr. 458; Eberle v. Mayer, 1 Rawle, 366; Levy v. Wallis, 4 Dall. 167; Chancellor v. Phillips, 4 Dall. 218; Casher v. Peterson, 1 South. 317; Sterling v. Van Cleve, 7 Halst. 285; Cox v. Jackson, 1 Hay. (N. C.) 423; Howell v. Alkyn, 2 Rawle, 282.

[2] Doty v. Turner, 8 Johns. 20; Rew v. Barber, 3 Cow. 272; Russell v. Gibbs, 5 Cow. 390; Cumberland Bank v. Hann, 4 Harrison, 166; Sterling v. Van Cleve, 7 Halst. 285; Howell v. Alkyn, 2 Rawle, 282; Cox v. M'Dougal, 2 Yeates, 434; Perit v. Webster, 2 Yeates, 524; *Contra*, Bucknal v. Roiston, Prec. Ch. 285; Commonwealth v. Stremback, 3 Rawle, 341; Berry v. Smith, 3 Wash. C. C. 60; Lewis v. Smith, 2 S. & R. 142; Parker v. Waugh, 34 Mo. 340.

[3] Matthews v. Warne, 6 Halst. 295; Williamson v. Johnston, 7 Halst. 86; Barnes v. Billington, 1 Wash. C. C. 29; Farrington v. Sinclair, 15 Johns. 428; Knox v. Summers, 4 Yeates, 477; Guardians v. Lawrence, 4 Yeates, 194; Swigert v. Thomas, 7 Dana, 220; Earl's Appeal, 13 Penn. 483; Cook v. Wood, 1 Harrison, 254; Cumberland Bank v. Hann, 4 Harrison, 166; Bingham v. Young, 10 Penn. 395; *vide* Adams v. Moseley, 3 Fla. 322.

[4] Russell v. Gibbs, 5 Cow. 390; Society v. Hitchcock, 2 Browne, 333; Smith's Appeal, 2 Penn. 331; Cumberland Bank v. Hann, 4 Harrison, 166; Herkimer Co. Bank v. Brown, 6 Hill, 232; Thompson v. Van Vechten, 5 Abb. Pr. 458; *vide* Weir v. Hale, 3 W. & S. 285.

time is unreasonably long, the execution will be void.[1] Merely adjourning a sale does not amount to a waiver,[2] especially when it is done for the purpose of investigating a claim to the property, which is brought forward on the day appointed for the sale.[3] A sale of wheat growing in the ground may be postponed until it is fit to be reaped.[4] When hides are in vats undergoing the process of tanning, the sale may be postponed until the process is complete.[5]

REMEDY AGAINST JUDGMENT.—A fraudulent judgment may be attacked collaterally, for it is void as against creditors.[6] It may also be set aside upon an application to the court that rendered it.[7] Such application can only be made by a judgment creditor.[8] When it is made by a proper party the court may direct an issue to try the question of fraud.[9] The issue must be in regard to the alleged fraud and not in regard to the amount due.[10] If the judgment is found to

---

[1] Lovick v. Crowder, 8 B. & C. 132; s. c. 2 Man. Ry. 84; Rice v. Serjeant, 7 Mod. 37; Doty v. Turner, 8 Johns. 20; Russell v. Gibbs, 5 Cow. 390; Benjamin v. Smith, 4 Wend. 332; Earl's Appeal, 13 Penn. 483; Cumberland Bank v. Hann, 4 Harrison, 166; Berry v. Smith, 3 Wash. C. C. 60.

[2] Paton v. Westervelt, 12 N. Y. Leg. Obs. 7.

[3] Bush's Appeal, 65 Penn. 363.

[4] Whipple v. Foot, 2 Johns. 418.

[5] Power v. Van Buren, 7 Cow. 560.

[6] Imray v. Magnay, 11 M. & W. 267; Wilhelmi v. Leonard, 13 Iowa, 330; Burns v. Morse, 6 Paige, 108; Hackett v. Manlove, 14 Cal. 85; *vide* Tyler v. Leeds, 2 Stark. 218.

[7] Frasier v. Frasier, 9 Johns. 80; Austin v. Brown, 1 Harrison, 268.

[8] Wintringham v. Wintringham, 20 Johns. 296.

[9] Whiting v. Johnston, 11 S. & R. 328; Clark v. Douglas, 62 Penn. 408; Frasier v. Frasier, 9 Johns. 80; M'Neal v. Smith, 1 Yeates, 552; Geist v. Geist, 2 Penn. 441; Sommer v. Sommer, 1 Watts, 303.

[10] Numan v. Knapp, 5 Binn. 73.

be fraudulent it can not be vacated on the record, for it is good between the parties.[1] The doctrine that a purchaser *pendente lite* is bound by a judgment does not apply in favor of a fraudulent judgment.[2]

REMEDY AGAINST EXECUTION.—A fraudulent execution, or an execution issued upon a fraudulent judgment may be treated as null and void.[3] As the mandate of the writ to the sheriff is to bring the money into court, the court has jurisdiction to determine the priorities between conflicting executions, and may set aside an execution that is fraudulent.[4] It may decide the question in a summary way,[5] but if there is any doubt upon the question of fraud, it directs an issue to try it.[6] The sheriff is not bound to try the question of fraud or to decide which of two creditors should have the preference, but he ought to stand indifferent between the parties and not lend himself to either. If he lends his aid to one party and withholds it from the other, he must stand or fall by the rights of the party to whom he lends his aid.[7] In an action against the sheriff for making a false return evidence of fraud in a prior judgment or execution is admissible when he has

---

[1] Dougherty's Estate, 9 W. & S. 189; Thompson's Appeal, 57 Penn. 185.

[2] Falconer v. Jones, 3 Dev. 334; Haywood v. Sledge, 3 Dev. 338.

[3] Lovick v. Crowder, 8 B. & C. 132; s. c. 2 Man. & Ry. 84; Christopherson v. Burton, 3 Exch. 160; s. c. 18 L. J. Exch. 60; Boardman v. Keeler, 1 Aik. 158; Farrington v. Sinclair, 15 Johns. 429.

[4] Posey v. Underwood, 1 Hill, 262; Sutton v. Pettus, 4 Rich. 163; Lovick v. Crowder, 2 Man. & Ry. 84; s. c. 8 B. & C. 132; Warmoll v. Young, 5 B. & C. 660; s. c. 8 D. & R. 442; Williamson v. Johnston, 7 Halst. 86.

[5] Williamston v. Johnston, 7 Halst. 86.

[6] Barber v. Mitchell, 2 Dowl. P. C. 574; Matthews v. Warne, 6 Halst. 295; Williamston v. Johnston, 7 Halst. 86.

[7] Warmoll v. Young, 5 B. & C. 660; s. c. 8 D. & R. 442.

notice of the fraud or could have discovered it by reasonable diligence.[1] Notice to the deputy is notice to the sheriff himself.[2]

ATTACHMENTS.— There must be an actual seizure to constitute a valid attachment, and the property must not be left under the control of the debtor.[3] If it can not be removed without great injury, as hides in a vat, or paper in the process of being manufactured, or iron ore in an open field, a removal may be dispensed with, but the sheriff must use due diligence to prevent it from being withdrawn from his control.[4] An actual removal is not indispensable. The debtor may, with the permission of the sheriff, be allowed to use such articles as will not be injured by the use.[5] Such use, however, is a badge of fraud.[6] Delay in enforcing an attachment is also evidence of fraud.[7] A prior attachment may be set aside for fraud upon the motion of a subsequent attaching creditor.[8]

---

[1] Imray v. Magnay, 11 M. & W. 267 ; Christopherson v. Burton, 3 Exch. 160 ; s. c. 18 L. J. Exch. 60 ; Fairfield v. Baldwin, 12 Pick. 388 ; Warmoll v. Young, 5 B. & C. 660 ; s. c. 8 D. & R. 442 ; vide Kempland v. Macaulay, Peake, 65.

[2] Imray v. Magnay, 11 M. & W. 267.

[3] Baldwin v. Jackson, 12 Mass. 131.

[4] Mills v. Camp, 14 Conn. 219 ; Hemminway v. Wheeler, 14 Pick. 408.

[5] Baldwin v. Jackson, 12 Mass. 131; Train v. Wellington, 12 Mass. 495.

[6] Burrows v. Stoddard, 3 Conn. 160.

[7] Reed v. Ennis, 4 Abb. Pr. 393.

[8] Smith v. Gettinger, 3 Geo. 140; Harding v. Harding, 25 Vt. 487; Blaisdell v. Ladd, 14 N. H. 129; Buckman v. Buckman, 4 N. H. 319; Webster v. Harper, 7 N. H. 594; Pike v. Pike, 24 N. H. 384; vide Whipple v. Cass, 8 Iowa, 126.

CHAPTER XXI.

EXECUTORS DE SON TORT.

WHEN GRANTEE IS.—When the grantee retains,[1] or takes the property after the death of the debtor, he may be charged as executor *de son tort*.[2] This is the only way in which the property can be reached, because in no other way can a judgment be obtained establishing the debt and authorizing process against the property as that of the deceased debtor. Unless the property, therefore, could be reached in this way, the creditors would be without remedy at law. There may be both a rightful executor and an executor *de son tort* at the same time,[3] and if the rightful executor is also a creditor, he may sue the executor *de son tort*, and recover his debt, and the fact that he is rightful executor will not obstruct his action.[4]

---

[1] Howland v. Dews, R. M. Charlt. 383.

[2] Rol. Abr. 549, 13 H. 4 f. 4, pl. 9; Stokes' Case, 3 Leon. 57; Stamford's Case, 1 Dal. 94; s. c. 2 Leon. 223; Kitchin v. Dixon, Gouldsb. 116, pl. 12; Edwards v. Harben, 2 T. R. 587; Dorsey v. Smithson, 6 H. & J. 61; Yardley v. Arnold, 1 Car. & M. 434; Sturdevant v. Davis, 9 Ired. 365; Allen v. Kimball, 15 Me. 116; Crunkleton v. Wilson, 1 Browne, 360; Densler v. Edwards, 5 Ala. 31; Wilcox v. Watson, Cro. Eliz. 405; Clayton v. Tucker, 20 Geo. 452; Howland v. Dews, R. M. Charlt. 383; Warren v. Hall, 6 Dana, 450; *vide* King v. Lyman, 1 Root, 104.

[3] Dorsey v. Smithson, 6 H. & J. 61; Foster v. Wallace, 2 Mo. 231; Chamberlayne v. Temple, 2 Rand. 384; Howland v. Dews, R. M. Charlt. 383.

[4] Dorsey v. Smithson, 6 H. & J. 61; Shields v. Anderson, 3 Leigh, 729; Osborne v. Moss, 7 Johns. 161.

It is only in the case of personal property that the grantee can be so charged, for an intermeddling with the real estate of the deceased will not make him an executor *de son tort*.[1] It has also been held that he can not be so charged when the property has been sold before the decease of the debtor, although he retains the proceeds.[2] He is as responsible when he applies the property to his own use as if he applies it to other uses not sanctioned by law.[3]

How sued.—An executor *de son tort* may be sued wherever he may be found without reference to the jurisdiction in which the intermeddling with the property took place. A person who takes the property of the decedent in one State and there sells it without legal authority, and removes to another without having disbursed the proceeds in payment of debts or otherwise legally accounted for them, may be charged as executor *de son tort* in the latter State.[4] An executor *de son tort* is, in most respects, considered and treated as executor, and all lawful acts which he does, or payments which he makes in a due course of administration are allowed to him. The same form of action is used against him. He is not described as a wrongful executor, but simply alleged to be the executor. He may be joined with the rightful executor in an action against them. He, therefore, can plead any plea which a rightful executor may. The form of the judgment upon the plea of *ne unques executor* is *de bonis testatoris si vel non de bonis propriis*.[5] He can not, however, de-

---

[1] King v. Lyman, 1 Root, 104.

[2] Morrill v. Morrill, 13 Me. 415.

[3] Stephens v. Barnett, 7 Dana, 257.

[4] Densler v. Edwards, 5 Ala. 31.

[5] Howland v. Dews, R. M. Charlt. 383 ; Stephens v. Barnett, 7 Dana, 257.

rive any benefit from his wrongful act, and consequently can not retain for his debt.[1]

WHEN GRANTEE IS HEIR OR ADMINISTRATOR.—In
case of a fraudulent conveyance of land to the person
who becomes the debtor's heir, the deed is deemed void
and he takes as heir,[2] so far as creditors are concerned
and is liable for the debts of his ancestor. If the
transfer in such a case consists of personal property, he
may be considered as holding it either as heir or executor *de son tort*.[3] When the grantee is also devisee the
property may be considered as assets by devise.[4] If
the grantee is also executor the property is assets in his
hands.[5] Property fraudulently conveyed is a part of the
deceased debtor's estate,[6] and constitutes legal and not
equitable assets.[7] When the grantee is neither heir
nor devisee, nor personal representative, the only remedy of the creditor is against the thing granted or the
grantee.[8]

---

[1] Shields v. Anderson, 3 Leigh, 729.

[2] Humberton v. Howgill, Hob. 72 ; O'Connor v. Bernard, 2 Jo. 654 ;
Harrison v. Campbell, 6 Dana, 263.

[3] Warren v. Hall, 6 Dana, 450.

[4] Manhattan Co. v. Osgood, 15 Johns. 162; s. c. 3 Cow. 612.

[5] Burckmyers v. Mairs, Riley, 208; Marr v. Rucker, 1 Humph. 348;
Jackson v. Bowley, 1 Car. & M. 97; *vide* Backhouse v. Jett, 1 Brock.
500.

[6] Anon. 2 Rol. Rep. 173.

[7] Shee v. French, 3 Drew. 716.

[8] Ralls v. Graham, 4 Mon. 120; Harrison v. Campbell, 6 Dana, 263.

CHAPTER XXII.

No injunction to prevent sale.—It is only by the acquisition of a lien that a creditor has any vested or specified right in the property of his debtor. Be fore such lien is acquired the debtor has full dominion over his property. He may convert one species of property into another, and he may alienate to a purchaser. The rights of the debtor and those of the creditors are thus defined by positive rules, and the point at which the power of the debtor ceases and the rights of the creditors commence is clearly established. A creditor without such lien can not obtain an injunction to prevent the debtor from disposing of his property, although he has reason to apprehend that such disposition may be fraudulent.[1]

Actions against grantee.—If a fraudulent disposition has actually been made by the debtor of his property, a creditor can not, in the absence of special legislation, bring an action in assumpsit,[2] or on the case,[3] against those who combined and colluded with

---

[1] Uhl v. Dillon, 10 Md. 500; Rich v. Levy, 16 Md. 74; Hubbard v. Hubbard, 14 Md. 356; Moran v. Dawes, Hopk. 365; Wiggins v. Armstrong, 2 Johns. Ch. 144; Brooks v. Stone, 11 Abb. Pr. 220; s. c. 19 How. Pr. 395.

[2] Aspinwall v. Jones, 17 Mo. 209; Kelsey v. Murphy, 26 Penn. 78.

[3] Adler v. Fenton, 24 How. 407; Lamb v. Stone, 11 Pick. 527; Wellington v. Small, 3 Cush. 145; Smith v. Blake, 1 Day, 258; Green v. Kim-

him.   Assumpsit will not lie, for there is neither an express promise nor a privity from which the law will
imply a promise to pay the debt of the creditor.   An
action on the case can not be supported because the
damages are too contingent and remote.   As a creditor
has no special title in or to the property of the debtor,
the only proof of loss or injury which he could make
would be that the debtor had fraudulently conveyed it
away without receiving any value for it with the intent to avoid the payment of his demand, and that he
had no other means of obtaining payment.   Upon such
proof he would not be entitled to recover the amount
of his debt, for that would still be subsisting, and
might yet be collected.   Nor would he be entitled to recover the value of the property conveyed, for to that he
has no better claim than other creditors.   The only loss
or injury which could be shown would be that he has
been deprived of a chance or possibility of obtaining
payment from that property.   The loss would not even
be so great as this, for he might still have a chance of
reaching the property or its proceeds in the hands of
the fraudulent holder.   The value of his chance to secure it and have it applied to the payment of his debt
while in the hands of the debtor is all that he has lost
and would be the only basis upon which a jury would
be authorized to estimate his damages.   There are no
data, tables, or other means by which such a chance can
be estimated.   The loss or injury is too uncertain and
remote for legal estimation.   The action can only be
maintained by proof of a direct, certain, and material

---

ble, 6 Blackf. 552; Gardiner v. Sherrod, 2 Hawks. 173; Moody v. Burton,
27 Me. 427; Mowry v. Schroder, 4 Strobh. 69; *Contra*, Penrod v. Morrison, 2 Penna. 126; Mott v. Danforth, 6 Watts, 304; Meredith v. Benning,
1 H. & M. 585; Hopkins v. Beebe, 26 Penn. 85; Kelsey v. Murphy, 26
Penn. 78.

injury. If the creditor, however, has a lien upon the property which has been defeated by the transfer, his damages are sufficiently direct to sustain the action.[1]

CHANGE OF REMEDY.—When the debtor institutes proceedings to reach the property fraudulently conveyed, he may resort to the remedy in force at the time the transfer was made, or any remedy which has been subsequently given. His rights are not affected by the fact that by a subsequent improvement or alteration in the law a better and more effectual or different mode of reaching the property has been created.[2]

ACTIONS AT LAW.—A fraudulent transfer is void at law as well as in equity. It is treated as a nullity everywhere, and a court of law takes cognizance of the fraud as well a court of equity. In suits at law the question is generally tried in a suit against the sheriff for a false return if he omits to levy, or in an action of trespass or trover if he improperly levies upon the goods of a third person, or by an action directly against the execution creditor for directing the levy, or in trover or detinue against the purchaser at the sheriff's sale, or in an attachment suit. In relation to real estate the question is usually tried in an action of ejectment by the purchaser under the sheriff against the tenant in possession claiming under the disputed title. There are some instances where the remedy at law is deficient. Thus there is no remedy at law when the property can not be taken on execution or by attachment. In some States it is also held that property fraudulently purchased in the name of another can not be reached in an

---

[1] Smith v. Tonstall, Carthew, 3; Yates v. Joyce, 11 Johns. 136; Adams v. Paige, 7 Pick. 542; Pickett v. Pickett, 2 Hill Ch. 470.

[2] Blenkinsopp v. Blenkinsopp, 1 D. M. & G. 495; s. c. 12 Beav. 568; s. c. 21 L. J. Ch. 401.

action at law.[1]   In general, however, relief may be had
at law as well as in equity, and the determination of the
question of fraud can not be withdrawn from the forum
which the creditor selects.[2]   Fraud may be given in
evidence under a general issue which raises the question
of title to the property.[3]   When a bond of conveyance
is fraudulent, its validity can only be tested by a sale
and not by an attachment.[4]

BILL IN EQUITY.—The remedy most frequently used
is a bill in equity, because a court of equity sifts the
conscience of the parties and removes the cloud from
the title.   Fraud constitutes the most ancient foundation of its jurisdiction,[5] and is a sufficient ground
for its interposition.   It may grant relief although
there is ample remedy at law, for no relief is adequate except that which removes the fraudulent title.[6]
The relief in equity is different and may be more

---

[1] Howe v. Bishop, 3 Met. 26; Garfield v. Hatmaker, 15 N. Y. 475;
Page v. Goodman, 8 Ired. Eq. 16; Worth v. York, 13 Ired. 206; Davis
v. M'Kinney, 5 Ala. 719; Davis v. Tibbetts, 39 Me. 279; Gray v. Faris, 7
Yerg. 155; Dewey v. Long, 25 Vt. 564; Gowing v. Rich, 1 Ired. 553;
Garrett v. Rhame, 9 Rich. 407; Jimmerson v. Duncan, 3 Jones, (N. C.) 537;
Low v. Marco, 53 Me. 45; Webster v. Folsom, 58 Me. 230; Hamilton v.
Cone, 99 Mass. 478; Contra, Guthrie v. Gardner, 9 Wend. 414; Arnot v.
Beadle, 1 Hill. & D. 181; Tevis v. Doe, 3 Ind. 129; Pennington v. Clif-
ton, 11 Ind. 162; Kimmel v. M'Right, 2 Penn. 38; Coleman v. Cocke, 6
Rand. 618; Cecil Bank v. Snively, 23 Md. 253; Cutter v. Griswold, Walk.
Ch. 437; Roe v. Irwin, 32 Geo. 39; Godding v. Brackett, 34 Me. 27;
Hunt v. Blodgett, 17 Ill. 583.

[2] Marriott v. Givens, 8 Ala. 694.

[3] Gooch's Case, 5 Co. 60; Ashby v. Minnitt, 8 A. & E. 121.

[4] Stewart v. Coder, 11 Penn. 90.

[5] Hungerford v. Earle, 2 Vern. 261; Hartshorne v. Eames, 31 Me. 93;
Lillard v. M'Gee, 4 Bibb. 165.

[6] Tappan v. Evans, 11 N. H. 311; Bennett v. Musgrove, 2 Ves. Sr. 51;
Dodge v. Griswold, 8 N. H. 425; Blenkinsopp v. Blenkinsopp, 1 D. M. &
G. 495; Sheafe v. Sheafe, 40 N. H. 516; Jones v. Henry, 3 Litt. 427;
Mountford v. Taylor, 6 Ves. 788; Lewkner v. Freeman, 2 Freem. 236;

beneficial than that given by the law. But jurisdiction is not assumed upon the ground either that the subject is appropriate to a court of equity as a court of peculiar jurisdiction, or because that court proceeds upon an interpretation of the statute distinct and different from that given at law.[1] On the contrary it is entertained in equity notwithstanding it exists at law, and thus entertained because such deceitful practices dishonest in their concoction, progress, and consummation are so abhorrent to every tribunal of justice that every tribunal has authority and is bound to relieve against them according to their respective capacities and methods of proceeding, and because the relief peculiar to a court of equity is more perfect than at law.[2]

WHEN NO REMEDY AT LAW.—There are some cases where a remedy will be given in equity even though there is none at law. If the debtor fraudulently purchases property in the name of another, equity treats the grantee as trustee for the creditors, and subjects the property to their demands.[3] A court of equity will

Planters' Bank v. Walker, 7 Ala. 926; Sheppard v. Iverson, 12 Ala. 97; Traip v. Gould, 15 Me. 82; Bean v. Smith, 2 Mason, 252; Lillard v. M'Gee, 4 Bibb. 165; Buck v. Sherman, 2 Doug. 176; Fowler v. McCartney, 27 Miss. 509; Cook v. Johnson, 1 Beasley, 51; Musselman v. Kent, 33 Ind. 452; Cox v. Dunham, 4 Halst. Ch. 594; Swift v. Avents, 4 Cal. 390; Brandon v. Gowring, 6 Rich. Eq. 5; Abbey v. Banks, 31 Miss. 43; Phillips v. Wesson, 16 Geo. 137.

[1] Russell v. Hammond, 1 Atk. 13.

[2] Dobson v. Erwin, 1 Dev. & Bat. 569.

[3] Godbold v. Lambert, 8 Rich. Eq. 155; Odenheimer v. Hanson, 4 M'Lean, 437; Patterson v. Campbell, 9 Ala. 933; State Bank v. Harrow, 26 Iowa, 426; Smith v. McCann, 24 How. 398; Gardiner Bank v. Wheaton, 8 Me. 373; Smith v. Parker, 41 Me. 452; Bertrand v. Elder, 23 Ark. 494; Corey v. Greene, 51 Me. 114; Marshall v. Marshall, 2 Bush. 415; Brown v. M'Donald, 1 Hill Ch. 297; Halbert v. Grant, 4 Mon. 580; Dockray v. Mason, 48 Me. 178; Bay v. Cook, 31 Ill. 336; Belford v. Crane, 1

also afford a remedy against *choses in action*, stock, and other species of property not liable to an execution at law. Any distinction between property which may and property which may not be taken on execution is inconsistent with the rights which result from the relation of debtor and creditor, and has no foundation in just reasoning. It makes the rights of the creditors depend upon the form and character which the fraud or caprice of the debtor may give to his property. It is difficult to perceive any solid reason why the intangible property and effects of a debtor shall not be subjected to the payment of his debts equally with his chattels, which may be the subject of seizure a u sale under an execution at law. The abstract rights of the creditors are as perfect in the one case as in the other. The spirit of an enlightened jurisprudence requires that the property rights and interests of a debtor, whatever may be their form, if they have an ascertained value, shall be subject to the payment of his debts. Any other rule leads to fraud upon the creditors and encourages dishonesty in the debtor, who would only have to convert his property into the bond or promissory note of a third person or into stock of some kind and then settle the same upon his family in order to obtain a perfect immunity from his creditors.[1] A court of equity, therefore, for the

---

C. E. Green, 265 ; Peay v. Sublet, 1 Mo. 449 ; Newell v. Morgan, 2 Harring. 225 ; Demaru v. Driskell, 3 Blackf. 115 ; McDowell v. Cochran, 11 Ill. 31 ; Walcott v. Almy, 6 McLean, 23 ; Gentry v. Harper, 2 Jones Eq. 177 ; Rucker v. Abell, 8 B. Mon. 566 ; Gordon v. Lowell, 21 Me. 251.

[1] Wright v. Petrie, 1 S. & M. Ch. 282 ; Green v. Tantum, 4 C. E. Green, 105 ; s. c. 6 C. E. Green, 364 ; Alexander v. Tams, 13 Ill. 221 ; Odenheimer v. Hanson, 4 McLean, 437 ; Tappan v. Evans, 11 N. H. 311 ; Chase v. Searles, 45 N. H. 511 ; Weed v. Pierce, 9 Cow. 722 ; Taylor v. Jones, 2 Atk. 600 ; Catchings v. Manlove, 39 Miss. 655 ; Partridge v. Gopp, Ambl. 596 ; Hadden v. Spader, 5 Johns. Ch. 280 ; s. c. 20 Johns. 554 ; Hartshorne v. Eames, 31 Me. 93 ; West v. Saunders, 1 A. K. Marsh. 108 ; Bean v. Smith, 2 Mason,

purpose of enforcing justice, holds the fraudulent grantee as the trustee of those whom he defrauds, and takes jurisdiction to administer this trust.[1] Wherever *choses in action*, or other property of a similar character are liable to execution or attachment, the jurisdiction of a court of equity is unquestionable.[2]

CREDITOR MUST HAVE LIEN.—A fraudulent transfer is valid against all persons except those who proceed to appropriate the property by due course of law to the satisfaction of the grantor's debts. As it is valid against a simple contract creditor, such creditor can not ask the aid of a court of equity to set aside the transfer, for it does not interfere with his rights. Equity has jurisdiction of fraud, but it does not collect debts. A creditor must establish his demand at law, and obtain a lien upon the property, before the transfer interferes with his rights or he has any title to claim relief in equity.[3] No creditor can be said to be delayed, hin-

---

252; Harlan v. Barnes, 5 Dana, 219; Bay Iron Co. v. Goodall, 39 N. H. 221; Chase v. Searles, 45 N. H. 511; Treadwell v. Brown, 44 N. H. 551; Smithier v. Lewis, 1 Vern. 398; Anon. 1 Eq. Abr. 132; Sargent v. Salmond, 27 Me. 539; Greer v. Wright, 6 Gratt. 154; Manchester v. McKee, 4 Gilman, 511; *Contra*, Dundas v. Dutens, 1 Ves. Jr. 196; s. c. 2 Cox, 235; Rider v. Kidder, 10 Ves. 360; s. c. 12 Ves. 202; s. c. 13 Ves. 123; Matthews v. Feaver, 1 Cox, 278; Grogan v. Cooke, 2 Ball. & B. 233; Sims v. Thomas, 12 A. & E. 536; s. c. 4 P. & D. 233; s. c. 9 L. J. (N. S.) 2 B. 399; Norcutt v. Dodd, 1 Cr. & Ph. 100; Duffin v. Furness, Sel. Cas. Ch. 77; Caillaud v. Estwick, 1 Anst. 381; Stewart v. English, 6 Ind. 176; Cosby v. Ross, 3 J. J. Marsh. 290; Winebrenner v. Weisiger, 3 Mon. 32; Crozier v. Young, 3 Mon. 157; Bickley v. Norris, 2 Brev. 252. In some States this remedy is regulated by statute, but such statutes are generally considered as merely declaratory.

[1] Bean v. Smith, 2 Mason, 252.

[2] Patterson v. Campbell, 9 Ala. 933; Wright v. Petrie, 1 S. & M. Ch. 282.

[3] Meux v. Anthony, 11 Ark. 411; Smith v. Hurst, 10 Hare, 30; M'Kinley v. Combs, 1 Mon. 105; Griffith v. Bank, 6 G. & J. 424; Day v. Washburn, 24 How. 352; Jones v. Green, 1 Wall. 330; Coleman v. Croker, 1 Ves. Jr. 160; Collins v. Burton, 4 De G. & J. 612; Angell v. Draper, 1 Vern. 399; Brinkerhoff v. Brown, 4 Johns. Ch. 671; s. c. 6 Johns. Ch. 139;

dered, or defrauded by any conveyance until some property out of which he has a specific right to be satisfied
is withdrawn from his reach by a fraudulent conveyance. Such specific right does not exist until he has
bound the property by judgment or by judgment and
execution as the case may be, and has shown that he is
defrauded by the conveyance in consequence of not
being able to procure satisfaction of his debt in a due
course of law. Then, and then only, he acquires a specific right to be satisfied out of the property conveyed,
and shows that he is a creditor, and is delayed, hindered,
and defrauded by the conveyance. When a party has
thus brought himself within the the the terms of the statute,
he is entitled to the assistance of a court of equity to
remove the impediment to his legal rights. In this respect there is no distinction between the creditors of an
individual and the creditors of a partnership.[1]

Webster v. Clark, 25 Me. 313; Webster v. Withey, 25 Me. 326; Coleman v.
Cocke, 6 Rand. 618; Halbert v. Grant, 4 Mon. 580; Carter v. Bennett, 4 Fla.
283; Barrow v. Bailey, 5 Fla. 9; Hendricks v. Robinson, 2 Johns. Ch. 283;
s. c. 17 Johns. 438; Beck v. Burdett, 1 Paige, 305; Jones v. Green, 1 Wall.
330; Cropsey v. McKinney, 30 Barb. 47; Neustadt v. Joel, 2 Duer, 530;
Willets v. Vandenburgh, 34 Barb. 424; Williams v. Brown, 4 Johns. Ch.
682; Lawton v. Levy, 2 Edw. 197; Reubens v. Joel, 13 N. Y. 488; Greenwood v. Brodhead, 8 Barb. 593; Hall v. Joiner, 1 Rich. (N. S.) 186; Allen
v. Camp, 1 Mon. 231; Horner v. Zimmerman, 45 Ill. 14; Stone v. Manning,
2 Scam. 530; Rhodes v. Cousins, 6 Rand. 188; Tate v. Liggatt, 2 Leigh,
84; Kelso v. Blackburn, 3 Leigh, 299; Taylor v. Robinson, 7 Allen, 253;
Ishmael v. Parker, 13 Ill. 324; Duberry v. Clifton, Cooke, 328; Lister v.
Turner, 5 Hare, 281; Colman v. Croker, 1 Ves. Jr. 160. It has recently
been decided in England that a creditor at large may file a bill but that
the court will only set the transfer aside and leave him to pursue his remedy at law; Reese River Mining Co. v. Atwell, L. R. 7 Eq. 347. In the
following States the right to file a bill is given to a simple contract creditor by statute, viz., Maryland, Code, Art. 16, sec. 35; Virginia, Code, ch.
179, sec. 2; West Virginia, Code, ch. 133; Tenn. Code, §§ 4288, 4289; vide
Crompton v. Anthony, 13 Allen, 33.

[1] Dunlevy v. Tallmadge, 32 N. Y. 457; s. c. 29 How. Pr. 397; s. c. 18
Abb. Pr. 48; Young v. Frier, 1 Stockt. 465; vide Lawton v. Levy, 2 Edw.
97.

WHAT LIENS SUFFICIENT.—The claim for relief rests upon the fact that the creditor has acquired a specific lien upon the property, and that the obstruction interposed prevents a sale at a fair valuation. The bill is filed to remove the obstruction in order that the creditor may obtain a full price for the property. He must, therefore, proceed at law until he obtains such lien. In the case of land a judgment alone is commonly sufficient.[1] An execution, however, must be issued in order to obtain a lien on personal property.[2] If the execution is returned the lien is lost and a bill can not then be filed.[3] Another execution, however, may be issued, and the lien thus acquired will be sufficient to support a bill.[4] A lien by attachment,[5] or warrant of distress,[6] is as good as a lien by execution. Mere garnishment is not sufficient.[7] A party to whom a judgment is assigned

[1] Vasser v. Henderson, 40 Miss. 519; McCalmont v. Lawrence, 1 Blatch. 232; Gates v. Boomer, 17 Wis. 455; Cornell v. Radway, 22 Wis. 260; Mohawk Bank v. Atwater, 2 Paige, 54 ; Clarkson v. De Peyster, 3 Paige, 320; Shaw v. Dwight, 27 N. Y. 244; Dargan v. Waring, 11 Ala. 988; Newman v. Willetts, 52 Ill. 98; Weightman v. Hatch, 17 Ill. 281. In the following cases it has been held that an execution must be issued: N. A. Ins. Co. v. Graham, 5 Sandf. 197; McCullough v. Colby, 5 Bosw. 477; s. c. 4 Bosw. 603; Dana v. Haskill, 41 Me. 25.

[2] Jones v. Green, 1 Wall. 330; Clark v. Banner, 1 Dev. & Bat. Eq. 608; Anon. Eq. Cas. Abr. 77, pl. 14; Thurmond v. Reese, 3 Kelly, 449; Stephens v. Beall, 4 Geo. 319 ; Heye v. Bolles, 33 How. Pr. 266.

[3] Forbes v. Logan, 4 Bosw. 475; Watrous v. Lathrop, 4 Sandf. 700 ; vide Williams v. Hubbard, Walk. Ch. 28.

[4] Cuyler v. Moreland, 7 Paige, 273.

[5] Hunt v. Field, 1 Stockt. 36; Heyneman v. Dannenberg, 6 Cal. 376; Castle v. Bader, 23 Cal. 75; Dodge v. Griswold, 8 N. H. 425; Stone v. Anderson, 26 N. H. 506 ; Heye v. Bolles, 2 Daly, 231; Falconer v. Freeman, 4 Sandf. Ch. 565; Scales v. Scott, 13 Cal. 76; Greenleaf v. Mumford, 19 Abb. Pr. 469; s. c. 30 How. Pr. 30; vide Martin v. Michael, 23 Mo. 50; Melville v. Brown, 1 Harrison, 363; Mills v. Block, 30 Barb. 549; Mechanics' Bank v. Dakin, 28 How. Pr. 502.

[6] Allen v. Camp, 1 Mon. 231; vide Belknap v. Hastings, 1 Denio, 190.

[7] Bigelow v. Andress, 31 Ill. 322.

33

after the issuing of an execution need not have a new execution issued.[1]

RETURN OF EXECUTION UNSATISFIED WHEN PROPERTY NOT LIABLE AT LAW.—There are several exceptions to the rule which requires the creation of a lien prior to the filing of a bill in equity. One exception is where the property is such that it can not be taken on an execution at law. The creditor's right to relief in such case depends upon the fact of his having exhausted his legal remedies without being able to obtain satisfaction. The best and the only evidence of this is the actual return of an execution unsatisfied. The creditor must obtain judgment, issue an execution, and procure a return of *nulla bona* before he can file a bill in equity to obtain satisfaction out of the property of the debtor which can not be reached at law.[2] A return before the return day of the writ is sufficient if the bill is not filed until after the return day.[3] Whether a return before the return day is sufficient alone, is a point upon which the decisions vary.[4] If property purchased in the name of another is not liable to an execution at law, there must be a return of the execution.[5]

---

[1] Hastings v. Palmer, Clarke, 52.

[2] Beck v. Burdett, 1 Paige, 305; Heacock v. Durand, 42 Ill. 230; Clarkson v. De Peyster, 3 Paige, 320; Crippen v. Hudson, 13 N. Y. 161; McElwain v. Willis, 9 Wend. 548; Taylor v. Persee, 15 How. Pr. 417; Beach v. White, Walk. Ch. 495; Tappan v. Evans, 11 N. H. 311; Williams v. Hubbard, Walk. Ch. 28; Brown v. Bank, 31 Miss. 454; Chittenden v. Brewster, 2 Wall. 191; Jones v. Green, 1 Wall. 330; Green v. Tantum, 4 C. E. Green, 105; s. c. 6 C. E. Green, 364; Griffin v. Nitcher, 57 Me. 270; McCartney v. Bostwick, 31 Barb. 390; s. c. 32 N. Y. 53.

[3] Forbes v. Waller, 4 Bosw. 475; s. c. 25 N. Y. 430; Reynaud v. O'Brien, 35 N. Y. 99; s. c. 25 How. Pr. 67; Suydam v. Beals, 4 McLean, 12; Knauth v. Bassett, 34 Barb. 31.

[4] Forbes v. Waller, 25 N. Y. 430; s. c. 4 Bosw. 475; s. c. 25 How. Pr. 166; Bowen v. Parkhurst, 24 Ill. 257; *vide* Reynaud v. O'Brien, 25 How. Pr. 67; s. c. 35 N. Y. 99; Beach v. White, Walk. Ch. 495.

[5] Des Brisay v. Hogan, 53 Me. 554; Corey v. Greene, 51 Me. 114. Under

SECOND EXECUTION.—Where the right to file a bill to reach property not liable to seizure at law once exists by the return of an execution unsatisfied, if the debtor has either real or personal property which is a proper subject of sale on execution, but which is fraudulently transferred or incumbered for the purpose of protecting it from the execution of the creditor, and has other property which can only be reached by the aid of a court of equity, the creditor may sue out a second execution so as to obtain a specific lien upon the property which is subject to a sale thereon, and may then file a bill for the double purpose of removing the obstruction which has been fraudulently interposed against the execution at law, and also to reach other property of the debtor which can not be sold on the second execution.[1]

KIND OF JUDGMENTS.—A bill may be filed to enforce a decree in equity,[2] or a magistrate's judgment,[3] or a judgment by confession,[4] as well as a regular judgment at law. A judgment in an attachment suit when the debtor has not been summoned,[5] or a foreign judgment,[6]

---

the New York statutes there is, in such a case, a resulting trust, which may be reached by simple contract creditors; McCartney v. Bostwick, 32 N. Y. 53; s. c. 31 Barb. 390; Wood v. Robinson, 22 N. Y. 564; *vide* Ocean Natl. Bank v. Olcott, 46 N. Y. 12.

[1] Cuyler v. Moreland, 7 Paige, 273; Wright v. Petrie, 1 S. & M. Ch. 282.

[2] Farnsworth v. Straster, 12 Ill. 482; Clarkson v. De Peyster, 3 Paige, 320; Weightman v. Hatch, 17 Ill. 281.

[3] Bailey v. Burton, 8 Wend. 339; Crippen v. Hudson, 13 N. Y. 161; Harlan v. Barnes, 5 Dana, 219; Newdigate v. Lee, 9 Dana, 17; Ballentine v. Beall, 3 Scam. 203.

[4] Neusbaum v. Klein, 24 N. Y. 325.

[5] Manchester v. McKee, 4 Gilman, 511; *vide* Bailey v. Burton, 8 Wend. 339.

[6] McCartney v. Bostwick, 31 Barb. 390; s. c. 32 N. Y. 53; Farned v. Harris, 11 S. & M. 366; Berryman v. Sullivan, 13 S. & M. 65; *vide* Tarbell v. Griggs, 3 Paige, 207; Bullitt v. Taylor, 34 Miss. 708.

or process that is void is not sufficient.[1] Where a judgment is recovered against joint debtors upon service of process on any number less than the whole, a bill can not be maintained to interfere with any disposition of the separate property of those who have not been served,[2] but a transfer of the joint property may be set aside.[3] In such case, however, the persons who have not been served should be made parties.[4]

EQUITABLE DEMAND.—A second exception to the rule which requires a party to obtain a lien is in the case of a claim which is purely equitable and such as a court of equity will take cognizance of in the first instance. A party who holds such a claim may, when he looks altogether and exclusively to a court of equity and files a bill to enforce his demand, add a prayer for an auxilliary decree to remove obstructions fraudulently interposed to defeat or embarrass the remedial action of the court.[5]

WHEN DEBTOR DIES.—A third exception to the rule which requires a lien, is in a case where the debtor dies before a judgment is obtained against him. In such a case an action against his executor or administrator would be useless, for a judgment would not be evidence for any purpose against the grantee, and after as well as before its rendition an action against the grantee would necessarily be upon the original debt,

---

[1] Guerin v. Hunt, 6 Min. 375; s. c. 8 Minn. 477.

[2] Bilhofer v. Heubach, 15 Abb. Pr. 143; Field v. Chapman, 15 Abb. Pr. 434; s. c. 14 Abb. Pr. 133.

[3] Bilhofer v. Heubach, 15 Abb. Pr. 143.

[4] Howard v. Sheldon, 11 Paige, 558.

[5] Halbert v. Grant, 4 Mon. 580; Waller v. Todd, 3 Dana, 503; *vide* Williams v. Tipton, 5 Humph. 66; McDermott v. Blois, R. M. Charlt. 281.

and not upon the judgment.[1] An action against his
heirs would be equally nugatory, for they are only liable to creditors to the extent, interest, and right in the
real estate which descends to them from the debtor. A
fraudulent deed, however, binds the heirs as well as the
debtor, and upon an issue of *riens per descent* the judgment would be in their favor.[2] A court of equity,
however, is authorized by the principles which regulate
its jurisdiction to interpose at whatever point in the
progress of the legal remedy, it may appear that the
creditor is actually obstructed by the fraudulent transfer or its consequences. As there is no person at law
against whom a judgment can be obtained so as to affect
the property, the demand is dependent on equity for
its ascertainment and enforcement. A court of equity
will, therefore, take jurisdiction though there is no
judgment.[3] A bill in such a case is not an application
for the exercise of the auxiliary jurisdiction of the
court, but is a part of its original jurisdiction in
equity.[4]

EXECUTOR DE SON TORT.—This is the reason why it

---

[1] Loomis v. Tifft. 16 Barb. 541; Bireley v. Staley, 5 G. & J. 432.

[2] Loomis v. Tifft, 16 Barb. 541.

[3] Harrison v. Campbell, 6 Dana, 263; Bay v. Cook, 31 Ill. 336; Trippe
v. Ward, 2 Kelly, 304; Lynch v. Raleigh, 3 Ind. 273; Hagan v. Walker,
14 How. 29; Frazer v. Western, 1 Barb. Ch. 220; s. c. 1 How. App. Cas.
448; Loomis v. Tifft, 16 Barb. 541; Steere v. Hoagland, 39 Ill. 264; Watts
v. Gayle, 20 Ala. 817; Pharis v. Leachman, 20 Ala. 662; Bireley v. Staley,
5 G. & J. 432; Snodgrass v. Andrews, 30 Miss. 472; Winn v. Barnett, 31
Miss. 653; McDowell v. Cochran, 11 Ill. 31; O'Brien v. Coulter, 2 Blackf.
421; Merry v. Fremon, 44 Mo. 518; Chamberlayne v. Temple, 2 Rand,
384; *vide* Parstowe v. Weedon, 1 Eq. Cas. Abr. 149; Brunsden v. Stratton,
Prec. Ch. 520; Brown v. McDonald, 1 Hill Ch. 297; Scriven v. Bostwick,
2 McCord. Ch. 410; Mugge v. Ewing, 54 Ill. 236.

[4] Hagan v. Walker, 14 How. 29; Frazer v. Western, 1 Barb. Ch. 220;
s. c. 1 How. App. Cas. 448; Hampson v. Sumner, 18 Ohio, 444; Mc-
Naughtin v. Lamb, 2 Ind. 642; Snodgrass v. Andrews, 30 Miss. 472.

is not necessary in the case of personal property to bind it by an action against the grantee as executor *de son tort*. All the creditors have a specific right to be satisfied out of the property of their deceased debtor in the hands of his executor or administrator, if there is a rightful executor or administrator, or, if not, in the hands of his executor *de son tort*, or if there is a rightful executor or administrator, and also an executor *de son tort* out of the debtor's property in the hands of the latter, if there are not sufficient assets in the hands of the former. This is in the nature of a lien, and the executor or administrator and executor *de son tort* are in the nature of trustees for the creditors. A creditor has a right, therefore, to go originally into a court of equity against the grantee as executor *de son tort* for a discovery, account, and satisfaction out of the assets in his hands, and in that suit to establish his demand and to show that he can not get satisfaction otherwise, and so is hindered, delayed, and defrauded.[1]

NON-RESIDENTS.—Whether judgment must be obtained against a non-resident before a bill can be filed is a point upon which the decisions vary.[2]

WHEN OBJECTION MAY BE TAKEN.—The objection that a party has not obtained a lien or exhausted his remedy at law is one that may be taken at the hearing,[3] and is not obviated by the rendition of a judgment after the filing of the bill.[4]

WHEN RELIEF GRANTED.—A bill may be filed as soon as a deed is executed, although it has not

---

[1] Chamberlayne v. Temple, 2 Rand. 384.

[2] Anderson v. Bradford, 5 J. J. Marsh. 69; Scott v. M'Millen, 1 Litt. 302; Greenway v. Thomas, 14 Ill. 271.

[3] Tappan v. Evans, 11 N. H. 311; Meux v. Anthony, 11 Ark. 411; Brown v. Bank, 31 Miss. 454.

[4] Brown v. Bank, 31 Miss. 454.

been delivered or accepted, for the creditor is not bound to levy upon the property and take the risk of the litigation that may ensue.[1] A court of equity will interpose to prevent the use of a fraudulent judgment,[2] but will not vacate it.[3] The right to impeach a fraudulent transfer is not affected by the fact that the debtor may have other property. The creditor has the choice of the part upon which he will levy and the debtor can not take away the election.[4] If the creditor, however, has a security, that may be first applied to his debt before other property is appropriated towards its payment, he may be compelled to exhaust the security.[5] A court of equity exercises some discretion,[6] and will not interfere where there is an improper combination between the debtor and the creditor to the prejudice of the grantee.[7]

DEBTOR'S BANKRUPTCY.—If the debtor is declared a bankrupt, the title to the property vests in his assignee. Creditors can not levy upon it,[8] or claim property which has otherwise been fraudulently withheld.[9] The assignee may file a bill in equity to set aside a fraudulent conveyance,[10] and this right is vested in him exclusive-

---

[1] Gasper v. Bennett, 12 How. Pr. 417.

[2] Shaw v. Dwight, 27 N. Y. 244; Burns v. Morse, 6 Paige, 108; Clark v. Bailey, 2 Strobh. Eq. 143.

[3] Kaupe v. Bridge, 2 Robt. 459.

[4] Vasser v. Henderson, 40 Miss. 519; Wadsworth v. Havens, 3 Wend. 411; Wadsworth v. Williams, 100 Mass. 126; Gaylord v. Coruch, 5 Day, 223; Botsford v. Beers, 11 Conn. 369; vide Eigleberger v. Kibler, 1 Hill. Ch. 113; M'New v. Smith, 5 Gratt. 84.

[5] Coutts v. Greenhow, 2 Munf. 363; s. c. 4 H. & M. 485.

[6] Bennett v. Musgrove, 2 Ves. Sr. 52.

[7] Hemphill v. Hemphill, 34 Miss. 68.

[8] Williams v. Merritt, 103 Mass. 184.

[9] Codman v. Freeman, 3 Cush. 306; vide Hollinshed v. Allen, 17 Penn. 275.

[10] Carr v. Hilton, 1 Curt. 230; Pratt v. Curtis, 6 B. R. 139; Bradshaw v. Klein, 1 B. R. 146; Shirley v. Long, 6 Rand. 735; Shackleford v. Col-

ly.[1] If a creditor, however, has obtained a lien, he may continue the prosecution of a suit instituted prior to the commencement of the proceedings in bankruptcy.[2] When the bill is filed by the assignee the creditors are equitable though not necessary parties, and may be joined.[3] If the assignee declines to act, the creditors may file a bill and make him a party defendant.[4] They may also proceed in the same way when an administrator who is authorized by law to institute such proceedings declines to do so.[5]

OTHER PARTIES.—A receiver appointed under proceedings supplemental to an execution,[6] and the sheriff, when he has levied an attachment,[7] may file a bill. An assignee holding under a voluntary assignment can not.[8] A party who has purchased at a sale under an execution may file a bill to remove the cloud on his title and the impediment to his quiet enjoyment of the property.[9]

---

lier, 6 Bush. 149; Englebert v. Blanjot, 2 Whart. 240; Weber v. Samuel, 7 Penn. 500.

[1] *In re* Meyers, 2 Bt. 424; s. c. 1 B. R. 162; Stewart v. Isidor et al. 5 Abb. Pr. (N. S.) 68; s. c. 1 B. R. 129; Goodwin v. Sharkey, 5 Abb. Pr. (N. S.) 64; Thomas v. Phillips, 9 Penn. 355.

[2] Sedgwick v. Menck, 6 Blatch. 156; s. c. 1 B. R. 204; Stewart v. Isidor, 5 Abb. Pr. (N. S.) 68; s. c. 1 B. R. 129; Payne v. Able, 7 Bush. 344; Goldsmith v. Russell, 5 D. M. & G. 547; Storm v. Waddell, 2 Sandf. Ch. 494; Tichenor v. Allen, 13 Gratt. 15; Felter v. Cirode, 4 B. Mon. 482; *vide* Smith v. Gordon, 6 Law Rep. 313.

[3] Boone v. Hall, 7 Bush, 66.

[4] Sands v. Codwise, 4 Johns. 536.

[5] Bate v. Graham, 11 N. Y. 237.

[6] Porter v. Williams, 9 N. Y. 142; s. c. 12 How. Pr. 107; Hamlin v. Wright, 23 Wis. 491.

[7] Kelly v. Lane, 42 Barb. 594; s. c. 18 Abb. Pr. 229; s. c. 28 How. Pr. 128.

[8] Bishop v. Halsey, 3 Abb. Pr. 400; *vide* Garretson v. Brown, 2 Dutch. 425; Simpson v. Warren, 55 Me. 18; Swift. v. Thompson, 9 Conn. 63.

[9] Bailey v. Burton, 8 Wend. 339; Frakes v. Brown, 2 Blackf. 295; Har-

JOINDER OF PARTIES COMPLAINANT.—One creditor may file a bill in his own name and for his own benefit, and need not make other creditors standing in the same situation parties.[1] It is immaterial if there is an older judgment which constitutes a lien upon the property, for the oldest judgment at law will have the preference notwithstanding any decree which may be made in a suit to which the owner of that judgment is not a party.[2] The sheriff and the creditor may unite, for each has an interest in preventing a multiplicity of suits and having the whole matter closed by a single controversy.[3] Several creditors may join in filing a bill, for they have similar rights with respect to the property of their debtor. It is, therefore, proper for them to unite in the same suit for effecting the same end. Such a bill is not multifarious, for it relates to one subject matter.[4] The fact that one creditor may be entitled to additional and further relief forms no objection to their uniting in a bill for the purpose of obtaining the relief to which they are all entitled.[5] The bill may be filed on behalf of those who institute the proceedings alone or on behalf of all who may choose to come in and participate in the proceedings.[6] A creditor and an administrator

---

rison v. Kramer, 3 Iowa, 543; Gerrish v. Mace, 9 Gray, 250; *Contra,* Thigpen v. Pitt, 1 Jones Eq. 49.

[1] Grover v. Wakeman, 11 Wend. 187; s. c. 4 Paige, 23; Baker v. Bartol, 6 Cal. 483; Edmeston v. Lyde, 1 Paige, 637; Ballentine v. Beall, 3 Scam. 203.

[2] Grover v. Wakeman, 4 Paige, 23; s. c. 11 Wend. 187.

[3] Adams v. Davidson, 10 N. Y. 309.

[4] Lentilhon v. Moffat, 1 Edw. 451; Waller v. Todd, 3 Dana, 503; Comstock v. Rayford, 1 S. & M. 423; Gannard v. Eslava, 20 Ala. 732; Brinkerhoff v. Brown, 6 Johns. Ch. 139; Clarkson v. De Peyster, 3 Paige, 320; Ruffing v. Tilton, 12 Ind. 259.

[5] Clarkson v. De Peyster, 3 Paige, 320.

[6] Edmonstone v. Lyde, 1 Paige, 637; Bireley v. Staley, 5 G. & J. 432.

of the grantee can not unite in the same bill to set aside a gift made prior to the grant.[1] The assignor of a judgment may join with the assignee.[2]

JOINDER OF PARTIES DEFENDANT.—Creditors who have liens may file a bill after the appointment of a receiver, and make him a party.[3] The debtor is a necessary party, for it is his debt that is sought to be collected, and his fraudulent conduct that requires investigation. The title also remains in him for the benefit of creditors.[4] If the debtor is deceased, an administrator should be appointed,[5] and made a party defendant, so as to account for the assets that may come to his hands.[6] The debtor's heirs need not be made parties, for they have no interest in the property.[7]

The grantee is a necessary party.[8] If there is more than one grantee, then all the grantees must be made parties.[9] When the fraudulent conveyance consists of

---

[1] Coleman v. Pinkard, 2 Humph. 185.

[2] Beach v. White, Walk. Ch. 495.

[3] Gere v. Dibble, 17 How. Pr. 31.

[4] Lovejoy v. Irelan, 17 Md. 525; Gaylords v. Kelshaw, 1 Wall. 81; Sewall v. Russell, 2 Paige, 175; Beardsley Scythe Co. v. Foster, 36 N. Y. 561; s. c. 34 How. Pr. 97; Lawrence v. Bank, 35 N. Y. 320; s. c. 3 Robt. 142.

[5] Bachman v. Sepulveda, 39 Cal. 688; Scriven v. Bostick, 2 McCord Ch. 410; *Contra*, Bireley v. Staley, 5 G. & J. 432.

[6] Peaslee v. Barney, 1 Chip. 331; Chamberlayne v. Temple, 2 Rand. 384; Simpson v. Simpson, 7 Humph. 275; Pharis v. Leachman, 20 Ala. 662; Bachman v. Sepulveda, 39 Cal. 388; McDowell v. Cochran, 11 Ill. 31; Barton v. Bryant, 2 Ind. 189; Cobb v. Norwood, 11 Tex. 556; Snodgrass v. Andrews, 30 Miss. 472; *vide* Merry v. Fremon, 44 Mo. 518; Dockray v. Mason, 48 Me. 178; Cornell v. Redway, 22 Wis. 260; Jackson v. Forrest, 2 Barb. Ch. 676.

[7] Smith v. Grim, 26 Penn. 95.

[8] Rock v. Dade, May on Fraud, 519; Taylor v. Wyld, 8 Beav. 159; Hightower v. Mustian, 8 Geo. 506; Tichenor v. Allen, 13 Gratt. 15; Edmeston v. Lyde, 1 Paige, 637; Winchester v. Crandall, 1 Clarke, 371; *vide* Sockman v. Sockman, 18 Ohio, 362.

[9] Ward v. Hollins, 14 Md. 158.

an assignment, the creditors whose debts are provided
for in it are not necessary parties.[1] A person through
whom the title has passed from the debtor to the
grantee is a proper party.[2] Those who had interests
in the property prior to the transfer,[3] and the grantor
of property which has been fraudulently purchased in
the name of another,[4] and a purchaser *pendente lite*,[5]
are not necessary parties. Several grantees claiming
different portions of the property by distinct conveyances may be joined, for the object is to obtain satisfaction out of such property and this is single.[6] So also
where the judgment is joint and separate conveyances
are made by each of the debtors, all the grantees may
be united.[7] If a proper decree can be made consistent
with the general scope of the bill without causing any
embarrassment to any of the parties as to any other rights
which they may have or the parties or the court in executing the decree, the bill will not be dismissed at the
hearing for multifariousness.[8] The facts which give
jurisdiction to the court and a right to relief must be
plainly and succinctly stated. The amount and character of the debt should be set forth, for a decree can not
be rendered for other particulars and causes of action
not mentioned or alluded to in the pleadings.[9]

---

[1] Grover v. Wakeman, 4 Paige, 23; s. c. 11 Wend. 187; Irwin v. Keen,
3 Whart. 347; M'Kinley v. Combs, 1 Mon. 105; Therasson v. Hickok, 37
Vt. 454.

[2] Bennett v. McGuire, 58 Barb. 625.

[3] Venable v. Bank, 2 Pet. 107; Erfort v. Consalus, 47 Mo. 208.

[4] Ballentine v. Beall, 3 Scam. 203.

[5] Schaferman v. O'Brien, 28 Md. 565.

[6] Hamlin v. Wright, 23 Wis. 491; Chase v. Searles, 45 N. H. 511;
Brinkerhoff v. Brown, 6 Johns. Ch. 139; Fellows v. Fellows, 4 Cow. 682;
Allen v. Montgomery R. R. Co. 11 Ala. 437; Snodgrass v. Andrews, 30
Miss. 472; North v. Bradway, 9 Minn. 183; Boyd v. Hoyt, 5 Paige,
65.

[7] Planters' Bank v. Walker, 7 Ala. 926.

[8] Hays v. Doane, 3 Stockt. 84.

[9] Waltball v. Rives, 34 Ala. 91; Strike v. M'Donald, 2 H. & G. 191.

AVERMENTS OF BILL.—The bill must aver the facts which give a lien or confer jurisdiction without a lien.[1] If it is filed by simple contract creditors, it should be filed on behalf of all the creditors.[2] The fact that the debtor has transferred his property must be specifically and formally alleged,[3] and a description of the property must also be given.[4] In order to create a *lis pendens* the bill must be so definite in the description that any one reading it can learn thereby what property is intended to be made the subject of litigation.[5] An amended bill for this purpose only operates from the time of the service of process under it.[6]

BILL SHOULD STATE FACTS.—No particular form of the bill or formal specific allegations are necessary, but facts must be stated from which the inference may be drawn that the aid of a court of equity is required to obtain satisfaction of the debt. It is not enough to show that the debtor has made a fraudulent disposition of his property. The creditor must show that such disposition embarrasses him in obtaining satisfaction of his debt, for if the debtor has other property sufficient to satisfy the debt, there is no necessity for the creditor to resort to equity.[7] When the debtor is deceased, the bill must allege a deficiency[8] of the personal assets. An exhaustion of them, however, need not be alleged.[9]

---

[1] McElwain v. Willis, 9 Wend. 548 ; Beardsley Scythe Co. v. Foster, 36 N. Y. 561 ; s. c. 34 How. Pr. 97.

[2] Reese River Ming. Co. v. Atwell L. R. 7 Eq. 347 ; Barton v. Bryant, 2 Ind. 189 ; Strike v. M'Donald, 2 H. & G. 191.

[3] McElwain v. Willis, 9 Wend. 548.

[4] King v. Trice, 3 Ired. Eq. 568.

[5] Miller v. Sherry, 2 Wall. 237 ; McCauley v. Rodes, 7 B. Mon. 462.

[6] Miller v. Sherry, 2 Wall. 237.

[7] Dunham v. Cox, 2 Stockt. 437 ; Harris v. Taylor, 15 Cal. 348.

[8] State Bank v. Ellis, 30 Ala. 478 ; Quarles v. Grigsby, 31 Ala. 172.

[9] McLaughlin v. Bank of Potomac, 7 How. 220.

CHARGE OF FRAUD.—Fraud must be charged,[1] and this should in general be done by setting forth the facts which constitute the fraud.[2] Fraud may be sufficiently averred by setting forth the particular manner in which the act was done and the particular end and design to be accomplished. Where the facts thus stated show that a fraud was designed and perpetrated that may be a sufficient averment of the fraud, although the bill does not state the conclusion which the law itself will draw that the act was fraudulent.[3] When the transfer was made for a valuable consideration, there must be an allegation that the grantee participated in the fraud.[4] When the complainant apprehends that the defendant will plead the statute of limitations against him, he should aver in his bill that the fraud has been discovered within such a period previous to the commencement of the suit as will prevent the bar.[5] Certainty to a common intent is all that is required in chancery pleadings. The accuracy which would exclude every other conclusion is not required.[6]

INDORSER. DECREE MUST CONFORM TO BILL.—An indorser who has taken up the note which constituted the debt can not have a pending bill in the name of the holder prosecuted for his use, for the payment to

---

[1] Richardson v. Horton, 7 Beav. 112.

[2] Prentice v. Madden, 4 Chand. 170; Catchings v. Manlove, 39 Miss. 655; Kinder v. Macy, 7 Cal. 206; Meeker v. Harris, 19 Cal. 278; Harris v. Taylor, 15 Cal. 348; Jessup v. Hulse, 29 Barb. 539; Hovey v. Holcomb, 11 Ill. 660.

[3] Hovey v. Holcomb, 11 Ill. 660; Catchings v. Manlove, 39 Miss. 655; Moreland v. Atchinson, 34 Tex. 351.

[4] Klein v. Horine, 47 Ill. 430.

[5] McLure v. Ashby, 7 Rich. Eq. 430; Erickson v. Quinn, 3 Lans. 299; s. c. 47 N. Y. 410; Carr v. Hilton, 1 Curt. 230, 390; Shannon v. White, 6 Rich. Eq. 96.

[6] Pope v. Wilson, 7 Ala. 690.

the holder put an end to the suit.[1] No decree can be founded upon evidence, and in relation to matters which are not put in issue between the parties. A creditor can not impeach a transfer on a ground not taken in his bill.[2] When a bill has been filed by a simple contract creditor to enforce the trust arising from an assignment he may, after obtaining judgment, and upon a subsequent discovery of fraud, file a supplemental bill to set aside the assignment, for the subject matter of both the original and supplemental bill is the debt due to the complainant and the trust fund out of which he seeks payment.[3]

PLEADING.—When a bill is defective for want of proper parties, and this defect appears on its face, it is liable to a demurrer,[4] but if the defect does not appear on its face, the objection can only be taken by plea or answer disclosing who are proper parties.[5] No matter can be pleaded in bar of the discovery merely when it would be equally valid as a defence to the relief.[6] It is the right of the defendant to verify his answer by an affidavit, and the complainant can not deprive him of it by waiving an answer under oath.[7] The grantee is the party who is interested in defeating the suit, and he can not be prejudiced by the conduct of the debtor.

---

[1] Heighe v. Farmers' Bank, 5 H. & J. 68.

[2] Roberts v. Gibson, 6 H. & J. 116; Tripp v. Vincent, 3 Barb. Ch. 613; Bailey v. Ryder, 10 N. Y. 363; Hovey v. Holcomb, 11 Ill. 660; Parkhurst v. McGraw, 24 Miss. 134; Nicholson v. Leavitt, 4 Sandf. 252; Myers v. Sheriff, 21 La. An. 172; Bachman v. Sepulveda, 39 Cal. 688; Ontario Bank v. Root, 3 Paige, 478.

[3] Baker v. Bartol, 6 Cal. 483.

[4] Hightower v. Mustian, 8 Geo. 506.

[5] Bay Iron Co. v. Goodall, 39 N. H. 221; M'Kinley v. Combs, 1 Mon. 105.

[6] Brownell v. Curtis, 10 Paige, 210.

[7] Clements v. Moore, 6 Wall. 299.

The fact that the debtor suffers the bill to be taken *pro confesso*,[1] or admits the fraud in his answer,[2] will not affect the grantee. Whether a party can protect himself from making a discovery on the ground that he will thereby subject himself to a criminal prosecution or a forfeiture can not be considered as yet settled.[3] To so much of the bill as is material and necessary for the defendant to answer, he must speak directly and without evasion. He must answer the charge not merely literally but confess or traverse the substance of each charge positively and with certainty, and particular precise charges must be answered particularly and precisely and not in a general manner, even though a general denial may amount to a full denial of the charges.[4]

SUPPLEMENTAL ANSWER.—An answer can not be amended. The practice is to permit the defendant, upon a proper case, to file a supplemental answer, thus giving the complainant the benefit of the original answer with the explanations or denials contained in the supplemental answer. Under such an answer, if the defendant by mistake or misapprehension of the facts, or of his rights, has made an admission in his original answer which is inconsistent with the truth, he has an opportunity by proofs to show the truth and thus re-

---

[1] Sands v. Hildreth, 2 Johns. Ch. 35; s. c. 14 Johns. 493; Hollister v. Loud, 2 Mich. 309.

[2] Glenn v. Grover, 3 Md. 212; Scheitlin v. Stone, 43 Barb. 634; s. c. 29 How. Pr. 355; Kittering v. Parker, 8 Ind. 44; Hord v. Rust, 4 Bibb. 231.

[3] Bunn v. Bunn, 3 New Rep. 679; s. c. 12 W. R. 561; Wich v. Parker, 22 Beav. 59; Michael v. Gay, 1 F. & F. 409; Bay Iron Co. v. Goodall, 39 N. H. 221; *vide* Reg v. Smith, 6 Cox. C. C. 31; Creswell & Cokes Case, 2 Leon. 8.

[4] Barrow v. Bailey, 5 Fla. 9; Croft v. Arthur, 3 Dessau. 223; Phippen v. Durham, 8 Gratt. 457; Bailey v. Nicoll, 1 Edw. 32.

lieve himself from the consequences of his mistake.[1]
When a supplemental bill is filed after the original
bill has been answered, the answer to the supplemental
bill must be restricted to the matters stated in it, for
the defendant has no right, under pretext of answering
the supplemental bill, to add to or amend his answer to
the original bill.[2] A party who claims protection as a
purchaser without notice of the fraud, must deny notice
fully and particularly, and such denial must extend to
the time of paying the money and receiving the transfer.[3]

MATTERS RESPONSIVE TO THE BILL IS EVIDENCE.—
Statements in the answer responsive to the averments
in the bill are evidence in favor of the defendant,[4] but
averments which are not responsive to the bill must be
sustained by proof.[5] Statements which consists of explanations or qualifications of an admission are responsive,[6] but when the answer admits a fact and insists
upon a distinct fact by way of avoidance, the fact admitted is established, but the fact insisted upon must
be proved; otherwise the admission stands as if the
fact in avoidance had not been averred.[7]

---

[1] Hughes v. Bloomer, 9 Paige, 269.

[2] Richards v. Swan, 7 Gill. 366; s. c. 2 Md. Ch. 111.

[3] Miller v. Fraley, 21 Ark. 22; Byers v. Fowler, 12 Ark. 218; Stanton v.
Green, 34 Miss. 576.

[4] Dewey v. Littlejohn, 2 Ired. Eq. 495; Pomeroy v. Manin, 2 Paine,
476; Blow v. Gage, 44 Ill. 208; Phettiplace v. Sayles, 4 Mason, 312;
Glenn v. Randall, 2 Md. Ch. 220; Green v. Tanner, 8 Met. 411; Hartshorne v. Eames, 31 Me. 93.

[5] Sanborn v. Kittredge, 20 Vt. 632; McNeal v. Glenn, 4 Md. 87; s. c.
3 Md. Ch. 349; Grover v. Wakeman, 4 Paige, 23; s. c. 11 Wend. 187.

[6] Glenn v. Randall, 2 Md. Ch. 220; Eastman v. M'Alpin, 1 Kelly, 157;
Glenn v. Grover, 3 Md. 212; s. c. 3 Md. Ch. 29.

[7] Clements v. Moore, 6 Wall. 299; Randall v. Phillips, 3 Mason, 378;
Cummings v. McCullough, 5 Ala. 324; Brown v. M'Donald, 1 Hill. Ch.
297; Hampson v. Sumner, 18 Ohio, 444; Stanton v. Green, 34 Miss. 576.

How DENIAL MAY BE OVERCOME.—A denial of fraud in the answer is not conclusive.[1] An answer, however, which is responsive to the bill and denies the allegations made therein in regard to the motives and intentions of the parties is conclusive, unless it is overcome by the testimony of two witnesses, or of one witness with corroborating circumstances.[2] If the answer, however, admits facts from which a conclusive presumption of a fraudulent intent must be drawn, the denial of the answer is overcome.[3] A positive denial will not prevail against admissions in the answer of facts which show that the transfer was fraudulent.[4] Pregnant or slight circumstances, however, are not sufficient.[5] When there is a general denial of all fraud, facts specifically and particularly charged in the bill can not be taken to be true although they are not denied in the answer, for objections to the answer for the want of particularity and fulness should be taken by exceptions to its sufficiency.[6]

---

[1] How v. Camp, Walk. Ch. 427; Miller v. Tolleson, Harp. Ch. 145; Edginton v. Williams, Wright, 439; Griffin v. Wardlaw, Harp. Ch. 481; Burtus v. Tisdall, 4 Barb. 571; Dick v. Grissom, 1 Freem. Ch. (Miss.) 428.

[2] Moffatt v. McDowell, 1 McCord Ch. 434; Myers v. Kinzie, 26 Ill. 36; Blow v. Gage, 44 Ill. 208; Feigley v. Feigley, 7 Md. 537; Glenn v. Grover, 3 Md. 212; Green v. Tanner, 8 Met. 411; Gray v. Faris, 7 Yerg. 155; Allen v. Mower, 17 Vt. 61; Allen v. White, 17 Vt. 69; Jenison v. Graves, 4 Blackf. 440; Clark v. Bailey, 2 Strobh. Ev. 143; Parkhurst v. McGraw, 24 Miss. 134; Kittering v. Parker, 8 Ind. 44; Culbertson v. Luckey, 13 Iowa, 12; Wright v. Wheeler, 14 Iowa, 8; Wightman v. Hart, 37 Ill. 123; Walter v. McNabb, 1 Heisk, 703.

[3] Grover v. Wakeman, 11 Wend. 187; s. c. 4 Paige, 23; Cunningham v. Freeborn, 11 Wend. 241; Fiedler v. Day, 2 Sandf. 594; Cook v. Johnson, 1 Beasley, 51.

[4] Robinson v. Stewart, 10 N. Y. 189; Belford v. Crane, 1 C. E. Green, 265; Litchfield v. Pelton, 6 Barb. 187.

[5] Glenn v. Grover, 3 Md. 212; How v. Camp. Walk. Ch. 427.

[6] Parkman v. Welch, 19 Pick. 231; Waterbury v. Sturtevant, 18 Wend. 353; McRea v. Branch Bank, 29 How. 376.

To give the defendant, however, the full benefit of an answer, so far as to require more than one witness to control it, the answer must be direct and specific as to the matter charged in the bill. So in weighing the whole evidence in the case the fact that the defendant only answers generally will operate against him wherever the bill charges him with particular acts of fraud. The circumstance that the defendant omits to deny the facts in the same explicit manner as they are charged raises the presumption that the appeal to his conscience has been somewhat effectual, and that he proposes shielding himself under a denial of the legal effect of his actions rather than to deny under oath the particular acts imputed to him.[1] When the cause is heard on bill and answer, all pertinent facts stated in the answer must be taken to be true.[2] The practice of permitting other creditors to come in and make themselves parties to a creditor's bill and thereby obtain the benefit, assuming at the same time their portion of the costs and expenses is well settled.[3]

STATUTE OF LIMITATIONS.—The statute of limitations is never considered as an objection to the payment of a claim unless it is specially relied on.[4] The plea may be set up as a bar to the demand,[5] or to the title to the property. Such a plea can not be put in after a defence has been made to the

---

[1] Parkman v. Welch, 19 Pick. 231; Waterbury v. Sturtevant, 18 Wend. 353; Hawkins v. Alston, 4 Ired. Eq. 137; Enders v. Swayne, 8 Dana, 103; Gamble v. Johnson, 9 Mo. 605.

[2] Heydock v. Stanhope, 1 Curt. 471; Heacock v. Durand, 42 Ill. 230.

[3] Myers v. Fenn, 5 Wall. 205; Strike v. M'Donald, 2 H. & G. 191; s. c. 1 Bland, 57.

[4] Strike v. M'Donald, 2 H. & G. 191.

[5] McDowell v. Goldsmith, 6 Md. 319; s. c. 2 Md. Ch. 370; Lott v. De Graffenreid, 10 Rich. Eq. 346; M'Clenney, v. M'Clenney, 3 Tex. 192.

claim.[1] In determining its sufficiency the substance of the objection must govern rather than the form in which it is presented.[2] The original complainant may rely upon the statute of limitations in opposition to the claims of other creditors who come in after the institution of the suit.[3] The plea of the statute of limitations in the answer will not apply to claims that are filed subsequently. The defence as to such claims must be taken by exceptions.[4] The complainant's claim to relief is to be referred to his right at the time of filing the bill, and if it was well founded and in full force at the time, it will not be barred by lapse of time during the pendency of the suit.[5] The statute continues to run against other creditors until they come in by filing their petition or the vouchers of their claims.[6] If a judgment is recovered against the debtor after the transfer, but before the claim is barred, the original claim becomes merged in the judgment, and the plea of limitations against the original claim will not avail.[7] If the claim, however, is barred before judgment a confession of judgment by the debtor after the transfer will not defeat the plea.[8]

LIMITATIONS AS TO TITLE.—There is a conflict among

---

[1] Williams v. Banks, 19 Md. 22.

[2] McDowell v. Goldsmith, 24 Md. 214.

[3] Strike v. M'Donald, 2 H. & G. 191; McDowell v. Goldsmith, 6 Md. 319; s. c. 2 Md. Ch. 370; s. c. 24 Md. 214.

[4] Williams v. Banks, 11 Md. 198; McDowell v. Goldsmith, 24 Md. 214.

[5] Hunt v. Knox, 34 Miss. 655.

[6] Strike v. McDonald, 2 H. & G. 191; s. c. 1 Bland, 57; McDowell v. Goldsmith, 6 Md. 319; s. c. 2 Md. Ch. 370; s. c. 24 Md. 214.

[7] Schaferman v. O'Brien, 28 Md. 565; Williams v. Banks, 11 Md. 198; s. c. 19 Md. 22.

[8] McDowell v. Goldsmith, 24 Md. 214; vide Jones v. Read, 1 Humph. 335.

the decisions as to the time from which the statute begins to run so as to bar a claim to the title of the property. In some it is held to run only from the time of
an actual levy upon the property,[1] while in others it is
held to run from the rendition of a judgment.[2] When
the property is such that it can not be taken on execution, the statute does not begin to run until after the
recovery of a judgment and the return of an execution
unsatisfied.[3] If the grantee is also administrator, he
can not plead the statute of limitations.[4]

LIMITATIONS RUN ONLY FROM DISCOVERY.—The statute
of limitations is not obligatory upon a court of equity,
and does not apply to proceedings in equity, except so
far as the court deems it conducive to the ends of justice to apply it in analogy to the rules which prevail in
a court of law. As the court only acts on this analogy
because of its subserviency to the ends of justice, it
does not follow the statute when such a course would
be obviously subversive of justice. In equity, therefore,
the statute does not commence to run until the discovery of the fraud.[5] A denial of notice of the fraud is

---

[1] Peterson v. Williamson, 2 Dev. 326; Pickett v. Pickett, 3 Dev. 6;
Hoke v. Henderson, 3 Dev. 12; Dobson v. Erwin, 4 Dev. & Bat. 201;
Beach v. Catlin, 4 Day, 284; Law v. Smith, 4 Ind. 56; Belt v. Raguet, 27
Tex. 471; vide Scriven v. Bostwick, 2 McCord Ch. 410; Musselman v.
Kent, 33 Ind. 452.

[2] Jones v. Read, 1 Humph. 355; Porter v. Cocke, Peck. 30; Blanton
v. Whitaker, 11 Humph. 313; Compton v. Perry, 23 Tex. 414; Reynolds
v. Lansford, 16 Tex. 286; Martel v. Somers, 26 Tex. 551; vide Wilson v.
Buchanan, 7 Gratt. 334; Bank v. Ballard, 12 Rich. 259; Reeves v. Dougherty, 7 Yerg. 222; Dodd v. McCraw, 8 Ark. 83; Marr v. Rucker, 1
Humph. 348.

[3] Gates v. Andrews, 37 N. Y. 637; Eyre v. Beebe, 28 How. Pr. 333.

[4] Stephens v. Barnett, 7 Dana, 257.

[5] McLure v. Ashby, 7 Rich. Eq. 430; Eigleberger v. Kibler, 1 Hill
Ch. 113; Martin v. Smith, 1 Dillon, 85; s. c. 4 B. R. 83; s. c. 3 A. L. T.
(C. R.) 190.

a negative proposition. The affirmative is with the party who asserts the fact of notice and whose interest it is to establish that fact. The burden of proof, therefore, rests upon the defendant.[1]

Mere suspicion of fraud is not sufficient. It is necessary to bring home to the creditor a knowledge of the facts constituting the fraud. The statute only begins to run from the time when a knowledge of the facts constituting the fraud, or the means by which a knowledge of those facts might, by proper diligence have been obtained.[2] Positive information, however, is not required. The notice will be sufficient to prevent the suspension of the statute, if it be such as would put a reasonably diligent man upon the inquiry. Nor must the aggrieved party wait until he has discovered evidence by which he may establish the fraud in a court of justice. If he has knowledge that a fraud has been committed, though that knowledge is confined to himself, he must proceed diligently, for the statute in such case will not be suspended.[3] The ignorance of an executor will not prevent the running of the statute when the facts were known to the testator.[4] Independently of the statute, delay alone may be sufficient to deprive the complainant of his right to recover.[5]

THE DECREE.—The decree can only be made to affect the transfers which the bill alleges to be fraudulent.[6] After the transfer is declared void, the court may

---

[1] McClure v. Ashby, 7 Rich. Eq. 430; Shannon v. White, 6 Rich. Eq. 96 ; vide Erickson v. Quinn, 3 Lans. 299; s. c. 47 N. Y. 410 ; Carr v. Hilton, 1 Curt. 390, 230.

[2] Shannon v. White, 6 Rich. Eq. 96 ; Abbey v. Bank, 31 Miss. 434 ; Snodgrass v. Bank, 25 Ala. 161 ; Erickson v. Quinn, 47 N. Y. 410; s. c. 3 Lans. 299.

[3] McClure v. Ashby 7 Rich. Eq. 430.

[4] Lott v. De Graffenreid, 10 Rich. Eq. 346.

[5] Huston v. Cantril, 11 Leigh, 136.

[6] Wilson v. Horr, 15 Iowa, 489.

leave the creditor to enforce his execution at law when the property can be so reached, or, having assumed jurisdiction of the cause and subject matter, may proceed to do full and complete justice by directing a sale of the property.[1] When a creditor brings a suit to procure a satisfaction of his own claim only, the action ends as soon as he is satisfied and no decree can be made affecting any surplus that may remain in the grantee's hands.[2] If several creditors are parties to the proceedings, the proceeds will be distributed according to the priorities of the various parties, for the funds remain subject to the same liens as the property before the sale.[3]

CREDITORS AT LARGE.—Upon a bill filed by simple contract creditors, a distribution is made ratably among all the creditors, preserving, however, the rights of those who have liens upon the property.[4]

LIENS.—The filing of a bill by a judgment creditor, and the service of process create a lien in equity upon the effects of the debtor. This has been aptly termed an equitable levy.[5] To constitute a lien, the bill must

---

[1] Scouton v. Bender, 3 How. Pr. 185; Yoder v. Standiford, 7 Mon. 478; Planters' Bank v. Walker, 7 Ala. 926; Hunt v. Knox, 34 Miss. 655; Chatauque Bank v. White, 6 N. Y. 236; s. c. 6 Barb. 589; McCalmont v. Lawrence, 1 Blatch. 232; *vide* Higgins v. York Building Co. 2 Atk. 107; Hendrickson v. Winne, 3 How. Pr. 127.

[2] Ward v. Enders, 29 Ill. 519; Ballentine v. Beall, 3 Scam. 203; Kaupe v. Bridge, 2 Robt. 459; Bostwick v. Menck, 40 N. Y. 383.

[3] Codwise v. Gelston, 10 Johns. 507.

[4] Day v. Washburn, 24 How. 352; Robinson v. Stewart, 10 N. Y. 189; Barton v. Bryant, 2 Ind. 189; McNaughtin v. Lamb, 2 Ind. 642.

[5] Chittenden v. Brewster, 2 Wall. 191; Hartshorne v. Eames, 31 Me. 93; Newell v. Morgan, 2 Harring. 225; Newdegate v. Lee, 9 Dana, 17; Bank v. Burke, 4 Blackf. 141; Ballentine v. Beall, 3 Scam. 203; Spader v. Davis, 5 Johns. Ch. 280; Albany Bank v. Schermerhorn, 1 Clarke, 297;

be filed against the grantee and not against the debtor alone.[1] The filing of the bill must also be followed up by service of process.[2] If creditors file separate bills, they are entitled to priority of payment in the order in which they commence their suits.[3] When the property can not be taken on execution, it is not the return of an execution unsatisfied, but the filing of a bill, that gives a lien. If the party whose execution is first returned unsatisfied delays, a subsequent execution will gain a preference by superior vigilance in filing a bill.[4] The filing of a bill will also give a prior lien upon the personal estate of the debtor when there has not been an actual levy. The lien is created by the issuing of the execution, and the filing of the bill gives it a priority.[5]

SUBJECT TO OTHER LIENS.—The equitable lien created by the filing of a bill is subject to any valid lien which may happen to exist in favor of any other creditor at the time of the service of the process.[6] In the case of land it is subject to prior legal liens created by

---

Jeffries v. Cochrane, 47 Barb. 557 ; Cummings v. McCullough, 5 Ala. 324; Moffat v. Ingham, 7 Dana, 495 ; Barrett v. Reed, Wright, 700 ; Peacock v. Tompkins, Meigs, 317 ; Gracey v. Davis, 3 Strobh. Eq. 55 ; Stanton v. Keyes, 14 Ohio St. R. 443; Maiders v. Culver, 1 Duvall, 164; vide Peacock v. Tompkins, Meigs, 317 ; Chase v. Searles, 45 N. H. 511.

[1] Fields v. Sands, 8 Bosw. 685 ; Conger v. Sands, 19 How. Pr. 8.

[2] Boynton v. Rawson, 1 Clarke, 584.

[3] Hone v. Henriquez, 13 Wend. 240; s. c. 2 Edw. 120; Moffat v. Ingham, 7 Dana, 495 ; Fields v. Sands, 8 Bosw. 685 ; Boynton v. Rawson, 1 Clarke, 584.

[4] Weed v. Pierce, 9 Cow. 722; Edmeston v. Lyde, 1 Paige, 637; Beck v. Burdett, 1 Paige, 305 ; Grover v. Wakeman, 4 Paige, 23 ; s. c. 11 Wend. 187.

[5] Scouton v. Bender, 3 How. Pr. 185 ; Weed v. Pierce, 9 Cow. 722; Albany Bank v. Schermerhorn, Clarke, 297.

[6] Scouton v. Bender, 3 How. Pr. 185 ; Lane v. Lutz, 1 Keyes, 203 ; Haleys v. Williams, 1 Leigh, 140 ; Hubbs v. Bancroft, 4 Ind. 388.

judgments rendered against the debtor.[1] A judgment rendered after the filing of the bill, and prior to the divesting of the title, is also a lien upon the land.[2] After the appointment of a receiver, no lien can be acquired, for the debtor's title is then divested.[3] The title of a a party who purchases from the receiver does not relate back to the judgment lien of the creditor who filed the bill, but is subject to all liens existing at the time of the appointment of the receiver in favor of persons who are not parties to the proceedings.[4]

COSTS.—Costs are peculiarly within the discretion of the court. They are usually allowed to the successful party.[5] In cases of constructive fraud they may be paid out of the fund.[6] When the transaction is such as would naturally induce a creditor to call for an explanation, the bill may be dismissed without costs if he is unsuccessful.[7] If the case is one of peculiar hardship to the creditor,[8] or if the conduct of the defendant does

---

[1] Chatauque Bank v. Risley, 19 N. Y. 369 ; Scouton v. Bender, 3 How Pr. 185; Albany Bank v. Schermerhorn, 1 Clarke, 297; vide Dargan v. Waring, 11 Ala. 988; Lyon v. Robbins, 46 Ill. 276; Miller v. Sherry, 2 Wall. 237.

[2] Watson v. R. R. Co. 6 Abb. Pr. (N. S.) 91.

[3] Albany Bank v. Schermerhorn, 1 Clarke, 297; Chatauque Bank v. White, 6 N. Y. 236 ; s. c. 6 Barb. 589.

[4] Chatauque Bank v. Risley, 19 N. Y. 369.

[5] Webb v. Daggett, 2 Barb. 9 ; How v. Camp, Walk. Ch. 427.

[6] Grover v. Wakeman, 11 Wend. 187; s. c. 4 Paige, 23 ; Saunders v. Turbeville, 2 Humph. 272; Fiedler v. Day, 2 Sandf. 594; Erickson v. Quinn, 47 N. Y. 410.

[7] White v. Sansom, 3 Atk. 410; Houghton v. Tate, 3 Y. & J. 486; Holmes v. Penney, 3 K. & J. 90; Townsend v. Westacott, 4 Beav. 58; Hale v. Saloon Omnibus Co. 4 Drew. 492 ; Magawley's Trust, 5 De G. & S. 1; McArthur v. Hoysradt, 11 Paige, 495; Jacks v. Tunno, 3 Dessau, 1; Cunningham v. Freeborn, 11 Wend. 241; Stern v. Fisher, 32 Barb. 198; Cox v. Platt, 32 Barb. 126 ; s. c. 19 How. Pr. 121; Niolon v. Douglass, 2 Hill. Ch. 443; Pomeroy v. Manin, 2 Paine, 476; Webb v. Daggett, 2 Barb. 9; Wakefield v. Gibbon, 1 Giff. 401.

[8] Hickman v. Quinn, 6 Yerg. 96.

not meet with the approbation of the court,[1] each party may be directed to pay his own costs. A purchaser who has failed mainly through a defect in his answer may be ordered to pay his own costs alone.[2] The costs of a person who is a necessary party may be allowed out of the fund when he has not been guilty of fraud.[3] Except in case of a gross abuse of the trust, an assignee claiming under a voluntary assignment is not usually charged with costs.[4] In the case of a creditor's bill, the counsel fees for the complainant's solicitor may be allowed out of the fund.[5]

---

[1] Clark v. Bailey, 2 Strobh. Eq. 143; Miller v. Halsey, 4 Abb. Pr. (N. S.) 28.

[2] Byers v. Fowler, 12 Ark. 218.

[3] Norcutt v. Dodd, 1 Cr. & Ph. 100; Townsend v. Westacott, 4 Beav. 58.

[4] Webb v. Daggett, 2 Barb. 9.

[5] Strike v. M'Donald, 2 H. & G. 191; Goldsmith'v. Russell, 5 D. M. & G. 547.

CHAPTER XXIII.

EVIDENCE.

PROOF OF INDEBTEDNESS.—Before any person can assail a transfer as fraudulent he must show either that he is a creditor of the grantor or represents creditors.[1] For the purpose of establishing such indebtedness the admissions of the grantor made prior to the transfer at a time when he had no interest to make false admissions, are competent evidence against him and all who claim under him either mediately or immediately by a subsequent title.[2] His declarations,[3] notes,[4] and accounts,[5] are *prima facie* evidence of the existence of the debts they respectively purport to represent. But admissions made after the transfer are not competent evidence.[6]

JUDGMENTS.—The record of a judgment rendered

---

[1] Garnons v. Knight, 5 B. & C. 671; Candler v. Fisher, 11 Md. 332; Mahany v. Lazier, 16 Md. 69; Conillard v. Duncan, 6 Allen, 440; Stanbro v. Hopkins, 28 Barb. 265; Ingram v. Phillips, 3 Strobh. Ch. 565.

[2] Richards v. Swan, 7 Gill. 366; Gamble v. Johnson, 9 Mo. 605; High v. Nelms, 14 Ala. 350; Satterwhite v. Hicks, Busbee, 105; Hale v. Smith, 6 Me. 416; Dubose v. Young, 14 Ala. 139; Goodgame v. Cole, 12 Ala. 77.

[3] Ragan v. Kennedy, 1 Tenn. 91; Satterwhite v. Hicks, Busbee, 105.

[4] High v. Nelms, 14 Ala. 350; Foster v. Wallace, 2 Mo. 231; Feagan v. Cureton, 19 Geo. 404.

[5] Richards v. Swan, 7 Gill. 366.

[6] Redfield v. Buck, 35 Conn. 328; Hitt v. Ormsbee, 12 Ill. 166; Townsend v. Westacott, 2 Beav. 340.

against the debtor is competent evidence against the grantee to establish the existence of the debt. It is not competent evidence against third parties of the facts upon which the judgment is founded, but is evidence of the existence of the judgment itself, and is also *prima facie* evidence of the existence of the indebtedness.[1] There is a distinction between a mere admission of the debtor and a judgment, for the record of a judgment rendered after the transfer is sufficient evidence of the debt.[2] A judgment rendered against the debtor's administrator, whether domestic,[3] or foreign,[4] is not competent evidence against the grantee. If a judgment is by confession the creditor must prove it to be for a just debt.[5] In this respect there is a distinction between a judgment obtained in due course of law and a judgment obtained by the consent of the debtor. The law presumes the former to be founded upon a valuable consideration and rendered for a just debt, but indulges no such presumption in favor of the latter.

ONLY PRIMA FACIE AS AGAINST GRANTEE.—The evidence of the existence of the debt whether in the form of an admission, or note, or judgment, is only *prima facie* evidence of an indebtedness as against the grantee

---

[1] Railroad Co. v. Kyle, 5 Bosw. 587; Law v. Payson, 32 Me. 521; Garrigues v. Harris, 17 Penn. 344; Garland v. Rives, 4 Rand. 282; Feagan v. Cureton, 19 Geo. 404; Vogt v. Ticknor, 48 N. H. 242; Easley v. Dye, 14 Ala. 158; Clayton v. Brown, 30 Geo 490; Snodgrass v. Bank, 25 Ala. 161; Reed v. Davis, 5 Pick. 388; Prescott v. Hayes, 43 N. H. 593; Tappan v. Nutting, Brayt. 137; Hinde v. Longworth, 11 Wheat. 199.

[2] Young v. Pate, 4 Yerg. 164.

[3] McDowell v. Goldsmith, 24 Md. 214; Baker v. Welch, 4 Mo. 484; Osgood v. Manhattan Co. 3 Cow. 612; *Contra*, M'Laughlin v. Bank of Potomac, 7 How. 220; Chamberlayne v. Temple, 2 Rand. 384.

[4] King v. Clarke, 2 Hill Ch. 611.

[5] Sanders v. ———, Holt, 327; s. c. Skinner, 586; Botts v. Cozine, Hoff. Ch. 79.

and it is always competent for him to impeach the debt either as to its existence, its *bona fide* character, its date, or its continuance.[1] He may inquire into the grounds of a judgment and show that it does not give the party who holds it a right as against him to impeach the transfer.[2] He may show that the debt,[3] or the judgment,[4] has been paid, or that there were mutual claims which could have been made the subject of a set-off, and by this means be mutually cancelled,[5] or that the debt was barred by the statute of limitations before the commencement of the suit in which the judgment was obtained,[6] or that the judgment is being used for the benefit of the debtor.[7] The right to impeach, however, does not extend so far as to give him the right to retry an issue which has been litigated and determined between the parties in accordance with the forms and principles of law without fraud or collusion.[8]

LIMITED TO PLEADINGS.—Evidence to establish the fraud must be confined to the pleadings, for the facts which the pleadings admit can not be varied or contra-

---

[1] Boutwell v. McClure, 30 Vt. 674.

[2] Miller v. Miller, 23 Me. 22 ; Taylor v. Eubanks, 3 A. K. Marsh. 239; Miller v. Johnson, 27 Md. 6; Warner v. Dove, 33 Md. 579; Posten v. Posten, 4 Whart. 27; Church v. Chapin, 35 Vt. 223 ; Hall v. Hamlin, 2 Watts, 354; Mattingly v. Nye, 8 Wall. 370; Ingalls v. Brooks, 29 Vt. 398; Bruggerman v. Hoerr, 7 Minn. 337; Sargent v. Salmond, 27 Me. 539 ; Caswell v. Caswell, 28 Me. 232; Carter v. Bennett, 4 Fla. 283; King v. Tharp, 26 Iowa, 283; Esty v. Long, 41 N. H. 103 ; Jenness v. Berry, 17 N. H. 549; *Contra,* Starr v. Starr, 1 Ohio, 321.

[3] Mattingly v. Nye, 8 Wall. 370.

[4] Boutwell v. McClure, 30 Vt. 674.

[5] Warner v. Percy, 22 Vt. 155.

[6] Warner v. Dove, 33 Md. 579 ; McDowell v. Goldsmith, 24 Md. 214.

[7] Feagan v. Cureton, 19 Geo. 404.

[8] Sidensparker v. Sidensparker, 52 Me. 481; Ferguson v. Kumler, 11 Minn. 104.

dicted. The only purpose of evidence is to establish what is alleged by one party and denied by the other.[1] To establish the controverted facts proof is the end and evidence is the means. Proof establishes the truth. Evidence only tends towards it. Any pertinent and legitimate facts conducing to the proof of a litigated fact are evidence of it, either weaker or stronger, according to their entire character and complexion.[2] Evidence which tends to prove an issue, contributes to its establishment and assists in giving a leaning to the mind in its consideration or determination. That which is directed to an end, however, may not necessarily attain it. It may be received as evidence if it has this tendency, but it is not to be treated as conclusive or as necessarily warranting the fact which it tends to establish. Evidence, however, may be so direct and positive as to amount to proof itself, but in general it consists of facts which, while they do not necessarily establish the controverted fact, tend to justify the inference of its existence.[3]

ADMISSIBILITY.—In questions of fraud a wide range of evidence is allowed.[4] Fraud assumes many shapes, disguises and subterfuges, and is generally so secretly hatched that it can only be detected by a consideration of facts and circumstances which are not unfrequently trivial, remote, and disconnected. A wide latitude of evidence is, therefore, allowed in order that it may be detected and exposed. This principle arises from necessity and is established for the protection of society

[1] Parkhurst v. McGraw, 24 Miss. 134.
[2] Miles v. Edelen, 1 Duvall, 270.
[3] Davenport v. Cummings, 15 Iowa, 219.
[4] Covanhovan v. Hart, 21 Penn. 495; Garrigues v. Harris, 17 Penn. 344.

and the benefit of morals. Each detached piece of evidence is not rejected as it is offered, because it is apparently trivial.[1] Any fact however slight, if at all relevant to the issue is admissible.[2] It is not easy to draw the precise line separating those circumstances which are fairly admissible from those which ought to be excluded. The true test, however, is whether the evidence can throw light upon the transaction or is altogether irrelevant.[3] Evidence which has no connection with the matters in issue but merely tends to create a personal prejudice against one of the parties should be excluded.[4] So also if the whole evidence taken together would merely raise a suspicion, it may be rejected.[5]

EVIDENCE OF SECRET TRUST.—Sometimes the proof of the fraudulent intent depends upon the establishment of a secret trust between the parties, and in all cases when a fraud is established the grantee is treated as a trustee for the creditors. Such a trust, however, is not a trust between the parties to the transaction to be set up and enforced by the *cestui que trust* or his representatives. It is a question of fraud by reason of a secret trust with fraudulent intent as affecting the validity of the transfer. Hence the doctrines of the law as to the proof of a trust, whether it may be by parol or must be by writing, are not involved. The question is one of fraudulent intent and such intent

---

[1] Blue v. Penniston, 27 Mo. 272.

[2] Waters v. Dashiell, 1 Md. 455 ; Curtis v. Moore, 20 Md. 93; Balto. & Ohio R. R. Co. v. Hoge, 34 Penn. 214.

[3] Zerbe v. Miller, 16 Penn. 488 ; Heath v. Page, 63 Penn. 108 ; Blue v. Penniston, 27 Mo. 272 ; Wright v. Linn, 16 Tex. 34.

[4] Carr v. Gale, Daveis, 328 ; Davenport v. Wright, 51 Penn. 292.

[5] Boylston v. Carver, 11 Mass. 515.

may be proved by any kind of evidence by which fraud may be proved.[1]

RES GESTÆ.—In questions of fraud or *bona fides* an adequate judgment can in general only be formed by having a perfect view of the whole transaction and this includes the conversation which forms a part of it. The language which is used on any occasion forms a part of the *res gestæ*. The declarations and acts of the debtor made before the transfer and contemporaneous with it are admissible.[2] They are admissible in evidence in favor of the grantee,[3] as well as of creditors. The acts,[4] and declarations of the grantee,[5] which accompany the transfer stand on the same footing as those of the debtor. So far as the acts and declarations of the parties form a part of and assist in giving character to the transaction, they constitute a part of the *res gestæ*, and are competent evidence.[6] When admitted they do not

---

[1] McLane v. Johnson, 43 Vt. 48; Starr v. Starr, 1 Ohio, 321; Hills v. Elliott, 12 Mass. 26; Blair v. Alston, 26 Ark. 41.

[2] McDowell v. Goldsmith, 6 Md. 319; s. c. 2 Md. Ch. 370; Waters v. Riggin, 19 Md. 536; Badger v. Story, 16 N. H. 168; Angier v. Ash, 26 N. H. 99; Goodgame v. Cole, 12 Ala. 77; Elliott v. Stoddard, 98 Mass. 145; Sackett v. Spencer, 65 Penn. 89; York County Bank v. Carter, 38 Penn. 446; Merrill v. Meachum, 5 Day, 341; Cook v. Swan, 5 Conn. 140; Crary v. Sprague, 12 Wend. 41; Gamble v. Johnson, 9 Mo. 605; Hardee v. Langford, 6 Fla. 13; Potter v. McDowell, 31 Mo. 62; Marsh v. Davis, 24 Vt. 363; Hoose v. Robbins, 18 La. An. 648; Heath v. Page, 63 Penn. 108; Weil v. Silverstone, 6 Bush. 698; Peck v. Crouse, 46 Barb. 151; McLane v. Johnson, 43 Vt. 48; Pomeroy v. Bailey, 43 N. H. 118; Wilson v. Forsyth, 24 Barb. 105; M'Kinney v. Rhoads, 5 Watts, 343; Wykoff v. Carr, 8 Mich. 44; Bates v. Ableman, 13 Wis. 644; *vide* Alexander v. Gould, 1 Mass. 165; Reichart v. Castator, 5 Binn. 109.

[3] Elliott v. Stoddard, 98 Mass. 145; Sackett v. Spencer, 65 Penn. 89; Sweetzer v. Mead, 5 Mich. 107; *vide* Gruber v. Boyles, 1 Brev. 266; U. S. v. Mertz, 2 Watts, 406; College v. Powell, 12 Gratt. 372.

[4] Cuyler v. McCartney, 40 N. Y. 221; s. c. 33 Barb. 165.

[5] Boyden v. Moore, 11 Pick. 362.

[6] Claytor v. Anthony, 6 Rand. 285.

conclusively establish the fraud, but are to be considered in connection with other evidence and to be governed as to their effect by the usual rules of the law.[1]

CONTEMPORANEOUS ACTS AND DECLARATIONS.—In
order to invalidate a transfer for a valuable consideration, it must be shown that it was made with a
fraudulent intent on the part of the debtor, and
that the grantee had notice of this intent, and participated in it. These propositions are, in some measure, independent of each other, inasmuch as there
may be a fraudulent intent on the part of the debtor
which may not be known to the grantee though proof
of both must concur to establish the right of a creditor
to recover. The evidence to prove these several propositions may be of different kinds and drawn from different sources. It may apply separately to the two
branches of the case. Evidence in regard to the conduct and declarations of the debtor prior to the transfer
is admissible to prove the fraud on his part, and if this
is proved, the knowledge of it on the part of the
grantee may be proved by any circumstances tending
to show a participation in the designs of the debtor.
These acts and declarations may be proved without
proving knowledge on the part of the grantee of the
particular acts and declarations from which the fraudulent intent is to be inferred.[2] It is upon this principle

---

[1] McDowell v. Goldsmith, 6 Md. 319; s. c. 2 Md. Ch. 370.

[2] Bridge v. Eggleston, 14 Mass. 245; Clarke v. Waite, 12 Mass. 439;
Foster v. Hall, 12 Pick. 89; Blake v. White, 13 N. H. 267; Heath v. Page,
63 Penn. 108; Howe v. Reed, 12 Me. 515; Landecker v. Houghtaling, 7
Cal. 391; Mansir v. Crosby, 6 Gray, 334; Gillet v. Phelps, 12 Wis. 392;
Davis v. Stern, 15 La. An. 177; Grooves v. Steele, 2 La. An. 480; Gray v.
St. John, 35 Ill. 222; Winchester v. Charter, 97 Mass. 140; Sarle v. Arnold,
7 R. I. 582; Cook v. Moore, 11 Cush. 213; Kimmel v. M'Right, 2 Penn.
38; Farmers' Bank v. Douglass, 11 S. & M. 469; Guidry v. Grivot, 2 Martin (N. S.) 13; Chase v. Walters, 28 Iowa, 460; Wright v. Linn, 16 Tex.

that fraudulent transfers to other persons, at or about the time of the transfer, may be shown.[1] There is, moreover, a probable connection in a series of sales nearly at the same time, the result of which is to strip a man of his available property. If such evidence were not admissible, it would be in the power of parties, by subdividing such transactions, to altogether destroy the force of the evidence resulting from their general character.[2]

LIMITATION OF RULE.—The rule that distinct frauds may be shown is limited, however, to such frauds as are contemporaneous, or at most nearly so, and does not embrace dealings which are so remote in point of time as to throw no light upon the matter in issue between the parties.[3] The admissibility of such evidence is to

34; Lynde v. McGregor, 13 Allen, 172; McElfatrick v. Hicks, 21 Penn. 404; Booth v. Bunce, 33 N. Y. 139; Trezevant v. Courtenay, 23 La. An. 628; Chase v. Chase, 105 Mass. 385; *Contra*, Beach v. Catlin, 4 Day, 284; Reed v. Smith, 14 Ala. 380; Oden v. Rippettoe, 4 Ala. 68; Partelo v. Harris, 26 Conn. 480; Pettibone v. Phelps, 13 Conn. 445; Jones v. Norris, 2 Ala. 526; Adams v. Foley, 4 Iowa, 44; Prior v. White, 12 Ill. 261; Curtis v. Moore, 20 Md. 93.

[1] Livermore v. Northrop, 44 N. Y. 107; Crow v. Ruby, 5 Mo. 484; Cummings v. McCullough, 5 Ala. 324; Cram v. Mitchell, 1 Sandf. Ch. 251; Guerin v. Hunt, 6 Minn. 375; Lehmer v. Herr, 1 Duvall, 360; Blake v. White, 13 N. H. 267; Hills v. Hoitt, 18 N. H. 603; Whittier v. Varney, 10 N. H. 291; Van Kirk v. Wilds, 11 Barb. 520; Angrave v. Stone, 45 Barb. 35; Benning v. Nelson, 23 Ala. 801; Fisher v. True, 38 Me. 534; Howe v. Reed, 12 Me. 515; Ford v. Williams, 3 B. Mon. 550; Zerbe v. Miller, 16 Penn. 488; Deakers v. Temple, 41 Penn. 234; Sarle v. Arnold, 7 R. I. 582; Warren v. Williams, 52 Me. 343; Taylor v. Robinson, 2 Allen, 562; *vide* Brett v. Catlin, 57 Barb. 404; Mower v. Hanford, 6 Minn. 535; Christopher v. Covington, 2 B. Mon. 357.

[2] Pierce v. Hoffman, 24 Vt. 525.

[3] Cohn v. Mulford, 15 Cal. 50; Staples v. Smith, 48 Me. 470; Huntzinger v. Harper, 44 Penn. 204; McAulay v. Earnhart, 1 Jones, (N. C.) 502; Imray v. Magnay, 11 M. & W. 267; Flagg v. Willington, 6 Me. 386; Boyd v. Brown, 17 Pick. 453; Cook v. Swan, 5 Conn. 140; Blake v. Howard, 11 Me. 202.

35

be determined according to the degree of its relation to the transfer in controversy. It need not take place immediately with it, provided it is calculated to unfold the nature and quality of the fact it is intended to explain, and so to harmonize with it as to constitute one transaction. Within these limits the rule may be considered as only an enlarged application of the principles which admits the acts and declarations which constitute a part of the *res gestœ*. Prior declarations which are subsequently adopted and acted upon by the grantee are admissible upon other grounds.[1]

DECLARATIONS OF CONSPIRATORS.—When several persons are engaged in a common enterprise, each is responsible for the declarations as well as the acts of the others. If the connection and purpose are first established, the declarations of one of the parties, while engaged in the prosecution of this purpose, may be received against the others. They are admissible as a part of the *res gestœ*. They constitute parts of the transaction on which the rights of the creditors depend. The statements of a person who has participated in an act are not considered as mere hearsay but as legitimate evidence of the act done,[2] and are thus competent evidence against the others.[3] It constitutes no objection to the

---

[1] Cuyler v. McCartney, 40 N. Y. 221; s. c. 33 Barb. 165.

[2] Stovall v. Farmers' Bank, 8 S. & M. 305.

[3] Jenne v. Joslyn, 41 Vt. 478; McDowell v. Rissell, 37 Penn. 164; Lee v. Lamprey, 43 N. H. 13; M'Kee v. Gilchrist, 3 Watts, 230; Rogers v. Hall, 4 Watts, 359; Gibbs v. Neely, 7 Watts, 305; Trimble v. Turner, 13 S. & M. 348; Tuttle v. Turner, 28 Tex. 759; Hartman v. Diller, 62 Penn. 37; Bredin v. Bredin, 3 Penn. 81; Kelsey v. Murphy, 26 Penn. 78; Stewart v. Johnson, 3 Harrison, 87; Caldwell v. Williams, 1 Ind. 405; Cuyler v. McCartney, 40 N. Y. 221; Waterbury v. Sturtevant, 18 Wend. 353; Reitenbach v. Reitenbach, 1 Rawle. 362; Claytor v. Anthony, 6 Rand. 285; Abney v. Kingsland, 10 Ala. 355; Eaton v. Cooper, 29 Vt. 444; Borland v. Mayo, 8 Ala. 104; Stovall v. Farmers' Bank, 8 S. & M. 305.

admissibility of such declarations that the plan was concocted before the party against whom they are offered
became an associate. By connecting himself with the
others and aiding in the execution of their plan, he
adopts their prior acts and declarations so far as they
constitute a part of the *res gestœ*, as much as if he had
been present and assented to each successive step in
carrying out and consummating the fraud.[1]

CONSPIRACY MUST BE ESTABLISHED.—Before such declarations can be given in evidence, however, there
must be proof of the confederacy. In order to ascertain
whether they are admissible, it devolves upon the court
to determine for itself whether other facts are sufficiently
proved, and whether these facts are *prima facie* sufficient proof that the parties have combined to effect the
fraudulent design. If it finds that there is such proof
it admits the declarations as fit evidence to be considered by the jury, in forming their judgment on the
whole case, who may nevertheless negative the combination.[2] The combination can not be established by
the declarations themselves, for a species of evidence
which is in its nature inadmissible, unless some other
fact is proved, can not be used to establish the fact the
proof of which is an indispensable condition of its own
admissibility. They, therefore, can not even be heard
until a foundation is laid for their introduction, by
proper proof, that the debtor and grantee were engaged
in a conspiracy to defraud creditors.[3] Mere proof that
they have concurred in a transfer does not establish it,
for it only shows a common intent, but not a common

---

[1] Stewart v. Johnson, 3 Harrison, 87.

[2] Claytor v. Anthony, 6 Rand. 285.

[3] Cuyler v. McCartney, 40 N. Y. 221; Claytor v. Anthony, 6 Rand.
285; Abney v. Kingsland, 10 Ala. 355.

intent to defraud.[1] A very slight degree of concert or collusion, however, is sufficient.[2] The retention of possession,[3] or a statement of the debtor showing a fraudulent intent made so near the grantee that he might, and most probably did, hear it, are sufficient.[4] The retention of possession, however, must be of such a character as to raise a presumption of a fraudulent intent.[5]

SUBSEQUENT DECLARATIONS.—The existence of the fraudulent intent must always be proved by evidence, which is competent as against the grantee. The acts and declarations of the debtor, however, made after the transfer, have not, in the absence of any proof of a conspiracy, any tendency to prove the cause or motive of the act. After the transfer is consummated the debtor becomes a stranger to the title for all purposes, and his acts and declarations are no more binding on the grantee than are those of any stranger to the transaction. They are in their nature hearsay and irrelevant. No person, moreover, should be allowed to defeat his transfer by his own acts or words.[6] If the declarations

---

[1] Cuyler v. McCartney, 40 N. Y. 221.

[2] Hartman v. Diller, 62 Penn. 37.

[3] Caldwell v. Williams, 1 Ind. 405; Borland v. Mayo, 8 Ala. 104; Waterbury v. Sturtevant, 18 Wend. 353.

[4] Stovall v. Farmers' Bank, 8 S. & M. 305.

[5] Abney v. Kingsland, 10 Ala. 355.

[6] Miner v. Phillips, 42 Ill. 128; Babb v. Clemson, 12 S. & R. 328; Clements v. Moore, 6 Wall. 299; Foster v. Wallace, 2 Mo. 231; Steward v. Thomas, 35 Mo. 202; Hessing v. McCloskey, 37 Ill. 341; Visher v. Webster, 13 Cal. 58; Lewis v. Wilcox, 6 Nev. 215; Peck v. Crouse, 46 Barb, 151; Vance v. Smith, 2 Heisk. 343; Ogden v. Peters, 15 Barb. 560; Bogert v. Haight, 9 Paige, 297; Ball v. Loomis, 29 N. Y. 412; Savery v. Spaulding, 8 Iowa, 239; Norton v. Kearney, 10 Wis. 443; Myers v. Kinzie, 26 Ill. 36; Wynne v. Glidewell, 17 Ind. 446; Bates v. Ableman, 13 Wis. 644; Burt v. McKinstry, 4 Minn. 204; Pickett v. Pickett, 3 Dev. 6; Edgell v. Bennett, 7 Vt. 534; Gamble v. Johnson, 9 Mo. 605; Humphries

or acts are made or done with the assent of the grantee,[1] or if the debtor is produced as a witness,[2] then they may be used as evidence upon other grounds and not merely as intrinsically competent of themselves.

DECLARATIONS IN POSSESSION.—When the debtor remains in possession of the property, his acts and declarations are competent evidence against the grantee. The possession is a part of the *res gestæ*, and the nature and character of the possession is an important point of inquiry. The acts and declarations connected with it and forming a part of its attendant circumstances are collateral indications of its nature, extent, and purpose. They are admissible, not because any peculiar credit is due to the party in possession, but because they qualify and characterize the very fact to be investigated.[3] The

---

v. McCraw, 9 Ark. 91; Scott v. Heilager, 14 Penn. 238; Reed v. Smith, 14 Ala. 380; Foote v. Cobb, 18 Ala. 585; Strong v. Brewer, 17 Ala. 706; McElfatrick v. Hicks, 21 Penn. 402; Wolf v. Carothers, 3 S. & R. 240; Gridley v. Bingham, 51 Ill. 153; Taylor v. Robinson, 2 Allen, 562; Derby v. Gallup, 5 Minn. 119; Lormore v. Campbell, 60 Barb. 62; Pier v. Duff, 63 Penn. 59; Sackett v. Spencer, 65 Penn. 89; Cohn v. Mulford, 15 Cal. 50; Zimmerman v. Lamb, 7 Minn. 421; Winchester v. Charter, 97 Mass. 140; Aldrich v. Earle, 13 Gray, 578; Sutter v. Lackmann, 39 Mo. 91; Shaw v. Robertson, 12 Minn. 445; Miner v. Phillips, 42 Ill. 128; Pulliam v. Newberry, 41 Ala. 168; Weinrich v. Porter, 47 Mo. 293; Ragan v. Kennedy, 1 Tenn. 91; Clark v. Johnson, 5 Day, 373; Phillips v. Eamer, 1 Esp. 355; Glenn v. Grover, 3 Md. 212; Collumb v. Read, 24 N. Y. 505; Cuyler v. McCartney, 40 N. Y. 221.

[1] Kendall v. Hughes, 7 B. Mon. 368.

[2] Borland v. Mayo, 8 Ala. 104; Venable v. Bank, 2 Pet. 107.

[3] Askew v. Reynolds, 1 Dev. & Bat. 367; Marsh v. Hampton, 5 Jones, (N. C.) 382; Goodgame v. Cole, 12 Ala. 77; Cole v. Varner, 31 Ala. 244; Pomeroy v. Bailey, 43 N. H. 118; Ragan v. Kennedy, 1 Tenn. 91; Peck v. Land, 2 Kelly, 1; Paper Works v. Willett, 1 Robt. 131; Helfrich v. Stem, 17 Penn. 143; Carnahan v. Wood, 2 Swan, 500; Abney v. Kingsland, 10 Ala. 355; Waggoner v. Cooley, 17 Ill. 239; Currie v. Hart, 2 Sandf. Ch. 353; Adams v. Davidson, 10 N. Y. 309; Jacobs v. Remsen, 36 N. Y. 668; Babb v. Clemson, 10 S. & R. 419; s. c. 12 S. & R. 328; Blake

principle applies to personal as well as real property,[1] and extends to the declarations of any person in possession.[2] The possession, however, must be actual and not merely constructive, and inconsistent with the title of the grantee.[3] The acts and declarations are admissible in favor of the grantee as well as of creditors.[4] But before they can be received, the possession must be shown to the satisfaction of the court.[5] They are not, moreover, admissible to every conceivable extent. As the ground of their admission is to explain the possession, they are limited to such as are explanatory of it. Anything beyond this is no part of the thing done, and consequently is inadmissible,[6] unless it is competent for some other reason.

RELATIONS OF THE PARTIES AND EVENTS CONNECTED WITH THE TRANSFER.—It is always competent to show what precedes and follows the transfer, the relations of the parties both prior and subsequent, and all the facts and circumstances surrounding it.[7] It is upon this

---

v. White, 13 N. H. 267; Foster v. Woodfin, 11 Ired. 339; Robinson v. Pitzer, 3 W. Va. 335; Redfield v. Buck, 35 Conn. 328; Caldwell v. Rose, 1 Smith, 190; Reed v. Smith, 14 Ala. 380; Farnsworth v. Bell, 5 Sneed, 531; Neal v. Peden, 1 Head, 546; Grant v. Lewis, 14 Wis. 487; Deakers v. Temple, 41 Penn. 234; Carrollton Bank v. Cleveland, 15 La. An. 616; Willies v. Farley, 3 C. & P. 395; Wilbur v. Strickland, 1 Rawle, 458; Grant v. Lewis, 14 Wis. 487; Blake v. Graves, 18 Iowa, 312; Cahoon v. Marshall, 25 Cal. 197.

[1] McBride v. Thompson, 8 Ala. 650.

[2] Walcott v. Keith, 22 N. H. 196; Kendall v. Hughes, 7 B. Mon. 368.

[3] Trotter v. Watson, 6 Humph. 509; Donaldson v. Johnson, 2 Chand. 160; Ford v. Williams, 13 N. Y. 577; Mayer v. Clark, 40 Ala. 259.

[4] Waters v. Riggin, 19 Md. 536; Walcott v. Keith, 22 N. H. 196; Upson v. Raiford, 29 Ala. 188; vide Williams v. Kelsey, 6 Geo. 365.

[5] Thomas v. De Graffenreid, 17 Ala. 602.

[6] Abney v. Kingsland, 10 Ala. 355; McBride v. Thompson, 8 Ala. 650; Borland v. Mayo, 8 Ala. 104; Christopher v. Covington, 2 B. Mon. 357; vide Burckmyer v. Maris, Riley, 208.

[7] Erfort v. Consalus, 47 Mo. 208.

ground that evidence of other contemporaneous transfers between the same parties is admissible.[1] It must, however, be shown that they were so connected with the transfer in controversy as to make it apparent that the parties had a common purpose in both.[2] The principles applies also to subsequent transfers.[3] But even though fraud is proved in other transfers it is not conclusive.[4] The whole conduct of the parties with reference to the property transferred may be shown as bearing upon the question of good faith or fraudulent intent. It is true that the fraud must be in the inception of the transaction, but the subsequent acts are calculated to explain the motives which actuated the parties at the beginning and give tone to the original purpose.[5] Such subsequent acts are also admissible in favor of the grantee.[6] The transfer, however, must be judged by its terms and in the light of the contemporaneous and subsequent acts of the parties. These furnish the data for the determination of the intent and motives with which it was made.[7]

---

[1] Van Kirk v. Wilds, 11 Barb. 520; Amsden v. Manchester, 40 Barb. 158; Gibbs v. Neely, 7 Watts, 305; M'Ilvoy v. Kennedy, 2 Bibb. 380; Benham v. Cary, 11 Wend. 83; Cumming v. Fryer, Dudley, 182; Trotter v. Watson, 6 Humph. 509; Pierson v. Tom, 1 Tex. 577; Helfrich v. Stem, 17 Penn. 143; Belt v. Raguet, 27 Tex. 471; Price v. Mahoney, 24 Iowa, 582; Erfort v. Consalus, 47 Mo. 208; McCabe v. Brayton, 38 N. Y. 196.

[2] Williams v. Robbins, 15 Gray, 590; Sutter v. Lackman, 39 Mo. 91.

[3] Lynde v. McGregor, 13 Allen, 172.

[4] Collumb v. Read, 24 N. Y. 505.

[5] Flanigan v. Lampman, 12 Mich. 58; Dallam v. Renshaw, 26 Mo. 533; Wilson v. Ferguson, 10 How. Pr. 175; Wright v. Linn, 16 Tex. 34; Forbes v. Waller, 25 N. Y. 430; Carr v. Gate, Davies, 328; Snodgrass v. Bank, 25 Ala. 161; Blue v. Penniston, 27 Mo. 272; Warren v. Williams, 52 Me. 343.

[6] Cecil Bank v. Snively, 23 Md. 253; Helfrich v. Stem, 17 Penn. 143; Graham v. Lockhart, 8 Ala. 9; Creagh v. Savage, 14 Ala. 454.

[7] Forbes v. Waller, 25 N. Y. 430.

CONTEMPORANEOUS ACTS.—Evidence of the condition and acts of the parties at and about the time of the transfer is competent, for it serves to show the reasonableness of their conduct and to throw light upon their motives. It may be shown that the grantor was indebted,[1] or intoxicated,[2] or that the grantee was unable to purchase the property,[3] or that the statements in a written instrument are false,[4] or that receipts between the parties are fraudulent,[5] or that the debtor made the transfer known,[6] or that he concealed a part of his property.[7] Evidence of the character either of the debtor[8] or of the grantee[9] is not admissible, for character is not directly put in issue by the nature of the controversy. A verdict setting aside the transfer for fraud in another suit between other parties,[10] or the issuing of an attachment by another creditor, is not competent evidence.[11] Heavy purchases immediately preceding the

---

[1] Hanet v. Dundass, 4 Penn. 178; Manhattan Co. v. Osgood, 15 Johns. 162; Covanhovan v. Hart, 21 Penn. 495; Helfrich v. Stem, 17 Penn. 143; Smith v. Henry, 2 Bailey, 118; Williams v. Banks, 11 Md. 198; Mills v. Howeth, 19 Tex. 257; Waters v. Dashiell, 1 Md. 455; King v. Bailey, 6 Mo. 575.

[2] Delaware v. Ensign, 21 Barb. 85.

[3] Borland v. Mayo, 8 Ala. 104; Demerritt v. Miles, 22 N. H. 523; M'Ilvoy v. Kennedy, 2 Bibb, 380; Hyman v. Bailey, 13 La. An., 450; Amsden v. Manchester, 40 Barb. 158; Belt v. Raguet, 27 Tex. 471; Stebbins v. Miller, 12 Allen, 591; *vide* Derby v. Gallup, 5 Minn. 119; Cook v. Swan, 5 Conn. 140.

[4] Peake v. Stout, 8 Ala. 647.

[5] Balt. & Ohio R. R. Co. v. Hoge, 34 Penn. 214.

[6] Paper Works v. Willett, 1 Robt. 131.

[7] Wilson v. Forsyth, 24 Barb. 105; Guerin v. Hunt, 8 Minn. 477.

[8] Gutzweiler v. Lackman, 23 Mo. 168; Church v. Drummond, 7 Ind. 17.

[9] M'Kinney v. Rhoads, 5 Watts. 343; Holmesley v. Hogue, 2 Jones, (N. C.) 391.

[10] Mower v. Hanford, 6 Minn. 535.

[11] Miner v. Phillips, 42 Ill. 128.

transfer may be shown.[1] The declarations of one
grantee are not admissible against another who holds
with him as tenant in common.[2] The fact of an attorney's advice to the grantee may be shown.[3]

WITNESS CANNOT TESTIFY TO ANOTHER'S INTENT.—
The intent with which an act is done is to be ascertained from the circumstances surrounding it, and from
the acts and declarations of the parties, and is therefore
a deduction or inference from facts; consequently a
witness cannot testify in regard to the intentions of another, for he must speak of facts within his own knowledge, and not of inferences that he may draw from facts
that may be known to him.[4] The debtor[5] and the grantee[6]
may each testify in regard to his own intentions. Such
testimony on the part of the debtor is not regarded as
anything more than an expression of his opinion
as to the character of the transaction, and is not conclusive,[7] and unless it is supported by other evidence, is

---

[1] Curtis v. Moore, 20 Md. 93.

[2] Manhattan Co. v. Osgood, 3 Cow. 612; s. c. 15 Johns. 162; Graham
v. Lockhart, 8 Ala, 9; Governor v. Campbell, 17 Ala. 566; Cuyler v. Mc-
Cartney, 40 N. Y. 221.

[3] Goodgame v. Cole, 12 Ala. 77; Nicholson v. Leavitt, 4 Sandf. 252;
Fisher v. True, 38 Me. 534; *vide* Lee v. Lamprey, 43 N. H. 13.

[4] Peake v. Stout, 8 Ala. 647; Spaulding v. Strang, 36 Barb. 310; Mattison v. Demarest, 4 Robt. 161.

[5] Forbes v. Waller, 4 Bosw. 475; s. c. 25 N. Y. 430; s. c. 25 How. Pr.
166; Paper Works v. Willett, 1 Robt. 131; Law v. Payson, 32 Me. 521;
Seymour v. Beach, 4 Vt. 493; Wolf v. Carothers, 3 S. & R. 240; Miner v.
Phillips, 42 Ill. 123; Spaulding v. Strang, 36 Barb. 310; Forbes v. Logan,
4 Bosw. 475; Matthews v. Poultney, 33 Barb. 127; Seymour v. Wilson, 14
N. Y. 567; Watkins v. Wallace, 19 Mich. 567.

[6] Bedell v. Chase, 34 N. Y. 386; Paxton v. Boyce, 1 Tex. 317; Edwards v. Currier, 43 Me. 474; Wheelden v. Wilson, 44 Me. 1; Potter v.
McDowell, 31 Mo. 62.

[7] Bates v. Ableman, 13 Wis. 644; Newman v. Cordell, 43 Barb. 448;
Loker v. Haynes, 11 Mass. 498; Brown v. Osgood, 25 Me. 505; Griffin v. Marquardt, 21 N. Y. 121; Keteltas v. Wilson, 36 Barb. 298; s. c. 23 How. Pr. 69.

entitled to but little weight.[1] His mere suppositions in regard to his solvency are inadmissible.[2] Declarations of mere abstract opinions—as, for instance, that a man ought to secure something for his family—are irrelevant.[3]

RECITALS IN DEEDS ARE PRIMA FACIE.—As the presumption is always in favor of fairness, the statement of the payment of the consideration in an instrument is *prima facie* evidence of the fact.[4] It is, however, the lowest species of *prima facie* evidence, inasmuch as the same motives which would induce parties to make and execute a fraudulent conveyance, would induce them to insert an acknowledgment of the payment and receipt of the consideration;[5] and therefore where there is any evidence of fraud, there must be other proof of the

---

[1] Atwood v. Impson, 5 C. E. Green, 150; Work v. Ellis, 50 Barb. 512; Kittering v. Parker, 8 Ind. 44; Borland v. Walker, 7 Ala. 269.

[2] Ogden v. Peters, 15 Barb. 560.

[3] Whiting v. Johnson, 11 S. & R. 328.

[4] Glenn v. Grover, 3 Md. 212; Farringer v. Ramsay, 2 Md. 365; s. c. 4 Md. Ch. 33; Glenn v. Randall, 2 Md. Ch. 220; Moore v. Blondheim, 19 Md. 172; Stockett v. Holliday, 9 Md. 480; Mayfield v. Kilgour, 31 Md. 240; Marden v. Babcock, 2 Met. 99; Every v. Edgerton, 7 Wend. 259; Foster v. Hall, 12 Pick. 89; Lutton v. Hesson, 18 Penn. 109; Clark v. Depew, 25 Penn. 509; Hundley v. Buckner, 6 S. & M. 70; Hempstead v. Johnston, 18 Ark. 123; Brown v. Bartee, 10 S. & M. 268; Splawn v. Martin, 17 Ark. 146; Brinley v. Spring, 7 Me. 241; Merrell v. Williamson, 35 Ill. 529; Gates v. Labeaume, 19 Mo. 17; Mandel v. Peay, 20 Ark. 325; Rindekoff v. Guggenheim, 3 Cold. 284; Shontz v. Brown, 27 Penn. 123; *Contra*, Merrill v. Locke, 41 N. H. 486; Kimball v. Fenner, 12 N. H. 248; Prescott v. Hayes, 43 N. H. 593; Belknap v. Wendell, 21 N. H. 175; Ferguson v. Clifford, 37 N. H. 86; Claywell v. McGimpsie, 4 Dev. 89; Feimester v. McRorie, 12 Ired. 287; Governor v. Campbell, 17 Ala. 566; Branch Bank v. Kinsey, 5 Ala. 9; McCain v. Wood, 4 Ala. 258; McGintry v. Reeves, 10 Ala. 137; McCaskle v. Amarine, 12 Ala. 17; Dolin v. Gardner, 15 Ala. 758; Ferguson v. Gilbert, 16 Ohio St. R. 88; Vogt v. Ticknor, 48 N. H. 242; Brown v. Knox, 6 Mo. 302; College v. Powell, 12 Gratt, 372; Crow v. Ruby, 5 Mo. 484.

[5] Clapp v. Tirrill, 20 Pick. 247; Clark v. Depew, 25 Penn. 509.

consideration.[1] The declarations of the debtor, not made in the presence of the grantee, are not admissible to prove the consideration.[2] Proof cannot be given of the payment of the consideration after the commence· ment of the suit.[3]

WHEN PROOF OF CONSIDERATION MATERIAL.—A deed executed in good faith passes the interest of·the grantor in the property to the grantee, whether any consider· ation is actually paid or not as between the parties to it.[4] It is only when an instrument is assailed by cred· itors that the amount and character of the consider· ation become material. In such controversies it is a leading principle that no evidence is admissible which contradicts the deed or changes its character.[5] The kind of consideration determines whether the instrument belongs to the class of deeds known as bargains and sales, or covenants to stand seized to uses, and to which ever class it belongs its character cannot be changed by parol evidence.[6]

WHEN EVIDENCE OF CONSIDERATION MATERIAL.—If no consideration is expressed in a deed, evidence of a consideration may be given.[7] If the deed purports to

---

[1] Whitaker v. Garnett, 3 Bush. 402 ; Redfield Manuf. Co. v. Dysart, 62 Penn. 62 ; Allen v. Cowan, 28 Barb. 99 ; Rogers v. Hall, 4 Watts, 359 ; Zerbe v. Miller, 16 Penn. 488 ; Mead v. Phillips, 1 Sandf. Ch. 83.

[2] Yardley v. Arnold, 1 Car. & M. 434 ; Hooper v. Edwards, 18 Ala. 280 ; Colquitt v. Thomas, 8 Geo. 258 ; Taylor v. Moore, 2 Rand. 563 ; Coole v. Braham, 3 Exch. 183 ; U. S. v. Mertz, 2 Watts, 406 ; Whiting v. Johnson, 11 S. & R. 328 ; Wilson v. Hillhouse, 14 Iowa, 199.

[3] Angrave v. Stone, 45 Barb. 35.

[4] Bank v. Housman, 6 Paige, 526 ; Doe v. Hurd, 8 Blackf. 310 ; Jackson v. Garnsey, 16 Johns. 189 ; Cunningham v. Dwyer, 23 Md. 219.

[5] Betts v. Union Bank, 1 H. & G. 175.

[6] Cunningham v. Dwyer, 23 Md. 219.

[7] Peacock v. Monk, 1 Ves. Sr. 127 ; Howell v. Elliott, 1 Dev. 76 ; Banks v. Brown, 1 Riley Ch. 131 ; s. c. 2 Hill Ch. 558.

be for a valuable consideration, evidence may be given of an additional consideration of the same kind as that so set forth.[1] This additional consideration may consist either of money paid to the grantor's creditors,[2] or an indebtedness due to the grantee,[3] or a liability as indorser,[4] or the grantee's note,[5] or a claim for damages,[6] or future advances,[7] or any other valuable consideration.[8] A mere secret parol trust to apply the property to the benefit of the grantor's creditors is not sufficient.[9] A mere nominal consideration may, according to circumstances, constitute a voluntary deed,[10] or a deed founded upon a valuable consideration.[11]

FROM OTHER PARTIES.—It is not necessary that the proof should show that the consideration passed immediately from the grantee to the grantor. If A. bargains for land with B., and pays the agreed price, and at A.'s request the deed is made to C. without

---

[1] Anderson v. Tydings, 3 Md. Ch. 167; Bullard v. Briggs, 7 Pick. 533; Banks v. Brown, 1 Riley Ch. 131; s. c. 2 Hill Ch. 558; Cunningham v. Dwyer, 23 Md. 219; McNeal v. Glenn, 4 Md. 87; s. c. 3 Md. Ch. 349.

[2] Glenn v. Randall, 2 Md. Ch. 220; Waters v. Riggin, 19 Md. 536.

[3] Anderson v. Tydings, 3 Md. Ch. 167; Buffum v. Green, 5 N. H. 71; Cunningham v. Dwyer, 23 Md. 219; Credle v. Carrawan, 64 N. C. 422.

[4] McKinster v. Babcock, 26 N. Y. 378.

[5] Mayfield v. Kilgour, 31 Md. 240.

[6] Fellows v. Emperor, 13 Barb. 92.

[7] Craig v. Tippin, 2 Sandf. Ch. 78; Bank v. Finch, 3 Barb. Ch. 293; Lawrence v. Tucker, 23 How. 14; Cole v. Albers, 1 Gill. 412; Shirras v. Craig, 7 Cranch, 34.

[8] Tyler v. Carlton, 7 Me. 175.

[9] Jones v. Slubey, 5 H. & J. 372; Bireley v. Staley, 5 G. & J. 432; Pettibone v. Stevens, 15 Conn. 19.

[10] Baxter v. Sewell, 3 Md. 334; s. c. 2 Md. Ch. 447; Walker v. Burrows, 1 Atk. 93; Wickes v. Clarke, 8 Paige, 161; Ridgeway v. Underwood, 4 Wash. C. C. 129; McKinley v. Combs, 1 Mon. 105; Felder v. Harper, 12 Ala. 612.

[11] Cunningham v. Dwyer, 23 Md. 219; Harvey v. Alexander, 1 Rand. 219.

any fraudulent intent, C. may maintain his title to the property by proving the consideration so paid. Even if the design of the conveyance were that C. should hold the land in trust for A., but he has executed no writing by which that trust can be legally proved, still the title of C. can not be impeached by a creditor of B. on that account, for a declaration of trust may at any time afterwards be executed, or A. may confide in the integrity of C., and it is a matter only between A. and C. whether the trust be executed or not. In the case supposed B. has obtained the value of his land, and his creditors are not necessarily injured.[1]

CONTEMPORANEOUS DEEDS. — For the purpose of repelling any imputation of fraud it may be shown that a deed was made in consideration of another instrument of the same date. Whether they constitute parts of the same transaction depends upon all the surrounding circumstances of each particular case, and not upon the simple fact whether they are or are not, by express references, grafted into, or connected with each other, and is generally a question of fact.[2]

NOTES AND JUDGMENTS.—Evidence may be given to show what was the consideration of a note which purports to be for value received.[3] A judgment confessed in the name of one person may be shown by parol to have been given for debts due to others.[4]

CONSIDERATION CANNOT BE VARIED.—A deed pur-

---

[1] Bullard v. Briggs, 7 Pick. 533; Harvey v. Alexander, 1 Rand. 219.
[2] Harman v. Richards, 10 Hare, 81; Gale v. Williamson, 8 M. & W. 405; Keen v. Preston, 24 Md. 395; Belt v. Raguet, 27 Tex. 471.
[3] Harris v. Alcock, 10 G. & J. 226.
[4] Insurance Co. v. Wallis, 23 Md. 173; Harris v. Alcock, 10 G. &. J. 226; Groshen v. Thomas, 20 Md. 234.

porting to be for a valuable consideration cannot be set up as a gift.[1] If it purports to be given for love and affection, proof of a valuable consideration is inadmissible. The statement of a particular consideration imports the whole consideration, and is a negative to any other, and such evidence would, if admitted, vary the consideration, and consequently is not competent.[2] Under the expression " other good causes and considerations," the considerations of love and affection may be shown.[3] A difference between the debts described as the consideration of a deed and those offered in evidence, either as to names, debts, or amounts, does not necessarily affect the validity of the instrument, but at most merely furnishes grounds for an unfavorable presumption.[4]

EVIDENCE BY GRANTEE.—The grantee may prove his ignorance of the grantor's insolvency.[5] The debtor's schedules in bankruptcy[6] and his prior offers to sell the property to other persons,[7] are not competent evidence. It may be shown that up to the time of the transfer the debtor was applying his means in discharge of his debts.[8] A letter from the debtor to him notifying him of the execution of a mortgage in his favor is admis-

---

[1] Hildreth v. Sands, 2 Johns. Ch. 35 ; Betts v. Union Bank, 1 H. & G. 175 ; Rollins v. Mooers, 25 Me. 192 ; vide Brackett v. Wait, 4 Vt. 389.

[2] Ellinger v. Crowl, 17 Md. 361 ; McNeal v. Glenn, 4 Md. 87 ; s. c. 3 Md. Ch. 349 ; Hinds v. Longworth, 11 Wheat, 199 ; Baxter v. Sewell, 3 Md. 334 ; s. c. 2 Md. Ch. 447 ; Bean v. Smith, 2 Mason 252 ; vide Henderson v. Dodd, 1 Bailey Ch. 138.

[3] Pomeroy v. Bailey, 43 N. H. 118.

[4] Graham v. Lockhart, 8 Ala. 9 ; Pomeroy v. Manin, 2 Paine, 476.

[5] Filley v. Register, 4 Minn. 391.

[6] Carr v. Gale, Daveis, 328.

[7] Tifts v. Bunker, 55 Me. 178 ; Fisher v. True, 38 Me. 534.

[8] Mower v. Hanford, 6 Minn. 535.

sible.[1] Proof may be given of declarations made by the grantee prior to the transfer of an intention to assist the debtor to evade the claims of his creditors.[2]

BURDEN OF PROOF.—It is a universal principal both at law and in equity that the law never presumes fraud. *Odiosa et inhonesta non sunt in lege præsumenda et in facto quod se habet ad bonum et malum de bono quam malo præsumendum est.* The burden of proof, therefore, rests upon the creditors whenever they assail a transfer for fraud.[3] It is not necessary, however, to establish it by direct and positive proof, for this can seldom be done. Generally the first effort of a man who intends to commit a fraud is to throw a veil over the transaction, to shield it against assault, and baffle all attempts at detection. No man willingly furnishes the evidence of his own turpitude. Fraud is, for this reason, rarely perpetrated openly and in broad daylight. It is committed in secret, and privately, and usually hedged in and surrounded by all the guards which can be invoked to prevent discovery and exposure. Its operations are frequently circuitous and difficult of detection. It is, therefore, usually established by circumstantial evidence.[4]

---

[1] Sweetzer v. Mead, 5 Mich. 107.

[2] Foster v. Thompson, 5 Gray, 453; Helfrich v. Sten, 17 Penn. 143.

[3] Thornton v. Hook, 36 Cal. 223; Foster v. Hall, 12 Pick. 89; Nichols v. Patten, 18 Me. 231; Blaisdell v. Cowell, 14 Me. 370; Fifield v. Gaston, 12 Iowa, 218; Bell v. Hill, 1 Hay. (N. C.) 72; Sutton v. Lackman, 39 Mo. 91; Elliott v. Stoddard, 98 Mass. 145.

[4] Bullock v. Narrott, 49 Ill. 62; Kempner v. Churchill, 8 Wall. 362; Floyd v. Goodwin, 8 Yerg. 484; Sibly v. Hood, 3 Mo. 206; Wright v. Grover, 27 Ill. 426; King v. Mocn, 42 Mo. 551; Newman v. Cordell, 43 Barb. 448; Hicks v. Stone, 13 Minn. 434; Pope v. Andrews, 1 S. & M. Ch. 135; Land v. Jeffries, 5 Rand. 599; Rogers v. Hall, 4 Watts, 359; Curtis v. Moore, 20 Md. 93; McConihe v. Sawyer, 12 N. H. 396; Floyd v. Goodwin, 8 Yerg. 484; Kane v. Drake, 27 Ind. 29.

MODE OF PROOF.—No transfer is fraudulent unless it is made with an intent to delay, hinder or defraud creditors, and this intent is an emotion of the mind, and can usually be shown only by the acts and declarations of the party.[1] These acts and declarations, and all the concomitant circumstances, must be established, and then the motive may be deduced from them in accordance with those principles which are shown by experience and observation to rule human conduct.[2] The proof in each case will consequently depend upon its own circumstances.[3] It usually consists of many items of evidence which, standing detached and alone, would be immaterial, but which, in connection with others, tend to illustrate and shed light upon the character of the transaction, and show the position in which the parties stand and their motives, conduct, and relations to each other. *Quæ tingula non prosunt, juncta juvant.* Although the evidence is generally circumstantial it is often as potent as direct testimony. Sometimes a combination of circumstances characterize a transaction so plainly and so clearly as to stamp upon it unerring and indelible marks of fraud which can not be mistaken, and the transaction itself present phases so remarkable and peculiar that no fair-minded person can hesitate to pronounce it fraudulent. These *indicia* are often the clearest proof and quite as reliable as positive evidence.[4]

FRAUD MAY BE PRESUMED.—It is sometimes said that fraud can never be presumed, but the fact that it is generally established by circumstantial evidence,

---

[1] Babcock v. Eckler, 24 N. Y. 623.

[2] Filley v. Register, 4 Minn. 391.

[3] Huff v. Roane, 22 Ark. 184.

[4] Newman v. Cordell, 43 Barb. 448; Boies v. Henney, 32 Ill. 130.

shows that this expression is incorrect. The law never presumes fraud, but fraud itself may be established by inference the same as any other fact. Presumptions are of two kinds, legal and natural. Allegations of fraud are sometimes supported by one, and sometimes by the other, and are seldom, almost never, sustained by that direct and plenary proof which excludes all presumption. Fraud is established by mere presumption of law, when the necessary consequence of an act is to delay or defraud. A natural presumption is the deduction of one fact from another. When creditors are about to be cheated, it is very uncommon for the perpetrators to proclaim their purpose and call in witnesses to see it done. A resort to presumptive evidence, therefore, becomes absolutely necessary to protect the rights of honest men from this as from other invasions. Fraud in the transfer of goods or land may be shown by the same amount of proof as will establish any other fact in its own nature as likely to exist. In any case the number and cogency of the circumstances from which guilt may be inferred are proportioned to the original improbability of the offence. The frequency of frauds upon creditors, the difficulty of detection, the powerful motives which tempt an insolvent man to commit it and the plausible casuistry with which it is sometimes reconciled to the consciences even of persons whose previous lives have been without reproach, are considerations which prevent its classification among the grossly improbable violations of moral duty, and often permit it to be presumed from facts which may seem slight. How much evidence is required to raise a presumption of actual fraud can not be determined according to any inflexible rule.[1]

---

[1] Kaine v. Weigley, 22 Penn. 179; Kendall v. Hughes, 7 B. Mon. 368; Reed v. Noxon, 48 Ill. 323; Colquitt v. Thomas, 8 Geo. 258.

36

AMOUNT OF PROOF.—While the law abhors fraud, it is also unwilling to impute it on slight and trivial evidence and thereby cast an unjust reproach upon the character of the parties.[1] Such an imputation is grave in its character and can only be sustained on satisfactory proof. If the evidence is so conflicting that no conclusion can be reached, the transaction must be sustained, upon the principle that the burden of proof is on the party who assails it, and if he does no more than create an equilibrium, he fails to make ou this case.[2] Mere suspicion leading to no certain results is not sufficient.[3] A legal title will not be divested upon mere conjectures or evidence loose and indeterminate in its character.[4] Fraud will never be imputed when the circumstances and facts upon which it is predicated may consist with honesty and purity of intention.[5]

NOT INCONSISTENT WITH OTHER THEORY.—It is not necessary, however, that the proofs tending to the conclusion of fraud should be incapable of being accounted for upon any other hypothesis. There is no rule of evidence or principle of law which requires that the circumstances must be of so conclusive a nature and

---

[1] Thompson v. Sanders, 6 J. J. Marsh. 94; Blow v. Gage, 44 Ill. 208.

[2] Kaine v. Weigley, 22 Penn. 179.

[3] Parkhurst v. McGraw, 24 Miss. 134; Blow v. Gage, 44 Ill. 208; Waddingham v. Loker, 44 Mo. 132; Bartlett v. Blake, 37 Me. 124; Belk v. Massey, 11 Rich. 614; Roberts v. Guernsey, 3 Grant, 237; Phettiplace v. Sayles, 4 Mason, 312; Hale v. Saloon Omnibus Co. 4 Drew. 492; s. c. 28 L. J. Ch. 777; Thompson v. Sanders, 6 J. J. Marsh. 94; Glenn v. Grover, 3 Md. 212; s. c. 3 Md. Ch. 29; Faringer v. Ramsay, 2 Md. 365; s. c. 4 Md. Ch. 33; Buck v. Sherman, 2 Doug. (Mich.) 176; White v. Trotter, 14 S. & M. 30; Hoose v. Robbins, 18 La. An. 648; King v. Moon, 42 Mo. 551; Waterman v. Donalson, 43 Ill. 29.

[4] Fifield v. Gaston, 12 Iowa, 218.

[5] Stiles v. Lightfoot, 26 Ala. 443; Lyman v. Cessford, 15 Iowa, 229; Dallam v. Renshaw, 26 Mo. 533.

tendency as to exclude every other hypothesis than the one sought to be established in order to authorize the inference of fraud from circumstantial evidence. If the evidence is admissible as conducing in any degree to the proof of the fact, the only legal test applicable to it upon such an issue is its sufficiency to satisfy the mind and conscience and produce a satisfactory conviction or belief.[1] What amount or weight of evidence is sufficient proof of a fraudulent intent is not a matter of legal definition.

MUST BE SATISFACTORY.—The proof, however, must be clear and satisfactory.[2] It must be so strong and cogent as to satisfy a man of sound judgment of the truth of the allegation.[3] Circumstances affording a strong presumption are sufficient,[4] but the presumption must be drawn from pregnant facts and not from far fetched probabilities.[5] Inferences are to be drawn from such facts not singly but as a whole.[6] As an allegation of fraud is against the presumption of honesty, it requires stronger proof than if no such presumption existed. As it is against a presumption of fact, perhaps often a slight one, it requires somewhat more evidence than would suffice to prove the acknowledgment of an obligation or the delivery of a chattel.[7] It is not necessary, however, that the fraud shall be proved beyond a reasonable doubt. Issues of fact in civil cases are determined by a preponderance of testimony, and the rule

---

[1] Linn v. Wright, 18 Tex. 317.

[2] King v. Moon, 42 Mo. 551 ; Fifield v. Gaston, 12 Iowa, 218.

[3] Henry v. Henry, 8 Barb. 588.

[4] Parkhurst v. McGraw, 24 Miss. 134 ; Hempstead v. Johnston, 18 Ark. 123.

[5] Paxton v. Boyce, 1 Tex. 317.

[6] Stebbins v. Miller, 12 Allen, 591.

[7] Hatch v. Bayley, 12 Cush. 27.

applies as well to cases in which fraud is imputed as to any other. If the evidence produces a rational belief, it can not be discarded although some doubt remains.[1] The payment of a full price does not purify a transaction but is entitled to great weight when the proof of fraud is not clear.[2]

SAME RULE IN EQUITY AS AT LAW.— In the proof of a fraudulent intent the same general rule prevails in equity as at law. The law does not presume fraud, but it must be established by evidence. A court of equity is also governed by the same principles as a court of law in drawing inferences from the testimony placed before it. The difficulty of demonstrating the intention from the overt acts and conduct of the parties furnish no reason for the assertion of the power by a judge guided by no more certain rule than his own arbitrary conclusions to presume a fraudulent intent from his own vague suspicions of the nature and character of the transaction unassisted and uncontrolled by any certain and fixed principles. The character of a transaction is not thus dependent on the peculiar notions of the judge as to what will constitute good or ill faith.[3] The only exception to the rule is where the price given by the grantee is inadequate. When a transfer is of such indecisive and dubious aspect that it can not either be entirely suppressed or entirely supported with satisfaction, a court of equity may allow it to stand as a security for the amount actually paid and let the creditors in upon

---

[1] Ford v. Chambers, 19 Cal. 143; Bryant v. Simoneau, 5 Ill. 324; McConihe v. Sawyer, 12 N. H. 396; Rice v. Dignowithy, 4 S. & M. 57; Watkins v. Wallace, 19 Mich. 57.

[2] Kittering v. Parker, 8 Ind. 44.

[3] Wilson v. Lott, 5 Fla. 305; vide King v. Moon, 42 Mo. 551; Hempstead v. Johnson, 18 Ark. 123.

the balance. The creditors thus get what in equity and good conscience they ought to have and the grantee ought not to withhold from them.[1]

---

[1] Boyd v. Dunlap, 1 Johns. Ch. 478; Bigelow v. Ayrault, 46 Barb. 143; Herne v. Meeres, 1 Vern. 465; s. c. 2 Bro. C. C. 177, n.; Bean v. Smith, 2 Mason, 252; McArthur v. Hoysradt, 11 Paige, 495; Barrow v. Bailey, 5 Fla. 9; Scott v. Winship, 20 Geo. 429; Farmers' Bank v. Long, 7 Bush. 337; M'Meekin v. Edmonds, 1 Hill. Ch. 288; Garland v. Rives, 4 Rand. 282; Barnwell v. Ward, 1 Atk. 260; Clements v. Moore, 6 Wall. 299; Drury v. Cross, 7 Wall. 299; Doughten v. Gray, 2 Stockt. 323; Bennett v. Musgrove, 2 Ves. 51; Ward v. Shallet, 2 Ves. 16; Trimble v. Ratcliffe, 9 B. Mon. 511; s. c. 12 B. Mon. 32.

CHAPTER XXIV.

EXTENT OF GRANTEE'S LIABILITY.

DECREE MUST CONFORM TO BILL.—A creditor can not subject any property to the satisfaction of his demand which he does not claim by his bill.[1] The decree against the grantee must in general be for a surrender of the property, and not for an absolute sum.[2]

GRANTEE NOT LIABLE AFTER SURRENDER. — An honest man will not accept a fraudulent conveyance, and a party who holds property fraudulently will, as soon as he comes to a sense of his moral duty, restore it to those to whom it belongs. He ought generally to give it back to the debtor, in order that it may be applied to his debts if wanted, or to his benefit if not necessary for that purpose. Although the law for the purpose of discouraging fraud will not compel him to restore it to the debtor, yet no person who possesses a sense of justice or honesty will retain it. The relation between the grantee and creditors is different; there is no express obligation between them. The creditors, however, ought to receive their debts, and the law gives them a claim to the property, and charges the grantee as a trustee, in consequence of his possession. The trust is not express, but arises by operation of law, in consequence of his having in his hands that which ought to be applied to the satis-

---

[1] Bozman v. Draughan, 3 Stew. 243.
[2] Bozman v. Draughan, 3 Stew. 243; Greer v. Wright, 6 Gratt. 154.

faction of their demands. It depends, therefore, on the possession of the property. If the grantee, there-fore, divests himself in good faith of that which he could not retain without dishonesty before the right of the creditors to call him to an account accrues, there is nothing remaining upon which to raise a trust, and the relation of trustee ceases.[1] The grantee for the same reason can not be held to account for the prop-erty, or the proceeds arising from a sale of it, which have been applied by him in good faith to the pay-ment of the debts of the grantor.[2] In this respect there is no distinction between a transfer which is fraudulent in fact and one which is fraudulent in law.[3] Unless the commencement of the suit gives notice of the cause of action, the grantee will be protected for payments made before such notice is given.[4]

PROCEEDS.—The grantee is construed to be a trustee for the creditors, and as such is responsible for all his acts in disposing of the property fraudulently conveyed to him. If he has parted with it he must account for the value. *Is autem dolo malo emit, bona fide autem ementi vendidit, in solidum pretium rei quod accepit tenebitur.*[5] A court of equity follows the pro-

---

[1] Swift v. Holdridge, 10 Ohio, 230 ; Stickney v. Crane, 35 Vt. 89; *vide* Baker v. Bartol, 6 Cal. 483.

[2] Bostwick v. Beizer, 10 Abb. Pr. 197 ; Collumb v. Read, 24 N. Y. 505 ; Grover v. Wakeman 4 Paige, 23 ; s. c., 11 Wend. 187 ; Ames v. Blunt, 5 Paige, 13 ; Strong v. Skinner, 4 Barb. 546 ; Averill v. Loucks, 6 Barb. 470 ; *in re* Wilson, 4 Penn. 430 ; Weber v. Samuel, 7 Penn. 499 ; Kaupe v. Bridge, 2 Robt. 459 ; Cummings v. McCullough, 5 Ala. 324 ; Butler v. Jaffray, 12 Ind. 504 ; Stickney v. Crane, 35 Vt. 89 ; Therasson v. Hickok, 37 Vt. 454 ; White v. Banks, 21 Ala. 705 ; How v. Camp, Walk. Ch. 427 ; Bryant v. Young, 21 Ala. 264 ; *vide* Barcroft v. Snodgrass, 1 Cold. 430.

[3] Ames v. Blunt, 5 Paige, 13.

[4] Weber v. Samuel, 7 Penn. 499.

[5] *Dig Lib*, 42 *tit.* 9.

ceeds of the property and affords a remedy by turning
the legal owner into a trustee for the benefit of creditors.[1] The proceeds may be followed into any property
in which it has been invested so far as it can be traced.[2]
The grantee is liable for property which he has converted to his own use.[3] If he sells the property and
receives insufficient security, the loss falls upon him,
and not upon the creditors.[4] If he impedes the creditors by unnecessary litigation, he will be held to make
good all loss which may be occasioned by his unjust
interference.[5] When he gives notes as a consideration
for the transfer, he furnishes the debtor with facilities
for defrauding his creditors, and will, therefore, be held
liable for the notes that are misapplied.[6] If the property has been mixed with other property of the grantee
so that the proceeds can not be ascertained, he may be
charged with the value and interest thereon.[7]

---

[1] Halbert v. Grant, 4 Mon. 580; Wright v. Hancock, 3 Munf. 521;
Hopkirk v. Randolph, 2 Brock. 132; How v. Camp, Walk. Ch. 427;
Grimsley v. Hooker, 3 Jones Eq. 41; Backhouse v. Jett, 1 Brock. 500;
Bryant v. Young, 21 Ala. 264; Van Winkle v. Smith, 26 Miss. 491;
Swinford v. Rogers, 23 Cal. 233; Jones v. Reeder, 22 Ind. 111; Davis v.
Gibbon, 24 Iowa, 257; Ames v. Blunt, 5 Paige, 13; Keep v. Sanderson, 12
Wis. 352; Kelly v. Lane, 42 Barb. 594; s. c., 18 Abb. Pr. 229; s. c., 28
How. Pr. 128; Hawkins v. Alston, 4 Ired. Eq. 137; McGill v. Harman, 2
Jones Eq. 179; Brown v. Godsey, 2 Jones Eq. 417; Clements v. Moore, 6
Wall. 299; vide Kaupe v. Bridge, 2 Robt. 459. The proceeds can not be
reached by an action at law. Lawrence v. Bank, 35 N. Y. 320; Simpson
v. Simpson, 7 Humph. 275; Tubb v. Williams, 7 Humph. 367; Campbell
v. Erie R. R. Co. 46 Barb. 540; Childs v. Derrick, 1 Yerg. 79; Richards
v. Ewing, 11 Humph. 327; Contra, Abney v. Kingsland, 10 Ala. 355;
Carvill v. Stout, 10 Ala. 796; Lynch v. Welsh, 3 Penn. 294; Heath v.
Paige, 63 Penn. 108; French v. Breidelman, 2 Grant, 319.

[2] Clements v. Moore, 6 Wall. 299; McGill v. Harman, 2 Jones Eq. 179.

[3] Van Winkle v. Smith, 26 Miss. 491; How v. Camp, Walk. Ch. 427.

[4] Robinson v. Boyd, 17 Mich. 128.

[5] Watson v. Kennedy, 3 Strobbs. Eq. 1.

[6] Clements v. Moore, 6 Wall. 299.

[7] Steere v. Hoagland, 50 Ill. 377.

INSURANCE.—The creditors have no claim to the money paid to him upon a policy of insurance taken out by him upon the property. He holds the legal title by an unimpeachable right as against all the world except the creditors, and the contingency does not affect his right to obtain an insurance on the property in his own name and for his own benefit. His insurable interest is perfect and complete. An insurance is a valid contract which he has the right to make, and the benefit which accrues to him from it can not be defeated by creditors on the ground that he holds the property by a title which in a certain contingency may be defeasible. The money received on the policy does not stand in the place of the property destroyed. It is in no proper or just sense the proceeds of the property. It is a sum paid by the insurer in consideration of a certain premium as an indemnity for the loss of the property in which the insured has a legal and insurable interest. This indemnity can not be taken away by setting up a contingent right or title in the property.[1]

RENTS AND PROFITS.—The grantee may also be charged with the rents and profits that have accrued from the property. *Et fructus non tantum qui percepti sunt verum etiam hi qui percipi potuerunt a fraudatore, veniunt. Partum quoque in hanc actionem venire, puto verius esse. Præterea generaliter sciendum est ex hac actione restitutionem fieri oportere in pristinum statum, sive res fuerunt sive obligationes, ut perinde omnia revocentur ac si liberatio facta non esset. Propter quod etiam medii temporis commodum quod quis consequeretur liberatione non facta, præstandum erit dum usuræ non præstentur si in stipulatum deductae non fuerunt ; aut si talis contractus fuit in quo usuræ deberi potuerunt etiam non deductæ. Haec*

---

[1] Lerow v. Wilmarth, 9 Allen, 382.

actio post annum de eo quod ad eum pervenit adversus quem actio movetur, competit ; iniquum enim prœtor putavit, in lucro morari eum qui lucrum sensit ex fraude; idcirco lucrum ei extorquendum putavit. Sive igitur ipse fraudator sit ad quem pervenit, sive alius quivis, competit actio in id quod ad eum pervenit, dolove malo ejus factum est quominus perveniret.[1] *Non solum autem ipsam rem alienatam restitui oportet, sed et fructus qui alienationis tempore terrœ cohœrent, quia in bonis fraudatoris fuerunt. Item eos qui post inchoatum judicium recepti sint. Medio autem tempore perceptos in restitutionem non venire.*[2] *Fructus autem fundo cohœsisse non satis intelligere se, Labeo ait, utrum duntaxat qui maturi an etiam qui immaturi fuerint, prœtor significet. Cœterum etiam si de his senserit qui maturi fuerint, nihilo magis possessionem restitui oportere. Nam cum fundus alienaretur, quod ad eum fructusque ejus attineret, unam quandam rem fuisse, id est, fundum cujus omnis generis alienationem fructus sequi. Nec eum qui hyberno tempore habuerit fundum centum, si sub tempus messis, vindemiœve, fructus ejus vendere possit decem, idcirco duas res, id est, fundum centum et fructus decem, eum habere intelligendum; sed unam, id est, fundum centum; sicut is quoque unam rem haberet qui separatim solum œdium vendere possit.*[3]

FROM WHAT TIME PROFITS ARE COMPUTED.—It certainly is not consonant with the principles of the law that the grantee should derive any advantage from his fraud. Consequently, he may be compelled to account for the profits from the time of the transfer.[4]   An

---

[1] *Dig. Lib.*, 42 tit. 9, §§ 20, 21, 24.
[2] *Dig. Lib.*, 42 tit. 9.
[3] *Dig. Lib.*, 42 tit. 9.
[4] Strike v. M'Donald, 2 H. & G. 191; Kipp v. Hanna, 2 Bland, 26; Mead

account may also be taken of what has been received as compensation for the use of the property.[1] The grantee should not be charged with the increased rent and profits arising from improvements made by him.[2]

THE AMOUNT. — When the grantee has merely received money on a voluntary bond, he is only liable for the amount received.[3]   If the grantee has merely received a loan, and is innocent of all fraud, he will only be compelled to pay the money at the time and in the manner he agreed to pay it to the debtor.[4]   When the property is allowed to stand as indemnity for the amount paid by the grantee, he will be charged with interest on the excess above the real value from the day of the transfer.[5]

NO INDEMNITY IN CASE OF ACTUAL FRAUD.—*Si debitor in fraudem creditorum minore pretio fundum scienti emptori vendiderit ; deinde hi quibus de revocando eo actio datur, eum petant ; quæsitum est an pretium restituere debeant ? Proculus existimat, omnimodo restituendum esse fundum etiam si pretium non solvatur. Et rescriptum est secundum Proculi sententiam. Ex his colligi potest ne quidem portionem emptori reddendam*

---

v. Coombs, 4 C. E. Green, 112; How v. Camp, Walk. Ch. 427; *vide* Sands v. Codwise, 4 Johns. 536; Robinson v. Stewart, 10 N. Y. 189; Bean v. Smith, 2 Mason, 252; Ringgold v. Waggoner, 14 Ark. 69; King v. Wilcox, 11 Paige, 589; Blow v. Maynard, 2 Leigh, 29; Higgins v. York Building Co. 2 Atk. 107; Croft v. Arthur, 3 Dessau. 223 ; Backhouse v. Jett, 1 Brock. 500; Pharis v. Leachman, 20 Ala. 662 ; Brown v. M'Donald, 1 Hill Ch. 297.

[1] Shields v. Anderson, 3 Leigh, 729; *Contra*, Simpson v. Simpson, 7 Humph. 275.

[2] King v. Wilcox, 11 Paige, 589.

[3] Hopkirk v. Randolph, 2 Brock. 132.

[4] Weed v. Pierce, 9 Cow. 722.

[5] Drury v. Cross, 7 Wall. 299; Wilson v. Horr, 15 Iowa, 489.

*ex pretio, Posse tamen dici, eam rem apud arbitrum ex
causa animadvertendam ut si nummi soluti in bonis
exstent, jubeat eos reddi ; quia ea ratione nemo fraude-
tur.*[1]

A transfer tainted with actual fraud is absolutely
void, although it is founded upon a valuable consideration. Such is the doctrine at law, and in cases of actual
fraud equity follows the law and gives relief to the full
extent to which a court of law would give relief. There
is no instance of any reimbursement or indemnity
afforded by a court of equity to a *particeps criminis* in
a case of positive fraud. No right can be deduced from
a fraudulent act. Every one who engages in a fraudulent scheme forfeits all right to protection either at law
or in equity. The law does not so far countenance
fraudulent contracts as to protect the perpetrator to the
extent of his investment. This doctrine is supported by
every principle of morality and justice, as well as by
the principles of sound policy. No party should be
permitted to join in a conspiracy to cheat another with
impunity. The law, therefore, will not permit the
transfer to stand as a security for the amount paid to
the debtor,[2] or for the sums subsequently paid to
creditors,[3] even though he thereby pays off a mortgage.[4]

---

[1] *Dig. Lib.* 42, § 14.

[2] M'Kee v. Gilchrist, 3 Watts, 230; Stovall v. Farmers' Bank, 8 S. &
M. 305 ; Holland v. Cruft, 20 Pick. 321 ; Sands v. Codwise, 4 Johns. 536 ;
How v. Camp, Walk. Ch. 427; Pettibone v. Stevens, 15 Conn. 19;
Moore v. Tarlton, 5 Ala. 444 ; Marriot v. Givens, 8 Ala. 694; Goodwin v.
Hammond, 13 Cal 168; Bibb v. Baker, 17 B. Mon. 292 ; Bleakley's Ap-
peal, 66 Penn. 187 ; Miller v. Tolleson, Harp. Ch. 145; Brooks v. Caugh-
ran, 3 Head, 464.

[3] Williamson v. Goodwyn, 9 Gratt. 503 ; Wood v. Hunt, 38 Barb. 302 ;
Borland v. Walker, 7 Ala. 269; Bean v. Smith, 2 Mason, 252.

[4] Pettus v. Smith, 4 Rich. Eq. 197; Wiley v. Knight, 27 Ala.
336.

No allowance can be made to an assignee for his services under a fraudulent assignment,[1] or for the sum paid to counsel after the lien of the creditors had attached.[2]

No SET-OFF.—If the grantee is also a creditor, he can not set off his debt against the demand upon him for the property. As the transfer is void his title fails. He is deemed to have come by the property wrongfully, and to permit him to hold it by setting off his own debt against it, would be giving effect to a transfer condemned by the law. It can not be done without a sacrifice of the principle. The doctrine of set-off is founded in natural justice, and never is applied to a case where the party comes by property wrongfully. He can no more be allowed his set-off against property acquired by a fraudulent deed than if he had acquired it tortiously.[3] Upon the same principle a creditor who has assented to a fraudulent assignment can not set off his claim against the proceeds of property placed in his hands to sell as an auctioneer.[4] It has, however, been held that, when the property has been sold and the creditors seek the proceeds, the amount due to the grantee may be retained.[5]

DEBT OF GRANTEE.—A fraudulent judgment cannot

---

[1] Hastings v. Spencer, 1 Curt. 504; Brown v. Warren, 43 N. H. 430; vide Bishop v. Catlin, 28 Vt. 71.

[2] Hastings v. Spencer, 1 Curt. 504.

[3] Riggs v. Murray, 2 Johns. Ch. 565; s. c. 15 Johns. 571; Harris v. Sumner, 2 Pick. 129; Burtus v. Tisdall, 4 Barb. 571; Bean v. Smith, 2 Mason, 252; M'Kee v. Gilchrist, 3 Watts, 230; Wright v. Hancock, 3 Munf. 521; Thompson v. Drake, 3 B. Mon. 565; Wilson v. Horr, 15 Iowa, 489; Price v. Masterson, 35 Ala. 483; Foster v. Grigsby, 1 Bush, 86; vide Goddard v. Hapgood, 25 Vt. 351; Bishop v. Catlin, 28 Vt. 71; Brown v. Warren, 43 N. H. 430.

[4] Hone v. Henriquez, 13 Wend. 240; s. c. 2 Edw. 120.

[5] Tubb v. Williams, 7 Humph. 367; Peacock v. Tompkins, Meigs, 317.

even be used to collect the amount that is due to the
party to whom it is given.[1]   A fraudulent transfer does
not extinguish a debt due to the grantee, but as soon
as it is set aside the debt becomes available, and
the grantee is then entitled to share in the fund
the same as any other creditor holding the same
rank.[2]

INDEMNITY IN CASE OF CONSTRUCTIVE FRAUD.—When
a transfer is not tainted with actual fraud, but is fraudulent merely by construction of law, it will be allowed
to stand as security for the money advanced by the
grantee.[3]   This is especially true when a conveyance is
set aside in equity on the ground that it is partially
voluntary,[4] or of such a suspicious character that it will
not do to let it stand while the proof will not warrant
the court in setting it aside altogether.[5]   The grantee

---

[1] Cleveland v. R. R. Co. 7 A. L. Reg. 537.

[2] Robinson v. Stewart, 10 N. Y. 189; Dickinson v. Way, 3 Rich. Eq.
412; Riggs v. Murray, 2 Johns. Ch. 565; s. c. 15 Johns. 571; Johnston v.
Bank, 3 Stroth. Eq. 263; Yoder v. Sandiford, 7 Mon. 478; vide White v.
Graves, 7 J. J. Marsh. 523; Miller v. Tolleson, Harp. Ch. 145, Garland v.
Rives, 4 Rand. 282; Fryer v. Bryan, 2 Hill Ch. 56; Pettibone v. Stevens,
15 Conn. 19.

[3] Alley v. Connell, 3 Head, 578; Wood v. Goff, 7 Bush, 59; Dohoney
v. Dohoney, 7 Bush, 217; M'Meekin v. Edmonds, 1 Hill Ch. 288;
Herschfeldt v. George, 6 Mich. 456; Tripp v. Vincent, 8 Paige, 176;
Neuffer v. Pardue, 3 Sneed, 191; Weedon v. Hawes, 13 Conn. 50; Sanford
v. Wheeler, 13 Conn. 165; Short v. Tinsley, 1 Met. (Ky.) 397; Scouton v.
Bender, 8 How. Pr. 185; Anderson v. Fuller, 1 McMullan Ch. 27;
Clements v. Moore, 6 Wall. 299; Drury v. Cross, 7 Wall. 299; Brown v.
M'Donald, 1 Hill Ch. 297; Parker v. Holmes, 2 Hill Ch. 93.

[4] College v. Powell, 12 Gratt. 372; Worthington v. Bullitt, 6 Md. 172;
Crumbaugh v. Kugler, 2 Ohio St. R. 373; Herschfeldt v. George, 6 Mich.
456; Church v. Chapin, 35 Vt. 223; Corlett v. Radcliffe, 14 Moore P. C.
121.

[5] Boyd v. Dunlap, 1 Johns. Ch. 478; Bigelow v. Ayrault, 46 Barb 143;
Herne v. Meeres, 1 Vern. 465; Clements v. Moore, 6 Wall. 299; Bean v.
Smith, 2 Mason, 252; Doughten v. Gray, 2 Stockt. 323.

of property which has been partially paid for
by the debtor, may be allowed for all payments
made by him, for in such a case he is substituted to the rights of the vendor, whose title he
took.[1] Compensation for services may also be allowed.[2]

PARTNER, FEME COVERT.—A partner who accepts a
fraudulent transfer of the partnership property from
his copartner, may be remitted to his lien as a partner
and thus secured in all his real advances for the firm.[3]
If a *feme covert* participates in the fraud of her husband
in a conveyance, the consideration of which is the
relinquishment of her right of dower, the fraud by reason
of her coverture can not be imputed to her, and the
transfer will stand as security for her dower.[4] The
rents and profits will be deemed equivalent to the
interest,[5] or deducted from the amount to be re-
funded.[6]

EXPENDITURES.—When the transfer is tainted with
actual fraud no allowance can be made for improvements.[7] It would seem, however, to be just and reasonable to allow expenditures as an offset to rents and

---

[1] Gardiner Bank v. Wheaton, 8 Me. 373; Ogle v. Lichteberger, 1 A.
L. Reg. 121.

[2] Brown v. M'Donald, 1 Hill Ch. 297; Gardiner Bank v. Wheaton, 8
Me. 373.

[3] Thompson v. Drake, 3 B. Mon. 565.

[4] Blanton v. Taylor, Gilmer, 209; Quarles v. Lacy, 4 Munf. 251; College v. Powell, 12 Gratt. 372; Taylor v. Moore, 2 Rand. 563; Ward v.
Crotty, 4 Met. (Ky.) 59.

[5] Brown v. M'Donald, 1 Hill Ch. 297.

[6] Gardiner Bank v. Wheaton, 8 Me. 373.

[7] Strike v. M'Donald, 2 H. & G. 191; s. c. 1 Bland. 57; High v. Nelms,
14 Ala. 350; *vide* How v. Camp Walk. Ch. 427; King v. Wilcox, 11
Paige, 589.

profits,[1] especially when they have been made to pay taxes.[2] *Sed cum aliquo modo, scilicet ut sumptus facti deducantur ; nam arbitrio judicis non prius cogendus est rem restituere quam si impensas necessarias consequatur. Idemque erit probandum et si quis alius sumptus ex voluntate fidejussorum creditorumque fecerit.*[3] A donee who has taken possession and made improvements under a parol promise of a gift is entitled to compensation for improvements.[4] An assignee claiming under a voluntary assignment is allowed all his necessary expenses and disbursements in collecting the debts and converting the property into money.[5]

APPORTIONMENT.—The whole amount in the hands of the grantee may be appropriated to the payment of the debts, although there may be other persons equally liable,[6] for the creditor is not bound to apportion his debt among the various grantees. But, where all the grantees are convened, and all the materials for an apportionment are before the court, the demand will be apportioned among the responsible parties, if it can be done without any material delay or injury to the creditor. This will be done, however, with a reservation of the right to the creditor to resort for satisfaction to all the parties responsible to him to the full extent of

---

[1] Croft v. Arthur, 3 Dessau. 223 ; Rucker v. Abell, 8 B. Mon. 566 ; Byers v. Fowler, 12 Ark. 218; *vide* Strike v. M'Donald, 2 H. & G. 191 ; s. c. 1 Bland, 57.

[2] How v. Camp, Walk. Ch. 427; King v. Wilcox, 11 Paige, 589; *vide* Strike v. M'Donald, 2 H. & G. 191; s. c. 1 Bland, 57.

[3] *Dig. Lib.* 42 *tit.* 9, § 20.

[4] Rucker v. Abell, 8 B. Mon. 566.

[5] Strong v. Skinner, 4 Barb. 546; Bishop v. Catlin, 28 Vt. 71; Brown v. Warren, 43 N. H. 430; Therasson v. Hickok, 37 Vt. 454.

[6] Hopkirk v. Randolph, 2 Brock. 132; Van Wyck v. Seward, 18 Wend. 375.

their liabilities respectively in the event of his failing, from insolvency or any other cause, to procure satisfaction from any of the parties of their due proportion of his demand.[1] The surplus which may remain after the payment of the debt and costs belongs to the grantee.[2] The grantee may retain what is exempt from execution.[3]

---

[1] Chamberlayne v. Temple, 2 Rand. 384; Brice v. Myers, 5 Ohio, 121.

[2] Wood v. Hunt, 38 Barb. 302; Birtch v. Elliott, 3 Ind. 99; King v. Tharp, 26 Iowa, 283; Allen v. Trustees, 102 Mass. 262; Freeman v. Burnham, 36 Conn. 469; Norton v. Norton, 5 Cush. 524; Bostwick v. Minck, 40 N. Y. 383.

[3] Martel v. Somers, 26 Tex. 551.

CASES FROM THE YEAR BOOKS.

En briefe de Det port vers deux execut's **J. B.** les queux diont per Horton, que le dit J. B. en sa vie doner touts ses biens a eux y un fait q' ils monstre avant sans c' q' ils averont l'admistrac' des aut's biens, etc., judgem't si acc'. Trem. mesme cel done fuit fait y fraude et colluss' pur ouster no' et aut's as queux il fuit dettor de nostr' action prist, etc., per q' nous priom' nr'e det. Horton dist q' le done fuit fait bona fide sans ascun tiel, etc., prist & sic ad patriam quod nota.—13 *Henry IV, f.* 4.

En un bill de trespass dun chival et iiij. vach a tort prises, etc., port vers T. de W. et R. de N. Les queux plede de rien culp : trove fuit y Enquest, que le dit R. avoit rec' vers J. B. rrs, en la Court de P., per que le dit T. come baily, etc., prist mesms les vaches en nosm dexec. et les livera a mesm cesty R. et amesna a chastel de P. Et oustr' ils dis. que mesms les bestes fur' les bestes le dit J. B. jour de judgment rendu ; mes il les dona puis y fait a mesm cesty qui ore se pl' y fraud a delaier l'exec. Et ils fur' opposez de la Court a dire qui prist les profits de mesms les bestes en le mean temps. Qui dis. Sir, le donor. Thorp ; jeo entend ceo don de nul valu, et jeo tien q' ce'y a qui tiel don fuit fait le fist fors gardein des bestes al' oepz l'autre' quia fraus & dolus, &c. Car autrement en aur' jamais home exec. des chat' ; y q' prenes rien y vostre bill.—*Li. As.* 101, *f.* 72.

CASES FROM THE YEAR BOOKS.

TRANSLATION.

In a writ for debt brought against two executors of J. B. they say by Horton that the said J. B., in his life, gave them all his property, by a deed of which they make profert withóut their having the administration of the other property. Judgment *si actio*.

Trem. This same gift was made fraudulently and collusively to oust us and others, to whom he was a debtor, from our action. Ready, etc. Wherefore we pray for our debt.

Horton says that the gift was made in good faith without any such, etc. Ready, and so to the country, *quod nota*.

In a bill for trespass for one horse and four cows tortiously seized, &c., brought against T. of W. and R. of N., who plead not guilty: it was found by inquest that the said R. had recovered against J. B. rrs. in the court of P., on authority of which the said T., as bailiff, etc., took the said cows in execution and delivered them to R. and carried them to the castle of P. Furthermore, they say that the said beasts were the beasts of the said J. B. on the day when the judgment was rendered, but he gave them afterwards by deed to him who is now plaintiff fraudulently to delay execution. And they were interrogated by the court as to this point; who received the profits of the beasts in the meantime? They said, Sir, the donor.

Thorpe. I consider the gift null and void, and hold that he to whom such a gift was made became only keeper of the beasts for the use of the other, because fraud and deceit, &c. For otherwise a man would never have execution on chattels; wherefore take nothing by your bill.

En le chancery un bill fuit abatu pur non suffic. del matter, et le pl' dit q' cel bill fuit misconceive; mes il mr'a pur son matter q. J. B. que est jades baron le def. achata del pere le pl' q' execut' il est a Brig, certein bn's al value de C marks, etc. Et puis m' cestuy J. B. vient en Engleterre et p' defraudr' son dettor fist un done de ses bn's a un tiel, etc., mes il continua, son possess. et prist Westm. et morust, et ses bn's. continua en le poss. la feme, etc., et puis el prist m' cestuy q' est supp' destre def. al baron, et ala en Lond; et emport m' le bn's ove luy et est seisie et poss. de eux, etc., le quel matter, &c. Et priom' q' il rn'd a cel matter et bill, et il aver copy de ceo et issint agard le court, quod nota, &c.—16 *Edw. IV, folio* 9.

Scire facias des dams' recouer' le vicont ret' que le defendant au' vend ces chateaux en fraude de tolt' lexecucion. ꟼ Scroop : home puit bien auer vendu ces chateaux cy bien apres jugement come deuaunt sauns ce que exec' se fra deux chatcaux.—*Fitzherbert's Abdgt., Execution pl.* 108.

ꟼ Det y Belk. si home recouera dam' et le defendant alien ses bn's y fraude la issue poet estre prise s' c' et si soit troue le pl' au'a executio del bn's alien y fraud qd non negat. —*Brook's Abr., Collusion, pl.* 9.

In chancery a bill was dismissed as insufficient in substance, and the plaintiff said that the bill was misconceived, but he showed for his substance that J. B., who was the former husband of the defendant, bought of the plaintiff's father, whose executor he is at Brig, certain property, of the value of one hundred marks, &c. And afterwards the same J. B. came to England, and to defraud his creditors made a gift of his property to a certain person, &c., but he continued his possession and took refuge at Westminster and died, and his property continued in the possession of his wife, &c., and afterwards she married the person who is supposed to be defendant, and went to London and took the said property with her, and is seized and possessed of it, &c., which substance, &c. And we pray that he makes answer to this matter and bill, and that he have copy of it, and thus the court awarded, *quod nota,* &c.

Scire facias for damages recovered. The sheriff returns that the defendant had fraudulently sold the chattels to prevent execution.

Scroop. These chattels might very well have been sold as well after judgment as before, provided that execution on the chattels had not already issued.

Debt by Belk. If a man recover damages, and the defendant alienate his goods fraudulently, the issue may be taken on that, and, if it be found, the plaintiff can have execution on the goods fraudulently alienated ; *quod non negat.*

APPENDIX.

STATUTES OF THE VARIOUS STATES.

ENGLAND.

50 E. III, Cap. 6.

Item. Because that divers people inherit of divers tenements, borrowing divers goods in money or in merchandise of divers people of this realm, do give their tenements and chattels to their friends, by collusion thereof to have the profits at their will, and after do flee to the franchise of *Westminster*, of *St. Martin le Grand*, of *London*, or other such privileged places, and there do live a great time with an high countenance of another man's goods, and profits of the said tenements and chattels, till the said creditors shall be bound to take a small parcel of their debt, and release the remnant; it is ordained and assented, that if it be found that such gifts be so made by collusion, that the said creditors shall have execution of the said tenements and chattels as if no such gift had been made.

3 H. VII, Cap. 4.

Item. That where oftentimes deeds of gift of goods and chattels have been made, to the intent to defraud their creditors of their duties, and that the person or persons that maketh the said deed of gift goeth to the sanctuary, or other places privileged, and occupieth and liveth with the said goods and chattels, their creditors being unpaid; it is ordained, enacted, and established by the assent of the Lords Spiritual and Temporal, and at the request of the Commons in the said Parlia-

ment assembled, and by the authority of the same, that all
deeds of gift of goods and chattels made or to be made of
trust, to the use of that person or persons that made the same
deed or gift, be void and of none effect.

13 Eliz., Cap. 5.

For the avoiding and abolishing of feigned, covinous, and
fraudulent feoffments, gifts, grants, alienations, conveyances,
bonds, suits, judgments, and executions, as well of lands and
tenements, as of goods and chattels, more commonly used and
practised in these days, than hath been seen or heard of heretofore; which feoffments, gifts, grants, alienations, conveyances,
bonds, suits, judgments, and executions, have been, and are
devised and contrived of malice, fraud, covin, collusion, or
guile, to the end, purpose, and intent, to delay, hinder, or defraud creditors and others of their just and lawful actions, suits,
debts, accounts, damages, penalties, forfeitures, heriots, mortuaries, and reliefs, not only to the let or hindrance of the due
course and execution of law and justice, but also to the overthrow of all true and plain dealing, bargaining, and chevisance
between man and man, without the which no commonwealth or
civil society can be maintained or continued:

II. Be it therefore declared, ordained, and enacted by the
authority of this present Parliament, that all and every feoffment, gift, grant, alienation, bargain, and conveyance of lands,
tenements, hereditaments, goods, and chattels, or any of them,
or of any lease, rent, common, or other profit or charge out of
the same lands, tenements, hereditaments, goods, and chattels,
or any of them, by writing or otherwise; and all and every
bond, suit, judgment, and execution, at any time had or made
sithence the beginning of the Queen's Majesty's reign that now
is, or at any time hereafter to be had or made, to or for any
intent or purpose before declared and expressed, shall be from
henceforth deemed and taken (only as against that person or
persons, his or their heirs, successors, executors, administrators,
and assigns, and every of them, whose actions, suits, debts,
accounts, damages, penalties, forfeitures, heriots, mortuaries,
and reliefs, by such guileful, covinous or fraudulent devices and

practices as is aforesaid, are, shall, or might be in any wise disturbed, hindered, delayed, or defrauded), to be clearly and utterly void, frustrate, and of none effect; any pretence, color, feigned consideration, expressing of use, or any other matter or thing to the contrary notwithstanding.

III. And be it further enacted by the authority aforesaid, that all and every the parties to such feigned, covinous, or fraudulent feoffment, gift, grant, alienation, bargain, conveyance, bonds, suits, judgments, executions, and other things before expressed, and being privy and knowing of the same, or any of them, which at any time after the tenth day of June next coming, shall wittingly and willingly put in use, avow, maintain, justify, or defend the same, or any of them, as true, simple, and done, had or made *bona fide*, and upon good consideration; or shall alien, or assign any the lands, tenements, goods, leases, or other things before mentioned, to him or them conveyed, as is aforesaid, or any part thereof, shall incur the penalty and forfeiture of one year's value of the said lands, tenements, and hereditaments, leases, rents, commons, or other profits, of or out of the same; and the whole value of said goods and chattels, and also so much money as are or shall be contained in any such covinous and feigned bond; one moiety whereof to be the Queen's Majesty, her heirs and successors, and the other moiety to the party or parties grieved by such feigned and fraudulent feoffment, grant, alienation, bargain, conveyance, bonds, suits, judgments, executions, leases, rents, commons, profits, charges, and other things aforesaid, to be recovered in any of the Queen's Courts of Record, by action of debt, bill, plaint, or information, wherein no essoin, protection, or wager of law shall be admitted for the defendant or defendants; and also being thereof lawfully convicted, shall suffer imprisonment for one half year without bail or mainprise.

VI. Provided also, and it be enacted by the authority aforesaid, that this act, or anything therein contained, shall not extend to any estate or interest in lands, tenements, hereditaments, leases, rents, commons, profits, goods, or chattels, had, made, conveyed or assured, or hereafter to be had, made, conveyed, or assured; which estate or interest, is or shall be upon good consideration, and *bona fide* lawfully conveyed or assured to any person or persons, or bodies politick or corporate, not having at the time of such conveyance or assurance to them made, any manner of notice or knowledge of such covin, fraud, or collusion, as is aforesaid; any thing before mentioned to the contrary hereof notwithstanding.

VII. This Act to endure unto the end of the first session of the next Parliament.

Note.—This Act was made perpetual by 29 Eliz., cap 5.

VERMONT.
Chapter 113.

§ 32. All fraudulent and deceitful conveyances of houses, lands, tenements, or hereditaments, or of goods and chattels, all bonds, bills, notes, contracts and agreements, all suits, judgments, and executions, made or had to avoid any right, debt, or duty of any other person, shall as against the party or parties only whose right, debt, or duty is attempted to be avoided, their heirs, executors, administrators, or assigns be null and void.

§ 33. All the parties to such fraudulent and deceitful conveyances (of houses, &c.), and to all such suits, &c., as are mentioned in the preceding section, who, being priory thereto, shall justify the same to have been made, had, or executed *bona fide*, and upon good consideration, or who shall alien or assign any such houses, &c., so conveyed to him, or them as aforesaid, shall forfeit the value of such houses, &c., and the value of such goods and chattels, also so much money as is mentioned in such covinous bond, bill, &c.; which forfeitures shall be equally divided between the party aggrieved and the county in which such offence is committed, to be secured by action on the case founded on this statute.

§ 34. In any action brought on the preceding section of this chapter, all persons being parties or privies to such fraudulent and deceitful conveyances may be joined as party defendants in such action.

Chapter 34.

§ 48. If any person who is summoned as a trustee shall have in his possession any goods, effects, or credits of the principal defendant, which he holds by a conveyance or title that is void as to the creditors of the defendant, he may be adjudged a trustee on account of such goods, effects or credit, although the principal defendant could not have maintained an action therefore against him.

Chapter 65.

§ 28. All fraudulent and deceitful deeds, conveyances and alienations of lands, or of any estate or interest therein, and every charge upon lands, or upon the rents and profits thereof, procured, made, or suffered, with intent to avoid any right, debt, or duty of any person shall as against such person whose right, debt, or duty shall be so intended to be avoided, his heirs or assigns, be utterly void.

RHODE ISLAND.

§ 2. Every gift, grant, or conveyance of lands, tenements, hereditaments, goods, or chattels, or of any rent, interest or profit out of the same, by writing or otherwise, and every note, bill, bond, contract, suit, judgment, or execution, had or made and contrived, of fraud, covin, collusion, or guile, to the intent or purpose to delay, hinder, or defraud creditors of their just and lawful actions, suits, debts, accounts, damages or just demands of what nature soever ; or to deceive or defraud those who shall purchase *bona fide* the same lands, tenements, hereditaments, goods, or chattels, or any rent, interest, or profit out of them, shall be henceforth deemed and taken as against the person or persons, his, her, or their heirs, successors, executors, administrators, or assigns, and every of them, whose debts, suits, demands, estates, rights, or interests, by such guileful and covinous devices and practices as aforesaid, shall or might be in any wise injured, disturbed, hindered, delayed, or defrauded, to be clearly and utterly void ; any pretence, color, feigned consideration, expressing of use, or any other matter or thing to the contrary notwithstanding.—*Page* 22, *Public Laws of Rhode Island.*

CONNECTICUT.

Be it enacted by the Senate and House of Representatives in General Assembly convened:

§ 1. That all fraudulent and deceitful conveyances of lands and tenements, or any interest in them, or, of goods and chattels, and all bonds, suits, judgments, executions, or contracts, made with intent to avoid any debt, or duty, of others, shall be utterly void, as against those persons only, their heirs, executors, administrators or assigns, whose debt, or duty, is endeavored to be avoided, notwithstanding any consideration upon which such contract may be pretended to have been made.

§ 2. And all the parties to such fraudulent contract knowing the fraud, who shall willingly justify the same, as being made *bona fide*, and on good consideration, shall forfeit one year's value of the land, and the whole value of the goods and chattels, and as much money as shall be contained in such fraudulent bond or contract, one-half to the party aggrieved, who shall sue for the same, and prosecute the suit to effect, and the other half to the treasury of the State.—*Revised Statutes of Conn., Title* 20.

NEW YORK.

§ 1. All deeds of gift, all conveyances, and all transfers or assignments, verbal or written, of goods, chattels, or things in action, made in trust for the use of the person making the same, shall be void as against the creditors, existing or subsequent, of such person.

§ 5. Every sale made by a vendor, of goods and chattels in his possession or under his control, and every assignment of goods and chattels by way of mortgage or security, or upon any condition whatever, unless the same be accompanied by an immediate delivery, and be followed by an actual and continued change of possession of the things sold, mortgaged or assigned, shall be presumed to be fraudulent and void as against the creditors of the vendor, or creditors of the person making such assignment, or subsequent purchasers in good faith ; and shall be conclusive evidence of fraud, unless it shall be made to appear, on the part of the persons claiming under such sale or assignment, that the same was made in good faith, and without any intent to defraud such creditors or purchasers.—*Title 2, Revised Statutes of New York.*

§ 1. Every conveyance or assignment, in writing or otherwise, of any estate or interest in lands, or in goods or things in action, or of any rents or profits issuing therefrom, and every charge upon lands, goods, or things in action, or upon the rents or profits thereof, made with the intent to hinder, delay, or defraud creditors or other persons of their lawful suits, damages, forfeitures, debts, or demands, and every bond or other evidence of debt given, suit commenced, decree or judgment suffered, with the like intent, as against the persons so hindered, delayed or defrauded, shall be void.

§ 3. Every conveyance, charge, instrument or proceeding declared to be void, by the provisions of this chapter, as against creditors and purchasers, shall be equally void against the heirs, successors, personal representatives or assignees of such creditors and purchasers.

§ 4. The question of fraudulent intent in all cases arising under the provisions of this chapter, shall be deemed a question of fact and not of law; nor shall any conveyance or charge be adjudged fraudulent as against creditors or purchasers, solely on the ground, that it was not founded on a valuable consideration.

§ 5. The provisions of this chapter shall not be construed in any manner, to affect or impair the title of a purchaser for a valuable consideration, unless it shall appear, that such purchaser had previous notice of the fraudulent intent of his immediate grantor, or of the fraud rendering void the title of such grantor.—*Title 3, Revised Statutes of New York.*

NEW JERSEY.

1. Every deed of gift, and conveyance of goods and chattels, made or to be made, in trust to the use of the person or persons, making the same deed of gift or conveyance, shall be, and hereby is declared to be void and of no effect.

2. And for the avoiding and abolishing of all feigned, covinous, and fraudulent feoffments, gifts, grants, alienations,

conveyances, bonds, suits, judgments and executions, as well of lands and tenements, as goods and chattels, which have been and are devised and contrived of malice, fraud, covin, collusion, or guile, to the end, purpose and intent, to delay, hinder or defraud creditors, and others of their just and lawful actions, suits, debts, accounts, damages, penalties, forfeitures and demands, not only to the let or hindrance of the due course and execution of law and justice, but also to the overthrow of all true and plain dealing, agreements, bargains, contracts and traffic between man and man, without which no commonwealth or civil society can be maintained or continued : All and every feoffment, gift, grant, alienation, bargain and conveyance of lands, tenements, hereditaments, goods and chattels, or any of them, or of any lease, rent, common or other profit or charge out of the same lands, tenements, hereditaments, goods and chattels, or any of them, by writing or otherwise, and all and every bond, suit, judgment and execution, at any time heretofore had or made, or hereafter to be had or made, to or for any intent or purpose before declared and expressed, shall be deemed and taken, (only as against that person or those persons, his, her, or their heirs, successors, executors, administrators, and assigns, and every of them, whose actions, suits, debts, accounts, damages, penalties, forfeitures and demands, by such guileful, covinous or fraudulent devices, and practices, as aforesaid, are or shall, or may be in anywise disturbed, hindered, or defeated,) to be clearly and utterly void, frustrate, and of no effect ; any pretence, color, feigned consideration, expressing of use, or any other matter or thing to the contrary notwithstanding.

4. All and every the parties to such feigned, covinous, and fraudulent feoffment, gift, grant, alienation, bargain, lease, charge, conveyance, bonds, suits, judgments, executions, and other things before expressed, or being privy to and knowing of the same, or any of them, who at any time hereafter, shall wittingly and willingly put in use, avow, maintain, justify or defend the same, or any of them, as true, simple, and done, had or made, *bona fide*, and upon good consideration, or shall alien or assign, any the lands, tenements, goods, leases, or other things before mentioned, to him, her, or them conveyed as

aforesaid, or any part thereof, shall incur the penalty and forfeiture of one year's value of the said lands, tenements and hereditaments, leases, rents, commons or other profits, of or out of the same, and the whole value of the said goods and chattels, and also so much money as is or shall be contained in any such covinous and feigned bond; the one moiety whereof to be to the State, and the other moiety to the party or parties grieved by such feigned and fraudulent feoffment, gift, grant, alienation, bargain, conveyance, bonds, suits, judgments, executions, leases, rents, commons, profits, charges, and other things aforesaid; to be recovered in any court of record by action of debt, bill, plaint or information.

6. This act, or anything therein contained, shall not extend to, or be construed to impeach, defeat, make void or fraustrate any conveyance, assignment of lease assurance, grant, charge, lease, estate, interest or limitation of use or uses, of, in, to, or out of any lands, tenements or hereditaments, goods or chattels, at any time heretofore had or made, or hereafter to be had or made, upon or for good consideration, and *bona fide*, to any person or persons, bodies politic or corporate, not having, at the time of such conveyance or assurance to him, her, or them made, any manner of notice or knowledge of such covin, fraud or collusion, as aforesaid; and also that no lawful mortgage made, or to be made, *bona fide*, and without fraud or covin, and upon good consideration, shall be impeached or impaired, by force of this act; but every such mortgage shall stand in like force and effect, as the same should have done if this act had never been made; anything before in this act to the contrary notwithstanding.—*The Laws of New Jersey, Nixon's Digest,* 304.

[Nov. 26th, 1794, R. S. 499.]

VIRGINIA.

1. Every gift, conveyance, assignment, or transfer of, or charge upon, any estate, real or personal, every suit commenced, or decree, judgment, or execution suffered or obtained, and every bond or other writing given, with intent to delay, hinder, or defraud creditors, purchasers, or other persons, of or from what they are or may be lawfully entitled to, shall as to

such creditors, purchasers, or other persons, their representatives or assigns, be void. This section shall not effect the title of a purchaser for valuable consideration, unless it appear that he had notice of the fraudulent intent of his immediate grantor, or of the fraud rendering void the title of such grantor.

2. Every gift, conveyance, assignment, transfer, or charge, which is not upon consideration deemed valuable in law, shall be void as to creditors whose debts shall have been contracted at the time it was made, but shall not, on that account merely, be void as to creditors, whose debts shall have been contracted, or as to purchasers who shall have purchased, after it was made; and though it be decreed to be void as to a prior creditor, because voluntary, it shall not for that cause be decreed to be void as to subsequent creditors or purchasers.—*Chap. CXVIII, Code of Virginia*, 1860.

WEST VIRGINIA.

1. Every gift, conveyance, assignment, or transfer of, or charge upon any estate, real or personal, every suit commenced, or decree, judgment, or execution suffered or obtained, and every bond or other writing given, with intent to delay, hinder, or defraud creditors, purchasers, or other persons, or of from what they are or may be lawfully entitled to shall as to such creditors, purchasers, or other persons, their representatives or assigns be void. This section shall not affect the title of a purchaser for valuable consideration, unless it appear that he had notice of the fraudulent intent of his immediate grantor, or of the fraud rendering void the title of such grantor.

2. Every gift, conveyance, assignment, transfer, or charge, which is not upon consideration deemed valuable in law, shall be void as to creditors, whose debts shall have been contracted at the time it was made, but shall not, on that account merely, be void as to creditors whose debts shall have been contracted, or as to purchasers who shall have purchased after it was made; and though it be decreed to be void as to a prior creditor, because voluntary, it shall not for that cause be decreed to be void as to subsequent creditors or purchasers.—*Chap. LXXIV, Code of West Virginia*, 1868.

NORTH CAROLINA.

1. For avoiding and abolishing feigned, covinous, and fraudulent gifts, grants, alienations, conveyances, bonds, suits, judgments, and executions, as well of lands and tenements as of goods and chattels, which may be contrived and devised of fraud, to the purpose and intent to delay, hinder, and defraud creditors and others of their just and lawful actions and debts.

2. *Be it enacted*, That every gift, grant, alienation, bargain, and conveyance of lands, tenements, hereditaments, goods and chattels, by writing or otherwise, and every bond, suit, judg- ment, and execution, at any time had or made, to or for any intent or purpose last before declared and expressed, shall be deemed and taken (only as against that person, his heirs, ex- ecutors, administrators, and assigns, whose actions, debts, ac- counts, damages, penalties, and forfeitures, by such covinous or fraudulent devices and practices aforesaid, are, shall, or might be in any way disturbed, hindered, delayed or de- frauded), to be utterly void and of no effect; any pretence, color, feigned consideration, expressing of use, or any other matter or thing to the contrary notwithstanding.

3. No voluntary gift or settlement of property by one in- debted, shall be deemed or taken to be void in law as to creditors of the donor or settler prior to such gift or settlement, by reason merely of such indebtedness, if property, at the time of making such gift or settlement, fully sufficient and available for the satisfaction of all his then creditors, be retained by such donor or settler; but the indebtedness of the donor or settler at such time shall be held and taken, as well with re- spect to creditors prior as creditors subsequent to such gift or settlement, to be evidence only from which an intent to delay, hinder, or defraud creditors may be inferred; and in any trial at law shall, as such, be submitted by the court to the jury, with such observations as may be right and proper.

4. Nothing contained in the foregoing sections shall be construed to impeach or make void any conveyance, interest, limitation of use or uses, of or in any lands or tenements, goods or chattels, *bona fide* made, upon any for good consideration, to

38

any person not having notice of such fraud.—*Chap.* 50, *Revised Code of North Carolina.*

GEORGIA.

§ 1942. The following acts by debtors shall be fraudulent in law against creditors, and as to them null and void, viz:

1. [Every assignment or transfer by a debtor, insolvent at the time, of real or personal property, or choses in action of any description to any person, either in trust or for the benefit of, or in behalf of creditors, where any trust or benefit is reserved to the assignor or any person for him.]

2. Every conveyance of real or personal estate by writing or otherwise, and every bond, suit, judgment, and execution, or contract of any description, had or made with intention to delay or defraud creditors, and such intention known to the party taking; a *bona fide* transaction on a valuable consideration, and without notice or grounds for reasonable suspicion shall be valid.

Every voluntary deed or conveyance, not for a valuable consideration, made by a debtor insolvent at the time of such conveyance.

§ 1943. A debtor may prefer one creditor to another, and to that end he may *bona fide* give a lien by mortgage or other legal means, or he may sell in payment of the debt, or he may transfer negotiable papers as collateral security, the surplus in such cases not being reserved for his own benefit or that of any other favored creditor, to the exclusion of other creditors.
—*Article II, Code of Georgia,* 1868.

FLORIDA.

§ 1. Every feoffment, gift, grant, alienation, bargain, sale, conveyance, transfer and assignment of lands, tenements, hereditaments, and other goods and chattels, or any of them, or any lease, rent, use, common or other profit, benefit or charge whatever, out of lands, tenements, hereditaments, or other goods and chattels, or any of them, by writing or otherwise, and every bond, note, contract, suit, judgment and execution, which shall at any time hereafter be had, made or executed, contrived or devised, of fraud, covin, collusion, or guile, to the end, purpose or intent to delay, hinder, or defraud creditors or others of their just and lawful actions, suits, debts, accounts, damages, demands, penalties, or forfeitures, shall be from henceforth, as against the person or persons, or body politic or corporate, his, her or their heirs, successors, executors, administrators and assigns, and every of them so intended to be delayed, hindered or defrauded, deemed, held, adjudged and taken, to be utterly void, fraustrate, and of none effect; any pretence, color, feigned consideration, expressing of use, or any other matter or thing to the contrary notwithstanding:

Provided, That the foregoing section of this act, or anything therein contained, shall not extend to any estate or interest in lands, tenements, hereditaments, leases, rents, uses, commons, profits, goods or chattels, which shall be had, made, conveyed, or assured, if such estate or interest shall be upon good consideration, and *bona fide*, lawfully conveyed or assured to any person or persons, body politic or corporate, not having at the time of such conveyance or assurance to them made, any manner of notice or knowledge of such covin, fraud or collusion, as aforesaid, anything in the said section to the contrary notwithstanding.—*Chap. XXVII, Bush's Digest of the Statute Law of Florida.*

ALABAMA.

§ 1550. All deeds of gift, all conveyances, transfers and assignments, verbal or written, of goods, chattels or things in action, made in trust for the use of the person making the same, are void against creditors, existing or subsequent, of such person.

§ 1554. All conveyances or assignments, in writing or otherwise, of any estate or interest in real or personal property, and every charge upon the same, made with intent to hinder, delay or defraud creditors, purchasers, or other persons, of their lawful suits, damages, forfeitures, debts, or demands; and every bond or other evidence of debt given, suit commenced, decree or judgment suffered, with the like intent, against the persons who are or may be so hindered, delayed, or defrauded, their heirs, personal representatives and assigns, are void.— *Chap. IV, Article I, Code of Alabama.*

TEXAS.

Art. 3876. [1.] Be it further enacted, That every gift, grant or conveyance of lands, slaves, tenements, hereditaments, goods or chattels, or of any rent, common or profit out of the same, by writing or otherwise, and every bond, suit, judgment or execution had or made and contrived of malice, fraud, covin, collusion or guile, to the intent or purpose to delay, hinder or defraud creditors of their just and lawful actions, suits, debts, accounts, damages, penalties or forfeitures, or to defraud, or to deceive those who shall purchase the same lands, slaves, tenements or hereditaments, or any rent, profit or commodity out of them, shall be from henceforth deemed and taken only as against the person or persons, his or her or their successors, executors, administrators or assigns, and every of them, whose debts, suits, demands, estates, interests, by such guileful and covinous devices and practices as is aforesaid, shall or might be in any wise disturbed, hindered, delayed or defrauded, to be clearly and utterly void; any pretence, color, feigned consideration, expressing of use, or any other matter or thing to the contrary notwithstanding.

Art. 3877. [3.] Be it further enacted, That the second section of this Act shall not extend to any estate or interest in any lands, goods, chattels, slaves, or any rents, common or profit out of the same, which shall be upon good consideration and *bona fide* lawfully conveyed or assured to any person or persons, bodies politic or corporate.—*Act of January 18th,* 1840, *Laws of Texas, Paschal's Digest.*

OHIO.

§ 1. Be it enacted by the General Assembly of the State of Ohio: That all deeds of gifts and conveyances of goods and chattels, made in trust to the use of the person or persons making the same, shall be, and hereby are declared to be void and of no effect.

§ 2. That every gift, grant or conveyance of lands, tenements, hereditaments, rents, goods or chattels, and every bond, judgment or execution, made or obtained with intent to defraud creditors of their just and lawful debts or damages, or to defraud or to deceive the person or persons who shall purchase such lands, tenements, hereditaments, rents, goods or chattels, shall be deemed utterly void and of no effect.—*Chap.* 47, *Revised Statutes of Ohio.*

KENTUCKY.

§ 1. Be it enacted by the General Assembly of the Commonwealth of Kentucky: That every gift, conveyance, assignment or transfer of, or charge upon any estate, real or personal, or right or thing in action, or any rent or profit thereof made with the intent to delay, hinder or defraud creditors, purchasers or other persons, and every bond or other evidence of debt given, suit commenced, decree or judgment suffered, with like intent, shall be void as against such creditors, purchasers, and other persons.

This section shall not affect the title of a purchaser for valuable consideration, unless it appear that he had notice of the fraudulent intent of his immediate grantor, or of the fraud rendering void the title of such grantor.

§ 2. Every gift, conveyance, assignment, transfer or charge made by a debtor of or upon any of his estate, without valuable consideration therefor, shall be void as to all his then existing liabilities, but shall not, on that account alone, be void as to creditors whose debts or demands are thereafter contracted, or as to purchasers with notice of the voluntary alienation or charge; and though it be adjudged to be void as to a prior creditor, it shall not therefore be decreed to be void as to such subsequent creditors or purchasers.—*Chap.* 40, *Revised Statutes of Kentucky.*

TENNESSEE.

Every gift, grant, conveyance of lands, tenements, hereditaments, goods or chattels, or of any rent, common or profit out of the same, by writing or otherwise, and every bond, suit, judgment or execution, had or made and contrived of malice, fraud, covin, collusion or guile, to the intent or purpose to delay, hinder or defraud creditors of their just and lawful actions, suits, debts, accounts, damages, penalties, forfeitures, or to defraud or deceive those who shall purchase the same lands, tenements or hereditaments, or any rent, profit or commodity out of them, shall be deemed and taken only as against the person, his heirs, successors, executors, administrators and assigns, whose debts, suits, demands, estates or interests by such guileful and covinous practices, as aforesaid, shall or might be in any wise disturbed, hindered, delayed or defrauded, to be clearly and utterly void; any pretence, color, feigned consideration expressing of use or any other matter or thing to the contrary notwithstanding.—*Statutes of Tennessee*, 1 *Thompson & Steger*, § 1759.

INDIANA.

§ VIII. Every sale made by a vendor of goods in his possession, or under his control, unless the same be accompanied by immediate delivery, and be followed by an actual change of the possession of the things sold, shall be presumed to be fraudulent and void, as against the creditors of the vendor, or subsequent purchasers in good faith, unless it shall be made to appear, that the same was made in good faith, and without any intent to defraud such creditors or purchasers.

§ IX. The term "creditors" as used in the last section, shall be construed to include all persons who shall be creditors of the vendor or assignor, at any time whilst such goods were in his possession or under his control.

§ XVII. All conveyances or assignments in writing or otherwise, of any estate in lands, or of goods, or things in action, every charge upon lands, goods, or things in action, and all bonds, contracts, evidences of debt, judgments, decrees, made or suffered with the intent to hinder, delay, or defraud creditors, or other persons of their lawful damages, forfeitures, debts, or demands, shall be void as to the person sought to be defrauded.

§ XVIII. All deeds of gift, conveyances, transfers, or assignments, verbal or written, of goods or things in action, made in trust for the use of the person making the same, shall be void as against creditors existing or subsequent, of such person.

§ XIX. Every conveyance, charge, instrument, act or proceeding, declared by the provisions of this act to be void, as against creditors or purchasers, shall be void against the heirs, personal representatives or assignees of such creditors or purchasers.

§ XX. The provisions of this act shall not be construed to affect the title of a purchaser for a valuable consideration, unless it shall appear that such purchaser had previous notice of the fraudulent intent of his immediate grantor, or assignor, or of the fraud rendering void the title of such grantor, or assignor.

§ XXI. The question of fraudulent intent, in all cases arising under the provisions of this act, shall be deemed a question of fact, nor shall any conveyance or charge be adjudged fraudulent, as against creditors or purchasers, solely on the ground that it was not founded on a valuable consideration.—*Chap.* 66, *Statutes of Indiana.*

ILLINOIS.

Every gift, grant or conveyance of lands, tenements, hereditaments, goods or chattels, or of any rent, common or profit of the same, by writing or otherwise, and every bond, suit, judgment or execution had and made, or contrived of malice, fraud, covin, collusion or guile, to the intent or purpose to delay, hinder, or defraud creditors of their just and lawful actions, suits, debts, accounts, damages, penalties or forfeitures, or to defraud or deceive those who shall purchase the same lands, tenements or hereditaments, or any rent, profit or commodity out of them, shall be from thenceforth deemed and taken only as against the person or persons, his, her, or their heirs, successors, executors, administrators, or assigns, and every of them, whose debts, suits, demands, estates and interests, by such guileful and covinous devices and practices as aforesaid shall, or might be in anywise disturbed, hindered, delayed, or defrauded, to be clearly and utterly void; any pretence, color feigned consideration, expression of use, or any other matter or thing to the contrary notwithstanding; and moreover, if a conveyance be of goods and chattels, and be not on consideration, deemed valuable in law, it shall be taken to be fraudulent unless the same be by will duly proved and recorded, or by deed in writing, acknowledged or proved, if the same deed includes land also, in such manner as conveyances of land are by law directed to be acknowledged or proved by two witnesses, before any court of record in the county wherein one of the parties lives, within eight months after the execution thereof, or unless possession shall really and *bona fide* remain with the donee; and in like manner where any loan of goods and chattels shall be pretended to have been made to any person, with whom, or those claiming under him, possession shall have remained for the space of five years, without demand made and pursued by due process at law, on the part of the pretended lender, or where any reservation or limitation shall be pretended to have been made of an use or property by way of condition, remainder, or otherwise, in goods or chattels, the possession whereof shall have remained in another, as aforesaid, the same shall be taken as to creditors and purchasers of the person aforesaid so remaining in possession, to be fraudulent, and that the absolute property is with the possession, unless such loan, reservation or limitation of use or property were declared, by will or deed in writing, proved and recorded as aforesaid.—*Gross Statutes, Illinois* (1869), § 3, *page* 302 ; *Revised Statutes, chap.* 44, § 2.

WISCONSIN.

§ 1. All deeds of gift, all conveyances, and all transfers or assignments, verbal or written, of goods, chattels, or things in action, made in trust for the use of the person making the same, shall be void as against the creditors, existing or subsequent, of such person.

§ 5. Every sale made by a vendor, of goods and chattels in his possession or under his control, and every assignment of goods and chattels, unless the same be accompanied by an immediate delivery, and be followed by an actual and continued change of possession of the things sold or assigned, shall be presumed to be fraudulent and void, as against the creditors of the vendor, or the creditors of the person making such assignment, or subsequent purchasers in good faith; and shall be conclusive evidence of fraud, unless it shall be made to appear, on the part of the persons claiming under such sale or assignment, that the same was made in good faith, and without any intent to defraud such creditors or purchasers.—*Chap. CVII, Revised Statutes of Wisconsin*, 1858.

§ 1. Every conveyance or assignment, in writing or otherwise, of any estate or interest in lands, or in goods or things in action, or of any rents or profits issuing therefrom, and every charge upon lands, goods, or things in action, or upon the rents or profits thereof, made with the intent to hinder, delay, or defraud creditors or other persons of their lawful actions, damages, forfeitures, debts, or demands, and every bond, or other evidence of debt given, actions commenced, order or judgment suffered, with the like intent, as against the persons so hindered, delayed, or defrauded, shall be void.

§ 4. The question of fraudulent intent, in all cases arising under the provisions of this title, shall be deemed a question of fact, and not of law, nor shall any conveyance or charge be adjudged fraudulent as against creditors or purchasers, solely on the ground that it was not founded on a valuable consideration.

§ 5. The provisions of this title shall not be construed in any manner to affect or impair the title of a purchaser for a valuable consideration, unless it shall appear that such purchaser had previous notice of the fraudulent intent of his immediate grantor, or of the fraud rendering void the the title of such grantor.—*Chap. CVIII, Revised Statutes of Wisconsin*, 1858.

MICHIGAN.

§ 1. All deeds of gift, all conveyances, and all transfers or assignments, verbal or written, of goods, chattels or things in in action, made in trust for the use of the person making the same, shall be void as against the creditors, existing or subsequent, of such person.

§ 7. Every sale made by a vendor, of goods and chattels in his possession or under his control, and every assignment of goods and chattels by way of mortgage or security, or upon any condition whatever, unless the same be accompanied by an immediate delivery, and be followed by an actual and continued change of possession of the things sold, mortgaged or assigned, shall be presumed to be fraudulent and void, as against the creditors of the vendor, or the creditors of the person making such assignment, or subsequent purchasers in good faith, and shall be conclusive evidence of fraud, unless it shall be made to appear, on the part of the persons claiming under such sale or assignment, that the same was made in good faith, and without any intent to defraud such creditors or purchasers.—*Chap.* 81, *Revised Statutes of Michigan.*

§ 1. Every conveyance or assignment, in writing or otherwise, of any estate or interest in lands, or in goods or things in action, or of any rents or profits issuing therefrom, and any charge upon lands, goods or things in action, or upon the rents and profits thereof, made with the intent to hinder, delay or defraud creditors or other persons of their lawful suits, damages, forfeitures, debts or demands, and every bond or other evidence of debt given, suit commenced, decree or judgment suffered, with like intent as against the persons so hindered, delayed or defrauded, shall be void.

§ 3. Every conveyance, charge, instrument or proceeding, declared by law to be void as against creditors or purchasers, shall be equally void as against the heirs, successors, personal representatives or assigns of such creditors and purchasers.

§ 4. The question of fraudulent intent, in all cases arising under this, or either of the last two preceding chapters, shall be deemed a question of fact, and not of law.

§ 5. None of the provisions of this, or the last two preceding chapters, shall be construed in any manner to affect or impair the title of a purchaser for a valuable consideration, unless it shall appear that he had previous notice of the fraudulent intent of his immediate grantor, or of the fraud rendering void the title of such grantor.—*Chap.* 82, *Revised Statutes of Michigan.*

MINNESOTA.

§ 14. All deeds of gifts, all conveyances, and all transfers or assignments, verbal or written, of goods, chattels, or things in action, made in trust for the use of the person making the same, shall be void as against the creditors existing or subsequent of such person.

§ 15. Every sale made by a vendor of goods and chattels in his possession or made under his control, and every assignment of goods and chattels, unless the same is accompanied by an immediate delivery, and followed by an actual and continued change of possession of the things sold or assigned, shall be presumed to be fraudulent and void as against the creditors of the vendor or assignor, or subsequent purchasers in good faith unless those claiming under such sale or assignment make it appear that the same was made in good faith and without any intent to hinder, delay, or defraud such creditors or purchasers.

§ 16. The term "creditors" as used in the preceding section, includes all persons who are creditors of the vendor or assignee, at any time while such goods and chattels remain in his possession or under his control.

§ 17. Nothing contained in the two preceding sections shall apply to contracts of bottomry or respondentia, nor assignments or hypothecations of vessels or goods at sea, or in foreign ports, or without this State : *provided* the assignee or mortgagee takes possession of such vessel or goods as soon as possible, after the arrival thereof within this State.

§ 18. Every conveyance or assignment in writing or otherwise of any estate or interest in lands, or of any rents or profits issuing therefrom, and every charge upon lands or upon the rents or profits thereof, made with the intent to hinder, delay, or defraud creditors or other persons of their lawful actions, damages, forfeitures, debts, or demands, and every bond or other evidence of debt given, actions commenced, order or judgment suffered, with the like intent as against the persons so hindered, delayed or defrauded, shall be void.

§ 19. Every conveyance, charge, instrument, or proceeding declared to be void by the provisions of this and the two preceding titles, as against creditors or purchasers, shall be equally void against the heirs, successors, personal representatives, or assignees of such creditors or purchasers.

§ 20. The question of fraudulent intent in all cases, arising under the provisions of this title shall be deemed a question of fact and not of law, and no conveyance or charge shall be adjudged fraudulent as against creditors solely on the ground that it was not founded on a valuable consideration.

§ 21. The provisions of this title shall not be construed in any manner to affect or impair the title of a purchaser for a valuable consideration unless it appears that such purchaser had previous notice of the fraudulent intent of his immediate grantor, or the fraud rendering void the title of such grantor.

§ 22. The term " conveyance," as used in this chapter, shall be construed to embrace every instrument in writing, except a last will and testament, whatever may be its form, and by whatever name it may be known in law, by which any estate or interest in lands is created, aliened, assigned, or surrendered.—*Chap. XLI, Tit. 3, page 335, Minnesota Revised Statutes*, 1866.

OREGON.

§ 49. Every conveyance or assignment in writing or otherwise, of any estate or interest in lands or in goods, or things in action, or of any rents or profits issuing therefrom, and every charge upon lands, goods, or things in action, or upon the rents or profits thereof, made with the intent to hinder, delay, or defraud creditors or other persons of their lawful suits, damages, forfeitures, debts, or demands, and every bond or other evidence of debt given, suit commenced, decree or judgment suffered with the like intent as against the persons so hindered, delayed or defrauded shall be void.—*Drady's Statutes, Oregon Code*, 656.

ARKANSAS.

§ 3. Every deed of gift and conveyance of goods and chattels in trust to the use of the person so making such deed of gift or conveyance, is declared to be void as against creditors existing and subsequent purchasers.

§ 4. Every conveyance or assignment, in writing or otherwise of any estate or interest in lands, or in goods and chattels, or things in action, or of any rents issuing therefrom, and every charge upon lands, goods, or things in action, or upon the rents and profits thereof, and every bond, suit, judgment, decree, or execution made or contrived with the intent to hinder, delay, or defraud creditors or other persons of their lawful actions, damages, forfeitures, debts, or demands, as against creditors and purchasers prior and subsequent, shall be void.

§ 9. This act shall not extend to any estate or interest in any lands or tenements, goods or chattels, or any rents or profits out of the same, which shall be upon a valuable consideration and *bona fide* and lawfully conveyed; nor shall this act be construed to avoid any deed or sale to a subsequent *bona fide* purchaser from the grantee for valuable consideration and without any notice of fraud.—*Chap.* 73, *Digest of the Statutes of Arkansas.*

MISSOURI.

§ 1. Every deed of gift and conveyance of goods and chattels in trust, to the use of the person so making such deed of gift or conveyance, is declared to be void as against creditors existing and subsequent, and purchasers.

§ 2. Every conveyance or assignment in writing or otherwise, of any estate or interest in lands, or in goods and chattels, or in things in action, or of any rents and profits issuing therefrom, and every charge upon lands, goods, or things in action, or upon the rents and profits thereof, and every bond, suit, judgment, decree, or execution, made or contrived with the intent to hinder, delay, or defraud creditors of their lawful actions, damages, forfeitures, debts, or demands, (or to defraud or deceive those who shall purchase the same lands, tenements, hereditaments, or any rent, profit, or commodity issuing [out] of them), shall be from henceforth deemed and taken as against said creditors and purchasers prior and subsequent, to be clearly and utterly void.

§ 7. This Act shall not extend to any estate or interest in any lands, tenements, or hereditaments, goods or chattels, or any rents, profits, or commons out of the same, which shall be upon valuable consideration and *bona fide* and lawfully conveyed ; nor shall it be construed to avoid any deed as against any subsequent *bona fide* purchaser from the grantee for valuable consideration, and without any notice of fraud.

§ 10. Every sale made by a vendor of goods and chattels in his possession, or under his control, unless the same be accompanied by delivery in a reasonable time (regard being had to the situation of the property), and be followed by an actual and continued change of the possession of the things sold, shall be held to be fraudulent and void as against the creditors of the vendor or subsequent purchasers in good faith.—1 *Waggner's Missouri Statutes*, 279 *et seq.*

KANSAS.

Be it enacted by the Legislature of the State of Kansas :

§ 1. All gifts and conveyances of goods and chattels, made in trust to the use of the person or persons making the same, shall be void and of no effect.

§ 2. Every gift, grant, or conveyance of lands, tenements, hereditaments, rents, goods, or chattels, and every bond, judgment, or execution, made or obtained, with intent to hinder, delay, or defraud creditors of their just and lawful debts or damages, or to defraud, or to deceive the person or persons who shall purchase such lands, tenements, hereditaments, rents, goods, or chattels, shall be deemed utterly void and of no effect.

§ 3. Every sale or conveyance of personal property unaccompanied by an actual and continued change of possession, shall be deemed to be void as against purchasers without notice and existing or subsequent creditors, until it is shown that such sale was made in good faith and upon sufficient consideration. This section shall not interfere with the provisions of law relating to chattel mortgages.—*Chap.* 43, *General Statutes of Kansas*, 1868.

GENERAL INDEX.

INDEX.

39

VOLUNTARY CONVEYANCES—*continued.*
>by person in debt, 288.
>mere indebtedness, 289.
>comparative indebtedness, 291.
>by insolvent, 292.
>which leaves donor insolvent, 293.
>insolvency not necessary, 293.
>effect to defraud, 294.
>solvency determined by event, 294.
>demands to be met, 295.
>proof must be clear, 295.
>such as prudent man would make, 296.
>ordinary course of events, 296.
>nominal assets, 297.
>hazards of business, 297.
>property must be accessible, 298.
>incumbered property, 298.
>property where donor resides, 298.
>different kinds of property, 299.
>solvency determined by result, 299.
>negligence of creditors, 300.
>accident, 300.
>improvidence, 301.
>no secret trust, 301.
>valid when donor has ample means, 302.
>partially voluntary, 303.
>when valid against subsequent creditors, 324.
>void against prior is void against subsequent, 326.
>continuous indebtedness, 327.
>when subsequent creditors may impeach, 329.
>participation by subsequent creditors, 329.

WAGES, of child, 258, 272.
>of wife, 258, 272.
>of debtor, 269.
>of child after emancipation, 272.

WIFE. See HUSBAND AND WIFE.

WITNESS may testify to his own intent, 553.
>cannot testify to intent of another, 553.
>effect of omission to produce, 95.

www.ingramcontent.com/pod-product-compliance
Lightning Source LLC
Chambersburg PA
CBHW021938220326
41599CB00010BA/283